SOCIAL ETHICS

Morality and
Social Policy

SOCIAL ETHICS

Morality and Social Policy

FOURTH EDITION

Thomas A. Mappes

Frostburg State University

Jane S. Zembaty

University of Dayton

McGraw-Hill, Inc.
New York St. Louis San Francisco Auckland Bogotá
Caracas Lisbon London Madrid Mexico City Milan
Montreal New Delhi San Juan Singapore
Sydney Tokyo Toronto

This book is printed on acid-free paper.

SOCIAL ETHICS
Morality and Social Policy

7 8 9 0 DOC DOC 9 0 9 8 7 6

ISBN 0-07-040133-0

This book was set in Times Roman by The Clarinda Company.
The editors were Cynthia Ward and James R. Belser;
the production supervisor was Kathryn Porzio.
The cover was designed by Carla Bauer.
R. R. Donnelley & Sons Company was printer and binder.

Library of Congress Cataloging-in-Publication Data

Mappes, Thomas A.
Social ethics: morality and social policy / Thomas A. Mappes,
Jane S. Zembaty. — 4th ed.
p.   cm.
Includes bibliographical references.
ISBN 0-07-040133-0
1. Social ethics.   2. United States—Social policy.   3. United
States—Moral conditions.   I. Zembaty, Jane S.   II. Title.
HM216.M27   1992
170—dc20   91-11542

About the authors

Thomas A. Mappes, professor of philosophy at Frostburg State University (Maryland), is the author of several articles and is the coeditor (with Jane S. Zembaty) of *Biomedical Ethics* (3/e, 1991). In 1985, the Frostburg State University Foundation presented him with the Faculty Achievement Award for Teaching.

Jane S. Zembaty, professor of philosophy at the University of Dayton, specializes in classical Greek philosophy and social ethics. In addition to *Biomedical Ethics,* her published work includes articles on Greek philosophy, such as "Plato's *Republic* and Greek Morality on Lying."

Contents

Preface

Is the death penalty a morally acceptable type of punishment? Is the interest of human beings in eating meat sufficient to justify the way in which we raise and slaughter animals? Do more affluent individuals and countries have a moral obligation to eliminate starvation and malnutrition among the needy? Is society justified in enacting laws that limit individual liberty in sexual matters? What obligations, if any, does society have to undo some of the self-perpetuating inequalities caused by past racial and sexual discrimination?

The way we answer such moral questions and the social policies we adopt in keeping with our answers will directly affect our lives. It is not surprising, therefore, that discussions of these and other contemporary moral issues often involve rhetorical arguments whose intent is to elicit highly emotional, unreflective responses. This book is designed to provide material that will encourage a reflective and critical examination of some contemporary moral problems. To achieve this end, we have developed chapters that bring the central issues into clear focus, while allowing the supporting arguments for widely diverse positions to be presented by those who embrace them.

With the appearance of this fourth edition, we are confident that *teachability* will continue to be the most salient characteristic of *Social Ethics*. All of the editorial features employed in earlier editions to enhance teachability have been retained in the fourth. An introduction to each chapter both sets the ethical issues and scans the various positions together with their supporting argumentation. Every selection is prefaced by a headnote that provides both biographical data on the author and a short statement of some of the key points or arguments to be found in the selection. Every selection is followed by questions whose purpose is to elicit further critical analysis and discussion. Finally, each chapter concludes with a short annotated bibliography designed to guide the reader in further research.

We have tried to provide readings that are free of unnecessary technical jargon and yet introduce serious moral argumentation. Further, in order to emphasize the connection of contemporary moral problems with matters of social policy, we have liberally incorporated relevant legal opinions. We have taken substantial editorial license by deleting almost all the numerous citations that usually attend legal writing in order to render the legal opinions maximally readable to the nonlegal eye. Those interested in further legal research can check the appropriate credit lines for the necessary bibliographical data to locate the cases in their original form. We should also note that, where appropriate, both in legal cases and in other readings, we have renumbered footnotes.

We would be remiss not to express our indebtedness to all those whose work is reprinted in these pages. We are also indebted to Joy Kroeger-Mappes, Frostburg State University, for her helpful critical comments, and to the following reviewers who provided us with very useful reactions and suggestions: Edwin B. Allaire, University of Texas, Austin; Fred J. Blomgren, Monroe Community College; Paul Carrick, Harrisburg Area Community College; Allen Davidoff, University of Cincinnatti; David B. Fletcher, Wheaton College; Robert Good, Rider College; Richard J. Hall, Michigan State University; Karen Hanson, Indiana University; Harold Hatt, Phillips University; Robert Hollinger, Iowa State University; Richard Lippke, James Madison University; Don Marquis, University of Kansas; Alistair Moles, California State University–Sacramento; Charles Pinches, University of Central Arkansas; Nelson Potter, University of Nebraska; Mary Ellen Ross, Trinity University; Tara Smith, University of Texas; Kathy Squadrito, Purdue University; Mark Timmons, Memphis State University; and Robert S. Trotter, William Jewell College. Shelley Drees, Michelle Benson, and Linda McKinley deserve thanks for their help with manuscript preparation, Matt Walls deserves thanks for his valuable assistance in proofreading, and we continue to be grateful to the reference librarians at both the University of Dayton and Frostburg State University.

Thomas A. Mappes
Jane S. Zembaty

SOCIAL ETHICS

Morality and
Social Policy

CHAPTER 1

Abortion

Attention in this chapter is focused primarily on the issue of the ethical (moral) acceptability of abortion. Some attention is also given to the social policy aspects of abortion, especially in conjunction with developments in the United States Supreme Court.

ABORTION: THE ETHICAL ISSUE

Discussions of the ethical acceptability of abortion often take for granted (1) an awareness of the various kinds of reasons that may be given for having an abortion and (2) a basic acquaintance with the biological development of a human fetus.

1   Reasons for Abortion

Why would a woman have an abortion? The following catalog, not meant to provide an exhaustive survey, is sufficient to indicate that there is a wide range of potential reasons for abortion.

(a) In certain extreme cases, if the fetus is allowed to develop normally and come to term, the pregnant woman herself will die.

(b) In other cases it is not the woman's life but her health, physical or mental, that will be severely endangered if the pregnancy is allowed to continue.

(c) There are also cases in which the pregnancy will probably, or surely, produce a severely impaired child.

(d) There are others in which the pregnancy is the result of rape or incest.[1]

(e) There are instances in which the pregnant woman is unmarried and there will be the social stigma of illegitimacy.

(f) There are other instances in which having a child, or having another child, will be an unbearable financial burden.

---

[1]The expression "therapeutic abortion" suggests abortion for medical reasons. Accordingly, abortions corresponding to (a), (b), and (c) are usually said to be therapeutic. More problematically, abortions corresponding to (d) have often been identified as therapeutic. Perhaps it is presumed that pregnancies resulting from rape or incest are traumatic, thus a threat to mental health. Or perhaps calling such an abortion "therapeutic" is just a way of indicating that it is thought to be justifiable.

(g) Certainly common, and perhaps most common of all, are those instances in which having a child will interfere with the happiness of the woman, or the joint happiness of a couple, or even the joint happiness of a family unit that already includes children. Here there are almost endless possibilities. The woman may desire a professional career. A couple may be content and happy together and feel their relationship would be damaged by the intrusion of a child. Parents may have older children and not feel up to raising another child, and so forth.

2   The Biological Development of a Human Fetus

During the course of a human pregnancy, in the nine-month period from conception to birth, the product of conception undergoes a continual process of change and development. *Conception* takes place when a male germ cell (the spermatozoon) combines with a female germ cell (the ovum), resulting in a single cell (the single-cell zygote), which embodies the full genetic code, twenty-three pairs of chromosomes. The single-cell zygote soon begins a process of cellular division. The resultant multicell zygote, while continuing to grow and beginning to take shape, proceeds to move through the fallopian tube and then to undergo gradual *implantation* at the uterine wall. The unborn entity is formally designated a zygote up until the time that implantation is complete, almost two weeks after conception. Thereafter, until the end of the eighth week, roughly the point at which brain waves can be detected, the unborn entity is formally designated an *embryo*. It is in this embryonic period that organ systems and other human characteristics begin to undergo noticeable development. From the end of the eighth week until birth, the unborn entity is formally designated a *fetus*. (The term "fetus," however, is commonly used as a general term to designate the unborn entity, whatever its stage of development.) Two other points in the development of the fetus are especially noteworthy as relevant to discussions of abortion, but these points are usually identified by reference to gestational age as calculated not from conception but from the first day of the woman's last menstrual period. Accordingly, somewhere between the twelfth and the sixteenth week there usually occurs *quickening,* the point at which the woman begins to feel the movements of the fetus. And somewhere in the neighborhood of the twenty-fourth week, *viability* becomes a realistic possibility. Viability is the point at which the fetus is capable of surviving outside the womb.

With the facts of fetal development in view, it may be helpful to indicate the various medical techniques of abortion. Early (first trimester) abortions were at one time performed by *dilatation and curettage* (D&C) but are now commonly performed by *uterine aspiration,* also called "suction curettage." The D&C features the stretching (dilatation) of the cervix and the scraping (curettage) of the inner walls of the uterus. Uterine aspiration simply involves sucking the fetus out of the uterus by means of a tube connected to a suction pump. Later abortions require *dilatation and evacuation* (D&E), *induction techniques,* or *hysterotomy.* In the D&E, which is the abortion procedure commonly used in the early stages of the second trimester, a forceps is used to dismember the fetus within the uterus; the fetal remains are then withdrawn through the cervix. In one commonly employed induction technique, a saline solution injected into the amniotic cavity induces labor, thus expelling the fetus. Another induction technique employs prostaglandins (hormonelike substances) to induce labor. Hysterotomy—in essence a miniature cesarean section—is a major surgical procedure and is uncommonly employed in the United States.

A brief discussion of fetal development together with a cursory survey of various reasons for abortion has prepared the way for a formulation of the ethical issue of abortion in its broadest terms. *Up to what point of fetal development, if any,* and *for what reasons, if any, is abortion ethically acceptable?* Some hold that abortion is *never* ethically acceptable, or at most is acceptable only where abortion is necessary to save the life of the pregnant woman. This view is frequently termed the *conservative* view on abortion. Others hold that abortion is *always* ethically acceptable—at any point of fetal development and for any of the standard reasons. This view is frequently termed the *liberal* view on abortion. Still others are anxious to defend more *moderate* views, holding that abortion is ethically acceptable up to a certain point of fetal development *and/or* holding that some reasons provide a sufficient justification for abortion whereas others do not.

THE CONSERVATIVE VIEW AND THE LIBERAL VIEW

The *moral status* of the fetus has been a pivotal issue in discussions of the ethical acceptability of abortion. The concept of moral status is commonly explicated in terms of rights. On this construal, to say that a fetus has moral status is to say that the fetus has rights. What kinds of rights, if any, does the fetus have? Does it have the same rights as more visible humans, and thus *full moral status,* as conservatives typically contend? Does it have no rights, and thus *no (significant) moral status,* as liberals typically contend? (Or perhaps, as some moderates argue, does the fetus have a subsidiary or *partial moral status,* however this is to be conceptualized?) If the fetus has no rights, the liberal is prone to argue, then it does not have any more right to life than a piece of tissue such as an appendix, and an abortion is no more morally objectionable than an appendectomy. If the fetus has the same rights as any other human being, the conservative is prone to argue, then it has the same right to life as the latter, and an abortion, except perhaps when the pregnant woman's life is endangered, is as morally objectionable as any other murder.

Discussions of the moral status of the fetus often refer directly to the biological development of the fetus and pose the question: At what point in the continuous development of the fetus do we have a human life? In the context of such discussions, "human" implies full moral status, "nonhuman" implies no (significant) moral status, and any notion of partial moral status is systematically excluded. To distinguish the human from the nonhuman, to "draw the line," and to do so in a nonarbitrary way, is the central concern. The *conservative* on abortion typically holds that the line must be drawn at conception. Usually the conservative argues that conception is the only point at which the line can be nonarbitrarily drawn. Against attempts to draw the line at points such as implantation, quickening, viability, or birth, considerations of continuity in the development of the fetus are pressed. The conservative is sometimes said to employ "slippery-slope arguments," that is, to argue that a line cannot be securely drawn anywhere along the path of fetal development. It is said that the line will inescapably slide back to the point of conception to find objective support—by reference to the fact that the full genetic code is present subsequent to conception, whereas it is not present prior to conception.

With regard to "drawing the line," the *liberal* typically contends that the fetus remains nonhuman even in its most advanced stages of development. The liberal, of course, does not mean to deny that a fetus is biologically a human fetus. Rather the claim is that the fetus is not human in any morally significant sense—it has no (significant) moral status. This point is often made in terms of the concept of personhood. Mary Anne Warren, who defends the liberal view on abortion in one of this chapter's selections, argues that the fetus is not a person. She also contends that the fetus bears so little resemblance to a person that it cannot be said to have a significant right to life. It is important to notice that, as Warren analyzes the concept of personhood, even a newborn baby is not a person. This conclusion, as might be expected, prompts Warren to a consideration of the moral justifiability of infanticide, an issue closely related to the problem of abortion.

Though the conservative view on abortion is most commonly predicated on the straightforward contention that the fetus is a person from conception, other lines of argument are sometimes advanced in its defense. One conservative, advancing what might be labeled the "presumption argument," writes:

> In being willing to kill the embryo, we accept responsibility for killing what we must admit *may* be a person. There is some reason to believe it is—namely the *fact* that it is a living, human individual and the inconclusiveness of arguments that try to exclude it from the protected circle of personhood.
>
> *To be willing to kill what for all we know could be a person is to be willing to kill it if it is a person.* And since we cannot absolutely settle if it is a person except by a metaphysical postulate, for all practical purposes we must hold that to be willing to kill the embryo is to be willing to kill a person.[2]

In accordance with this line of argument, though it may not be possible to show conclusively that the fetus is a person from conception, we must presume that it is. Another line of argument that is sometimes advanced in defense of the conservative view emphasizes the potential rather than the actual personhood of the fetus. Even if the fetus is not a person, it is said, there can be no doubt that it is a potential person. Accordingly, by virtue of its potential personhood, the fetus must be accorded a right to life. Mary Anne Warren, in response to this line of argument, argues that the potential personhood of the fetus provides no basis for the claim that it has a significant right to life.

In one of the readings in this chapter, Don Marquis argues for a very conservative view on abortion, although he does not argue for what is commonly referred to as "the" conservative view on abortion. Whereas the standard conservative is committed to a "sanctity-of-life" viewpoint, according to which the lives of all biologically human beings (assuming their moral innocence) are considered immune from attack,

---

[2]Germain Grisez, *Abortion: The Myths, the Realities, and the Arguments* (New York: Corpus Books, 1970), p. 306.

Marquis bases his opposition to abortion on a distinctive theory about the wrongness of killing. Although Marquis claims that there is a strong moral presumption against abortion, and although he clearly believes that the vast majority of abortions are seriously immoral, he is not committed to the standard conservative contention that the only possible exception is the case in which abortion is necessary to save the life of the pregnant woman.

MODERATE VIEWS

The conservative and liberal views, as explicated, constitute two extreme poles on the spectrum of ethical views of abortion. Each of the extreme views is marked by a formal simplicity. The conservative proclaims abortion to be immoral, irrespective of the stage of fetal development and irrespective of alleged justifying reasons. The one exception, admitted by some conservatives, is the case in which abortion is necessary to save the life of the pregnant woman.[3] The liberal proclaims abortion to be morally acceptable, irrespective of the stage of fetal development.[4] Moreover, there is no need to draw distinctions between those reasons that are sufficient to justify abortion and those that are not. No justification is needed. The *moderate,* in vivid contrast to both the conservative and the liberal, is unwilling to sweepingly condemn or condone abortion. Some abortions are morally justifiable; some are morally objectionable. In some moderate views, the stage of fetal development is a relevant factor in the assessment of the moral acceptability of abortion. In other moderate views, the alleged justifying reason is a relevant factor in the assessment of the moral acceptability of abortion. In still other moderate views, both the stage of fetal development and the alleged justifying reason are relevant factors in the assessment of the moral acceptability of abortion.

[3]One especially prominent conservative view is associated with the Roman Catholic Church. In accordance with Catholic moral teaching, the *direct* killing of innocent human life is forbidden. Hence, abortion is forbidden. Even if the pregnant woman's life is in danger, perhaps because her heart or kidney function is inadequate, abortion is impermissible. In two special cases, however, procedures resulting in the death of the fetus are allowable. In the case of an ectopic pregnancy, where the developing fetus is lodged in the fallopian tube, the fallopian tube may be removed. In the case of a pregnant woman with a cancerous uterus, the cancerous uterus may be removed. In these cases, the death of the fetus is construed as *indirect* killing, the foreseen but unintended by-product of a surgical procedure designed to protect the life of the woman. If the distinction between direct and indirect killing is a defensible one (and this is a controversial issue), it might still be suggested that the distinction is not rightly applied in the Roman Catholic view of abortion. For example, some critics contend that abortion may be construed as indirect killing, indeed an allowable form of indirect killing, in at least all cases where it is necessary to save the life of the pregnant woman. For one helpful exposition and critical analysis of the Roman Catholic position on abortion, see Daniel Callahan, *Abortion: Law, Choice and Morality* (New York: Macmillan, 1970), chap. 12, pp. 409–447.

[4]In considering the liberal contention that abortions are morally acceptable irrespective of the stage of fetal development, we should take note of an ambiguity in the concept of abortion. Does "abortion" refer merely to the termination of a pregnancy in the sense of detaching the fetus from the pregnant woman, or does "abortion" entail the death of the fetus as well? Whereas the abortion of a *previable* fetus entails its death, the "abortion" of a *viable* fetus, by means of hysterotomy (a miniature cesarean section), does not entail the death of the fetus and would seem to be tantamount to the birth of a baby. With regard to the "abortion" of a *viable* fetus, liberals can defend the woman's right to detach the fetus from her body without contending that the woman has the right to insist on the death of the child.

Moderate views have been developed in accordance with the following clearly identifiable strategies:

1   Moderation of the Conservative View

One strategy for generating a moderate view presumes the typical conservative contention that the fetus has full moral status from conception. What is denied, however, is that we must conclude to the moral impermissibility of abortion in *all* cases. In one of this chapter's readings, Jane English attempts to moderate the conservative view in just this way. She argues that certain abortion cases may be assimilated to cases of self-defense. Thus, for English, on the presumption that the fetus from conception has full moral status, some reasons are sufficient to justify abortion whereas others are not.

2   Moderation of the Liberal View

A second strategy for generating a moderate view presumes the liberal contention that the fetus has no (significant) moral status even in the latest stages of pregnancy. What is denied, however, is that we must conclude to the moral permissibility of abortion in *all* cases. It might be said, in accordance with this line of thought, that even though abortion does not violate the rights of the fetus (which is presumed to have no rights), the practice of abortion remains ethically problematic because of its negative social consequences. Such an argument seems especially forceful in the later stages of pregnancy, when the fetus increasingly resembles a newborn infant. It is argued that very late abortions have a brutalizing effect on those involved and, in various ways, lead to the breakdown of attitudes associated with respect for human life. Jane English, in an effort to moderate the liberal view, advances an argument of this general type. Even if the fetus is not a person, she holds, it is gradually becoming increasingly personlike. Appealing to a "coherence of attitudes," she argues that abortion demands more weighty justifying reasons in the later stages of pregnancy than it does in the earlier stages.

3   Moderation in "Drawing the Line"

A third strategy for generating a moderate view, in fact a whole range of moderate views, is associated with "drawing-the-line" discussions. Whereas the conservative typically draws the line between human (having full moral status) and nonhuman (having no moral status) at conception, and the liberal typically draws that same line at birth (or sometime thereafter), a moderate view may be generated by drawing the line somewhere between these two extremes. For example, the line might be drawn at implantation, at the point where brain activity begins, at quickening, at viability, etc. Whereas drawing the line at implantation would tend to generate a rather "conservative" moderate view, drawing the line at viability would tend to generate a rather "liberal" moderate view. Wherever the line is drawn, it is the burden of any such moderate view to show that the point specified is a nonarbitrary one. Once such a point has been specified, however, it might be argued that abortion is ethically acceptable before that point and ethically unacceptable after that point. Or further stipulations may be added in accordance with strategies (1) and (2) above.

L. W. Sumner is committed in this chapter to the development of a moderate view in accordance with this third strategy. He argues that the fetus has no significant moral standing (status) prior to the point at which it becomes *sentient*—that is, capable of feeling pleasure and pain. With the emergence of sentience, however, he attributes (full) moral standing to the fetus. Thus he "draws the line" at this particular point of fetal development. Although Sumner considers all abortions morally permissible prior to this point, he does not consider all abortions morally impermissible subsequent to this point. In essence, then, he is also committed to an application of strategy (1).

4 Moderation in the Assignment of Moral Status

A fourth strategy for generating a moderate view depends on assigning the fetus some sort of subsidiary or *partial moral status*. Although this approach is not reflected in the readings in this chapter,[5] it seems to have some measure of intuitive plausibility. It would seem, however, that anyone who defends a moderate view based on the concept of partial moral status must first of all face the problem of explicating the nature of such partial moral status. A second and closely related problem is that of showing how the interests of those with partial moral status are to be weighed against the interests of those with full moral status.

ABORTION AND SOCIAL POLICY

In the United States, the Supreme Court's decision in *Roe v. Wade* (1973) has been the focal point of the social policy debate over abortion. This case had the effect, for all practical purposes, of legalizing "abortion on request." The Court held that it was unconstitutional for a state to have laws prohibiting the abortion of a previable fetus. According to the Court, a woman has a constitutionally guaranteed right to decide to terminate a pregnancy (prior to viability), although a state, for reasons related to maternal health, may restrict the manner and circumstances in which abortions are performed subsequent to the end of the first trimester. The reasoning underlying the Court's holding in *Roe* can be found in the majority opinion reprinted in this chapter.

Since the action of the Court in *Roe* had the practical effect of establishing a woman's legal right to choose whether or not to abort, it was enthusiastically received by "right-to-choose" forces. On the other hand, "right-to-life" forces, committed to the conservative view on the morality of abortion, vehemently denounced the Court for "legalizing murder." In response to *Roe,* right-to-life forces adopted a number of political strategies. The most significant of these strategies will be discussed here.

Right-to-life forces originally worked for the enactment of a constitutional amendment directly overruling *Roe*. The proposed "Human Life Amendment"—declaring the personhood of the fetus—was calculated to achieve the legal prohibition

---

[5]Daniel Callahan embraces this approach in *Abortion: Law, Choice and Morality,* chap. 14, pp. 493–501.

of abortion, allowing an exception only for abortions necessary to save the life of a pregnant woman. Right-to-life support also emerged for the idea of a constitutional amendment allowing Congress and/or each state to decide whether to restrict abortion. (If this sort of amendment were enacted, it would undoubtedly have the effect of prohibiting abortion or at least severely restricting it in a number of states.) Right-to-choose forces reacted in strong opposition to these proposed constitutional amendments. In their view, any effort to achieve the legal prohibition of abortion represents an illicit attempt by one group (conservatives on abortion) to impose their moral views on those who have different views. Thus, to some extent the justifiability of restrictive abortion laws is bound up with a much broader question: Is it justifiable to employ the law in an effort to 'enforce morality'? (Cf. the discussion of the principle of legal moralism in Chapter 6.)

In 1980, right-to-life forces were notably successful in achieving a more limited political aim, the cutoff of Medicaid funding for abortion. Medicaid is a social program designed to provide public funds to pay for the medical care of impoverished people. At issue in *Harris v. McRae,* decided by the Supreme Court in 1980, was the constitutionality of the so-called Hyde Amendment, legislation that had passed Congress with vigorous right-to-life support. The Hyde Amendment, in the version considered by the Court, restricted federal Medicaid funding to (1) cases in which the pregnant woman's life is endangered and (2) cases of rape and incest. The Court, in a five-to-four decision, upheld the constitutionality of the Hyde Amendment. According to the Court, a woman's right to an abortion does not entail *the right to have society fund the abortion.* But if there is no constitutional obstacle to the cutoff of Medicaid funding for abortion, it must still be asked if society's refusal to fund the abortions of poor women is an ethically sound social policy. Considerations of social justice are often pressed by those who argue that it is not.

In the wake of *Roe,* right-to-life forces made recurrent efforts to secure the passage of statutes designed (in various ways) to place obstacles in the path of women seeking an abortion. In *Akron v. Akron Center for Reproductive Health* (1983), the Supreme Court considered the constitutionality of a local ordinance of this sort. The most important provisions of the ordinance were (1) the requirement that any abortion subsequent to the first trimester be performed in a hospital (as opposed to a clinic), (2) the requirement that the attending physician (as opposed to other trained personnel) personally inform the patient of a host of particulars concerning fetal development, the emotional and physical risks of abortion, etc., "in order to insure . . . truly informed consent," and (3) the requirement that a physician not perform an abortion until twenty-four hours after a consent form had been signed by the pregnant woman. In a six-to-three decision, the Court reaffirmed *Roe v. Wade* and declared each of the ordinance's provisions unconstitutional. The Court called attention to the additional financial burdens created by provisions (1) and (3) in invalidating them. Although endorsing the importance of informed consent, the Court emphasized two problems related to provision (2). First, "the information required is designed not to inform the woman's consent but rather to persuade her to withhold it altogether." Second, a physician may legitimately delegate the counseling task to another qualified individual.

With the decision of the Supreme Court in *Webster v. Reproductive Health Services* (1989), right-to-life forces celebrated a dramatic victory. Two crucial provisions of a Missouri statute were upheld. One provision bans the use of *public* facilities and *public* employees in the performance of abortions. Another requires physicians to perform tests to determine the viability of any fetus believed to be twenty weeks or older. In essence, *Webster* represents for right-to-life forces the first benefits of a long-term strategy: to undermine *Roe v. Wade* by controlling (through the political process) the appointment of new Supreme Court justices. From the perspective of right-to-choose forces, of course, the *Webster* decision is a deeply disturbing one, since it seems to indicate the present Court's willingness to retreat from *Roe*. The opinion of Chief Justice William H. Rehnquist in *Webster* is reprinted in this chapter.

The recent emergence of RU 486, a drug developed in France, has further complicated the social policy debate over abortion in the United States. RU 486 functions to terminate early pregnancy. Research on its employment presently indicates that the drug, when used within forty-nine days of a missed menstrual period, is 96 percent effective in inducing menses and thereby terminating pregnancy. Although there have been some reports of minor side effects (e.g., heavier bleeding, nausea, and fatigue), there are no apparent long-term negative effects. Worries about safety aside, RU 486 has been warmly endorsed by right-to-choose forces. If the drug were to become legally available in the United States, it would largely "privatize" abortion decisions. Of course, right-to-life forces are bitterly opposed to the legal availability of RU 486. They refer to the drug as a "human pesticide" and denounce its employment as "chemical warfare on the unborn."

Thomas A. Mappes

On the Moral and Legal Status of Abortion

Mary Anne Warren

Mary Anne Warren is associate professor of philosophy at San Francisco State University. Among her published articles are "Secondary Sexism and Quota Hiring," "Do Potential People Have Moral Rights?" and "Is Androgyny the Answer to Sexual Stereotyping?" She is also the author of *The Nature of Woman: An Encyclopedia and Guide to the Literature* (1980) and *Gendercide: The Implications of Sex Selection* (1985).

Warren, defending the liberal view on abortion, promptly distinguishes two senses of the term "human": (1) One is *human in the genetic sense* when one is a member of the biological species *Homo sapiens.* (2) One is *human in the moral sense* when one is a full-fledged member of the moral community. Warren attacks the

Reprinted with the permission of the author and the publisher from *The Monist,* vol. 57, no. 1 (January 1973). "Postscript on Infanticide" reprinted with permission of the author from Richard Wasserstrom, ed., *Today's Moral Problems* (New York: Macmillan, 1975).

presupposition underlying the standard conservative argument against abortion—that the fetus is human in the moral sense. She contends that the moral community, the set of beings with full and equal moral rights, consists of all and only people (persons). (Thus she takes the concept of personhood to be equivalent to the concept of humanity in the moral sense.) After analyzing the concept of person, she concludes that a fetus is so unlike a person as to have no significant right to life. Nor, she argues, does the fetus's *potential* for being a person provide us any basis for ascribing to it any significant right to life. It follows, she contends, that a woman's right to obtain an abortion is absolute. Abortion is morally justified at any stage of fetal development. It also follows, she contends, that no legislation against abortion can be justified on the grounds of protecting the rights of the fetus. In a concluding postscript, Warren briefly assesses the moral justifiability of infanticide.

The question which we must answer in order to produce a satisfactory solution to the problem of the moral status of abortion is this: How are we to define the moral community, the set of beings with full and equal moral rights, such that we can decide whether a human fetus is a member of this community or not? What sort of entity, exactly, has the inalienable rights to life, liberty, and the pursuit of happiness? Jefferson attributed these rights to all *men,* and it may or may not be fair to suggest that he intended to attribute them *only* to men. Perhaps he ought to have attributed them to all human beings. If so, then we arrive, first, at [John] Noonan's problem of defining what makes a being human, and, second, at the equally vital question which Noonan does not consider, namely, What reason is there for identifying the moral community with the set of all human beings, in whatever way we have chosen to define that term?

1   ON THE DEFINITION OF "HUMAN"

One reason why this vital second question is so frequently overlooked in the debate over the moral status of abortion is that the term "human" has two distinct, but not often distinguished, senses. This fact results in a slide of meaning, which serves to conceal the fallaciousness of the traditional argument that since (1) it is wrong to kill innocent human beings, and (2) fetuses are innocent human beings, then (3) it is wrong to kill fetuses. For if "human" is used in the same sense in both (1) and (2) then, whichever of the two senses is meant, one of these premises is question-begging. And if it is used in two different senses then of course the conclusion doesn't follow.

Thus, (1) is a self-evident moral truth,[1] and avoids begging the question about abortion, only if "human being" is used to mean something like "a full-fledged member of the moral community." (It may or may not also be meant to refer exclusively to members of the species *Homo sapiens*.) We may call this the *moral* sense of "human." It is not to be confused with what we will call the *genetic* sense, i.e., the sense in which *any* member of the species is a human being, and no member of any other species could be. If (1) is acceptable only if the moral sense is intended, (2) is non-question-begging only if what is intended is the genetic sense.

In "Deciding Who Is Human," Noonan argues for the classification of fetuses with human beings by pointing to the presence of the full genetic code, and the potential capacity for rational thought.[2] It is clear that what he needs to show, for his version of the traditional argument to be valid, is that fetuses are human in the moral sense, the sense in which it is analytically true that all human beings have full moral rights. But, in the absence of any argument showing that whatever is genetically human is also morally human, and he gives none, nothing more than genetic humanity can be demonstrated by the presence of the human genetic code. And, as we will see, the *potential* capacity for rational thought can at most show that an entity has the potential for *becoming* human in the moral sense.

2 DEFINING THE MORAL COMMUNITY

Can it be established that genetic humanity is sufficient for moral humanity? I think that there are very good reasons for not defining the moral community in this way. I would like to suggest an alternative way of defining the moral community, which I will argue for only to the extent of explaining why it is, or should be, self-evident. The suggestion is simply that the moral community consists of all and only *people,* rather than all and only human beings;[3] and probably the best way of demonstrating its self-evidence is by considering the concept of personhood, to see what sorts of entity are and are not persons, and what the decision that a being is or is not a person implies about its moral rights.

What characteristics entitle an entity to be considered a person? This is obviously not the place to attempt a complete analysis of the concept of personhood, but we do not need such a fully adequate analysis just to determine whether and why a fetus is or isn't a person. All we need is a rough and approximate list of the most basic criteria of personhood, and some idea of which, or how many, of these an entity must satisfy in order to properly be considered a person.

In searching for such criteria, it is useful to look beyond the set of people with whom we are acquainted, and ask how we would decide whether a totally alien being was a person or not. (For we have no right to assume that genetic humanity is necessary for personhood.) Imagine a space traveler who lands on an unknown planet and encounters a race of beings utterly unlike any he has ever seen or heard of. If he wants to be sure of behaving morally toward these beings, he has to somehow decide whether they are people, and hence have full moral rights, or whether they are the sort of thing which he need not feel guilty about treating as, for example, a source of food.

How should he go about making this decision? If he has some anthropological background, he might look for such things as religion, art, and the manufacturing of tools, weapons, or shelters, since these factors have been used to distinguish our human from our prehuman ancestors, in what seems to be closer to the moral than the genetic sense of "human." And no doubt he would be right to consider the presence of such factors as good evidence that the alien beings were people, and morally human. It would, however, be overly anthropocentric of him to take the absence of these things as adequate evidence that they were not, since we can imagine people who have progressed beyond, or evolved without ever developing, these cultural characteristics.

I suggest that the traits which are most central to the concept of personhood, or humanity in the moral sense, are, very roughly, the following:

1 consciousness (of objects and events external and/or internal to the being), and in particular the capacity to feel pain;

2 reasoning (the *developed* capacity to solve new and relatively complex problems);

3 self-motivated activity (activity which is relatively independent of either genetic or direct external control);

4 the capacity to communicate, by whatever means, messages of an indefinite variety of types, that is, not just with an indefinite number of possible contents, but on indefinitely many possible topics;

5 the presence of self-concepts, and self-awareness, either individual or racial, or both.

Admittedly, there are apt to be a great many problems involved in formulating precise definitions of these criteria, let alone in developing universally valid behavioral criteria for deciding when they apply. But I will assume that both we and our explorer know approximately what (1)–(5) mean, and that he is also able to determine whether or not they apply. How, then, should he use his findings to decide whether or not the alien beings are people? We needn't suppose that an entity must have *all* of these attributes to be properly considered a person; (1) and (2) alone may well be sufficient for personhood, and quite probably (1)–(3) are sufficient. Neither do we need to insist that any one of these criteria is *necessary* for personhood, although once again (1) and (2) look like fairly good candidates for necessary conditions, as does (3), if "activity" is construed so as to include the activity of reasoning.

All we need to claim, to demonstrate that a fetus is not a person, is that any being which satisfies *none* of (1)–(5) is certainly not a person. I consider this claim to be so obvious that I think anyone who denied it, and claimed that a being which satisfied none of (1)–(5) was a person all the same, would thereby demonstrate that he had no notion at all of what a person is—perhaps because he had confused the concept of a person with that of genetic humanity. If the opponents of abortion were to deny the appropriateness of these five criteria, I do not know what further arguments would convince them. We would probably have to admit that our conceptual schemes were indeed irreconcilably different, and that our dispute could not be settled objectively.

I do not expect this to happen, however, since I think that the concept of a person is one which is very nearly universal (to people), and that it is common to both pro-abortionists and antiabortionists, even though neither group has fully realized the relevance of this concept to the resolution of their dispute. Furthermore, I think that on reflection even the antiabortionists ought to agree not only that (1)–(5) are central to the concept of personhood, but also that it is a part of this concept that all and only people have full moral rights. The concept of a person is in part a moral concept; once we have admitted that *x* is a person we have recognized, even if we have not agreed to respect, *x's* right to be treated as a member of the moral community. It is true that the claim that *x is a human being* is more commonly voiced as part of an appeal to treat *x* decently than is the claim that *x* is a person, but this is either because "human being" is here used in the sense which implies personhood, or because the genetic and moral senses of "human" have been confused.

Now if (1)–(5) are indeed the primary criteria of personhood, then it is clear that genetic humanity is neither necessary nor sufficient for establishing that an entity is a person. Some human beings are not people, and there may well be people who are not human beings. A man or woman whose consciousness has been permanently obliterated but who remains alive is a human being which is no longer a person; defective human beings, with no appreciable mental capacity, are not and presumably never will be people; and a fetus is a human being which is not yet a person, and which therefore cannot coherently be said to have full moral rights. Citizens of the next century should be prepared to recognize highly advanced, self-aware robots or computers, should such be developed, and intelligent inhabitants of other worlds, should such be found, as people in the fullest sense, and to respect their moral rights. But to ascribe full moral rights to an entity which is not a person is as absurd as to ascribe moral obligations and responsibilities to such an entity.

3 FETAL DEVELOPMENT AND THE RIGHT TO LIFE

Two problems arise in the application of these suggestions for the definition of the moral community to the determination of the precise moral status of a human fetus. Given that the paradigm example of a person is a normal adult human being, then (1) How like this paradigm, in particular how far advanced since conception, does a human being need to be before it begins to have a right to life by virtue, not of being fully a person as of yet, but of being *like* a person? and (2) To what extent, if any, does the fact that a fetus has the *potential* for becoming a person endow it with some of the same rights? Each of these questions requires some comment.

In answering the first question, we need not attempt a detailed consideration of the moral rights of organisms which are not developed enough, aware enough, intelligent enough, etc., to be considered people, but which resemble people in some respects. It does seem reasonable to suggest that the more like a person, in the relevant respects, a being is, the stronger is the case for regarding it as having a right to life, and indeed the stronger its right to life is. Thus we ought to take seriously the suggestion that, insofar as "the human individual develops biologically in a continuous fashion . . . the rights of a human person might develop in the same way."[4] But we must keep in mind that the attributes which are relevant in determining whether or not an entity is enough like a person to be regarded as having some of the same moral rights are no different from those which are relevant to determining whether or not it is fully a person—i.e., are no different from (1)–(5)—and that being genetically human, or having recognizably human facial and other physical features, or detectable brain activity, or the capacity to survive outside the uterus, are simply not among these relevant attributes.

Thus it is clear that even though a seven- or eight-month fetus has features which make it apt to arouse in us almost the same powerful protective instinct as is commonly aroused by a small infant, nevertheless it is not significantly more personlike than is a very small embryo. It is *somewhat* more personlike; it can apparently feel and respond to pain, and it may even have a rudimentary form of consciousness, insofar as its brain is quite active. Nevertheless, it seems safe to say that it is not fully conscious, in the way that an infant of a few months is, and that it cannot reason, or communicate messages of indefinitely many sorts, does not engage in self-motivated activity, and has no self-awareness. Thus, in the *relevant* respects, a fetus, even a fully developed one, is considerably less personlike than is the average mature mammal, indeed the average fish. And I think that a rational person must conclude that if the right to life of a fetus is to be based upon its resemblance to a person, then it cannot be said to have any more right to life than, let us say, a newborn guppy (which also seems to be capable of feeling pain), and that a right of that magnitude could never override a woman's right to obtain an abortion, at any stage of her pregnancy.

There may, of course, be other arguments in favor of placing legal limits upon the stage of pregnancy in which an abortion may be performed. Given the relative safety of the new techniques of artificially inducing labor during the third trimester, the danger to the woman's life or health is no longer such an argument. Neither is the fact that people tend to respond to the thought of abortion in the later stages of pregnancy with emotional repulsion, since mere emotional responses cannot take the place of moral reasoning in determining what ought to be permitted. Nor, finally, is the frequently heard argument that legalizing abortion, especially late in the pregnancy, may erode the level of respect for human life, leading, perhaps, to an increase in unjustified euthanasia and other crimes. For this threat, if it is a threat, can be better met by educating people to the kinds of moral distinctions which we are making here than by limiting access to abortion (which limitation may, in its disregard for the rights of women, be just as damaging to the level of respect for human rights).

Thus, since the fact that even a fully developed fetus is not personlike enough to have any significant right to life on the basis of its personlikeness shows that no legal restrictions upon the stage of pregnancy in which an abortion may be performed can be justified on the grounds that we should protect the rights of the older fetus, and since there is no other apparent justification for such restrictions, we may conclude that they are entirely unjustified. Whether or not it would be *indecent* (whatever that means) for a woman in her seventh month to obtain an abortion just to avoid having to postpone a trip to Europe, it would not, in itself, be *immoral,* and therefore it ought to be permitted.

4   POTENTIAL PERSONHOOD AND THE RIGHT TO LIFE

We have seen that a fetus does not resemble a person in any way which can support the claim that it has even some of the same rights. But what about its *potential,* the fact that if nurtured and allowed to develop naturally it will very probably become a person? Doesn't that alone give it at least some right to life? It is hard to deny that the fact that an entity is a potential person is a strong prima facie reason for not destroying it; but we need not conclude from this that a potential person has a right to life, by virtue of that potential. It may be that our feeling that it is better, other things being equal, not to destroy a potential person is better explained by the fact that potential people are still (felt to be) an invaluable resource, not to be lightly squandered. Surely, if every speck of dust were a potential person, we would be much less apt to conclude that every potential person has a right to become actual.

Still, we do not need to insist that a potential person has no right to life whatever. There may well be something immoral, and not just imprudent, about wantonly destroying potential people, when doing so isn't necessary to protect anyone's rights. But even if a potential person does have some prima facie right to life, such a right could not possibly outweigh the right of a woman to obtain an abortion, since the rights of any actual person invariably outweigh those of any potential person, whenever the two conflict. Since this may not be immediately obvious in the case of a human fetus, let us look at another case.

Suppose that our space explorer falls into the hands of an alien culture, whose scientists decide to create a few hundred thousand or more human beings, by breaking his body into its component cells, and using these to create fully developed human beings, with, of course, his genetic code. We may imagine that each of these newly created men will have all of the original man's abilities, skills, knowledge, and so on, and also have an individual self-concept, in short that each of them will be a bona fide (though hardly unique) person. Imagine that the whole project will take only seconds, and that its chances of success are extremely high, and that our explorer knows all of this, and also knows that these people will be treated fairly. I maintain that in such a situation he would have every right to escape if he could, and thus to deprive all of these potential people of their potential lives; for his right to life outweighs all of theirs together, in spite of the fact that they are all genetically human, all innocent, and all have a very high probability of becoming people very soon, if only he refrains from acting.

Indeed, I think he would have a right to escape even if it were not his life which the alien scientists planned to take, but only a year of his freedom, or, indeed, only a day. Nor would he be obligated to stay if he had gotten captured (thus bringing all these people-potentials into existence) because of his own carelessness, or even if he had done so deliberately, knowing the consequences. Regardless of how he got captured, he is not morally obligated to remain in captivity for *any* period of time for the sake of permitting any number of potential people to come into actuality, so great is the margin by which one actual person's right to liberty outweighs whatever right to life even a hundred thousand potential people have. And it seems reasonable to conclude that the rights of a woman will outweigh by a similar margin whatever right to life a fetus may have by virtue of its potential personhood.

Thus, neither a fetus's resemblance to a person, nor its potential for becoming a person provides any basis whatever for the claim that it has any significant right to life. Consequently, a woman's right to protect her health, happiness, freedom, and even her life,[5] by terminating an unwanted pregnancy, will always override whatever right to life it may be appropriate to ascribe to a fetus, even a fully developed one.

And thus, in the absence of any overwhelming social need for every possible child, the laws which restrict the right to obtain an abortion, or limit the period of pregnancy during which an abortion may be performed, are a wholly unjustified violation of a woman's most basic moral and constitutional rights.[6]

POSTSCRIPT ON INFANTICIDE

Since the publication of this article, many people have written to point out that my argument appears to justify not only abortion, but infanticide as well. For a newborn infant is not significantly more personlike than an advanced fetus, and consequently it would seem that if the destruction of the latter is permissible so too must be that of the former. Inasmuch as most people, regardless of how they feel about the morality of abortion, consider infanticide a form of murder, this might appear to represent a serious flaw in my argument.

Now, if I am right in holding that it is only people who have a full-fledged right to life, and who can be murdered, and if the criteria of personhood are as I have described them, then it obviously follows that killing a new-born infant isn't murder. It does *not* follow, however, that infanticide is permissible, for two reasons. In the first place, it would be wrong, at least in this country and in this period of history, and other things being equal, to kill a new-born infant, because even if its parents do not want it and would not suffer from its destruction, there are other people who would like to have it, and would, in all probability, be deprived of a great deal of pleasure by its destruction. Thus, infanticide is wrong for reasons analogous to those which make it wrong to wantonly destroy natural resources, or great works of art.

Secondly, most people, at least in this country, value infants and would much prefer that they be preserved, even if foster parents are not immediately available. Most of us would rather be taxed to support orphanages than allow unwanted infants to be destroyed. So long as there are people who want an infant preserved, and who are willing and able to provide the means of caring for it, under reasonably humane conditions, it is *ceteris paribus,* wrong to destroy it.

But, it might be replied, if this argument shows that infanticide is wrong, at least at this time and in this country, doesn't it also show that abortion is wrong? After all, many people value fetuses, are disturbed by their destruction, and would much prefer that they be preserved, even at some cost to themselves. Furthermore, as a potential source of pleasure to some foster family, a fetus is just as valuable as an infant. There is, however, a crucial difference between the two cases: so long as the fetus is unborn, its preservation, contrary to the wishes of the pregnant woman, violates her rights to freedom, happiness, and self-determination. Her rights override the rights of those who would like the fetus preserved, just as if someone's life or limb is threatened by a wild animal, his right to protect himself by destroying the animal overrides the rights of those who would prefer that the animal not be harmed.

The minute the infant is born, however, its preservation no longer violates any of its mother's rights, even if she wants it destroyed, because she is free to put it up for adoption. Consequently, while the moment of birth does not mark any sharp discontinuity in the degree to which an infant possesses the right to life, it does mark the end of its mother's right to determine its fate. Indeed, if abortion could be performed without killing the fetus, she would never possess the right to have the fetus destroyed, for the same reasons that she has no right to have an infant destroyed.

On the other hand, it follows from my argument that when an unwanted or defective infant is born into a society which cannot afford and/or is not willing to care for it, then its destruction is permissible. This conclusion will, no doubt, strike many people as heartless and immoral; but remember that the very existence of people who feel this way, and who are willing and able to provide care for unwanted infants, is reason enough to conclude that they would be preserved.

NOTES

1 Of course, the principle that it is (always) wrong to kill innocent human beings is in need of many other modifications, e.g., that it may be permissible to do so to save a greater number of other innocent human beings, but we may safely ignore these complications here.

2 John Noonan, "Deciding Who is Human," *Natural Law Forum,* 13 (1968), 135.

3 From here on, we will use "human" to mean genetically human, since the moral sense seems closely connected to, and perhaps derived from, the assumption that genetic humanity is sufficient for membership in the moral community.

4 Thomas L. Hayes, "A Biological View," *Commonweal,* 85 (March 17, 1967), 677–78; quoted by Daniel Callahan, in *Abortion: Law, Choice and Morality* (London: Macmillan & Co., 1970).

5 That is, insofar as the death rate, for the woman, is higher for childbirth than for early abortion.

6 My thanks to the following people, who were kind enough to read and criticize an earlier version of this paper: Herbert Gold, Gene Glass, Anne Lauterbach, Judith Thomson, Mary Mothersill, and Timothy Binkley.

QUESTIONS

1 Would you endorse Warren's analysis of the concept of personhood?

2 Does the fetus, even if it is not an *actual* person, have a serious right to life on the grounds that it is a *potential* person?

3 Is a newborn infant a person? In any case, are there any circumstances in which infanticide would be morally permissible?

Abortion and the Concept of a Person

Jane English

Jane English (1947–1978) was a philosopher whose life came to a tragic end, at the age of thirty-one, in a mountain-climbing accident on the Matterhorn. She had taught at the University of North Carolina, Chapel Hill, and had published such articles as "Justice between Generations" and "Sex Equality in Sports." She was also the editor of *Sex Equality* (1977) and the coeditor of *Feminism and Philosophy* (1977).

English begins by arguing that one of the central issues in the abortion debate, whether a fetus is a person, cannot be decisively resolved. However, she contends, whether we presume that the fetus is or is not a person, we must arrive at a moderate stance on the problem of abortion. In an effort to moderate the *conservative* view, English argues that it is unwarranted to conclude, from the presumption that the fetus is a person, that abortion is always morally impermissible. Reasoning on the basis of a self-defense model, she finds abortion morally permissible in many cases. In an effort to moderate the *liberal* view, English argues that it is unwarranted to conclude, from the presumption that the fetus is not a person, that abortion is always morally permissible. Even if the fetus is not a person, she argues, the similarity between a fetus and a baby is sufficient to make abortion problematic in the later stages of pregnancy.

The abortion debate rages on. Yet the two most popular positions seem to be clearly mistaken. Conservatives maintain that a human life begins at conception and that therefore abortion must be wrong because it is murder. But not all killings of humans are murders. Most notably, self defense may justify even the killing of an innocent person.

Liberals, on the other hand, are just as mistaken in their argument that since a fetus does not become a person until birth, a woman may do whatever she pleases in and to her own body. First, you cannot do as you please with your own body if it affects other people adversely.[1] Second, if a fetus is not a person, that does not imply that you can do to it anything you wish. Animals, for example, are not persons, yet to kill or torture them for no reason at all is wrong.

At the center of the storm has been the issue of just when it is between ovulation and adulthood that a person appears on the scene. Conservatives draw the line at conception, liberals at birth. In this paper I first examine our concept of a person and conclude that no single criterion can capture the concept of a person and no sharp line can be drawn. Next I argue that if a fetus is a person, abortion is still justifiable in many cases; and if a fetus is not a person, killing it is still wrong in many cases. To a large extent, these two solutions are in agreement. I conclude that our concept of a person cannot and need not bear the weight that the abortion controversy has thrust upon it.

Reprinted with permission of the publisher from the *Canadian Journal of Philosophy,* vol. 5, no. 2 (October 1975), pp. 233–243.

I

The several factions in the abortion argument have drawn battle lines around various proposed criteria for determining what is and what is not a person. For example, Mary Anne Warren[2] lists five features (capacities for reasoning, self-awareness, complex communication, etc.) as her criteria for personhood and argues for the permissibility of abortion because a fetus falls outside this concept. Baruch Brody[3] uses brain waves. Michael Tooley[4] picks having-a-concept-of-self as his criterion and concludes that infanticide and abortion are justifiable, while the killing of adult animals is not. On the other side, Paul Ramsey[5] claims a certain gene structure is the defining characteristic. John Noonan[6] prefers conceived-of-humans and presents counterexamples to various other candidate criteria. For instance, he argues against viability as the criterion because the newborn and infirm would then be non-persons, since they cannot live without the aid of others. He rejects any criterion that calls upon the sorts of sentiments a being can evoke in adults on the grounds that this would allow us to exclude other races as non-persons if we could just view them sufficiently unsentimentally.

These approaches are typical: foes of abortion propose sufficient conditions for personhood which fetuses satisfy, while friends of abortion counter with necessary conditions for personhood which fetuses lack. But these both presuppose that the concept of a person can be captured in a strait jacket of necessary and/or sufficient conditions.[7] Rather, "person" is a cluster of features, of which rationality, having a self concept and being conceived of humans are only part.

What is typical of persons? Within our concept of a person we include, first, certain biological factors: descended from humans, having a certain genetic makeup, having a head, hands, arms, eyes, capable of locomotion, breathing, eating, sleeping. There are psychological factors: sentience, perception, having a concept of self and of one's own interests and desires, the ability to use tools, the ability to use language or symbol systems, the ability to joke, to be angry, to doubt. There are rationality factors: the ability to reason and draw conclusions, the ability to generalize and to learn from past experience, the ability to sacrifice present interests for greater gains in the future. There are social factors: the ability to work in groups and respond to peer pressures, the ability to recognize and consider as valuable the interests of others, seeing oneself as one among "other minds," the ability to sympathize, encourage, love, the ability to evoke from others the responses of sympathy, encouragement, love, the ability to work with others for mutual advantage. Then there are legal factors: being subject to the law and protected by it, having the ability to sue and enter contracts, being counted in the census, having a name and citizenship, the ability to own property, inherit, and so forth.

Now the point is not that this list is incomplete, or that you can find counterinstances to each of its points. People typically exhibit rationality, for instance, but someone who was irrational would not thereby fail to qualify as a person. On the other hand, something could exhibit the majority of these features and still fail to be a person, as an advanced robot might. There is no single core of necessary and sufficient features which we can draw upon with the assurance that they constitute what really makes a person; there are only features that are more or less typical.

This is not to say that no necessary or sufficient conditions can be given. Being alive is a necessary condition for being a person, and being a U.S. Senator is sufficient. But rather than falling inside a sufficient condition or outside a necessary one, a fetus lies in the penumbra region where our concept of a person is not so simple. For this reason I think a conclusive answer to the question whether a fetus is a person is unattainable.

Here we might note a family of simple fallacies that proceed by stating a necessary condition for personhood and showing that a fetus has that characteristic. This is a form of the fallacy of affirming the consequent. For example, some have mistakenly reasoned from the premise that a fetus is human (after all, it is a human fetus rather than, say, a canine fetus), to the conclusion that it is *a* human. Adding an equivocation on "being," we get the fallacious argument that since a fetus is something both living and human, it is a human being.

Nonetheless, it does seem clear that a fetus has very few of the above family of characteristics, whereas a newborn baby exhibits a much larger proportion of them—and a two-year-old has even more. Note that one traditional anti-abortion argument has centered on pointing out the many ways in which a fetus resembles a baby. They emphasize its development ("It already has ten fingers. . . .") without mentioning its dissimilarities to adults (it still has gills and a tail). They also try to evoke the sort of sympathy on our part that we only feel toward other persons ("Never to laugh . . . or feel the sunshine?"). This all seems to be a relevant way to argue, since its purpose is to persuade us that a fetus satisfies so many of the important features on the list that it ought to be treated as a person. Also note that a fetus near the time of birth satisfies many more of these factors than a fetus in the early months of development. This could provide reason for making distinctions among the different stages of pregnancy, as the U.S. Supreme Court has done.[8]

Historically, the time at which a person has been said to come into existence has varied widely. Muslims date personhood from fourteen days after conception. Some medievals followed Aristotle in placing ensoulment at forty days after conception for a male fetus and eighty days for a female fetus.[9] In European common law since the Seventeenth Century, abortion was considered the killing of a person only after quickening, the time when a pregnant woman first feels the fetus move on its own. Nor is this variety of opinions surprising. Biologically, a human being develops gradually. We shouldn't expect there to be any specific time or sharp dividing point when a person appears on the scene.

For these reasons I believe our concept of a person is not sharp or decisive enough to bear the weight of a solution to the abortion controversy. To use it to solve that problem is to clarify *obscurum per obscurius.*

II

Next let us consider what follows if a fetus is a person after all. Judith Jarvis Thomson's landmark article, "A Defense of Abortion,"[10] correctly points out that some additional argumentation is needed at this point in the conservative argument to bridge the gap between the premise that a fetus is an innocent person and the conclusion that killing it is always wrong. To arrive at this conclusion, we would need the additional premise that killing an innocent person is always wrong. But killing an innocent person is sometimes permissible, most notably in self defense. Some examples may help draw out our intuitions or ordinary judgments about self defense.

Suppose a mad scientist, for instance, hypnotized innocent people to jump out of the bushes and attack innocent passers-by with knives. If you are so attacked, we agree you have a right to kill the attacker in self defense, if killing him is the only way to protect your life or to save yourself from serious injury. It does not seem to matter here that the attacker is not malicious but himself an innocent pawn, for your killing of him is not done in a spirit of retribution but only in self defense.

How severe an injury may you inflict in self defense? In part this depends upon the severity of the injury to be avoided: you may not shoot someone merely to avoid having your clothes torn. This might lead one to the mistaken conclusion that the defense may only equal the threatened injury in severity; that to avoid death you may kill, but to avoid a black eye you may only inflict a black eye or the equivalent. Rather, our laws and customs seem to say that you may create an injury somewhat, but not enormously, greater than the injury to be avoided. To fend off an attack whose outcome would be as serious as rape, a severe beating or the loss of a finger, you may shoot; to avoid having your clothes torn, you may blacken an eye.

Aside from this, the injury you may inflict should only be the minimum necessary to deter or incapacitate the attacker. Even if you know he intends to kill you, you are not justified in shooting him if you could equally well save yourself by the simple expedient of running away. Self defense is for the purpose of avoiding harms rather than equalizing harms.

Some cases of pregnancy present a parallel situation. Though the fetus is itself innocent, it may pose a threat to the pregnant woman's well-being, life prospects or health, mental or physical. If the pregnancy presents a slight threat to her interests, it seems self defense cannot justify abortion. But if the threat is on a par with a serious beating or the loss of a finger, she may kill the fetus that poses such a threat, even if it is an innocent person. If a lesser harm to the fetus could have the same defensive effect, killing it would not be justified. It is unfortunate that the only way to free the woman from the pregnancy entails the death of the fetus (except in very late stages of pregnancy). Thus a self defense model supports Thomson's point that the woman has a right only to be freed from the fetus, not a right to demand its death.[11]

The self defense model is most helpful when we take the pregnant woman's point of view. In the pre-Thomson literature, abortion is often framed as a question for a third party: do you, a doctor, have a right to choose between the life of the woman and that of the fetus? Some have claimed that if you were a passer-by who witnessed a struggle between the innocent hypnotized attacker and his equally innocent victim, you would have no reason to kill either in defense of the other. They have concluded that the self defense model implies that a woman may attempt to abort herself, but that a doctor should not assist her. I think the position of the third party is somewhat more complex. We do feel some inclination to intervene on behalf of the victim rather than the attacker, other things equal. But if both parties are innocent, other factors come into consideration. You would rush to the aid of your husband whether he was attacker or attackee. If a hypnotized famous violinist were attacking a skid row bum, we would try to save the individual who is of more value to society. These considerations would tend to support abortion in some cases.

But suppose you are a frail senior citizen who wishes to avoid being knifed by one of these innocent hypnotics, so you have hired a bodyguard to accompany you. If you are attacked, it is clear we believe that the bodyguard, acting as your agent, has a right to kill the attacker to save you from a serious beating. Your rights of self defense are transferred to your agent. I suggest that we should similarly view the doctor as the pregnant woman's agent in carrying out a defense she is physically incapable of accomplishing herself.

Thanks to modern technology, the cases are rare in which pregnancy poses as clear a threat to a woman's bodily health as an attacker brandishing a switchblade. How does self defense fare when more subtle, complex and long-range harms are involved?

To consider a somewhat fanciful example, suppose you are a highly trained surgeon when you are kidnapped by the hypnotic attacker. He says he does not intend to harm you but to take you back to the mad scientist who, it turns out, plans to hypnotize you to have a permanent mental block against all your knowledge of medicine. This would automatically destroy your career which would in turn have a serious adverse impact on your family, your personal relationships and your happiness. It seems to me that if the only way you can avoid this outcome is to shoot the innocent attacker, you are justified in so doing. You are defending yourself from a drastic injury to your life prospects. I think it is no exaggeration to claim that unwanted pregnancies (most obviously among teenagers) often have such adverse life-long consequences as the surgeon's loss of livelihood.

Several parallels arise between various views on abortion and the self defense model. Let's suppose further that these hypnotized attackers only operate at night, so that it is well known that they can be avoided completely by the considerable inconvenience of never leaving your house after dark. One view is that since you could stay home at night, therefore if you go out and are selected by one of these hypnotized people, you have no right to defend yourself. This parallels the view that abstinence is the only acceptable way to avoid pregnancy. Others might hold that you ought to take along some defense such as Mace which will deter the hypnotized person without killing him, but that if this defense fails, you are obliged to submit to the resulting injury, no matter how severe it is. This parallels the view that contraception is all right but abortion is always wrong, even in cases of contraceptive failure.

A third view is that you may kill the hypnotized person only if he will actually kill you, but not if he will only injure you. This is like the position that abortion is permissible only if it is required to save a woman's life. Finally we have the view that it is all right to kill the attacker, even if only to avoid a very slight inconvenience to yourself and even if you knowingly walked down the very street where all these incidents have been taking place without taking along any Mace or protective escort. If we assume that a fetus is a person, this is the analogue of the view that abortion is always justifiable, "on demand."

The self defense model allows us to see an important difference that exists between abortion and infanticide, even if a fetus is a person from conception. Many have argued that the only way to justify abortion without justifying infanticide would be to find some characteristic of personhood that is acquired at birth. Michael Tooley, for one, claims infanticide is justifiable because the really significant characteristics of person are acquired some time after birth. But all such approaches look to characteristics of the developing human and ignore the relation between the fetus and the woman. What if, after birth, the presence of an infant or the need to support it posed a grave threat to the woman's sanity or life prospects? She could escape this threat by the simple expedient of running away. So a solution that does not entail the death of the infant is available. Before birth, such solutions are not available because of the biological dependence of the fetus on the woman. Birth is the crucial point not because of any characteristics the fetus gains, but because after birth the woman can defend herself by a means less drastic than killing the infant. Hence self defense can be used to justify abortion without necessarily thereby justifying infanticide.

III

On the other hand, supposing a fetus is not after all a person, would abortion always be morally permissible? Some opponents of abortion seem worried that if a fetus is not a full-fledged person, then we are justified in treating it in any way at all. However, this does not follow. Non-persons do get some consideration in our moral code, though of course they do not have the same rights as persons have (and in general they do not have moral responsibilities), and though their interests may be overridden by the interests of persons. Still, we cannot just treat them in any way at all.

Treatment of animals is a case in point. It is wrong to torture dogs for fun or to kill wild birds for no reason at all. It is wrong Period, even though dogs and birds do not have the same rights persons do. However, few people think it is wrong to use dogs as experimental animals, causing them considerable suffering in some cases, provided that the resulting research will probably bring discoveries of great benefit to people. And most of us think it all right to kill birds for food or to protect our crops. People's rights are different from the consideration we give to animals, then, for it is wrong to experiment on people, even if others might later benefit a great deal as a result of their suffering. You might volunteer to be a subject, but this would be supererogatory; you certainly have a right to refuse to be a medical guinea pig.

But how do we decide what you may or may not do to non-persons? This is a difficult problem, one for which I believe no adequate account exists. You do not want to say, for instance, that torturing dogs is all right whenever the sum of its effects on people is good—when it doesn't warp the sensibilities of the torturer so much that he mistreats people. If that were the case, it would be all right to torture dogs if you did it in private, or if the torturer lived on a desert island or died soon afterward, so that his actions had no effect on people. This is an inadequate account, because whatever moral consideration animals get, it has to be indefeasible, too. It will have to be a general proscription of certain actions, not merely a weighing of the impact on people on a case-by-case basis.

Rather, we need to distinguish two levels on which consequences of actions can be taken into account in moral reasoning. The traditional objections to Utilitarianism focus on the fact that it operates solely on the first level, taking all the consequences into account in particular cases only. Thus Utilitarianism is open to "desert island" and "lifeboat" counterexamples because these cases are rigged to make the consequences of actions severely limited.

Rawls' theory could be described as a teleological sort of theory, but with teleology operating on a higher level.[12] In choosing the principles to regulate society from the original position, his hypothetical choosers make their decision on the basis of the total consequences of various systems. Furthermore, they are constrained to choose a general set of rules which people can readily learn and apply. An ethical theory must operate by generating a set of sympathies and attitudes toward others which reinforces the functioning of that set of moral principles. Our prohibition against killing people operates by means of certain moral sentiments including sympathy, compassion and guilt. But if these attitudes are to form a coherent set, they carry us further: we tend to perform supererogatory actions, and we tend to feel similar compassion toward person-like non-persons.

It is crucial that psychological facts play a role here. Our psychological constitution makes it the case that for our ethical theory to work, it must prohibit certain treatment of non-persons which are significantly person-like. If our moral rules allowed people to treat some person-like non-persons in ways we do not want people to be treated, this would undermine the system of sympathies and attitudes that makes the ethical system work. For this reason, we would choose in the original position to make mistreatment of some sorts of animals wrong in general (not just wrong in the cases with public impact), even though animals are not themselves parties in the original position. Thus it makes sense that it is those animals whose appearance and behavior are most like those of people that get the most consideration in our moral scheme.

It is because of "coherence of attitudes," I think, that the similarity of a fetus to a baby is very significant. A fetus one week before birth is so much like a newborn baby in our psychological space that we cannot allow any cavalier treatment of the former while expecting full sympathy and nurturative support for the latter. Thus, I think that anti-abortion forces are indeed giving their strongest arguments when they point to the similarities between a fetus and a baby, and when they try to evoke our emotional attachment to and sympathy for the fetus. An early horror story from New York about nurses who were expected to alternate between caring for six-week premature infants and disposing of viable 24-week aborted fetuses is just that—a horror story. These beings are so much alike that no one can be asked to draw a distinction and treat them so very differently.

Remember, however, that in the early weeks after conception, a fetus is very much unlike a person. It is hard to develop these feelings for a set of genes which doesn't yet have a head, hands, beating heart, response to touch or the ability to move by itself. Thus it seems to me that the alleged "slippery slope" between conception and birth is not so very slippery. In the early stages of pregnancy, abortion can hardly be compared to murder for psychological reasons, but in the latest stages it is psychologically akin to murder.

Another source of similarity is the bodily continuity between fetus and adult. Bodies play a surprisingly central role in our attitudes toward persons. One has only to think of the philosophical literature on how far physical identity suffices for personal identity or Wittgenstein's remark that the best picture of the human soul is the human body. Even after death, when all agree the body is no longer a person, we still observe elaborate customs of respect for the human body; like people who torture dogs, necrophiliacs are not to be trusted with people.[13] So it is appropriate that we show respect to a fetus as the body continuous with the body of a person. This is a degree of resemblance to persons that animals cannot rival.

Michael Tooley also utilizes a parallel with animals. He claims that it is always permissible to drown newborn kittens and draws conclusions about infanticide.[14] But it is only permissible to drown kittens when their survival would cause some hardship. Perhaps it would be a burden to feed and house six more cats or to find other homes for them. The alternative of letting them starve produces even more suffering than the drowning. Since the kittens get their rights second-hand, so to speak, *via* the need for coherence in our attitudes, their interests are often overridden by the interests of full-fledged persons. But if their survival would be no inconvenience to people at all, then it is wrong to drown them, *contra* Tooley.

Tooley's conclusions about abortion are wrong for the same reason. Even if a fetus is not a person, abortion is not always permissible, because of the resemblance of a fetus to a person. I agree with Thomson that it would be wrong for a woman who is seven months pregnant to have an abortion just to avoid having to postpone a trip to Europe. In the early months of pregnancy when the fetus hardly resembles a baby at all, then, abortion is permissible whenever it is in the interests of the pregnant woman or her family. The reasons would only need to outweigh the pain and inconvenience of the abortion itself. In the middle months, when the fetus comes to resemble a person, abortion would be justifiable only when the continuation of the pregnancy or the birth of the child would cause harms—physical, psychological, economic or social—to the woman. In the late months of pregnancy, even on our current assumption that a fetus is not a person, abortion seems to be wrong except to save a woman from significant injury or death.

The Supreme Court has recognized similar gradations in the alleged slippery slope stretching between conception and birth. To this point, the present paper has been a discussion of the moral status of abortion only, not its legal status. In view of the great physical, financial and sometimes psychological costs of abortion, perhaps the legal arrangement most compatible with the proposed moral solution would be the absence of restrictions, that is, so-called abortion "on demand."

So I conclude, first, that application of our concept of a person will not suffice to settle the abortion issue. After all, the biological development of a human being is gradual. Second, whether a fetus is a person or not, abortion is justifiable early in pregnancy to avoid modest harms and seldom justifiable late in pregnancy except to avoid significant injury or death.[15]

NOTES

1 We also have paternalistic laws which keep us from harming our own bodies even when no one else is affected. Ironically, antiabortion laws were originally designed to protect pregnant women from a dangerous but tempting procedure.

2 Mary Anne Warren, "On the Moral and Legal Status of Abortion," *Monist 57* (1973), p. 55.

3 Baruch Brody, "Fetal Humanity and the Theory of Essentialism," in Robert Baker and Frederick Elliston, eds., *Philosophy and Sex* (Buffalo, N.Y., 1975).

4 Michael Tooley, "Abortion and Infanticide," *Philosophy and Public Affairs* 2 (1971).

5 Paul Ramsey, "The Morality of Abortion," in James Rachels, ed., *Moral Problems* (New York, 1971).

6 John Noonan, "Abortion and the Catholic Church: A Summary History," *Natural Law Forum* 12 (1967), pp. 125–131.

7 Wittgenstein has argued against the possibility of so capturing the concept of a game, *Philosophical Investigations* (New York, 1958), §66–71.

8 Not because the fetus is partly a person and so has some of the rights of persons, but rather because of the rights of person-like non-persons. This I discuss in part III below.

9 Aristotle himself was concerned, however, with the different question of when the soul takes form. For historical data, see Jimmye Kimmey, "How the Abortion Laws Happened," *Ms.* 1 (April, 1973), pp. 48ff, and John Noonan, *loc. cit.*

10 J. J. Thomson, "A Defense of Abortion," *Philosophy and Public Affairs* 1 (1971).

11 *Ibid.,* p. 52.

12 John Rawls, *A Theory of Justice* (Cambridge, Mass., 1971), §3–4.

13 On the other hand, if they can be trusted with people, then our moral customs are mistaken. It all depends on the facts of psychology.

14 *Op. cit.,* pp. 40, 60–61.

15 I am deeply indebted to Larry Crocker and Arthur Kuflik for their constructive comments.

QUESTIONS

1 Is English successful in her effort to moderate both the conservative view and the liberal view on abortion?

2 Is the following a justifiable criticism? In moderating the conservative view, English winds up with a rather "conservative" moderate view, whereas in moderating the liberal view, she winds up with a rather "liberal" moderate view. Therefore, she is not successful in showing that the problem of abortion can be effectively resolved without first establishing whether or not the fetus is a person.

Why Abortion Is Immoral

Don Marquis

Don Marquis is professor of philosophy at the University of Kansas. He specializes in applied ethics and medical ethics. His published articles include "Leaving Therapy to Chance," "An Argument that All Prerandomized Clinical Trials Are Unethical," and "Harming the Dead."

Marquis argues that abortion, with rare exceptions, is seriously immoral. He bases this conclusion on a theory that he presents and defends about the wrongness of killing. In his view, killing another adult human being is wrong precisely because the victim is deprived of all the value—"activities, projects, experiences, and enjoyments"—of his or her future. Since abortion deprives a typical fetus of a "future like ours," he contends, the moral presumption against abortion is as strong as the presumption against killing another adult human being.

The view that abortion is, with rare exceptions, seriously immoral has received little support in the recent philosophical literature. No doubt most philosophers affiliated with secular institutions of higher education believe that the anti-abortion position is either a symptom of irrational religious dogma or a conclusion generated by seriously confused philosophical argument. The purpose of this essay is to undermine this general belief. This essay sets out an argument that purports to show, as well as any argument in ethics can show, that abortion is, except possibly in rare cases, seriously immoral, that it is in the same moral category as killing an innocent adult human being.

This argument is based on a major assumption: If fetuses are in the same category as adult human beings with respect to the moral value of their lives, then the *presumption* that any particular abortion is immoral is exceedingly strong. Such a presumption could be overridden only by considerations more compelling than a woman's right to privacy. The defense of this assumption is beyond the scope of this essay.[1]

Furthermore, this essay will neglect a discussion of whether there are any such compelling considerations and what they are. Plainly there are strong candidates: abortion before implantation, abortion when the life of a woman is threatened by a pregnancy or abortion after rape. The casuistry of these hard cases will not be explored in this essay. The purpose of this essay is to develop a general argument for the claim that, subject to the assumption above, the overwhelming majority of deliberate abortions are seriously immoral. . . .

. . . A necessary condition of resolving the abortion controversy is a . . . theoretical account of the wrongness of killing. After all, if we merely believe, but do not understand, why killing adult human beings such as ourselves is wrong, how could we conceivably show that abortion is either immoral or permissible? . . .

Reprinted, as slightly modified by the author, with permission of the author and the publisher from the *Journal of Philosophy*, vol. 86 (April 1989).

In order to develop such an account, we can start from the following unproblematic assumption concerning our own case: it is wrong to kill *us*. Why is it wrong? Some answers can be easily eliminated. It might be said that what makes killing us wrong is that a killing brutalizes the one who kills. But the brutalization consists of being inured to the performance of an act that is hideously immoral; hence, the brutalization does not explain the immorality. It might be said that what makes killing us wrong is the great loss others would experience due to our absence. Although such hubris is understandable, such an explanation does not account for the wrongness of killing hermits, or those whose lives are relatively independent and whose friends find it easy to make new friends.

A more obvious answer is better. What primarily makes killing wrong is neither its effect on the murderer nor its effect on the victim's friends and relatives, but its effect on the victim. The loss of one's life is one of the greatest losses one can suffer. The loss of one's life deprives one of all the experiences, activities, projects, and enjoyments that would otherwise have constituted one's future. Therefore, killing someone is wrong, primarily because the killing inflicts (one of) the greatest possible losses on the victim. To describe this as the loss of life can be misleading, however. The change in my biological state does not by itself make killing me wrong. The effect of the loss of my biological life is the loss to me of all those activities, projects, experiences, and enjoyments which would otherwise have constituted my future personal life. These activities, projects, experiences, and enjoyments are either valuable for their own sakes or are means to something else that is valuable for its own sake. Some parts of my future are not valued by me now, but will come to be valued by me as I grow older and as my values and capacities change. When I am killed, I am deprived both of what I now value which would have been part of my future personal life, but also what I would come to value. Therefore, when I die, I am deprived of all of the value of my future. Inflicting this loss on me is ultimately what makes killing me wrong. This being the case, it would seem that what makes killing *any* adult human being prima facie seriously wrong is the loss of his or her future.[2]

How should this rudimentary theory of the wrongness of killing be evaluated? It cannot be faulted for deriving an 'ought' from an 'is', for it does not. The analysis assumes that killing me (or you, reader) is prima facie seriously wrong. The point of the analysis is to establish which natural property ultimately explains the wrongness of the killing, given that it is wrong. A natural property will ultimately explain the wrongness of killing, only if (1) the explanation fits with our intuitions about the matter and (2) there is no other natural property that provides the basis for a better explanation of the wrongness of killing. This analysis rests on the intuition that what makes killing a particular human or animal wrong is what it does to that particular human or animal. What makes killing wrong is some natural effect or other of the killing. Some would deny this. For instance, a divine-command theorist in ethics would deny it. Surely this denial is, however, one of those features of divine–command theory which renders it so implausible.

The claim that what makes killing wrong is the loss of the victim's future is directly supported by two considerations. In the first place, this theory explains why we regard killing as one of the worst of crimes. Killing is especially wrong, because it deprives the victim of more than perhaps any other crime. In the second place, people with AIDS or cancer who know they are dying believe, of course, that dying is a very bad thing for them. They believe that the loss of a future to them that they would otherwise have experienced is what makes their premature death a very bad thing for them. A better theory of the wrongness of killing would require a different natural property associated with killing which better fits with the attitudes of the dying. What could it be?

The view that what makes killing wrong is the loss to the victim of the value of the victim's future gains additional support when some of its implications are examined. In the first place, it is incompatible with the view that it is wrong to kill only beings who are biologically human. It is possible that there exists a different species from another planet whose members have a future like ours. Since having a future like that is what makes killing someone wrong, this theory entails that it would be wrong to kill members of such a species. Hence, this theory is opposed to the claim that only life that is biologically human has great moral worth, a claim which many anti-abortionists have seemed to adopt. This opposition, which this theory has in common with personhood theories, seems to be a merit of the theory.

In the second place, the claim that the loss of one's future is the wrong-making feature of one's being killed entails the possibility that the futures of some actual nonhuman mammals on our own planet are sufficiently like ours that it is seriously wrong to kill them also. Whether some animals do have the same right to life as human beings depends on adding to the account of the wrongness of killing some additional account of just what it is about my future or the futures of other adult human beings which makes it wrong to kill us. No such additional account will be offered in this essay. Undoubtedly, the provision of such an account would be a very difficult matter. Undoubtedly, any such account would be quite controversial. Hence, it surely should not reflect badly on this sketch of an elementary theory of the wrongness of killing that it is indeterminate with respect to some very difficult issues regarding animal rights.

In the third place, the claim that the loss of one's future is the wrong-making feature of one's being killed does not entail, as sanctity of human life theories do, that active euthanasia is wrong. Persons who are severely and incurably ill, who face a future of pain and despair, and who wish to die will not have suffered a loss if they are killed. It is, strictly speaking, the value of a human's future which makes killing wrong in this theory. This being so, killing does not necessarily wrong some persons who are sick and dying. Of course, there may be other reasons for a prohibition of active euthanasia, but that is another matter. Sanctity-of-human-life theories seem to hold that active euthanasia is seriously wrong even in an individual case where there seems to be good reason for it independently of public policy considerations. This consequence is most implausible, and it is a plus for the claim that the loss of a future of value is what makes killing wrong that it does not share this consequence.

In the fourth place, the account of the wrongness of killing defended in this essay does straightforwardly entail that it is prima facie seriously wrong to kill children and infants, for we do presume that they have futures of value. Since we do believe that it is wrong to kill defenseless little babies, it is important that a theory of the wrongness of killing easily account for this. Personhood theories of the wrongness of killing, on the other hand, cannot straightforwardly account for the wrongness of killing infants and young children. Hence, such theories must add special ad hoc accounts of the wrongness of killing the young. The plausibility of such ad hoc theories seems to be a function of how desperately one wants such theories to work. The claim that the primary wrong-making feature of a killing is the loss to the victim of the value of its future accounts for the wrongness of killing young children and infants directly; it makes the wrongness of such acts as obvious as we actually think it is. This is a further merit of this theory. Accordingly, it seems that this value of a future-like-ours theory of the wrongness of killing shares strengths of both sanctity-of-life and personhood accounts while avoiding weaknesses of both. In addition, it meshes with a central intuition concerning what makes killing wrong.

The claim that the primary wrong-making feature of a killing is the loss to the victim of the value of its future has obvious consequences for the ethics of abortion. The future of a standard fetus includes a set of experiences, projects, activities, and such which are identical with the futures of adult human beings and are identical with the futures of young children. Since the reason that is sufficient to explain why it is wrong to kill human beings after the time of birth is a reason that also applies to fetuses, it follows that abortion is prima facie seriously morally wrong.

This argument does not rely on the invalid inference that, since it is wrong to kill persons, it is wrong to kill potential persons also. The category that is morally central to this analysis is the category of having a valuable future like ours; it is not the category of personhood. The argument to the conclusion that abortion is prima facie seriously morally wrong proceeded independently of the notion of person or potential person or any equivalent. Someone may wish to start with this analysis in terms of the value of a human future, conclude that abortion is, except perhaps in rare circumstances, seriously morally wrong, infer that fetuses have the right to life, and then call fetuses "persons" as a result of their having the right to life. Clearly, in this case, the category of person is being used to state the *conclusion* of the analysis rather than to generate the *argument* of the analysis.

The structure of this anti-abortion argument can be both illuminated and defended by comparing it to what appears to be the best argument for the wrongness of the wanton infliction of pain on animals. This latter argument is based on the assumption that it is prima facie wrong to inflict pain on me (or you, reader). What is the natural property associated with the infliction of pain which makes such infliction wrong? The obvious answer seems to be that the infliction of pain causes suffering and that suffering is a misfortune. The suffering caused by the infliction of pain is what makes the wanton infliction of pain on me wrong. The wanton infliction of pain on other adult humans causes suffering. The wanton infliction of pain on animals causes suffering. Since causing suffering is what makes the wanton infliction of pain wrong and since the wanton infliction of pain on animals causes suffering, it follows that the wanton infliction of pain on animals is wrong.

This argument for the wrongness of the wanton infliction of pain on animals shares a number of structural features with the argument for the serious prima facie wrongness of abortion. Both arguments start with an obvious assumption concerning what it is wrong to do to me (or you, reader). Both then look for the characteristic or the consequence of the wrong action which makes the action wrong. Both recognize that the wrong-making feature of these immoral actions is a property of actions sometimes directed at individuals other than postnatal human beings. If the structure of the argument for the wrongness of the wanton infliction of pain on animals is sound, then the structure of the argument for the prima facie serious wrongness of abortion is also sound, for the structure of the two arguments is the same. The structure common to both is the key to the explanation of how the wrongness of abortion can be demonstrated without recourse to the category of person. In neither argument is that category crucial. . . .

Of course, this value of a future-like-ours argument, if sound, shows only that abortion is prima facie wrong, not that it is wrong in any and all circumstances. Since the loss of the future to a standard fetus, if killed, is, however, at least as great a loss as the loss of the future to a standard adult human being who is killed, abortion, like ordinary killing, could be justified only by the most compelling reasons. The loss of one's life is almost the greatest misfortune that can happen to one. Presumably abortion could be justified in some circumstances, only if the loss consequent on failing to abort would be at least as great. Accordingly, morally permissible abortions will be rare indeed unless, perhaps, they occur so early in pregnancy that a fetus is not yet definitely an individual. Hence, this argument should be taken as showing that abortion is presumptively very seriously wrong, where the presumption is very strong—as strong as the presumption that killing another adult human being is wrong. . . .

In this essay, it has been argued that the correct ethic of the wrongness of killing can be extended to fetal life and used to show that there is a strong presumption that any abortion is morally impermissible. If the ethic of killing adopted here entails, however, that contraception is also seriously immoral, then there would appear to be a difficulty with the analysis of this essay.

But this analysis does not entail that contraception is wrong. Of course, contraception prevents the actualization of a possible future of value. Hence, it follows from the claim that futures of value should be maximized that contraception is prima facie immoral. This obligation to maximize does not exist, however; furthermore, nothing in the ethics of killing in this paper entails that it does. The ethics of killing in this essay would entail that contraception is wrong only if something were denied a human future of value by contraception. Nothing at all is denied such a future by contraception, however.

Candidates for a subject of harm by contraception fall into four categories: (1) some sperm or other, (2) some ovum or other, (3) a sperm and an ovum separately, and (4) a sperm and an ovum together. Assigning the harm to some sperm is utterly arbitrary, for no reason can be given for making a sperm the subject of harm rather than an ovum. Assigning the harm to some ovum is utterly arbitrary, for no reason can be given for making an ovum the subject of harm rather than a sperm. One might attempt to avoid these problems by insisting that contraception deprives both the sperm and the ovum separately of a valuable future like ours. On this alternative, too many futures are lost. Contraception was supposed to be wrong, because it deprived us of one future of value, not two. One might attempt to avoid this problem by holding that contraception deprives the combination of sperm and ovum of a valuable future like ours. But here the definite article misleads. At the time of contraception, there are hundreds of millions of sperm, one (released) ovum and millions of possible combinations of all of these. There is no actual combination at all. Is the subject of the loss to be a merely possible combination? Which one? This alternative does not yield an actual subject of harm either. Accordingly, the immorality of contraception is not entailed by the loss of a future-like-ours argument simply because there is no nonarbitrarily identifiable subject of the loss in the case of contraception. . . .

The purpose of this essay has been to set out an argument for the serious presumptive wrongness of abortion subject to the assumption that the moral permissibility of abortion stands or falls on the moral status of the fetus. Since a fetus possesses a property, the possession of which in adult human beings is sufficient to make killing an adult human being wrong, abortion is wrong. This way of dealing with the problem of abortion seems superior to other approaches to the ethics of abortion, because it rests on an ethics of killing which is close to self-evident, because the crucial morally relevant property clearly applies to fetuses, and because the argument avoids the usual equivocations on 'human life', 'human being', or 'person'. The argument rests neither on religious claims nor on Papal dogma. It is not subject to the objection of "speciesism." Its soundness is compatible with the moral permissibility of euthanasia and contraception. It deals with our intuitions concerning young children.

Finally, this analysis can be viewed as resolving a standard problem—indeed, *the* standard problem—concerning the ethics of abortion. Clearly, it is wrong to kill adult human beings. Clearly, it is not wrong to end the life of some arbitrarily chosen single human cell. Fetuses seem to be like arbitrarily chosen human cells in some respects and like adult humans in other respects. The problem of the ethics of abortion is the problem of determining the fetal property that settles this moral controversy. The thesis of this essay is that the problem of the ethics of abortion, so understood, is solvable.

NOTES

1 Judith Jarvis Thomson has rejected this assumption in a famous essay, "A Defense of Abortion," *Philosophy and Public Affairs* 1, #1 (1971), 47–66.

2 I have been most influenced on this matter by Jonathan Glover, *Causing Death and Saving Lives* (New York: Penguin, 1977), ch. 3; and Robert Young, "What Is So Wrong with Killing People?" *Philosophy,* LIV, 210 (1979): 515–528.

QUESTIONS

1 If the wrongness of killing derives from the fact that the victim is deprived of the value of his or her future, does it follow that it is less wrong to kill someone fifty years old than it is

to kill someone twenty years old? If so, does this implication suggest that there is some deficiency in Marquis's theory about the wrongness of killing?

2 Does Marquis provide a satisfactory response to the possible objection that his theory about the wrongness of killing implies that contraception is morally wrong?

3 If Marquis's basic approach is accepted, which abortions could still be considered morally justified?

Abortion: A Moderate View

L. W. Sumner

L. W. Sumner is professor of philosophy at the University of Toronto. He is the author of *Abortion and Moral Theory* (1981) and *The Moral Foundation of Rights* (1987). His published articles include "The Good and the Right," "Rights Denaturalized," and "Animal Welfare and Animal Rights."

The moderate view advanced by Sumner is based on his contention that the developing fetus gains moral standing (status) when it becomes *sentient,* that is, capable of feeling pleasure and pain. He provisionally locates this "threshold" somewhere in the second trimester and draws a fundamental distinction between prethreshold and postthreshold abortions. In his view, prethreshold abortions are morally unproblematic whereas postthreshold abortions are "morally equivalent to the decision to commit infanticide." He insists, however, that even postthreshold abortions can be justified for what he calls "therapeutic" and "eugenic" reasons. Sumner also outlines and argues for a moderate social policy on abortion.

. . . Let us say that a being has *moral standing* if it merits moral consideration in its own right and not just in virtue of its relations with other beings. To have moral standing is to be more than a mere thing or item of property. What, more precisely, moral standing consists in can be given different interpretations; thus, it might be the possession of some set of basic moral rights, or the requirement that one be treated as an end and not merely as a means, or the inclusion of one's interest in a calculus of social welfare. However it is interpreted, whether a being is accorded moral standing must make a great difference in the way in which we take that being into account in our moral thinking. Whether a fetus is accorded moral standing must therefore make a great difference in the way in which we think about abortion. An account of the moral status of abortion must be supported by an account of the moral status of the fetus.

There is also a political question concerning abortion to which we need an answer. Every society must decide how, if at all, it will regulate the practice of abortion. . . .

THE ESTABLISHED VIEWS

. . . The abortion debate in most of the Western democracies has been dominated by two positions that are so well entrenched that they may be called the established views. The liberal view supports what is popularly known as the "pro-choice" position on abortion. At its heart is the contention that the fetus at every stage of pregnancy has no moral standing. From this premise it follows that although abortion kills the fetus it does not wrong it, since a being with no moral standing cannot be wronged. Abortion at all stages of pregnancy lacks a victim; circumstantial differences aside, it is the moral equivalent of contraception. The decision to seek an abortion, therefore, can properly be left to a woman's discretion. There is as little justification for legal regulation of abortion as there is for such regulation of contraception. The only defensible abortion policy is a permissive policy. The conservative view, however, supports what is popularly known as the "pro-life" position on abortion. At its heart is the contention that the fetus at every stage of pregnancy has full moral standing—the same status as an adult human being. From this premise it follows that because abortion kills the fetus it also wrongs it. Abortion at all stages of pregnancy has a victim; circumstantial differences aside, it is the moral equivalent of infanticide (and of other forms of homicide as well). The decision to seek an abortion, therefore, cannot properly be left to a woman's discretion. There is as much justification for legal regulation of abortion as there is for such regulation of infanticide. The only defensible abortion policy is a restrictive policy.

. . . We should note an important feature that [these views] share. On the substantive issue that is at the heart of the matter, liberals and conservatives occupy positions that are logical contraries, the latter holding that all fetuses have standing and the former that none do. Although contrary positions cannot both be true, they can both be false. From a logical point of view, it is open to someone to hold that some fetuses have standing while others do not. Thus while the established views occupy the opposite extremes along the spectrum of possible positions on this issue, there is a logical space between them. This logical space reflects the fact that each of the established views offers a *uniform* account of the moral status of the fetus—each, that is, holds that all fetuses have the same status, regardless of any respects in which they might differ. The most obvious respect in which fetuses can differ is in their gestational age and thus their level of development. During the normal course of pregnancy, a fetus gradually evolves from a tiny one-celled organism into a medium-sized and highly complex organism consisting of some six million differentiated cells. Both of the established views are committed to holding that all of the beings at all stages of this transition have precisely the same moral status. The gestational age of the fetus at the time of abortion is thus morally irrelevant on both views. So also is the reason for the abortion. This is irrelevant on the liberal view because no reason is necessary to justify abortion at any stage of pregnancy and equally irrelevant on the conservative view because no reason is sufficient to do so. The established views, therefore, despite their differences, agree on two very important matters: the moral irrelevance of both when and why an abortion is performed.

This agreement places the established views at odds with both common practice and common opinion in most of the Western democracies. A moderate abortion policy regulates abortion either by imposing a time limit or by stipulating recognized grounds (or both). The abortion policies of virtually all of the Western democracies (and many other countries as well) now contain one or both of these constraints. But neither of the established views can provide any support for a moderate policy. Further, in countries with moderate policies there generally exists a broad public consensus supporting such policies. Opinion polls typically disclose majority agreement on the relevance both of the timing of an abortion and of the grounds for it. On the question of timing there is widespread agreement that early abortions are less problematic than late ones. Abortion may be induced within the first two weeks following conception by an intrauterine device or a "morning after" pill, both of which will prevent the implantation of a blastocyst. Most people seem to find nothing objectionable in the use of these abortifacients. At the opposite extreme, abortion may be induced during the sixth month of pregnancy (or even later) by saline injection or hysterotomy. Most people seem to have some qualms about the use of these techniques at such an advanced stage of pregnancy. On the question of grounds there is widespread agreement that some grounds are less problematic than others. The grounds commonly cited for abortion may be conveniently divided into four categories: therapeutic (risk to the life or health of the mother), eugenic (risk of fetal deformity), humanitarian (pregnancy resulting from the commission of some crime, such as rape or incest), and socioeconomic (e.g., poverty, desertion, family size). Popular support for abortion on therapeutic grounds tends to be virtually unanimous (especially when the risk is particularly serious), but this unanimity gradually diminishes as we move through the other categories until opinion is about evenly divided concerning socioeconomic grounds. Whatever the detailed breakdown of opinion on these issues, there is a widely shared conviction that it does matter both when and why an abortion is performed. Since these are the very factors whose relevance is denied by both of the established views, there is a serious gap between those views and current public opinion.

The existence of this gap is not in itself a reason for rejecting either of the established views. The majority may simply be mistaken on these issues, and the dominance of moderate policies may reflect nothing more than the fact that they are attractive political compromises when the public debate has been polarized by the established views. Neither political practice nor public opinion can provide a justification for a moderate view of abortion or a moderate abortion policy. But the gap does provide us with a motive for exploring the logical space between the established views a little more carefully. . . .

A MODERATE VIEW

. . . There are various obstacles in the path of developing a moderate view of abortion. For one thing, any such view will lack the appealing simplicity of the established views. Both liberals and conservatives begin by adopting a simple account of the moral status of the fetus and end by supporting a simple abortion policy. A moderate account of the moral status of the fetus and a moderate abortion policy will inevitably be more complex. Further, a moderate account of the moral status of the fetus, whatever its precise shape, will draw a boundary between those fetuses that have moral standing and those that do not. It will then have to show that the location of this boundary is not arbitrary. Finally, a moderate view may seem nothing more than a compromise between the more extreme positions that lacks any independent rationale of its own.

These obstacles may, however, be less formidable than they appear. Although the complexity of a moderate view may render it harder to sell in the marketplace of ideas, it may otherwise be its greatest asset. It should be obvious by now that the moral issues raised by the peculiar nature of the fetus, and its peculiar relationship with its mother, are not simple. It would be surprising therefore if a simple resolution of them were satisfactory. The richer resources of a complex view may enable it to avoid some of the less palatable implications of its simpler rivals. The problem of locating a nonarbitrary threshold is easier to deal with when we recognize that there can be no sharp breakpoint in the course of human development at which moral standing is suddenly acquired. The attempt to define such a breakpoint [is] the fatal mistake of the naive versions of the liberal and conservative views. If, as seems likely, an acceptable criterion of moral standing is built around some characteristic that is acquired gradually during the normal course of human development, then moral standing will also be acquired gradually during the normal course of human development. In that case, the boundary between those beings that have moral standing and those that do not will be soft and slow rather than hard and fast. The more sophisticated and credible versions of the established views also pick out stages of development rather than precise breakpoints as their thresholds of moral standing; the only innovation of a moderate view is to locate this stage somewhere during pregnancy. The real challenge to a moderate view, therefore, is to show that it can be well grounded, and thus that it is not simply a way of splitting the difference between two equally unattractive options.

[A] critique of the established views [can equip] us with specifications for the design of a moderate alternative to them. The fundamental flaw of the established views [is] their adoption of a uniform account of the moral status of the fetus. A moderate view of abortion must therefore be built on a *differential* account of the moral status of the fetus, awarding moral standing to some fetuses and withholding it from others. The further defects of the established views impose three constraints on the shape of such a differential account. It must explain the moral relevance of the gestational age of the fetus at the time of abortion and thus must correlate moral status with level of fetal development. It must also explain the moral relevance, at least at some stages of pregnancy, of the reason for which an abortion is performed. And finally it must preserve the distinction between the moral innocuousness of contraception and the moral seriousness of infanticide. When we combine these specifications, we obtain the rough outline of a moderate view. Such a view will identify the stage of pregnancy during which the fetus gains moral standing. Before that threshold, abortion will be as morally innocuous as contraception and no grounds will be needed to justify it. After the threshold, abortion will be as morally serious as infanticide and some special grounds will be needed to justify it (if it can be justified at this stage at all).

A moderate view is well grounded when it is derivable from an independently plausible criterion of moral standing. It is not difficult to construct a criterion that will yield a threshold somewhere during pregnancy.[1] Let us say that a being is sentient when it has the capacity to experience pleasure and pain and thus the capacity for enjoyment and suffering. Beings that are self-conscious or rational are generally (though perhaps not necessarily) also sentient, but many sentient beings lack both self-consciousness and rationality. A sentience criterion of moral standing thus sets a lower standard than that shared by the established views. Such a criterion will accord moral standing to the mentally handicapped regardless of impairments of their cognitive capacities. It will also accord moral standing to many, perhaps most, nonhuman animals.

The plausibility of a sentience criterion would be partially established by tracing out its implications for moral contexts other than abortion. But it would be considerably enhanced if such a criterion could also be given a deeper grounding. Such a grounding can be supplied by what seems a reasonable conception of the nature of morality. The moral point of view is just one among many evaluative points of view. It appears to be distinguished from the others in two respects: its special concern for the interest, welfare, or well-being of creatures and its requirement of impartiality. Adopting the moral point of view requires in one way or another according equal consideration to the interests of all beings. If this is so, then a being's having an interest to be considered is both necessary and sufficient for its having moral standing. While the notion of interest or welfare is far from transparent, its irreducible core appears to be the capacity for enjoyment and suffering: all and only beings with this capacity have an interest or welfare that the moral point of view requires us to respect. But then it follows easily that sentience is both necessary and sufficient for moral standing. . . .

When we apply a sentience criterion to the course of human development, it yields the result that the threshold of moral standing is the stage during which the capacity to experience pleasure and pain is first required. This capacity is clearly possessed by a newborn infant (and a full-term fetus) and is clearly not possessed by a pair of gametes (or a newly fertilized ovum). It is therefore acquired during the normal course of gestation. But when? A definite answer awaits a better understanding than we now possess of the development of the fetal nervous system and thus of fetal consciousness. We can, however, venture a provisional answer. It is standard practice to divide the normal course of gestation into three trimesters of thirteen weeks each. It is likely that a fetus is unable to feel pleasure or pain at the beginning of the second trimester and likely that it is able to do so at the end of that trimester. If this is so, then the threshold of sentience, and thus also the threshold of moral standing, occurs sometime during the second trimester.

We can now fill in our earlier sketch of a moderate view of abortion. A fetus acquires moral standing when it acquires sentience, that is to say at some stage in the second trimester of pregnancy. Before that threshold, when the fetus lacks moral standing, the decision to seek an abortion is morally equivalent to the decision to employ contraception; the effect in both cases is to prevent the existence of a being with moral standing. Such decisions are morally innocuous and should be left to the discretion of the parties involved. Thus, the liberal view of abortion, and a permissive abortion policy, are appropriate for early (prethreshold) abortions. After the threshold, when the fetus has moral standing, the decision to seek an abortion is morally equivalent to the decision to commit infanticide; the effect in both cases is to terminate the existence of a being with moral standing. Such decisions are morally serious and should not be left to the discretion of the parties involved (the fetus is now one of the parties involved).

It should follow that the conservative view of abortion and a restrictive abortion policy are appropriate for late (post-threshold) abortions. But this does not follow. Conservatives hold that abortion, because it is homicide, is unjustified on any grounds. This absolute position is indefensible even for post-threshold fetuses with moral standing. Of the four categories of grounds for abortion, neither humanitarian nor socioeconomic grounds will apply to post-threshold abortions, since a permissive policy for the period before the threshold will afford women the opportunity to decide freely whether they wish to continue their pregnancies. Therapeutic grounds will however apply, since serious risks to maternal life or health may materialize after the threshold. If they do, there is no justification for refusing an abortion. A pregnant woman is providing life support for another being that is housed within her body. If continuing to provide that life support will place her own life or health at serious risk, then she cannot justifiably be compelled to do so, even though the fetus has moral standing and will die if deprived of that life support. Seeking an abortion in such circumstances is a legitimate act of self-preservation.

A moderate abortion policy must therefore include a therapeutic ground for post-threshold abortions. It must also include a eugenic ground. Given current technology, some tests for fetal abnormalities can be carried out only in the second trimester. In many cases, therefore, serious abnormalities will be detected only after the fetus has passed the threshold. Circumstantial differences aside, the status of a severely deformed post-threshold fetus is the same as the status of a severely deformed newborn infant. The moral issues concerning the treatment of such newborns are themselves complex, but there appears to be a good case for selective infanticide in some cases. If so, then there is an even better case for late abortion on eugenic grounds, since here we must also reckon in the terrible burden of carrying to term a child that a woman knows to be deformed.

A moderate abortion policy will therefore contain the following ingredients: a time limit that separates early from late abortions, a permissive policy for early abortions, and a policy for late abortions that incorporates both therapeutic and eugenic grounds. This blueprint leaves many smaller questions of design to be settled. The grounds for late abortions must be specified more carefully by determining what is to count as a serious risk to maternal life or health and what is to count as a serious fetal abnormality. While no general formulation of a policy can settle these matters in detail, guidelines can and should be supplied. A policy should also specify the procedure that is to be followed in deciding when a particular case has met these guidelines.

But most of all, a moderate policy must impose a defensible time limit. As we saw earlier, from the moral point of view there can be no question of a sharp breakpoint. Fetal development unfolds gradually and cumulatively, and sentience like all other capacities is acquired slowly and by degrees. Thus we have clear cases of pre-sentient fetuses in the first trimester and clear cases of sentient fetuses in the third trimester. But we also have unclear cases, encompassing many (perhaps most) second-trimester fetuses. From the moral point of view, we can say only that in these cases the moral status of the fetus, and thus the moral status of abortion, is indeterminate. This sort of moral indeterminacy occurs also at later stages of human development, for instance when we are attempting to fix the age of consent or of competence to drink or drive. We do not pretend in these latter cases that the capacity in question is acquired overnight on one's sixteenth or eighteenth birthday, and yet for legal purposes we must draw a sharp and determinate line. Any such line will be somewhat arbitrary, but it is enough if it is drawn within the appropriate threshold stage. So also in the case of a time limit for abortion, it is sufficient if the line for legal purposes is located within the appropriate threshold stage. A time limit anywhere in the second trimester is therefore defensible, at least until we acquire the kind of information about fetal development that will enable us to narrow the threshold stage and thus to locate the time limit with more accuracy. . . .

NOTES

1 The sentience criterion is defended in my *Abortion and Moral Theory* (Princeton, N.J.: Princeton University Press, 1981), 128–46.

QUESTIONS

1 If sentience is the "threshold" of moral standing for a developing fetus, is it necessary to conclude that a sentient fetus has *full* moral standing (status)?
2 Are "prethreshold abortions" as morally unproblematic as Sumner believes?
3 In your judgment, are Sumner's views on the morality of abortion too conservative, too liberal, or "just right"? What about his views on abortion social policy?

Majority Opinion in *Roe v. Wade*
Justice Harry A. Blackmun

Harry A. Blackmun, associate justice of the United States Supreme Court, is a graduate of Harvard University Law School. After some fifteen years in private practice he became legal counsel to the Mayo Clinic (1950–1959). Justice Blackmun also served as United States circuit judge (1959–1970) before his appointment in 1970 to the Supreme Court.

In this case, a pregnant single woman, suing under the fictitious name of Jane Roe, challenged the constitutionality of the existing Texas criminal abortion law.

United States Supreme Court. 410 U.S. 113 (1973).

According to the Texas Penal Code, the performance of an abortion, except to save the life of the mother, constituted a crime that was punishable by a prison sentence of two to five years. At the time this case was finally resolved by the Supreme Court, abortion legislation varied widely from state to state. Some states, principally New York, had already legalized abortion on demand. Most other states, however, had legalized various forms of therapeutic abortion but had retained some measure of restrictive abortion legislation.

Justice Blackmun, writing an opinion concurred in by six other justices, argues that a woman's decision to terminate a pregnancy is encompassed by a *right to privacy*—but only up to a certain point in the development of the fetus. As the right to privacy is not an absolute right, it must yield at some point to the state's legitimate interests. Justice Blackmun contends that the state has a legitimate interest in protecting the health of the pregnant woman and that this interest becomes compelling at approximately the end of the first trimester in the development of the fetus. He also contends that the state has a legitimate interest in protecting potential life and that this interest becomes compelling at the point of viability.

It is . . . apparent that at common law, at the time of the adoption of our Constitution, and throughout the major portion of the 19th century, abortion was viewed with less disfavor than under most American statutes currently in effect. Phrasing it another way, a woman enjoyed a substantially broader right to terminate a pregnancy than she does in most States today. At least with respect to the early stage of pregnancy, and very possibly without such a limitation, the opportunity to make this choice was present in this country well into the 19th century. Even later, the law continued for some time to treat less punitively an abortion procured in early pregnancy. . . .

Three reasons have been advanced to explain historically the enactment of criminal abortion laws in the 19th century and to justify their continued existence.

It has been argued occasionally that these laws were the product of a Victorian social concern to discourage illicit sexual conduct. Texas, however, does not advance this justification in the present case, and it appears that no court or commentator has taken the argument seriously. . . .

A second reason is concerned with abortion as a medical procedure. When most criminal abortion laws were first enacted, the procedure was a hazardous one for the woman. This was particularly true prior to the development of antisepsis. Antiseptic techniques, of course, were based on discoveries by Lister, Pasteur, and others first announced in 1867, but were not generally accepted and employed until about the turn of the century. Abortion mortality was high. Even after 1900, and perhaps until as late as the development of antibiotics in the 1940's, standard modern techniques such as dilatation and curettage were not nearly so safe as they are today. Thus it has been argued that a State's real concern in enacting a criminal abortion law was to protect the pregnant woman, that is, to restrain her from submitting to a procedure that placed her life in serious jeopardy.

Modern medical techniques have altered this situation. Appellants and various *amici* refer to medical data indicating that abortion in early pregnancy, that is, prior to the end of first trimester, although not without its risk, is now relatively safe. Mortality rates for women undergoing early abortions, where the procedure is legal, appear to be as low as or lower than the rates for normal childbirth. Consequently, any interest of the State in protecting the woman from an inherently hazardous procedure, except when it would be equally dangerous for her to forgo it, has largely disappeared. Of course, important state interests in the area of health and medical standards do remain. The State has a legitimate interest in seeing to it that abortion, like any other medical procedure, is performed under circumstances that insure maximum safety for the patient. This interest obviously extends at least to the performing physician and his staff, to the facilities involved, to the availability of after-care, and to adequate provision for any complication or emergency that might arise. The prevalence of high mortality rates at illegal "abortion mills" strengthens, rather than weakens, the State's interest in regulating the conditions under which abortions are performed. Moreover, the risk to the woman increases as her pregnancy continues. Thus the State retains a definite interest in protecting the woman's own health and safety when an abortion is performed at a late stage of pregnancy.

The third reason is the State's interest—some phrase it in terms of duty—in protecting prenatal life. Some of the argument for this justification rests on the theory that a new human life is present from the moment of conception. The State's interest and general obligation to protect life then extends, it is argued, to prenatal life. Only when the life of the pregnant mother herself is at stake, balanced against the life she carries within her, should the interest of the embryo or fetus not prevail. Logically, of course, a legitimate state interest in this area need not stand or fall on acceptance of the belief that life begins at conception or at some other point prior to live birth. In assessing the State's interest, recognition may be given to the less rigid claim that as long as at least *potential* life is involved, the State may assert interests beyond the protection of the pregnant woman alone.

Parties challenging state abortion laws have sharply disputed in some courts the contention that a purpose of these laws, when enacted, was to protect prenatal life. Pointing to the absence of legislative history to support the contention, they claim that most state laws were designed solely to protect the woman. Because medical advances have lessened this concern, at least with respect to abortion in early pregnancy, they argue that with respect to such abortions the laws can no longer be justified by any state interest. There is some scholarly support for this view of original purpose. The few state courts called upon to interpret their laws in the late 19th and early 20th centuries did focus on the State's interest in protecting the woman's health rather than in preserving the embryo and fetus. . . .

The Constitution does not explicitly mention any right of privacy. In a line of decisions, however, going back perhaps as far as *Union Pacific R. Co. v. Botsford* (1891), the Court has recognized that a right of personal privacy, or a guarantee of certain areas or zones of privacy, does exist under the Constitution. In varying contexts the Court or individual Justices have indeed found at least the roots of that right in the First Amendment, . . . in the Fourth and Fifth Amendments . . . in the penumbras of the Bill of Rights . . . in the Ninth Amendment . . . or in the concept of liberty guaranteed by the first section of the Fourteenth Amendment. . . . These decisions make it clear that only personal rights that can be deemed "fundamental" or "implicit in the concept of ordered liberty," . . . are included in this guarantee of personal privacy. They also make it clear that the right has some extension to activities relating to marriage, . . . procreation, . . . contraception, . . . family relationships, . . . and child rearing and education. . . .

This right of privacy, whether it be founded in the Fourteenth Amendment's concept of personal liberty and restrictions upon state action, as we feel it is, or, as the District Court determined, in the Ninth Amendment's reservation of rights to the people, is broad enough to encompass a woman's decision whether or not to terminate her pregnancy. . . .

. . . [A]ppellants and some *amici* argue that the woman's right is absolute and that she is entitled to terminate her pregnancy at whatever time, in whatever way, and for whatever reason she alone chooses. With this we do not agree. Appellants' arguments that Texas either has no valid interest at all in regulating the abortion decision, or no interest strong enough to support any limitation upon the woman's sole determination, is unpersuasive. The Court's decisions recognizing a right of privacy also acknowledge that some state regulation in areas protected by that right is appropriate. As noted above, a state may properly assert important interests in safe-guarding health, in maintaining medical standards, and in protecting potential life. At some point in pregnancy, these respective interests become sufficiently compelling to sustain regulation of the factors that govern the abortion decision. The privacy right involved, therefore, cannot be said to be absolute. . . .

We therefore conclude that the right of personal privacy includes the abortion decision, but that this right is not unqualified and must be considered against important state interests in regulation.

We note that those federal and state courts that have recently considered abortion law challenges have reached the same conclusion. . . .

Although the results are divided, most of these courts have agreed that the right of privacy, however based, is broad enough to cover the abortion decision; that the right, nonetheless, is not absolute and is subject to some limitations; and that at some point the state interests as to protection of health, medical standards, and prenatal life, become dominant. We agree with this approach. . . .

The appellee and certain *amici* argue that the fetus is a "person" within the language and meaning of the Fourteenth Amendment. In support of this they outline at length and in detail the well-known facts of fetal development. If this suggestion of personhood is established, the appellant's case, of course, collapses, for the fetus' right to life is then guaranteed specifically by the Amendment. The appellant conceded as much on reargument. On the other hand, the appellee conceded on reargument that no case could be cited that holds that a fetus is a person within the meaning of the Fourteenth Amendment. . . .

All this, together with our observation, *supra,* that throughout the major portion of the 19th century prevailing legal abortion practices were far freer than they are today, persuades us that the word "person," as used in the Fourteenth Amendment, does not include the unborn. . . . Indeed, our decision in *United States v. Vuitch*

(1971) inferentially is to the same effect, for we there would not have indulged in statutory interpretation favorable to abortion in specified circumstances if the necessary consequence was the termination of life entitled to Fourteenth Amendment protection.

. . . As we have intimated above, it is reasonable and appropriate for a State to decide that at some point in time another interest, that of health of the mother or that of potential human life, becomes significantly involved. The woman's privacy is no longer sole and any right of privacy she possesses must be measured accordingly.

Texas urges that, apart from the Fourteenth Amendment, life begins at conception and is present throughout pregnancy, and that, therefore, the State has a compelling interest in protecting that life from and after conception. We need not resolve the difficult question of when life begins. When those trained in the respective disciplines of medicine, philosophy, and theology are unable to arrive at any consensus, the judiciary, at this point in the development of man's knowledge, is not in a position to speculate as to the answer.

It should be sufficient to note briefly the wide divergence of thinking on this most sensitive and difficult question. There has always been strong support for the view that life does not begin until live birth. This was the belief of the Stoics. It appears to be the predominant, though not the unanimous, attitude of the Jewish faith. It may be taken to represent also the position of a large segment of the Protestant community, insofar as that can be ascertained; organized groups that have taken a formal position on the abortion issue have generally regarded abortion as a matter for the conscience of the individual and her family. As we have noted, the common law found greater significance in quickening. Physicians and their scientific colleagues have regarded that event with less interest and have tended to focus either upon conception or upon live birth or upon the interim point at which the fetus becomes "viable," that is, potentially able to live outside the mother's womb, albeit with artificial aid. Viability is usually placed at about seven months (28 weeks) but may occur earlier, even at 24 weeks. . . .

In areas other than criminal abortion the law has been reluctant to endorse any theory that life, as we recognize it, begins before live birth or to accord legal rights to the unborn except in narrowly defined situations and except when the rights are contingent upon live birth. . . . In short, the unborn have never been recognized in the law as persons in the whole sense.

In view of all this, we do not agree that, by adopting one theory of life, Texas may override the rights of the pregnant woman that are at stake. We repeat, however, that the State does have an important and legitimate interest in preserving and protecting the health of the pregnant woman, whether she be a resident of the State or a nonresident who seeks medical consultation and treatment there, and that it has still *another* important and legitimate interest in protecting the potentiality of human life. These interests are separate and distinct. Each grows in substantiality as the woman approaches term and, at a point during pregnancy, each becomes "compelling."

With respect to the State's important and legitimate interest in the health of the mother, the "compelling" point, in the light of present medical knowledge, is at approximately the end of the first trimester. This is so because of the now established medical fact . . . that until the end of the first trimester mortality in abortion is less than mortality in normal childbirth. It follows that, from and after this point, a State may regulate the abortion procedure to the extent that the regulation reasonably relates to the preservation and protection of maternal health. Examples of permissible state regulation in this area are requirements as to the qualifications of the person who is to perform the abortion; as to the licensure of that person; as to the facility in which the procedure is to be performed, that is, whether it must be a hospital or may be a clinic or some other place of less-than-hospital status; as to the licensing of the facility; and the like.

This means, on the other hand, that, for the period of pregnancy prior to this "compelling" point, the attending physician, in consultation with his patient, is free to determine, without regulation by the State, that in his medical judgment the patient's pregnancy should be terminated. If that decision is reached, the judgment may be effectuated by an abortion free of interference by the State.

With respect to the State's important and legitimate interest in potential life, the "compelling" point is at viability. This is so because the fetus then presumably has the capability of meaningful life outside the mother's womb. State regulation protective of fetal life after viability thus has both logical and biological justifications. If the State is interested in protecting fetal life after viability, it may go so far as to proscribe abortion during that period except when it is necessary to preserve the life or health of the mother. . . .

To summarize and repeat:

1 A state criminal abortion statute of the current Texas type, that excepts from criminality only a *life saving* procedure on behalf of the mother, without regard to pregnancy stage and without recognition of the other interests involved, is violative of the Due Process Clause of the Fourteenth Amendment.

(a) For the stage prior to approximately the end of the first trimester, the abortion decision and its effectuation must be left to the medical judgment of the pregnant woman's attending physician.

(b) For the stage subsequent to approximately the end of the first trimester, the State, in promoting its interest in the health of the mother, may, if it chooses, regulate the abortion procedure in ways that are reasonably related to maternal health.

(c) For the stage subsequent to viability the State, in promoting its interest in the potentiality of human life, may, if it chooses, regulate, and even proscribe, abortion except where it is necessary, in appropriate medical judgment, for the preservation of the life or health of the mother.

2 The State may define the term "physician," as it has been employed [here], to mean only a physician currently licensed by the State, and may proscribe any abortion by a person who is not a physician as so defined.

. . . The decision leaves the State free to place increasing restrictions on abortion as the period of pregnancy lengthens, so long as those restrictions are tailored to the recognized state interests. The decision vindicates the right of the physician to administer medical treatment according to his professional judgment up to the points where important state interests provide compelling justifications for intervention. Up to those points the abortion decision in all its aspects is inherently, and primarily, a medical decision, and basic responsibility for it must rest with the physician. If an individual practitioner abuses the privilege of exercising proper medical judgment, the usual remedies, judicial and intraprofessional, are available. . . .

QUESTIONS

1 Justice Blackmun contends that the state's legitimate interest in protecting the health of the mother becomes *compelling* at the end of the first trimester. Does the Court's choice of this particular point as "compelling" have any substantial justification, or is the choice fundamentally arbitrary?

2 Justice Blackmun contends that the state's legitimate interest in protecting potential life becomes *compelling* at the point of viability. Does the Court's choice of this particular point as "compelling" have any substantial justification, or is the choice fundamentally arbitrary?

3 Justice Blackmun *explicitly* disavows entering into philosophical speculation on the problem of the beginning of human life. To what extent could it be said that he *implicitly* takes a philosophical position on this problem?

Opinion in *Webster v. Reproductive Health Services*

Justice William H. Rehnquist

William H. Rehnquist, chief justice of the United States Supreme Court, is a graduate of Stanford University Law School. In 1969, after spending a number of years in private practice, he became assistant attorney general, Office of Legal Counsel, United States Department of Justice. He was appointed to the Supreme Court in 1972 and became chief justice of the Court in 1986.

At issue in this case is the constitutionality of certain provisions of a Missouri statute designed to place restrictions on abortion. Of special importance are provisions banning the use of *public* facilities and *public* employees in the performance of abortions and a provision requiring physicians to perform tests to determine the viability of any fetus believed to be twenty weeks or older.

In announcing the judgment of a bitterly divided Court, Chief Justice Rehnquist argues that just as it is constitutionally acceptable for a state to refuse to fund abortions directly (e.g., through Medicaid), it is constitutionally acceptable for a state to prohibit the use of public facilities and employees in the performance of abortions. In upholding the constitutionality of the viability-testing provision, he maintains that this provision "permissibly furthers" the state's interest in protecting potential human life. Chief Justice Rehnquist also argues that the present case does not call for a reexamination of *Roe v. Wade,* but he makes very clear his view that the *Roe* trimester framework is both "unsound in principle and unworkable in practice."

United States Supreme Court. 109 S.Ct. 3040 (1989).

This appeal concerns the constitutionality of a Missouri statute regulating the performance of abortions. The United States Court of Appeals for the Eighth Circuit struck down several provisions of the statute on the ground that they violated this Court's decision in *Roe v. Wade* (1973) and cases following it. We noted probable jurisdiction and now reverse.

I

In June 1986, the Governor of Missouri signed into law Missouri Senate Committee Substitute for House Bill No. 1596 (hereinafter Act or statute), which amended existing state law concerning unborn children and abortions. The Act consisted of 20 provisions, 5 of which are now before the Court. The first provision, or preamble, contains "findings" by the state legislature that "[t]he life of each human being begins at conception," and that "unborn children have protectable interests in life, health, and well-being." The Act further requires that all Missouri laws be interpreted to provide unborn children with the same rights enjoyed by other persons, subject to the Federal Constitution and this Court's precedents. Among its other provisions, the Act requires that, prior to performing an abortion on any woman whom a physician has reason to believe is 20 or more weeks pregnant, the physician ascertain whether the fetus is viable by performing "such medical examinations and tests as are necessary to make a finding of the gestational age, weight, and lung maturity of the unborn child." The Act also prohibits the use of public employees and facilities to perform or assist abortions not necessary to save the mother's life, and it prohibits the use of public funds, employees, or facilities for the purpose of "encouraging or counseling" a woman to have an abortion not necessary to save her life.

In July 1986, five health professionals employed by the State and two nonprofit corporations brought this class action in the United States District Court for the Western District of Missouri to challenge the constitutionality of the Missouri statute. Plaintiffs, appellees in this Court, sought declaratory and injunctive relief on the ground that certain statutory provisions violated the First, Fourth, Ninth, and Fourteenth Amendments to the Federal Constitution. . . .

Plaintiffs filed this suit "on their own behalf and on behalf of the entire class consisting of facilities and Missouri licensed physicians or other health care professionals offering abortion services or pregnancy counseling and on behalf of the entire class of pregnant females seeking abortion services or pregnancy counseling within the State of Missouri." The two nonprofit corporations are Reproductive Health Services, which offers family planning and gynecological services to the public, including abortion services up to 22 weeks "gestational age,"[1] and Planned Parenthood of Kansas City, which provides abortion services up to 14 weeks gestational age. . . .

Several weeks after the complaint was filed, the District Court temporarily restrained enforcement of several provisions of the Act. . . .

The Court of Appeals for the Eighth Circuit affirmed, with one exception not relevant to this appeal. The Court of Appeals determined that Missouri's declaration that life begins at conception was "simply an impermissible state adoption of a theory of when life begins to justify its abortion regulations." Relying on *Colautti* v.

Franklin (1979), it further held that the requirement that physicians perform viability tests was an unconstitutional legislative intrusion on a matter of medical skill and judgment. The Court of Appeals invalidated Missouri's prohibition on the use of public facilities and employees to perform or assist abortions not necessary to save the mother's life. It distinguished our decisions in *Harris* v. *McRae* (1980) and *Maher* v. *Roe* (1977), on the ground that " '[t]here is a fundamental difference between providing direct funding to effect the abortion decision and allowing staff physicians to perform abortions at an existing publicly owned hospital.' " The Court of Appeals struck down the provision prohibiting the use of public funds for "encouraging or counseling" women to have nontherapeutic abortions, for the reason that this provision was both overly vague and inconsistent with the right to an abortion enunciated in *Roe* v. *Wade. . . .*

II

Decision of this case requires us to address four sections of the Missouri Act: (a) the preamble; (b) the prohibition on the use of public facilities or employees to perform abortions; (c) the prohibition on public funding of abortion counseling; and (d) the requirement that physicians conduct viability tests prior to performing abortions. We address these *seriatim.*

A

The Act's preamble, as noted, sets forth "findings" by the Missouri legislature that "[t]he life of each human being begins at conception," and that "[u]nborn children have protectable interests in life, health, and well-being." The Act then mandates that state laws be interpreted to provide unborn children with "all the rights, privileges, and immunities available to other persons, citizens, and residents of this state," subject to the Constitution and this Court's precedents. In invalidating the preamble, the Court of Appeals relied on this Court's dictum that " 'a State may not adopt one theory of when life begins to justify its regulation of abortions.' " It rejected Missouri's claim that the preamble was "abortion-neutral," and "merely determine[d] when life begins in a nonabortion context, a traditional state prerogative." The court thought that "[t]he only plausible inference" from the fact that "every remaining section of the bill save one regulates the performance of abortions" was that "the state intended its abortion regulations to be understood against the backdrop of its theory of life."

The State contends that the preamble itself is precatory and imposes no substantive restrictions on abortions. . . .

. . . Certainly the preamble does not by its terms regulate abortion or any other aspect of appellees' medical practice. The Court has emphasized that *Roe* v. *Wade* "implies no limitation on the authority of a State to make a value judgment favoring childbirth over abortion." The preamble can be read simply to express that sort of value judgment.

We think the extent to which the preamble's language might be used to interpret other state statutes or regulations is something that only the courts of Missouri can definitively decide. . . .

It will be time enough for federal courts to address the meaning of the preamble should it be applied to restrict the activities of appellees in some concrete way. . . . We therefore need not pass on the constitutionality of the Act's preamble.

B

Section 188.210 provides that "[i]t shall be unlawful for any public employee within the scope of his employment to perform or assist an abortion, not necessary to save the life of the mother," while §188.215 makes it "unlawful for any public facility to be used for the purpose of performing or assisting an abortion not necessary to save the life of the mother." The Court of Appeals held that these provisions contravened this Court's abortion decisions. We take the contrary view.

As we said earlier this Term . . . , "our cases have recognized that the Due Process Clauses generally confer no affirmative right to governmental aid, even where such aid may be necessary to secure life, liberty, or property interests of which the government itself may not deprive the individual." In *Maher* v. *Roe, supra,* the Court upheld a Connecticut welfare regulation under which Medicaid recipients received payments for medical services related to childbirth, but not for nontherapeutic abortions. The Court rejected the claim that this unequal subsidization of childbirth and abortion was impermissible under *Roe* v. *Wade.* As the Court put it:

> "The Connecticut regulation before us is different in kind from the laws invalidated in our previous abortion decisions. The Connecticut regulation places no obstacles—absolute or otherwise—in the pregnant woman's path to an abortion. An indigent woman who desires an abortion suffers no disadvantage as a consequence of Connecticut's decision to fund childbirth; she continues as before to be dependent on private sources for the service she desires. The State may have made childbirth a more attractive alternative, thereby influencing the woman's decision, but it has imposed no restriction on access to abortions that was not already there. The indigency that may make it difficult—and in some cases, perhaps, impossible—for some women to have abortions is neither created nor in any way affected by the Connecticut regulation."

Relying on *Maher,* the Court in *Poelker* v. *Doe* (1977) held that the city of St. Louis committed "no constitutional violation . . . in electing, as a policy choice, to provide publicly financed hospital services for childbirth without providing corresponding services for nontherapeutic abortions."

More recently, in *Harris* v. *McRae* (1980), the Court upheld "the most restrictive version of the Hyde Amendment," which withheld from States federal funds under the Medicaid program to reimburse the costs of abortions, " 'except where the life of the mother would be endangered if the fetus were carried to term.' " As in *Maher* and *Poelker,* the Court required only a showing that Congress' authorization of "reimbursement for medically necessary services generally, but not for certain medically necessary abortions" was rationally related to the legitimate governmental goal of encouraging childbirth.

The Court of Appeals distinguished these cases on the ground that "[t]o prevent access to a public facility does more than demonstrate a political choice in favor of childbirth; it clearly narrows and in some cases forecloses the availability of abortion to women." The court reasoned that the ban on the use of public facilities "could prevent a woman's chosen doctor from performing an abortion because of his un-privileged status at other hospitals or because a private hospital adopted a similar anti-abortion stance." It also thought that "[s]uch a rule could increase the cost of obtaining an abortion and delay the timing of it as well."

We think that this analysis is much like that which we rejected in *Maher, Poelker,* and *McRae.* As in those cases, the State's decision here to use public facilities and staff to encourage childbirth over abortion "places no governmental obstacle in the path of a woman who chooses to terminate her pregnancy." Just as Congress' refusal to fund abortions in *McRae* left "an indigent woman with at least the same range of choice in deciding whether to obtain a medically necessary abortion as she would have had if Congress had chosen to subsidize no health care costs at all," Missouri's refusal to allow public employees to perform abortions in public hospitals leaves a pregnant woman with the same choices as if the State had chosen not to operate any public hospitals at all. The challenged provisions only restrict a woman's ability to obtain an abortion to the extent that she chooses to use a physician affiliated with a public hospital. This circumstance is more easily remedied, and thus considerably less burdensome, than indigency, which "may make it difficult—and in some cases, perhaps, impossible—for some women to have abortions" without public funding. Having held that the State's refusal to fund abortions does not violate *Roe* v. *Wade,* it strains logic to reach a contrary result for the use of public facilities and employ-ees. If the State may "make a value judgment favoring childbirth over abortion and . . . implement that judgment by the allocation of public funds," surely it may do so through the allocation of other public resources, such as hospitals and medical staff. . . .

. . . Thus we uphold the Act's restrictions on the use of public employees and facilities for the performance or assistance of nontherapeutic abortions.

C

The Missouri Act contains three provisions relating to "encouraging or counseling a woman to have an abortion not necessary to save her life." Section 188.205 states that no public funds can be used for this purpose; § 188.210 states that public em-ployees cannot, within the scope of their employment, engage in such speech; and § 188.215 forbids such speech in public facilities. The Court of Appeals did not con-sider § 188.205 separately from §§ 188.210 and 188.215. It held that all three of these provisions were unconstitutionally vague, and that "the ban on using public funds, employees, and facilities to encourage or counsel a woman to have an abor-tion is an unacceptable infringement of the woman's fourteenth amendment right to choose an abortion after receiving the medical information necessary to exercise the right knowingly and intelligently."

Missouri has chosen only to appeal the Court of Appeals' invalidation of the public funding provision, § 188.205. A threshold question is whether this provision reaches primary conduct, or whether it is simply an instruction to the State's fiscal officers not to allocate funds for abortion counseling. We accept, for purposes of decision, the State's claim that § 188.205 "is not directed at the conduct of any physician or health care provider, private or public," but "is directed solely at those persons responsible for expending public funds."

Appellees contend that they are not "adversely" affected under the State's interpretation of § 188.205, and therefore that there is no longer a case or controversy before us on this question. . . . A majority of the Court agrees with appellees that the controversy over § 188.205 is now moot. . . .

D

Section 188.029 of the Missouri Act provides:

"Before a physician performs an abortion on a woman he has reason to believe is carrying an unborn child of twenty or more weeks gestational age, the physician shall first determine if the unborn child is viable by using and exercising that degree of care, skill, and proficiency commonly exercised by the ordinarily skillful, careful, and prudent physician engaged in similar practice under the same or similar conditions. In making this determination of viability, the physician shall perform or cause to be performed such medical examinations and tests as are necessary to make a finding of the gestational age, weight, and lung maturity of the unborn child and shall enter such findings and determination of viability in the medical record of the mother."

As with the preamble, the parties disagree over the meaning of this statutory provision. The State emphasizes the language of the first sentence, which speaks in terms of the physician's determination of viability being made by the standards of ordinary skill in the medical profession. Appellees stress the language of the second sentence, which prescribes such "tests as are necessary" to make a finding of gestational age, fetal weight, and lung maturity.

The Court of Appeals read § 188.029 as requiring that after 20 weeks "doctors *must* perform tests to find gestational age, fetal weight and lung maturity." The court indicated that the tests needed to determine fetal weight at 20 weeks are "unreliable and inaccurate" and would add $125 to $250 to the cost of an abortion. It also stated that "amniocentesis, the only method available to determine lung maturity, is contrary to accepted medical practice until 28–30 weeks of gestation, expensive, and imposes significant health risks for both the pregnant woman and the fetus."

We must first determine the meaning of § 188.029 under Missouri law. Our usual practice is to defer to the lower court's construction of a state statute, but we believe the Court of Appeals has "fallen into plain error" in this case. " 'In expounding a statute, we must not be guided by a single sentence or member of a sentence, but look to the provisions of the whole law, and to its object and policy.' " The Court of Appeals' interpretation also runs "afoul of the well-established principle that statutes will be interpreted to avoid constitutional difficulties."

We think the viability-testing provision makes sense only if the second sentence is read to require only those tests that are useful to making subsidiary findings as to viability. If we construe this provision to require a physician to perform those tests needed to make the three specified findings *in all circumstances,* including when the physician's reasonable professional judgment indicates that the tests would be irrelevant to determining viability or even dangerous to the mother and the fetus, the second sentence of § 188.029 would conflict with the first sentence's *requirement* that a physician apply his reasonable professional skill and judgment. It would also be incongruous to read this provision, especially the word "necessary," to require the performance of tests irrelevant to the expressed statutory purpose of determining viability. It thus seems clear to us that the Court of Appeals' construction of § 188.029 violates well-acepted canons of statutory interpretation used in the Missouri courts. . . .

The viability-testing provision of the Missouri Act is concerned with promoting the State's interest in potential human life rather than in maternal health. Section 188.029 creates what is essentially a presumption of viability at 20 weeks, which the physician must rebut with tests indicating that the fetus is not viable prior to performing an abortion. It also directs the physician's determination as to viability by specifying consideration, if feasible, of gestational age, fetal weight, and lung capacity. The District Court found that "the medical evidence is uncontradicted that a 20-week fetus is *not* viable," and that "23½ to 24 weeks gestation is the earliest point in pregnancy where a reasonable possibility of viability exists." But it also found that there may be a 4-week error in estimating gestational age, which supports testing at 20 weeks.

In *Roe* v. *Wade,* the Court recognized that the State has "important and legitimate" interests in protecting maternal health and in the potentiality of human life. During the second trimester, the State "may, if it chooses, regulate the abortion procedure in ways that are reasonably related to maternal health." After viability, when the State's interest in potential human life was held to become compelling, the State "may, if it chooses, regulate, and even proscribe, abortion except where it is necessary, in appropriate medical judgment, for the preservation of the life or health of the mother."

In *Colautti* v. *Franklin, supra,* upon which appellees rely, the Court held that a Pennsylvania statute regulating the standard of care to be used by a physician performing an abortion of a possibly viable fetus was void for vagueness. But in the course of reaching that conclusion, the Court reaffirmed its earlier statement in *Planned Parenthood of Central Missouri* v. *Danforth* (1976), that " 'the determination of whether a particular fetus is viable is, and must be, a matter for the judgement of the responsible attending physician.' " The dissent ignores the statement in *Colautti* that "neither the legislature nor the courts may proclaim one of the elements entering into the ascertainment of viability—be it weeks of gestation or fetal weight or any other single factor—as the determinant of when the State has a compelling interest in the life or health of the fetus." To the extent that § 188.029 regulates the method for determining viability, it undoubtedly does superimpose state regulation on the medical determination of whether a particular fetus is viable. The Court of Appeals and the District Court thought it unconstitutional for this reason. To the extent that the viability tests increase the cost of what are in fact second-trimester abortions, their validity may also be questioned under *Akron* v. *Akron Center for Reproductive Health* (1983), where the Court held that a requirement that second trimester abortions must be performed in hospitals was invalid because it substantially increased the expense of those procedures.

We think that the doubt cast upon the Missouri statute by these cases is not so much a flaw in the statute as it is a reflection of the fact that the rigid trimester analysis of the course of a pregnancy enunciated in *Roe* has resulted in subsequent cases like *Colautti* and *Akron* making constitutional law in this area a virtual Procrustean bed. Statutes specifying elements of informed consent to be provided abortion patients, for example, were invalidated if they were thought to "structur[e] . . . the dialogue between the woman and her physician." *Thornburgh* v. *American College of Obstetricians and Gynecologists* (1986). As the dissenters in *Thornburgh* pointed out, such a statute would have been sustained under any traditional standard of judicial review, or for any other surgical procedure except abortion.

Stare decisis is a cornerstone of our legal system, but it has less power in constitutional cases, where, save for constitutional amendments, this Court is the only body able to make needed changes. We have not refrained from reconsideration of a prior construction of the Constitution that has proved "unsound in principle and unworkable in practice." We think the *Roe* trimester framework falls into that category.

In the first place, the rigid *Roe* framework is hardly consistent with the notion of a Constitution cast in general terms, as ours is, and usually speaking in general principles, as ours does. The key elements of the *Roe* framework—trimesters and viability—are not found in the text of the Constitution or in any place else one would expect to find a constitutional principle. Since the bounds of the inquiry are essentially indeterminate, the result has been a web of legal rules that have become increasingly intricate, resembling a code of regulations rather than a body of constitutional doctrine. As JUSTICE WHITE has put it, the trimester framework has left this Court to serve as the country's "*ex officio* medical board with powers to approve or disapprove medical and operative practices and standards throughout the United States."

In the second place, we do not see why the State's interest in protecting potential human life should come into existence only at the point of viability, and that there should therefore be a rigid line allowing state regulation after viability but prohibiting it before viability. The dissenters in *Thornburgh,* writing in the context of the *Roe* trimester analysis, would have recognized this fact by positing against the "fundamental right" recognized in *Roe* the State's "compelling interest" in protecting potential human life throughout pregnancy. . . .

The tests that § 188.029 requires the physician to perform are designed to determine viability. The State here has chosen viability as the point at which its interest in potential human life must be safeguarded. It is true that the tests in question increase the expense of abortion, and regulate the discretion of the physician in determining the viability of the fetus. Since the tests will undoubtedly show in many cases that the fetus is not viable, the tests will have been performed for what were in fact second-trimester abortions. But we are satisfied that the requirement of these tests permissibly furthers the State's interest in protecting potential human life, and we therefore believe § 188.029 to be constitutional.

The dissent takes us to task for our failure to join in a "great issues" debate as to whether the Constitution includes an "unenumerated" general right to privacy as recognized in cases such as *Griswold* v. *Connecticut* (1965) and *Roe.* But *Griswold* v. *Connecticut,* unlike *Roe,* did not purport to adopt a whole framework, complete with detailed rules and distinctions, to govern the cases in which the asserted liberty interest would apply. As such, it was far different from the opinion, if not the holding, of *Roe* v. *Wade,* which sought to establish a constitutional framework for judging state regulation of abortion during the entire term of pregnancy. That framework sought to deal with areas of medical practice traditionally subject to state regulation, and it sought to balance once and for all by reference only to the calendar the claims of the State to protect the fetus as a form of human life against the claims of a woman to decide for herself whether or not to abort a fetus she was carrying. The experience of the Court in applying *Roe* v. *Wade* in later cases suggests to us that there is wisdom in not unnecessarily attempting to elaborate the abstract differences between a "fundamental right" to abortion, as the Court described it in *Akron,* a "limited fundamental constitutional right," which JUSTICE BLACKMUN's dissent today treats *Roe* as having established, or a liberty interest protected by the Due Process Clause, which we believe it to be. The Missouri testing requirement here is reasonably designed to ensure that abortions are not performed where the fetus is viable— an end which all concede is legitimate—and that is sufficient to sustain its constitutionality.

The dissent also accuses us, *inter alia,* of cowardice and illegitimacy in dealing with "the most politically divisive domestic legal issue of our time." There is no doubt that our holding today will allow some governmental regulation of abortion that would have been prohibited under the language of cases such as *Colautti* v. *Franklin* and *Akron* v. *Akron Center for Reproductive Health, Inc., supra.* But the goal of constitutional adjudication is surely not to remove inexorably "politically divisive" issues from the ambit of the legislative process, whereby the people through their elected representatives deal with matters of concern to them. The goal of constitutional adjudication is to hold true the balance between that which the Constitution puts beyond the reach of the democratic process and that which it does not. We think we have done that today. The dissent's suggestion that legislative bodies, in a Nation where more than half of our population is women, will treat our decision today as an invitation to enact abortion regulation reminiscent of the dark ages not only misreads our views but does scant justice to those who serve in such bodies and the people who elect them.

III

Both appellants and the United States as *Amicus Curiae* have urged that we overrule our decision in *Roe* v. *Wade.* The facts of the present case, however, differ from those at issue in *Roe.* Here, Missouri has determined that viability is the point at which its interest in potential human life must be safeguarded. In *Roe,* on the other hand, the Texas statute criminalized the performance of *all* abortions, except when the mother's life was at stake. This case therefore affords us no occasion to revisit the holding of *Roe*, which was that the Texas statute unconstitutionally infringed the right to an abortion derived from the Due Process Clause, and we leave it undisturbed. To the extent indicated in our opinion, we would modify and narrow *Roe* and succeeding cases.

Because none of the challenged provisions of the Missouri Act properly before us conflict with the Constitution, the judgment of the Court of Appeals is *Reversed.*

NOTES

1 The Act defines "gestational age" as the "length of pregnancy as measured from the first day of the woman's last menstrual period."

QUESTIONS

1 It is constitutionally permissible for a state to ban the use of *public* facilities and *public* employees in the performance of abortions, but is it advisable for a state to do so? Is it advisable for a state to refuse to provide Medicaid funding for abortions?
2 What would be the basic elements of an ideal social policy on abortion? Why?

SUGGESTED ADDITIONAL READINGS FOR CHAPTER 1

BOLTON, MARTHA BRANDT: "Responsible Women and Abortion Decisions." In Onora O'Neill and William Ruddick, eds., *Having Children: Philosophical and Legal Reflections on Parenthood.* New York: Oxford University Press, 1979, pp. 40–51. In defending a moderate view on the morality of abortion, Bolton emphasizes the importance of contextual features in the life of a pregnant woman. She argues that the decision to bear a child must "fit" into a woman's life and make sense in terms of her responsibilities to her family and to the larger society.

BRODY, BARUCH: "On the Humanity of the Foetus." In Robert L. Perkins, ed., *Abortion: Pro and Con.* Cambridge, Mass.: Schenkman, 1974, pp. 69–90. Brody critically examines the various proposals for "drawing the line" on the humanity of the fetus, ultimately suggesting that the most defensible view would draw the line at the point where fetal brain activity begins.

ENGELHARDT, H. TRISTRAM, JR.: "The Ontology of Abortion." *Ethics,* vol. 84, April 1974, pp. 217–234. Engelhardt focuses attention on the issue of "whether or to what extent the fetus is a person." He argues that, strictly speaking, a human person is not present until the later stages of infancy. However, he finds the point of viability significant in that, with viability, an infant can play the social role of "child" and thus be treated "as if it were a person."

FEINBERG, JOEL: "Abortion." In Tom Regan, ed., *Matters of Life and Death.* New York: Random House, 1980, pp. 183–217. In this long essay, Feinberg analyzes the strengths and weaknesses of alternative views of the moral status of the fetus. He also considers the extent to which abortion is morally justifiable *if* it is granted that the fetus is a person.

FEINBERG, JOEL, ed.: *The Problem of Abortion,* 2d ed. Belmont, Calif.: Wadsworth, 1984. This excellent anthology features a wide range of articles on the moral justifiability of abortion.

HUMBER, JAMES M.: "Abortion: The Avoidable Moral Dilemma." *Journal of Value Inquiry,* vol. 9, Winter 1975, pp. 282–302. Humber, defending the conservative view on the morality of abortion, examines and rejects what he identifies as the major defenses of abortion. He also contends that proabortion arguments are typically so poor that they can only be viewed as "after-the-fact-rationalizations."

LANGERAK, EDWARD A.: "Abortion: Listening to the Middle." *Hastings Center Report,* vol. 9, October 1979, pp. 24–28. Langerak suggests a theoretical framework for a moderate view that incorporates two "widely shared beliefs": (1) that there is something about the fetus *itself* that makes abortion morally problematic and (2) that late abortions are significantly more problematic than early abortions.

NOONAN, JOHN T., JR.: "An Almost Absolute Value in History." In John T. Noonan, Jr., ed., *The Morality of Abortion: Legal and Historical Perspectives.* Cambridge, Mass.: Harvard University Press, 1970, pp. 51–59. In this well-known statement of the conservative view on the morality of abortion, Noonan argues that conception is the only objectively based and nonarbitrary point at which to "draw the line" between the nonhuman and the human.

ROSS, STEVEN L.: "Abortion and the Death of the Fetus." *Philosophy and Public Affairs,* vol. 11, Summer 1982, pp. 232–245. Ross draws a distinction between abortion as the termination of pregnancy and abortion as the termination of the life of the fetus. He proceeds to defend abortion in the latter sense, insisting that it is justifiable for a woman to desire not only the termination of pregnancy but also the death of the fetus.

THOMSON, JUDITH JARVIS: "A Defense of Abortion." *Philosophy and Public Affairs,* vol. 1, Fall 1971, pp. 47–66. In this widely discussed article, Thomson attempts to "moderate the conservative view." For the sake of argument, she grants the premise that the fetus (from conception) is a person. Still, she argues, under certain conditions abortion remains morally permissible.

TOOLEY, MICHAEL: *Abortion and Infanticide.* New York: Oxford University Press, 1983. In this long book, Tooley defends the liberal view on the morality of abortion. He insists that the question of the morality of abortion cannot be satisfactorily resolved "in isolation from the questions of the morality of infanticide and of the killing of nonhuman animals."

CHAPTER 2

Surrogate Motherhood and Reproductive Technology

Reproductive technology provides a spectrum of possibilities for the relief of human infertility. Despite this obvious benefit, the employment of such technology is the subject of continuing ethical debate. The readings in this chapter deal especially with ethical issues associated with two technologically assisted ways of dealing with infertility—surrogate motherhood and *in vitro* fertilization (IVF).

REPRODUCTIVE TECHNOLOGIES AND THE TREATMENT OF INFERTILITY

Human reproduction, as it naturally occurs, is characterized by sexual intercourse, tubal fertilization, implantation in the uterus, and subsequent *in utero* gestation. The expression "reproductive technologies" can be understood as applicable to an array of technical procedures that would replace the various steps in the natural process of reproduction, to a lesser or greater extent.

Artificial insemination is a procedure that replaces sexual intercourse as a means of achieving tubal fertilization. Artificial insemination has long been available, primarily as a means of overcoming infertility on the part of a male, usually a husband. It is sometimes possible that the husband's infertility may be overcome by AIH, artificial insemination with the sperm of the *husband*. More often, the couple must turn to AID, artificial insemination with the sperm of a *donor*. AID has also been employed when it has been established that the husband carries a mutant gene that would place a couple's offspring at genetic risk. Moreover, it has been suggested, most prominently in the work of the well-known geneticist Hermann J. Muller,[1] that

---

[1]See, for example, Hermann J. Muller, "Means and Aims in Human Genetic Betterment," in T. M. Sonneborn, ed., *The Control of Human Heredity and Evolution* (New York: Macmillan, 1965), pp. 100–122.

AID be voluntarily employed as a way of achieving the aims of positive eugenics.[2] Muller recommended the formation of sperm banks, which would collect and store the sperm of men judged to be "outstanding" in various ways. His idea was that an "enlightened" couple who desired a child would have recourse to one of these banks in order to arrange for the wife's artificial insemination. Another controversial use of AID is its employment by unmarried women. Probably even more controversial is the employment of artificial insemination within the context of a *surrogate motherhood arrangement*. In the most typical case, a wife's infertility motivates a couple to seek out a so-called surrogate mother. The surrogate agrees to be artificially inseminated with the husband's sperm, in order to bear a child for the couple.

In vitro fertilization (IVF) literally means fertilization "in glass." The sperm of a husband (or a donor) is united, in a laboratory, with the ovum of a wife (or a donor). Whereas artificial insemination is a technically simple procedure, IVF followed by embryo transfer (to the uterus for implantation) is a system of reproductive technology that features a high degree of technical sophistication. The first documented "test tube baby," Louise Brown, was born in England in July 1978. Her birth was the culmination of years of collaboration between a gynecologist, Patrick Steptoe, and an embryologist, Robert Edwards. This pioneering team developed methods for obtaining mature eggs from a woman's ovaries (via a minor surgical procedure called a laparoscopy), effectively fertilizing eggs in the laboratory, cultivating them to the eight-cell stage, and then transferring a developing embryo to the uterus for implantation.

Reproductive centers throughout the United States now provide *in vitro* procedures for the treatment of infertility. Although success rates continue to be somewhat unimpressive, it is expected that they will improve as techniques are further refined. An important development in this regard is the achievement of the first frozen embryo birth by an Australian team in 1984. Since it is now also possible, with the use of fertility drugs, to harvest a crop of mature eggs (perhaps ten or so) from a woman's ovaries, embryos frozen at the eight-cell stage can be thawed over a period of several months in an effort to achieve a successful implantation. Of course, the freezing of embryos is a technique that seems to suggest a number of ominous possibilities. But the freezing of unfertilized eggs, which at face value seems preferable to the freezing of embryos, has proven to be technically more difficult.

IVF followed by embryo transfer is a system of reproductive technology that replaces not only sexual intercourse but also tubal fertilization in the natural process of reproduction. But consider also the future possibility of dispensing with implantation and *in utero* gestation as well. There seems to be no theoretical obstacle to totally artificial gestation, which would take place within the confines of an artificial womb. If *ectogenesis,* the process of artificial gestation, becomes a reality, then the combination of IVF and ectogenesis would provide us with a system of reproductive technology in which each element in the natural process of reproduction has been effectively replaced. At the present time, however, IVF (accompanied by embryo transfer)

---

[2]Roughly, positive eugenics aims at enhancing the genetic heritage of the species, whereas negative eugenics aims at preventing deterioration of the gene pool.

is seen primarily as a means of overcoming female infertility, especially infertility due to obstruction of the fallopian tubes.

One important spinoff of IVF technology is a procedure known as GIFT, that is, gamete intrafallopian transfer. In this procedure, eggs are obtained as they would be for IVF, but instead of being fertilized *in vitro,* the eggs are placed together with sperm in the fallopian tube (or tubes) where it is hoped that fertilization will take place *in vivo* (i.e., in the living situation). Although there is some risk of ectopic pregnancy in GIFT, the success rates for this procedure seem to be slightly higher than the success rates for IVF in combination with embryo transfer.

In contrast to a woman whose infertility can be traced to fallopian-tube obstruction, consider a woman whose ovaries are either absent or nonfunctional. Since she has no ova, she cannot produce genetic offspring. If her uterus is functional, however, there is no biological obstacle to her bearing a child. Let us suppose that she very much wants to bear a child that is her husband's genetic offspring. Her problem can be addressed by some form of *egg donation,* and there are three major possibilities to consider:[3] (1) IVF of a donor egg with the husband's sperm, followed by embryo transfer to the wife. (2) Artificial insemination of an egg donor with the husband's sperm, producing *in vivo* fertilization; nonsurgical removal of the embryo via lavage (a washing out) of the donor's uterus; recovery of the embryo and transfer to the uterus of the wife.[4] (3) Transfer of a donor egg together with the husband's sperm to the wife's fallopian tube, thus employing GIFT in an effort to achieve tubal fertilization and subsequent implantation.

In the case just discussed, a woman has a functional uterus but nonfunctional ovaries. Consider now the converse case: a woman has functional ovaries but a nonfunctional uterus. Perhaps she has had a hysterectomy. She is capable of becoming, in a manner of speaking, the *genetic* but not the *gestational* mother of a child. Now, suppose that she and her husband desire a child "of their own." This situation gives rise to the possibility of a surrogate motherhood arrangement somewhat different than the kind predicated upon artificial insemination. In this case, IVF could be employed to fertilize the wife's egg with the husband's sperm. The embryo could then be transferred to the uterus of a surrogate who would agree to bear the child for the couple.

One other proposed scheme of reproductive technology is based on *cloning,* a form of asexual reproduction. Many scientists believe that the techniques necessary for successful human cloning will be available in the not too distant future. Accordingly, the following sequence of events can be imagined: A mature human egg will be obtained from a woman and enucleated in a laboratory—that is, the nucleus of the egg cell will be removed. Meanwhile, a body cell from a donor (who might be anyone including the woman who has provided the egg) will be obtained and enucleated. The resultant nucleus, which contains the donor's heretofore unique genotype, will undergo a process calculated to activate its dormant genes and then be inserted

---

[3]Some form of egg donation might also be considered when a woman's own ova would place her offspring at risk for genetic disease.
[4]To date, the success rates for this technique have not been impressive. There is also a risk of unwanted pregnancy on the part of the donor, because lavage might fail to wash out the embryo.

into the egg cell. From this point, the renucleated egg will develop in the way that a newly fertilized egg ordinarily develops. Implantation (not necessarily into the uterus of the woman from whom the original egg was obtained) and subsequent *in utero* gestation will then lead to the birth of a human "clone." In contrast to off-spring resulting from sexual reproduction, where the resultant genotype is the result of contributions by two parents, the "clone" will have the same genotype as his or her "parent."

ETHICAL CONCERNS

To what extent, if at all, is it ethically acceptable to employ the various reproductive technologies just discussed? A host of ethical concerns have been expressed about these technologies, and a brief survey of the most prominent of these concerns should prove helpful.

Most of the ethical opposition to artificial insemination derives from religious views. AID especially has been attacked on the grounds that it illicitly separates pro-creation from the marriage relationship. Inasmuch as AID introduces a third party (the sperm donor) into a marriage relationship, it has been called a form of adultery. Even AIH, which cannot be accused of separating procreation from the marriage relationship, has not uniformly escaped attack. Some religious ethicists have gone so far as to contend that procreation is morally illicit whenever it is not the product of personal lovemaking. Although these sorts of objections frequently recur in discussions of IVF, the various forms of egg donation, and cloning, they seem to have little force for those who do not share the basic worldview from which they proceed.

In one of this chapter's selections, Herbert T. Krimmel argues that it is wrong for a person to create a child with the intention of abdicating parental responsibility for it. The argument is meant to apply both to egg donation and sperm donation. Krim-mel also objects to an unmarried woman resorting to AID, on the grounds that it is unfair to intentionally deprive a child of a father. But his primary concern is to de-velop the case against surrogate motherhood.

Three other selections in this chapter deal with the controversial practice of sur-rogate motherhood. In one, excerpted from the New Jersey Supreme Court opinion in the celebrated Baby M case, *commercial* surrogacy contracts—that is, those that provide for a fee to be paid to the surrogate—are held to be invalid and unenforce-able in the State of New Jersey. At present, however, the legal status of surrogacy contracts varies from state to state, and legislatures continue to struggle with the so-cial policy aspects of surrogacy. One option is for a state simply to recognize surro-gacy contracts as valid and legally enforceable. Another option—at the other end of the spectrum—is for the state to prohibit anyone from entering into a surrogacy con-tract. Yet another option is for the state to prohibit commercial surrogacy contracts. Bonnie Steinbock argues in this chapter against the legal prohibition of commercial surrogacy contracts, although she insists on the importance of state regulation. Bar-bara Katz Rothman presents a very different point of view. Her opposition to the whole idea of surrogacy is explicitly based on an appeal to feminist values. Rothman is careful to point out, however, that there is significant disagreement among feminists on this issue.

Some of the ethical opposition to IVF is based on the perceived "unnaturalness" of the procedure. Closely related is the charge that the procedure depersonalizes or dehumanizes procreation. Other opponents of IVF have argued that we must abstain from any intervention that inflicts unknown risks on developing offspring. Another recurrent argument against IVF is that its acceptance by society will lead to the acceptance of more and more objectionable developments in reproductive technology.

In addition to arguments advanced in support of a wholesale rejection of *in vitro* fertilization, a number of concerns having a more limited scope can be identified. Some commentators have been quite willing to endorse the employment of IVF and embryo transfer within the framework of a marital relationship but find any third-party involvement, such as egg donation or surrogate motherhood, objectionable. Other critics object primarily to a frequent concomitant of *in vitro* procedures, the discarding of embryos considered unneeded or unsuitable for implantation. (Those who consider even an early embryo a person are especially vocal on this score.) Although the practice of freezing embryos offers a partial solution to the problem of surplus embryos, some would argue that, in this case, the "solution" creates more problems than it solves.

Two readings in this chapter focus directly on the ethics of IVF. In providing an overall defense of this reproductive technology, Peter Singer rejects many of the standard arguments against it. He also contends that there is no ethical problem with freezing *early* embryos, discarding them, or using them for research purposes. Susan Sherwin, in a very different spirit, works out a critique of IVF within the framework of feminist ethics. From a feminist point of view, she maintains, use of this technology is morally problematic for a number of closely related reasons. Although there is a diversity of views in the feminist community about the ethics of IVF, many feminists believe that the availability of IVF (and other reproductive technologies) is at best a mixed blessing for women.

In terms of ethical acceptability, cloning would seem to be the most problematic of all the reproductive technologies. Whereas the fundamental value of the other reproductive technologies under discussion can be located in the relief of infertility, the connection between cloning and the relief of infertility is more tenuous. Related to this consideration is the argument that cloning is the reproductive technology most likely to be misused, to the detriment of society. Of course, the stock charges against reproductive technology—that it is "unnatural" and depersonalizes reproduction— are also raised against cloning. But probably the most important arguments against cloning are those that emphasize psychological and social difficulties associated with a clone's manner of origin and lack of genetic uniqueness. One other noteworthy argument calls attention to the biological danger that would attend widespread cloning. Widespread cloning would have the effect of limiting the variety of genotypes in the species and thus limit species adaptability in the face of changing circumstances.

Thomas A. Mappes

The Case Against Surrogate Parenting

Herbert T. Krimmel

Herbert T. Krimmel is professor of law at Southwestern University School of Law, Los Angeles. His areas of specialization include jurisprudence and bioethics. He is the author of "Surrogate Mother Arrangements from the Perspective of the Child" and the coauthor of "Abortion: An Inspection into the Nature of Human Life and Potential Consequences of Legalizing Its Destruction."

In Krimmel's view, it is fundamentally wrong to separate the decision to create a child from the decision to be a parent to it. He does not object to the surrogate mother's role as host for a developing child, but he maintains that it is unethical for her to create a child (via the provision of an ovum) with the intention of abdicating all parental responsibilities. (For analogous reasons, he considers the donation of sperm in AID to be unethical.) "The procreator should desire the child for its own sake, and not as a means to attaining some other end." If surrogate motherhood arrangements are accepted by society, he maintains, there is a great danger that we will come to view children as commodities. He also argues that acceptance of surrogate motherhood arrangements would have other negative social consequences, most notably an increased stress upon the family structure. But his opposition to the legalization of surrogate motherhood arrangements is based first and foremost on his conviction that it is morally wrong for a person "to create a child, not because she desired it, but because it could be useful to her."

Is it ethical for someone to create a human life with the intention of giving it up? This seems to be the primary question for both surrogate mother arrangements and artificial insemination by donor (AID), since in both situations a person who is providing germinal material does so only upon assurance that someone else will assume full responsibility for the child he or she helps to create.

THE ETHICAL ISSUE

In analyzing the ethics of surrogate mother arrangements, it is helpful to begin by examining the roles the surrogate mother performs. First, she acts as a procreator in providing an ovum to be fertilized. Second, after her ovum has been fertilized by the sperm of the man who wishes to parent the child, she acts as host to the fetus, providing nurture and protection while the newly conceived individual develops.

I see no insurmountable moral objections to the functions the mother performs in this second role as host. Her actions are analogous to those of a foster mother or of a wet-nurse who cares for a child when the natural mother cannot or does not do so. Using a surrogate mother as a host for the fetus when the biological mother cannot

Reprinted with permission of the author and the publisher from *Hastings Center Report,* vol. 13 (October 1983), pp. 35–39.

bear the child is no more morally objectionable than employing others to help educate, train, or otherwise care for a child. Except in extremes, where the parent relinquishes or delegates responsibilities for a child for trivial reasons, the practice would not seem to raise a serious moral issue.

I would argue, however, that the first role that the surrogate mother performs—providing germinal material to be fertilized—does pose a major ethical problem. The surrogate mother provides her ovum, and enters into a surrogate mother arrangement, with the clear understanding that she is to avoid responsibility for the life she creates. Surrogate mother arrangements are designed to separate in the mind of the surrogate mother the decision to create a child from the decision to have and raise that child. The cause of this dissociation is some other benefit she will receive, most often money. In other words, her desire to create a child is born of some motive other than the desire to be a parent. This separation of the decision to create a child from the decision to parent it is ethically suspect. The child is conceived not because he is wanted by his biological mother, but because he can be useful to someone else. He is conceived in order to be given away.

At their deepest level, surrogate mother arrangements involve a change in motive for creating children: from a desire to have them for their own sake, to a desire to have them because they can provide some other benefit. The surrogate mother creates a child with the intention to abdicate parental responsibilities. Can we view this as ethical? My answer is no. I will explain why by analyzing various situations in which surrogate mother arrangements might be used.

WHY MOTIVE MATTERS

Let's begin with the single parent. A single woman might use AID, or a single man might use a surrogate mother arrangement, if she or he wanted a child but did not want to be burdened with a spouse. Either practice would intentionally deprive the child of a mother or a father. This, I assert, is fundamentally unfair to the child.

Those who disagree might point to divorce or to the death of a parent as situations in which a child is deprived of one parent and must rely solely or primarily upon the other. The comparison, however, is inapt. After divorce or the death of a parent, a child may find herself with a single parent due to circumstances that were unfortunate, unintended, and undesired. But when surrogate mother arrangements are used by a single parent, depriving the child of a second parent is one of the intended and desired effects. It is one thing to ask how to make the best of a bad situation when it is thrust upon a person. It is different altogether to ask whether one may intentionally set out to achieve the same result. The morality of identical results (for example, killings) will oftentimes differ depending upon whether the situation is invited by, or involuntarily thrust upon, the actor. Legal distinctions following and based upon this ethical distinction are abundant. The law of self-defense provides a notable example.

Since a woman can get pregnant if she wishes whether or not she is married, and since there is little that society can do to prevent women from creating children even if their intention is to deprive the children of a father, why should we be so concerned about single men using surrogate mother arrangements if they too want a child but not a spouse? To say that women can intentionally plan to be unwed mothers is not to condone the practice. Besides, society will hold the father liable in a paternity action if he can be found and identified, which indicates some social concern that people should not be able to abdicate the responsibilities that they incur in generating children. Otherwise, why do we condemn the proverbial sailor with a pregnant girlfriend in every port?

In many surrogate mother arrangements, of course, the surrogate mother will not be transferring custody of the child to a single man, but to a couple: the child's biological father and a stepmother, his wife. What are the ethics of surrogate mother arrangements when the child is taken into a two-parent family? Again, surrogate mother arrangements and AID pose similar ethical questions: The surrogate mother transfers her parental responsibilities to the wife of the biological father, while with AID the sperm donor relinquishes his interest in the child to the husband of the biological mother. In both cases the child is created with the intention of transferring the responsibility for its care to a new set of parents. The surrogate mother situation is more dramatic than AID since the transfer occurs after the child is born, while in the case of AID the transfer takes place at the time of the insemination. Nevertheless, the ethical point is the same: creating children for the purpose of transferring them. For a surrogate mother the question remains: Is it ethical to create a child for the purpose of transferring it to the wife of the biological father?

At first blush this looks to be little different from the typical adoption, for what is an adoption other than a transfer of responsibility from one set of parents to another? The analogy is misleading, however, for two reasons. First, it is difficult to imagine anyone conceiving children for the purpose of putting them up for adoption. And, if such a bizarre event were to occur, I doubt that we would look upon it with moral approval. Most adoptions arise either because an undesired conception is brought to term, or because the parents wanted to have the child, but find that they are unable to provide for it because of some unfortunate circumstances that develop after conception.

Second, even if surrogate mother arrangements were to be classified as a type of adoption, not all offerings of children for adoption are necessarily moral. For example, would it be moral for parents to offer their three-year-old for adoption because they are bored with the child? Would it be moral for a couple to offer for adoption their newborn female baby because they wanted a boy?

Therefore, even though surrogate mother arrangements may in some superficial ways be likened to adoption, one must still ask whether it is ethical to separate the decision to create children from the desire to have them. I would answer no. The procreator should desire the child for its own sake, and not as a means to attaining some other end. Even though one of the ends may be stated altruistically as an attempt to bring happiness to an infertile couple, the child is still being used by the surrogate. She creates it not because she desires it, but because she desires something from it.

To sanction the use and treatment of human beings as means to the achievement of other goals instead of as ends in themselves is to accept an ethic with a tragic past, and to establish a precedent with a dangerous future. Already the press has reported the decision of one couple to conceive a child for the purpose of using it as a bone marrow donor for its sibling (*Los Angeles Times,* April 17, 1979, p. I-2). And the bioethics literature contains articles seriously considering whether we should clone human beings to serve as an inventory of spare parts for organ transplants and articles that foresee the use of comatose human beings as self-replenishing blood banks and manufacturing plants for human hormones. How far our society is willing to proceed down this road is uncertain, but it is clear that the first step to all these practices is the acceptance of the same principle that the Nazis attempted to use to justify their medical experiments at the Nuremberg War Crimes Trials: that human beings may be used as means to the achievement of other goals, and need not be treated as ends in themselves.

But why, it might be asked, is it so terrible if the surrogate mother does not desire the child for its own sake, when under the proposed surrogate mother arrangements there will be a couple eagerly desiring to have the child and to be its parents? That this argument may not be entirely accurate will be illustrated in the following section, but the basic reply is that creating a child without desiring it fundamentally changes the way we look at children—instead of viewing them as unique individual personalities to be desired in their own right, we may come to view them as commodities or items of manufacture to be desired because of their utility. A recent newspaper account describes the business of an agency that matches surrogate mothers with barren couples as follows:

> Its first product is due for delivery today. Twelve others are on the way and an additional 20 have been ordered. The "company" is Surrogate Mothering Ltd. and the "product" is babies.[1]

The dangers of this view are best illustrated by examining what might go wrong in a surrogate mother arrangement, and most important, by viewing how the various parties to the contract may react to the disappointment.

WHAT MIGHT GO WRONG

Ninety-nine percent of the surrogate mother arrangements may work out just fine: the child will be born normal, and the adopting parents (that is, the biological father and his wife) will want it. But, what happens when, unforeseeably, the child is born deformed? Since many defects cannot be discovered prenatally by amniocentesis or other means, the situation is bound to arise. Similarly, consider what would happen if the biological father were to die before the birth of the child. Or if the "child" turns out to be twins or triplets. Each of these instances poses an inevitable situation where the adopting parents may be unhappy with the prospect of getting the child or children. Although legislation can mandate that the adopting parents take the child or children in whatever condition they come or whatever the situation, provided the surrogate mother has abided by all the contractual provisions of the surrogate mother arrangement, the important point for our discussion is the attitude that the surrogate mother or the adopting parent might have. Consider the example of the deformed child.

When I participated in the Surrogate Parent Foundation's inaugural symposium in November 1981, I was struck by the attitude of both the surrogate mothers and the adopting parents to these problems. The adopting parents worried, "Do we have to take such a child?" and the surrogate mothers said in response, "Well, we don't want to be stuck with it." Clearly, both groups were anxious not [to] be responsible for the "undesirable child" born of the surrogate mother arrangement. What does this portend?

It is human nature that when one pays money, one expects value. Things that one pays for have a way of being seen as commodities. Unavoidable in surrogate mother arrangements are questions such as: "Did I get a good one?" We see similar behavior with respect to the adoption of children: comparatively speaking, there is no shortage of black, Mexican-American, mentally retarded, or older children seeking homes; the shortage is in attractive, intelligent-looking Caucasian babies. Similarly, surrogate mother arrangements involve more than just the desire to have a child. The desire is for a certain type of child.

But, it may be objected, don't all parents voice these same concerns in the normal course of having children? Not exactly. No one doubts or minimizes the pain and disappointment parents feel when they learn that their child is born with some genetic or congenital birth defect. But this is different from the surrogate mother situation, where neither the surrogate mother situation, where neither the surrogate mother nor the adopting parents may feel responsible, and both sides may feel that they have a legitimate excuse not to assume responsibility for the child. The surrogate mother might blame the biological father for having "defective sperm," as the adopting parents might blame the surrogate mother for a "defective ovum" or for improper care of the fetus during pregnancy. The adopting parents desire a normal child, not *this* child in any condition, and the surrogate mother doesn't want it in any event. So both sides will feel threatened by the birth of an "undesirable child." Like bruised fruit in the produce bin of a supermarket, this child is likely to become an object of avoidance.

Certainly, in the natural course of having children a mother may doubt whether she wants a child if the father has died before its birth; parents may shy away from a defective infant, or be distressed at the thought of multiple births. Nevertheless, I believe they are more likely to accept these contingencies as a matter of fate. I do not think this is the case with surrogate mother arrangements. After all, in the surrogate mother arrangement the adopting parents can blame someone outside the marital relationship. The surrogate mother has been hosting this child all along, and she is delivering it. It certainly *looks* far more like a commodity than the child that arrives in the natural course within the family unit.

A DANGEROUS AGENDA

Another social problem, which arises out of the first, is the fear that surrogate mother arrangements will fall prey to eugenic concerns. Surrogate mother contracts typically have clauses requiring genetic tests of the fetus and stating that the surrogate mother must have an abortion (or keep the child herself) if the child does not pass these tests.

In the last decade we have witnessed a renaissance of interest in eugenics. This, coupled with advances in biomedical technology, has created a host of abuses and new moral problems. For example, genetic counseling clinics now face a dilemma: amniocentesis, the same procedure that identifies whether a fetus suffers from certain genetic defects, also discloses the sex of a fetus. Genetic counseling clinics have reported that even when the fetus is normal, a disproportionate number of mothers abort female children. Aborting normal fetuses simply because the prospective parents desire children of a certain sex is one result of viewing children as commodities. The recent scandal at the Repository for Germinal Choice, the so-called "Nobel Sperm Bank," provides another chilling example. Their first "customer" was, unbeknownst to the staff, a woman who "had lost custody of two other children because they were abused in an effort to 'make them smart.' "[2] Of course, these and similar evils may occur whether or not surrogate mother arrangements are allowed by law. But to the extent that they promote the view of children as commodities, these arrangements contribute to these problems. There is nothing wrong with striving for betterment, as long as it does not result in intolerance to that which is not perfect. But I fear that the latter attitude will become prevalent.

Sanctioning surrogate mother arrangements can also exert pressures upon the family structure. First, as was noted earlier, there is nothing technically to prevent the use of surrogate mother arrangements by single males desiring to become parents. Indeed, single females can already do this with AID or even without it. But even if legislation were to limit the use of the surrogate mother arrangement to infertile couples, other pressures would occur: namely the intrusion of a third adult into the marital community. I do not think that society is ready to accept either single parenting or quasi-adulterous arrangements as normal.

Another stress on the family structure arises within the family of the surrogate mother. When the child is surrendered to the adopting parents it is removed not only from the surrogate mother, but also from her family. They too have interests to be considered. Do not the siblings of that child have an interest in the fact that their little baby brother has been "given" away? One woman, the mother of a medical student who had often donated sperm for artificial insemination, expressed her feelings to me eloquently. She asked, "I wonder how many grandchildren I have that I have never seen and never been able to hold or cuddle."

Intrafamily tensions can also be expected to result in the family of the adopting parents due to the asymmetry of relationship the adopting parents will have toward the child. The adopting mother has no biological relationship to the child, whereas the adopting father is also the child's biological father. Won't this unequal biological claim on the child be used as a wedge in childrearing arguments? Can't we imagine the father saying, "Well, he is my son, not yours"? What if the couple eventually gets divorced? Should custody in a subsequent divorce between the adopting mother and the biological father be treated simply as a normal child custody dispute? Or should the biological relationship between father and child weigh more heavily? These questions do not arise in typical adoption situations since both parents are equally unrelated biologically to the child. Indeed, in adoption there is symmetry. The surrogate mother situation is more analogous to second marriages, where the children of one party by a prior marriage are adopted by the new spouse. Since asymmetry in second marriage situations causes problems, we can anticipate similar difficulties arising from surrogate mother arrangements.

There is also the worry that the offspring of a surrogate mother arrangement will be deprived of important information about his or her heritage. This also happens with adopted children or children conceived by AID, who lack information about their biological parents, which could be important to them medically. Another less popularly recognized problem is the danger of half-sibling marriages, where the child of the surrogate mother unwittingly falls in love with a half sister or brother. The only way to avoid these problems is to dispense with the confidentiality of parental records; however, the natural parents may not always want their identity disclosed.

The legalization of surrogate mother arrangements may also put undue pressure upon poor women to use their bodies in this way to support themselves and their families. Analogous problems have arisen in the past with the use of paid blood donors. And occasionally the press reports someone desperate enough to offer to sell an eye or some other organ. I believe that certain things should be viewed as too important to be sold as commodities, and I hope that we have advanced from the time when parents raised children for profitable labor, or found themselves forced to sell their children.

While many of the social dilemmas I have outlined here have their analogies in other present-day occurrences such as divorced families or in adoption, every addition is hurtful. Legalizing surrogate mother arrangements will increase the frequency of these problems, and put more stress on our society's shared moral values.

[CONCLUSION]

An infertile couple might prefer to raise a child with a biological relationship to the husband, rather than to raise an adopted child who has no biological relationship to either the husband or the wife. But does the marginal increase in joy that they might therefore experience outweigh the potential pain that they, or the child conceived in such arrangements, or others might suffer? Does their preference outweigh the social costs and problems that the legalization of surrogate mothering might well engender? I honestly do not know. I don't even know on what hypothetical scale such interests could be weighed and balanced. But even if we could weigh such interests, and even if personal preference outweighed the costs, I still would not be able to say that we could justify achieving those ends by these means; that ethically it would be permissible for a person to create a child, not because she desired it, but because it could be useful to her. . . .

NOTES

1 Bob Dvorchak, "Surrogate Mothers: Pregnant Idea Now a Pregnant Business," *Los Angeles Herald Examiner,* December 27, 1983, p. A1.
2 "2 Children Taken from Sperm Bank Mother," *Los Angeles Times,* July 14, 1982; p. I-3; "The Sperm Bank Scandal," *Newsweek* 24 (July 26, 1982).

QUESTIONS

1 Is it morally wrong for a person to provide genetic material (via sperm or egg donation) for the creation of a child with the explicit intention of transferring parental responsibility to someone else?

2 Would it be unfair to the resulting child for a single woman to make use of AID or a single man to make use of a surrogate mother arrangement?

3 Do surrogate motherhood arrangements encourage the view that children are commodities? Do they threaten the structure of the family?

Opinion in the *Matter of Baby M*

Justice Robert N. Wilentz

Robert N. Wilentz is chief justice of the New Jersey Supreme Court. A graduate of Columbia University Law School, he was admitted to the New Jersey bar in 1952 and appointed chief justice in 1979.

This case developed when Mary Beth Whitehead entered into a commercial surrogacy agreement with a married couple (Elizabeth and William Stern) and subsequently decided not to surrender the child to them. The original trial court in New Jersey ruled that the surrogacy contract was valid. It also ordered termination of Whitehead's parental rights, awarded sole custody of the child to Mr. Stern, and authorized adoption by Mrs. Stern.

Chief Justice Wilentz, writing for a unanimous New Jersey Supreme Court, argues that the surrogacy contract is invalid and unenforceable in New Jersey because it conflicts with both the statutes and public policies of that state. Although consideration of the best interests of the child leads him to award primary custody to the Sterns, he finds no basis for the termination of Whitehead's parental rights and therefore holds that she is entitled to visitation.

In this matter the Court is asked to determine the validity of a contract that purports to provide a new way of bringing children into a family. For a fee of $10,000, a woman agrees to be artificially inseminated with the semen of another woman's husband; she is to conceive a child, carry it to term, and after its birth surrender it to the natural father and his wife. The intent of the contract is that the child's natural mother will thereafter be forever separated from her child. The wife is to adopt the child, and she and the natural father are to be regarded as its parents for all purposes. The contract providing for this is called a "surrogacy contract," the natural mother inappropriately called the "surrogate mother."

We invalidate the surrogacy contract because it conflicts with the law and public

New Jersey Supreme Court (1988). Reprinted with permission from 109 N.J. 396. Copyright © 1988 by West Publishing Co.

policy of this State. While we recognize the depth of the yearning of infertile couples to have their own children, we find the payment of money to a "surrogate" mother illegal, perhaps criminal, and potentially degrading to women. Although in this case we grant custody to the natural father, the evidence having clearly proved such custody to be in the best interests of the infant, we void both the termination of the surrogate mother's parental rights and the adoption of the child by the wife/stepparent. We thus restore the "surrogate" as the mother of the child. We remand the issue of the natural mother's visitation rights to the trial court, since that issue was not reached below and the record before us is not sufficient to permit us to decide it *de novo.*

We find no offense to our present laws where a woman voluntarily and without payment agrees to act as a "surrogate" mother, provided that she is not subject to a binding agreement to surrender her child. Moreover, our holding today does not preclude the Legislature from altering the current statutory scheme, within constitutional limits, so as to permit surrogacy contracts. Under current law, however, the surrogacy agreement before us is illegal and invalid.

FACTS

In February 1985, William Stern and Mary Beth Whitehead entered into a surrogacy contract. It recited that Stern's wife, Elizabeth, was infertile, that they wanted a child, and that Mrs. Whitehead was willing to provide that child as the mother with Mr. Stern as the father.

The contract provided that through artificial insemination using Mr. Stern's sperm, Mrs. Whitehead would become pregnant, carry the child to term, bear it, deliver it to the Sterns, and thereafter do whatever was necessary to terminate her maternal rights so that Mrs. Stern could thereafter adopt the child. Mrs. Whitehead's husband, Richard,[1] was also a party to the contract; Mrs. Stern was not. Mr. Whitehead promised to do all acts necessary to rebut the presumption of paternity under the Parentage Act. Although Mrs. Stern was not a party to the surrogacy agreement, the contract gave her sole custody of the child in the event of Mr. Stern's death. Mrs. Stern's status as a nonparty to the surrogate parenting agreement presumably was to avoid the application of the baby-selling statute to this arrangement.

Mr. Stern, on his part, agreed to attempt the artificial insemination and to pay Mrs. Whitehead $10,000 after the child's birth, on its delivery to him. In a separate contract, Mr. Stern agreed to pay $7,500 to the Infertility Center of New York ("ICNY"). The Center's advertising campaigns solicit surrogate mothers and encourage infertile couples to consider surrogacy. ICNY arranged for the surrogacy contract by bringing the parties together, explaining the process to them, furnishing the contractual form, and providing legal counsel.

The history of the parties' involvement in this arrangement suggests their good faith. William and Elizabeth Stern were married in July 1974, having met at the University of Michigan, where both were Ph.D. candidates. Due to financial considerations and Mrs. Stern's pursuit of a medical degree and residency, they decided to defer starting a family until 1981. Before then, however, Mrs. Stern learned that she might have multiple sclerosis and that the disease in some cases renders pregnancy a serious health risk. Her anxiety appears to have exceeded the actual risk, which current medical authorities assess as minimal. Nonetheless that anxiety was evidently quite real, Mrs. Stern fearing that pregnancy might precipitate blindness, paraplegia, or other forms of debilitation. Based on the perceived risk, the Sterns decided to forego having their own children. The decision had special significance for Mr. Stern. Most of his family had been destroyed in the Holocaust. As the family's only survivor, he very much wanted to continue his bloodline.

Initially the Sterns considered adoption, but were discouraged by the substantial delay apparently involved and by the potential problem they saw arising from their age and their differing religious backgrounds. They were most eager for some other means to start a family.

The paths of Mrs. Whitehead and the Sterns to surrogacy were similar. Both responded to advertising by ICNY. The Sterns' response, following their inquiries into adoption, was the result of their long-standing decision to have a child. Mrs. Whitehead's response apparently resulted from her sympathy with family members and others who could have no children (she stated that she wanted to give another couple the "gift of life"); she also wanted the $10,000 to help her family. . . .

. . . The two couples met to discuss the surrogacy arrangement and decided to go forward. On February 6, 1985, Mr. Stern and Mr. and Mrs. Whitehead executed the surrogate parenting agreement. After several artificial inseminations over a period of months, Mrs. Whitehead became pregnant. The pregnancy was uneventful and on March 27, 1986, Baby M was born.

Not wishing anyone at the hospital to be aware of the surrogacy arrangement, Mr. and Mrs. Whitehead appeared to all as the proud parents of a healthy female child. Her birth certificate indicated her name to be Sara Elizabeth Whitehead and her father to be Richard Whitehead. In accordance with Mrs. Whitehead's request, the Sterns visited the hospital unobtrusively to see the newborn child.

Mrs. Whitehead realized, almost from the moment of birth, that she could not part with this child. She had felt a bond with it even during pregnancy. Some indication of the attachment was conveyed to the Sterns at the hospital when they told Mrs. Whitehead what they were going to name the baby. She apparently broke into tears and indicated that she did not know if she could give up the child. She talked about how the baby looked like her other daughter, and made it clear that she was experiencing great difficulty with the decision.

Nonetheless, Mrs. Whitehead was, for the moment, true to her word. Despite powerful inclinations to the contrary, she turned her child over to the Sterns on March 30 at the Whiteheads' home.

The Sterns were thrilled with their new child. They had planned extensively for its arrival, far beyond the practical furnishing of a room for her. It was a time of joyful celebration—not just for them but for their friends as well. The Sterns looked forward to raising their daughter, whom they named Melissa. While aware by then that Mrs. Whitehead was undergoing an emotional crisis, they were as yet not cognizant of the depth of that crisis and its implications for their newly-enlarged family.

Later in the evening of March 30, Mrs. Whitehead became deeply disturbed, disconsolate, stricken with unbearable sadness. She had to have her child. She could not eat, sleep, or concentrate on anything other than her need for her baby. The next day she went to the Sterns' home and told them how much she was suffering.

The depth of Mrs. Whitehead's despair surprised and frightened the Sterns. She told them that she could not live without her baby, that she must have her, even if only for one week, that thereafter she would surrender her child. The Sterns, concerned that Mrs. Whitehead might indeed commit suicide, not wanting under any circumstances to risk that, and in any event believing that Mrs. Whitehead would keep her word, turned the child over to her. It was not until four months later, after a series of attempts to regain possession of the child, that Melissa was returned to the Sterns, having been forcibly removed from the home where she was then living with Mr. and Mrs. Whitehead, the home in Florida owned by Mary Beth Whitehead's parents.

The struggle over Baby M began when it became apparent that Mrs. Whitehead could not return the child to Mr. Stern. Due to Mrs. Whitehead's refusal to relinquish the baby, Mr. Stern filed a complaint seeking enforcement of the surrogacy contract. He alleged, accurately, that Mrs. Whitehead had not only refused to comply with the surrogacy contract but had threatened to flee from New Jersey with the child in order to avoid even the possibility of his obtaining custody. The court papers asserted that if Mrs. Whitehead were to be given notice of the application for an order requiring her to relinquish custody, she would, prior to the hearing, leave the state with the baby. And that is precisely what she did. After the order was entered, *ex parte,* the process server, aided by the police, in the presence of the Sterns, entered Mrs. Whitehead's home to execute the order. Mr. Whitehead fled with the child, who had been handed to him through a window while those who came to enforce the order were thrown off balance by a dispute over the child's current name.

The Whiteheads immediately fled to Florida with Baby M. They stayed initially with Mrs. Whitehead's parents, where one of Mrs. Whitehead's children had been living. For the next three months, the Whiteheads and Melissa lived at roughly twenty different hotels, motels, and homes in order to avoid apprehension. From time to time Mrs. Whitehead would call Mr. Stern to discuss the matter; the conversations, recorded by Mr. Stern on advice of counsel, show an escalating dispute about rights, morality, and power, accompanied by threats of Mrs. Whitehead to kill herself, to kill the child, and falsely to accuse Mr. Stern of sexually molesting Mrs. Whitehead's other daughter.

Eventually the Sterns discovered where the Whiteheads were staying, commenced supplementary proceedings in Florida, and obtained an order requiring the Whiteheads to turn over the child. Police in Florida enforced the order, forcibly removing the child from her grandparents' home. She was soon thereafter brought to New Jersey and turned over to the Sterns. The prior order of the court, issued *ex parte,* awarding custody of the child to the Sterns *pendente lite,* was reaffirmed by the trial court after consideration of the certified representations of the parties (both represented by counsel) concerning the unusual sequence of events that had unfolded. Pending final judgment, Mrs. Whitehead was awarded limited visitation with Baby M.

The Sterns' complaint, in addition to seeking possession and ultimately custody of the child, sought enforcement of the surrogacy contract. Pursuant to the contract, it asked that the child be permanently placed in their custody, that Mrs. Whitehead's parental rights be terminated, and that Mrs. Stern be allowed to adopt the child, *i.e.,* that, for all purposes, Melissa become the Sterns' child.

The trial took thirty-two days over a period of more than two months. . . . Soon after the conclusion of the trial, the trial court announced its opinion from the bench. 217 *N.J.Super.* 313 (1987). It held that the surrogacy contract was valid; ordered that Mrs. Whitehead's parental rights be terminated and that sole custody of the child be granted to Mr. Stern; and, after hearing brief testimony from Mrs. Stern, immediately entered an order allowing the adoption of Melissa by Mrs. Stern, all in accordance with the surrogacy contract. Pending the outcome of the appeal, we granted a continuation of visitation to Mrs. Whitehead, although slightly more limited than the visitation allowed during the trial.

Although clearly expressing its view that the surrogacy contract was valid, the trial court devoted the major portion of its opinion to the question of the baby's best interests. . . .

On the question of best interests . . . the court's analysis of the testimony was perceptive, demonstrating both its understanding of the case and its considerable experience in these matters. We agree substantially with both its analysis and conclusions on the matter of custody.

The court's review and analysis of the surrogacy contract, however, is not at all in accord with ours. . . .

INVALIDITY AND UNENFORCEABILITY OF SURROGACY CONTRACT

We have concluded that this surrogacy contract is invalid. Our conclusion has two bases: direct conflict with existing statutes and conflict with the public policies of this State, as expressed in its statutory and decisional law.

One of the surrogacy contract's basic purposes, to achieve the adoption of a child through private placement, though permitted in New Jersey "is very much disfavored." Its use of money for this purpose—and we have no doubt whatsoever that the money is being paid to obtain an adoption and not, as the Sterns argue, for the personal services of Mary Beth Whitehead—is illegal and perhaps criminal. In addition to the inducement of money, there is the coercion of contract: the natural mother's irrevocable agreement, prior to birth, even prior to conception, to surrender the child to the adoptive couple. Such an agreement is totally unenforceable in private placement adoption. Even where the adoption is through an approved agency, the formal agreement to surrender occurs only *after* birth . . . , and then, by regulation, only after the birth mother has been offered counseling. Integral to these invalid provisions of the surrogacy contract is the related agreement, equally invalid, on the part of the natural mother to cooperate with, and not to contest, proceedings to terminate her parental rights, as well as her contractual concession, in aid of the adoption, that the child's best interests would be served by awarding custody to the natural father and his wife—all of this before she has even conceived, and, in some cases, before she has the slightest idea of what the natural father and adoptive mother are like.

The foregoing provisions not only directly conflict with New Jersey statutes, but also offend long-established State policies. These critical terms, which are at the heart of the contract, are invalid and unenforceable; the conclusion therefore follows, without more, that the entire contract is unenforceable.

A   Conflict with Statutory Provisions

The surrogacy contract conflicts with: (1) laws prohibiting the use of money in connection with adoptions; (2) laws requiring proof of parental unfitness or abandonment before termination of parental rights is ordered or an adoption is granted; and (3) laws that make surrender of custody and consent to adoption revocable in private placement adoptions. . . .

B   Public Policy Considerations

The surrogacy contract's invalidity, resulting from its direct conflict with the above statutory provisions, is further underlined when its goals and means are measured against New Jersey's public policy. The contract's basic premise, that the natural parents can decide in advance of birth which one is to have custody of the child, bears no relationship to the settled law that the child's best interests shall determine custody. . . . The surrogacy contract guarantees permanent separation of the child from one of its natural parents. Our policy, however, has long been that to the extent possible, children should remain with and be brought up by both of their natural parents. . . .

The surrogacy contract violates the policy of this State that the rights of natural parents are equal concerning their child, the father's right no greater than the mother's. . . . The whole purpose and effect of the surrogacy contract was to give the father the exclusive right to the child by destroying the rights of the mother.

The policies expressed in our comprehensive laws governing consent to the surrender of a child stand in stark contrast to the surrogacy contract and what it implies. . . .

Under the contract, the natural mother is irrevocably committed before she knows the strength of her bond with her child. She never makes a totally voluntary, informed decision, for quite clearly any decision prior to the baby's birth is, in the most important sense, uninformed, and any decision after that, compelled by a pre-existing contractual commitment, the threat of a lawsuit, and the inducement of a $10,000 payment, is less than totally voluntary. Her interests are of little concern to those who controlled this transaction. . . .

Worst of all, however, is the contract's total disregard of the best interests of the child. There is not the slightest suggestion that any inquiry will be made at any time to determine the fitness of the Sterns as custodial parents, of Mrs. Stern as an adoptive parent, their superiority to Mrs. Whitehead, or the effect on the child of not living with her natural mother.

This is the sale of a child, or, at the very least, the sale of a mother's right to her child, the only mitigating factor being that one of the purchasers is the father. Almost every evil that prompted the prohibition on the payment of money in connection with adoptions exists here. . . .

The main difference [between an adoption and a surrogacy contract], that the unwanted pregnancy is unintended while the situation of the surrogate mother is voluntary and intended, is really not significant. Initially, it produces stronger reactions of sympathy for the mother whose pregnancy was unwanted than for the surrogate mother, who "went into this with her eyes wide open." On reflection, however, it appears that the essential evil is the same, taking advantage of a woman's circumstances (the unwanted pregnancy or the need for money) in order to take away her child, the difference being one of degree.

In the scheme contemplated by the surrogacy contract in this case, a middle man, propelled by profit, promotes the sale. Whatever idealism may have motivated any of the participants, the profit motive predominates, permeates, and ultimately governs the transaction. The demand for children is great and the supply small. The availability of contraception, abortion, and the greater willingness of single mothers to bring up their children has led to a shortage of babies offered for adoption. The situation is ripe for the entry of the middleman who will bring some equilibrium into the market by increasing the supply through the use of money.

Intimated, but disputed, is the assertion that surrogacy will be used for the benefit of the rich at the expense of the poor. In response it is noted that the Sterns are not rich and the Whiteheads not poor. Nevertheless, it is clear to us that it is unlikely that surrogate mothers will be as proportionately numerous among those women in the top twenty percent income bracket as among those in the bottom twenty percent. Put differently, we doubt that infertile couples in the low-income bracket will find upper income surrogates.

In any event, even in this case one should not pretend that disparate wealth does not play a part simply because the contrast is not the dramatic "rich versus poor." At the time of trial, the Whiteheads' net assets were probably negative—Mrs. Whitehead's own sister was foreclosing on a second mortgage. Their income derived from Mr. Whitehead's labors. Mrs. Whitehead is a homemaker, having previously held part-time jobs. The Sterns are both professionals, she a medical doctor, he a biochemist. Their combined income when both were working was about $89,500 a year and their assets sufficient to pay for the surrogacy contract arrangements.

The point is made that Mrs. Whitehead *agreed* to the surrogacy arrangement, supposedly fully understanding the consequences. Putting aside the issue of how compelling her need for money may have been, and how significant her understanding of the consequences, we suggest that her consent is irrelevant. There are, in a civilized society, some things that money cannot buy. In America, we decided long ago that merely because conduct purchased by money was "voluntary" did not mean that it was good or beyond regulation and prohibition. Employers can no longer buy labor at the lowest price they can bargain for, even though that labor is "voluntary," or buy women's labor for less money than paid to men for the same job, or purchase the agreement of children to perform oppressive labor, or purchase the agreement of workers to subject themselves to unsafe or unhealthful working conditions. There are, in short, values that society deems more important than granting to wealth whatever it can buy, be it labor, love, or life. Whether this principle recommends prohibition of surrogacy, which presumably sometimes results in great satisfaction to all of the parties, is not for us to say. We note here only that, under existing law, the fact that Mrs. Whitehead "agreed" to the arrangement is not dispositive.

The long-term effects of surrogacy contracts are not known, but feared—the impact on the child who learns her life was bought, that she is the offspring of someone who gave birth to her only to obtain money; the impact on the natural mother as the full weight of her isolation is felt along with the full reality of the sale of her body and her child; the impact on the natural father and adoptive mother once they realize the consequences of their conduct. Literature in related areas suggests these are substantial considerations, although, given the newness of surrogacy, there is little information.

The surrogacy contract is based on principles that are directly contrary to the objectives of our laws. It guarantees the separation of a child from its mother; it looks to adoption regardless of suitability; it totally ignores the child; it takes the child from the mother regardless of her wishes and her maternal fitness; and it does all of this, it accomplishes all of its goals, through the use of money.

Beyond that is the potential degradation of some women that may result from this arrangement. In many cases, of course, surrogacy may bring satisfaction, not only to the infertile couple, but to the surrogate mother herself. The fact, however, that many women may not perceive surrogacy negatively but rather see it as an opportunity does not diminish its potential for devastation to other women.

In sum, the harmful consequences of this surrogacy arrangement appear to us all too palpable. In New Jersey the surrogate mother's agreement to sell her child is void. Its irrevocability infects the entire contract, as does the money that purports to buy it.

TERMINATION

We have already noted that under our laws termination of parental rights cannot be based on contract, but may be granted only on proof of the statutory requirements. That conclusion was one of the bases for invalidating the surrogacy contract. Although excluding the contract as a basis for parental termination, we did not explicitly deal with the question of whether the statutory bases for termination existed. We do so here.

As noted before, if termination of Mrs. Whitehead's parental rights is justified, Mrs. Whitehead will have no further claim either to custody or to visitation, and adoption by Mrs. Stern may proceed pursuant to the private placement adoption statute. If termination is not justified, Mrs. Whitehead remains the legal mother, and even if not entitled to custody, she would ordinarily be expected to have some rights of visitation. . . .

Nothing in this record justifies a finding that would allow a court to terminate Mary Beth Whitehead's parental rights under the statutory standard. It is not simply that obviously there was no "intentional abandonment or very substantial neglect of parental duties without a reasonable expectation of reversal of that conduct in the future," quite the contrary, but furthermore that the trial court never found Mrs. Whitehead an unfit mother and indeed affirmatively stated that Mary Beth Whitehead had been a good mother to her other children. . . .

CUSTODY

Having decided that the surrogacy contract is illegal and unenforceable, we now must decide the custody question without regard to the provisions of the surrogacy contract that would give Mr. Stern sole and permanent custody. . . .

. . . The question of custody in this case, as in practically all cases, assumes the fitness of both parents, and no serious contention is made in this case that either is unfit. The issue here is which life would be *better* for Baby M, one with primary custody in the Whiteheads or one with primary custody in the Sterns.

The circumstances of this custody dispute are unusual and they have provoked some unusual contentions. The Whiteheads claim that even if the child's best interests would be served by our awarding custody to the Sterns, we should not do so, since that will encourage surrogacy contracts—contracts claimed by the Whiteheads, and we agree, to be violative of important legislatively-stated public policies. Their position is that in order that surrogacy contracts be deterred, custody should remain in the surrogate mother unless she is unfit, regardless of the best interests of the child. We disagree. Our declaration that this surrogacy contract is unenforceable and illegal is sufficient to deter similar agreements. We need not sacrifice the child's interests in order to make that point sharper. . . .

Our custody conclusion is based on strongly persuasive testimony contrasting both the family life of the Whiteheads and the Sterns and the personalities and characters of the individuals. The stability of the Whitehead family life was doubtful at the time of trial. Their finances were in serious trouble (foreclosure by Mrs. Whitehead's sister on a second mortgage was in process). Mr. Whitehead's employment, though relatively steady, was always at risk because of his alcoholism, a condition that he seems not to have been able to confront effectively. Mrs. Whitehead had not worked for quite some time, her last two employments having been part-time. One of the Whiteheads' positive attributes was their ability to bring up two children, and apparently well, even in so vulnerable a household. Yet substantial question was raised even about that aspect of their home life. The expert testimony contained criticism of Mrs. Whitehead's handling of her son's educational difficulties. Certain of the experts noted that Mrs. Whitehead perceived herself as omnipotent and omniscient concerning her children. She knew what they were thinking, what they wanted, and she spoke for them. As to Melissa, Mrs. Whitehead expressed the view that she alone knew what that child's cries and sounds meant. Her inconsistent stories about various things engendered grave doubts about her ability to explain honestly and sensitively to Baby M—and at the right time—the nature of her origin. Although faith in professional counseling is not a *sine qua non* of parenting, several experts believed that Mrs. Whitehead's contempt for professional help, especially professional psychological help, coincided with her feelings of omnipotence in a way that could be devastating to a child who most likely will need such help. In short, while love and affection there would be, Baby M's life with the Whiteheads promised to be too closely controlled by Mrs. Whitehead. The prospects for wholesome, independent psychological growth and development would be at serious risk.

The Sterns have no other children, but all indications are that their household and their personalities promise a much more likely foundation for Melissa to grow and thrive. There *is* a track record of sorts—during the one-and-a-half years of custody Baby M has done very well, and the relationship between both Mr. and Mrs. Stern and the baby has become very strong. The household is stable, and likely to remain so. Their finances are more than adequate, their circle of friends supportive, and their marriage happy. Most important, they are loving, giving, nurturing, and open-minded people. They have demonstrated the wish and ability to nurture and protect Melissa, yet at the same time to encourage her independence. Their lack of experience is more than made up for by a willingness to learn and to listen, a willingness that is enhanced by their professional training, especially Mrs. Stern's experience as a pediatrician. They are honest; they can recognize error, deal with it, and learn from it. They will try to determine rationally the best way to cope with problems in their relationship with Melissa. When the time comes to tell her about her origins, they will probably have found a means of doing so that accords with the best interests of Baby M. All in all, Melissa's future appears solid, happy, and promising with them.

Based on all of this we have concluded, independent of the trial court's identical conclusion, that Melissa's best interests call for custody in the Sterns. . . .

VISITATION

The trial court's decision to terminate Mrs. Whitehead's parental rights precluded it from making any determination on visitation. Our reversal of the trial court's order, however, requires delineation of Mrs. Whitehead's rights to visitation. It is apparent to us that this factually sensitive issue, which was never addressed below, should not be determined *de novo* by this Court. We therefore remand the visitation issue to the trial court for an abbreviated hearing and determination. . . .

We have decided that Mrs. Whitehead is entitled to visitation at some point, and that question is not open to the trial court on this remand. The trial court will determine what kind of visitation shall be granted to her, with or without conditions, and when and under what circumstances it should commence. . . .

CONCLUSION

. . . We have found that our present laws do not permit the surrogacy contract used in this case. Nowhere, however, do we find any legal prohibition against surrogacy when the surrogate mother volunteers, without any payment, to act as a surrogate and is given the right to change her mind and to assert her parental rights. Moreover, the Legislature remains free to deal with this most sensitive issue as it sees fit, subject only to constitutional constraints. . . .

NOTES

1 Subsequent to the trial court proceedings, Mr. and Mrs. Whitehead were divorced, and soon thereafter Mrs. Whitehead remarried. Nevertheless, in the course of this opinion we will make reference almost exclusively to the facts as they existed at the time of trial, the facts on which the decision we now review was reached. We note moreover that Mr. Whitehead remains a party to this dispute. For these reasons, we continue to refer to appellants as Mr. and Mrs. Whitehead.

QUESTIONS

1 Are commercial surrogacy contracts tantamount to baby selling?
2 Do you agree with the custody decision made by Justice Wilentz in this case?
3 Would the New Jersey legislature be well advised to pass a statute making commercial surrogacy contracts legally valid and enforceable?

Surrogate Motherhood as Prenatal Adoption

Bonnie Steinbock

Bonnie Steinbock is associate professor of philosophy at the State University of New York at Albany. She is the editor of *Killing and Letting Die* (1980). Her published articles include "The Intentional Termination of Life," "Prenatal Wrongful Death," and "Drunk Driving."

Steinbock maintains that commercial surrogacy contracts should not be prohibited by the state. She argues that it is unjustifiably paternalistic for the state to ban surrogacy in an effort to protect the potential surrogate from a choice that may later be regretted. She also argues that concerns about a negative psychological impact on potential offspring are insufficient to warrant an outright ban. Moreover, in her view, commercial surrogacy is neither inherently exploitive nor inconsistent with human dignity. In dealing with the charge that commercial surrogacy amounts to baby selling, she insists that payment to the surrogate can be understood as compensation for "the risks, sacrifice, and discomfort the surrogate undergoes during pregnancy." Although Steinbock considers the legal prohibition of surrogacy contracts to be incompatible with a proper regard for the value of individual freedom, she believes that the practice of surrogacy should be regulated by the state. In particular, she would insist that surrogacy contracts be structured so as to allow the surrogate a postnatal waiting period during which she would be free to change her mind and keep the child.

The recent case of "Baby M" has brought surrogate motherhood to the forefront of American attention. Ultimately, whether we permit or prohibit surrogacy depends on

From *Law, Medicine, and Health Care*, vol. 16 (Spring 1988). Reprinted with permission of the publisher (American Society of Law and Medicine).

what we take to be good reasons for preventing people from acting as they wish. A growing number of people want to be, or hire, surrogates; are there legitimate reasons to prevent them? Apart from its intrinsic interest, the issue of surrogate motherhood provides us with an opportunity to examine different justifications for limiting individual freedom.

. . . I examine claims that surrogacy is ethically unacceptable because it is exploitive, inconsistent with human dignity, or harmful to the children born of such arrangements. I conclude that these reasons justify restrictions on surrogate contracts, rather than an outright ban. . . .

SHOULD SURROGACY BE PROHIBITED?

On June 27, 1988, Michigan became the first state to outlaw commercial contracts for women to bear children for others.[1] Yet making a practice illegal does not necessarily make it go away: witness black-market adoption. The legitimate concerns that support a ban on surrogacy might be better served by careful regulation. However, some practices, such as slavery, are ethically unacceptable, regardless of how carefully regulated they are. Let us consider the arguments that surrogacy is intrinsically unacceptable.

Paternalistic Arguments

These arguments against surrogacy take the form of protecting a potential surrogate from a choice she may later regret. As an argument for banning surrogacy, as opposed to providing safeguards to ensure that contracts are freely and knowledgeably undertaken, this is a form of paternalism.

At one time, the characterization of a prohibition as paternalistic was a sufficient reason to reject it. The pendulum has swung back, and many people are willing to accept at least some paternalistic restrictions on freedom. Gerald Dworkin points out that even Mill made one exception to his otherwise absolute rejection of paternalism: he thought that no one should be allowed to sell himself into slavery, because to do so would be to destroy his future autonomy.

This provides a narrow principle to justify some paternalistic interventions. To preserve freedom in the long run, we give up the freedom to make certain choices, those that have results that are "far-reaching, potentially dangerous and irreversible."[2] An example would be a ban on the sale of crack. Virtually everyone who uses crack becomes addicted and, once addicted, a slave to its use. We reasonably and willingly give up our freedom to buy the drug, to protect our ability to make free decisions in the future.

Can a Dworkinian argument be made to rule out surrogacy agreements? Admittedly, the decision to give up a child is permanent, and may have disastrous effects on the surrogate mother. However, many decisions may have long-term, disastrous effects (e.g., postponing childbirth for a career, having an abortion, giving a child up for adoption). Clearly we do not want the state to make decisions for us in all these matters. Dworkin's argument is rightly restricted to paternalistic interferences that protect the individual's autonomy or ability to make decisions in the future. Surrogacy does not involve giving up one's autonomy, which distinguishes it from both the crack and selling-oneself-into-slavery examples. Respect for individual freedom requires us to permit people to make choices they may later regret.

Moral Objections

. . . We must all agree that a practice that exploits people or violates human dignity is immoral. However, it is not clear that surrogacy is guilty on either count.

Exploitation   The mere fact that pregnancy is *risky* does not make surrogate agreements exploitive, and therefore morally wrong. People often do risky things for money; why should the line be drawn at undergoing pregnancy? The usual response is to compare surrogacy and kidney-selling. The selling of organs is prohibited because of the potential for coercion and exploitation. But why should kidney-selling be viewed as intrinsically coercive? A possible explanation is that no one would do it, unless driven by poverty. The choice is both forced and dangerous, and hence coercive.

The situation is quite different in the case of the race-car driver or stuntman. We do not think that they are *forced* to perform risky activities for money: they freely choose to do so. Unlike selling one's kidneys, these are activities that we can understand (intellectually, anyway) someone choosing to do. Movie stuntmen, for example, often enjoy their work, and derive satisfaction from doing it well. Of course they "do it for the money," in the sense that they would not do it without compensation; few people are willing to work "for free." The element of coercion is missing, however, because they enjoy the job, despite the risks, and could do something else if they chose.

The same is apparently true of most surrogates. "They choose the surrogate role primarily because the fee provides a better economic opportunity than alternative occupations, but also because they enjoy being pregnant and the respect and attention that it draws."[3] Some may derive a feeling of self-worth from an act they regard as highly altruistic: providing a couple with a child they could not otherwise have. If these motives are present, it is far from clear that the surrogate is being exploited. Indeed, it seems objectionally paternalistic to insist that she is.

Human Dignity   It may be argued that even if womb-leasing is not necessarily exploitive, it should still be rejected as inconsistent with human dignity. But why? As John Harris points out, hair, blood, and other tissue is often donated or sold; what is so special about the uterus?[4]

Human dignity is more plausibly invoked in the strongest argument against surrogacy, namely, that it is the sale of a child. Children are not property, nor can they be bought or sold. It could be argued that surrogacy is wrong because it is analogous to slavery, and so is inconsistent with human dignity.

However, there are important differences between slavery and a surrogate agreement. The child born of a surrogate is not treated cruelly or deprived of freedom or resold; none of the things that make slavery so awful are part of surrogacy. Still, it may be thought that simply putting a market value on a child is wrong. Human life has intrinsic value; it is literally priceless. Arrangements that ignore this violate our deepest notions of the value of human life. It is profoundly disturbing to hear in a television documentary on surrogacy the boyfriend of a surrogate say, quite candidly, "We're in it for the money."

[The trial court judge in the Baby M case] accepted the premise that producing a child for money denigrates human dignity, but he denied that this happens in a surrogate agreement. Ms. Whitehead was not paid for the surrender of the child to the father: she was paid for her willingness to be impregnated and carry Mr. Stern's child to term. The child, once born, is his biological child. "He cannot purchase what is already his."[5]

This is misleading, and not merely because Baby M is as much Ms. Whitehead's child as Mr. Stern's. It is misleading because it glosses over the fact that the surrender of the child was part—indeed, the whole point—of the agreement. If the surrogate were paid merely for being willing to be impregnated and carrying the child to term, then she would fulfill the contract upon giving birth. She could take the money *and* the child. Mr. Stern did not agree to pay Ms. Whitehead merely to *have* his child, but to provide him with a child. The New Jersey Supreme Court held that this violated New Jersey's laws prohibiting the payment or acceptance of money in connection with adoption.

One way to remove the taint of baby-selling would be to limit payment to medical expenses associated with the birth or incurred by the surrogate during pregnancy (as is allowed in many jurisdictions, including New Jersey, in ordinary adoptions). Surrogacy could be seen, not as baby-selling, but as a form of adoption. Nowhere did the Supreme Court find any legal prohibition against surrogacy when there is no payment, and when the surrogate has the right to change her mind and keep the child. However, this solution effectively prohibits surrogacy, since few women would become surrogates solely for self-fulfillment or reasons of altruism.

The question, then, is whether we can reconcile paying the surrogate, beyond her medical expenses, with the idea of surrogacy as prenatal adoption. We can do this by separating the terms of the agreement, which include surrendering the infant at birth to the biological father, from the justification for payment. The payment should be seen as compensation for the risks, sacrifice, and discomfort the surrogate undergoes during pregnancy. This means that if, through no fault on the part of the surrogate, the baby is stillborn, she should still be paid in full, since she has kept her part of the bargain. (By contrast, in the Stern-Whitehead agreement, Ms. Whitehead was to receive only $1,000 for a stillbirth).[6] If, on the other hand, the surrogate changes her mind and decides to keep the child, she would break the agreement, and would not be entitled to any fee or to compensation for expenses incurred during pregnancy. . . .

. . . There are sound moral and policy . . . reasons to provide a postnatal waiting period in surrogate agreements. As the Baby M case makes painfully clear, the surrogate may underestimate the bond created by gestation and the emotional trauma caused by relinquishing the baby. Compassion requires that we acknowledge these findings, and not deprive a woman of the baby she has carried because, before conception, she underestimated the strength of her feelings for it. Providing a waiting period, as in ordinary postnatal adoptions, will help protect women from making irrevocable mistakes, without banning the practice.

Some may object that this gives too little protection to the prospective adoptive parents. They cannot be sure that the baby is theirs until the waiting period is over. While this is hard on them, a similar burden is placed on other adoptive parents. If the absence of a guarantee serves to discourage people from entering surrogacy agreements, that is not necessarily a bad thing, given all the risks inherent in such contracts. In addition, this requirement would make stricter screening and counseling of surrogates essential, a desirable side-effect.

Harm to Others

Paternalistic and moral objections to surrogacy do not seem to justify an outright ban. What about the effect on the offspring of such contracts? We do not yet have solid data on the effects of being a "surrogate child." Any claim that surrogacy creates psychological problems in the children is purely speculative. But what if we did discover that such children have deep feelings of worthlessness from learning that their natural mothers deliberately created them with the intention of giving them away? Might we ban surrogacy as posing an unacceptable risk of psychological harm to the resulting children?

Feelings of worthlessness are harmful. They can prevent people from living happy, fulfilling lives. However, a surrogate child, even one whose life is miserable because of these feelings, cannot claim to have been harmed by the surrogate agreement. Without the agreement, the child would never have existed. Unless she is willing to say that her life is not worth living because of these feelings, that she would be better off never having been born, she cannot claim to have been harmed by being born of a surrogate mother.

Elsewhere I have argued that children can be *wronged* by being brought into existence, even if they are not, strictly speaking, *harmed*.[7] They are wronged if they are deprived of the minimally decent existence to which all citizens are entitled. We owe it to our children to see that they are not born with such serious impairments that their most basic interests will be doomed in advance. If being born to a surrogate is a handicap of this magnitude, comparable to being born blind or deaf or severely mentally retarded, then surrogacy can be seen as wronging the offspring. This would be a strong reason against permitting such contracts. However, it does not seem likely. Probably the problems arising from surrogacy will be like those faced by adopted children and children whose parents divorce. Such problems are not trivial, but neither are they so serious that the child's very existence can be seen as wrongful.

If surrogate children are neither harmed nor wronged by surrogacy, it may seem that the argument for banning surrogacy on grounds of its harmfulness to the offspring evaporates. After all, if the children themselves have no cause for complaint, how can anyone else claim to reject it on their behalf? Yet it seems extremely counter-intuitive to suggest that the risk of emotional damage to the children born of such arrangements is not even relevant to our deliberations. It seems quite reasonable and proper—even morally obligatory—for policy-makers to think about the possible detrimental effects of new reproductive technologies, and to reject those likely to create physically or emotionally damaged people. The explanation for this must involve the idea that it is wrong to bring people into the world in a harmful condition, even if they are not, strictly speaking, harmed by having been brought into existence. Should evidence emerge that surrogacy produces children with serious psychological problems, that would be a strong reason for banning the practice.

There is some evidence on the effect of surrogacy on the other children of the surrogate mother. One woman reported that her daughter, now seventeen, who was eleven at the time of the surrogate birth, "is still having problems with what I did, and as a result she is still angry with me." She explains: "Nobody told me that a child could bond with a baby while you're still pregnant. I didn't realize then that all the times she listened to his heartbeat and felt his legs kick that she was becoming attached to him."[8]

A less sentimental explanation is possible. It seems likely that her daughter, seeing one child given away, was fearful that the same might be done to her. We can expect anxiety and resentment on the part of children whose mothers give away a brother or sister. The psychological harm to these children is clearly relevant to a determination of whether surrogacy is contrary to public policy. At the same time, it should be remembered that many things, including divorce, remarriage, and even moving to a new neighborhood, create anxiety and resentment in children. We should not use the effect on children as an excuse for banning a practice we find bizarre or offensive.

CONCLUSION

There are many reasons to be extremely cautious of surrogacy. I cannot imagine becoming a surrogate, nor would I advise anyone else to enter into a contract so fraught with peril. But the fact that a practice is risky, foolish, or even morally distasteful is not sufficient reason to outlaw it. It would be better for the state to regulate the practice, and minimize the potential for harm, without infringing on the liberty of citizens.

NOTES

1 *New York Times,* June 28, 1988, A20.
2 Gerald Dworkin, "Paternalism," in R. A. Wasserstrom, ed., *Morality and the Law* (Belmont, Cal.: Wadsworth, 1971); reprinted in J. Feinberg and H. Gross, eds., *Philosophy of Law,* 3d ed. (Belmont, Cal.: Wadsworth, 1986), 265.
3 John Robertson, "Surrogate Mothers: Not So Novel after All," *Hastings Center Report,* 13, no. 5 (1983): 29; citing P. Parker, "Surrogate Mother's Motivations: Initial Findings," *American Journal of Psychiatry,* 140 (1983): 1.
4 J. Harris, *The Value of Life* (London: Routledge & Kegan Paul, 1985), 144.

5 In re Baby "M," 217 N.J. Super. 372, 525 A.2d 1157 (1987).
6 George Annas, "Baby M: Babies (and Justice) for Sale," *Hastings Center Report,* 17, no. 3 (1987): 14.
7 Bonnie Steinbock, "The Logical Case for 'Wrongful Life'," *Hastings Center Report,* 16, no. 2 (1986): 15.
8 "Baby M Case Stirs Feelings of Surrogate Mothers," *New York Times,* March 2, 1987, B1.

QUESTIONS

1 Is commercial surrogacy relevantly similar to selling a kidney? Is commercial surrogacy relevantly similar to prostitution?
2 Should commercial surrogacy contracts be prohibited by law?
3 Would you endorse Steinbock's idea that commercial surrogacy contracts should always contain a provision allowing the surrogate a postnatal waiting period during which she can change her mind and keep the child? How long would this period be? Thirty days? Sixty days? Six months?

Surrogacy: A Question of Values

Barbara Katz Rothman

Barbara Katz Rothman is professor of sociology at Baruch College and the Graduate Center of the City University of New York. She is the author of *In Labor: Women and Power in the Birthplace* (1982), *The Tentative Pregnancy: Prenatal Diagnosis and the Future of Mother-hood* (1986), and *Recreating Motherhood: Ideology and Technology in a Patriarchal Society* (1989).

Rothman contrasts the values that underlie her opposition to surrogacy with the values that underlie the opposition of religious leaders to surrogacy. She rejects traditional arguments against surrogacy, namely, that it is "unnatural" and that it violates the "sanctity of the family." Instead, as a feminist, Rothman bases her opposition to surrogacy on two principal values. First, she insists on the centrality of relationships in general and the special importance of the relationship that is created by a woman's experience of pregnancy. Second, she places great importance on a woman maintaining control over her own body. Since Rothman conceptualizes the fetus as part of a woman's body, she insists that a woman can "never bear anybody else's baby."

People—friends, colleagues, maybe especially family—keep pointing out to me, with a bemused air, how strange it is to find me arguing on the same side as religious leaders in the debate on surrogacy arrangements. I too occasionally find some amusement in the "strange bedfellows" phenomenon. Indeed, with carefully

Reprinted with permission of the publisher from *Conscience,* vol. 7 (May/June 1987), pp. 1–4.

groomed "happy surrogates" and their equally wellgroomed brokers placed on a TV or radio show by a professional public relations firm, I often find myself, side by side with some priest or rabbi, brought in by a producer to give a "balanced" view. So we argue the problems of surrogacy, sandwiched between car commercials, wine cooler ads, and other signs of the times.

The "tag" they use to identify me on television—the white line of print that shows up on the screen, but that I never get to see in the studio—sometimes reads "author," rarely reads "sociologist," but most often reads "feminist." So there we are, "feminist" and "priest" or "rabbi" arguing the same, antisurrogacy side.

However, it is only on the very surface that I am on the same side as these religious leaders. We may have landed on the same side as this particular fence, but we have taken very different paths to get here, and we are headed in very different directions. The values that I use in my opposition to surrogacy are fundamentally different from those the [religious leaders are] using, and the goals I seek are just as different. Strangely enough, in many ways my values are much the same as those used by those of my feminist colleagues who have come to an opposite conclusion. So rather than just presenting conclusions—the deeply damaging nature of so-called "surrogacy" arrangements as I see it—I want to use this opportunity to explore these issues of values.

The arguments against surrogacy that come out of traditional religious contexts most often rest on two basic principles: first, that surrogacy is "unnatural" because it goes against the nature of women and especially of mothers; and second, that it violates the sanctity of the family. Feminists are a lot less sure about just what is "natural" for women, but on the whole, we have concluded that the institution of motherhood as it exists in our society is pretty far from any natural state. Feminists are not about to get caught up in any "maternal instincts" arguments. Women end pregnancies with abortions, or end their motherhood by giving a baby up for adoption, when that is what they feel they need to do. Being pregnant does not necessarily mean a woman is going to mother and raise the child that might be born of that pregnancy, nor are we going to claim that only a birth mother can mother and nurture a baby. We know that loving people, men as well as women, can provide all the warm, caring, loving nurturance a baby needs.

Feminists are also not concerned with maintaining the "sanctity of the family," a pleasant-enough-sounding phrase that has been used to cover an awful lot of damage. That was the argument offered to allow men to beat their wives and children, the argument used to stop funding day care centers, and the argument used most generally to stop women from controlling their own lives and their own bodies. The "family" whose "sanctity" is being maintained is the patriarchal, male-dominated family. Feminists have a different sense of family; we need to protect the single young mother and her child, the lesbian couple and their children, and the gay man's family. As feminists, we are concerned not with the control, ownership, and kinship issues of the traditional family, but with the *relationships* that people establish with one another, both with adults and with children.

Why then, as feminist, do I oppose the surrogacy relationship? The "liberal" wing of feminism does not necessarily oppose these contracts. As long as the women entering into them do so of their own volition, with fully informed consent, and as long as they maintain their control over their own bodies throughout the pregnancies, some feminists have said that surrogacy contracts should be supported by the state. Some go as far as Lori Andrews, for instance, a noted liberal feminist, who says that these contracts should be binding, with absolutely no opportunity for the mother to change her mind. Andrews says that it is important for women to be held to *these* contracts if women are ever to be taken seriously in legal contracts.

What then are the objections that I, as a more radical feminist, as a socialist feminist, raise to surrogacy? More importantly, on what values—values more basic to me than "a deal's a deal"—am I basing my objections?

My values place relationships as central. Rather than the ownership or kinship ties that appear to epitomize the "traditional" or patriarchal family, I value the interpersonal relations people establish. A man does not own his wife, nor does he have ownership rights over the child she produces of her body. Men may own their sperm, but children are not sperm grown up. Children are not "owned," and they are certainly not to be available for sale. On the other hand, children do not enter the world from Mars or out of a black box. Children, as it says in the books for children, come from mothers. They enter the world in a relationship—a physical, social, and emotional relationship with the woman in whose body they have been nurtured. The nurturance of pregnancy is a relationship, one that develops as a fetus becomes more and more a baby.

That does not mean that the maternal relationship cannot be ended, nor does it mean that the relationship is the most overwhelming, all-powerful relationship on earth. In fact, we know it to be a fairly fragile relationship. The intimacy that a mother and her baby experience can be easily lost if they are separated. If a woman chooses to end this relationship, so be it. When a mother chooses to give a baby up to others who want to raise that baby as their own, she is doing what we have all done in our lives: ending a relationship. Sometimes this is done with less, and sometimes with more pain, but rarely is it an easy thing for a mother to do. The relationship that a woman has established by the time she births her baby has more weight, in my value system, than claims of genetic ties, of contracts signed, or of down payments made.

When I make this argument with traditionally oriented people, I am often asked if this doesn't contradict my ideas about a woman's right to abort an unwanted pregnancy. Not at all, I think. When a woman chooses an abortion, she is choosing not to enter into a maternal relationship. Women want access to safe abortions as quickly as possible, before a relationship can be begun. In sum, in my value system, I am placing the woman, her experiences and her relationships, at the very heart of my understanding of all pregnancies.

The second value I bring as a feminist to my understanding of surrogacy contracts is the value of women's bodily autonomy, control over their bodies—and I see the fetus as part of a woman's body. Traditional patriarchal values would see the fetus as part of its father's body—his "seed" planted in a woman's body. In a patriarchal system, the father—or the state or church—are held to have special control over a woman's body and life because of the fetus that she can bear. As a feminist, I reject that.

The fetus is *hers*. Women never bear anybody else's baby: not their husbands', not the state's, and not the purchaser's in a surrogacy contract. Every woman bears her *own* baby. I believe that to be true regardless of the source of the sperm, and regardless also of the source of the egg.

Most of the surrogacy arrangements we have seen so far, like the Stern-Whitehead case, were done not with elaborate new reproductive technology, but with the very old and very simple technology of artificial insemination. The "surrogate" has been the mother in every possible way to the baby she bore, but some newer technologies allow eggs to be transferred from woman to woman—allowing a woman to be pregnant with a fetus grown of another woman's egg.

The [Catholic] Church rejects technology. I do not. When technology is used to allow a woman to enter motherhood with a pregnancy, in just the way that artificial insemination has been used to allow an infertile man to become a social father beginning with a pregnancy, I have no problem with it. My concern is when that technology is used in a so-called surrogacy arrangement—when the birth mother (the pregnant woman) is declared to be only a "rented womb" or a "surrogate," and the "real" mother is declared to be the woman who donated the egg. By making it possible for black and brown women to be used to bear white babies, this technology will bring the costs of surrogacy down and the controls on surrogates up. Some of us fear the development of "baby farming", with babies being produced on a "Holly Farms" or "Perdue" model.

The Church objects to the technology because the Church values the fertilized egg itself as an object it believes to be human. I object when women are "used," when parts of women are put up for sale or hire, and when our relationships are discounted in favor of genetic ties and monetary ties.

The liberal feminists who would allow surrogacy contracts still demand rights of bodily autonomy for the so-called surrogate. The compromise position that they maintain is that it is indeed her body, and she must have all decision-making control over her pregnancy, but it is not her baby in her body if she has contracted it away. I feel that that kind of "compromise" does a profound disservice to women. I cannot ever believe that a woman is pregnant with someone else's baby. That idea is repugnant to me—it reduces the woman to a container. Also, I do not think that that kind of compromise—saying the pregnancy is indeed hers, but the fetus/baby theirs (the purchasers)—can be workable. The "preciousness" of the very wanted, very expensive baby will far outweigh the value given to the "cheap labor" of the surrogate.

We are encouraging the development of "production standards" in pregnancy— standards that will begin with the hired pregnancy, but grow to include all pregnancies. This is the inevitable result of thinking of pregnancy not as a relationship between a woman and her fetus, but as a service she provides for others, and of thinking of the woman herself not as a person, but as the container for another, often more valued, person.

So, yes, I agree with the patriarchal religious leaders who say that the state should not recognize surrogacy arrangements, but no, we're not really on the same side. Strange world, isn't it?

QUESTIONS

1 Would you endorse both the feminist values identified by Rothman and the opposition to surrogacy that she bases on those values?
2 If a married couple provides sperm and egg for IVF and the resultant embryo is implanted in a surrogate who later changes her mind about giving up the child, who should have the presumption of custody?

Creating Embryos

Peter Singer

Peter Singer is professor of philosophy and director of the Centre for Human Bioethics at Monash University, Victoria, Australia. He is the author of such books as *Animal Liberation* (1975) and *Practical Ethics* (1980). He is the coauthor of *Should the Baby Live?* (1985) and the editor of *Applied Ethics* (1986).

Singer identifies seven distinct objections that have been made to the use of IVF even in the "simple case"—a case in which a married couple is infertile, only eggs and sperm provided by the couple are involved, and all resulting embryos are transferred to the uterus of the wife. He takes some of these objections more seriously than others but ultimately concludes that none should "count against going ahead" with IVF in the simple case. Singer then considers a number of variations on the simple case, and he identifies the moral status of the embryo as an underlying issue of great importance. In his view, early embryos have no moral status because they are incapable of feeling pain or pleasure. Accordingly, he finds no ethical problem with freezing early embryos, discarding them, or using them for research purposes.

The treatment of human embryos became a matter of public controversy in July 1978. That month saw the birth of Louise Brown, the first human being to have developed from an embryo which at some point in its existence was outside a human body. This marked the beginning of what can properly be called a revolution in human reproduction. The point is not that *in vitro* fertilization (the technique used to make possible the birth of Louise Brown) is itself so extraordinary. On the contrary, *in vitro* fertilization, or IVF, can be seen as simply a way of overcoming certain forms of infertility, such as blocked fallopian tubes. In this sense, IVF is no more revolutionary than a microsurgical operation to remove the blockage in the tubes. But IVF is revolutionary because it brings the embryo out of the human body. Once the embryo is in the open, human beings can observe it, manipulate it, and make

From *Ethical Issues at the Outset of Life* (1987), edited by William B. Weil, Jr. and Martin Benjamin, pp. 43–51, 57–59, 60–62. Based on work done together with Deane Wells and previously published in *Making Babies* (1985). Reprinted with permission of Charles Scribner's Sons, an imprint of Macmillan Publishing Company. Copyright © 1984, 1985 Peter Singer and Deane Wells.

life-or-death decisions about it. These possibilities make IVF, and its future applications, a subject of the utmost moral importance.

Consider what has already happened, all within the first decade after Brown. Women who do not produce eggs have been given eggs by other women who do; they have then given birth to babies to whom they are genetically entirely unrelated (1).

Embryos have been frozen in liquid nitrogen, stored for more than a year, thawed, and then transferred to women who have given birth to normal children. In one case, two "twins"—that is, children conceived from eggs produced by a single ovulatory cycle—were born 16 months apart. Another case illustrated the pitfalls of embryo freezing: two embryos, in storage in a Melbourne laboratory, were orphaned when their parents were killed in a plane crash, apparently leaving no instructions regarding the disposition of their embryos (1).

Scientists have begun to speculate on the medical purposes to which embryos might be put. Dr. Robert Edwards, the scientist who, together with Patrick Steptoe, made it possible for Louise Brown to be born, has suggested that if embryos could be grown for about 17 days, we could take from them developing blood cells which would have the potential to overcome such fatal diseases as sickle cell anemia and perhaps leukemia (2).

There was a time when our ethical codes could slowly adapt to changing circumstances. Those days are gone. We have to decide, right now, whether the moral status of embryos is such that it is wrong to freeze them or experiment upon them. We have also to make an immediate decision on whether there is any objection to allowing some women to carry and bring to birth embryos to which they have no genetic link. We have, at most, until the end of the century to decide how to handle new technologies for selecting and manipulating embryos, technologies that will force us to ask which human qualities are most desirable. We must start by acquainting ourselves with the new techniques and deciding which of them should form part of the society in which we live.

IVF: THE SIMPLE CASE

The so-called simple case of IVF is that in which a married, infertile couple use an egg taken from the wife and sperm taken from the husband, and all embryos created are inserted into the womb of the wife. This case allows us to consider the ethics of IVF in itself, without the complications of the many other issues that can arise in different circumstances. Then we can go on to look at these complications separately.

The Technique

The technique itself is now well known and is fast becoming a routine part of infertility treatment in many countries. The infertile woman is given a hormone treatment to induce her ovaries to produce more than one egg in her next cycle. Her hormone levels are carefully monitored to detect the precise moment at which the eggs are ripening. At this time the eggs are removed. This is usually done by laparoscopy, a minor operation in which a fine tube is inserted into the woman's abdomen and the egg is sucked out up the tube. A laparoscope, a kind of periscope illuminated by fiber optics, is also inserted into the abdomen so that the surgeon can locate the place where the ripe egg is to be found. Instead of laparoscopy, some IVF teams are now using ultrasound techniques, which eliminate the need for a general anesthetic.

Once the eggs have been collected they are placed in culture in small glass dishes known as petri dishes, not in test tubes despite the popular label of "test-tube babies." Sperm is then obtained from the male partner by means of masturbation and placed with the egg. Fertilization follows in at least 80 percent of the ripe eggs. The resulting embryos are allowed to cleave once or twice and are usually transferred to the woman some 48 to 72 hours after fertilization. The actual transfer is done via the vagina and is a simple procedure.

It is after the transfer, when the embryo is back in the uterus and beyond the scrutiny of medical science, that things are most likely to go wrong. Even with the most experienced IVF teams, the majority of embryos transferred fail to implant in the uterus. One pregnancy for every five transfers is currently considered to be a good working average for a competent IVF team. Many of the newer teams fail to achieve anything like this rate. Nevertheless, there are so many units around the world now practicing IVF that thousands of babies have been produced as a result of the technique. IVF has ceased to be experimental and is now a routine, if still "last resort" method of treating some forms of infertility.

Objections to the Simple Case

There is some opposition to IVF even in the simple case. The most frequently heard objections are as follows:

1 IVF is unnatural.
2 IVF is risky for the offspring.
3 IVF separates the procreative and the conjugal aspects of marriage and so damages the marital relationship.
4 IVF is illicit because it involves masturbation.
5 Adoption is a better solution to the problem of childlessness.
6 IVF is an expensive luxury and the resources would be better spent elsewhere.
7 IVF allows increased male control over reproduction and hence threatens the status of women in the community.

We can deal swiftly with the first four of these objections. If we were to reject medical advances on the grounds that they are "unnatural" we would be rejecting modern medicine as a whole, for the very purpose of the medical enterprise is to resist the ravages of nature which would otherwise shorten our lives and make them much less pleasant. If anything is in accordance with the nature of our species, it is the application of our intelligence to overcome adverse situations in which we find ourselves. The application of IVF to infertile couples is a classic example of this application of human intelligence.

The claim that IVF is risky for the offspring is one that was argued with great force before IVF became a widely used technique. It is sufficient to note that the results of IVF so far have happily refuted these fears. The most recent Australian figures, for example, based on 934 births, indicate that the rate of abnormality was 2.7%, which is very close to the national average of 1.5%. When we take into account the greater average age of women seeking IVF, as compared with the childbearing population as a whole, it does not seem that the *in vitro* technique itself adds to the risk of an abnormal offspring. This view is reinforced by the fact that the abnormalities were all ones that arise with the ordinary method of reproduction; there have been no new "monsters" produced by IVF (3). Perhaps we still cannot claim with statistical certainty that the risk of defect is no higher with IVF than with the more common method of conception; but if the risk is higher at all, it would appear to be only very slightly higher, and still within limits which may be considered acceptable.

The third and fourth objections have been urged by spokesmen for certain religious groups, but they are difficult to defend outside the confines of particular religions. Few infertile couples will take seriously the view that their marital relationship will be damaged if they use the technique which offers them the best chance of having their own child. It is in any case extraordinarily paternalistic for anyone else to tell a couple that they should not use IVF because it will harm their marriage. That, surely, is for them to decide.

The objection to masturbation comes from a similar source and can be even more swiftly dismissed. Religious prohibitions on masturbation are taboos from past times which even religious spokesmen are beginning to consider outdated. Moreover, even if one could defend a prohibition on masturbation for sexual pleasure—perhaps on the (very tenuous) ground that sexual activity is wrong unless it is directed either toward procreation or toward the strengthening of the bond between marriage partners—it would be absurd to extend a prohibition with that kind of rationale to a case in which masturbation is being used in the context of a marriage and precisely in order to make reproduction possible. (The fact that some religions do persist in regarding masturbation as wrong, even in these circumstances, is indicative of the folly of an ethical system based on absolute rules, irrespective of the circumstances in which those rules are being applied, or the consequences of their application.)

Overpopulation and the Allocation of Resources

The next two objections, however, deserve more careful consideration. In an overpopulated world in which there are so many children who cannot be properly fed and cared for, there is something incongruous about using all the ingenuity of modern medicine to create more children. And similarly, when there are so many deaths caused by preventable diseases, is there not something wrong with the priorities which lead us to develop expensive techniques for overcoming the relatively less serious problem of infertility?

These objections are sound to the following extent: in an ideal world we would find loving families for unwanted children before we created additional children; and in an ideal world we would clear up all the preventable ill-health and malnutrition-related diseases before we went on to tackle the problem of infertility. But is it appropriate to ask, of IVF alone, whether it can stand the test of measurement against what we would do in an ideal world? In an ideal world, none of us would consume more than our fair share of resources. We would not drive expensive cars while others die for the lack of drugs costing a few cents. We would not eat a diet rich in wastefully produced animal products while others cannot get enough to nourish their bodies. We cannot demand more of infertile couples than we are ready to demand of ourselves. If fertile couples are free to have large families of their own, rather than adopt destitute children from overseas, infertile couples must also be free to do what they can to have their own families. In both cases, overseas adoption, or perhaps the adoption of local children who are unwanted because of some impairment, should be considered; but if we are not going to make this compulsory in the former case, it should not be made compulsory in the latter.

There is a further question: to what extent do infertile couples have a right to assistance from community medical resources? Again, however, we must not single out IVF for harsher treatment than we give to other medical techniques. If tubal surgery is available and covered by one's health insurance, or is offered as part of a national health scheme, then why should IVF be treated any differently? And if infertile couples can get free or subsidized psychiatry to help them overcome the psychological problems of infertility, there is something absurd about denying them free or subsidized treatment which could overcome the root of the problem, rather than the symptoms. By today's standards, after all, IVF is not an inordinately expensive medical technique; and there is no country, as far as I know, which limits its provision of free or subsidized health care to those cases in which the patient's life is in danger. Once we extend medical care to cover cases of injury, incapacity, and psychological distress, IVF has a strong claim to be included among the range of free or subsidized treatments available.

The Effect on Women

The final objection is one that has come from some feminists. In a recently published collection of essays by women titled *Test-Tube Women: What Future for Motherhood?,* several contributors are suspicious of the new reproductive technology. None is more hostile than Robyn Rowland, an Australian sociologist, who writes:

> Ultimately the new technology will be used for the benefit of men and to the detriment of women. Although technology itself is not always a negative development, the real question has always been—who controls it? Biological technology is in the hands of men (4).

And Rowland concludes with a warning as dire as any uttered by the most conservative opponents of IVF:

> What may be happening is the last battle in the long war of men against women. Women's position is most precarious . . . we may find ourselves without a product of any kind with which to bargain. For the history of "mankind" women have been seen in terms of their value as child-bearers. We have to ask, if that last power is taken and controlled by men, what role is envisaged for women in the new world? Will women become obsolete? Will

we be fighting to retain or reclaim the right to bear children—has patriarchy conned us once again? I urge you sisters to be vigilant (4).

I can see little basis for such claims. For a start, women have figured quite prominently in the leading IVF teams in Britain, Australia, and the United States: Jean Purdy was an early colleague of Edwards and Steptoe in the research that led to the birth of Louise Brown; Linda Mohr has directed the development of embryo freezing at the Queen Victoria Medical Centre in Melbourne; and in the United States Georgeanna Jones and Joyce Vargyas have played leading roles in the groundbreaking clinics in Norfolk, Virginia, and at the University of Southern California, respectively. It seems odd for a feminist to neglect the contributions these women have made.

Even if one were to grant, however, that the technology remains predominantly in male hands, it has to be remembered that it was developed in response to the needs of infertile couples. From interviews I have conducted and meetings I have attended, my impression is that while both partners are often very concerned about their childlessness, in those cases in which one partner is more distressed than the other by this situation, that partner is usually the woman. Feminists usually accept that this is so, attributing it to the power of social conditioning in a patriarchal society; but the origin of the strong female desire for children is not really what is in question here. The question is: in what sense is the new technology an instrument of male domination over women? If it is true that the technology was developed at least as much in response to the needs of women as in response to the needs of men, then it is hard to see why a feminist should condemn it.

It might be objected that whatever the origins of IVF and no matter how benign it may be when used to help infertile couples, the further development of techniques such as ectogenesis—the growth of the embryo from conception totally outside the body, in an artificial womb—will reduce the status of women. Again, it is not easy to see why this should be so. Ectogenesis will, if it is ever successful, provide a choice for women. Shulamith Firestone argued several years ago in her influential feminist work *The Dialectic of Sex* (5) that this choice will remove the fundamental biological barrier to complete equality. Hence Firestone welcomed the prospect of ectogenesis and condemned the low priority given by our male-dominated society to research in this area.

Firestone's view is surely more in line with the drive to sexual equality than the position taken by Rowland. If we argue that to break the link between women and childbearing would be to undermine the status of women in our society, what are we saying about the ability of women to obtain true equality in other spheres of life? I am not so pessimistic about the abilities of women to achieve equality with men across the broad range of human endeavor. For that reason I think women will be helped, rather than harmed, by the development of a technology which makes it possible for them to have children without being pregnant. As Nancy Breeze, a very differently inclined contributor to the same collection of essays, puts it:

> Two thousand years of morning sickness and stretch marks have not resulted in liberation for women or children. If you should run into a Petri dish, it could turn out to be your best friend. So rock it; don't knock it! (6)

So to sum up this discussion of the ethics of the simple case of IVF: the ethical objections urged against IVF under these conditions are not strong. They should not count against going ahead with IVF when it is the best way of overcoming infertility and when the infertile couple are not prepared to consider adoption as a means of overcoming their problem. There is, admittedly, a serious question about how much of the national health budget should be allocated to this area. But then, there are serious questions about the allocation of resources in other areas of medicine as well.

IVF: OTHER CASES

IVF can be used in circumstances that differ from those of the simple case in the following respects:

1 The couple may not be legally married; or there may be no couple at all, the patient being a single woman.

2 The couple may not be infertile but may wish to use IVF for some other reason, for instance because the woman carries a genetic defect.

3 The sperm, or the egg, or both, may come from another person, not from the couple themselves.

4 Some of the embryos created may not be inserted into the womb of the wife; instead they may be frozen and stored for later use, or donated to others, or used for research, or simply discarded.

All of these variations on the simple case raise potentially difficult issues. I say "potentially difficult" because in some cases the difficulties arise only once we consider the more extreme instances. For instance, there are no good grounds for discriminating against couples who are not legally married but have a long-standing de facto relationship; on the other hand one would need to consider more carefully whether to allow a single woman to make use of IVF. It is true that single fertile women are entirely free to procreate as irresponsibly as they like; yet the doctor who assists an infertile woman to do the same must take some care that the child in whose creation he or she is assisting will grow up in circumstances that are compatible with a good start in life. A single mother may well be able to provide such circumstances, but it is at least appropriate for the doctor to make some inquiries before going ahead.

IVF for fertile couples when the woman carries a serious genetic defect is scarcely problematic; if we would allow artificial insemination when the man has a similar defect, we should also allow IVF when the woman is the carrier. Here too, however, there is a question about how far we should go. What if the defect is a very minor one? What if there is no defect at all, but the woman wants a donor egg from a friend whose intelligence or beauty she considers superior to her own? A California sperm bank is already offering selected women the sperm of Nobel Prize-winning scientists. It is only a matter of time before eggs are offered in the same manner. Nevertheless it seems clear that as long as IVF is in short supply, those who are infertile or who carry a serious genetic defect should have the first claim upon it. . . .

The use of donor sperm, eggs, and embryos raises further questions. There is a precedent in the use of donor sperm in artificial insemination. The lesson that has been learned here is that there is a great need for counseling the couple because there may be psychological problems when one parent is not the genetic parent of the child. There is also the question of whether the child is to be told of her or his genetic origins. Many adopted persons now consider that they have a right to full information about their genetic parents. There is a strong case for saying that the same applies to people born as a result of the use of donor sperm or eggs, and that non-identifying data about the donor should be released to the parents, with a view to the child being informed at a later stage.

The most controversial of these issues is that of the moral status of the embryo; this is the question at stake when we consider whether to create more embryos than we are willing to put back into the womb at one time. Disposing of the embryos, or using them for research purposes, runs counter to the view held by some that the embryo is a human being with the same right to life as any other human being. Even embryo freezing does little to placate those who take this view, since on present indications the chances of a frozen embryo surviving to become a living child are not high. But, religious doctrines apart, is it plausible to hold that the embryo has a right to life? The moral status of the embryo is perhaps the most fundamental of all the moral issues raised by the reproduction revolution. Many people believe it to be an insoluble philosophical problem, one on which we just have to take our stand, more or less arbitrarily, without hope of persuading those of a different view. I believe, on the contrary, that the issue is amenable to rational discussion. . . .

THE MORAL STATUS OF THE EMBRYO

. . . [A]ttempts to argue that the early embryo has a right to life [can be shown to be inadequate]. It remains only to say something positive about when in its development the embryo may acquire rights.

The answer must depend on the actual characteristics of the embryo. The minimal characteristic which is needed to give the embryo a claim to consideration is sentience, or the capacity to feel pain or pleasure. Until the embryo reaches that point, there is nothing we can do to the embryo which causes harm to *it*. We can, of course, damage it in such a way as to cause harm to the person it will become, if it lives, but if it never becomes a person, the embryo has not been harmed, because its total lack of awareness means that it can have no interest in becoming a person.

Once an embryo may be capable of feeling pain, there is a clear case for very strict controls over the experimentation which can be done with it. At this point the embryo ranks, morally, with other creatures who are conscious but not self-conscious. Many nonhuman animals come into this category, and in my view they have often been unjustifiably made to suffer in scientific research. We should have stringent controls over research to ensure that this cannot happen to embryos, just as we should have stringent controls to ensure that it cannot happen to animals.

Practical Implications of the Moral Status of Embryos

The conclusion to draw from this is that as long as the parents give their consent, there is no ethical objection to discarding a very early embryo. If the early embryo can be used for significant research, so much the better. What is crucial is that the embryo not be kept beyond the point at which it has formed a brain and a nervous system, and might be capable of suffering. Two government committees—the Warnock Committee in Britain (7) and the Waller Committee in Victoria, Australia (8)—have recently recommended that research on embryos should be allowed, but only up to 14 days after fertilization. This is the period at which the so-called "primitive streak," the first indication of the development of a nervous system, begins to form, and up to this stage there is certainly no possibility of the embryo feeling anything at all. In fact, the 14-day limit is unnecessarily conservative. A limit of, say, 28 days would still be very much on the safe side of the best estimates of when the embryo may be able to feel pain; but such a limit would, in contrast to the 14-day limit, allow research on embryos at the stage at which some of the more specialized cells have begun to form. As we saw earlier, this research would, according to Robert Edwards, have the potential to cure such terrible diseases as sickle cell anemia and leukemia (2).

As for freezing the embryo with a view to later implantation, the question here is essentially one of risk. If freezing carries no special risk of abnormality, there seems to be nothing objectionable about it. With embryo freezing, this appears to be the case. The ethical objections some people have to freezing embryos has led to the suggestion that it would be better to freeze eggs (7); for this and other reasons there has been a considerable research effort directed at freezing eggs. Human eggs are more difficult to freeze than human embryos, and until recently it had not proved possible to freeze them in a manner which allowed fertilization after thawing. In December 1985, however, an IVF team at Flinders University, in Adelaide, South Australia, announced that it had succeeded in obtaining a pregnancy from an egg which had been frozen and thawed before being fertilized (9). The technique used involved stripping away a protective outer layer from the egg, so that it would take up a chemical which would protect it during the freezing process. This technique does overcome the ethical problems some find in freezing embryos, but it does so at the cost of introducing a new potential cause of risk to the offspring, the risk that the chemicals absorbed by the egg may have some harmful effect (10). Whether or not this risk proves to be a real one, from the point of view of ethics, one may doubt whether the risk is worth running, if the primary reason for running it is to avoid objections, which we have now seen to be ill-founded, to the freezing of embryos.

Going beyond the simple case does bring us into a more ethically controversial area, but there is no overall case against applying IVF outside the restricted ambit of the simple case. The essential point is to consider each additional step carefully before it is taken. Some steps will prove unwise, but others will be beneficial and not open to any well-grounded objections. . . .

REFERENCES

1 Singer P, Wells D. Making babies. New York: Scribner's, 1985.
2 Edwards R G. Paper presented at the Fourth World Congress on IVF. Melbourne, Australia, Nov 22, 1985.

3 Abstract. Proceedings of the Fifth Scientific Meeting of the Fertility Society of Australia, Adelaide, Dec. 2–6, 1986.

4 Rowland R. Reproductive technologies: the final solution to the woman question? In: Arditti R, Klein RD, Minden S, eds, Test-tube women: what future for motherhood? London: Pandora, 1984.

5 Firestone S. The dialectic of sex. New York: Bantam, 1971.

6 Breeze N. Who is going to rock the petri dish? In: Arditti R, Klein RD, Minden S, eds, Test-tube women: what future for motherhood? London: Pandora, 1984.

7 Warnock M (Chairperson). Report of the Committee of Inquiry into Human Fertilisation and Embryology. London: Her Majesty's Stationery Office, 1984, p 66.

8 Waller L (Chairman). Victorian Government Committee to Consider the Social, Ethical and Legal Issues Arising from In Vitro Fertilization. Report on the disposition of embryos produced by in vitro fertilization. Melbourne: Victorian Government Printer, 1984, p 47.

9 The Australian, Dec 19, 1985.

10 Trounson A. Paper presented at the Fourth World Congress on IVF, Melbourne, Australia, Nov 22, 1985.

QUESTIONS

1 Is there any compelling reason to believe that the employment of IVF in the "simple case" is immoral?

2 Is it morally legitimate to freeze early embryos, discard them, or use them for research purposes?

Feminist Ethics and *in Vitro* Fertilization

Susan Sherwin

Susan Sherwin is professor of philosophy at Dalhousie University, Halifax, Nova Scotia. She is coeditor of *Moral Problems in Medicine* (1976; 2d ed., 1983). Her published articles include "The Concept of a Person in the Context of Abortion," "A Feminist Approach to Ethics," and "Feminist Ethics and Medical Ethics: Two Different Approaches to Contextual Ethics."

Sherwin outlines the nature of feminist ethics and provides a critique of IVF within that theoretical framework. From a feminist point of view, she maintains, IVF is morally problematic for a number of closely related reasons, including the following: (1) Although the desires of infertile couples for access to IVF are understandable and worthy of sympathetic regard, such desires themselves emerge from social arrangements and cultural values that are deeply oppressive to women. (2) IVF technology gives the appearance of providing women with increased reproductive freedom but in reality threatens women with a significant decrease of reproductive freedom. Sherwin also insists that those who find themselves in moral

Reprinted with permission of the author and the publisher from *Canadian Journal of Philosophy,* suppl. vol. 13 (1987), pp. 276–284.

opposition to IVF have a responsibility to support medical and social developments
that would reduce the perceived need of couples for IVF.

Many authors from all traditions consider it necessary to ask why it is that some
couples seek IVF technology so desperately. Why is it so important to so many people to produce their 'own' child? On this question, theorists in the analytic tradition
seem to shift to previously rejected ground and suggest that this is a natural, or at
least a proper, desire. Englehardt, for example, says, 'The use of technology in the
fashioning of children is integral to the goal of rendering the world congenial to persons.'[1] Bayles more cautiously observes that 'A desire to beget for its own sake . . .
is probably irrational'; nonetheless, he immediately concludes, 'these techniques for
fulfilling that desire have been found ethically permissible.'[2] R. G. Edwards and
David Sharpe state the case most strongly: 'the desire to have children must be
among the most basic of human instincts, and denying it can lead to considerable
psychological and social difficulties.'[3] Interestingly, although the recent pronounce-
ment of the Catholic Church assumes that 'the desire for a child is natural,'[4] it denies
that a couple has a right to a child: 'The child is not an object to which one has a
right.'[5]

Here, I believe, it becomes clear why we need a deeper sort of feminist analysis.
We must look at the sort of social arrangements and cultural values that underlie the
drive to assume such risks for the sake of biological parenthood. We find that the
capitalism, racism, sexism, and elitism of our culture have combined to create a set
of attitudes which views children as commodities whose value is derived from their
possession of parental chromosomes. Children are valued as privatized commodities,
reflecting the virility and heredity of their parents. They are also viewed as the responsibility of their parents and are not seen as the social treasure and burden that
they are. Parents must tend their needs on pain of prosecution, and, in return, they
get to keep complete control over them. Other adults are inhibited from having
warm, stable interactions with the children of others—it is as suspect to try to hug
and talk regularly with a child who is not one's own as it is to fondle and hang long-
ingly about a car or a bicycle which belongs to someone else—so those who wish to
know children well often find they must have their own.

Women are persuaded that their most important purpose in life is to bear and raise
children; they are told repeatedly that their life is incomplete, that they are lacking in
fulfillment if they do not have children. And, in fact, many women do face a barren
existence without children. Few women have access to meaningful, satisfying jobs.
Most do not find themselves in the centre of the romantic personal relationships
which the culture pretends is the norm for heterosexual couples. And they have been
socialized to be fearful of close friendships with others—they are taught to distrust
other women, and to avoid the danger of friendship with men other than their husbands. Children remain the one hope for real intimacy and for the sense of accomplishment which comes from doing work one judges to be valuable.

To be sure, children can provide that sense of self worth, although for many
women (and probably for all mothers at some times) motherhood is not the romanti-

cized satisfaction they are led to expect. But there is something very wrong with a culture where childrearing is the only outlet available to most women in which to pursue fulfillment. Moreover, there is something wrong with the ownership theory of children that keeps other adults at a distance from children. There ought to be a variety of close relationships possible between children and adults so that we all recognize that we have a stake in the well-being of the young, and we all benefit from contact with their view of the world.

In such a world, it would not be necessary to spend the huge sums on designer children which IVF requires while millions of other children starve to death each year. Adults who enjoyed children could be involved in caring for them whether or not they produced them biologically. And, if the institution of marriage survives, women and men would marry because they wished to share their lives together, not because the men needed someone to produce heirs for them and women needed financial support for their children. That would be a world in which we might have reproductive freedom of choice. The world we now live in has so limited women's options and self-esteem, it is legitimate to question the freedom behind women's demand for this technology, for it may well be largely a reflection of constraining social perspectives.

Nonetheless, I must acknowledge that some couples today genuinely mourn their incapacity to produce children without IVF and there are very significant and unique joys which can be found in producing and raising one's own children which are not accessible to persons in infertile relationships. We must sympathize with these people. None of us shall live to see the implementation of the ideal cultural values outlined above which would make the demand for IVF less severe. It is with real concern that some feminists suggest that the personal wishes of couples with fertility difficulties may not be compatible with the overall interests of women and children.

Feminist thought, then, helps us to focus on different dimensions of the problem than do other sorts of approaches. But, with this perspective, we still have difficulty in reaching a final conclusion on whether to encourage, tolerate, modify, or restrict this sort of reproductive technology. I suggest that we turn to the developing theories of feminist ethics for guidance in resolving this question.[6]

In my view, a feminist ethics is a moral theory that focusses on relations among persons as well as on individuals. It has as a model an inter-connected social fabric, rather than the familiar one of isolated, independent atoms; and it gives primacy to bonds among people rather than to rights to independence. It is a theory that focusses on concrete situations and persons and not on free-floating abstract actions.[7] Although many details have yet to be worked out, we can see some of its implications in particular problem areas such as this.

It is a theory that is explicitly conscious of the social, political, and economic relations that exist among persons; in particular, as a feminist theory, it attends to the implications of actions or policies on the status of women. Hence, it is necessary to ask questions from the perspective of feminist ethics in addition to those which are normally asked from the perspective of mainstream ethical theories. We must view issues such as this one in the context of the social and political realities in which they arise, and resist the attempt to evaluate actions or practices in isolation (as traditional responses in biomedical ethics often do). Thus, we cannot just address the question of IVF per se without asking how IVF contributes to general patterns of women's oppression. As Kathryn Pyne Addelson has argued about abortion,[8] a feminist perspective raises questions that are inadmissable within the traditional ethical frameworks, and yet, for women in a patriarchal society, they are value questions of greater urgency. In particular, a feminist ethics, in contrast to other approaches in biomedical ethics, would take seriously the concerns just reviewed which are part of the debate in the feminist literature.

A feminist ethics would also include components of theories that have been developed as 'feminine ethics,' as sketched out by the empirical work of Carol Gilligan.[9] (The best example of such a theory is the work of Nel Noddings in her influential book *Caring*.)[10] In other words, it would be a theory that gives primacy to interpersonal relationships and woman-centered values such as nurturing, empathy, and co-operation. Hence, in the case of IVF, we must care for the women and men who are so despairing about their infertility as to want to spend the vast sums and risk the associated physical and emotional costs of the treatment, in pursuit of 'their own children.' That is, we should, in Noddings' terms, see their reality as our own and address their very real sense of loss. In so doing, however, we must also consider the implications of this sort of solution to their difficulty. While meeting the perceived desires of some women—desires which are problematic in themselves, since they are so compatible with the values of a culture deeply oppressive to women—this technology threatens to further entrench those values which are responsible for that oppression. A larger vision suggests that the technology offered may, in reality, reduce women's freedom and, if so, it should be avoided.

A feminist ethics will not support a wholly negative response, however, for that would not address our obligation to care for those suffering from infertility; it is the responsibility of those who oppose further implementation of this technology to work towards the changes in the social arrangements that will lead to a reduction of the sense of need for this sort of solution. On the medical front, research and treatment ought to be stepped up to reduce the rates of peral sepsis and gonorrhea which often result in tubal blockage, more attention should be directed at the causes and possible cures for male infertility, and we should pursue techniques that will permit safe reversible sterilization providing women with better alternatives to tubal ligation as a means of fertility control; these sorts of technology would increase the control of many women over their own fertility and would be compatible with feminist objectives. On the social front, we must continue the social pressure to change the status of women and children in our society from that of breeder and possession respectively; hence, we must develop a vision of society as community where all participants are valued members, regardless of age or gender. And we must challenge the notion that having one's wife produce a child with his own genes is sufficient cause for the wives of men with low sperm counts to be expected to undergo the physical and emotional assault such technology involves.

Further, a feminist ethics will attend to the nature of the relationships among those concerned. Annette Baier has eloquently argued for the importance of developing an ethics of trust,[11] and I believe a feminist ethics must address the question of the degree of trust appropriate to the relationships involved. Feminists have noted that women have little reason to trust the medical specialists who offer to respond to their reproductive desires, for, commonly women's interests have not come first from the medical point of view.[12] In fact, it is accurate to perceive feminist attacks on reproductive technology as expressions of the lack of trust feminists have in those who control the technology. Few feminists object to reproductive technology per se; rather they express concern about who controls it and how it can be used to further exploit women. The problem with reproductive technology is that it concentrates power in reproductive matters in the hands of those who are not directly involved in the actual bearing and rearing of the child; i.e., in men who relate to their clients in a technical, professional, authoritarian manner. It is a further step in the medicalization of pregnancy and birth which, in North America, is marked by relationships between pregnant women and their doctors which are very different from the traditional relationships between pregnant women and midwives. The latter relationships fostered an atmosphere of mutual trust which is impossible to replicate in hospital deliveries today. In fact, current approaches to pregnancy, labour, and birth tend to view the mother as a threat to the fetus who must be coerced to comply with medical procedures designed to ensure delivery of healthy babies at whatever cost necessary to the mother. Frequently, the fetus-mother relationship is medically characterized as adversarial and the physicians choose to foster a sense of alienation and passivity in the role they permit the mother. However well IVF may serve the interests of the few women with access to it, it more clearly serves the interests (be they commercial, professional, scholarly, or purely patriarchal) of those who control it.

Questions such as these are a puzzle to those engaged in the traditional approaches to ethics, for they always urge us to separate the question of evaluating the morality of various forms of reproductive technology in themselves, from questions about particular uses of that technology. From the perspective of a feminist ethics, however, no such distinction can be meaningfully made. Reproductive technology is not an abstract activity, it is an activity done in particular contexts and it is those contexts which must be addressed.

Feminist concerns [make] clear the difficulties we have with some of our traditional ethical concepts; hence, feminist ethics directs us to rethink our basic ethical notions. Autonomy, or freedom of choice, is not a matter to be determined in isolated instances, as is commonly assumed in many approaches to applied ethics. Rather it is a matter that involves reflection on one's whole life situation. The freedom of choice feminists appeal to in the abortion situation is freedom to define one's status as childbearer, given the social, economic, and political significance of reproduction for women. A feminist perspective permits us to understand that reproductive freedom includes control of one's sexuality, protection against coerced sterilization (or iatrogenic sterilization, e.g. as caused by the Dalkon Shield), and the existence of a social and economic network of support for the children we may choose to bear. It is the freedom to redefine our roles in society according to our concerns and needs as women.

In contrast, the consumer freedom to purchase technology, allowed only to a few couples of the privileged classes (in traditionally approved relationships), seems to entrench further the patriarchal notions of woman's role as childbearer and of heterosexual monogamy as the only acceptable intimate relationship. In other words, this sort of choice does not seem to foster autonomy for women on the broad scale. IVF is a practice which seems to reinforce sexist, classist, and often racist assumptions of our culture; therefore, on our revised understanding of freedom, the contribution of this technology to the general autonomy of women is largely negative.

We can now see the advantage of a feminist ethics over mainstream ethical theories, for a feminist analysis explicitly accepts the need for a political component to our understanding of ethical issues. In this, it differs from traditional ethical theories and it also differs from a simply feminine ethics approach, such as the one Noddings offers, for Noddings seems to rely on individual relations exclusively and is deeply suspicious of political alliances as potential threats to the pure relation of caring. Yet, a full understanding of both the threat of IVF, and the alternative action necessary should we decide to reject IVF, is possible only if it includes a political dimension reflecting on the role of women in society.

From the point of view of feminist ethics, the primary question to consider is whether this and other forms of reproductive technology threaten to reinforce the lack of autonomy which women now experience in our culture—even as they appear, in the short run, to be increasing freedom. We must recognize that the interconnections among the social forces oppressive to women underlie feminists' mistrust of this technology which advertises itself as increasing women's autonomy.[13] The political perspective which directs us to look at how this technology fits in with general patterns of treatment for women is not readily accessible to traditional moral theories, for it involves categories of concern not accounted for in those theories—e.g. the complexity of issues which makes it inappropriate to study them in isolation from one another, the role of oppression in shaping individual desires, and potential differences in moral status which are connected with differences in treatment.

It is the set of connections constituting women's continued oppression in our society which inspires feminists to resurrect the old slippery slope arguments to warn against IVF. We must recognize that women's existing lack of control in reproductive matters begins the debate on a pretty steep incline. Technology with the potential to further remove control of reproduction from women makes the slope very slippery indeed. This new technology, though offered under the guise of increasing reproductive freedom, threatens to result, in fact, in a significant decrease in freedom, especially since it is a technology that will always include the active involvement of designated specialists and will not ever be a private matter for the couple or women concerned.

Ethics ought not to direct us to evaluate individual cases without also looking at the implications of our decisions from a wide perspective. My argument is that a theory of feminist ethics provides that wider perspective, for its different sort of methodology is sensitive to both the personal and the social dimensions of issues. For that reason, I believe it is the only ethical perspective suitable for evaluating issues of this sort.

NOTES

1 H. Tristram Englehardt, *The Foundations of Bioethics* (Oxford: Oxford University Press 1986), 239

2 Michael Bayles, *Reproductive Ethics* (Englewood Cliffs, NJ: Prentice-Hall 1984) 31

3 Robert G. Edwards and David J. Sharpe, 'Social Values and Research in Human Embryology,' *Nature* 231 (May 14, 1971), 87

4 Joseph Card Ratzinger and Alberto Bovone, 'Instruction on Respect for Human Life in its Origin and on the Dignity of Procreation: Replies to Certain Questions of the Day' (Vatican City: Vatican Polyglot Press 1987), 33

5 Ibid., 34

6 Many authors are now working on an understanding of what feminist ethics entail. Among the Canadian papers I am familiar with, are Kathryn Morgan's 'Women and Moral Madness,' Sheila Mullett's 'Only Connect: The Place of Self-Knowledge in Ethics,' both in this volume, and Leslie Wilson's 'Is a Feminine Ethics Enough?' *Atlantis* (forthcoming).

7 Susan Sherwin, 'A Feminist Approach to Ethics,' *Dalhousie Review* 64, 4 (Winter 1984–85) 704–13

8 Kathryn Pyne Addelson, 'Moral Revolution,' in Marilyn Pearsall, ed., *Women and Values* (Belmont, CA: Wadsworth 1986), 291–309

9 Carol Gilligan, *In a Different Voice* (Cambridge, MA: Harvard University Press 1982)

10 Nel Noddings, *Caring* (Berkeley: University of California Press 1984)

11 Annette Baier, 'What Do Women Want in a Moral Theory?' *Nous* 19 (March 1985) 53–64, and 'Trust and Antitrust,' *Ethics* 96 (January 1986) 231–60

12 Linda Williams presents this position particularly clearly in her invaluable work 'But What Will They Mean for Women? Feminist Concerns About the New Reproductive Technologies,' No. 6 in the *Feminist Perspective* Series, CRIAW.

13 Marilyn Frye vividly describes the phenomenon of inter-relatedness which supports sexist oppression by appeal to the metaphor of a bird cage composed of thin wires, each relatively harmless in itself, but, collectively, the wires constitute an overwhelming barrier to the inhabitant of the cage. Marilyn Frye, *The Politics of Reality: Essays in Feminist Theory* (Trumansburg, NY: The Crossing Press 1983), 4–7

QUESTIONS

1 Do the desires of infertile couples for access to IVF typically emerge, as Sherwin maintains, from social arrangements and cultural values that are deeply oppressive to women?

2 On balance, does IVF technology enhance or restrict the reproductive freedom of women?

SUGGESTED ADDITIONAL READINGS FOR CHAPTER 2

HOLMES, HELEN BEQUAERT: "In Vitro Fertilization: Reflections on the State of the Art." *Birth,* vol. 15, September 1988, pp. 134–145. Holmes provides an account of the various steps in the current clinical practice of IVF and embryo transfer. She calls attention to a wide array of risks, clinical problems, and ethical issues.

HULL, RICHARD T., ed.: *Ethical Issues in the New Reproductive Technologies.* Belmont, Calif.: Wadsworth, 1990. This anthology provides useful material on artificial insemination, IVF, and surrogate motherhood.

HUMBER, JAMES M., and ROBERT F. ALMEDER, eds.: *Biomedical Ethics Reviews 1983.* Clifton, N.J.: Humana, 1983. Section II of this book (pp. 45–90) contains two long articles on surrogate motherhood. In "Surrogate Gestation: Law and Morality," Theodore M. Benditt concludes that "there is not much of a legal case or moral case" against surrogate gestation. In an exploratory essay, "Surrogate Motherhood: The Ethical Implications," Lisa H. Newton identifies and discusses five areas of moral concern.

Law, Medicine and Health Care, vol. 16, Spring/Summer 1988. This special issue is entirely dedicated to surrogate motherhood. Articles are organized under the headings of (1) civil liberties, (2) ethics, and (3) women's autonomy. Material is also provided on the case of Baby M.

MALM, HEIDI: "Paid Surrogacy: Arguments and Responses." *Public Affairs Quarterly,* vol. 3, April 1989, pp. 57–66. Malm critiques and rejects five arguments intended to show that commercial surrogacy contracts should be prohibited.

McCORMICK, RICHARD A.: "Reproductive Technologies: Ethical Issues." *Encyclopedia of Bioethics* (1978), vol. 4, pp. 1454–1464. McCormick reviews the ethical issues associated with artificial insemination, IVF, and cloning. In an extensive discussion of artificial insemination, he makes clear the views of various religious ethicists.

OVERALL, CHRISTINE: *Ethics and Human Reproduction: A Feminist Analysis.* Boston: Allen & Unwin, 1987. Overall embraces a feminist perspective on reproductive ethics and contrasts a feminist approach with nonfeminist and antifeminist approaches. Chapter 6 deals with surrogate motherhood and Chapter 7 deals with artificial reproduction.

PURDY, LAURA M.: "Surrogate Mothering: Exploitation or Empowerment?" *Bioethics,* vol. 3, January 1989, pp. 18–34. Purdy argues against the view that surrogate mothering is necessarily immoral. She acknowledges the danger that surrogate mothering could deepen the exploitation of women but also insists that surrogacy has the potential to empower women.

TIEFEL, HANS O.: "Human *In Vitro* Fertilization: A Conservative View." *Journal of the American Medical Association,* vol. 247, June 18, 1982, pp. 3235–3242. Tiefel contends that "the decisive objection to clinical uses of [IVF] lies in the possible and even likely risk of greater than normal harm to offspring." He also argues that nonclinical (purely experimental) uses of IVF are morally unjustifiable, because such uses fail to accord due respect to human embryos.

WARREN, MARY ANNE: "IVF and Women's Interests: An Analysis of Feminist Concerns." *Bioethics,* vol. 2, January 1988, pp. 37–57. Warren argues that, although IVF (and other reproductive technologies) "pose some significant dangers for women, it would be wrong to conclude that women's interests demand an end to IVF and other reproductive research." In an effort to guard against a possible negative impact on the interests of women, she insists that IVF is not an adequate overall social response to the problem of involuntary infertility.

CHAPTER 3

Euthanasia

The moral justifiability of euthanasia is not a newly emerging issue, but it is an issue that is debated with a new intensity in contemporary times. Recent advances in biomedical technology have made it possible to prolong human life in ways undreamed of by past generations of medical practitioners. As a result, it is not unusual to find a person who has lived a long and useful life now permanently incapable of functioning in any recognizably human fashion. Biological life continues; but some find it tempting to say that human life, in any meaningful sense, has ceased. In one case the patient is in an irreversible coma, reduced to a vegetative existence. In another case the patient's personality has completely deteriorated. In still another case the patient alternates inescapably between excruciating pain and drug-induced stupor. In each of these cases, the quality of human life has deteriorated. There is no longer any capacity for creative employment, intellectual pursuit, or the cultivation of interpersonal relationships. In short, in each of these three cases life seems to have been rendered meaningless in the sense that the individual has lost all capacity for normal human satisfactions. In the first case there is simply no consciousness, which is a necessary condition for deriving satisfaction. In the second case consciousness has been dulled to such an extent that there is no longer any capacity for satisfaction. In the third case excruciating pain and sedation combine to undercut the possibility of satisfaction.

At the other end of the spectrum of life, we are confronted with the severely impaired newborn child. In some tragic cases, a child seems to have no significant potential for meaningful human life. For example, an anencephalic child, one born with a partial or total absence of the brain, has no prospect for human life as we know it. Biomedical technology is sometimes sufficient to sustain or at least temporarily prolong the life of a severely impaired newborn, depending on the particular nature of the child's medical condition, but one question commands attention. Is the child better off dead?

Religious people pray and nonreligious people hope that death will come quickly to themselves or to loved ones who are in the midst of terminal illnesses and forced to endure pain and/or indignity. The same attitudes often prevail in the face of tragically compromised newborns. The prevalence of these attitudes seems to confirm the truth, however sad, that some human beings, by virtue of their medical condition, are better off dead. But if it is true that someone is better off dead, then mercy is on the side of death, and the issue of euthanasia comes to the fore. Euthanasia, in its various forms, is the subject of discussion in this chapter.

THE MORAL JUSTIFIABILITY OF EUTHANASIA

Discussions of the moral justifiability of euthanasia often involve reference to distinctions that are themselves controversial. Such distinctions include that between ordinary and extraordinary means of prolonging life, that between killing and allowing to die, and that between active and passive euthanasia. Indeed, the very concept of euthanasia is controversial. In accordance with what might be called the "narrow construal of euthanasia," euthanasia is equivalent to mercy *killing*. In this view, if a physician administers a lethal dose of a drug to a terminally ill patient (on grounds of mercy), this act is a paradigm of euthanasia. If, on the other hand, a physician *allows the patient to die* (e.g., by withholding or withdrawing a respirator), this does not count as euthanasia. In accordance with what might be called the "broad construal of euthanasia," the category of euthanasia encompasses both killing and allowing to die (on grounds of mercy). Those who adopt the broad construal of euthanasia often distinguish between active euthanasia (i.e., killing) and passive euthanasia (i.e., allowing to die). Although there seem to be clear cases of killing (e.g., the lethal dose) and clear cases of allowing to die (e.g., withholding or withdrawing a respirator), there are more troublesome cases as well. Suppose a physician administers pain medication with the knowledge that the patient's life will be shortened as a result. A case of killing? Suppose a physician withholds "ordinary means" of life support, whatever that might be. A case of allowing to die? Sometimes it is even said that *withdrawing* life-sustaining treatment is active ("pulling the plug!") in a way that *withholding* it is not, but it is implausible to think that there is an important moral difference between withdrawing and withholding life-sustaining treatment.

The historically important distinction between ordinary and extraordinary means of prolonging life is perhaps especially problematic. The idea that extraordinary means are not mandatory, whereas ordinary means are, has been embraced in many quarters. The language of "extraordinary means" is sometimes found in "living wills," judicial opinions, and codelike statements expressing principles of medical ethics. In addition, some philosophers continue to defend the moral importance of the distinction between ordinary and extraordinary means, but many contemporary commentators believe that the distinction is of no fundamental importance, even if ambiguities of meaning can be clearly resolved.

There is one further distinction, itself relatively uncontroversial, that plays an important role in discussions of euthanasia. *Voluntary* euthanasia proceeds with the (informed) consent of the person involved. *Involuntary* euthanasia proceeds without the consent of the person involved, when the person involved is *incapable* of (informed) consent.[1] The possibility of involuntary euthanasia might arise, for example, in the case of a comatose adult. The much discussed case of Karen Ann Quinlan is a

---

[1]Some authors, such as Stephen G. Potts in this chapter, distinguish among voluntary, nonvoluntary, and involuntary euthanasia. When this threefold distinction is made, euthanasia would be "nonvoluntary" if the person involved were *incapable of consent* and "involuntary" if it were to take place *against the will* of the person involved.

case of this sort.[2] The possibility of involuntary euthanasia might also arise with regard to adults who have for any number of reasons (e.g., Alzheimer's disease) lost their decision-making capacity, and it might arise with regard to children. Indeed, a very prominent variety of involuntary euthanasia involves severely impaired newborns. When the voluntary/involuntary distinction is combined with the active/passive distinction, it is clear that four types of euthanasia can be generated: (1) active voluntary euthanasia, (2) passive voluntary euthanasia, (3) active involuntary euthanasia, and (4) passive involuntary euthanasia.

A very common view on the morality of euthanasia, so common that it might justifiably be termed the "standard view," may be explicated as follows: Withholding or withdrawing life-sustaining treatment is morally acceptable (under certain specifiable conditions), but mercy killing is never morally acceptable. Those who operate in accordance with the narrow conception of euthanasia would express the standard view by saying that withholding or withdrawing life-sustaining treatment can be morally acceptable, but *euthanasia* is never morally acceptable. Those who operate in accordance with the broad conception of euthanasia would express the standard view by saying that *passive euthanasia* is morally acceptable (under certain specifiable conditions), but *active euthanasia* is never morally acceptable. The standard view, especially as expressed in a 1973 formulation by the American Medical Association (AMA), is vigorously attacked by James Rachels in one of this chapter's readings. Thomas D. Sullivan accuses Rachels of misconstruing the sense behind the standard view. Sullivan offers a defense of the standard view. Rachels, in turn, criticizes Sullivan's reliance on the distinction between intentional and nonintentional terminations of life and the distinction between ordinary and extraordinary means of life support.

The withholding or withdrawing of life-sustaining treatment in the case of terminally ill patients is surely an established part of medical practice. Moreover, several religious traditions explicitly acknowledge the morality of this practice. In addition, it is widely believed that a patient has the moral (and legal) right to refuse any medical treatment, a right that would encompass the refusal of life-sustaining treatment. Thus, there is a substantial body of opinion, perhaps something close to a consensus view, maintaining the moral legitimacy of withholding or withdrawing life-sustaining treatment in the case of terminally ill patients. There is no such consensus view on the morality of *mercy killing,* which will be referred to here as "active euthanasia."

Those who argue for the moral legitimacy of active euthanasia emphasize consid-

---

[2]In the Quinlan case, Joseph Quinlan, the father of comatose twenty-one-year-old Karen Ann Quinlan, sought to be appointed guardian of the person and property of his daughter. As guardian, he would then authorize the discontinuance of the mechanical respirator that was thought to be sustaining the vital life processes of his daughter. Judge Muir of the Superior Court of New Jersey decided against the request of Joseph Quinlan. *In re Quinlan,* 137 N.J. Super 227 (1975). Justice Hughes of the Supreme Court of New Jersey overturned the lower court's decision. *In re Quinlan,* 70 N.J. 10, 335 A. 2d 647 (1976). When the respirator was finally withdrawn, Karen Ann Quinlan proved capable of breathing on her own. She remained alive in a "persistent vegetative state" for about ten years.

erations of humaneness. In the case of *voluntary* active euthanasia, the humanitarian appeal is often conjoined with an appeal to the primacy of individual autonomy. Thus the case for the morality of voluntary active euthanasia incorporates two basic arguments: (1) It is cruel and inhumane to refuse the plea of a terminally ill person that his or her life be mercifully ended in order to avoid future suffering and indignity. (2) Individual choice should be respected to the extent that it does not result in harm to others. Since no one is harmed by terminally ill patients' undergoing active euthanasia, a decision to have one's life ended in this fashion should be respected.

In defending the moral legitimacy of active euthanasia in this chapter, Rachels appeals directly to humanitarian considerations, but he also constructs an argument based on the golden rule. Typically, those who argue against the moral legitimacy of active euthanasia rest their case on one or both of the following strategies of argument: (1) They appeal to some "sanctity of life" principle to the effect that the intentional termination of (innocent) human life is always immoral. Sullivan advances this sort of argument in his defense of the standard view. (2) They advance a rule-utilitarian argument to the effect that any systematic acceptance of active euthanasia would lead to damaging consequences for society (e.g., via a lessening of respect for human life). This second sort of argument recurs in discussions of the legalization of active euthanasia.

ACTIVE EUTHANASIA AND SOCIAL POLICY

Should active euthanasia be legalized? If so, in what form or forms and with what safeguards? Although active euthanasia is presently illegal in all fifty states, proposals for its legalization have been recurrently advanced. Most commonly, it is the legalization of *voluntary* active euthanasia that has been proposed.

There are some who consider active euthanasia in any form intrinsically immoral (sometimes on overtly religious grounds) and for this reason are opposed to the legalization of voluntary active euthansia. Others, such as Stephen G. Potts in this chapter, see nothing intrinsically wrong with individual acts of voluntary active euthansia, but still stand opposed to any systematic social policy that would permit its practice. It is said, for example, that the risk of abuse is too great and that patients would needlessly die when mistakenly thought to be incurably ill. It is also said that the legalization of *voluntary* active euthanasia would lead us down a slippery slope to the legalization of *involuntary* euthanasia. Those who support the legalization of voluntary active euthanasia recognize that some bad consequences may result from such legislation. However, they typically seek to establish that potential dangers are minimal.

Two specific models for the legalization of voluntary active euthanasia are discussed in this chapter. One model is provided by a set of guidelines under which voluntary active euthanasia is presently permitted in the Netherlands. Another model is provided by the provisions of the "Humane and Dignified Death Act," a California legislative proposal. In one of this chapter's selections, Marcia Angell clarifies the difference between these two models. She also argues that the risk of abuse would be much greater in the proposed California legislation than it is in the Dutch system. In the course of her discussion, Angell refers to some of the standard arguments for and against the legalization of voluntary active euthanasia.

TREATMENT DECISIONS FOR INCOMPETENT PATIENTS

The rigors of incurable illness and the dying process frequently deprive previously competent patients of their decision-making capacity. How can a person best ensure that his or her personal wishes with regard to life-sustaining treatment will be honored even if decision-making capacity is lost? Although communication of one's attitudes about various forms of life-sustaining treatment to one's physician, family, and friends surely provides some measure of protection, it is frequently asserted that the most effective protection comes through the formation of *advance directives.*

There are two basic types of advance directives, and each has legal status in most but not all states. In executing an *instructional* directive, a person specifies instructions about her or his care in the event that decision-making capacity is lost. Such a directive dealing specifically with the dying process and refusal of various forms of life-sustaining treatment is usually called "a living will." In executing a *proxy* directive, a person specifies a surrogate decision maker to make health-care decisions for him or her in the event that decision-making capacity is lost. The legal mechanism for executing a proxy directive is called a "durable power of attorney." Since purging ambiguities from even the most explicit written directives is difficult, as is foreseeing all the contingencies that might give rise to a need for treatment decisions, many commentators recommend the execution of a durable power of attorney even if a person has already executed a living will.

If a patient lacks decision-making capacity, a surrogate decision maker must be identified, and this will ordinarily be a member of the family or a close personal friend. If the patient has provided instructional directives, the surrogate is of course expected to follow them, but often enough a surrogate decision maker must function in the absence of instructional directives. In applying the *substituted judgment* standard, the surrogate decision maker is expected to consider the patient's preferences and values and make the decision that the patient would make if she or he were able to choose. If no reliable basis exists to infer what the patient would have chosen, then the surrogate decision maker is expected to retreat to the *best interests* standard. In applying the best interests standard, the surrogate decision maker is expected to choose what a rational person in the patient's circumstances would choose.

In the case of *Cruzan v. Director, Missouri Department of Health* (1990), the United States Supreme Court considered for the first time a "right-to-die" case. Nancy Cruzan, a woman in her mid-twenties, was injured in an automobile accident and ultimately reduced to existence in a persistent vegetative state. Cruzan's parents, in an effort to exercise substituted judgment on her behalf, sought court authorization to terminate her artificial nutrition and hydration. But the State of Missouri contended that nutrition and hydration should not be terminated because there was no "clear and convincing evidence" that termination of treatment is what Nancy Cruzan would have wanted in such circumstances. The Supreme Court ultimately sided with the State of Missouri and ruled against the Cruzans. An excerpt from Justice Rehnquist's majority opinion in the *Cruzan* case appears in this chapter.

Thomas A. Mappes and Jane S. Zembaty

Active and Passive Euthanasia

James Rachels

James Rachels is professor of philosophy at the University of Alabama in Birmingham. Specializing in ethics, he is the author of such articles as "Why Privacy Is Important," "On Moral Absolutism," and "Can Ethics Provide Answers?" He is also the author of *The Elements of Moral Philosophy* (1986) and *The End of Life: Euthanasia and Morality* (1986), and he is the editor of *Understanding Moral Philosophy* (1976).

Rachels identifies the standard (conventional) view on the morality of euthanasia as the doctrine which permits passive euthanasia but rejects active euthanasia. He then argues that the conventional doctrine may be challenged for four reasons. First, active euthanasia is in many cases more humane than passive euthanasia. Second, the conventional doctrine leads to decisions concerning life and death on irrelevant grounds. Third, the doctrine rests on a distinction between killing and letting die that itself has no moral importance. Fourth, the most common arguments in favor of the doctrine are invalid.

The distinction between active and passive euthanasia is thought to be crucial for medical ethics. The idea is that it is permissible, at least in some cases, to withhold treatment and allow a patient to die, but it is never permissible to take any direct action designed to kill the patient. This doctrine seems to be accepted by most doctors, and it is endorsed in a statement adopted by the House of Delegates of the American Medical Association on December 4, 1973:

> The intentional termination of the life of one human being by another—mercy killing—is contrary to that for which the medical profession stands and is contrary to the policy of the American Medical Association.
>
> The cessation of the employment of extraordinary means to prolong the life of the body when there is irrefutable evidence that biological death is imminent is the decision of the patient and/or his immediate family. The advice and judgment of the physician should be freely available to the patient and/or his immediate family.

However, a strong case can be made against this doctrine. In what follows, I will set out some of the relevant arguments, and urge doctors to reconsider their views on this matter.

Reprinted with permission from *The New England Journal of Medicine,* vol. 292, no. 2 (Jan. 9, 1975), pp. 78–80.

To begin with a familiar type of situation, a patient who is dying of incurable cancer of the throat is in terrible pain, which can no longer be satisfactorily alleviated. He is certain to die within a few days, even if present treatment is continued, but he does not want to go on living for those days since the pain is unbearable. So he asks the doctor for an end to it, and his family joins in the request.

Suppose the doctor agrees to withhold treatment, as the conventional doctrine says he may. The justification for his doing so is that the patient is in terrible agony, and since he is going to die anyway, it would be wrong to prolong his suffering needlessly. But now notice this. If one simply withholds treatment, it may take the patient longer to die, and so he may suffer more than he would if more direct action were taken and a lethal injection given. This fact provides strong reason for thinking that, once the initial decision not to prolong his agony has been made, active euthanasia is actually preferable to passive euthanasia, rather than the reverse. To say otherwise is to endorse the option that leads to more suffering rather than less, and is contrary to the humanitarian impulse that prompts the decision not to prolong his life in the first place.

Part of my point is that the process of being "allowed to die" can be relatively slow and painful, whereas being given a lethal injection is relatively quick and painless. Let me give a different sort of example. In the United States about one in 600 babies is born with Down's syndrome. Most of these babies are otherwise healthy— that is, with only the usual pediatric care, they will proceed to an otherwise normal infancy. Some, however, are born with congenital defects such as intestinal obstructions that require operations if they are to live. Sometimes, the parents and the doctor will decide not to operate, and let the infant die. Anthony Shaw describes what happens then:

> . . . When surgery is denied [the doctor] must try to keep the infant from suffering while natural forces sap the baby's life away. As a surgeon whose natural inclination is to use the scalpel to fight off death, standing by and watching a salvageable baby die is the most emotionally exhausting experience I know. It is easy at a conference, in a theoretical discussion, to decide that such infants should be allowed to die. It is altogether different to stand by in the nursery and watch as dehydration and infection wither a tiny being over hours and days. This is a terrible ordeal for me and the hospital staff—much more so than for the parents who never set foot in the nursery.[1]

I can understand why some people are opposed to all euthanasia, and insist that such infants must be allowed to live. I think I can also understand why other people favor destroying these babies quickly and painlessly. But why should anyone favor letting "dehydration and infection wither a tiny being over hours and days?" The doctrine that says that a baby may be allowed to dehydrate and wither, but may not be given an injection that would end its life without suffering, seems so patently cruel as to require no further refutation. The strong language is not intended to offend, but only to put the point in the clearest possible way.

My second argument is that the conventional doctrine leads to decisions concerning life and death made on irrelevant grounds.

Consider again the case of the infants with Down's syndrome who need operations for congenital defects unrelated to the syndrome to live. Sometimes, there is no operation, and the baby dies, but when there is no such defect, the baby lives on. Now, an operation such as that to remove an intestinal obstruction is not prohibitively difficult. The reason why such operations are not performed in these cases is, clearly, that the child has Down's syndrome and the parents and doctor judge that because of that fact it is better for the child to die.

But notice that this situation is absurd, no matter what view one takes of the lives and potentials of such babies. If the life of such an infant is worth preserving, what does it matter if it needs a simple operation? Or, if one thinks it better that such a baby should not live on, what difference does it make that it happens to have an unobstructed intestinal tract? In either case, the matter of life and death is being decided on irrelevant grounds. It is the Down's syndrome, and not the intestines, that is the issue. The matter should be decided, if at all, on that basis, and not be allowed to depend on the essentially irrelevant question of whether the intestinal tract is blocked.

What makes this situation possible, of course, is the idea that when there is an intestinal blockage, one can "let the baby die," but when there is no such defect there is nothing that can be done, for one must not "kill" it. The fact that this idea leads to such results as deciding life or death on irrelevant grounds is another good reason why the doctrine should be rejected.

One reason why so many people think that there is an important moral difference between active and passive euthanasia is that they think killing someone is morally worse than letting someone die. But is it? Is killing, in itself, worse than letting die? To investigate this issue, two cases may be considered that are exactly alike except that one involves killing whereas the other involves letting someone die. Then, it can be asked whether this difference makes any difference to the moral assessments. It is important that the cases be exactly alike, except for this one difference, since otherwise one cannot be confident that it is this difference and not some other that accounts for any variation in the assessments of the two cases. So, let us consider this pair of cases:

In the first, Smith stands to gain a large inheritance if anything should happen to his six-year-old cousin. One evening while the child is taking his bath, Smith sneaks into the bathroom and drowns the child, and then arranges things so that it will look like an accident.

In the second, Jones also stands to gain if anything should happen to his six-year-old cousin. Like Smith, Jones sneaks in planning to drown the child in his bath. However, just as he enters the bathroom Jones sees the child slip and hit his head, and fall face down in the water. Jones is delighted; he stands by, ready to push the child's head back under if it is necessary, but it is not necessary. With only a little thrashing about the child drowns all by himself, "accidentally," as Jones watches and does nothing.

Now Smith killed the child, whereas Jones "merely" let the child die. That is the only difference between them. Did either man behave better, from a moral point of view? If the difference between killing and letting die were in itself a morally important matter, one should say that Jones's behavior was less reprehensible than

Smith's. But does one really want to say that? I think not. In the first place, both men acted from the same motive, personal gain, and both had exactly the same end in view when they acted. It may be inferred from Smith's conduct that he is a bad man, although that judgment may be withdrawn or modified if certain further facts are learned about him—for example, that he is mentally deranged. But would not the very same thing be inferred about Jones from his conduct? And would not the same further considerations also be relevant to any modification of this judgment? More-over, suppose Jones pleaded, in his own defense, "After all, I didn't do anything ex-cept just stand there and watch the child drown. I didn't kill him; I only let him die." Again, if letting die were in itself less bad than killing, this defense should have at least some weight. But it does not. Such a "defense" can only be regarded as a gro-tesque perversion of moral reasoning. Morally speaking, it is no defense at all.

Now, it may be pointed out, quite properly, that the cases of euthanasia with which doctors are concerned are not like this at all. They do not involve personal gain or the destruction of normally healthy children. Doctors are concerned only with cases in which the patient's life is of no further use to him, or in which the patient's life has become or will soon become a terrible burden. However, the point is the same in these cases: the bare difference between killing and letting die does not, in itself, make a moral difference. If a doctor lets a patient die, for humane rea-sons, he is in the same moral position as if he had given the patient a lethal injection for humane reasons. If his decision was wrong—if, for example, the patient's illness was in fact curable—the decision would be equally regrettable no matter which method was used to carry it out. And if the doctor's decision was the right one, the method used is not in itself important.

The AMA policy statement isolates the crucial issue very well; the crucial issue is "the intentional termination of the life of one human being by another." But after identifying this issue, and forbidding "mercy killing," the statement goes on to deny that the cessation of treatment is the intentional termination of a life. This is where the mistake comes in, for what is the cessation of treatment, in these circumstances, if it is not "the intentional termination of the life of one human being by another?" Of course, it is exactly that, and if it were not, there would be no point to it.

Many people will find this judgment hard to accept. One reason, I think, is that it is very easy to conflate the question of whether killing is, in itself, worse than letting die, with the very different question of whether most actual cases of killing are more reprehensible than most actual cases of letting die. Most actual cases of killing are clearly terrible (think, for example, of all the murders reported in the newspapers), and one hears of such cases every day. On the other hand, one hardly ever hears of a case of letting die, except for the actions of doctors who are motivated by humani-tarian reasons. So one learns to think of killing in a much worse light than of letting die. But this does not mean that there is something about killing that makes it in itself worse than letting die, for it is not the bare difference between killing and let-ting die that makes the difference in these cases. Rather, the other factors—the mur-derer's motive of personal gain, for example, contrasted with the doctor's humanitar-ian motivation—account for different reactions to the different cases.

I have argued that killing is not in itself any worse than letting die; if my contention is right, it follows that active euthanasia is not any worse than passive euthanasia. What arguments can be given on the other side? The most common, I believe, is the following:

"The important difference between active and passive euthanasia is that, in passive euthanasia, the doctor does not do anything to bring about the patient's death. The doctor does nothing, and the patient dies of whatever ills already afflict him. In active euthanasia, however, the doctor does something to bring about the patient's death: he kills him. The doctor who gives the patient with cancer a lethal injection has himself caused his patient's death; whereas if he merely ceases treatment, the cancer is the cause of the death."

A number of points need to be made here. The first is that it is not exactly correct to say that in passive euthanasia the doctor does nothing, for he does do one thing that is very important: he lets the patient die. "Letting someone die" is certainly different, in some respects, from other types of action—mainly in that it is a kind of action that one may perform by way of not performing certain other actions. For example, one may let a patient die by way of not giving medication, just as one may insult someone by way of not shaking his hand. But for any purpose of moral assessment, it is a type of action nonetheless. The decision to let a patient die is subject to moral appraisal in the same way that a decision to kill him would be subject to moral appraisal: it may be assessed as wise or unwise, compassionate or sadistic, right or wrong. If a doctor deliberately let a patient die who was suffering from a routinely curable illness, the doctor would certainly be to blame for what he had done, just as he would be to blame if he had needlessly killed the patient. Charges against him would then be appropriate. If so, it would be no defense at all for him to insist that he didn't "do anything." He would have done something very serious indeed, for he let his patient die.

Fixing the cause of death may be very important from a legal point of view, for it may determine whether criminal charges are brought against the doctor. But I do not think that this notion can be used to show a moral difference between active and passive euthanasia. The reason why it is considered bad to be the cause of someone's death is that death is regarded as a great evil—and so it is. However, if it has been decided that euthanasia—even passive euthanasia—is desirable in a given case, it has also been decided that in this instance death is no greater an evil than the patient's continued existence. And if this is true, the usual reason for not wanting to be the cause of someone's death simply does not apply.

Finally, doctors may think that all of this is only of academic interest—the sort of thing that philosophers may worry about but that has no practical bearing on their own work. After all, doctors must be concerned about the legal consequences of what they do, and active euthanasia is clearly forbidden by the law. But even so, doctors should also be concerned with the fact that the law is forcing upon them a moral doctrine that may well be indefensible, and has a considerable effect on their practices. Of course, most doctors are not now in the position of being coerced in this matter, for they do not regard themselves as merely going along with what the law requires. Rather, in statements such as the AMA policy statement that I have quoted, they are endorsing this doctrine as a central point of medical ethics. In that statement, active euthanasia is condemned not merely as illegal but as "contrary to that for which the medical profession stands," whereas passive euthanasia is approved. However, the preceding considerations suggest that there is really no moral difference between the two, considered in themselves (there may be important moral differences in some cases in their *consequences,* but, as I pointed out, these differences may make active euthanasia, and not passive euthanasia, the morally preferable option). So, whereas doctors may have to discriminate between active and passive euthanasia to satisfy the law, they should not do any more than that. In particular, they should not give the distinction any added authority and weight by writing it into official statements of medical ethics.

NOTES

1 A. Shaw: "Doctor, Do We Have a Choice?" *The New York Times Magazine,* Jan. 30, 1972, p. 54.

QUESTIONS

1 If you were a physician, what would you do when the parents of a baby with Down's syndrome and an intestinal obstruction decided against surgery? Would you let the baby slowly die from dehydration and starvation, would you take some active step to end the baby's life, or would you take the case to court to force the surgery? How would you justify your decision?
2 Can the conventional doctrine on active and passive euthanasia be defended against Rachels's arguments?

Active and Passive Euthanasia: An Impertinent Distinction?

Thomas D. Sullivan

Thomas D. Sullivan is professor of philosophy at the College of St. Thomas in St. Paul, Minnesota. He is the author of "Between Thoughts and Things: The Status of Meaning" and "Adequate Evidence for Religious Assent" and the coauthor of "Benevolence and Absolute Prohibitions." He is also the author of an article on abortion, "In Defense of Total Regard."

Sullivan, responding directly to Rachels, offers a defense of the standard (traditional) view on the morality of euthanasia. Sullivan charges Rachels with misconstruing the sense behind the traditional view. On Sullivan's analysis, the traditional view is not dependent on the distinction between killing and letting die. Rather, it simply forbids the *intentional* termination of life, whether by killing or letting die. The cessation of *extraordinary* means, he maintains, is morally permissible because, though death is foreseen, it need not be intended.

From *Human Life Review,* vol. III, no. 3 (Summer 1977), pp. 40–46. Reprinted with permission of the publisher (The Human Life Foundation, Inc., 150 East 35th Street, New York, NY 10016).

Because of recent advances in medical technology, it is today possible to save or prolong the lives of many persons who in an earlier era would have quickly perished. Unhappily, however, it often is impossible to do so without committing the patient and his or her family to a future filled with sorrows. Modern methods of neurosurgery can successfully close the opening at the base of the spine of a baby born with severe myelomeningocoele, but do nothing to relieve the paralysis that afflicts it from the waist down or to remedy the patient's incontinence of stool and urine. Antibiotics and skin grafts can spare the life of a victim of severe and massive burns, but fail to eliminate the immobilizing contractions of arms and legs, the extreme pain, and the hideous disfigurement of the face. It is not surprising, therefore, that physicians and moralists in increasing number recommend that assistance should not be given to such patients, and that some have even begun to advocate the deliberate hastening of death by medical means, provided informed consent has been given by the appropriate parties.

The latter recommendation consciously and directly conflicts with what might be called the "traditional" view of the physician's role. The traditional view, as articulated, for example, by the House of Delegates of the American Medical Association in 1973, declared:

> The intentional termination of the life of one human being by another—mercy killing—is contrary to that for which the medical profession stands and is contrary to the policy of the American Medical Association.
>
> The cessation of the employment of extra-ordinary means to prolong the life of the body when there is irrefutable evidence that biological death is imminent is the decision of the patient and/or his immediate family. The advice and judgment of the physician should be freely available to the patient and/or his immediate family.

Basically this view involves two points: (1) that it is impermissible for the doctor or anyone else to terminate intentionally the life of a patient, but (2) that it is permissible in some cases to cease the employment of "extraordinary means" of preserving life, even though the death of the patient is a foreseeable consequence.

Does this position really make sense? Recent criticism charges that it does not. The heart of the complaint is that the traditional view arbitrarily rules out all cases of intentionally acting to terminate life, but permits what is in fact the moral equivalent, letting patients die. This accusation has been clearly articulated by James Rachels in a widely-read article that appeared in a recent issue of the *New England Journal of Medicine,* entitled "Active and Passive Euthanasia."[1] By "active euthanasia" Rachels seems to mean *doing something* to bring about a patient's death, and by "passive euthanasia," not doing anything, i.e., just letting the patient die. Referring to the A.M.A. statement, Rachels sees the traditional position as always forbidding active euthanasia, but permitting passive euthanasia. Yet, he argues, passive euthanasia may be in some cases morally indistinguishable from active euthanasia, and in other cases even worse. To make his point he asks his readers to consider the case of a Down's syndrome baby with an intestinal obstruction that easily could be remedied through routine surgery. Rachels comments:

> I can understand why some people are opposed to all euthanasia, and insist that such infants must be allowed to live. I think I can also understand why other people favor destroy-

ing these babies quickly and painlessly. But why should anyone favor letting 'dehydration and infection wither a tiny being over hours and days?' The doctrine that says that a baby may be allowed to dehydrate and wither, but may not be given an injection that would end its life without suffering, seems so patently cruel as to require no further refutation.[2]

Rachels' point is that decisions such as the one he describes as "patently cruel" arise out of a misconceived moral distinction between active and passive euthanasia, which in turn rests upon a distinction between killing and letting die that itself has no moral importance.

> One reason why so many people think that there is an important moral difference between active and passive euthanasia is that they think killing someone is morally worse than letting someone die. But is it? . . . To investigate this issue, two cases may be considered that are exactly alike except that one involves killing whereas the other involves letting someone die. Then, it can be asked whether this difference makes any difference to the moral assessments. . . .
>
> In the first, Smith stands to gain a large inheritance if anything should happen to his six-year-old cousin. One evening while the child is taking his bath, Smith sneaks into the bathroom and drowns the child, and then arranges things so that it will look like an accident.
>
> In the second, Jones also stands to gain if anything should happen to his six-year-old cousin. Like Smith, Jones sneaks in planning to drown the child in his bath. However, just as he enters the bathroom Jones sees the child slip and hit his head, and fall face down in the water. Jones is delighted; he stands by, ready to push the child's head back under if it is necessary, but it is not necessary. With only a little thrashing about the child drowns all by himself, "accidentally," as Jones watches and does nothing.[3]

Rachels observes that Smith killed the child, whereas Jones "merely" let the child die. If there's an important moral distinction between killing and letting die, then, we should say that Jones' behavior from a moral point of view is less reprehensible than Smith's. But while the law might draw some distinctions here, it seems clear that the acts of Jones and Smith are not different in any important way, or, if there is a difference, Jones' action is even worse.

In essence, then, the objection to the position adopted by the A.M.A. of Rachels and those who argue like him is that it endorses a highly questionable moral distinction between killing and letting die, which, if accepted, leads to indefensible medical decisions. Nowhere does Rachels quite come out and say that he favors active euthanasia in some cases, but the implication is clear. Nearly everyone holds that it is sometimes pointless to prolong the process of dying and that in those cases it is morally permissible to let a patient die even though a few hours or days could be salvaged by procedures that would also increase the agonies of the dying. But if it is impossible to defend a general distinction between letting people die and acting to terminate their lives directly, then it would seem that active euthanasia also may be morally permissible.

Now what shall we make of all this? It *is* cruel to stand by and watch a Down's baby die an agonizing death when a simple operation would remove the intestinal obstruction, but to offer the excuse that in failing to operate we didn't *do* anything to bring about death is an example of moral evasiveness comparable to the excuse Jones would offer for his action of "merely" letting his cousin die. Furthermore, it is true that if someone is trying to bring about the death of another human being, then it makes little difference from the moral point of view if his purpose is achieved by action or by malevolent omission, as in the cases of Jones and Smith.

But if we acknowledge this, are we obliged to give up the traditional view expressed by the A.M.A. statement? Of course not. To begin with, we are hardly obliged to assume the Jones-like role Rachels assigns the defender of the traditional view. We have the option of operating on the Down's baby and saving its life. Rachels mentions that possibility only to hurry past it as if that is not what his opposition would do. But, of course, that is precisely the course of action most defenders of the traditional position would choose.

Secondly, while it may be that the reason some rather confused people give for upholding the traditional view is that they think killing someone is always worse than letting them die, nobody who gives the matter much thought puts it that way. Rather they say that killing someone is clearly morally worse than not killing them, and killing them can be done by acting to bring about their death or by refusing ordinary means to keep them alive in order to bring about the same goal.

What I am suggesting is that Rachels' objections leave the position he sets out to criticize untouched. It is worth noting that the jargon of active and passive euthanasia—and it is jargon—does not appear in the resolution. Nor does the resolution state or imply the distinction Rachels attacks, a distinction that puts a moral premium on overt behavior—moving or not moving one's parts—while totally ignoring the intentions of the agent. That no such distinction is being drawn seems clear from the fact that the A.M.A. resolution speaks approvingly of ceasing to use extra-ordinary means in certain cases, and such withdrawals might easily involve bodily movement, for example unplugging an oxygen machine.

In addition to saddling his opposition with an indefensible distinction it doesn't make, Rachels proceeds to ignore one that it does make—one that is crucial to a just interpretation of the view. Recall the A.M.A. allows the withdrawal of what it calls extra-ordinary means of preserving life; clearly the contrast here is with ordinary means. Though in its short statement those expressions are not defined, the definition Paul Ramsey refers to as standard in his book, *The Patient as Person,* seems to fit.

> Ordinary means of preserving life are all medicines, treatments, and operations, which offer a reasonable hope of benefit for the patient and which can be obtained and used without excessive expense, pain, and other inconveniences.
>
> Extra-ordinary means of preserving life are all those medicines, treatments, and operations which cannot be obtained without excessive expense, pain, or other inconvenience, or which, if used, would not offer a reasonable hope of benefit.[4]

Now with this distinction in mind, we can see how the traditional view differs from the position Rachels mistakes for it. The traditional view is that the intentional termination of human life is impermissible, irrespective of whether this goal is brought about by action or inaction. Is the action or refraining *aimed* at producing a death? Is the termination of life *sought, chosen or planned?* Is the intention deadly? If so, the act or omission is wrong.

But we all know it is entirely possible that the unwillingness of a physician to use extra-ordinary means for preserving life may be prompted not by a determination to bring about death, but by other motives. For example, he may realize that further treatment may offer little hope of reversing the dying process and/or be excruciating, as in the case when a massively necrotic bowel condition in a neonate is out of control. The doctor who does what he can to comfort the infant but does not submit it to further treatment or surgery may foresee that the decision will hasten death, but it certainly doesn't follow from that fact that he intends to bring about its death. It is, after all, entirely possible to foresee that something will come about as a result of one's conduct without intending the consequence or side effect. If I drive downtown, I can foresee that I'll wear out my tires a little, but I don't drive downtown with the intention of wearing out my tires. And if I choose to forego my exercises for a few days, I may think that as a result my physical condition will deteriorate a little, but I don't omit my exercise with a view to running myself down. And if you have to fill a position and select Green, who is better qualified for the post than her rival Brown, you needn't appoint Mrs. Green with the intention of hurting Mr. Brown, though you may foresee that Mr. Brown will feel hurt. And if a country extends its general education programs to its illiterate masses, it is predictable the suicide rate will go up, but even if the public officials are aware of this fact, it doesn't follow that they initiate the program with a view to making the suicide rate go up. In general, then, it is not the case that all the foreseeable consequences and side effects of our conduct are necessarily intended. And it is because the physician's withdrawal of extra-ordinary means can be otherwise motivated than by a desire to bring about the predictable death of the patient that such action cannot categorically be ruled out as wrong.

But the refusal to use ordinary means is an altogether different matter. After all, what is the point of refusing assistance which offers reasonable hope of benefit to the patient without involving excessive pain or other inconvenience? How could it be plausibly maintained that the refusal is not motivated by a desire to bring about the death of the patient? The traditional position, therefore, rules out not only direct actions to bring about death, such as giving a patient a lethal injection, but malevolent omissions as well, such as not providing minimum care for the newborn.

The reason the A.M.A. position sounds so silly when one listens to arguments such as Rachels' is that he slights the distinction between ordinary and extra-ordinary means and then drums on cases where *ordinary* means are refused. The impression is thereby conveyed that the traditional doctrine sanctions omissions that are morally indistinguishable in a substantive way from direct killings, but then incomprehensibly refuses to permit quick and painless termination of life. If the traditional doctrine would approve of Jones' standing by with a grin on his face while his young cousin drowned in a tub, or letting a Down's baby wither and die when ordinary means are available to preserve its life, it would indeed be difficult to see how anyone could defend it. But so to conceive the traditional doctrine is simply to misunderstand it. It is not a doctrine that rests on some supposed distinction between "active" and "passive euthanasia," whatever those words are supposed to mean, nor on a distinction between moving and not moving our bodies. It is simply a prohibition against intentional killing, which includes both direct actions and malevolent omissions.

To summarize—the traditional position represented by the A.M.A. statement is not incoherent. It acknowledges, or more accurately, insists upon the fact that withholding ordinary means to sustain life may be tantamount to killing. The traditional position can be made to appear incoherent only by imposing upon it a crude idea of killing held by none of its more articulate advocates.

Thus the criticism of Rachels and other reformers, misapprehending its target, leaves the traditional position untouched. That position is simply a prohibition of murder. And it is good to remember, as C. S. Lewis once pointed out:

> No man, perhaps, ever at first described to himself the act he was about to do as Murder, or Adultery, or Fraud, or Treachery. . . . And when he hears it so described by other men he is (in a way) sincerely shocked and surprised. Those others "don't understand." If they knew what it had really been like for him, they would not use those crude "stock" names. With a wink or a titter, or a cloud of muddy emotion, the thing has slipped into his will as something not very extraordinary, something of which, rightly understood in all of his peculiar circumstances, he may even feel proud.[5]

I fully realize that there are times when those who have the noble duty to tend the sick and the dying are deeply moved by the sufferings of their patients, especially of the very young and the very old, and desperately wish they could do more than comfort and companion them. Then, perhaps, it seems that universal moral principles are mere abstractions having little to do with the agony of the dying. But of course we do not see best when our eyes are filled with tears.

NOTES

1 *The New England Journal of Medicine,* vol. 292 (Jan. 9, 1975), pp. 78–80. [Reprinted, this volume, pp. 110–115.]
2 *Ibid.,* pp. 78–79. [This volume, p. 111.]
3 *Ibid.,* p. 79. [This volume, p. 112.]
4 Paul Ramsey, *The Patient As Person* (New Haven and London: Yale University Press, 1970), p. 122. Ramsey abbreviates the definition first given by Gerald Kelly, S. J., *Medico-Moral Problems* (St. Louis, Mo.: The Catholic Hospital Association, 1958), p. 129.
5 C. S. Lewis, *A Preface to Paradise Lost* (London and New York: Oxford University Press, 1970), p. 126.

QUESTIONS

1 Is Sullivan correct in holding that the traditional position is "simply a prohibition of murder"?
2 Is the traditional view dependent on the distinction between killing and letting die (contra Sullivan)?
3 Would it be morally wrong for a physician to withdraw "extraordinary means" *with the explicit intention* of bringing about the death of a terminally ill patient who is in great pain? Would it always be morally wrong for a physician to withdraw "ordinary" means?

More Impertinent Distinctions and a Defense of Active Euthanasia

James Rachels

A biographical sketch of James Rachels is found on p. 110.

This selection falls into two major sections. In the first major section, Rachels responds to Sullivan; in the second, he develops arguments in support of the moral justifiability of active euthanasia. Rachels makes a new departure in responding to Sullivan. He presents two additional arguments against the standard (traditional) view on the morality of euthanasia. Rachels contends, first, that the traditional view is mistaken because it depends on an indefensible distinction between intentional and nonintentional terminations of life. Next he contends that the traditional view is mistaken because it depends on an indefensible distinction between ordinary and extraordinary means of treatment. Rachels's defense of active euthanasia rests on two arguments—the argument from mercy and the argument from the golden rule.

Many thinkers, including almost all orthodox Catholics, believe that euthanasia is immoral. They oppose killing patients in any circumstances whatever. However, they think it is all right, in some special circumstances, to allow patients to die by withholding treatment. The American Medical Association's policy statement on mercy killing supports this traditional view. In my paper "Active and Passive Euthanasia"[1] I argued, against the traditional view, that there is in fact no moral difference between killing and letting die—if one is permissible, then so is the other.

Professor Sullivan[2] does not dispute my argument; instead he dismisses it as irrelevant. The traditional doctrine, he says, does not appeal to or depend on the distinction between killing and letting die. Therefore, arguments against that distinction "leave the traditional position untouched."

Is my argument really irrelevant? I don't see how it can be. As Sullivan himself points out,

> Nearly everyone holds that it is sometimes pointless to prolong the process of dying and that in those cases it is morally permissible to let a patient die even though a few hours or days could be salvaged by procedures that would also increase the agonies of the dying. But if it is impossible to defend a general distinction between letting people die and acting to terminate their lives directly, then it would seem that active euthanasia also may be morally permissible.(117)

But traditionalists like Professor Sullivan hold that active euthanasia—the direct killing of patients—is *not* morally permissible; so, if my argument is sound, their view

Reprinted from Thomas A. Mappes and Jane S. Zembaty, eds., *Biomedical Ethics* (New York: Mc-Graw Hill, 1981), pp. 355–359. Copyright © 1978 by James Rachels. Also from Tom Regan, ed., *Matters of Life and Death: New Introductory Essays in Moral Philosophy.* Copyright © 1980 by Random House, Inc. Reprinted by permission of Random House, Inc.

must be mistaken. I cannot agree, then, that my argument "leaves the traditional position untouched."

However, I shall not press this point. Instead I shall present some further arguments against the traditional position, concentrating on those elements of the position which Professor Sullivan himself thinks most important. According to him, what is important is, first, that we should never *intentionally* terminate the life of a patient, either by action or omission, and second, that we may cease or omit treatment of a patient, knowing that this will result in death, only if the means of treatment involved are *extraordinary*.

INTENTIONAL AND NONINTENTIONAL TERMINATION OF LIFE

We can, of course, distinguish between what a person does and the intention with which he does it. But what is the significance of this distinction for ethics?

> The traditional view [says Sullivan] is that the intentional termination of human life is impermissible, irrespective of whether this goal is brought about by action or inaction. Is the action or refraining *aimed at* producing a death? Is the termination of life *sought, chosen or planned?* Is the intention deadly? If so, the act or omission is wrong.(118)

Thus on the traditional view there is a very definite sort of moral relation between act and intention. An act which is otherwise permissible may become impermissible if it is accompanied by a bad intention. The intention makes the act wrong.

There is reason to think that this view of the relation between act and intention is mistaken. Consider the following example. Jack visits his sick and lonely grandmother, and entertains her for the afternoon. He loves her and his only intention is to cheer her up. Jill also visits the grandmother, and provides an afternoon's cheer. But Jill's concern is that the old lady will soon be making her will; Jill wants to be included among the heirs. Jack also knows that his visit might influence the making of the will, in his favor, but that is no part of his plan. Thus Jack and Jill do the very same thing—they both spend an afternoon cheering up their sick grandmother—and what they do may lead to the same consequences, namely influencing the will. But their intentions are quite different.

Jack's intention was honorable and Jill's was not. Could we say on that account that what Jack did was right, but what Jill did was wrong? No; for Jack and Jill did the very same thing, and if they did the same thing, we cannot say that one acted rightly and the other wrongly.[3] Consistency requires that we assess similar actions similarly. Thus if we are trying to evaluate their *actions,* we must say about one what we say about the other.

However, if we are trying to assess Jack's *character,* or Jill's, things are very different. Even though their actions were similar, Jack seems admirable for what he did, while Jill does not. What Jill did—comforting an elderly sick relative—was a morally good thing, but we would not think well of her for it since she was only scheming after the old lady's money. Jack, on the other hand, did a good thing *and* he did it with an admirable intention. Thus we think well, not only of what Jack did, but of Jack.

The traditional view, as presented by Professor Sullivan, says that the intention with which an act is done is relevant to determining whether the act is right. The example of Jack and Jill suggests that, on the contrary, the intention is not relevant to deciding whether the *act* is right or wrong, but instead it is relevant to assessing the character of the person who does the act, which is very different.

Now let us turn to an example that concerns more important matters of life and death. This example is adapted from one used by Sullivan himself (119). A massively necrotic bowel condition in a neonate is out of control. Dr. White realizes that further treatment offers little hope of reversing the dying process and will only increase the suffering; so, he does not submit the infant to further treatment—even though he knows that this decision will hasten death. However, Dr. White does not seek, choose, or plan that death, so it is not part of his intention that the baby dies.

Dr. Black is faced with a similar case. A massively necrotic bowel condition in a neonate is out of control. He realizes that further treatment offers little hope of saving the baby and will only increase its suffering. He decides that it is better for the baby to die a bit sooner than to go on suffering pointlessly; so, with the intention of letting the baby die, he ceases treatment.

According to the traditional position, Dr. White's action was acceptable, but Dr. Black acted wrongly. However, this assessment faces the same problem we encountered before. Dr. White and Dr. Black did *the very same thing:* their handling of the cases was identical. Both doctors ceased treatment, knowing that the baby would die sooner, and both did so because they regarded continued treatment as pointless, given the infants' prospects. So how could one's action be acceptable and the other's not? There was, of course, a subtle difference in their *attitudes* toward what they did. Dr. Black said to himself, "I want this baby to die now, rather than later, so that it won't suffer more; so I won't continue the treatment." A defender of the traditional view might choose to condemn Dr. Black for this, and say that his character is defective (although I would not say that); but the traditionalist should not say that Dr. Black's *action* was wrong on that account, at least not if he wants to go on saying that Dr. White's action was right. A pure heart cannot make a wrong act right; neither can an impure heart make a right act wrong. As in the case of Jack and Jill, the intention is relevant, not to determining the rightness of actions, but to assessing the character of the people who act.

There is a general lesson to be learned here. The rightness or wrongness of an act is determined by the reasons for or against it. Suppose you are trying to decide, in this example, whether treatment should be continued. What are the reasons for and against this course of action? On the one hand, if treatment is ceased the baby will die very soon. On the other hand, the baby will die eventually anyway, even if treatment is continued. It has no chance of growing up. Moreover, if its life is prolonged, its suffering will be prolonged as well, and the medical resources used will be unavailable to others who would have a better chance of a satisfactory cure. In light of all this, you may well decide against continued treatment. But notice that there is no mention here of anybody's intentions. The intention you would have, if you decided to cease treatment, is not one of the things you need to consider. It is not among the reasons either for or against the action. That is why it is irrelevant to determining whether the action is right.

In short, a person's intention is relevant to an assessment of his character. The fact that a person intended so-and-so by his action may be a reason for thinking him a good or a bad person. But the intention is not relevant to determining whether the act itself is morally right. The rightness of the act must be decided on the basis of the objective reasons for or against it. It is permissible to let the baby die, in Sullivan's example, because of the facts about the baby's condition and its prospects—not because of anything having to do with anyone's intentions. Thus the traditional view is mistaken on this point.

ORDINARY AND EXTRAORDINARY MEANS OF TREATMENT

The American Medical Association policy statement says that life-sustaining treatment may sometimes be stopped if the means of treatment are "extraordinary"; the implication is that "ordinary" means of treatment may not be withheld. The distinction between ordinary and extraordinary treatments is crucial to orthodox Catholic thought in this area, and Professor Sullivan reemphasizes its importance: he says that, while a physician may sometimes rightly refuse to use extraordinary means to prolong life, "the refusal to use ordinary means is an altogether different matter."(119)

However, upon reflection it is clear that it is sometimes permissible to omit even very ordinary sorts of treatments.

> Suppose that a diabetic patient long accustomed to self-administration of insulin falls victim to terminal cancer, or suppose that a terminal cancer patient suddenly develops diabetes. Is he in the first case obliged to continue, and in the second case obliged to begin, insulin treatment and die painfully of cancer, or in either or both cases may the patient choose rather to pass into diabetic coma and an earlier death? . . . What of the conscious patient suffering from painful incurable disease who suddenly gets pneumonia? Or an old man slowly deteriorating who from simply being inactive and recumbent gets pneumonia: Are we to use antibiotics in a likely successful attack upon this disease which from time immemorial has been called "the old man's friend"?[4]

These examples are provided by Paul Ramsey, a leading theological ethicist. Even so conservative a thinker as Ramsey is sympathetic with the idea that, in such cases, life-prolonging treatment is not mandatory: the insulin and the antibiotics need not be used. Yet surely insulin and antibiotics are "ordinary" treatments by today's medical standards. They are common, easily administered, and cheap. There is nothing exotic about them. So it appears that the distinction between ordinary and extraordinary means does not have the significance traditionally attributed to it.

But what of the *definitions* of "ordinary" and "extraordinary" means which Sullivan provides? Quoting Ramsey, he says that

> Ordinary means of preserving life are all medicines, treatments, and operations, which offer a reasonable hope of benefit for the patient and which can be obtained and used without excessive expense, pain, and other inconveniences.

> Extra-ordinary means of preserving life are all those medicines, treatments, and operations which cannot be obtained without excessive expense, pain, or other inconvenience, or which, if used, would not offer a reasonable hope of benefit.(118)

Do these definitions provide us with a useful distinction—one that can be used in determining when a treatment is mandatory and when it is not?

The first thing to notice is the way the word "excessive" functions in these definitions. It is said that a treatment is extraordinary if it cannot be obtained without *excessive* expense or pain. But when is an expense "excessive"? Is a cost of $10,000 excessive? If it would save the life of a young woman and restore her to perfect health, $10,000 does not seem excessive. But if it would only prolong the life of Ramsey's cancer-stricken diabetic a short while, perhaps $10,000 is excessive. The point is not merely that what is excessive changes from case to case. The point is that what is excessive *depends on* whether it would be a good thing for the life in question to be prolonged.

Second, we should notice the use of the word "benefit" in the definitions. It is said that ordinary treatments offer a reasonable hope of *benefit* for the patient; and that treatments are extraordinary if they will not benefit the patient. But how do we tell if a treatment will benefit the patient? Remember that we are talking about life-prolonging treatments; the "benefit," if any, is the continuation of life. Whether continued life is a benefit depends on the details of the particular case. For a person with a painful terminal illness, a temporarily continued life may not be a benefit. For a person in irreversible coma, such as Karen Quinlan, continued biological existence is almost certainly not a benefit. On the other hand, for a person who can be cured and resume a normal life, life-sustaining treatment definitely is a benefit. Again, the point is that in order to decide whether life-sustaining treatment is a benefit we must *first* decide whether it would be a good thing for the life in question to be prolonged.

Therefore, these definitions do not mark out a distinction that can be used to help us decide when treatment may be omitted. We cannot by using the definitions identify which treatments are extraordinary, and then use that information to determine whether the treatment may be omitted. For the definitions require that we must *already* have decided the moral questions of life and death *before* we can answer the question of which treatments are extraordinary!

We are brought, then, to this conclusion about the distinction between ordinary and extraordinary means. If we apply the distinction in a straightforward, common-sense way, the traditional doctrine is false, for it is clear that it is sometimes permissible to omit ordinary treatments. On the other hand, if we define the terms as suggested by Ramsey and Sullivan, the distinction is useless in practical decision-making. In either case, the distinction provides no help in formulating an acceptable ethic of letting die.

To summarize what has been said so far, the distinction between killing and letting die has no moral importance; on that Professor Sullivan and I agree. He, however, contends that the distinctions between intentional and nonintentional termination of life, and ordinary and extraordinary means, must be at the heart of a correct moral view. I believe that the arguments given above refute this view. Those distinctions are no better than the first one. The traditional view is mistaken.

In my original paper I did not argue in favor of active euthanasia. I merely argued that active and passive euthanasia are equivalent: *if* one is acceptable, so is the other. However, Professor Sullivan correctly inferred that I do endorse active euthanasia. I believe that it is morally justified in some instances and that at least two strong arguments support this position. The first is the argument from mercy; the second is the argument from the golden rule.

THE ARGUMENT FROM MERCY

Preliminary Statement of the Argument

The single most powerful argument in support of euthanasia is the argument from mercy. It is also an exceptionally simple argument, at least in its main idea, which makes one uncomplicated point. Terminal patients sometimes suffer pain so horrible that it is beyond the comprehension of those who have not actually experienced it. Their suffering can be so terrible that we do not like even to read about it or think about it; we recoil even from the descriptions of such agony. The argument from mercy says: Euthanasia is justified because it provides an end to *that.*

The great Irish satirist Jonathan Swift took eight years to die, while, in the words of Joseph Fletcher, "His mind crumbled to pieces."[5] At times the pain in his blinded eyes was so intense he had to be restrained from tearing them out with his own hands. Knives and other potential instruments of suicide had to be kept from him. For the last three years of his life, he could do nothing but sit and drool; and when he finally died it was only after convulsions that lasted thirty-six hours.

Swift died in 1745. Since then, doctors have learned how to eliminate much of the pain that accompanies terminal illness, but the victory has been far from complete. So, here is a more modern example.

Stewart Alsop was a respected journalist who died in 1975 of a rare form of cancer. Before he died, he wrote movingly of his experiences as a terminal patient. Although he had not thought much about euthanasia before, he came to approve of it after rooming briefly with someone he called Jack:

> The third night that I roomed with Jack in our tiny double room in the solid-tumor ward of the cancer clinic of the National Institutes of Health in Bethesda, Md., a terrible thought occurred to me.
>
> Jack had a melanoma in his belly, a malignant solid tumor that the doctors guessed was about the size of a softball. The cancer had started a few months before with a small tumor in his left shoulder, and there had been several operations since. The doctors planned to remove the softball-sized tumor, but they knew Jack would soon die. The cancer had metastasized—it had spread beyond control.
>
> Jack was good-looking, about 28, and brave. He was in constant pain, and his doctor had prescribed an intravenous shot of a synthetic opiate—a pain-killer, or analgesic—every four hours. His wife spent many of the daylight hours with him, and she would sit or lie on his bed and pat him all over, as one pats a child, only more methodically, and this seemed to help control the pain. But at night, when his pretty wife had left (wives cannot stay overnight at the NIH clinic) and darkness fell, the pain would attack without pity.
>
> At the prescribed hour, a nurse would give Jack a shot of the synthetic analgesic, and

this would control the pain for perhaps two hours or a bit more. Then he would begin to moan, or whimper, very low, as though he didn't want to wake me. Then he would begin to howl, like a dog.

When this happened, either he or I would ring for a nurse, and ask for a pain-killer. She would give him some codeine or the like by mouth, but it never did any real good—it affected him no more than half an aspirin might affect a man who had just broken his arm. Always the nurse would explain as encouragingly as she could that there was not long to go before the next intravenous shot—"Only about 50 minutes now." And always poor Jack's whimpers and howls would become more loud and frequent until at last the blessed relief came.

The third night of this routine, the terrible thought occurred to me: "If Jack were a dog," I thought, "what would be done with him?" The answer was obvious: the pound, and chloroform. No human being with a spark of pity could let a living thing suffer so, to no good end.[6]

The NIH clinic is, of course, one of the most modern and best-equipped hospitals we have. Jack's suffering was not the result of poor treatment in some backward rural facility; it was the inevitable product of his disease, which medical science was powerless to prevent.

I have quoted Alsop at length not for the sake of indulging in gory details but to give a clear idea of the kind of suffering we are talking about. We should not gloss over these facts with euphemistic language, or squeamishly avert our eyes from them. For only by keeping them firmly and vividly in mind can we appreciate the full force of the argument from mercy: If a person prefers—and even begs for—death as the only alternative to lingering on *in this kind of torment,* only to die anyway after a while, then surely it is not immoral to help this person die sooner. As Alsop put it, "No human being with a spark of pity could let a living thing suffer so, to no good end."

The Utilitarian Version of the Argument

In connection with this argument, the utilitarians should be mentioned. They argue that actions and social policies should be judged right or wrong *exclusively* according to whether they cause happiness or misery; and they argue that when judged by this standard, euthanasia turns out to be morally acceptable. The utilitarian argument may be elaborated as follows:

1 Any action or social policy is morally right if it serves to increase the amount of happiness in the world or to decrease the amount of misery. Conversely, an action or social policy is morally wrong if it serves to decrease happiness or to increase misery.

2 The policy of killing, at their own request, hopelessly ill patients who are suffering great pain, would decrease the amount of misery in the world. (An example could be Alsop's friend Jack.)

3 Therefore, such a policy would be morally right.

The first premise of this argument, (1), states the Principle of Utility, which is the basic utilitarian assumption. Today most philosophers think that this principle is wrong, because they think that the promotion of happiness and the avoidance of misery are not the *only* morally important things. Happiness, they say, is only one among many values that should be promoted: freedom, justice, and a respect for people's rights are also important. To take one example: People *might* be happier if there were no freedom of religion; for, if everyone adhered to the same religious beliefs, there would be greater harmony among people. There would be no unhappiness caused within families by Jewish girls marrying Catholic boys, and so forth. Moreover, if people were brainwashed well enough, no one would mind not having freedom of choice. Thus happiness would be increased. But, the argument continues, even if happiness *could* be increased this way, it would not be right to deny people freedom of religion, because people have a right to make their own choices. Therefore, the first premise of the utilitarian argument is unacceptable.

There is a related difficulty for utilitarianism, which connects more directly with the topic of euthanasia. Suppose a person is leading a miserable life—full of more unhappiness than happiness—but does *not* want to die. This person thinks that a miserable life is better than none at all. Now I assume that we would all agree that the person should not be killed; that would be plain, unjustifiable murder. Yet it *would* decrease the amount of misery in the world if we killed this person—it would lead to an increase in the balance of happiness over unhappiness—and so it is hard to see how, on strictly utilitarian grounds, it could be wrong. Again, the Principle of Utility seems to be an inadequate guide for determining right and wrong. So we are on shaky ground if we rely on *this* version of the argument from mercy for a defense of euthanasia.

Doing What Is in Everyone's Best Interests

Although the foregoing utilitarian argument is faulty, it is nevertheless based on a sound idea. For even if the promotion of happiness and avoidance of misery are not the *only* morally important things, they are still very important. So, when an action or a social policy would decrease misery, that is *a* very strong reason in its favor. In the cases of voluntary euthanasia we are now considering, great suffering is eliminated, and since the patient requests it, there is no question of violating individual rights. That is why, regardless of the difficulties of the Principle of Utility, the utilitarian version of the argument still retains considerable force.

I want now to present a somewhat different version of the argument from mercy, which is inspired by utilitarianism but which avoids the difficulties of the foregoing version by not making the Principle of Utility a premise of the argument. I believe that the following argument is sound and proves that active euthanasia *can* be justified:

1 If an action promotes the best interests of *everyone* concerned, and violates *no one's* rights, then that action is morally acceptable.

2 In at least some cases, active euthanasia promotes the best interests of everyone concerned and violates no one's rights.

3 Therefore, in at least some cases active euthanasia is morally acceptable.

It would have been in everyone's best interests if active euthanasia had been employed in the case of Stewart Alsop's friend, Jack. First, and most important, it would have been in Jack's own interests, since it would have provided him with an easier, better death, without pain. (Who among us would choose Jack's death, if we had a choice, rather than a quick painless death?) Second, it would have been in the best interests of Jack's wife. Her misery, helplessly watching him suffer, must have been almost equal to his. Third, the hospital staff's best interests would have been served, since if Jack's dying had not been prolonged, they could have turned their attention to other patients whom they could have helped. Fourth, other patients would have benefited since medical resources would no longer have been used in the sad, pointless maintenance of Jack's physical existence. Finally, if Jack himself requested to be killed, the act would not have violated his rights. Considering all this, how can active euthanasia in this case be wrong? How can it be wrong to do an action that is merciful, that benefits everyone concerned, and that violates no one's rights?

THE ARGUMENT FROM THE GOLDEN RULE

"Do unto others as you would have them do unto you" is one of the oldest and most familiar moral maxims. Stated in just that way, it is not a very good maxim: Suppose a sexual pervert started treating others as he would like to be treated himself; we might not be happy with the results. Nevertheless, the basic idea behind the golden rule is a good one. The basic idea is that moral rules apply impartially to everyone alike; therefore, you cannot say that you are justified in treating someone else in a certain way unless you are willing to admit that that person would also be justified in treating *you* in that way if your positions were reversed.

Kant and the Golden Rule

The great German philosopher Immanuel Kant (1724–1804) incorporated the basic idea of the Golden Rule into his system of ethics. Kant argued that we should act only on rules that we are willing to have applied universally; that is, we should behave as we would be willing to have *everyone* behave. He held that there is one supreme principle of morality, which he called "the Categorical Imperative." The Categorical Imperative says:

> Act only according to that maxim by which you can at the same time will that it should become a universal law.[7]

Let us discuss what this means. When we are trying to decide whether we ought to do a certain action, we must first ask what general rule or principle we would be following if we did it. Then, we ask whether we would be willing for everyone to follow that rule, in similar circumstances. (This determines whether "the maxim of the act"—the rule we would be following—can be "willed" to be "a universal law.") If we would not be willing for the rule to be followed universally, then we should not follow it ourselves. Thus, if we are not willing for others to apply the rule to *us,* we ought not apply it to *them.*

In the eighteenth chapter of St. Matthew's gospel there is a story that perfectly illustrates this point. A man is owed money by another, who cannot pay, and so he has the debtor thrown into prison. But he himself owes money to the king and begs that *his* debt be forgiven. At first the king forgives the debt. However, when the king hears how this man has treated the one who owed him, he changes his mind and "delivers him unto the tormentors" until he can pay. The moral is clear: If you do not think that others should apply the rule "Don't forgive debts!" to *you,* then you should not apply it to others.

The application of all this to the question of euthanasia is fairly obvious. Each of us is going to die someday, although most of us do not know when or how. But suppose you were told that you would die in one of two ways, and you were asked to choose between them. First, you could die quietly, and without pain, from a fatal injection. Or second, you could choose to die of an affliction so painful that for several days before death you would be reduced to howling like a dog, with your family standing by helplessly, trying to comfort you, but going through its own psychological hell. It is hard to believe that any sane person, when confronted by these possibilities, would choose to have a rule applied that would force upon him or her the second option. And if we would not want such a rule, which excludes euthanasia, applied to us, then we should not apply such a rule to others.

Implications for Christians

There is a considerable irony here. Kant [himself] was personally opposed to active euthanasia, yet his own Categorical Imperative seems to sanction it. The larger irony, however, is for those in the Christian Church who have for centuries opposed active euthanasia. According to the New Testament accounts, Jesus himself promulgated the Golden Rule as the supreme moral principle—"This is the Law and the Prophets," he said. But if this is the supreme principle of morality, then how can active euthanasia be always wrong? If I would have it done to me, how can it be wrong for me to do likewise to others?

R. M. Hare has made this point with great force. A Christian as well as a leading contemporary moral philosopher, Hare has long argued that "universalizability" is one of the central characteristics of moral judgment. ('Universalizability' is the name he gives to the basic idea embodied in both the Golden Rule and the Categorical Imperative. It means that a moral judgment must conform to universal principles, which apply to everyone alike, if it is to be acceptable.) In an article called "Euthanasia: A Christian View," Hare argues that Christians, if they took Christ's teachings about the Golden Rule seriously, would not think that euthanasia is always wrong. He gives this (true) example:

> The driver of a petrol lorry [i.e., a gas truck] was in an accident in which his tanker over-turned and immediately caught fire. He himself was trapped in the cab and could not be freed. He therefore besought the bystanders to kill him by hitting him on the head, so that

he would not roast to death. I think that somebody did this, but I do not know what happened in court afterwards.

Now will you please all ask yourselves, as I have many times asked myself, what you wish that men should do to you if you were in the situation of that driver. I cannot believe that anybody who considered the matter seriously, as if he himself were going to be in that situation and had now to give instructions as to what rule the bystanders should follow, would say that the rule should be one ruling out euthanasia absolutely.[8]

We might note that *active* euthanasia is the only option here; the concept of passive euthanasia, in these circumstances, has no application. . . .

Professor Sullivan finds my position pernicious. In his penultimate paragraph he says that the traditional doctrine "is simply a prohibition of murder," and that those of us who think otherwise are confused, teary-eyed sentimentalists. But the traditional doctrine is not that. It is a muddle of indefensible claims, backed by tradition but not by reason.

NOTES

1 "Active and Passive Euthanasia," *The New England Journal of Medicine,* vol. 292 (Jan. 9, 1975), pp. 78–80. [Reprinted, this volume, pp. 110–115.]

2 "Active and Passive Euthanasia: An Impertinent Distinction?" *The Human Life Review,* vol. III (1977), pp. 40–46. Parenthetical references in the text are to this article [as reprinted in this volume, pp. 115–120.]

3 It might be objected that they did not "do the same thing," for Jill manipulated and deceived her grandmother, while Jack did not. If their actions are described in this way, then it may seem that "what Jill did" was wrong, while "what Jack did" was not. However, this description of what Jill did incorporates her intention into the description of the act. In the present context we must keep the act and the intention separate, in order to discuss the relation between them. If they *cannot* be held separate, then the traditional view makes no sense.

4 *The Patient as Person* (New Haven: Yale University Press, 1970), pp. 115–116.

5 *Morals and Medicine* (Boston: Beacon Press, 1960), p. 174.

6 "The Right to Die with Dignity," *Good Housekeeping,* August 1974, pp. 69, 130.

7 *Foundations of the Metaphysics of Morals,* p. 422.

8 *Philosophic Exchange* (Brockport, New York), II:I (Summer 1975), p. 45.

QUESTIONS

1 Can the moral importance of the distinction between ordinary and extraordinary means be defended against Rachels's critique?

2 Rachels asks, "How can it be wrong to do an action that is merciful, that benefits everyone concerned, and that violates no one's rights?" If you think that it can be wrong to perform such an action, what arguments would you offer against Rachels's argument from mercy?

3 Some people offer the following argument against euthanasia: It is always possible that a patient has been misdiagnosed or that a cure may be found for an apparently terminal illness; therefore, we can *never* be certain that a patient's condition is hopeless. Is this conclusion true? If so, does it lead to the further conclusion that euthanasia is morally wrong?

Euthanasia

Marcia Angell

Marcia Angell, M.D., is executive editor of *The New England Journal of Medicine*. She has written editorials such as "Disease as a Reflection of the Psyche" and "Respecting the Autonomy of Competent Patients." Her other published articles include "Cost Containment and the Physician" and "Medicine: The Endangered Patient-Centered Ethic."

Angell identifies the conditions under which (active) euthanasia is permitted in the Netherlands and calls attention to two major differences between the Dutch guidelines and the provisions of a California legislative proposal, the "Humane and Dignified Death Act." After reviewing some of the standard arguments both for and against legalizing euthanasia, she argues that the risk of abuse would be much greater in the proposed California legislation than it is in the Dutch system.

Over the past decade the issue of whether it is ever permissible to withhold life-sustaining treatment has been debated by doctors and ethicists and in the courts and state legislatures. Gradually, a consensus has emerged that it is indeed permissible and even mandatory to withhold life-sustaining treatment under certain circumstances.[1-3] Now attention has begun to turn toward the issue of euthanasia. Euthanasia means purposely terminating the life of a patient to prevent further suffering, and it is illegal. Thus, it is different from withholding life-sustaining treatment. It is also different from administering a drug, such as morphine, that may hasten death but has another purpose. For many, the beginning of a debate about euthanasia is ominous—a step down a slippery slope leading to widespread disregard for the value of human life. For others, it signifies an opportunity to deal more humanely and rationally with prolonged meaningless suffering. My purpose here is to provide some background on this issue and to present arguments for and against euthanasia.

In the Netherlands, euthanasia officially remains a crime, punishable by up to 12 years in prison, but it is practiced fairly commonly and openly there, protected by a body of case law and by strong public support. Estimates are that 5000 to 8000 Dutch lives are ended by euthanasia each year.[4] The Dutch Medical Association in 1984 suggested guidelines for performing euthanasia,[5] and in 1985 a government-appointed Commission on Euthanasia issued a report[6] that in essence endorsed the guidelines and recommended a change in the criminal code to permit euthanasia. Although a change is unlikely during the tenure of the present government, it will almost certainly be an important issue in the next general election. The guidelines under which euthanasia is performed in the Netherlands are stringent. Four essential conditions must be met: (1) The patient must be competent. This requirement excludes many groups of patients for whom the question of withholding life-sustaining treatment has been most contentious in the United States—such as patients with ad-

Reprinted with permission from *The New England Journal of Medicine*, vol. 319 (November 17, 1988), pp. 1348–1350.

vanced Alzheimer's disease, retarded patients, handicapped newborns, and patients, such as Karen Quinlan, who are in a persistent vegetative state. (2) The patient must request euthanasia voluntarily, consistently, and repeatedly over a reasonable time, and the request must be well documented. This requirement prevents euthanasia in response to an ill-considered or impulsive request. (3) The patient must be suffering intolerably, with no prospect of relief, although there needn't be a terminal disease. Thus, depression, for which there is treatment, would not be a reason for euthanasia, but amyotrophic lateral sclerosis might be. (4) Euthanasia must be performed by a physician in consultation with another physician not involved in the case; the usual method is to induce sleep with a barbiturate, followed by a lethal injection of curare.

In California this year, an unsuccessful effort was made to collect enough signatures on a petition to place a proposed law on the fall ballot that would legalize euthanasia.[7] This initiative was sponsored by Americans Against Human Suffering, the political arm of the Hemlock Society, an organization devoted to promoting the idea of appropriate euthanasia. In two important ways the provisions of the proposed law in California differed from the Dutch guidelines. First, they were more stringent than the Dutch guidelines in that they required a candidate for euthanasia to be terminally ill, with a life expectancy of less than six months with or without medical treatment. Second, they were more lax than the Dutch guidelines in that they permitted euthanasia by advance directive. A competent adult, healthy or not, could assign a durable power of attorney to authorize euthanasia if he became terminally ill and incompetent within seven years. Thus, unlike the situation in the Netherlands, euthanasia would be possible for incompetent as well as competent patients, provided they had once been competent; only children and those born mentally retarded would be excluded. Note that both the Dutch guidelines and the California proposal would preclude performing euthanasia at the sole discretion of a physician, as purportedly occurred in the case of Debbie.[8]

Most observers believe that the California initiative failed because of organizational problems, not voter sentiment. Public opinion polls have shown fairly consistently that about three fifths of the American public favor legalizing euthanasia under certain conditions (compared with about three quarters of the Dutch public).[9] Americans Against Human Suffering intends to repeat its effort to place the issue on the ballot in California in 1990 and also to make similar efforts in Washington, Oregon, and Florida.

What are the arguments for and against legalizing euthanasia? And where do doctors fit in? Arguments against euthanasia are more familiar than those for it. First, we have strong legal, religious, and cultural taboos against taking human life, almost regardless of the circumstances (wars, self-defense, and legal executions being the notable exceptions). These reflect the supreme value we place on human life, as well as a concern that any compromise of this position might lead to a general erosion of our respect for life. Thus, many would acknowledge that there may be circumstances in which euthanasia would be appropriate for an individual patient but would oppose it because it would tend to devalue life. Related to this argument is the fear that the devaluation would be selective, that euthanasia might occur too often among the weak and powerless in our society—that is, among the very old, the poor, or the handicapped. Lessons learned from the Nazis fuel this fear.

There is also concern that euthanasia could be abused not only by society at large but by individuals. Inevitably, despite safeguards (even as stringent as those in the Netherlands), there must be some vagueness in any language permitting euthanasia. For example, how do we define intolerable suffering? Exactly what is a voluntary, repeated, and consistent request? This vagueness reflects the variations and subtleties of the circumstances as well as the inadequacies of language. However, it makes it easy to imagine the ne'er-do-well nephew persuading his rich old uncle to request euthanasia.

Finally, doctors have their own set of special concerns about euthanasia. Many of us believe that euthanasia is appropriate under certain conditions and that it should indeed be legalized, but that we should not perform it ourselves. According to this view, doctors should only extend life, never shorten it, and patients must be in no doubt about what our function is. A poll of doctors released June 2 by the University of Colorado at Denver Center for Health Ethics and Policy showed that three fifths of them favored legalizing euthanasia, but nearly half of those would not perform it themselves.

The principal argument in favor of euthanasia is that it is more humane than forcing a patient to continue a life of unmitigated suffering. According to this view, there is no moral difference under some circumstances between euthanasia and withholding life-sustaining treatment. In both situations, the purpose is a merciful death, and the only practical difference is that withholding life-sustaining treatment entails more suffering because it takes longer. Furthermore, it requires an element of happenstance, such as the development of pneumonia for which there is treatment that could be withheld. Proponents of euthanasia also argue that it furthers the principle of individual self-determination, and that this enhances rather than diminishes respect for human life. They believe that it is contradictory to permit patients to refuse life-sustaining treatment, while not honoring their request for euthanasia.

If euthanasia were permissible, the best way to minimize the possibility of abuse would be to limit its availability, as in the Netherlands, to competent patients who request it because of their current situation and not because of a hypothetical future one. This would mean denying euthanasia to incompetent patients, even with an advance directive, and would thus sharply limit its use. Nevertheless, such a limitation may be the price of preventing abuse. Furthermore, it could be argued that the suffering of incompetent patients, certainly those in a persistent vegetative state, is experienced more by their families than by themselves.

If euthanasia were legalized, doctors morally opposed to it should not, of course, be required to perform it. On the other hand, doctors who believe in the desirability of euthanasia under certain conditions, but who would refuse to perform it, raise a different issue. Can they appropriately excuse themselves from a difficult part of what they consider good patient care? Would they favor the creation of a profession especially dedicated to performing euthanasia (a problematic and, I think, unsavory prospect)?

Whatever their view of the morality and appropriateness of legalizing euthanasia and of performing it, doctors should be prepared for its emergence as an important issue in the years ahead and should be ready to debate it. Perhaps, also, those who favor legalizing euthanasia but would not perform it should rethink their position. Our ability to extend life through new technologies will certainly grow, and with it will grow the dilemmas created by the extension of intractable suffering.

REFERENCES

1 President's Commission for the Study of Ethical Problems in Medicine and Biomedical and Behavioral Research. Deciding to forego life-sustaining treatment: a report on the ethical, medical, and legal issues in treatment decisions. Washington, D.C.: Government Printing Office, 1983.
2 Annas GJ, Glantz LH. The right of elderly patients to refuse life-sustaining treatment. Milbank Q 1986; 64:Suppl 2:95–162.
3 Current Opinions of the Council on Ethical and Judicial Affairs of the AMA—1986. Withholding or withdrawing life-prolonging treatment. Chicago: American Medical Association, 1986.
4 Pence GE. Do not go slowly into that dark night: mercy killing in Holland. Am J Med 1988; 84:139–41.
5 Central Committee of the Royal Dutch Medical Association. Vision on euthanasia. Med Contact 1984; 39:990–8.
6 Final report of the Netherlands State Commission on Euthanasia: an English summary. Bioethics 1987; 1:163–74.
7 The Humane and Dignified Death Act. California Civil Code, Title 10.5.
8 It's over, Debbie. JAMA 1988; 259:272.
9 Roper Organization of New York City. The 1988 Roper poll on attitudes toward active voluntary euthanasia. Los Angeles: National Hemlock Society, 1988.

QUESTIONS

1 Would you endorse a proposal to legalize (active) euthanasia in your state based on the model provided by the Dutch guidelines?
2 Would you endorse a proposal to legalize (active) euthanasia in your state based on the model provided by the California "Humane and Dignified Death" Act?

Objections to the Institutionalisation of Euthanasia

Stephen G. Potts

Stephen G. Potts, an English physician, is presently resident in psychiatry, Maudsley Hospital, London. His contributions to the literature of bioethics include "Persuading Pagans" and "Headaches in Britain over Brain Death Criteria."

Potts argues against any scheme that would institutionalize—that is, legalize—(voluntary, active) euthanasia. He identifies and briefly discusses a wide range of risks posed by legalization, and he insists that the burden of proof falls on the proponents of legalization. Potts endorses the "right to die" but insists that this right does not entail the right to receive assistance in suicide or the right to be killed.

[I am opposed] to any attempt to institutionalise euthanasia . . . because the risks of such institutionalisation are so grave as to outweigh the very real suffering of those who might benefit from it.

RISKS OF INSTITUTIONALISATION

Among the potential effects of a legalised practice of euthanasia are the following:

1   Reduced Pressure to Improve Curative or Symptomatic Treatment   If euthanasia had been legal forty years ago, it is quite possible that there would be no hospice movement today. The improvement in terminal care is a direct result of attempts made to minimise suffering. If that suffering had been extinguished by extinguishing the patients who bore it, then we may never have known the advances in the control of pain, nausea, breathlessness and other terminal symptoms that the last twenty years have seen.

Some diseases that were terminal a few decades ago are now routinely cured by newly developed treatments. Earlier acceptance of euthanasia might well have undercut the urgency of the research efforts which led to the discovery of those treatments. If we accept euthanasia now, we may well delay by decades the discovery of effective treatments for those diseases that are now terminal.

2   Abandonment of Hope   Every doctor can tell stories of patients expected to die within days who surprise everyone with their extraordinary recoveries. Every doctor has experienced the wonderful embarrassment of being proven wrong in their pessimistic prognosis. To make euthanasia a legitimate option as soon as the prog-

Reprinted with permission of the publisher from Stephen G. Potts, "Looking for the Exit Door: Killing and Caring in Modern Medicine," *Houston Law Review,* vol. 25 (1988), pp. 504–509, 510–511.

nosis is pessimistic enough is to reduce the probability of such extraordinary recoveries from low to zero.

3   Increased Fear of Hospitals and Doctors   Despite all the efforts at health education, it seems there will always be a transference of the patient's fear of illness from the illness to the doctors and hospitals who treat it. This fear is still very real and leads to large numbers of late presentations of illnesses that might have been cured if only the patients had sought help earlier. To institutionalise euthanasia, however carefully, would undoubtedly magnify all the latent fear of doctors and hospitals harbored by the public. The inevitable result would be a rise in late presentations and, therefore, preventable deaths.

4   Difficulties of Oversight and Regulation   Both the Dutch and the Californian proposals list sets of precautions designed to prevent abuses. They acknowledge that such abuses are a possibility. I am far from convinced that the precautions are sufficient to prevent either those abuses that have been foreseen or those that may arise after passage of the law. The history of legal "loopholes" is not a cheering one: Abuses might arise when the patient is wealthy and an inheritance is at stake, when the doctor has made mistakes in diagnosis and treatment and hopes to avoid detection, when insurance coverage for treatment costs is about to expire, and in a host of other circumstances.

5   Pressure on the Patient   Both sets of proposals seek to limit the influence of the patient's family on the decision, again acknowledging the risks posed by such influence. Families have all kinds of subtle ways, conscious and unconscious, of putting pressure on a patient to request euthanasia and relieve them of the financial and social burden of care. Many patients already feel guilty for imposing burdens on those who care for them, even when the families are happy to bear that burden. To provide an avenue for the discharge of that guilt in a request for euthanasia is to risk putting to death a great many patients who do not wish to die.

6   Conflict with Aims of Medicine   The pro-euthanasia movement cheerfully hands the dirty work of the actual killing to the doctors who, by and large, neither seek nor welcome the responsibility. There is little examination of the psychological stresses imposed on those whose training and professional outlook are geared to the saving of lives by asking them to start taking lives on a regular basis. Euthanasia advocates seem very confident that doctors can be relied on to make the enormous efforts sometimes necessary to save some lives, while at the same time assenting to requests to take other lives. Such confidence reflects, perhaps, a high opinion of doctors' psychic robustness, but it is a confidence seriously undermined by the shocking rates of depression, suicide, alcoholism, drug addiction, and marital discord consistently recorded among this group.

7   Dangers of Societal Acceptance   It must never be forgotten that doctors, nurses, and hospital administrators have personal lives, homes, and families, or that they are something more than just doctors, nurses or hospital administrators. They are *citizens* and a significant part of the society around them. I am very worried about what the institutionalisation of euthanasia will do to society, in general, and, particularly how much it will further erode our attachment to the sixth commandment. ["Thou shalt not kill."] How will we regard murderers? What will we say to the terrorist who justifies killing as a means to his political end when we ourselves justify killing as a means to a humanitarian end? I do not know and I daresay the euthanasia advocates do not either, but I worry about it and they appear not to. They need to justify their complacency.

8   The Slippery Slope   How long after acceptance of voluntary euthanasia will we hear the calls for nonvoluntary euthanasia? There are thousands of comatose or demented patients sustained by little more than good nursing care. They are an enormous financial and social burden. How soon will the advocates of euthanasia be arguing that we should "assist them in dying"—for, after all, they won't mind, will they?

How soon after *that* will we hear the calls for involuntary euthanasia, the disposal of the burdensome, the unproductive, the polluters of the gene pool? We must never forget the way the Nazi euthanasia programme made this progression in a few short years. "Oh, but they were barbarians," you say, and so they were, but not at the outset.

If developments in terminal care can be represented by a progression from the CURE mode of medical care to the CARE mode, enacting voluntary euthanasia legislation would permit a further progression to the KILL mode. The slippery slope argument represents the fear that, if this step is taken, then it will be difficult to avoid a further progression to the CULL mode, as illustrated:

CURE   The central aim of medicine
CARE   The central aim of terminal care once patients are beyond cure
KILL   The aim of the proponents of euthanasia for those patients beyond cure and not helped by care
CULL   The feared result of weakening the prohibition on euthanasia

I do not know how easy these moves will be to resist once voluntary euthanasia is accepted, but I have seen little evidence that the modern euthanasia advocates care about resisting them or even worry that they might be possible.

9   Costs and Benefits   Perhaps the most disturbing risk of all is posed by the growing concern over medical costs. Euthanasia is, after all, a very cheap service. The cost of a dose of barbiturates and curare and the few hours in a hospital bed that it takes them to act is minute compared to the massive bills incurred by many patients in the last weeks and months of their lives. Already in Britain, there is a serious under-provision of expensive therapies like renal dialysis and intensive care, with the result that many otherwise preventable deaths occur. Legalising euthanasia would save substantial financial resources which could be diverted to more "useful" treatments. These economic concerns already exert pressure to accept euthanasia, and, if accepted, they will inevitably tend to enlarge the category of patients for whom euthanasia is permitted.

Each of these objections could, and should, be expanded and pressed harder. I do not propose to do so now, for it is sufficient for my purposes to list them as *risks,* not inevitabilities. Several elements go into our judgment of the severity of a risk: the *probability* that the harm in question will arise (the odds), the *severity* of the harm in question (the stakes), and the ease with which the harm in question can be corrected (the *reversibility*). The institutionalisation of euthanasia is such a radical departure from anything that has gone before in Western society that we simply cannot judge the probability of any or all of the listed consequences. Nor can we rule any of them out. There must, however, be agreement that the severity of each of the harms listed is enough to give serious cause for concern, and the severity of all the harms together is enough to horrify. Furthermore, many of the potential harms seem likely to prove very difficult, if not impossible, to reverse by reinstituting a ban on euthanasia.

WEIGHING THE RISKS

For all these reasons, the burden of proof *must* lie with those who would have us gamble by legalising euthanasia. They should demonstrate beyond reasonable doubt that the dangers listed will not arise, just as chemical companies proposing to introduce a new drug are required to demonstrate that it is safe as well as beneficial. Thus far, the proponents of euthanasia have relied exclusively on the compassion they arouse with tales of torment mercifully cut short by death, and have made little or no attempt to shoulder the burden of proving that legalising euthanasia is safe. Until they make such an attempt and carry it off successfully, their proposed legislation must be rejected outright.

THE RIGHT TO DIE AND THE DUTY TO KILL

The nature of my arguments should have made it clear by now that I object, not so much to individual acts of euthanasia, but to institutionalising it as a practice. All the pro-euthanasia arguments turn on the individual case of the patient in pain, suffering at the center of an intolerable existence. They exert powerful calls on our compassion, and appeal to our pity, therefore, we assent too readily when it is claimed that such patients have a *"right to die"* as an escape from torment. So long as the right to die means no more than the right to refuse life-prolonging treatment and the right to rational suicide, I agree. The advocates of euthanasia want to go much further than this though. They want to extend the right to die to encompass the right to receive assistance in suicide and, beyond that, the right to be killed. Here, the focus shifts from the patient to the agent, and from the killed to the killer; but, the argument begins to break down because our compassion does not extend this far.

If it is true that there is a right to be assisted in suicide or a right to be killed, then it follows that someone, somewhere, has a *duty* to provide the assistance or to do the killing. When we look at the proposed legislation, it is very clear upon whom the advocates of euthanasia would place this duty: the doctor. It would be the doctor's job to provide the pills and the doctor's job to give the lethal injection. The regulation of euthanasia is meant to prevent anyone, other than the doctor, from doing it. Such regulation would ensure that the doctor does it with the proper precautions and consultations, and would give the doctor security from legal sanctions for doing it. The emotive appeal of euthanasia is undeniably powerful, but it lasts only so long as we can avoid thinking about who has to do the killing, and where, and when, and how. Proposals to institutionalise euthanasia force us to think hard about these things, and the chill that their contemplation generates is deep enough to freeze any proponent's ardor. . . .

[One final objection to the institutionalisation of euthanasia] relates to another set out above (#5. Pressure on the patient). The objection turns on the concern that many requests for euthanasia will not be truly voluntary because of pressure on the patient or the patient's fear of becoming a burden. There is a significant risk that legalising voluntary euthanasia out of respect for the *right* to die will generate many requests for euthanasia out of a perceived *duty* to die. . . .

QUESTIONS

1 Does Potts provide a compelling case against the legalization of voluntary active euthanasia?

2 Should voluntary active euthanasia be legalized? If so, in what form or forms and with what safeguards?

Majority Opinion in *Cruzan v. Director, Missouri Department of Health*

Justice William H. Rehnquist

A biographical sketch of Justice William H. Rehnquist is found on p. 45.

This case developed when the parents of Nancy Beth Cruzan—a woman existing in a persistent vegetative state subsequent to an automobile accident suffered at the age of twenty-five—sought authorization from a Missouri trial court to terminate their daughter's artificial nutrition and hydration. The trial court authorized termination of treatment, but the Supreme Court of Missouri reversed the decision of the trial court. The United States Supreme Court upheld the judgment of the Missouri Supreme Court.

Writing the majority opinion in a five-to-four decision, Justice Rehnquist acknowledges that a *competent* person has a constitutionally protected right to refuse lifesaving nutrition and hydration. However, in the case of an *incompetent* person, he argues, it is not unconstitutional for Missouri to insist that nutrition and

United States Supreme Court. 110 S.Ct. 2841 (1990).

hydration can be terminated only if there is "clear and convincing evidence" that termination of treatment is what the person would have wanted. Since this standard of proof has presumably not been satisfied in the case of Nancy Beth Cruzan, he concludes, the judgment of the Missouri Supreme Court is affirmed. (In subsequent developments, a Missouri court considered new evidence presented by Cruzan's parents and concluded that there was "clear and convincing evidence" that she would have chosen to terminate treatment. Nutrition and hydration were subsequently withheld and Nancy Cruzan died in December of 1990.)

Petitioner Nancy Beth Cruzan was rendered incompetent as a result of severe injuries sustained during an automobile accident. Co-petitioners Lester and Joyce Cruzan, Nancy's parents and co-guardians, sought a court order directing the withdrawal of their daughter's artificial feeding and hydration equipment after it became apparent that she had virtually no chance of recovering her cognitive faculties. The Supreme Court of Missouri held that because there was no clear and convincing evidence of Nancy's desire to have life-sustaining treatment withdrawn under such circumstances, her parents lacked authority to effectuate such a request. We . . . now affirm.

On the night of January 11, 1983, Nancy Cruzan lost control of her car as she traveled down Elm Road in Jasper County, Missouri. The vehicle overturned, and Cruzan was discovered lying face down in a ditch without detectable respiratory or cardiac function. Paramedics were able to restore her breathing and heartbeat at the accident site, and she was transported to a hospital in an unconscious state. An attending neurosurgeon diagnosed her as having sustained probable cerebral contusions compounded by significant anoxia (lack of oxygen). The Missouri trial court in this case found that permanent brain damage generally results after 6 minutes in an anoxic state; it was estimated that Cruzan was deprived of oxygen from 12 to 14 minutes. She remained in a coma for approximately three weeks and then progressed to an unconscious state in which she was able to orally ingest some nutrition. In order to ease feeding and further the recovery, surgeons implanted a gastrostomy feeding and hydration tube in Cruzan with the consent of her then husband. Subsequent rehabilitative efforts proved unavailing. She now lies in a Missouri state hospital in what is commonly referred to as a persistent vegetative state: generally, a condition in which a person exhibits motor reflexes but evinces no indications of significant cognitive function.[1] The State of Missouri is bearing the cost of her care.

After it had become apparent that Nancy Cruzan had virtually no chance of regaining her mental faculties her parents asked hospital employees to terminate the artificial nutrition and hydration procedures. All agree that such a removal would cause her death. The employees refused to honor the request without court approval. The parents then sought and received authorization from the state trial court for termination. The court found that a person in Nancy's condition had a fundamental right under the State and Federal Constitutions to refuse or direct the withdrawal of "death prolonging procedures." The court also found that Nancy's "expressed thoughts at age twenty-five in somewhat serious conversation with a housemate friend that if sick or injured she would not wish to continue her life unless she could live at least halfway normally suggests that given her present condition she would not wish to continue on with her nutrition and hydration."

The Supreme Court of Missouri reversed by a divided vote. The court recognized a right to refuse treatment embodied in the common-law doctrine of informed consent, but expressed skepticism about the application of that doctrine in the circumstances of this case. The court also declined to read a broad right of privacy into the State Constitution which would "support the right of a person to refuse medical treatment in every circumstance," and expressed doubt as to whether such a right existed under the United States Constitution. It then decided that the Missouri Living Will statute (1986) embodied a state policy strongly favoring the preservation of life. The court found that Cruzan's statements to her roommate regarding her desire to live or die under certain conditions were "unreliable for the purpose of determining her intent," "and thus insufficient to support the co-guardians claim to exercise substituted judgment on Nancy's behalf." It rejected the argument that Cruzan's parents were entitled to order the termination of her medical treatment, concluding that "no person can assume that choice for an incompetent in the absence of the formalities required under Missouri's Living Will statutes or the clear and convincing, inherently reliable evidence absent here." . . .

We granted certiorari to consider the question of whether Cruzan has a right under the United States Constitution which would require the hospital to withdraw life-sustaining treatment from her under these circumstances.

At common law, even the touching of one person by another without consent and without legal justification was a battery. Before the turn of the century, this Court observed that "[n]o right is held more sacred, or is more carefully guarded, by the common law, than the right of every individual to the possession and control of his own person, free from all restraint or interference of others, unless by clear and unquestionable authority of law." This notion of bodily integrity has been embodied in the requirement that informed consent is generally required for medical treatment. Justice Cardozo, while on the Court of Appeals of New York, aptly described this doctrine: "Every human being of adult years and sound mind has a right to determine what shall be done with his own body; and a surgeon who performs an operation without his patient's consent commits an assault, for which he is liable in damages." The informed consent doctrine has become firmly entrenched in American tort law.

The logical corollary of the doctrine of informed consent is that the patient generally possesses the right not to consent, that is, to refuse treatment. Until about 15 years ago and the seminal decision [of the New Jersey Supreme Court] in *In re Quinlan* (1976), the number of right-to-refuse-treatment decisions were relatively few. Most of the earlier cases involved patients who refused medical treatment forbidden by their religious beliefs, thus implicating First Amendment rights as well as common law rights of self-determination. More recently, however, with the advance of medical technology capable of sustaining life well past the point where natural forces would have brought certain death in earlier times, cases involving the right to refuse life-sustaining treatment have burgeoned.

In the *Quinlan* case, young Karen Quinlan suffered severe brain damage as the result of anoxia, and entered a persistent vegetative state. Karen's father sought judicial approval to disconnect his daughter's respirator. The New Jersey Supreme Court granted the relief, holding that Karen had a right of privacy grounded in the Federal Constitution to terminate treatment. Recognizing that this right was not absolute, however, the court balanced it against asserted state interests. Noting that the State's interest "weakens and the individual's right to privacy grows as the degree of bodily invasion increases and the prognosis dims," the court concluded that the state interests had to give way in that case. The court also concluded that the "only practical way" to prevent the loss of Karen's privacy right due to her incompetence was to allow her guardian and family to decide "whether she would exercise it in these circumstances."

After *Quinlan,* however, most courts have based a right to refuse treatment either solely on the common law right to informed consent or on both the common law right and a constitutional privacy right. . . .

. . . State courts have available to them for decision a number of sources—state constitutions, statutes, and common law—which are not available to us. In this Court, the question is simply and starkly whether the United States Constitution prohibits Missouri from choosing the rule of decision which it did. This is the first case in which we have been squarely presented with the issue of whether the United States Constitution grants what is in common parlance referred to as a "right to die." We follow the judicious counsel . . . that in deciding "a question of such magnitude and importance . . . it is the [better] part of wisdom not to attempt, by any general statement, to cover every possible phase of the subject."

The Fourteenth Amendment provides that no State shall "deprive any person of life, liberty, or property, without due process of law." The principle that a competent person has a constitutionally protected liberty interest in refusing unwanted medical treatment may be inferred from our prior decisions. In *Jacobson* v. *Massachusetts* (1905), for instance, the Court balanced an individual's liberty interest in declining an unwanted smallpox vaccine against the State's interest in preventing disease. . . .

Just this Term, in the course of holding that a State's procedures for administering antipsychotic medication to prisoners were sufficient to satisfy due process concerns, we recognized that prisoners possess "a significant liberty interest in avoiding the unwanted administration of antipsychotic drugs under the Due Process Clause of the Fourteenth Amendment." Still other cases support the recognition of a general liberty interest in refusing medical treatment.

But determining that a person has a "liberty interest" under the Due Process Clause does not end the inquiry;[2] "whether respondent's constitutional rights have been violated must be determined by balancing his liberty interests against the relevant state interests."

Petitioners insist that under the general holdings of our cases, the forced administration of life-sustaining medical treatment, and even of artificially-delivered food and water essential to life, would implicate a competent person's liberty interest. Although we think the logic of the cases [referred to] above would embrace such a liberty interest, the dramatic consequences involved in refusal of such treatment would inform the inquiry as to whether the deprivation of that interest is constitutionally permissible. But for purposes of this case, we assume that the United States Constitution would grant a competent person a constitutionally protected right to refuse lifesaving hydration and nutrition.

Petitioners go on to assert that an incompetent person should possess the same right in this respect as is possessed by a competent person. . . .

The difficulty with petitioners' claim is that in a sense it begs the question: an incompetent person is not able to make an informed and voluntary choice to exercise a hypothetical right to refuse treatment or any other right. Such a "right" must be exercised for her, if at all, by some sort of surrogate. Here, Missouri has in effect recognized that under certain circumstances a surrogate may act for the patient in electing to have hydration and nutrition withdrawn in such a way as to cause death, but it has established a procedural safeguard to assure that the action of the surrogate conforms as best it may to the wishes expressed by the patient while competent. Missouri requires that evidence of the incompetent's wishes as to the withdrawal of treatment be proved by clear and convincing evidence. The question, then, is whether the United States Constitution forbids the establishment of this procedural requirement by the State. We hold that it does not.

Whether or not Missouri's clear and convincing evidence requirement comports with the United States Constitution depends in part on what interests the State may properly seek to protect in this situation. Missouri relies on its interest in the protection and preservation of human life, and there can be no gainsaying this interest. As a general matter, the States—indeed, all civilized nations—demonstrate their commitment to life by treating homicide as serious crime. Moreover, the majority of States in this country have laws imposing criminal penalties on one who assists another to commit suicide. We do not think a State is required to remain neutral in the face of an informed and voluntary decision by a physically-able adult to starve to death.

But in the context presented here, a State has more particular interests at stake. The choice between life and death is a deeply personal decision of obvious and overwhelming finality. We believe Missouri may legitimately seek to safeguard the personal element of this choice through the imposition of heightened evidentiary requirements. It cannot be disputed that the Due Process Clause protects an interest in life as well as an interest in refusing life-sustaining medical treatment. Not all incompetent patients will have loved ones available to serve as surrogate decisionmakers. And even where family members are present, "[t]here will, of course, be some unfortunate situations in which family members will not act to protect a patient." A State is entitled to guard against potential abuses in such situations. Similarly, a State is entitled to consider that a judicial proceeding to make a determination regarding an incompetent's wishes may very well not be an adversarial one, with the added guarantee of accurate factfinding that the adversary process brings with it. Finally, we think a State may properly decline to make judgments about the "quality" of life that a particular individual may enjoy, and simply assert an unqualified interest in the preservation of human life to be weighed against the constitutionally protected interests of the individual.

In our view, Missouri has permissibly sought to advance these interests through the adoption of a "clear and convincing" standard of proof to govern such proceedings. "The function of a standard of proof, as that concept is embodied in the Due Process Clause and in the realm of factfinding, is to 'instruct the factfinder concerning the degree of confidence our society thinks he should have in the correctness of factual conclusions for a particular type of adjudication.' ". . .

We think it self-evident that the interests at stake in the instant proceedings are more substantial, both on an individual and societal level, than those involved in a run-of-the-mine civil dispute. But not only does the standard of proof reflect the importance of a particular adjudication, it also serves as "a societal judgment about how the risk of error should be distributed between the litigants." The more stringent the burden of proof a party must bear, the more that party bears the risk of an erroneous decision. We believe that Missouri may permissibly place an increased risk of an erroneous decision on those seeking to terminate an incompetent individual's life-sustaining treatment. An erroneous decision not to terminate results in a maintenance of the status quo; the possibility of subsequent developments such as advancements in medical science, the discovery of new evidence regarding the patient's intent, changes in the law, or simply the unexpected death of the patient despite the administration of life-sustaining treatment, at least create the potential that a wrong decision will eventually be corrected or its impact mitigated. An erroneous decision to withdraw life-sustaining treatment, however, is not susceptible of correction. . . .

In sum, we conclude that a State may apply a clear and convincing evidence standard in proceedings where a guardian seeks to discontinue nutrition and hydration of a person diagnosed to be in a persistent vegetative state. . . .

The Supreme Court of Missouri held that in this case the testimony adduced at trial did not amount to clear and convincing proof of the patient's desire to have hydration and nutrition withdrawn. In so doing, it reversed a decision of the Missouri trial court which had found that the evidence "suggest[ed]" Nancy Cruzan would not have desired to continue such measures, but which had not adopted the standard of "clear and convincing evidence" enunciated by the Supreme Court. The testimony adduced at trial consisted primarily of Nancy Cruzan's statements made to a housemate about a year before her accident that she would not want to live should she face life as a "vegetable," and other observations to the same effect. The observations did not deal in terms with withdrawal of medical treatment or of hydration and nutrition. We cannot say that the Supreme Court of Missouri committed constitutional error in reaching the conclusion that it did.[3]

Petitioners alternatively contend that Missouri must accept the "substituted judgment" of close family members even in the absence of substantial proof that their views reflect the views of the patient. . . .

No doubt is engendered by anything in this record but that Nancy Cruzan's mother and father are loving and caring parents. If the State were required by the United States Constitution to repose a right of "substituted judgment" with anyone, the Cruzans would surely qualify. But we do not think the Due Process Clause requires the State to repose judgment on these matters with anyone but the patient herself. Close family members may have a strong feeling—a feeling not at all ignoble or unworthy, but not entirely disinterested, either—that they do not wish to witness the continuation of the life of a loved one which they regard as hopeless, meaningless, and even degrading. But there is no automatic assurance that the view of close family members will necessarily be the same as the patient's would have been had she been confronted with the prospect of her situation while competent. All of the reasons previously discussed for allowing Missouri to require clear and convincing evidence of the patient's wishes lead us to conclude that the State may choose to defer only to those wishes, rather than confide the decision to close family members.

The judgment of the Supreme Court of Missouri is *Affirmed.*

NOTES

1 The State Supreme Court, adopting much of the trial court's findings, described Nancy Cruzan's medical condition as follows: ". . . In sum, Nancy is diagnosed as in a persistent vegetative state. She is not dead. She is not terminally ill. Medical experts testified that she could live another thirty years." . . .

2 Although many state courts have held that a right to refuse treatment is encompassed by a generalized constitutional right of privacy, we have never so held. We believe this issue is more properly analyzed in terms of a Fourteenth Amendment liberty interest. See *Bowers* v. *Hardwick* (1986).

3 The clear and convincing standard of proof has been variously defined in this context as "proof sufficient to persuade the trier of fact that the patient held a firm and settled commitment to the termination of life supports under the circumstances like those presented," and as evidence which "produces in the mind of the trier of fact a firm belief or conviction as to the truth of the allegations sought to be established, evidence so clear, direct and weighty and convincing as to enable [the factfinder] to come to a clear conviction, without hesitancy, of the truth of the precise facts in issue." . . .

QUESTIONS

1 If you were in a persistent vegetative state like Nancy Cruzan was, would you want artificial nutrition and hydration to be terminated?

2 If you were a citizen of Missouri, would you endorse a legislative proposal to recognize and honor the substituted judgment of close family members even in cases where there was no "clear and convincing evidence" that a now incompetent patient would have chosen to refuse life-sustaining treatment?

SUGGESTED ADDITIONAL READINGS FOR CHAPTER 3

BEAUCHAMP, TOM L.: "A Reply to Rachels on Active and Passive Euthanasia." In Tom L. Beauchamp and Seymour Perlin, eds., *Ethical Issues in Death and Dying.* Englewood Cliffs, N.J.: Prentice-Hall, 1978, pp. 246–258. Beauchamp suggests that rule-utilitarian considerations can provide a basis for defending the moral significance of the distinction between active and passive euthanasia.

"*Cruzan:* Clear and Convincing?" *Hastings Center Report,* vol. 20, September/October 1990, pp. 5–11. This set of six short articles provides critical reflections on the ruling of the United States Supreme Court in the *Cruzan* case.

DOWNING, A.B., ed.: *Euthanasia and the Right to Death: The Case for Voluntary Euthanasia.* New York: Humanities Press; London: Peter Owen, 1969. Two articles are especially notable in this collection of material on euthanasia. In "The Principle of Euthanasia," Antony Flew constructs "a general moral case for the establishment of a legal right" to voluntary (active) euthanasia. In a very well known article, "Euthanasia Legislation: Some Non-Religious Objections," Yale Kamisar argues against the legalization of voluntary (active) euthanasia.

KOHL, MARVIN, ed.: *Beneficent Euthanasia.* Buffalo, N.Y.: Prometheus, 1975. This anthology includes a number of helpful articles on the moral aspects of euthanasia. Also included are articles that provide statements of various religious positions on euthanasia. Other articles address the medical and legal aspects of euthanasia.

LYNN, JOANNE, ed.: *By No Extraordinary Means: The Choice to Forgo Life-Sustaining Food and Water.* Bloomington: Indiana University Press, 1986. This anthology provides a wide range of material on the issue of forgoing artificial nutrition and hydration.

MAY, WILLIAM E., et al.: "Feeding and Hydrating the Permanently Unconscious and Other Vulnerable Persons." *Issues in Law and Medicine,* vol. 3, Winter 1987, pp. 203–217. A group of ten authors argues that it is morally wrong to withhold or withdraw artificial nutrition and hydration from the permanently unconscious or from those who are seriously debilitated but nondying.

"Mercy, Murder, and Morality: Perspectives on Euthanasia." *Hastings Center Report,* vol. 19, January/February 1989, special supplement, pp. 1–32. This supplement contains nine articles on various aspects of (active) euthanasia. Especially noteworthy is an article by Daniel Callahan, "Can We Return Death to Disease?" Callahan argues against the morality of active euthanasia and defends the coherence and importance of the distinction between killing and allowing to die.

PRESIDENT'S COMMISSION FOR THE STUDY OF ETHICAL PROBLEMS IN MEDICINE AND BIOMEDICAL AND BEHAVIORAL RESEARCH. *Deciding to Forgo Life-Sustaining Treatment.* 1983. This valuable document provides a broad-based discussion of decision making regarding life-sustaining treatment.

STEINBOCK, BONNIE, ed.: *Killing and Letting Die.* Englewood Cliffs, N.J.: Prentice-Hall, 1980. This anthology provides a wealth of material on the killing–letting die distinction.

TRAMMELL, RICHARD L.: "Euthanasia and the Law." *Journal of Social Philosophy,* vol. 9, January 1978, pp. 14–18. Trammell contends that the legalization of voluntary positive (i.e., active) euthanasia would probably not "result in overall positive utility for the class of people eligible to choose." He emphasizes the unwelcome pressures that would be created by legalization.

WEIR, ROBERT F. *Selective Nontreatment of Handicapped Newborns: Moral Dilemmas in Neonatal Medicine.* New York: Oxford University Press, 1984. Weir surveys and critically analyzes a wide range of views (advanced by various pediatricians, attorneys, and ethicists) on the subject of selective nontreatment. He then presents and defends an overall policy for the guidance of decision making in this area.

CHAPTER 4

The Death Penalty

Strong convictions are firmly entrenched on both sides of the death penalty controversy. From one side, we hear in forceful tones that "murderers deserve to die." We are also told that no lesser punishment than the death penalty will suffice to deter potential murderers. From the other side of the controversy, in tones of equal conviction, we are told that the death penalty is a cruel and barbarous practice, effectively serving no purpose that could not be equally well served by a more humane punishment. "How long," it is asked, "must we indulge this uncivilized and pointless lust for revenge?" In the face of such strongly held but opposed views, each of us is invited to confront an important ethical issue, the morality of the death penalty. Before approaching the death penalty in its ethical dimensions, however, it may prove helpful to briefly discuss its constitutional dimensions. Many of the considerations raised in discussions of the constitutionality of the death penalty parallel those raised in discussions of its morality.

THE CONSTITUTIONALITY OF THE DEATH PENALTY

The Eighth Amendment to the Constitution of the United States explicitly prohibits the infliction of "cruel and unusual" punishment. If the death penalty is a cruel and unusual punishment, it is unconstitutional. But is it cruel and unusual? In a landmark case, *Furman v. Georgia* (1972), the Supreme Court ruled that the death penalty was unconstitutional *as then administered*. The Court did not comprehensively rule, however, that the death penalty was unconstitutional *by its very nature*. Indeed, subsequent developments in the Court have made clear that the death penalty is not unconstitutional—as long as it is administered in accordance with certain procedural requirements.

The decision reached in *Furman* was by a mere five-to-four majority. There was a basic divergence of viewpoint among those who voted with the majority. Both Justice Marshall and Justice Brennan argued straightforwardly that the death penalty is a cruel and unusual punishment *by its very nature*. From this perspective it would not matter how much the procedures of its administration might be modified. It would still remain a cruel and unusual punishment. Among the reasons advanced to support this contention, two are especially noteworthy. (1) The death penalty is excessive in the sense of being unnecessary; lesser penalties are capable of serving the desired legislative purpose. (2) The death penalty is abhorrent to currently existing moral values.

The other three justices (Douglas, White, and Stewart) who voted with the majority did not commit themselves to the position that the death penalty is unconstitutional *by its very nature.* Leaving this underlying issue unresolved, they simply advanced the more guarded contention that the death penalty was unconstitutional *as then administered.* In their view, the death penalty was unconstitutional primarily because it was being administered in an arbitrary and capricious manner. The essence of their argument can be reconstructed in the following way. The death penalty is, as a common matter of course, inflicted at the discretion of a jury (or sometimes a judge). The absence of explicit standards to govern the decision between life and death allows a wide range of unchecked prejudice to operate freely under the heading of "discretion." For example, "discretion" seems to render blacks more prone than whites to the death penalty. Such standardless discretion violates not only the Eighth Amendment but also the Fourteenth Amendment, which guarantees "due process of law."

As matters developed in the wake of *Furman,* it was the Court's objection to *standardless discretion* that provided an opening for the many individual states still anxious to retain the death penalty as a viable component of their legal systems. These states were faced with the challenge of devising procedures for inflicting the death penalty which would not be open to the charge of standardless discretion. Two such approaches gained prominence. (1) Some states (e.g., North Carolina) moved to dissolve the objection of standardless discretion by simply making the death penalty *mandatory* for certain crimes. (2) Other states (e.g., Georgia) took an equally obvious approach. It consisted in the effort to establish standards that would provide guidance for the jury (or the judge) in deciding between life and death.

Subsequent developments have made clear that the second approach is constitutionally acceptable whereas the first is not. In *Woodson v. North Carolina* (1976), the Court ruled (though by a mere five-to-four majority) that mandatory death sentences are unconstitutional. In *Gregg v. Georgia* (1976), however, the Court ruled (with only Justice Marshall and Justice Brennan dissenting) that the death penalty is not unconstitutional when imposed at the discretion of a jury for the *crime of murder,*[1] so long as appropriate safeguards are provided against any arbitrary or capricious imposition. Most important, there must be explicit standards established for the guidance of jury deliberations. The attitude of the Court in this regard is made clear by Justices Stewart, Powell, and Stevens in their opinion in *Gregg v. Georgia* (1976), which appears in this chapter. Also appearing in this chapter is the dissenting opinion of Justice Marshall.

---

[1] In *Gregg,* the Supreme Court considered only the constitutionality of imposing the death penalty for the *crime of murder.* In *Coker v. Georgia* (1977), 433 U.S. 584, the Court subsequently considered the constitutionality of imposing the death penalty for the *crime of rape.* Holding death to be a "grossly disproportionate" punishment for the crime of rape, the Court declared such an employment of the death penalty unconstitutional.

THE ETHICAL ISSUE

In any discussion of the morality of the death penalty, it is important to remember that the death penalty is a kind of punishment. Indeed, it is normally thought to be the most serious kind of punishment, hence the term "*capital* punishment." Most philosophers agree that punishment in general (as contrasted with capital punishment in particular) is a morally justified social practice. For one thing, however uneasy we might feel about inflicting harm on another person, it is hard to visualize a complex society managing to survive without an established legal system of punishment. However, to say that most philosophers agree that punishment in general is a morally justified social practice is not to say that there are no dissenters from this view. Some argue that it is possible to structure society in ways that would not necessitate commitment to a legal system of punishment as we know it. For example, might it not be that undesirable social behavior could be adequately kept in check by thera-peutic treatment rather than by traditional kinds of punishment? Such a system would certainly have the advantage of being more humane, but surely it is implausi-ble to believe that present therapeutic techniques are anywhere near adequate to the task. Perhaps future advances in the behavioral sciences will render such an alterna-tive more plausible. If so, it may one day be plausible to argue that the whole prac-tice of (nontherapeutic) punishment must be rejected on moral grounds. Still, for now, there is widespread agreement on the moral defensibility of punishment as an overall social practice. What stands out as an open and hotly debated ethical issue is whether or not the death penalty, as a distinctive kind of punishment, ought to con-tinue to play a role in our legal system of punishment.

Those in favor of retaining the death penalty are commonly called "retentionists." Retentionists differ among themselves regarding the kinds of cases in which they find it appropriate to employ the death penalty. They also differ among themselves regarding the supporting arguments they find acceptable. But anyone who supports the retention of the death penalty—for employment in whatever kinds of cases and for whatever reason—is by definition a retentionist. Those in favor of abolishing the death penalty are commonly called "abolitionists." Abolitionists, by definition, refuse to support any employment of the death penalty. Like the retentionists, how-ever, they differ among themselves concerning the supporting arguments they find acceptable.

There is one extreme, and not widely embraced, abolitionist line of thought. It is based on the belief that the sanctity of human life demands absolute nonviolence. On this view, killing of any kind, for any reason, is always and everywhere morally wrong. No one has the right to take a human life, not in self-defense, not in war, not in any circumstance. Thus, since the death penalty obviously involves a kind of kill-ing, it is a morally unacceptable form of punishment and must be abolished. This general view, which is associated with the Quakers and other pacifists, has struck most moral philosophers as implausible. Can we really think that killing, when it is the only course that will save oneself from an unprovoked violent assault, is morally wrong? Can we really think that it would be morally wrong to kill a terrorist if that were the *only* possible way of stopping him or her from exploding a bomb in the midst of a kindergarten class? The defender of absolute nonviolence is sometimes inclined to argue at this point that violence will only breed violence. There may indeed be much truth in this claim. Still, most people do not believe that such a claim provides adequate support for the contention that *all* killing is morally wrong, and if *some* killing is morally acceptable, perhaps the death penalty itself is morally acceptable. What arguments can be made on its behalf?

RETENTIONIST ARGUMENTS

Broadly speaking, arguments for the retention of the death penalty usually emphasize either (1) considerations of *justice* or (2) considerations of *social utility.* Those who emphasize considerations of justice typically develop their case along the following line: When the moral order is upset by the commission of some offense, it is only right that the disorder be rectified by punishment equal in intensity to the seriousness of the offense. This view is reflected in remarks such as "The scales of justice demand retribution" and "The offender must pay for the crime." Along this line, the philosopher Immanuel Kant (1724–1804) is famous for his unequivocal defense of the *lex talionis*—the law (principle) of retaliation, or as it is often expressed, "an eye for an eye." According to this principle, punishment is to be inflicted in a measure that will equalize the offense. And when the offense is murder, *only* capital punishment is sufficient to equalize it.

In one of this chapter's readings, Igor Primoratz argues for retention of the death penalty on retributive grounds. Stephen Nathanson, an abolitionist, provides a contrasting point of view. Nathanson argues that no adequate retributive rationale can be provided for the death penalty.

Although the demand for retribution continues to play a prominent role in the overall case for the death penalty, many retentionists (and obviously abolitionists as well) have come to feel quite uneasy with the notion of imposing the death penalty "because the wrongdoer *deserves* it." Perhaps this uneasiness can be traced, at least in part, to our growing awareness of the way in which social conditions, such as ghetto living, seem to spawn criminal activity. If so, then it seems that we have arrived at a point of intersection with a venerable—and vexing—philosophical problem, the problem of "freedom and determinism." Pure retributive thinking seems to presuppose a radical sense of human freedom and its correlate, a radical sense of personal responsibility and accountability for one's actions. This is undoubtedly why retentionists who espouse a retributive rationale often insist that the death penalty does not constitute a denial of the wrongdoer's dignity and worth as a human being. On the contrary, they say, the death penalty reaffirms the dignity and worth of a convicted murderer—by holding the person strictly responsible for the crime that has been committed and giving the person what she or he deserves. Of course, if someone is uneasy with the radical sense of human freedom that seems to underlie pure retributive thinking, he or she will surely be uneasy with the retributive rationale for retention of the death penalty. So let us turn our attention to the utilitarian side of the retentionist coin.

Since considerations of social utility are commonly advanced in defense of the practice of punishment in general, it is not surprising to find that they are also commonly advanced in defense of retaining the death penalty. Utilitarianism, as a distinct school of moral philosophy, locates the primary justification of punishment in its social utility. Utilitarians acknowledge that punishment consists in the infliction of evil on another person, but they hold that such evil is far outweighed by the future benefits that will accrue to society. Imprisonment, for example, might lead to such socially desirable effects as (1) *rehabilitation* of the criminal, (2) *incapacitation,* whereby we achieve temporary or permanent protection from the imprisoned criminal, and (3) *deterrence* of other potential criminals. When utilitarian considerations are recruited in support of the retention of the *death* penalty, it is clear that rehabilitation of the criminal can play no part in the case. But retentionists do frequently promote considerations of incapacitation and deterrence.

Accordingly, some retentionists appeal to considerations of incapacitation and argue that the death penalty is the only effective way to protect society from a certain subset of convicted murderers—namely, those who are at once *violence-prone and irreformable.* (Notice that an important difficulty here would be finding effective criteria for the recognition of those already convicted murderers who are truly violence-prone and irreformable.) Life imprisonment, it is said, cannot assure society of the needed protection, because even if "life imprisonment" were really life imprisonment, that is, even if a sentence of life imprisonment excluded the possibility of parole, violence-prone and irreformable inmates would still pose an imminent threat to prison guards and fellow inmates. Furthermore, escape is always possible. Thus, the death penalty is the only truly effective way of achieving societal protection.

Many retentionists think, however, that the strongest case for the death penalty can be made not on grounds of protecting society from already convicted murderers but rather on grounds of deterring would-be murderers. Because of the intense fear that most people have of death, it is argued, the death penalty functions as a uniquely effective deterrent. Although the threat of life imprisonment or even long-term imprisonment would surely be sufficient to deter many would-be murderers, the threat of execution would deter an even greater number. Thus the death penalty ought to be retained in our system of criminal justice because it is a more substantial deterrent than is life imprisonment.

With the appearance of this argument, the debate between retentionists and abolitionists becomes focused on a central factual issue. Is the death penalty indeed a more substantial deterrent than life imprisonment? Facts and figures often seem to dominate this particular aspect of the debate, and it is by no means easy to discern the true state of affairs. One retentionist argument, advanced by Ernest van den Haag in this chapter, takes as its starting point our very uncertainty. If we are unsure whether or not the death penalty is a uniquely effective deterrent, he argues, we are morally obliged to risk needlessly eradicating the lives of convicted murderers rather than risking the lives of innocent people who might become future murder victims. Jeffrey H. Reiman provides a counter to this particular retentionist argument and more generally provides an abolitionist perspective on the deterrence issue.

ABOLITIONIST ARGUMENTS

What can be said of the abolitionist case against the death penalty? Most abolitionists do not care to argue the extreme position, already discussed, of absolute nonviolence, yet they typically do want to commit themselves seriously to the "sanctity of human life." They emphasize the inherent worth and dignity of each individual and insist that the taking of a human life, while perhaps sometimes morally permissible, is a very serious matter and not to be permitted in the absence of weighty overriding reasons. At face value, they argue, the death penalty is cruel and inhumane; and since retentionists have failed to advance substantial reasons in its defense, it must be judged a morally unacceptable practice. Against retentionist arguments based on retribution as a demand of justice, abolitionists frequently argue that the "demand of justice" is nothing but a mask for a barbarous vengeance. Against retentionist arguments based on considerations of social utility, they simply argue that other more humane punishments will serve equally well. We do not need the death penalty to incapacitate convicted murderers because life imprisonment can provide us with a sufficient measure of societal protection. Also, since there is no reason to believe that the death penalty is a more effective deterrent than long-term imprisonment, retention cannot be justifed on the basis of considerations of deterrence.

In addition to advancing arguments that directly counter retentionist claims, abolitionists typically incorporate two further arguments into their overall case against the death penalty. The first of these arguments can be stated as follows: It is impossible to guarantee that mistakes will not be made in the administration of punishment, but this factor is especially important in the case of the death penalty, because only *capital* punishment is irrevocable. Thus only the death penalty eradicates the possibility of compensating an innocent person who has been wrongly punished. A second abolitionist argument focuses attention on patterns of discrimination in the administration of the death penalty. In our society, it is said, blacks are more likely to receive the death penalty than whites, and the poor and uneducated are more likely to receive the death penalty than the affluent and educated. A retentionist counter to each of these abolitionist arguments is provided by Primoratz.

Thomas A. Mappes

Opinion in *Gregg v. Georgia*

Justices
Potter Stewart,
Lewis F. Powell, Jr.,
and John Paul Stevens

Potter Stewart (1915–1985) and Lewis F. Powell, Jr., served as associate justices of the United States Supreme Court. John Paul Stevens continues to serve as associate justice of the Court. Justice Stewart, a graduate of Yale University Law School, spent some years in private practice, served as judge of the United States Court of Appeals, Sixth Circuit (1954–1958), and served on the Supreme Court from 1958 to 1981. Justice Powell, LL.B (Washington and Lee), LL.M (Harvard), practiced law in Richmond, Virginia, for nearly forty years prior to his appointment in 1971 to the Supreme Court. He retired from the Court in 1987. Justice Stevens, a graduate of Northwestern University School of Law, spent a number of years in private practice, served as judge of the United States Court of Appeals, Seventh Circuit (1970–1975), and was appointed to the Supreme Court in 1975.

The State of Georgia reacted to the Court's decision in *Furman v. Georgia* (1972) by drafting a death penalty statute calculated to avoid the Court's objection to standardless discretion. Georgia's approach, in contrast to the approach of those states that made the death penalty mandatory for certain crimes, embodied an effort to specify standards that would guide a jury (or a judge) in deciding between the death penalty and life imprisonment. In this case, with only Justice Marshall and Justice Brennan dissenting, the Court upheld the constitutionality of imposing the death penalty for the crime of murder under the law of Georgia.

Justices Stewart, Powell, and Stevens initially consider the contention that the death penalty for the crime of murder is, under all circumstances, cruel and unusual punishment, thus unconstitutional. On their analysis, a punishment is cruel and unusual if it fails to accord with "evolving standards of decency." Moreover, even if a punishment does accord with contemporary values, it must still be judged cruel and unusual if it fails to accord with the "dignity of man," the "basic concept underlying the Eighth Amendment." They take this second stipulation to rule out "excessive" punishment, identified as (1) that which involves the unnecessary and wanton infliction of pain or (2) that which is grossly out of proportion to the severity of the crime. In light of these considerations, Justices Stewart, Powell, and Stevens argue that the imposition of the death penalty for the crime of murder does not invariably violate the Constitution. They contend that legislative developments since *Furman* have made clear that the death penalty is acceptable to contemporary society. Moreover, they contend, the death penalty is not invariably excessive: (1) It may properly be considered necessary to achieve two principal social purposes—retribution and deterrence. (2) When the death penalty is imposed for the crime of murder, it may properly be considered not disproportionate to the severity of the crime.

Turning their attention to the death sentence imposed under the law of Georgia in this case, Justices Stewart, Powell, and Stevens maintain that a carefully drafted statute, ensuring "that the sentencing authority is given adequate information and

United States Supreme Court. 428 U.S. 153 (1976).

guidance," makes it possible to avoid imposing the death penalty in an arbitrary or capricious manner. The revised Georgia statutory system under which Gregg was sentenced to death, they conclude, does not violate the Constitution.

The issue in this case is whether the imposition of the sentence of death for the crime of murder under the law of Georgia violates the Eighth and Fourteenth Amendments.

I

The petitioner, Troy Gregg, was charged with committing armed robbery and murder. In accordance with Georgia procedure in capital cases, the trial was in two stages, a guilt stage and a sentencing stage. . . .

. . . The jury found the petitioner guilty of two counts of armed robbery and two counts of murder.

At the penalty stage, which took place before the same jury, . . . the trial judge instructed the jury that it could recommend either a death sentence or a life prison sentence on each count. . . . The jury returned verdicts of death on each count.

The Supreme Court of Georgia affirmed the convictions and the imposition of the death sentences for murder. . . . The death sentences imposed for armed robbery, however, were vacated on the grounds that the death penalty had rarely been imposed in Georgia for that offense. . . .

II

. . . The Georgia statute, as amended after our decision in *Furman v. Georgia* (1972), retains the death penalty for six categories of crime: murder, kidnaping for ransom or where the victim is harmed, armed robbery, rape, treason, and aircraft hijacking. . . .

III

We address initially the basic contention that the punishment of death for the crime of murder is, under all circumstances, "cruel and unusual" in violation of the Eighth and Fourteenth Amendments of the Constitution. In Part IV of this opinion, we will consider the sentence of death imposed under the Georgia statutes at issue in this case.

The Court on a number of occasions has both assumed and asserted the constitutionality of capital punishment. In several cases that assumption provided a necessary foundation for the decision, as the Court was asked to decide whether a particular method of carrying out a capital sentence would be allowed to stand under the Eighth Amendment. But until *Furman v. Georgia* (1972), the Court never confronted squarely the fundamental claim that the punishment of death always, regardless of the enormity of the offense or the procedure followed in imposing the sentence, is cruel and unusual punishment in violation of the Constitution. Although this issue was presented and addressed in *Furman,* it was not resolved by the Court. Four Justices would have held that capital punishment is not unconstitutional *per se;* two justices would have reached the opposite conclusion; and three Justices, while agreeing that the statutes then before the Court were invalid as applied, left open the question whether such punishment may ever be imposed. We now hold that the punishment of death does not invariably violate the Constitution.

A

The history of the prohibition of "cruel and unusual" punishment already has been reviewed at length. The phrase first appeared in the English Bill of Rights of 1689, which was drafted by Parliament at the accession of William and Mary. The English version appears to have been directed against punishments unauthorized by statute and beyond the jurisdiction of the sentencing court, as well as those disproportionate to the offense involved. The American draftsmen, who adopted the English phrasing in drafting the Eighth Amendment, were primarily concerned, however, with proscribing "tortures" and other "barbarous" methods of punishment.

In the earliest cases raising Eighth Amendment claims, the Court focused on particular methods of execution to determine whether they were too cruel to pass constitutional muster. The constitutionality of the sentence of death itself was not at issue, and the criterion used to evaluate the mode of execution was its similarity to "torture" and other "barbarous" methods. . . .

But the Court has not confined the prohibition embodied in the Eighth Amendment to "barbarous" methods that were generally outlawed in the 18th century. Instead, the Amendment has been interpreted in a flexible and dynamic manner. The Court early recognized that a "principle to be vital must be capable of wider application than the mischief which gave it birth." Thus the Clause forbidding "cruel and unusual" punishments "is not fastened to the obsolete but may acquire meaning as public opinion becomes enlightened by a humane justice." . . .

It is clear from the foregoing precedents that the Eighth Amendment has not been regarded as a static concept. As Mr. Chief Justice Warren said, in an oftquoted phrase, "[t]he Amendment must draw its meaning from the evolving standards of decency that mark the progress of a maturing society." Thus, an assessment of contemporary values concerning the infliction of a challenged sanction is relevant to the application of the Eighth Amendment. As we develop below more fully, this assessment does not call for a subjective judgment. It requires, rather, that we look to objective indicia that reflect the public attitude toward a given sanction.

But our cases also make clear that public perceptions of standards of decency with respect to criminal sanctions are not conclusive. A penalty also must accord with "the dignity of man," which is the "basic concept underlying the Eighth Amendment." This means, at least, that the punishment not be "excessive." When a form of punishment in the abstract (in this case, whether capital punishment may ever be imposed as a sanction for murder) rather than in the particular (the propriety of death as a penalty to be applied to a specific defendant for a specific crime) is under consideration, the inquiry into "excessiveness" has two aspects. First, the punishment must not involve the unnecessary and wanton infliction of pain. Second, the punishment must not be grossly out of proportion to the severity of the crime.

B

Of course, the requirements of the Eighth Amendment must be applied with an awareness of the limited role to be played by the courts. This does not mean that judges have no role to play, for the Eighth Amendment is a restraint upon the exercise of legislative power. . . .

But, while we have an obligation to insure that constitutional bounds are not overreached, we may not act as judges as we might as legislators. . . .

Therefore, in assessing a punishment selected by a democratically elected legislature against the constitutional measure, we presume its validity. We may not require the legislature to select the least severe penalty possible so long as the penalty selected is not cruelly inhumane or disproportionate to the crime involved. And a heavy burden rests on those who would attack the judgment of the representatives of the people.

This is true in part because the constitutional test is intertwined with an assessment of contemporary standards and the legislative judgment weighs heavily in ascertaining such standards. "[I]n a democratic society legislatures, not courts, are constituted to respond to the will and consequently the moral values of the people."

The deference we owe to the decisions of the state legislatures under our federal system is enhanced where the specification of punishments is concerned, for "these are peculiarly questions of legislative policy." Caution is necessary lest this Court become, "under the aegis of the Cruel and Unusual Punishment Clause, the ultimate arbiter of the standards of criminal responsibility . . . throughout the country." A decision that a given punishment is impermissible under the Eighth Amendment cannot be reversed short of a constitutional amendment. The ability of the people to express their preference through the normal democratic processes, as well as through ballot referenda, is shut off. Revisions cannot be made in the light of further experience.

C

In the discussion to this point we have sought to identify the principles and considerations that guide a court in addressing an Eighth Amendment claim. We now consider specifically whether the sentence of death for the crime of murder is a *per se* violation of the Eighth and Fourteenth Amendments to the Constitution. We note first that history and precedent strongly support a negative answer to this question.

The imposition of the death penalty for the crime of murder has a long history of acceptance both in the United States and in England. . . .

It is apparent from the text of the Constitution itself that the existence of capital punishment was accepted by the Framers. At the time the Eighth Amendment was ratified, capital punishment was a common sanction in every State. Indeed, the First

Congress of the United States enacted legislation providing death as the penalty for specified crimes. . . .

For nearly two centuries, this Court, repeatedly and often expressly, has recognized that capital punishment is not invalid *per se.* . . .

Four years ago, the petitioners in *Furman* and its companion cases predicated their argument primarily upon the asserted proposition that standards of decency had evolved to the point where capital punishment no longer could be tolerated. The petitioners in those cases said, in effect, that the evolutionary process had come to an end, and that standards of decency required that the Eighth Amendment be construed finally as prohibiting capital punishment for any crime regardless of its depravity and impact on society. This view was accepted by two Justices. Three other Justices were unwilling to go so far; focusing on the procedures by which convicted defendants were selected for the death penalty rather than on the actual punishment inflicted, they joined in the conclusion that the statutes before the Court were constitutionally invalid.

The petitioners in the capital cases before the Court today renew the "standards of decency" argument, but developments during the four years since *Furman* have undercut substantially the assumptions upon which their argument rested. Despite the continuing debate, dating back to the 19th century, over the morality and utility of capital punishment, it is now evident that a large proportion of American society continues to regard it as an appropriate and necessary criminal sanction.

The most marked indication of society's endorsement of the death penalty for murder is the legislative response to *Furman.* The legislatures of at least 35 States have enacted new statutes that provide for the death penalty for at least some crimes that result in the death of another person. And the Congress of the United States, in 1974, enacted a statute providing the death penalty for aircraft piracy that results in death. These recently adopted statutes have attempted to address the concerns expressed by the Court in *Furman* primarily (i) by specifying the factors to be weighed and the procedures to be followed in deciding when to impose a capital sentence, or (ii) by making the death penalty mandatory for specified crimes. But all of the post-*Furman* statutes make clear that capital punishment itself has not been rejected by the elected representatives of the people. . . .

The jury also is a significant and reliable objective index of contemporary values because it is so directly involved. The Court has said that "one of the most important functions any jury can perform in making . . . a selection [between life imprisonment and death for a defendant convicted in a capital case] is to maintain a link between contemporary community values and the penal system." It may be true that evolving standards have influenced juries in recent decades to be more discriminating in imposing the sentence of death. But the relative infrequency of jury verdicts imposing the death sentence does not indicate rejection of capital punishment *per se.* Rather, the reluctance of juries in many cases to impose the sentence may well reflect the humane feeling that this most irrevocable of sanctions should be reserved for a small number of extreme cases. Indeed, the actions of juries in many States since *Furman* are fully compatible with the legislative judgments, reflected in the new statutes, as to the continued utility and necessity of capital punishment in appropriate cases. At the close of 1974 at least 254 persons had been sentenced to death since *Furman,* and by the end of March 1976, more than 460 persons were subject to death sentences.

As we have seen, however, the Eighth Amendment demands more than that a challenged punishment be acceptable to contemporary society. The Court also must ask whether it comports with the basic concept of human dignity at the core of the Amendment. Although we cannot "invalidate a category of penalties because we deem less severe penalties adequate to serve the ends of penology," the sanction imposed cannot be so totally without penological justification that it results in the gratuitous infliction of suffering.

The death penalty is said to serve two principal social purposes: retribution and deterrence of capital crimes by prospective offenders.[1]

In part, capital punishment is an expression of society's moral outrage at particularly offensive conduct. This function may be unappealing to many, but it is essential in an ordered society that asks its citizens to rely on legal processes rather than self-help to vindicate their wrongs.

> The instinct of retribution is part of the nature of man, and channeling that instinct in the administration of criminal justice serves an important purpose in promoting the stability of a society governed by law. When people begin to believe that organized society is unwilling or unable to impose upon criminal offenders the punishment they "deserve," then there are sown the seeds of anarchy—of self-help, vigilante justice, and lynch law. *Furman v. Georgia* (Stewart, J., concurring).

"Retribution is no longer the dominant objective of the criminal law," but neither is it a forbidden objective nor one inconsistent with our respect for the dignity of men. Indeed, the decision that capital punishment may be the appropriate sanction in extreme cases is an expression of the community's belief that certain crimes are themselves so grievous an affront to humanity that the only adequate response may be the penalty of death.

Statistical attempts to evaluate the worth of the death penalty as a deterrent to crimes by potential offenders have occasioned a great deal of debate. The results simply have been inconclusive. . . .

Although some of the studies suggest that the death penalty may not function as a significantly greater deterrent than lesser penalties, there is no convincing empirical evidence either supporting or refuting this view. We may nevertheless assume safely that there are murderers, such as those who act in passion, for whom the threat of death has little or no deterrent effect. But for many others, the death penalty undoubtedly is a significant deterrent. There are carefully contemplated murders, such as murder for hire, where the possible penalty of death may well enter into the cold calculus that precedes the decision to act. And there are some categories of murder, such as murder by a life prisoner, where other sanctions may not be adequate.

The value of capital punishment as a deterrent of crime is a complex factual issue the resolution of which properly rests with the legislatures, which can evaluate the results of statistical studies in terms of their own local conditions and with a flexibility of approach that is not available to the courts. Indeed, many of the post-*Fur-*

man statutes reflect just such a responsible effort to define those crimes and those criminals for which capital punishment is most probably an effective deterrent.

In sum, we cannot say that the judgment of the Georgia Legislature that capital punishment may be necessary in some cases is clearly wrong. Considerations of federalism, as well as respect for the ability of a legislature to evaluate, in terms of its particular State, the moral consensus concerning the death penalty and its social utility as a sanction, require us to conclude, in the absence of more convincing evidence, that the infliction of death as a punishment for murder is not without justification and thus is not unconstitutionally severe.

Finally, we must consider whether the punishment of death is disproportionate in relation to the crime for which it is imposed. There is no question that death as a punishment is unique in its severity and irrevocability. When a defendant's life is at stake, the Court has been particularly sensitive to insure that every safeguard is observed. But we are concerned here only with the imposition of capital punishment for the crime of murder, and when a life has been taken deliberately by the offender,[2] we cannot say that the punishment is invariably disproportionate to the crime. It is an extreme sanction, suitable to the most extreme of crimes.

We hold that the death penalty is not a form of punishment that may never be imposed, regardless of the circumstances of the offense, regardless of the character of the offender, and regardless of the procedure followed in reaching the decision to impose it.

IV

We now consider whether Georgia may impose the death penalty on the petitioner in this case.

A

While *Furman* did not hold that the infliction of the death penalty *per se* violates the Constitution's ban on cruel and unusual punishments, it did recognize that the penalty of death is different in kind from any other punishment imposed under our system of criminal justice. Because of the uniqueness of the death penalty, *Furman* held that it could not be imposed under sentencing procedures that created a substantial risk that it would be inflicted in an arbitrary and capricious manner. . . .

Furman mandates that where discretion is afforded a sentencing body on a matter so grave as the determination of whether a human life should be taken or spared, that discretion must be suitably directed and limited so as to minimize the risk of wholly arbitrary and capricious action.

It is certainly not a novel proposition that discretion in the area of sentencing be exercised in an informed manner. We have long recognized that "[f]or the determination of sentences, justice generally requires . . . that there be taken into account the circumstances of the offense together with the character and propensities of the offender.". . .

Jury sentencing has been considered desirable in capital cases in order "to maintain a link between contemporary community values and the penal system—a link without which the determination of punishment could hardly reflect 'the evolving standards of decency that mark the progress of a maturing society.' " But it creates special problems. Much of the information that is relevant to the sentencing decision may have no relevance to the question of guilt, or may even be extremely prejudicial to a fair determination of that question. This problem, however, is scarcely insurmountable. Those who have studied the question suggest that a bifurcated procedure—one in which the question of sentence is not considered until the determination of guilt has been made—is the best answer. . . . When a human life is at stake and when the jury must have information prejudicial to the question of guilt but relevant to the question of penalty in order to impose a rational sentence, a bifurcated system is more likely to ensure elimination of the constitutional deficiencies identified in *Furman.*

But the provision of relevant information under fair procedural rules is not alone sufficient to guarantee that the information will be properly used in the imposition of punishment, especially if sentencing is performed by a jury. Since the members of a jury will have had little, if any, previous experience in sentencing, they are unlikely to be skilled in dealing with the information they are given. To the extent that this problem is inherent in jury sentencing, it may not be totally correctible. It seems clear, however, that the problem will be alleviated if the jury is given guidance regarding the factors about the crime and the defendant that the State, representing organized society, deems particularly relevant to the sentencing decision. . . .

While some have suggested that standards to guide a capital jury's sentencing deliberations are impossible to formulate, the fact is that such standards have been developed. When the drafters of the Model Penal Code faced this problem, they concluded "that it is within the realm of possibility to point to the main circumstances of aggravation and of mitigation that should be weighed *and weighed against each other* when they are presented in a concrete case.[3] While such standards are by necessity somewhat general, they do provide guidance to the sentencing authority and thereby reduce the likelihood that it will impose a sentence that fairly can be called capricious or arbitrary. Where the sentencing authority is required to specify the factors it relied upon in reaching its decision, the further safeguard of meaningful appellate review is available to ensure that death sentences are not imposed capriciously or in a freakish manner.

In summary, the concerns expressed in *Furman* that the penalty of death not be imposed in an arbitrary or capricious manner can be met by a carefully drafted statute that ensures that the sentencing authority is given adequate information and guidance. As a general proposition these concerns are best met by a system that provides for a bifurcated proceeding at which the sentencing authority is apprised of the information relevant to the imposition of sentence and provided with standards to guide its use of the information.

We do not intend to suggest that only the above-described procedures would be permissible under *Furman* or that any sentencing system constructed along these general lines would inevitably satisfy the concerns of *Furman,* for each distinct system must be examined on an individual basis. Rather, we have embarked upon this general exposition to make clear that it is possible to construct capital-sentencing systems capable of meeting *Furman's* constitutional concerns.

B

We now turn to consideration of the constitutionality of Georgia's capital-sentencing procedures. In the wake of *Furman,* Georgia amended its capital punishment statute, but chose not to narrow the scope of its murder provisions. Thus, now as before *Furman,* in Georgia "[a] person commits murder when he unlawfully and with malice aforethought, either express or implied, causes the death of another human being." All persons convicted of murder "shall be punished by death or by imprisonment for life."

Georgia did act, however, to narrow the class of murderers subject to capital punishment by specifying 10 statutory aggravating circumstances, one of which must be found by the jury to exist beyond a reasonable doubt before a death sentence can ever be imposed. In addition, the jury is authorized to consider any other appropriate aggravating or mitigating circumstances. The jury is not required to find any mitigating circumstance in order to make a recommendation of mercy that is binding on the trial court, but it must find a *statutory* aggravating circumstance before recommending a sentence of death.

These procedures require the jury to consider the circumstances of the crime and the criminal before it recommends sentence. No longer can a Georgia jury do as Furman's jury did: reach a finding of the defendant's guilt and then, without guidance or direction, decide whether he should live or die. Instead, the jury's attention is directed to the specific circumstances of the crime: Was it committed in the course of another capital felony? Was it committed for money? Was it committed upon a peace officer or judicial officer? Was it committed in a particularly heinous way or in a manner that endangered the lives of many persons? In addition, the jury's attention is focused on the characteristics of the person who committed the crime: Does he have a record of prior convictions for capital offenses? Are there any special facts about this defendant that mitigate against imposing capital punishment (*e.g.,* his youth, the extent of his cooperation with the police, his emotional state at the time of the crime). As a result, while some jury discretion still exists, "the discretion to be exercised is controlled by clear and objective standards so as to produce non-discriminatory application."

As an important additional safeguard against arbitrariness and caprice, the Georgia statutory scheme provides for automatic appeal of all death sentences to the State's Supreme Court. That court is required by statute to review each sentence of death and determine whether it was imposed under the influence of passion or prejudice, whether the evidence supports the jury's finding of a statutory aggravating circumstance, and whether the sentence is disproportionate compared to those sentences imposed in similar cases.

In short, Georgia's new sentencing procedures require as a prerequisite to the imposition of the death penalty, specific jury findings as to the circumstances of the crime or the character of the defendant. Moreover, to guard further against a situation comparable to that presented in *Furman,* the Supreme Court of Georgia compares each death sentence with the sentences imposed on similarly situated defendants to ensure that the sentence of death in a particular case is not disproportionate. On their face these procedures seem to satisfy the concerns of *Furman*. No longer should there be "no meaningful basis for distinguishing the few cases in which [the death penalty] is imposed from the many cases in which it is not.". . .

V

The basic concern of *Furman* centered on those defendants who were being condemned to death capriciously and arbitrarily. Under the procedures before the Court in that case, sentencing authorities were not directed to give attention to the nature or circumstances of the crime committed or to the character or record of the defendant. Left unguided, juries imposed the death sentence in a way that could only be called freakish. The new Georgia sentencing procedures, by contrast, focus the jury's attention on the particularized nature of the crime and the particularized characteristics of the individual defendant. While the jury is permitted to consider any aggravating or mitigating circumstances, it must find and identify at least one statutory aggravating factor before it may impose a penalty of death. In this way the jury's discretion is channeled. No longer can a jury wantonly and freakishly impose the death sentence; it is always circumscribed by the legislative guidelines. In addition, the review function of the Supreme Court of Georgia affords additional assurance that the concerns that prompted our decision in *Furman* are not present to any significant degree in the Georgia procedure applied here.

For the reasons expressed in this opinion, we hold that the statutory system under which Gregg was sentenced to death does not violate the Constitution. Accordingly, the judgment of the Georgia Supreme Court is affirmed.

NOTES

1 Another purpose that has been discussed is the incapacitation of dangerous criminals and the consequent prevention of crimes that they may otherwise commit in the future.

2 We do not address here the question whether the taking of the criminal's life is a proportionate sanction where no victim has been deprived of life—for example, when capital punishment is imposed for rape, kidnaping, or armed robbery that does not result in the death of any human being.

3 The Model Penal Code proposes the following standards: "(3) Aggravating Circumstances.

"(a) The murder was committed by a convict under sentence of imprisonment.

"(b) The defendant was previously convicted of another murder or of a felony involving the use or threat of violence to the person.

"(c) At the time the murder was committed the defendant also committed another murder.

"(d) The defendant knowingly created a great risk of death to many persons.

"(e) The murder was committed while the defendant was engaged or was an accomplice in the commission of, or an attempt to commit, or flight after committing or attempting to commit robbery, rape or deviate sexual intercourse by force or threat of force, arson, burglary or kidnapping.

"(f) The murder was committed for the purpose of avoiding or preventing a lawful arrest or effecting an escape from lawful custody.

"(g) The murder was committed for pecuniary gain.

"(h) The murder was especially heinous, atrocious or cruel, manifesting exceptional depravity.

"(4) Mitigating Circumstances.

"(a) The defendant has no significant history of prior criminal activity.

"(b) The murder was committed while the defendant was under the influence of extreme mental or emotional disturbance.

"(c) The victim was a participant in the defendant's homicidal conduct or consented to the homicidal act.

"(d) The murder was committed under circumstances which the defendant believed to provide a moral justification or extenuation for his conduct.

"(e) The defendant was an accomplice in a murder committed by another person and his participation in the homicidal act was relatively minor.

"(f) The defendant acted under duress or under the domination of another person.

"(g) At the time of the murder, the capacity of the defendant to appreciate the criminality [wrongfulness] of his conduct or to conform his conduct to the requirements of law was impaired as a result of mental disease or defect or intoxication.

"(h) The youth of the defendant at the time of the crime." ALI Model Penal Code § 210.6 (Proposed Official Draft 1962).

QUESTIONS

1 With regard to the imposition of the death penalty for the crime of murder, Justices Stewart, Powell, and Stevens write, "we cannot say that the punishment is invariably disproportionate to the crime." The Georgia statute under which Gregg was sentenced, however, retained the death penalty not only for the crime of murder but also for "kidnaping for ransom or where the victim is harmed, armed robbery, rape, treason, and aircraft hijacking." In your view, is the death penalty a disproportionate punishment for such crimes?

2 In note 3, we find a set of proposed model standards for the guidance of a jury in deciding whether a murderer warrants the death penalty or some lesser penalty, typically life imprisonment. Is the proposed set of aggravating circumstances (those whose presence should incline a jury toward the death penalty) defensible and complete? Is the proposed set of mitigating circumstances (those whose presence should incline a jury away from the death penalty) defensible and complete?

Dissenting Opinion in *Gregg V. Georgia*

Justice Thurgood Marshall

Thurgood Marshall, associate justice of the United States Supreme Court, is the first black ever to be appointed to the Supreme Court. Much of his distinguished private career was given over to providing legal counsel for groups dedicated to the advancement of civil rights. Justice Marshall also served as United States circuit judge (1961–1965) and United States solicitor general (1965–1967), before his appointment in 1967 to the Supreme Court.

United States Supreme Court. 428 U.S. 153 (1976).

Justice Marshall reaffirms the conclusion he had reached in *Furman v. Georgia* (1972): The death penalty is unconstitutional for two individually sufficient reasons. (1) It is excessive. (2) The American people, if fully informed, would consider it morally unacceptable. He insists that his conclusion in *Furman* has not been undercut by subsequent developments. Despite the fact that legislative activity since *Furman* would seem to indicate that the American people do not consider the death penalty morally unacceptable, Justice Marshall continues to maintain that the citizenry, *if fully informed,* would consider it morally unacceptable. At any rate, he maintains, the death penalty is unconstitutional because it is excessive, i.e., unnecessary to accomplish a legitimate legislative purpose. Neither deterrence nor retribution, the principal purposes asserted by Justices Stewart, Powell, and Stevens, can sustain the death penalty as nonexcessive in Justice Marshall's view. Since the available evidence does not show the death penalty to be a more effective deterrent than life imprisonment, he contends, the death penalty is not necessary to promote the goal of deterrence. Moreover, the death penalty is unnecessary to "further any legitimate notion of retribution." According to Justice Marshall, the notion that a murderer "deserves" death constitutes a denial of the wrongdoer's dignity and worth and thus is fundamentally at odds with the Eighth Amendment.

In *Furman v. Georgia* (1972) (concurring opinion), I set forth at some length my views on the basic issue presented to the Court in [this case]. The death penalty, I concluded, is a cruel and unusual punishment prohibited by the Eighth and Fourteenth Amendments. That continues to be my view.

I have no intention of retracing the "long and tedious journey" that led to my conclusion in *Furman.* My sole purposes here are to consider the suggestion that my conclusion in *Furman* has been undercut by developments since then, and briefly to evaluate the basis for my Brethren's holding that the extinction of life is a permissible form of punishment under the Cruel and Unusual Punishments Clause.

In *Furman* I concluded that the death penalty is constitutionally invalid for two reasons. First, the death penalty is excessive. And second, the American people, fully informed as to the purposes of the death penalty and its liabilities, would in my view reject it as morally unacceptable.

Since the decision in *Furman,* the legislatures of 35 States have enacted new statutes authorizing the imposition of the death sentence for certain crimes, and Congress has enacted a law providing the death penalty for air piracy resulting in death. I would be less than candid if I did not acknowledge that these developments have a significant bearing on a realistic assessment of the moral acceptability of the death penalty to the American people. But if the constitutionality of the death penalty turns, as I have urged, on the opinion of an *informed* citizenry, then even the enactment of new death statutes cannot be viewed as conclusive. In *Furman,* I observed that the American people are largely unaware of the information critical to a judgment on the morality of the death penalty, and concluded that if they were better informed they would consider it shocking, unjust, and unacceptable. A recent study, conducted after the enactment of the post-*Furman* statutes, has confirmed that the American people know little about the death penalty, and that the opinions of an informed public would differ significantly from those of a public unaware of the consequences and effects of the death penalty.

Even assuming, however, that the post-*Furman* enactment of statutes authorizing the death penalty renders the prediction of the views of an informed citizenry an uncertain basis for a constitutional decision, the enactment of those statutes has no bearing whatsoever on the conclusion that the death penalty is unconstitutional because it is excessive. An excessive penalty is invalid under the Cruel and Unusual Punishments Clause "even though popular sentiment may favor" it. The inquiry here, then, is simply whether the death penalty is necessary to accomplish the legitimate legislative purposes in punishment, or whether a less severe penalty—life imprisonment—would do as well.

The two purposes that sustain the death penalty as nonexcessive in the Court's view are general deterrence and retribution. In *Furman,* I canvassed the relevant data on the deterrent effect of capital punishment. The state of knowledge at that point, after literally centuries of debate, was summarized as follows by a United Nations Committee:

> "It is generally agreed between the retentionists and abolitionists, whatever their opinions about the validity of comparative studies of deterrence, that the data which now exist show no correlation between the existence of capital punishment and lower rates of capital crime."

The available evidence, I concluded in *Furman,* was convincing that "capital punishment is not necessary as a deterrent to crime in our society.". . .

. . . The evidence I reviewed in *Furman* remains convincing, in my view, that "capital punishment is not necessary as a deterrent to crime in our society." The justification for the death penalty must be found elsewhere.

The other principal purpose said to be served by the death penalty is retribution. The notion that retribution can serve as a moral justification for the sanction of death finds credence in the opinion of my Brothers STEWART, POWELL, and STEVENS. . . . It is this notion that I find to be the most disturbing aspect of today's unfortunate [decision].

The concept of retribution is a multifaceted one, and any discussion of its role in the criminal law must be undertaken with caution. On one level, it can be said that the notion of retribution or reprobation is the basis of our insistence that only those who have broken the law be punished, and in this sense the notion is quite obviously central to a just system of criminal sanctions. But our recognition that retribution plays a crucial role in determining who may be punished by no means requires approval of retribution as a general justification for punishment. It is the question whether retribution can provide a moral justification for punishment—in particular, capital punishment—that we must consider.

My Brothers STEWART, POWELL, and STEVENS offer the following explanation of the retributive justification for capital punishment:

> The instinct for retribution is part of the nature of man, and channeling that instinct in the administration of criminal justice serves an important purpose in promoting the stability of a society governed by law. When people begin to believe that organized society is unwilling or unable to impose upon criminal offenders the punishment they "deserve," then there are sown the seeds of anarchy—of self-help, vigilante justice, and lynch law.

This statement is wholly inadequate to justify the death penalty. As my Brother BRENNAN stated in *Furman,* "[t]here is no evidence whatever that utilization of imprisonment rather than death encourages private blood feuds and other disorders." It simply defies belief to suggest that the death penalty is necessary to prevent the American people from taking the law into their own hands.

In a related vein, it may be suggested that the expression of moral outrage through the imposition of the death penalty serves to reinforce basic moral values— that it marks some crimes as particularly offensive and therefore to be avoided. The argument is akin to a deterrence argument, but differs in that it contemplates the individual's shrinking from antisocial conduct, not because he fears punishment, but because he has been told in the strongest possible way that the conduct is wrong. This contention, like the previous one, provides no support for the death penalty. It is inconceivable that any individual concerned about conforming his conduct to what society says is "right" would fail to realize that murder is "wrong" if the penalty were simply life imprisonment.

The foregoing contentions—that society's expression of moral outrage through the imposition of the death penalty pre-empts the citizenry from taking the law into its own hands and reinforces moral values—are not retributive in the purest sense. They are essentially utilitarian in that they portray the death penalty as valuable because of its beneficial results. These justifications for the death penalty are inadequate because the penalty is, quite clearly I think, not necessary to the accomplishment of those results.

There remains for consideration, however, what might be termed the purely retributive justification for the death penalty—that the death penalty is appropriate, not because of its beneficial effect on society, but because the taking of the murderer's life is itself morally good. Some of the language of the opinion of my Brothers STEWART, POWELL, and STEVENS . . . appears positively to embrace this notion of retribution for its own sake as a justification for capital punishment. They state:

> [T]he decision that capital punishment may be the appropriate sanction in extreme cases is an expression of the community's belief that certain crimes are themselves so grievous an affront to humanity that the only adequate response may be the penalty of death.

They then quote with approval from Lord Justice Denning's remarks before the British Royal Commission on Capital Punishment:

> The truth is that some crimes are so outrageous that society insists on adequate punishment, because the wrong-doer deserves it, irrespective of whether it is a deterrent or not.

Of course, it may be that these statements are intended as no more than observations as to the popular demands that it is thought must be responded to in order to prevent anarchy. But the implication of the statements appears to me to be quite different—

namely, that society's judgment that the murderer "deserves" death must be re-spected not simply because the preservation of order requires it, but because it is appropriate that society make the judgment and carry it out. It is this latter notion, in particular, that I consider to be fundamentally at odds with the Eighth Amendment. The mere fact that the community demands the murderer's life in return for the evil he has done cannot sustain the death penalty, for as JUSTICES STEWART, POWELL, and STEVENS remind us, "the Eighth Amendment demands more than that a challenged punishment be acceptable to contemporary society." To be sustained under the Eighth Amendment, the death penalty must "compor[t] with the basic concept of hu-man dignity at the core of the Amendment;" the objective in imposing it must be "[consistent] with our respect for the dignity of [other] men." Under these standards, the taking of life "because the wrongdoer deserves it" surely must fail, for such a punishment has as its very basis the total denial of the wrongdoer's dignity and worth.

The death penalty, unnecessary to promote the goal of deterrence or to further any legitimate notion of retribution, is an excessive penalty forbidden by the Eighth and Fourteenth Amendments. I respectfully dissent from the Court's judgment upholding the [sentence] of death imposed upon the [petitioner in this case].

QUESTIONS

1 Is Justice Marshall correct in claiming that the American people, *if fully informed* about the death penalty, would consider it morally unacceptable?
2 Is the death penalty, as Justice Marshall claims, "unnecessary to promote the goal of deter-rence or to further any legitimate notion of retribution"?

A Life for a Life

Igor Primoratz

Igor Primoratz is senior lecturer in philosophy at the Hebrew University of Jerusalem. His many published articles on the topic of punishment include "Punishment and Utilitarianism" and "Punishment as Language." He is the author of *Justifying Legal Punishment* (1989), from which this selection is excerpted.

Primoratz endorses a retributive rationale for the retention of the death penalty and defends this rationale against commonly made abolitionist arguments. He rejects the idea that the death penalty violates a murderer's right to life and insists that there is no contradiction involved in a system of criminal law that prohibits murder and yet allows the state to administer the death penalty. He also defends the retributive rationale against arguments claiming to show that the death penalty is in reality a

From Igor Primoratz, *Justifying Legal Punishment* (1989), pp. 158–159, 161–166. Reprinted with the permission of Humanities Press International, Atlantic Highlands, NJ.

disproportionate penalty for the crime of murder. Finally, Primoratz argues that neither the possibility of executing an innocent person nor the discriminatory application of the death penalty can provide a credible basis for abolition.

. . . According to the retributive theory, consequences of punishment, however important from the practical point of view, are irrelevant when it comes to its justification; *the* moral consideration is its justice. Punishment is morally justified insofar as it is meted out as retribution for the offense committed. When someone has committed an offense, he deserves to be punished: it is just, and consequently justified, that he be punished. The offense is the sole ground of the state's right and duty to punish. It is also the measure of legitimate punishment: the two ought to be proportionate. So the issue of capital punishment within the retributive approach comes down to the question, Is this punishment ever proportionate retribution for the offense committed, and thus deserved, just, and justified?

The classic representatives of retributivism believed that it was, and that it was the only proportionate and hence appropriate punishment, if the offense was *murder*—that is, criminal homicide perpetrated voluntarily and intentionally or in wanton disregard of human life. In other cases, the demand for proportionality between offense and punishment can be satisfied by fines or prison terms;[1] the crime of murder, however, is an exception in this respect, and calls for the literal interpretation of the *lex talionis*. The uniqueness of this crime has to do with the uniqueness of the value which has been deliberately or recklessly destroyed. We come across this idea as early as the original formulation of the retributive view—the biblical teaching on punishment: "You shall accept no ransom for the life of a murderer who is guilty of death; but he shall be put to death."[2] The rationale of this command—one that clearly distinguishes the biblical conception of the criminal law from contemporaneous criminal law systems in the Middle East—is that man was not only created *by* God, like every other creature, but also, alone among all the creatures, *in the image of God:*

> That man was made in the image of God . . . is expressive of the peculiar and supreme worth of man. Of all creatures, Genesis 1 relates, he alone possesses this attribute, bringing him into closer relation to God than all the rest and conferring upon him the highest value. . . . This view of the uniqueness and supremacy of human life . . . places life beyond the reach of other values. The idea that life may be measured in terms of money or other property . . . is excluded. Compensation of any kind is ruled out. The guilt of the murderer is infinite because the murdered life is invaluable; the kinsmen of the slain man are not competent to say when he has been paid for. An absolute wrong has been committed, a sin against God which is not subject to human discussion. . . . Because human life is invaluable, to take it entails the death penalty.[3]

This view that the value of human life is not commensurable with other values, and that consequently there is only one truly equivalent punishment for murder, namely death, does not necessarily presuppose a theistic outlook. It can be claimed that, simply because we have to be alive if we are to experience and realize any other value at all, there is nothing equivalent to the murderous destruction of a human life except the destruction of the life of the murderer. Any other retribution, no matter how severe, would still be less than what is proportionate, deserved, and just. As long as the murderer is alive, no matter how bad the conditions of his life may be, there are always at least *some* values he can experience and realize. This provides a plausible interpretation of what the classical representatives of retributivism as a philosophical theory of punishment, such as Kant and Hegel, had to say on the subject.[4]

It seems to me that this is essentially correct. With respect to the larger question of the justification of punishment in general, it is the retributive theory that gives the right answer. Accordingly, capital punishment ought to be retained where it obtains, and reintroduced in those jurisdictions that have abolished it, although we have no reason to believe that, as a means of deterrence, it is any better than a very long prison term. It ought to be retained, or reintroduced, for one simple reason: that justice be done in cases of murder, that murderers be punished according to their deserts.

There are a number of arguments that have been advanced against this rationale of capital punishment. . . .

[One] abolitionist argument . . . simply says that capital punishment is illegitimate because it violates the right to life, which is a fundamental, absolute, sacred right belonging to each and every human being, and therefore ought to be respected even in a murderer.[5]

If any rights are fundamental, the right to life is certainly one of them; but to claim that it is absolute, inviolable under any circumstances and for any reason, is a different matter. If an abolitionist wants to argue his case by asserting an absolute right to life, she will also have to deny moral legitimacy to taking human life in war, revolution, and self-defense. This kind of pacifism is a consistent but farfetched and hence implausible position.

I do not believe that the right to life (nor, for that matter, any other right) is absolute. I have no general theory of rights to fall back upon here; instead, let me pose a question. Would we take seriously the claim to an absolute, sacred, inviolable right to life—coming from the mouth of a *confessed murderer?* I submit that we would not, for the obvious reason that it is being put forward by the person who confessedly denied another human being this very right. But if the murderer cannot plausibly claim such a right for himself, neither can *anyone else* do that in his behalf. This suggests that there is an element of reciprocity in our general rights, such as the right to life or property. I can convincingly claim these rights only so long as I acknowledge and respect the same rights of others. If I violate the rights of others, I thereby lose the same rights. If I am a murderer, I have no *right* to live.

Some opponents of capital punishment claim that a criminal law system which includes this punishment is contradictory, in that it prohibits murder and at the same time provides for its perpetration: "It is one and the same legal regulation which prohibits the individual from murdering, while allowing the state to murder. . . . This is obviously a terrible irony, an abnormal and immoral logic, against which everything in us revolts."[6]

This seems to be one of the more popular arguments against the death penalty, but it is not a good one. If it were valid, it would prove too much. Exactly the same might be claimed of other kinds of punishment: of prison terms, that they are "contradictory" to the legal protection of liberty; of fines, that they are "contradictory" to the legal protection of property. Fortunately enough, it is not valid, for it begs the question at issue. In order to be able to talk of the state as "murdering" the person it executes, and to claim that there is "an abnormal and immoral logic" at work here, which thrives on a "contradiction," one has to use the word "murder" in the very same sense—that is, in the usual sense, which implies the idea of the *wrongful* taking the life of another—both when speaking of what the murderer has done to the victim and of what the state is doing to him by way of punishment. But this is precisely the question at issue: whether capital punishment *is* "murder," whether it is wrongful or morally justified and right.

The next two arguments attack the retributive rationale of capital punishment by questioning the claim that it is only this punishment that satisfies the demand for proportion between offense and punishment in the case of murder. The first points out that any two human lives are different in many important respects, such as age, health, physical and mental capability, so that it does not make much sense to consider them equally valuable. What if the murdered person was very old, practically at the very end of her natural life, while the murderer is young, with most of his life still ahead of him, for instance? Or if the victim was gravely and incurably ill, and thus doomed to live her life in suffering and hopelessness, without being able to experience almost anything that makes a human life worth living, while the murderer is in every respect capable of experiencing and enjoying things life has to offer? Or the other way round? Would not the death penalty in such cases amount either to taking a more valuable life as a punishment for destroying a less valuable one, or *vice versa?* Would it not be either too much, or too little, and in both cases disproportionate, and thus unjust and wrong, from the standpoint of the retributive theory itself?[7]

Any plausibility this argument might appear to have is the result of a conflation of differences between, and value of, human lives. No doubt, any two human lives are *different* in innumerable ways, but this does not entail that they are not *equally valuable.* I have no worked-out general theory of equality to refer to here, but I do not think that one is necessary in order to do away with this argument. The modern humanistic and democratic tradition in ethical, social, and political thought is based on the idea that all human beings are equal. This finds its legal expression in the principle of equality of people under the law. If we are not willing to give up this principle, we have to stick to the assumption that, all differences notwithstanding, any two human lives, *qua* human lives, are equally valuable. If, on the other hand, we allow that, on the basis of such criteria as age, health, or mental or physical ability, it can be claimed that the life of one person is more or less valuable than the life of another, and we admit such claims in the sphere of law, including criminal law, we shall thereby give up the principle of equality of people under the law. In all consistency, we shall not be able to demand that property, physical and personal integrity, and all other rights and interests of individuals be given equal consideration in courts of law either—that is, we shall have to accept systematic discrimination between individuals on the basis of the same criteria across the whole field. I do not think anyone would seriously contemplate an overhaul of the whole legal system along these lines.

The second argument having to do with the issue of proportionality between murder and capital punishment draws our attention to the fact that the law normally provides for a certain period of time to elapse between the passing of a death sentence and its execution. It is a period of several weeks or months; in some cases it extends to years. This period is bound to be one of constant mental anguish for the condemned. And thus, all things considered, what is inflicted on him is disproportionately hard and hence unjust. It would be proportionate and just only in the case of "a criminal who had warned his victim of the date at which he would inflict a horrible death on him and who, from that moment onward, had confined him at his mercy for months."[8]

The first thing to note about this argument is that it does not support a full-fledged abolitionist stand; if it were valid, it would not show that capital punishment is *never* proportionate and just, but only that it is *very rarely* so. Consequently, the conclusion would not be that it ought to be abolished outright, but only that it ought to be restricted to those cases that would satisfy the condition cited above. Such cases do happen, although, to be sure, not very often; the murder of Aldo Moro, for instance, was of this kind. But this is not the main point. The main point is that the argument actually does not hit at capital punishment itself, although it is presented with that aim in view. It hits at something else: a particular way of carrying out this punishment, which is widely adopted in our time. Some hundred years ago and more, in the Wild West, they frequently hanged the man convicted to die almost immediately after pronouncing the sentence. I am not arguing here that we should follow this example today; I mention this piece of historical fact only in order to show that the interval between sentencing someone to death and carrying out the sentence is not a *part* of capital punishment itself. However unpalatable we might find those Wild West hangings, whatever objections we might want to voice against the speed with which they followed the sentencing, surely we shall not deny them the *description* of "executions." So the implication of the argument is not that we ought to do away with capital punishment altogether, nor that we ought to restrict it to those cases of murder where the murderer had warned the victim weeks or months in advance of what he was going to do to her, but that we ought to reexamine the procedure of carrying out this kind of punishment. We ought to weigh the reasons for having this interval between the sentencing and executing, against the moral and human significance of the repercussions such an interval inevitably carries with it.

These reasons, in part, have to do with the possibility of miscarriages of justice and the need to rectify them. Thus we come to the argument against capital punishment which, historically, has been the most effective of all: many advances of the abolitionist movement have been connected with discoveries of cases of judicial errors. Judges and jurors are only human, and consequently some of their beliefs and decisions are bound to be mistaken. Some of their mistakes can be corrected upon discovery; but precisely those with most disastrous repercussions—those which result in innocent people being executed—can never be rectified. In all other cases of mistaken sentencing we can revoke the punishment, either completely or in part, or at least extend compensation. In addition, by exonerating the accused we give moral satisfaction. None of this is possible after an innocent person has been executed; capital punishment is essentially different from all other penalties by being completely irrevocable and irreparable.[9] Therefore, it ought to be abolished.

A part of my reply to this argument goes along the same lines as what I had to say on the previous one. It is not so far-reaching as abolitionists assume; for it would be quite implausible, even fanciful, to claim that there have *never* been cases of murder which left no room whatever for reasonable doubt as to the guilt and full responsibility of the accused. Such cases may not be more frequent than those others, but they do happen. Why not retain the death penalty at least for them?

Actually, this argument, just as the preceding one, does not speak out against capital punishment itself, but against the existing procedures for trying capital cases. Miscarriages of justice result in innocent people being sentenced to death and executed, even in the criminal-law systems in which greatest care is taken to ensure that it never comes to that. But this does not stem from the intrinsic nature of the institution of capital punishment; it results from deficiencies, limitations, and imperfections of the criminal law procedures in which this punishment is meted out. Errors of justice do not demonstrate the need to do away with capital punishment; they simply make it incumbent on us to do everything possible to improve even further procedures of meting it out.

To be sure, this conclusion will not find favor with a diehard abolitionist. "I shall ask for the abolition of Capital Punishment until I have the infallibility of human judgement demonstrated to me," that is, as long as there is even the slightest possibility that innocent people may be executed because of judicial errors, Lafayette said in his day.[10] Many an opponent of this kind of punishment will say the same today. The demand to do away with capital punishment altogether, so as to eliminate even the smallest chance of that ever happening—the chance which, admittedly, would remain even after everything humanly possible has been done to perfect the procedure, although then it would be very slight indeed—is actually a demand to give a privileged position to murderers as against all other offenders, big and small. For if we acted on this demand, we would bring about a situation in which proportionate penalties would be meted out for all offenses, *except* for murder. Murderers would not be receiving the only punishment truly proportionate to their crimes, the punishment of death, but some other, lighter, and thus disproportionate penalty. All other offenders would be punished according to their deserts; only murderers would be receiving less than *they* deserve. In all other cases justice would be done in full; only in cases of the gravest of offenses, the crime of murder, justice would not be carried out in full measure. It is a great and tragic miscarriage of justice when an innocent person is mistakenly sentenced to death and executed, but systematically giving murderers advantage over all other offenders would also be a grave injustice. Is the fact that, as long as capital punishment is retained, there is a possibility that over a number of years, or even decades, an injustice of the first kind may be committed, unintentionally and unconsciously, reason enough to abolish it altogether, and thus end up with a system of punishments in which injustices of the second kind are perpetrated daily, consciously, and inevitably?[11]

There is still another abolitionist argument that actually does not hit out against capital punishment itself, but against something else. Figures are sometimes quoted which show that this punishment is much more often meted out to the uneducated and poor than to the educated, rich, and influential people; in the United States, much more often to blacks than to whites. These figures are adduced as a proof of the inherent injustice of this kind of punishment. On account of them, it is claimed that capital punishment is not a way of doing justice by meting out deserved punishment to murderers, but rather a means of social discrimination and perpetuation of social injustice.

I shall not question these findings, which are quite convincing, and anyway, there is no need to do that in order to defend the institution of capital punishment. For there seems to be a certain amount of discrimination and injustice not only in sentencing people to death and executing them, but also in meting out other penalties. The social structure of the death rows in American prisons, for instance, does not seem to be basically different from the general social structure of American penitentiaries. If this argument were valid, it would call not only for abolition of the penalty of death, but for doing away with other penalties as well. But it is not valid; as Burton Leiser has pointed out,

> . . . this is not an argument, either against the death penalty or against any other form of punishment. It is an argument against the unjust and inequitable distribution of penalties. If the trials of wealthy men are less likely to result in convictions than those of poor men, then something must be done to reform the procedure in criminal courts. If those who have money and standing in the community are less likely to be charged with serious offenses than their less affluent fellow citizens, then there should be a major overhaul of the entire system of criminal justice . . . But the maldistribution of penalties is no argument against any particular form of penalty.[12]

NOTES

1 Cf. I. Primoratz, *Justifying Legal Punishment* (Atlantic Highlands, N.J.: Humanities Press, 1989), pp. 85–94.

2 Numbers 35.31 (R.S.V.).

3 M. Greenberg, "Some Postulates of Biblical Criminal Law," in J. Goldin (ed.), *The Jewish Expression* (New York: Bantam, 1970), pp. 25–26. (Post-biblical Jewish law evolved toward the virtual abolition of the death penalty, but that is of no concern here.)

4 "There is no *parallel* between death and even the most miserable life, so that there is no equality of crime and retribution [in the case of murder] unless the perpetrator is judicially put to death" (I. Kant, "The Metaphysics of Morals," *Kant's Political Writings,* ed. H. Reiss, trans. H. B. Nisbet [Cambridge: Cambridge University Press, 1970], p. 156). "Since life is the full compass of a man's existence, the punishment [for murder] cannot simply consist in a 'value', for none is great enough, but can consist only in taking away a second life" (G. W. F. Hegel, *Philosophy of Right,* trans. T. M. Knox [Oxford: Oxford University Press, 1965], p. 247).

5 For an example of this view, see L. N. Tolstoy, *Smertnaya kazn i hristianstvo* (Berlin: I. P. Ladizhnikov, n.d.), pp. 40–41.

6 S. V. Vulović, *Problem smrtne kazne* (Belgrade: Geca Kon, 1925), pp. 23–24.

7 Cf. W. Blackstone, *Commentaries on the Laws of England,* 4th ed., ed. J. DeWitt Andrews (Chicago: Callaghan & Co., 1899), p. 1224.

8 A. Camus, "Reflections on the Guillotine," *Resistance, Rebellion and Death,* trans. J. O'Brien (London: Hamish Hamilton, 1961), p. 143.

9 For an interesting critical discussion of this point, see M. Davis, "Is the Death Penalty Irrevocable?," *Social Theory and Practice* 10 (1984).

10 Quoted in E. R. Calvert, *Capital Punishment in the Twentieth Century* (London: G. P. Putnam's Sons, 1927), p. 132.

11 For a criticism of this argument, see L. Sebba, "On Capital Punishment—A Comment," *Israel Law Review* 17 (1982), pp. 392–395.

12 B. M. Leiser, *Liberty, Justice and Morals: Contemporary Value Conflicts* (New York: Macmillan, 1973), p. 225.

QUESTIONS

1 Would you endorse a retributive rationale for the retention of the death penalty? If so, would you say that *all* murderers deserve to die or just *some?* If just some deserve to die, which ones?

2 If blacks are more likely to receive the death penalty than whites, if the poor and uneducated are more likely to receive the death penalty than the affluent and educated, do these facts constitute a compelling argument for abolition of the death penalty?

An Eye for an Eye?

Stephen Nathanson

Stephen Nathanson is professor of philosophy at Northeastern University. He is the author of articles such as "In Defense of 'Moderate Patriotism.' " He is also the author of *The Ideal of Rationality* (1985) and *An Eye for an Eye? The Morality of Punishing by Death* (1987), from which this selection is excerpted.

Nathanson, an abolitionist, distinguishes between *equality* retributivism and *proportional* retributivism and argues that neither of these retributive approaches can provide a justification for the death penalty. In his view: (1) Equality retributivism—committed to the principle that punishment should be equal to the crime ("an eye for an eye")—fails because it does not provide a systematically satisfactory criterion for determining appropriate punishment. (2) Proportional retributivism—committed to the principle that punishment should be proportional to the crime—fails because it does not require that murderers be executed. Nathanson also argues that a societal decision to abolish the death penalty would convey two important symbolic messages. First, we would thereby express our respect for the

Reprinted with permission of Rowman & Littlefield, Publishers, from Stephen Nathanson, *An Eye for an Eye?* (1987), pp. 72–77, 138–140, 145.

dignity of all human beings, even those guilty of murder. Second, in restraining the expression of our anger against murderers, we would reinforce the conviction that only defensive violence is justifiable.

Suppose we . . . try to determine what people deserve from a strictly moral point of view. How shall we proceed?

The most usual suggestion is that we look at a person's actions because what someone deserves would appear to depend on what he or she does. A person's actions, it seems, provide not only a basis for a moral appraisal of the person but also a guide to how he should be treated. According to the *lex talionis* or principle of "an eye for an eye," we ought to treat people as they have treated others. What people deserve as recipients of rewards or punishments is determined by what they do as agents.

This is a powerful and attractive view, one that appears to be backed not only by moral common sense but also by tradition and philosophical thought. The most famous statement of philosophical support for this view comes from Immanuel Kant, who linked it directly with an argument for the death penalty. Discussing the problem of punishment, Kant writes,

> What kind and what degree of punishment does legal justice adopt as its principle and standard? None other than the principle of equality . . . the principle of not treating one side more favorably than the other. Accordingly, any undeserved evil that you inflict on someone else among the people is one that you do to yourself. If you vilify, you vilify yourself; if you steal from him, you steal from yourself; if you kill him, you kill yourself. Only the law of retribution (*jus talionis*) can determine exactly the kind and degree of punishment.[1]

Kant's view is attractive for a number of reasons. First, it accords with our belief that what a person deserves is related to what he does. Second, it appeals to a moral standard and does not seem to rely on any particular legal or political institutions. Third, it seems to provides a measure of appropriate punishment that can be used as a guide to creating laws and instituting punishments. It tells us that the punishment is to be identical with the crime. Whatever the criminal did to the victim is to be done in turn to the criminal.

In spite of the attractions of Kant's view, it is deeply flawed. When we see why, it will be clear that the whole "eye for an eye" perspective must be rejected.

PROBLEMS WITH THE EQUAL PUNISHMENT PRINCIPLE

. . . [Kant's view] does not provide an adequate criterion for determining appropriate levels of punishment.

. . . We can see this, first, by noting that for certain crimes, Kant's view recommends punishments that are not morally acceptable. Applied strictly, it would require that we rape rapists, torture torturers, and burn arsonists whose acts have led to deaths. In general, where a particular crime involves barbaric and inhuman treat-

. s principle tells us to act barbarically and inhumanly in return. So, in
..ses, the principle generates unacceptable answers to the question of what
..itutes appropriate punishment.

This is not its only defect. In many other cases, the principle tells us nothing at all
about how to punish. While Kant thought it obvious how to apply his principle in the
case of murder, his principle cannot serve as a general rule because it does not tell us
how to punish many crimes. Using the Kantian version or the more common "eye
for an eye" standard, what would we decide to do to embezzlers, spies, drunken drivers, airline hijackers, drug users, prostitutes, air polluters, or persons who practice
medicine without a license? If one reflects on this question, it becomes clear that
there is simply no answer to it. We could not in fact design a system of punishment
simply on the basis of the "eye for an eye" principle.

In order to justify using the "eye for an eye" principle to answer our question
about murder and the death penalty, we would first have to show that it worked for a
whole range of cases, giving acceptable answers to questions about amounts of punishment. Then, having established it as a satisfactory general principle, we could apply it to the case of murder. It turns out, however, that when we try to apply the
principle generally, we find that it either gives wrong answers or no answers at all.
Indeed, I suspect that the principle of "an eye for an eye" is no longer even a principle. Instead, it is simply a metaphorical disguise for expressing belief in the death
penalty. People who cite it do not take it seriously. They do not believe in a kidnapping for a kidnapping, a theft for a theft, and so on. Perhaps "an eye for an eye" once
was a genuine principle, but now it is merely a slogan. Therefore, it gives us no
guidance in deciding whether murderers deserve to die.

In reply to these objections, one might defend the principle by saying that it does
not require that punishments be strictly identical with crimes. Rather, it requires only
that a punishment produce an amount of suffering in the criminal which is equal to
the amount suffered by the victim. Thus, we don't have to hijack airplanes belonging
to airline hijackers, spy on spies, etc. We simply have to reproduce in them the harm
done to others.

Unfortunately, this reply really does not solve the problem. It provides no answer
to the first objection, since it would still require us to behave barbarically in our
treatment of those who are guilty of barbaric crimes. Even if we do not reproduce
their actions exactly, any action which caused equal suffering would itself be barbaric. Second, in trying to produce equal amounts of suffering, we run into many
problems. Just how much suffering is produced by an airline hijacker or a spy? And
how do we apply this principle to prostitutes or drug users, who may not produce
any suffering at all? We have rough ideas about how serious various crimes are, but
this may not correlate with any clear sense of just how much harm is done.

Furthermore, the same problem arises in determining how much suffering a particular punishment would produce for a particular criminal. People vary in their tolerance of pain and in the amount of unhappiness that a fine or a jail sentence would
cause them. Recluses will be less disturbed by banishment than extroverts. Nature
lovers will suffer more in prison than people who are indifferent to natural beauty. A
literal application of the principle would require that we tailor punishments to indi-

vidual sensitivities, yet this is at best impractical. To a large extent, the legal system must work with standardized and rather crude estimates of the negative impact that punishments have on people.

The move from calling for a punishment that is identical to the crime to favoring one that is equal in the harm done is no help to us or to the defense of the principle. "An eye for an eye" tells us neither what people deserve nor how we should treat them when they have done wrong.

PROPORTIONAL RETRIBUTIVISM

The view we have been considering can be called "equality retributivism," since it proposes that we repay criminals with punishments equal to their crimes. In the light of problems like those I have cited, some people have proposed a variation on this view, calling not for equal punishments but rather for punishments which are *proportional* to the crime. In defending such a view as a guide for setting criminal punishments, Andrew von Hirsch writes:

> If one asks how severely a wrongdoer deserves to be punished, a familiar principle comes to mind: Severity of punishment should be commensurate with the seriousness of the wrong. Only grave wrongs merit severe penalties; minor misdeeds deserve lenient punishments. Disproportionate penalties are undeserved—severe sanctions for minor wrongs or vice versa. This principle has variously been called a principle of "proportionality" or "just deserts"; we prefer to call it commensurate deserts.[2]

Like Kant, von Hirsch makes the punishment which a person deserves depend on that person's actions, but he departs from Kant in substituting proportionality for equality as the criterion for setting the amount of punishment.

In implementing a punishment system based on the proportionality view, one would first make a list of crimes, ranking them in order of seriousness. At one end would be quite trivial offenses like parking meter violations, while very serious crimes such as murder would occupy the other. In between, other crimes would be ranked according to their relative gravity. Then a corresponding scale of punishments would be constructed, and the two would be correlated. Punishments would be proportionate to crimes so long as we could say that the more serious the crime was, the higher on the punishment scale was the punishment administered.

This system does not have the defects of equality retributivism. It does not require that we treat those guilty of barbaric crimes barbarically. This is because we can set the upper limit of the punishment scale so as to exclude truly barbaric punishments. Second, unlike the equality principle, the proportionality view is genuinely general, providing a way of handling all crimes. Finally, it does justice to our ordinary belief that certain punishments are unjust because they are too severe or too lenient for the crime committed.

The proportionality principle does, I think, play a legitimate role in our thinking about punishments. Nonetheless, it is no help to death penalty advocates, because it does not require that murderers be executed. All that it requires is that if murder is the most serious crime, then murder should be punished by the most severe punishment on the scale. The principle does not tell us what this punishment should be, however, and it is quite compatible with the view that the most severe punishment should be a long prison term.

This failure of the theory to provide a basis for supporting the death penalty reveals an important gap in proportional retributivism. It shows that while the theory is general in scope, it does not yield any *specific* recommendations regarding punishment. It tells us, for example, that armed robbery should be punished more severely than embezzling and less severely than murder, but it does not tell us how much to punish any of these. This weakness is, in effect, conceded by von Hirsch, who admits that if we want to implement the "commensurate deserts" principle, we must supplement it with information about what level of punishment is needed to deter crimes.[3] In a later discussion of how to "anchor" the punishment system, he deals with this problem in more depth, but the factors he cites as relevant to making specific judgments (such as available prison space) have nothing to do with what people deserve. He also seems to suggest that a range of punishments may be appropriate for a particular crime. This runs counter to the death penalty supporter's sense that death alone is appropriate for some murderers.[4]

Neither of these retributive views, then, provides support for the death penalty. The equality principle fails because it is not in general true that the appropriate punishment for a crime is to do to the criminal what he has done to others. In some cases this is immoral, while in others it is impossible. The proportionality principle may be correct, but by itself it cannot determine specific punishments for specific crimes. Because of its flexibility and open-endedness, it is compatible with a great range of different punishments for murder.[5] . . .

THE SYMBOLISM OF ABOLISHING THE DEATH PENALTY

What is the symbolic message that we would convey by deciding to renounce the death penalty and to abolish its use?

I think that there are two primary messages. The first is the most frequently emphasized and is usually expressed in terms of the sanctity of human life, although I think we could better express it in terms of respect for human dignity. One way we express our respect for the dignity of human beings is by abstaining from depriving them of their lives, even if they have done terrible deeds. In defense of human well-being, we may punish people for their crimes, but we ought not to deprive them of everything, which is what the death penalty does.

If we take the life of a criminal, we convey the idea that by his deeds he has made himself worthless and totally without human value. I do not believe that we are in a position to affirm that of anyone. We may hate such a person and feel the deepest anger against him, but when he no longer poses a threat to anyone, we ought not to take his life.

But, one might ask, hasn't the murderer forfeited whatever rights he might have had to our respect? Hasn't he, by his deeds, given up any rights that he had to decent treatment? Aren't we morally free to kill him if we wish?

These questions express important doubts about the obligation to accord any respect to those who have acted so deplorably, but I do not think that they prove that any such forfeiture has occurred. Certainly, when people murder or commit other crimes, they do forfeit some of the rights that are possessed by the law-abiding. They lose a certain right to be left alone. It becomes permissible to bring them to trial and, if they are convicted, to impose an appropriate—even a dreadful—punishment on them.

Nonetheless, they do not forfeit all their rights. It does not follow from the vileness of their actions that we can do anything whatsoever to them. This is part of the moral meaning of the constitutional ban on cruel and unusual punishments. No matter how terrible a person's deeds, we may not punish him in a cruel and unusual way. We may not torture him, for example. His right not to be tortured has not been forfeited. Why do these limits hold? Because this person remains a human being, and we think that there is something in him that we must continue to respect in spite of his terrible acts.

One way of seeing why those who murder still deserve some consideration and respect is by reflecting again on the idea of what it is to *deserve* something. In most contexts, we think that what people deserve depends on what they have done, intended, or tried to do. It depends on features that are qualities of individuals. The best person for the job deserves to be hired. The person who worked especially hard deserves our gratitude. We can call the concept that applies in these cases *personal* desert.

There is another kind of desert, however, that belongs to people by virtue of their humanity itself and does not depend on their individual efforts or achievements. I will call this impersonal kind of desert *human* desert. We appeal to this concept when we think that everyone deserves a certain level of treatment no matter what their individual qualities are. When the signers of the Declaration of Independence affirmed that people had inalienable rights to "life, liberty, and the pursuit of happiness," they were appealing to such an idea. These rights do not have to be earned by people. They are possessed "naturally," and everyone is bound to respect them.

According to the view that I am defending, people do not lose all of their rights when they commit terrible crimes. They still deserve some level of decent treatment simply because they remain living, functioning human beings. This level of moral desert need not be earned, and it cannot be forfeited. This view may sound controversial, but in fact everyone who believes that cruel and unusual punishment should be forbidden implicitly agrees with it. That is, they agree that even after someone has committed a terrible crime, we do not have the right to do anything whatsoever to him.

What I am suggesting is that by renouncing the use of death as a punishment, we express and reaffirm our belief in the inalienable, unforfeitable core of human dignity.

Why is this a worthwhile message to convey? It is worth conveying because this belief is both important and precarious. Throughout history, people have found innumerable reasons to degrade the humanity of one another. They have found qualities in others that they hated or feared, and even when they were not threatened by these people, they have sought to harm them, deprive them of their liberty, or take their lives from them. They have often felt that they had good reasons to do these things, and they have invoked divine commands, racial purity, and state security to support their deeds.

These actions and attitudes are not relics of the past. They remain an awful feature of the contemporary world. By renouncing the death penalty, we show our determination to accord at least minimal respect even to those whom we believe to be personally vile or morally vicious. This is, perhaps, why we speak of the *sanctity* of human life rather than its value or worth. That which is sacred remains, in some sense, untouchable, and its value is not dependent on its worth or usefulness to us. Kant expressed this ideal of respect in the famous second version of the Categorical Imperative: "So act as to treat humanity, whether in thine own person or in that of any other, in every case as an end withal, never as a means only." . . .

[THE SECOND SYMBOLIC MESSAGE]

. . . When the state has a murderer in its power and could execute him but does not, this conveys the idea that even though this person has done wrong and even though we may be angry, outraged, and indignant with him, we will nonetheless control ourselves in a way that he did not. We will not kill him, even though we could do so and even though we are angry and indignant. We will exercise restraint, sanctioning killing only when it serves a protective function.

Why should we do this? Partly out of a respect for human dignity. But also because we want the state to set an example of proper behavior. We do not want to encourage people to resort to violence to settle conflicts when there are other ways available. We want to avoid the cycle of violence that can come from retaliation and counter-retaliation. Violence is a contagion that arouses hatred and anger, and if unchecked, it simply leads to still more violence. The state can convey the message that the contagion must be stopped, and the most effective principle for stopping it is the idea that only defensive violence is justifiable. Since the death penalty is not an instance of defensive violence, it ought to be renounced.

We show our respect for life best by restraining ourselves and allowing murderers to live, rather than by following a policy of a life for a life. Respect for life and restraint of violence are aspects of the same ideal. The renunciation of the death penalty would symbolize our support of that ideal.

NOTES

1 Kant, *Metaphysical Elements of Justice,* translated by John Ladd (Indianapolis: Bobbs-Merrill, 1965), 101.

2 *Doing Justice* (New York: Hill & Wang, 1976), 66; reprinted in *Sentencing,* edited by H. Gross and A. von Hirsch (Oxford University Press, 1981), 243. For a more recent discussion and further defense by von Hirsch, see his *Past or Future Crimes* (New Brunswick, N.J.: Rutgers University Press, 1985).

3 Von Hirsch, *Doing Justice,* 93–94. My criticisms of proportional retributivism are not novel. For helpful discussions of the view, see Hugo Bedau, "Concessions to Retribution in

Punishment," in *Justice and Punishment,* edited by J. Cederblom and W. Blizek (Cambridge, Mass.: Ballinger, 1977), and M. Golding, *Philosophy of Law* (Englewood Cliffs, N.J.: Prentice Hall, 1975), 98–99.

4 See von Hirsch, *Past and Future Crimes,* ch. 8.

5 For more positive assessments of these theories, see Jeffrey Reiman, "Justice, Civilization, and the Death Penalty," *Philosophy and Public Affairs* 14 (1985):115–48; and Michael Davis, "How to Make the Punishment Fit the Crime," *Ethics* 93 (1983).

QUESTIONS

1 To what extent, if at all, should the principle of "an eye for an eye" be incorporated into our system of criminal justice?

2 Can a retributive rationale for retention of the death penalty be defended against the objections presented by Nathanson?

3 Does Nathanson's appeal to "the symbolism of abolishing the death penalty" provide a compelling argument for abolition? Could a retentionist develop a compelling argument based on the symbolism of *retaining* the death penalty?

Deterrence and Uncertainty

Ernest van den Haag

Ernest van den Haag is professor of jurisprudence and public policy at Fordham University. For many years, van den Haag maintained a private practice in psychoanalysis. He is the author of such works as *The Fabric of Society* (1957), *Political Violence and Civil Disobedience* (1972), and *Punishing Criminals: Concerning a Very Old and Painful Question* (1975).

The retentionist argument advanced by van den Haag is based on our uncertainty concerning the deterrent effect of the death penalty (whether or not it is a uniquely effective deterrent). According to his analysis, if we retain the death penalty, we run the risk of needlessly eradicating the lives of convicted murderers; perhaps the death penalty is *not* a uniquely effective deterrent. On the other hand, if we abolish the death penalty, we run the risk of innocent people becoming future murder victims; perhaps the death penalty *is* a uniquely effective deterrent. Faced with such uncertainty, van den Haag maintains, it is our moral obligation to retain the death penalty. "We have no right to risk additional future victims of murder for the sake of sparing convicted murderers."

. . . If we do not know whether the death penalty will deter others [in a uniquely effective way], we are confronted with two uncertainties. If we impose the death penalty, and achieve no deterrent effect thereby, the life of a convicted murderer has

Reprinted with permission of the publisher from the *Journal of Criminal Law, Criminology and Police Science,* vol. 60, no. 2 (1969).

been expended in vain (from a deterrent viewpoint). There is a net loss. If we impose the death sentence and thereby deter some future murderers, we spared the lives of some future victims (the prospective murderers gain too; they are spared punishment because they were deterred). In this case, the death penalty has led to a net gain, unless the life of a convicted murderer is valued more highly than that of the unknown victim, or victims (and the non-imprisonment of the deterred non-murderer).

The calculation can be turned around, of course. The absence of the death penalty may harm no one and therefore produce a gain—the life of the convicted murderer. Or it may kill future victims of murderers who could have been deterred, and thus produce a loss—their life.

To be sure, we must risk something certain—the death (or life) of the convicted man, for something uncertain—the death (or life) of the victims of murderers who may be deterred. This is in the nature of uncertainty—when we invest, or gamble, we risk the money we have for an uncertain gain. Many human actions, most commitments—including marriage and crime—share this characteristic with the deterrent purpose of any penalization, and with its rehabilitative purpose (and even with the protective).

More proof is demanded for the deterrent effect of the death penalty than is demanded for the deterrent effect of other penalties. This is not justified by the absence of other utilitarian purposes such as protection and rehabilitation; they involve no less uncertainty than deterrence.[1]

Irrevocability may support a demand for some reason to expect more deterrence than revocable penalties might produce, but not a demand for more proof of deterrence, as has been pointed out above. The reason for expecting more deterrence lies in the greater severity, the terrifying effect inherent in finality. Since it seems more important to spare victims than to spare murderers, the burden of proving that the greater severity inherent in irrevocability adds nothing to deterrence lies on those who oppose capital punishment. Proponents of the death penalty need show only that there is no more uncertainty about it than about greater severity in general.

The demand that the death penalty be proved more deterrent than alternatives can not be satisfied any more than the demand that six years in prison be proved to be more deterrent than three. But the uncertainty which confronts us favors the death penalty as long as by imposing it we might save future victims of murder. This effect is as plausible as the general idea that penalties have deterrent effects which increase with their severity. Though we have no proof of the positive deterrence of the penalty, we also have no proof of zero, or negative effectiveness. I believe we have no right to risk additional future victims of murder for the sake of sparing convicted murderers; on the contrary, our moral obligation is to risk the possible ineffectiveness of executions. However rationalized, the opposite view appears to be motivated by the simple fact that executions are more subjected to social control than murder. However, this applies to all penalties and does not argue for the abolition of any.

NOTES

1 Rehabilitation or protection are of minor importance in our actual penal system (though not in our theory). We confine many people who do not need rehabilitation and against whom we do not need protection (e.g., the exasperated husband who killed his wife); we release many unrehabilitated offenders against whom protection is needed. Certainly rehabilitation and protection are not, and deterrence is, the main actual function of legal punishment, if we disregard nonutilitarian purposes.

QUESTIONS

1 If we are unsure whether or not the death penalty is a uniquely effective deterrent, does our uncertainty favor retention, abolition, or neither?

2 Is the life of a convicted murderer worth as much as the life of a potential murder victim?

Civilization, Safety, and Deterrence

Jeffrey H. Reiman

Jeffrey H. Reiman is professor of philosophy and justice at The American University in Washington, D.C. He is the author of *In Defense of Political Philosophy* (1972) and *The Rich Get Richer and the Poor Get Prison* (3d ed., 1990). His many published articles include "The Fallacy of Libertarian Capitalism" and "The Marxian Critique of Criminal Justice."

Reiman challenges the following argument advanced by Ernest van den Haag: since the death penalty is ordinarily more feared than life imprisonment, it is reasonable to assume that the death penalty is a better deterrent than life imprisonment. Reiman calls this argument van den Haag's "common-sense argument" and presents four distinct reasons for rejecting it. In developing his third point, Reiman relies on the claim that abolition of the death penalty would have a civilizing impact on society, and thus he speaks of "a deterrent effect from *not executing*." This particular consideration, he maintains, can also be applied to refute the retentionist argument developed by van den Haag in the previous selection.

. . . By placing execution alongside torture in the category of things we will not do to our fellow human beings even when they deserve them, we broadcast the message that totally subjugating a person to the power of others *and* confronting him with the advent of his own humanly administered demise is too horrible to be done by civilized human beings to their fellows even when they have earned it: too horrible to do, and too horrible to be capable of doing. And I contend that broadcasting this message loud and clear would in the long run contribute to the general detestation of

From Jeffrey H. Reiman, "Justice, Civilization, and the Death Penalty: Answering van den Haag." *Philosophy and Public Affairs*, vol. 14 (Spring 1985). Excerpt, pp. 141–147, reprinted with permission of Princeton University Press.

murder and be, to the extent to which it worked itself into the hearts and minds of the populace, a deterrent. In short, refusing to execute murderers though they deserve it both reflects and continues the taming of the human species that we call civilization. Thus, I take it that the abolition of the death penalty, though it is a just punishment for murder, is part of the civilizing mission of modern states. . . .

Earlier I said that judging a practice too horrible to do even to those who deserve it does not exclude the possibility that it could be justified if necessary to avoid even worse consequences. Thus, were the death penalty clearly proven a better deterrent to the murder of innocent people than life in prison, we might have to admit that we had not yet reached a level of civilization at which we could protect ourselves without imposing this horrible fate on murderers, and thus we might have to grant the necessity of instituting the death penalty. But this is far from proven. The available research by no means clearly indicates that the death penalty reduces the incidence of homicide more than life imprisonment does. . . .

Conceding that it has not been proven that the death penalty deters more murders than life imprisonment, van den Haag has argued that neither has it been proven that the death penalty does *not* deter more murders, and thus we must follow common sense which teaches that the higher the cost of something, the fewer people will choose it, and therefore at least some potential murderers who would not be deterred by life imprisonment will be deterred by the death penalty. Van den Haag writes:

> . . . our experience shows that the greater the threatened penalty, the more it deters.
>
> . . . Life in prison is still life, however unpleasant. In contrast, the death penalty does not just threaten to make life unpleasant—it threatens to take life altogether. This difference is perceived by those affected. We find that when they have the choice between life in prison and execution, 99% of all prisoners under sentence of death prefer life in prison. . . .
>
> From this unquestioned fact a reasonable conclusion can be drawn in favor of the superior deterrent effect of the death penalty. Those who have the choice in practice . . . fear death more than they fear life in prison. . . . If they do, it follows that the threat of the death penalty, all other things equal, is likely to deter more than the threat of life in prison. One is most deterred by what one fears most. From which it follows that whatever statistics fail, or do not fail, to show, the death penalty is likely to be more deterrent than any other.[1]

Those of us who recognize how common-sensical it was, and still is, to believe that the sun moves around the earth, will be less willing than Professor van den Haag to follow common sense here, especially when it comes to doing something awful to our fellows. Moreover, there are good reasons for doubting common sense on this matter. Here are four:

1 From the fact that one penalty is more feared than another, it does not follow that the more feared penalty will deter more than the less feared, unless we know that the less feared penalty is not fearful enough to deter everyone who can be deterred—and this is just what we don't know with regard to the death penalty. Though I fear the death penalty more than life in prison, I can't think of any act that the death penalty would deter me from that an equal likelihood of spending my life in prison wouldn't deter me from as well. Since it seems to me that whoever would be deterred by a given likelihood of death would be deterred by an *equal* likelihood of life behind bars, I suspect that the common-sense argument only seems plausible because we evaluate it unconsciously assuming that potential criminals will face larger likelihoods of death sentences than of life sentences. If the likelihoods were equal, it seems to me that where life imprisonment was improbable enough to make it too distant a possibility to worry much about, a similar low probability of death would have the same effect. After all, we are undeterred by small likelihoods of death every time we walk the streets. And if life imprisonment were sufficiently probable to pose a real deterrent threat, it would pose as much of a deterrent threat as death. And this is just what most of the research we have on the comparative deterrent impact of execution versus life imprisonment suggests.

2 In light of the fact that roughly 500 to 700 suspected felons are killed by the police in the line of duty every year, and the fact that the number of privately owned guns in America is substantially larger than the number of households in America, it must be granted that anyone contemplating committing a crime *already* faces a substantial risk of ending up dead as a result. It's hard to see why anyone *who is not already deterred by this* would be deterred by the addition of the more distant risk of death after apprehension, conviction, and appeal. Indeed, this suggests that people consider risks in a much cruder way than van den Haag's appeal to common sense suggests—which should be evident to anyone who contemplates how few people use seatbelts (14% of drivers, on some estimates), when it is widely known that wearing them can spell the difference between life (outside prison) and death.

3 Van den Haag has maintained that deterrence doesn't work only by means of cost-benefit calculations made by potential criminals. It works also by the lesson about the wrongfulness of murder that is slowly learned in a society that subjects murderers to the ultimate punishment.[2] But if I am correct in claiming that the refusal to execute even those who deserve it has a civilizing effect, then the refusal to execute also teaches a lesson about the wrongfulness of murder. My claim here is admittedly speculative, but no more so than van den Haag's to the contrary. And my view has the added virtue of accounting for the failure of research to show an increased deterrent effect from executions *without having to deny the plausibility of van den Haag's common-sense argument that at least some additional potential murderers will be deterred by the prospect of the death penalty.* If there is a deterrent effect from *not executing,* then it is understandable that while executions will deter some murderers, this effect will be balanced out by the weakening of the deterrent effect of not executing, such that no net reduction in murders will result. And this, by the way, also disposes of van den Haag's argument that, in the absence of knowledge one way or the other on the deterrent effect of executions, we should execute murderers rather than risk the lives of innocent people whose murders might have been deterred if we had. If there is a deterrent effect of not executing, it follows that we risk innocent lives either way. And if this is so, it seems that the only reasonable course of action is to refrain from imposing what we know is a horrible fate.

4 Those who still think that van den Haag's common-sense argument for executing murderers is valid will find that the argument proves more than they bargained for. Van den Haag maintains that, in the absence of conclusive evidence on the relative deterrent impact of the death penalty versus life imprisonment, we must follow common sense and assume that if one punishment is more fearful than another, it will deter some potential criminals not deterred by the less fearful punishment. Since people sentenced to death will almost universally try to get their sentences changed to life in prison, it follows that death is more fearful than life imprisonment, and thus that it will deter some additional murderers. Consequently, we should institute the death penalty to save the lives these additional murderers would have taken. But, since people sentenced to be tortured to death would surely try to get their sentences changed to simple execution, the same argument proves that death-by-torture will deter still more potential murderers. Consequently, we should institute death-by-torture to save the lives these additional murderers would have taken. Anyone who accepts van den Haag's argument is then confronted with a dilemma: Until we have conclusive evidence that capital punishment is a greater deterrent to murder than life imprisonment, he must grant *either* that we should not follow common sense and not impose the death penalty; *or* we should follow common sense and torture murderers to death. In short, either we must abolish the electric chair or reinstitute the rack. Surely, this is the *reductio ad absurdum* of van den Haag's common-sense argument.

NOTES

1 Ernest van den Haag and John P. Conrad, *The Death Penalty: A Debate* (New York: Plenum Press, 1983), pp. 68–69.
2 Ibid., p. 63.

QUESTIONS

1 Is it reasonable to assume that the death penalty is a better deterrent than life imprisonment?
2 Is it plausible to believe that abolition of the death penalty would produce "a deterrent effect from not executing"?
3 Would you endorse either of the following claims? (1) We should abolish the death penalty unless retentionists can prove that it is a uniquely effective deterrent. (2) We should retain the death penalty unless abolitionists can prove that it is not a uniquely effective deterrent.

SUGGESTED ADDITIONAL READINGS FOR CHAPTER 4

BEDAU, HUGO ADAM: "Capital Punishment." In Tom Regan, ed., *Matters of Life and Death,* 2d ed. New York: Random House, 1986. Bedau, a prominent abolitionist, presents an expansive discussion of the morality of the death penalty. Part V of this long article is dedicated to a critical analysis and rejection of the view that considerations of retributive justice can provide an adequate justification for retention.
———, ed.: *The Death Penalty in America,* 3d ed. New York: Oxford University Press, 1982. This sourcebook provides a wealth of factual material relevant to the death penalty controversy. It also incorporates essays by both retentionists and abolitionists.
BERNS, WALTER: *For Capital Punishment.* New York: Basic, 1979. In this book, which provides a wide-ranging discussion of issues relevant to the death penalty controversy, Berns insists that capital punishment can be effectively defended on retributive grounds.

BLACK, CHARLES L., JR.: *Capital Punishment: The Inevitability of Caprice and Mistake,* 2d ed. New York: Norton, 1981. Black argues for abolition on the grounds that it is virtually impossible to eliminate arbitrariness and mistake from the numerous decisions that lead to the imposition of the death penalty.

DAVIS, MICHAEL: "Death, Deterrence, and the Method of Common Sense." *Social Theory and Practice,* vol. 7, Summer 1981, pp. 146–177. Davis argues that common sense is sufficient to establish the claim that death is the most effective deterrent. For other reasons, however, he is unwilling to endorse retention of the death penalty.

GOLDBERG, STEVEN: "On Capital Punishment." *Ethics,* vol. 85, October 1974, pp. 67–74. Goldberg, ultimately sympathetic to retention of the death penalty, focuses on the difficulties involved in the factual question of whether or not the death penalty is a uniquely effective deterrent.

MURPHY, JEFFRIE G.: *Punishment and Rehabilitation,* 2d ed. Belmont, Calif.: Wadsworth, 1985. This anthology provides a set of helpful readings on the philosophical aspects of punishment. Some explicit attention is paid to capital punishment.

NATHANSON, STEPHEN: *An Eye for an Eye? The Morality of Punishing by Death.* Totawa, N.J.: Rowman & Littlefield, 1987. Nathanson touches on all aspects of the death penalty controversy and constructs an overall case for abolition.

REIMAN, JEFFREY H.: "Justice, Civilization, and the Death Penalty: Answering van den Haag." *Philosophy and Public Affairs,* vol. 14, Spring 1985, pp. 115–148. Reiman argues that "abolition of the death penalty is part of the civilizing mission of modern states." In his view, although it is just to execute murderers, it is not unjust to forgo execution and punish murderers with long-term imprisonment. Counterarguments by Ernest van den Haag can be found in the same issue—"Refuting Reiman and Nathanson" (pp. 165–176).

VAN DEN HAAG, ERNEST, and JOHN P. CONRAD: *The Death Penalty: A Debate.* New York: Plenum, 1983. Van den Haag (a retentionist) and Conrad (an abolitionist) touch on all aspects of the death penalty controversy as they develop their respective cases and critically respond to each other's arguments.

WALLER, BRUCE N.: "From Hemlock to Lethal Injection: The Case for Self-Execution." *International Journal of Applied Philosophy,* vol. 4, Fall 1989, pp. 53–58. Waller argues that prisoners condemned to death should be allowed the alternative of killing themselves. He considers self-execution desirable because (1) it would cause less suffering and (2) it would show greater respect for the humanity of the prisoner.

CHAPTER 5

Sexual Morality

Individuals are sometimes described as having "loose morals" when their *sexual* behavior is out of line with what is considered morally appropriate. But assessments of morally appropriate sexual behavior vary enormously. Conventionalists consider sex morally appropriate only within the bounds of marriage. Some conventionalists even insist that there are substantial moral restrictions on sex *within marriage;* they are committed to the principle that sexual activity may not take place in a way that cuts off the possibility of procreation. More liberal thinkers espouse various degrees of permissiveness. Some would allow a full and open promiscuity; some would not. Some would allow homosexual behavior; some would not. In this chapter, various views on the topic of sexual morality are investigated.

CONVENTIONAL SEXUAL MORALITY

According to conventional sexual morality, sex is morally legitimate only within the bounds of marriage; nonmarital sex is immoral. The category of *nonmarital sex* is applicable to any sexual relation other than that between marriage partners. Thus it includes sexual relations between single people as well as adulterous sexual relations. Both religious and nonreligious arguments are advanced in support of conventional sexual morality, but our concern here is with the nonreligious arguments that are advanced in its defense.

One common defense of the traditional convention that sex is permissible only within the bounds of marriage is based on considerations of *social utility*. It takes the following form: A stable family life is absolutely essential for the proper raising of children and the consequent welfare of society as a whole. But the limitation of sex to marriage is a necessary condition of forming and maintaining stable family units. The availability of sex within marriage will reinforce the loving relationship between husband and wife, the *exclusive* availability of sex within marriage will lead most people to get married and to stay married, and the unavailability of extramarital sex will keep the marriage strong. Therefore, the convention that sex is permissible only within the bounds of marriage is solidly based on considerations of social utility.

This argument is attacked in many ways. Sometimes it is argued that stable family units are not really so essential. More commonly, it is argued that the availability of nonmarital sex does not really undercut family life. Whereas adultery might very well undermine a marital relationship, it is argued, premarital sex often prepares one for marriage. At any rate, it is pointed out, people continue to marry even after they have had somewhat free access to sexual relations.

Another prominent defense of conventional sexual morality is intimately bound up with *natural law theory,* an approach to ethics that is historically associated with the medieval philosopher and theologian Thomas Aquinas (1225–1274). The fundamental principle of natural law theory may be expressed in rather rough form as follows: Actions are morally appropriate insofar as they accord with our nature and end as human beings and morally inappropriate insofar as they fail to accord with our nature and end as human beings. With regard to sexual morality, Aquinas argues as follows:

> . . . the emission of semen ought to be so ordered that it will result in both the production of the proper offspring and in the upbringing of this offspring.
>
> It is evident from this that every emission of semen, in such a way that generation cannot follow, is contrary to the good for man. And if this be done deliberately, it must be a sin. Now, I am speaking of a way from which, *in itself,* generation could not result; such would be any emission of semen apart from the natural union of male and female. For which reason, sins of this type are called *contrary to nature.* . . .
>
> Likewise, it must also be contrary to the good for man if the semen be emitted under conditions such that generation could result but the proper upbringing would be prevented. . . .
>
> Now, it is abundantly evident that the female in the human species is not at all able to take care of the upbringing of offspring by herself, since the needs of human life demand many things which cannot be provided by one person alone. Therefore, it is appropriate to human nature that a man remain together with a woman after the generative act, and not leave her immediately to have such relations with another woman, as is the practice with fornicators. . . .
>
> Now, we call this society *matrimony.* Therefore, matrimony is natural for man, and promiscuous performance of the sexual act, outside matrimony, is contrary to man's good. For this reason, it must be a sin.[1]

According to Aquinas, procreation is the natural purpose or end of sexual activity. Accordingly, sexual activity is morally legitimate only when it accords with this fundamental aspect of human nature. Since sex is for the purpose of procreation, and since the proper upbringing of children can occur only within the framework of marriage, nonmarital sex violates the natural law; it is thereby immoral. In this way, then, Aquinas constructs a defense of conventional sexual morality.

Notice, however, that Aquinas is also committed to substantial restrictions on marital sex itself. Since procreation is the natural purpose or end of sexual activity, he contends, any sexual act that cuts off the possibility of procreation is "contrary to nature." It follows that such practices as oral intercourse, anal intercourse, "mutual masturbation," and the use of artificial birth control are illicit, even within marriage.

---

[1] Thomas Aquinas, *On the Truth of the Catholic Faith,* Book Three, "Providence," Part II, trans. Vernon J. Bourke (New York: Doubleday, 1956).

Of course, Aquinas also condemns masturbation and homosexual intercourse as "contrary to nature."

One common criticism of Aquinas's point of view on sexual morality centers on his insistence that sexual activity must not frustrate its natural purpose—procreation. Granted, it is said, procreation is in a biological sense the "natural" purpose of sex. Still, the argument goes, it is not clear that sexual activity cannot legitimately serve other important human purposes. Why cannot sex legitimately function as a means for the expression of love? Why, for that matter, cannot sex legitimately function simply as a source of intense (recreational) pleasure?

In contemporary times, Aquinas's point of view on sexual morality is continually reaffirmed in the formal teaching of the Roman Catholic Church. In the 1968 papal encyclical *Humanae Vitae,* artificial birth control is once again identified as immoral, a violation of the natural law: "Each and every marriage act must remain open to the transmission of life."[2] In a more recent Vatican document, reprinted in this chapter, the natural law framework of Aquinas is equally apparent: "The deliberate use of the sexual faculties outside of normal conjugal relations essentially contradicts its finality." "Homosexual acts are disordered by their very nature." "Masturbation is an intrinsically and seriously disordered act."

In one of this chapter's readings, Vincent C. Punzo provides a somewhat distinctive defense of conventional sexual morality. At the core of his argument is the idea of existential integrity. In Punzo's view, existential integrity is compromised whenever sexual intercourse is detached from the framework of commitment that is constitutive of marriage.

THE LIBERAL VIEW

In vivid contrast to conventional sexual morality is an approach that will be referred to here as the *liberal* view of sexual morality. Liberals reject as unfounded the conventionalist claim that nonmarital sex is immoral. They also reject the related claim (made by some conventionalists) that sex is immoral if it cuts off the possibility of procreation. Nor are liberals willing to accept the claim (defended by some nonconventionalists) that *sex without love* is immoral. Yet liberals insist that there are important moral restrictions on sexual activity. In the liberal view, sexual activity (like any other type of human activity) is morally objectionable to the extent that it is incompatible with a justified moral rule or principle. Accordingly, it is argued, the way to construct a defensible account of sexual morality is simply to work out the implications of relevant moral rules or principles in the area of sexual behavior.

In this vein, since it is widely acknowledged that the infliction of personal harm is morally objectionable, *some* sexual activity may be identified as immoral simply because it involves one person inflicting harm on another. For example, the seduction of a minor who does not even know "what it's all about" is morally objectionable on the grounds that the minor will almost inevitably be psychologically harmed. Rape,

---

[2]*Humanae Vitae* (1968), section 11. This encyclical is widely reprinted. See, for example, Robert Baker and Frederick Elliston, eds., *Philosophy and Sex* (Buffalo, N.Y.: Prometheus, 1975), pp. 131–149.

of course, is a moral outrage, in no small part because it typically involves the infliction of both physical and psychological harm. Its immorality, however, can also be
established by reference to another widely acknowledged (when properly understood) moral principle, roughly the principle that it is wrong for one person to "use"
another person.

Since the domain of sexual interaction seems to offer ample opportunity for "using" another person, the concept of using is worthy of special attention in this context. In one of this chapter's selections, Thomas A. Mappes attempts to clarify what
he calls the morally significant sense of "using another person." His ultimate aim is
to determine the conditions under which someone would be guilty of *sexually* using
another person, and the essence of his view is that the sexual using of another person
takes place whenever there is a violation of the requirement of *voluntary informed
consent* (to sexual interaction). Mappes especially emphasizes both *deception* and
coercion as mechanisms for the sexual using of another person.

Is nonmarital sex immoral? Is sex that cuts off the possibility of procreation immoral? Is sex without love immoral? According to the liberal, *no* sexual activity is
immoral unless some well-established moral rule or principle is transgressed. Does
one's sexual activity involve the infliction of harm on another? Does it involve the
using of another? Does it involve promise breaking, another commonly recognized
ground of moral condemnation? If the answer to such questions is no, the liberal
maintains, then the sexual activity in question is perfectly acceptable from a moral
point of view.

According to the liberal, then, we must conclude that nonmarital sex is, in many
cases, morally acceptable. Sexual partners may share some degree of mutual affection or love, or they may merely share a mutual desire to attain sexual satisfaction.
The sexual interaction may be heterosexual or homosexual. Or there may be no *inter*action at all; the sexual activity may be masturbation. But what about the morality
of adultery, an especially noteworthy type of nonmarital sex? As the marriage bond
is usually understood, the liberal might respond, there is present in cases of adultery
a distinctive ground of moral condemnation. To the extent that marriage involves a
pledge of sexual exclusivity, as is typically the case, then adulterous behavior seems
to involve a serious breaking of trust. However, the liberal would insist, if marriage
partners have entered upon a so-called open marriage, with no pledge of sexual exclusivity, then this special ground of moral condemnation evaporates.

If the liberal approach to sexual morality is correct, it is nevertheless important to
recognize that some particular sexual involvement could be morally acceptable and
yet unwise or imprudent, that is, not in a person's best long-term interests. An individual, for example, might very well decide to steer clear of casual sex, not because
it is immoral but because of a conviction (perhaps based on past experience) that it is
not productive of personal happiness.

THE SEX WITH LOVE APPROACH

There is one additional point of view on sexual morality that is sufficiently common
to warrant explicit recognition. One may, after all, find conventional sexual morality

unwarranted and yet be inclined to stop short of granting moral approval to the "promiscuity" that is found morally acceptable on the liberal view. This intermediate point of view can be identified as the *sex with love* approach. Defenders of this approach typically insist that sex without love reduces a humanly significant activity to a merely mechanical performance, which in turn leads to the disintegration (fragmentation) of the human personality. They differ among themselves, however, as to whether the love necessary to warrant a sexual relationship must be an *exclusive* love or whether it may be a *nonexclusive* love. Those who argue that it must be exclusive nevertheless grant that *successive* sexual liaisons are not objectionable. Those who argue that the love may be nonexclusive necessarily presume that a person is capable of simultaneously loving several persons. On their view, even *simultaneous* love affairs are not objectionable. Whether exclusive or nonexclusive love is taken to be the relevant standard, proponents of the sex with love approach usually argue that their view allows for sexual freedom in a way that avoids the alleged dehumanizing effects of mere promiscuity. Where sex and love remain united, it is argued, there is no danger of dehumanization and psychological disintegration. The liberal might respond: If psychological disintegration is a justifiable fear, which can be doubted, such a consideration shows not that sex without love is immoral but only that it is imprudent.

HOMOSEXUALITY, MORALITY, AND THE LAW

Is homosexual behavior immoral? While the advocate of conventional sexual morality vigorously condemns it, the liberal typically maintains that homosexual behavior is no more immoral in itself than heterosexual behavior. There are, however, a substantial number of people who reject conventional sexual morality but nevertheless remain morally opposed to homosexual behavior. Are such people correct in thinking that homosexual behavior is morally problematic in a way that heterosexual behavior is not? A homosexual, in the most generic sense, is a person (male or female) whose dominant sexual preference is for a person of the same sex. In common parlance, however, the term "homosexual" is often taken to designate a male, whereas the term "lesbian" is used to designate a female. It is apparently true that male homosexual behavior occasions a higher degree of societal indignation than female homosexual behavior, but it is implausible to believe that there is any morally relevant difference between the two.

There is no lack of invective against the homosexual and against homosexual behavior. For example, the following comments are often made: (1) "Homosexual behavior is repulsive and highly offensive." (2) "Homosexuality as a way of life is totally given over to promiscuity and is little susceptible of enduring human relationships." (3) "Homosexuals make the streets unsafe for our children." (4) "Homosexuality is a perversion, a sin against nature." (5) "If homosexual behavior is tolerated, the stability of family life will be threatened and the social fabric will be undermined." It is important to assess the extent to which such claims support the view that homosexual behavior is morally objectionable. With regard to (1), it may in fact be true that many people find homosexual behavior repulsive and offensive, but it is also true that many people find eating liver repulsive and offensive, and no one thinks that this fact establishes the conclusion that eating liver is morally objectionable. With regard to (2), it may be true that homosexuality is typically a promiscuous way of life, but it can be argued that society's attitude toward homosexuality is responsible for making homosexual relationships extremely difficult to sustain. With regard to (3), it may be true that *some* homosexuals prey upon children, and surely this is morally reprehensible, but still we find ourselves left with the more typical case in which homosexual relations take place between consenting adults.

Although the "unnaturalness argument" (4) is sometimes employed against such "perversions" as masturbation and (heterosexual) oral-genital sex practices, it is especially prominent as an argument against homosexual behavior. In one of this chapter's selections, Richard D. Mohr critically analyzes and rejects the contention that homosexual behavior is immoral because it is unnatural. He also provides a response to argument (5). Whereas proponents of (5) insist that homosexual behavior is a threat to social well-being, and thus cannot be tolerated, Mohr argues that societal acceptance of homosexuals and homosexual behavior would have beneficial rather than detrimental social consequences.

One of the central goals of the "gay liberation" movement is to achieve the decriminalization of homosexual behavior *between consenting adults in private*. Presently, however, homosexual behavior (even between consenting adults in private) remains a criminal offense in many states. These states have statutes that are often referred to as sodomy statutes. In the law, "sodomy" is roughly synonymous with "unnatural sex practices" or "crimes against nature." Accordingly, sodomy statutes typically prohibit both oral and anal intercourse, as well as other "crimes against nature," such as bestiality, i.e., sexual intercourse with animals. Though sodomy statutes apply to heterosexuals as well as homosexuals, they are usually enforced—if they are enforced at all—only against (male) homosexuals. The constitutionality of sodomy statutes is at issue in a Supreme Court case presented in this chapter, *Bowers v. Hardwick* (1986). In addition to constitutional questions, sodomy statutes also raise important questions about the wisdom and the ethical justification of laws that criminalize sexual conduct *between consenting adults in private*. For one thing, such laws seem, at least in part, to be designed to "enforce" conventional sexual morality. This is a dimension, however, that is more fully discussed in conjunction with the topic of pornography in Chapter 6.

Thomas A. Mappes

Vatican Declaration on Some Questions of Sexual Ethics

The title of this document is sometimes translated from the Latin as "Declaration on Certain Questions Concerning Sexual Ethics." The document itself was issued by the Sacred Congregation for the Doctrine of the Faith. It was approved by Pope Paul VI and first released for publication on January 15, 1976.

In this declaration, traditional Roman Catholic teaching is explicitly reaffirmed with regard to certain matters of sexual ethics. Both religious arguments (appeals to revealed truth) and philosophical arguments are advanced. (The philosophical arguments are developed within the framework of a natural law theory of ethics.) According to the document, there is an objective and unchanging moral order. Moral principles (including the principles of sexual morality) "have their origin in human nature itself." Accordingly, these principles may be known in two complementary ways: (1) through reason alone, via rational reflection on human nature, or (2) through divine revelation. After briefly explicating the natural law foundation of the traditional view that exercise of the sexual function is appropriate only within the marriage relationship, the document proceeds to reaffirm the immorality of premarital sex, homosexual behavior, and masturbation.

INTRODUCTION

Importance of Sexuality

1 The human person, according to the scientific disciplines of our day, is so deeply influenced by his sexuality that this latter must be regarded as one of the basic factors shaping human life. The person's sex is the source of the biological, psychological and spiritual characteristics which make the person male or female, and thus are extremely important and influential in the maturation and socialization of the individual. It is easy to understand, therefore, why matters pertaining to sex are frequently and openly discussed in books, periodicals, newspapers and other communications media.

Meanwhile, moral corruption is on the increase. One of the most serious signs of this is the boundless exaltation of sex. In addition, with the help of the mass media and the various forms of entertainment, sex has even invaded the field of education and infected the public mind.

In this situation, some educators, teachers and moralists have been able to contribute to a better understanding and vital integration of the special values and qualities proper to each sex. Others, however, have defended views and ways of acting which are in conflict with the true moral requirements of man, and have even opened the door to a licentious hedonism.

The result is that, within a few years' time, teachings, moral norms and habits of life hitherto faithfully preserved have been called into doubt, even by Christians. Many today are asking what they are to regard as true when so many current views are at odds with what they learned from the Church.

Occasion for This Declaration

2 In the face of this intellectual confusion and moral corruption the Church cannot stand by and do nothing. The issue here is too important in the life both of the individual and of contemporary society.[1]

Bishops see each day the ever increasing difficulties of the faithful in acquiring sound moral teaching, especially in sexual matters, and of pastors in effectively explaining that teaching. The bishops know it is their pastoral duty to come to the aid of the faithful in such a serious matter. Indeed, some outstanding documents have been published on the subject by some bishops and some episcopal conferences. But, since erroneous views and the deviations they produce continue to be broadcast everywhere, the Sacred Congregation for the Doctrine of the Faith in accordance with its role in the universal Church[2] and by mandate of the Supreme Pontiff, has thought it necessary to issue this Declaration.

I GENERAL CONSIDERATIONS

The Sources of Moral Knowledge

3 The men of our day are increasingly persuaded that their dignity and calling as human beings requires them to use their minds to discover the values and powers inherent in their nature, to develop these without ceasing and to translate them into action, so that they may make daily greater progress.

When it comes to judgments on moral matters, however, man may not proceed simply as he thinks fit. "Deep within, man detects the law of conscience—a law which is not self-imposed but which holds him to obedience. . . . For man has in his heart a law written by God. To obey it is the very dignity of man; according to it he will be judged."[3]

To us Christians, moreover, God has revealed his plan of salvation and has given us Christ, the Savior and sanctifier, as the supreme and immutable norm of life through his teaching and example. Christ himself has said: "I am the light of the world. No follower of mine shall ever walk in darkness; no, he shall possess the light of life."[4]

The authentic dignity of man cannot be promoted, therefore, except through adherence to the order which is essential to his nature. There is no denying, of course, that in the history of civilization many of the concrete conditions and relationships of human life have changed and will change again in the future but every moral evolution and every manner of life must respect the limits set by the immutable principles which are grounded in the constitutive elements and essential relations proper to the human person. These elements and relations are not subject to historical contingency.

The basic principles in question can be grasped by man's reason. They are contained in "the divine law—eternal, objective and universal—whereby God orders, directs and governs the entire universe and all the ways of the human community by a plan conceived in wisdom and love. God has made man a participant in this law, with the result that, under the gentle disposition of divine Providence, he can come to perceive ever more fully the truth that is unchanging."[5] This divine law is something we can know.

The Principles of Morality Are Perennial

4 Wrongly, therefore, do many today deny that either human nature or revealed law furnishes any absolute and changeless norm for particular actions except the general law of love and respect for human dignity. To justify this position, they argue that both the so-called norms of the natural law and the precepts of Sacred Scripture are simply products of a particular human culture and its expressions at a certain point in history.

But divine revelation and, in its own order, natural human wisdom show us genuine exigencies of human nature and, as a direct and necessary consequence, immutable laws which are grounded in the constitutive elements of human nature and show themselves the same in all rational beings.

Furthermore, the Church was established by Christ to be "the pillar and bulwark of truth."[6] With the help of the Holy Spirit she keeps a sleepless watch over the truths of morality and transmits them without falsification. She provides the authentic interpretation not only of the revealed positive law but also of "those principles of the moral order which have their origin in human nature itself"[7] and which relate to man's full development and sanctification. Throughout her history the Church has constantly maintained that certain precepts of the natural law bind immutably and without qualification, and that the violation of them contradicts the spirit and teaching of the Gospel.

The Fundamental Principles of Sexual Morality

5 Since sexual morality has to do with values which are basic to human and Christian life, the general doctrine we have been presenting applies to it. In this area there are principles and norms which the Church has always unhesitatingly transmitted as part of her teaching, however opposed they might be to the mentality and ways of the world. These principles and norms have their origin, not in a particular culture, but in knowledge of the divine law and human nature. Consequently, it is impossible for them to lose their binding force or to be called into doubt on the grounds of cultural change.

These principles guided Vatican Council II when it provided advice and directives for the establishment of the kind of social life in which the equal dignity of man and woman will be respected, even while the differences between them also are preserved.[8]

In speaking of the sexual nature of the human being and of the human generative powers, the Council observes that these are "remarkably superior to those found in lower grades of life."[9] Then it deals in detail with the principles and norms which apply to human sexuality in the married state and are based on the finality of the function proper to marriage.

In this context the Council asserts that the moral goodness of the actions proper to married life, when ordered as man's true dignity requires, "does not depend only on a sincere intention and the evaluating of motives, but must be judged by objective standards. These are drawn from the nature of the human person and of his acts, and have regard for the whole meaning of mutual self-giving and human procreation in the context of true love."[10]

These last words are a brief summation of the Council's teaching (previously set forth at length in the same document[11]) on the finality of the sexual act and on the chief norm governing its morality. It is respect for this finality which guarantees the moral goodness of the act.

The same principle, which the Church derives from divine revelation and from her authentic interpretation of the natural law, is also the source of her traditional teaching that the exercise of the sexual function has its true meaning and is morally good only in legitimate marriage.[12]

Limits of This Declaration

6 It is not the intention of this declaration to treat all abuses of the sexual powers nor to deal with all that is involved in the practice of chastity but rather to recall the Church's norms on certain specific points, since there is a crying need of opposing certain serious errors and deviant forms of behavior.

II SPECIFIC APPLICATIONS

Premarital Relations

7 Many individuals at the present time are claiming the right to sexual union before marriage, at least when there is a firm intention of marrying and when a love which both partners think of as already conjugal demands this further step which seems to them connatural. They consider this further step justified especially when external circumstances prevent the formal entry into marriage or when intimate union seems necessary if love is to be kept alive.

This view is opposed to the Christian teaching that any human genital act whatsoever may be placed only within the framework of marriage. For, however firm the intention of those who pledge themselves to each other in such premature unions, these unions cannot guarantee the sincerity and fidelity of the relationship between man and woman, and, above all, cannot protect the relationship against the changeableness of desire and determination.

Yet, Christ the Lord willed that the union be a stable one and he restored it to its original condition as founded in the difference between the sexes. "Have you not read that at the beginning the Creator made them male and female and declared, 'For this reason a man shall leave his father and mother and cling to his wife and the two shall become as one'? Thus they are no longer two but one flesh. Therefore, let no man separate what God has joined."[13]

St. Paul is even more explicit when he teaches that if unmarried people or widows cannot be continent, they have no alternative but to enter into a stable marital union: "It is better to marry than to be on fire."[14] For, through marriage the love of the spouses is taken up into the irrevocable love of Christ for his Church,[15] whereas unchaste bodily union[16] defiles the temple of the Holy Spirit which the Christian has become. Fleshly union is illicit, therefore, unless a permanent community of life has been established between man and woman.

Such has always been the Church's understanding of and teaching on the exercise of the sexual function.[17] She finds, moreover, that natural human wisdom and the lessons of history are in profound agreement with her.

Experience teaches that if sexual union is truly to satisfy the requirements of its own finality and of human dignity, love must be safeguarded by the stability marriage gives. These requirements necessitate a contract which is sanctioned and protected by society; the contract gives rise to a new state of life and is of exceptional importance for the exclusive union of man and woman as well as for the good of their family and the whole of human society. Premarital relations, on the other hand, most often exclude any prospect of children. Such love claims in vain to be conjugal since it cannot, as it certainly should, grow into a maternal and paternal love; or, if the pair do become parents, it will be to the detriment of the children, who are deprived of a stable environment in which they can grow up in a proper fashion and find the way and means of entering into the larger society of men.

Therefore, the consent of those entering into marriage must be externally manifested, and this in such a way as to render it binding in the eyes of society. The faithful, for their part, must follow the laws of the Church in declaring their marital consent; it is this consent that makes their marriage a sacrament of Christ.

Homosexuality

8 Contrary to the perennial teaching of the Church and the moral sense of the Christian people, some individuals today have, on psychological grounds, begun to judge indulgently or even simply to excuse homosexual relations for certain people.

They make a distinction which has indeed some foundation: between homosexuals whose bent derives from improper education or a failure of sexual maturation or habit or bad example or some similar cause and is only temporary or at least is not incurable; and homosexuals who are permanently such because of some innate drive or a pathological condition which is considered incurable.

The propensity of those in the latter class is—it is argued—so natural that it should be regarded as justifying homosexual relations within a sincere and loving communion of life which is comparable to marriage inasmuch as those involved in it deem it impossible for them to live a solitary life.

Objective Evil of Such Acts

As far as pastoral care is concerned, such homosexuals are certainly to be treated with understanding and encouraged to hope that they can some day overcome their difficulties and their inability to fit into society in a normal fashion. Prudence, too, must be exercised in judging their guilt. However, no pastoral approach may be taken which would consider these individuals morally justified on the grounds that such acts are in accordance with their nature. For, according to the objective moral order, homosexual relations are acts deprived of the essential ordination they ought to have.

In Sacred Scripture such acts are condemned as serious deviations and are even considered to be the lamentable effect of rejecting God.[18] This judgment on the part of the divinely inspired Scriptures does not justify us in saying that all who suffer from this anomaly are guilty of personal sin but it does show that homosexual acts are disordered by their very nature and can never be approved.

Masturbation

9 Frequently today we find doubt or open rejection of the traditional Catholic teaching that masturbation is a serious moral disorder. Psychology and sociology (it is claimed) show that masturbation, especially in adolescents, is a normal phase in the process of sexual maturation and is, therefore, not gravely sinful unless the individual deliberately cultivates a solitary pleasure that is turned in upon itself ("ipsation"). In this last case, the act would be radically opposed to that loving communion between persons of different sexes which (according to some) is the principal goal to be sought in the use of the sexual powers.

This opinion is contrary to the teaching and pastoral practice of the Catholic Church. Whatever be the validity of certain arguments of a biological and philosophical kind which theologians sometimes use, both the magisterium of the Church (following a constant tradition) and the moral sense of the faithful have unhesitatingly asserted that masturbation is an intrinsically and seriously disordered act.[19] The chief reason for this stand is that, whatever the motive, the deliberate use of the sexual faculty outside of normal conjugal relations essentially contradicts its finality. In such an act there is lacking the sexual relationship which the moral order requires, the kind of relationship in which "the whole meaning of mutual self-giving and human procreation" is made concretely real "in the context of true love."[20] Only within such a relationship may the sexual powers be deliberately exercised.

Even if it cannot be established that Sacred Scripture condemns this sin under a specific name, the Church's tradition rightly understands it to be condemned in the New Testament when the latter speaks of "uncleanness" or "unchasteness" or the other vices contrary to chastity and continence.

Sociological research can show the relative frequency of this disorder according to places, types of people and various circumstances which may be taken into account. It thus provides an array of facts. But facts provide no norm for judging the morality of human acts.[21] The frequency of the act here in question is connected with innate human weakness deriving from original sin, but also with the loss of the sense of God, with the moral corruption fostered by the commercialization of vice, with the unbridled license to be found in so many books and forms of public entertainment and with the forgetfulness of modesty, which is the safeguard of chastity.

In dealing with masturbation, modern psychology provides a number of valid and useful insights which enable us to judge more equitably of moral responsibility. They can also help us understand how adolescent immaturity (sometimes prolonged beyond the adolescent years) or a lack of psychological balance or habits can affect behavior, since they may make an action less deliberate and not always a subjectively serious sin. But the lack of serious responsibility should not be generally presumed; if it is, there is simply a failure to recognize man's ability to act in a moral way.

In the pastoral ministry, in order to reach a balanced judgment in individual cases account must be taken of the overall habitual manner in which the person acts, not only in regard to charity and justice, but also in regard to the care with which he observes the precept of chastity in particular. Special heed must be paid to whether he uses the necessary natural and supernatural helps which Christian asceticism recommends, in the light of long experience, for mastering the passions and attaining virtue. . . .

NOTES

1 See Vatican II, *Pastoral Constitution on the Church in the World of Today,* no. 47: *Acta Apostolicae Sedis* 58 (1966) 1067 [*The Pope Speaks* XI, 289–290].

2 See the Apostolic Constitution *Regimini Ecclesiae universae* (August 15, 1967), no. 29: *AAS* 59 (1967) 897 [*TPS* XII, 401–402].

3 *Pastoral Constitution on the Church in the World of Today,* no. 16: *AAS* 58 (1966) 1037 [*TPS* XI, 268].

4 *Jn* 8, 12.

5 *Declaration on Religious Freedom,* no. 3: *AAS* 58 (1966) 931 [*TPS* XI, 86].

6 *1 TM* 3, 15.

7 *Declaration on Religious Freedom,* no. 14: *AAS* 58 (1966) 940 [*TPS* XI, 93]. See also Pius XI, Encyclical *Casti Connubii* (December 31, 1930): *AAS* 22 (1930) 579–580; Pius XII, Address of November 2, 1954 *AAS* 46 (1954) 671–672 [*TPS* 1, 380–381]; John XXIII, Encyclical *Mater et Magistra* (May 25, 1961), no. 239: *AAS* 53 (1961) 457 [*TPS* VII, 388]; Paul VI, Encyclical *Humanae Vitae* (July 25, 1968), no. 4: *AAS* 60 (1968) 483 [*TPS* XIII, 331–332].

8 See Vatican II, *Declaration on Christian Education,* nos. 1 and 8: *AAS* 58 (1966) 729–730, 734–736 [*TPS* XI, 201–202, 206–207]; *Pastoral Constitution on the Church in the World of Today,* nos. 29, 60, 67: *AAS* 58 (1966) 1048–1049, 1080–1081, 1088–1089 [*TPS* XI, 276–277, 299–300, 304–305].

9 *Pastoral Constitution on the Church in the World of Today,* no. 51: *AAS* 58 (1966) 1072 [*TPS* XI, 293].

10 *Loc. cit.;* see also no. 49: *AAS* 58 (1966) 1069–1070 [*TPS* XI, 291–292].

11 See *Pastoral Constitution on the Church in the World of Today,* nos. 49–50: *AAS* 58 (1966) 1069–1072 [*TPS* XI, 291–293].

12 The present Declaration does not review all the moral norms for the use of sex, since they have already been set forth in the encyclicals *Casti Connubii* and *Humanae Vitae*.

13 *Mt* 19, 4–6.

14 *1 Cor* 7, 9.

15 See *Eph* 5, 25–32.

16 Extramarital intercourse is expressly condemned in *1 Cor* 5, 1; 6, 9; 7, 2; 10, 8; *Eph* 5, 5–7; *1 Tm* 1, 10; *Heb* 13, 4; there are explicit arguments given in *1 Cor* 6, 12–20.

17 See Innocent IV, Letter *Sub Catholicae professione* (March 6, 1254) (*DS* 835); Pius II, Letter *Cum sicut accepimus* (November 14, 1459) (*DS* 1367); Decrees of the Holy Office on September 24, 1665 (*DS* 2045) and March 2, 1679 (*DS* 2148); Pius XI, Encyclical *Casti Connubii* (December 31, 1930): *AAS* 22 (1930) 538–539.

18 *Rom* 1:24–27: "In consequence, God delivered them up in their lusts to unclean practices; they engaged in the mutual degradation of their bodies, these men who exchanged the truth of God for a lie and worshipped and served the creature rather than the Creator—blessed be he forever, amen! God therefore delivered them to disgraceful passions. Their women exchanged natural intercourse for unnatural, and the men gave up natural intercourse with women and burned with lust for one another. Men did shameful things with men, and thus received in their own persons the penalty for their perversity." See also what St. Paul says of sodomy in *1 Cor* 6, 9; *1 Tm* 1, 10.

19 See Leo IX, Letter *Ad splendidum nitentes* (1054) (*DS* 687–688); Decree of the Holy Office on March 2, 1679 (*DS* 2149); Pius XII, Addresses of October 8, 1953: *AAS* 45 (1953) 677–678, and May 19, 1956: *AAS* 48 (1956) 472–473.

20 *Pastoral Constitution on the Church in the World of Today,* no. 51: *AAS* 58 (1966) 1072 [*TPS* XI, 293].

21 See Paul VI, Apostolic Exhortation *Quinque iam anni* (December 8, 1970): *AAS* 63 (1971) 102 [*TPS* XV, 329]: "If sociological surveys are useful for better discovering the thought patterns of the people of a particular place, the anxieties and needs of those to whom we proclaim the word of God, and also the oppositions made to it by modern reasoning through the widespread notion that outside science there exists no legitimate form of knowledge, still the conclusions drawn from such surveys could not of themselves constitute a determining criterion of truth."

QUESTIONS

1 Is it plausible to maintain that unchanging moral principles "have their origin in human nature itself"? Is it plausible to maintain this especially with regard to principles of sexual morality?

2 Is masturbation immoral?

Sexual Morality and the Concept of Using Another Person

Thomas A. Mappes

Thomas A. Mappes is professor of philosophy at Frostburg State University, Maryland. He is the author of "What Is Personal Ethics and Should We Be Teaching More of It?" and the co-author of "Is Hume Really a Sceptic about Induction?" He is also coeditor (with Jane S. Zembaty) of *Biomedical Ethics* (3d ed., 1991).

Advocating a liberal approach to sexual morality, Mappes attempts to determine the conditions under which someone would be guilty of *sexually* using another person. On his view, the morally significant sense of "using another person" is best understood in reference to the notion of voluntary informed consent. Accordingly, his central thesis is that one person (A) is guilty of sexually using another person (B) "if and only if A intentionally acts in a way that violates the requirement that B's sexual interaction with A be based on B's voluntary informed consent." Mappes emphasizes the importance of deception and coercion as mechanisms for the sexual using of another person, but he also insists that such using can result from "taking advantage of someone's desperate situation."

The central tenet of *conventional* sexual morality is that nonmarital sex is immoral. A somewhat less restrictive sexual ethic holds that *sex without love* is immoral. If neither of these positions is philosophically defensible, and I would contend that neither is, it does not follow that there are no substantive moral restrictions on human sexual interaction. *Any* human interaction, including sexual interaction, may be judged morally objectionable to the extent that it transgresses a justified moral rule or principle. The way to construct a detailed account of sexual morality, it would seem, is simply to work out the implications of relevant moral rules or principles in the area of human sexual interaction.

As one important step in the direction of such an account, I will attempt to work out the implications of an especially relevant moral principle, the principle that it is wrong for one person to use another person. However ambiguous the expression "using another person" may seem to be, there is a determinate and clearly specifiable sense according to which using another person is morally objectionable. Once this morally significant sense of "using another person" is identified and explicated, the concept of using another person can play an important role in the articulation of a defensible account of sexual morality.

I   THE MORALLY SIGNIFICANT SENSE OF "USING ANOTHER PERSON"

Historically, the concept of using another person is associated with the ethical system of Immanuel Kant. According to a fundamental Kantian principle, it is morally wrong for A to use B *merely as a means* (to achieve A's ends). Kant's principle does not rule out A using B as a means, only A using B *merely* as a means, that is, in a way incompatible with respect for B as a person. In the ordinary course of life, it is surely unavoidable (and morally unproblematic) that each of us in numerous ways uses others as a means to achieve our various ends. A college teacher uses students as a means to achieve his or her livelihood. A college student uses instructors as a means of gaining knowledge and skills. Such human interactions, presumably based on the voluntary participation of the respective parties, are quite compatible with the idea of respect for persons. But respect for persons entails that each of us recognize the rightful authority of other persons (as rational beings) to conduct their individual lives as they see fit. We may legitimately recruit others to participate in the satisfaction of our personal ends, but they are used merely as a means whenever we undermine the voluntary or informed character of their consent to interact with us in some desired way. A coerces B at knife point to hand over $200. A uses B merely as a means. If A had requested of B a gift of $200, leaving B free to determine whether or not to make the gift, A would have proceeded in a manner compatible with respect for B as a person. C deceptively rolls back the odometer of a car and thereby manipulates D's decision to buy the car. C uses D merely as a means.

On the basis of these considerations, I would suggest that the morally significant sense of "using another person" is best understood by reference to the notion of *voluntary informed consent*. More specifically, A immorally uses B if and only if A intentionally acts in a way that violates the requirement that B's involvement with A's ends be based on B's voluntary informed consent. If this account is correct, using another person (in the morally significant sense) can arise in at least two important ways: via *coercion,* which is antithetical to voluntary consent, and via *deception,* which undermines the informed character of voluntary consent.

The notion of voluntary informed consent is very prominent in the literature of biomedical ethics and is systematically related to the much emphasized notion of (patient) autonomy. We find in the famous words of Supreme Court Justice Cardozo a ringing affirmation of patient autonomy. "Every human being of adult years and sound mind has a right to determine what shall be done with his own body." Because respect for individual autonomy is an essential part of respect for persons, if medical professionals (and biomedical researchers) are to interact with their patients (and research subjects) in an acceptable way, they must respect individual autonomy. That is, they must respect the self-determination of the patient/subject, the individual's right to determine what shall be done with his or her body. This means that they must not act in a way that violates the requirement of voluntary informed consent. Medical procedures must not be performed without the consent of competent patients; research on human subjects must not be carried out without the consent of the subjects involved. Moreover, consent must be voluntary; coercion undermines individual autonomy. Consent must also be informed; lying or withholding relevant information undercuts rational decision making and thereby undermines individual autonomy.

To further illuminate the concept of using that has been proposed, I will consider in greater detail the matter of research involving human subjects. In the sphere of researcher-subject interaction, just as in the sphere of human sexual interaction, there is ample opportunity for immorally using another person. If a researcher is engaged in a study that involves human subjects, we may presume that the "end" of the researcher is the successful completion of the study. (The researcher may desire this particular end for any number of reasons: the speculative understanding it will provide, the technology it will make possible, the eventual benefit of humankind, increased status in the scientific community, a raise in pay, etc.) The work, let us presume, strictly requires the use (employment) of human research subjects. The researcher, however, immorally uses other people only if he or she intentionally acts in a way that violates the requirement that the participation of research subjects be based on their voluntary informed consent.

Let us assume that in a particular case participation as a research subject involves some rather significant risks. Accordingly, the researcher finds that potential subjects are reluctant to volunteer. At this point, if an unscrupulous researcher is willing to resort to the immoral using of other people (to achieve his or her own ends), two manifest options are available—deception and coercion. By way of deception, the researcher might choose to lie about the risks involved. For example, potential subjects could be explicitly told that there are no significant risks associated with research participation. On the other hand, the researcher could simply withhold a full disclosure of risks. Whether pumped full of false information or simply deprived of relevant information, the potential subject is intentionally deceived in such a way as to be led to a decision that furthers the researcher's ends. In manipulating the decision making process of the potential subject in this way, the researcher is guilty of immorally using another person.

To explain how an unscrupulous researcher might immorally use another person via coercion, it is helpful to distinguish two basic forms of coercion.[1] "Occurrent" coercion involves the use of physical force. "Dispositional" coercion involves the threat of harm. If I am forcibly thrown out of my office by an intruder, I am the victim of occurrent coercion. If, on the other hand, I leave my office because an intruder has threatened to shoot me if I do not leave, I am the victim of dispositional coercion. The victim of occurrent coercion literally has no choice in what happens. The victim of dispositional coercion, in contrast, does intentionally choose a certain course of action. However, one's choice, in the face of the threat of harm, is less than fully voluntary.

It is perhaps unlikely that even an unscrupulous researcher would resort to any very explicit measure of coercion. Deception, it seems, is less risky. Still, it is well known that Nazi medical experimenters ruthlessly employed coercion. By way of occurrent coercion, the Nazis literally forced great numbers of concentration camp victims to participate in experiments that entailed their own death or dismemberment. And if some concentration camp victims "volunteered" to participate in Nazi research to avoid even more unspeakable horrors, clearly we must consider them victims of dispositional coercion. The Nazi researchers, employing coercion, immorally used other human beings with a vengeance.

II DECEPTION AND SEXUAL MORALITY

To this point, I have been concerned to identify and explicate the morally significant sense of "using another person." On the view proposed, A immorally uses B if and only if A intentionally acts in a way that violates the requirement that B's involvement with A's ends be based on B's voluntary informed consent. I will now apply this account to the area of human sexual interaction and explore its implications. For economy of expression in what follows, "using" (and its cognates) is to be understood as referring only to the morally significant sense.

If we presume a state of affairs in which A desires some form of sexual interaction with B, we can say that this desired form of sexual interaction with B is A's end. Thus A sexually *uses* B if and only if A intentionally acts in a way that violates the requirement that B's sexual interaction with A be based on B's voluntary informed consent. It seems clear then that A may sexually use B in at least two distinctive ways, (1) via coercion and (2) via deception. However, before proceeding to discuss deception and then the more problematic case of coercion, one important point must be made. In emphasizing the centrality of coercion and deception as mechanisms for the sexual using of another person, I have in mind sexual interaction with a fully competent adult partner. We should also want to say, I think, that sexual interaction with a child inescapably involves the sexual using of another person. Even if a child "consents" to sexual interaction, he or she is, strictly speaking, incapable of *informed* consent. It's a matter of being *incompetent* to give consent. Similarly, to the extent that a mentally retarded person is rightly considered incompetent, sexual interaction with such a person amounts to the sexual using of that person, unless someone empowered to give "proxy consent" has done so. (In certain circumstances, sexual involvement might be in the best interests of a mentally retarded person.) We can also visualize the case of an otherwise fully competent adult temporarily disordered by drugs or alcohol. To the extent that such a person is rightly regarded as temporarily incompetent, winning his or her "consent" to sexual interaction could culminate in the sexual using of that person.

There are a host of clear cases in which one person sexually uses another precisely because the former employs deception in a way that undermines the informed character of the latter's consent to sexual interaction. Consider this example. One person, A, has decided, as a matter of personal prudence based on past experience, not to become sexually involved outside the confines of a loving relationship. Another person, B, strongly desires a sexual relationship with A but does not love A. B, aware of A's unwillingness to engage in sex without love, professes love for A, thereby hoping to win A's consent to a sexual relationship. B's ploy is successful; A consents. When the smoke clears and A becomes aware of B's deception, it would be both appropriate and natural for A to complain, "I've been used."

In the same vein, here are some other examples. (1) Mr. A is aware that Ms. B will consent to sexual involvement only on the understanding that in time the two will be married. Mr. A has no intention of marrying Ms. B but says that he will. (2) Ms. C has herpes and is well aware that Mr. D will never consent to sex if he knows of her condition. When asked by Mr. D, Ms. C denies that she has herpes. (3). Mr. E knows that Ms. F will not consent to sexual intercourse in the absence of responsible birth control measures. Mr. E tells Ms. F that he has had a vasectomy, which is not the case. (4) Ms. G knows that Mr. H. would not consent to sexual involvement with a married woman. Ms. G is married but tells Mr. H that she is single. (5) Ms. I is well aware that Ms. J is interested in a stable lesbian relationship and will not consent to become sexually involved with someone who is bisexual. Ms. I tells Ms. J that she is exclusively homosexual, whereas the truth is that she is bisexual.

If one person's consent to sex is predicated on false beliefs that have been intentionally and deceptively inculcated by one's sexual partner in an effort to win the former's consent, the resulting sexual interaction involves one person sexually using another. In each of the above cases, one person explicitly *lies* to another. False information is intentionally conveyed to win consent to sexual interaction, and the end result is the sexual using of another person.

As noted earlier, however, lying is not the only form of deception. Under certain circumstances, the simple withholding of information can be considered a form of deception. Accordingly, it is possible to sexually use another person not only by (deceptively) lying about relevant facts but also by (deceptively) not disclosing relevant facts. If A has good reason to believe that B would refuse to consent to sexual interaction should B become aware of certain factual information, and if A withholds disclosure of this information in order to enhance the possibility of gaining B's consent, then, if B does consent, A sexually uses B via deception. One example will suffice. Suppose that Mr. A meets Ms. B in a singles bar. Mr. A realizes immediately that Ms. B is the sister of Ms. C, a woman that Mr. A has been sexually involved with for a long time. Mr. A, knowing that it is very unlikely that Ms. B will consent to sexual interaction if she becomes aware of Mr. A's involvement with her sister, decides not to disclose this information. If Ms. B eventually consents to sexual interaction, since her consent is the product of Mr. A's deception, it is rightly thought that she has been sexually used by him.

III COERCION AND SEXUAL MORALITY

We have considered the case of deception. The present task is to consider the more difficult case of coercion. Whereas deception functions to undermine the *informed* character of voluntary consent (to sexual interaction), coercion either obliterates consent entirely (the case of occurrent coercion) or undermines the voluntariness of consent (the case of dispositional coercion).

Forcible rape is the most conspicuous, and most brutal, way of sexually using another person via coercion.[2] Forcible rape may involve either occurrent coercion or dispositional coercion. A man who rapes a woman by the employment of sheer physical force, by simply overpowering her, employs occurrent coercion. There is literally no sexual *interaction* in such a case; only the rapist performs an action. In no sense does the woman consent to or participate in sexual activity. She has no choice in what takes place, or rather, physical force results in her choice being simply beside the point. The employment of occurrent coercion for the purpose of rape "objectifies" the victim in the strongest sense of that term. She is treated like a physical object. One does not interact with physical objects; one acts upon them. In a perfectly ordinary (not the morally significant) sense of the term, we "use" physical objects. But when the victim of rape is treated as if she were a physical object, there we have one of the most vivid examples of the immoral using of another person.

Frequently, forcible rape involves not occurrent coercion (or not *only* occurrent coercion) but dispositional coercion.[3] In dispositional coercion, the relevant factor is not physical force but the threat of harm. The rapist threatens his victim with immediate and serious bodily harm. For example, a man threatens to kill or beat a woman if she resists his sexual demands. She "consents," that is, she submits to his demands. He may demand only passive participation (simply not struggling against him) or he may demand some measure of active participation. Rape that employs dispositional coercion is surely just as wrong as rape that employs occurrent coercion, but there is a notable difference in the mechanism by which the rapist uses his victim in the two cases. With occurrent coercion, the victim's consent is entirely bypassed. With dispositional coercion, the victim's consent is not bypassed. It is coerced. Dispositional coercion undermines the *voluntariness* of consent. The rapist, by employing the threat of immediate and serious bodily harm, may succeed in bending the victim's will. He may gain the victim's "consent." But he uses another person precisely because consent is coerced.

The relevance of occurrent coercion is limited to the case of forcible rape. Dispositional coercion, a notion that also plays an indispensable role in an overall account of forcible rape, now becomes our central concern. Although the threat of immediate and serious bodily harm stands out as the most brutal way of coercing consent to sexual interaction, we must not neglect the employment of other kinds of threats to this same end. There are numerous ways in which one person can effectively harm, and thus effectively threaten, another. Accordingly, for example, consent to sexual interaction might be coerced by threatening to damage someone's reputation. If a person consents to sexual interaction to avoid a threatened harm, then that person has been sexually used (via dispositional coercion). In the face of a threat, of course, it remains possible that a person will refuse to comply with another's sexual demands. It is probably best to describe this sort of situation as a case not of coercion, which entails the *successful* use of threats to gain compliance, but of *attempted* coercion. Of course, the moral fault of an individual emerges with the *attempt* to coerce. A person who attempts murder is morally blameworthy even if the attempt fails. The same is true for someone who fails in an effort to coerce consent to sexual interaction.

Consider now each of the following cases:

Case 1 Mr. Supervisor makes a series of increasingly less subtle sexual overtures to Ms. Employee. These advances are consistently and firmly rejected by Ms. Employee. Eventually, Mr. Supervisor makes it clear that the granting of "sexual favors" is a condition of her continued employment.

Case 2 Ms. Debtor borrowed a substantial sum of money from Mr. Creditor, on the understanding that she would pay it back within one year. In the meantime, Ms. Debtor has become sexually attracted to Mr. Creditor, but he does not share her interest. At the end of the one-year period, Mr. Creditor asks Ms. Debtor to return the money. She says she will be happy to return the money so long as he consents to sexual interaction with her.

Case 3   Mr. Theatregoer has two tickets to the most talked-about play of the season. He is introduced to a woman whom he finds sexually attractive and who shares his interest in the theater. In the course of their conversation, she expresses disappointment that the play everyone is talking about is sold out; she would love to see it. At this point, Mr. Theatregoer suggests that she be his guest at the theater. "Oh, by the way," he says, "I always expect sex from my dates."

Case 4   Ms. Jetsetter is planning a trip to Europe. She has been trying for some time to develop a sexual relationship with a man who has shown little interest in her. She knows, however, that he has always wanted to go to Europe and that it is only lack of money that has deterred him. Ms. Jetsetter proposes that he come along as her traveling companion, all expenses paid, on the express understanding that sex is part of the arrangement.

Cases 1 and 2 involve attempts to sexually use another person whereas cases 3 and 4 do not. To see why this is so, it is essential to introduce a distinction between two kinds of proposals, viz., the distinction between *threats* and *offers.*[4] The logical form of a threat differs from the logical form of an offer in the following way. Threat: "If you *do not* do what I am proposing you do, I will bring about an *undesirable consequence* for you." Offer: "If you *do* what I am proposing you do, I will bring about a *desirable consequence* for you." The person who makes a threat attempts to gain compliance by attaching an undesirable consequence to the alternative of noncompliance. This person attempts to *coerce* consent. The person who makes an offer attempts to gain compliance by attaching a desirable consequence to the alternative of compliance. This person attempts not to coerce but to *induce* consent.

Since threats are morally problematic in a way that offers are not, it is not uncommon for threats to be advanced in the language of offers. Threats are represented as if they were offers. An armed assailant might say, "I'm going to make you an *offer*. If you give me your money, I will allow you to go on living." Though this proposal on the surface has the logical form of an offer, it is in reality a threat. The underlying sense of the proposal is this: "If you do not give me your money, I will kill you." If, in a given case, it is initially unclear whether a certain proposal is to count as a threat or an offer, ask the following question. Does the proposal in question have the effect of making a person *worse off upon noncompliance?* The recipient of an offer, upon noncompliance, *is not worse off* than he or she was before the offer. In contrast, the recipient of a threat, upon noncompliance, *is worse off* than he or she was before the threat. Since the "offer" of our armed assailant has the effect, upon noncompliance, of rendering its recipient worse off (relative to the preproposal situation of the recipient), the recipient is faced with a threat, not an offer.

The most obvious way for a coercer to attach an undesirable consequence to the path of noncompliance is by threatening to render the victim of coercion materially worse off than he or she has heretofore been. Thus a person is threatened with loss of life, bodily injury, damage to property, damage to reputation, etc. It is important to realize, however, that a person can also be effectively coerced by being threatened with the withholding of something (in some cases, what we would call a "benefit") to which the person is entitled. Suppose that A is mired in quicksand and is slowly but surely approaching death. When B happens along, A cries out to B for assistance. All B need do is throw A a rope. B is quite willing to accommodate A, "provided you pay me $100,000 over the next ten years." Is B making A an offer? Hardly! B, we must presume, stands under a moral obligation to come to the aid of a person in serious distress, at least when such assistance entails no significant risk, sacrifice of time, etc. A is entitled to B's assistance. Thus, in reality, B attaches an undesirable consequence to A's noncompliance with the proposal that A pay B $100,000. A is undoubtedly better off that B has happened along, but A is not rendered better off *by B's proposal.* Before B's proposal, A legitimately expected assistance from B, "no strings attached." In attaching a very unwelcome string, B's proposal effectively renders A worse off. What B proposes, then, is not an offer of assistance. Rather, B threatens A with the withholding of something (assistance) that A is entitled to have from B.

Since threats have the effect of rendering a person worse off upon noncompliance, it is ordinarily the case that a person does not welcome (indeed, despises) them. Offers, on the other hand, are ordinarily welcome to a person. Since an offer provides no penalty for noncompliance with a proposal but only an inducement for compliance, there is *in principle* only potential advantage in being confronted with an offer. In real life, of course, there are numerous reasons why a person may be less than enthusiastic about being presented with an offer. Enduring the presentation of trivial offers does not warrant the necessary time and energy expenditures. Offers can be both annoying and offensive; certainly this is true of some sexual offers. A person might also be unsettled by an offer that confronts him or her with a difficult decision. All this, however, is compatible with the fact that an offer is fundamentally welcome to a rational person in the sense that the *content* of an offer necessarily widens the field of opportunity and thus provides, in principle, only potential advantage.

With the distinction between threats and offers clearly in view, it now becomes clear why cases 1 and 2 do indeed involve attempts to sexually use another person whereas cases 3 and 4 do not. Cases 1 and 2 embody threats, whereas cases 3 and 4 embody offers. In case 1, Mr. Supervisor proposes sexual interaction with Ms. Employee and, in an effort to gain compliance, threatens her with the loss of her job. Mr. Supervisor thereby attaches an undesirable consequence to one of Ms. Employee's alternatives, the path of noncompliance. Typical of the threat situation, Mr. Supervisor's proposal has the effect of rendering Ms. Employee worse off upon noncompliance. Mr. Supervisor is attempting via (dispositional) coercion to sexually use Ms. Employee. The situation in case 2 is similar. Ms. Debtor, as *she* might be inclined to say, "offers" to pay Mr. Creditor the money she owes him *if* he consents to sexual interaction with her. In reality, Ms. Debtor is threatening Mr. Creditor, attempting to coerce his consent to sexual interaction, attempting to sexually use him. Though Mr. Creditor is not now in possession of the money Ms. Debtor owes him, he is *entitled* to receive it from her at this time. She threatens to deprive him of something to which he is entitled. Clearly, her proposal has the effect of rendering him worse off upon noncompliance. Before her proposal, he had the legitimate expectation, "no strings attached," of receiving the money in question.

Cases 3 and 4 embody offers; neither involves an attempt to sexually use another person. Mr. Theatregoer simply provides an inducement for the woman he has just met to accept his proposal of sexual interaction. He offers her the opportunity to see the play that everyone is talking about. In attaching a desirable consequence to the alternative of compliance, Mr. Theatregoer in no way threatens or attempts to coerce his potential companion. Typical of the offer situation, his proposal does not have the effect of rendering her worse off upon noncompliance. She now has a new opportunity; if she chooses to forgo this opportunity, she is no worse off. The situation in case 4 is similar. Ms. Jetsetter provides an inducement for a man that she is interested in to accept her proposal of sexual involvement. She offers him the opportunity to see Europe, without expense, as her traveling companion. Before Ms. Jetsetter's proposal, he had no prospect of a European trip. If he chooses to reject her proposal, he is no worse off than he has heretofore been. Ms. Jetsetter's proposal embodies an offer, not a threat. She cannot be accused of attempting to sexually use her potential traveling companion.

Consider now two further cases, 5 and 6, each of which develops in the following way. Professor Highstatus, a man of high academic accomplishment, is sexually attracted to a student in one of his classes. He is very anxious to secure her consent to sexual interaction. Ms. Student, confused and unsettled by his sexual advances, has begun to practice "avoidance behavior." To the extent that it is possible, she goes out of her way to avoid him.

Case 5 Professor Highstatus tells Ms. Student that, though her work is such as to entitle her to a grade of B in the class, she will be assigned a D unless she consents to sexual interaction.

Case 6 Professor Highstatus tells Ms. Student that, though her work is such as to entitle her to a grade of B, she will be assigned an A if she consents to sexual interaction.

It is clear that case 5 involves an attempt to sexually use another person. Case 6, however, at least at face value, does not. In case 5, Professor Highstatus *threatens* to deprive Ms. Student of the grade she deserves. In case 6, he *offers* to assign her a grade that is higher than she deserves. In case 5, Ms. Student would be worse off upon noncompliance with Professor Highstatus' proposal. In case 6, she would not be worse off upon noncompliance with his proposal. In saying that case 6 does not involve an attempt to sexually use another person, it is not being asserted that Professor Highstatus is acting in a morally legitimate fashion. In offering a student a higher grade than she deserves, he is guilty of abusing his institutional authority. He is under an obligation to assign the grades that students earn, as defined by the relevant course standards. In case 6, Professor Highstatus is undoubtedly acting in a morally reprehensible way, but in contrast to case 5, where it is fair to say that he both abuses his institutional authority *and* attempts to sexually use another person, we can plausibly say that in case 6 his moral failure is limited to abuse of his institutional authority.

There remains, however, a suspicion that case 6 might after all embody an attempt to sexually use another person. There is no question that the literal content of what Professor Highstatus conveys to Ms. Student has the logical form of an offer and not a threat. Still, is it not the case that Ms. Student may very well feel threatened? Professor Highstatus, in an effort to secure consent to sexual interaction, has announced that he will assign Ms. Student a higher grade than she deserves. Can she really turn him down without substantial risk? Is he not likely to retaliate? If she spurns him, will he not lower her grade or otherwise make it harder for her to succeed in her academic program? He does, after all, have power over her. Will he use it to her detriment? Surely he is not above abusing his institutional authority to achieve his ends; this much is abundantly clear from his willingness to assign a grade higher than a student deserves.

Is Professor Highstatus naive to the threat that Ms. Student may find implicit in the situation? Perhaps. In such a case, if Ms. Student reluctantly consents to sexual interaction, we may be inclined to say that he has *unwittingly* used her. More likely, Professor Highstatus is well aware of the way in which Ms. Student will perceive his proposal. He knows that threats need not be verbally expressed. Indeed, it may even be the case that he consciously exploits his underground reputation. "Everyone knows what happens to the women who reject Professor Highstatus's little offers." To the extent, then, that Professor Highstatus intends to convey a threat in case 6, he is attempting via coercion to sexually use another person.

Many researchers "have pointed out the fact that the possibility of sanctions for noncooperation is implicit in all sexual advances across authority lines, as between teacher and student."[5] I do not think that this consideration should lead us to the conclusion that a person with an academic appointment is obliged in all circumstances to refrain from attempting to initiate sexual involvement with one of his or her students. Still, since even "good faith" sexual advances may be ambiguous in the eyes of a student, it is an interesting question what precautions an instructor must take to avoid unwittingly coercing a student to consent to sexual interaction.

Much of what has been said about the professor/student relationship in an academic setting can be applied as well to the supervisor/subordinate relationship in an employment setting. A manager who functions within an organizational structure is required to evaluate fairly his or her subordinates according to relevant corporate or institutional standards. An unscrupulous manager, willing to abuse his or her institutional authority in an effort to win the consent of a subordinate to sexual interaction, can advance threats and/or offers related to the managerial task of employee evaluation. An employee whose job performance is entirely satisfactory can be threatened with an unsatisfactory performance rating, perhaps leading to termination. An employee whose job performance is excellent can be threatened with an unfair evaluation, designed to bar the employee from recognition, merit pay, consideration for promotion, etc. Such threats, when made in an effort to coerce employee consent to sexual interaction, clearly embody the attempt to sexually use another person. On the other hand, the manager who (abusing his or her institutional authority) offers to provide an employee with an inflated evaluation as an inducement for consent to sexual interaction does not, at face value, attempt to sexually use another person. Of course, all of the qualifications introduced in the discussion of case 6 above are applicable here as well.

IV THE IDEA OF A COERCIVE OFFER

In section III, I have sketched an overall account of sexually using another person *via coercion*. In this section, I will consider the need for modifications or extensions of the suggested account. As before, certain case studies will serve as points of departure.

Case 7   Ms. Starlet, a glamorous, wealthy, and highly successful model, wants nothing more than to become a movie superstar. Mr. Moviemogul, a famous producer, is very taken with Ms. Starlet's beauty. He invites her to come to his office for a screen test. After the screen test, Mr. Moviemogul tells Ms. Starlet that he is prepared to make her a star, on the condition that she agree to sexual involvement with him. Ms. Starlet finds Mr. Moviemogul personally repugnant; she is not at all sexually attracted to him. With great reluctance, she agrees to his proposal.

Has Mr. Moviemogul sexually used Ms. Starlet? No. He has made her an offer that she has accepted, however reluctantly. The situation would be quite different if it were plausible to believe that she was, before acceptance of his proposal, *entitled* to his efforts to make her a star. Then we could read case 7 as amounting to his threatening to deprive her of something to which she was entitled. But what conceivable grounds could be found for the claim that Mr. Moviemogul, before Ms. Starlet's acceptance of his proposal, is under an obligation to make her a star? He does not threaten her; he makes her an offer. Even if there are other good grounds for morally condemning his action, it is a mistake to think that he is guilty of coercing consent.

But some would assert that Mr. Moviemogul's offer, on the grounds that it confronts Ms. Starlet with an overwhelming inducement, is simply an example of a *coercive offer*. The more general claim at issue is that offers are coercive precisely inasmuch as they are extremely enticing or seductive. Though there is an important reality associated with the notion of a coercive offer, a reality that must shortly be confronted, we ought not embrace the view that an offer is coercive merely because it is extremely enticing or seductive. Virginia Held is a leading proponent of the view under attack here. She writes:

> A person unable to spurn an offer may act as unwillingly as a person unable to resist a threat. Consider the distinction between rape and seduction. In one case constraint and threat are operative, in the other inducement and offer. If the degree of inducement is set high enough in the case of seduction, there may seem to be little difference in the extent of coercion involved. In both cases, persons may act against their own wills.[6]

Certainly a rape victim who acquiesces at knife point is forced to act *against her will*. Does Ms. Starlet, however, act against her will? We have said that she consents "with great reluctance" to sexual involvement, but she does not act against her will. She *wants* very much to be a movie star. I might want very much to be thin. She regrets having to become sexually involved with Mr. Moviemogul as a means of achieving what she wants. I might regret very much having to go on a diet to lose weight. If we say that Ms. Starlet acts against her will in case 7, then we must say that I am acting against my will in embracing "with great reluctance" the diet I despise.

A more important line of argument against Held's view can be advanced on the basis of the widely accepted notion that there is a moral presumption against coercion. Held herself embraces this notion and very effectively clarifies it:

> . . . although coercion is not *always* wrong (quite obviously: one coerces the small child not to run across the highway, or the murderer to drop his weapon), there is a presumption against it. . . . This has the standing of a fundamental moral principle. . . .
>   What can be concluded at the moral level is that we have a *prima facie* obligation not to employ coercion.[7] [all italics hers]

But it would seem that acceptance of the moral presumption against coercion is not compatible with the view that offers become coercive precisely inasmuch as they become extremely enticing or seductive. Suppose you are my neighbor and regularly spend your Saturday afternoon on the golf course. Suppose also that you are a skilled gardener. I am anxious to convince you to do some gardening work for me and it must be done this Saturday. I offer you $100, $200, $300, . . . in an effort to make it worth your while to sacrifice your recreation and undertake my gardening. At some point, my proposal becomes very enticing. Yet, at the same time in no sense is my proposal becoming morally problematic. If my proposal were becoming coercive, surely our moral sense would be aroused.

Though it is surely not true that the extremely enticing character of an offer is sufficient to make it coercive, we need not reach the conclusion that no sense can be made out of the notion of a coercive offer. Indeed, there is an important social reality that the notion of a coercive offer appears to capture, and insight into this reality can be gained by simply taking note of the sort of case that most draws us to the language of "coercive offer." Is it not a case in which the recipient of an offer is in circumstances of genuine need, and acceptance of the offer seems to present the only realistic possibility for alleviating the need? Assuming that this sort of case is the heart of the matter, it seems that we cannot avoid introducing some sort of distinction between *genuine needs* and *mere wants*. Though the philosophical difficulties involved in drawing this distinction are not insignificant, I nevertheless claim that we will not achieve any clarity about the notion of a coercive offer, at least in this context, except in reference to it. Whatever puzzlement we may feel with regard to the host of borderline cases that can be advanced, it is nevertheless true, for example, that I *genuinely need* food and that I *merely want* a backyard tennis court. In the same spirit, I think it can be acknowledged by all that Ms. Starlet, though she *wants* very much to be a star, does not in any relevant sense *need* to be a star. Accordingly, there is little plausibility in thinking that Mr. Moviemogul makes her a coercive offer. The following case, in contrast, can more plausibly be thought to embody a coercive offer.

Case 8   Mr. Troubled is a young widower who is raising his three children. He lives in a small town and believes that it is important for him to stay there so that his children continue to have the emotional support of other family members. But economic times are tough. Mr. Troubled has been laid off from his job and has not been able to find another. His unemployment benefits have ceased and his relatives are in no position to help him financially. If he is unable to come up with the money for his mortgage payments, he will lose his rather modest house. Ms. Opportunistic lives in the same town. Since shortly after the death of Mr. Troubled's wife, she has consistently made sexual overtures in his direction. Mr. Troubled, for his part, does not care for Ms. Opportunistic and has made it clear to her that he is not interested in sexual involvement with her. She, however, is well aware of his present difficulties. To win his consent to a sexual affair, Ms. Opportunistic offers to make mortgage payments for Mr. Troubled on a continuing basis.

Is Ms. Opportunistic attempting to sexually use Mr. Troubled? The correct answer is yes, even though we must first accept the conclusion that her proposal embodies an offer and not a threat. If Ms. Opportunistic were threatening Mr. Troubled, her proposal would have the effect of rendering him worse off upon noncompliance. But this is not the case. If he rejects her proposal, his situation will not worsen; he will simply remain, as before, in circumstances of extreme need. It might be objected at this point that Ms. Opportunistic does in fact threaten Mr. Troubled. She threatens to deprive him of something to which he is entitled, namely, the alleviation of a genuine need. But this approach is defensible only if, before acceptance of her proposal, he is entitled to have his needs alleviated *by her.* And whatever Mr. Troubled and his children are entitled to from their society as a whole—they are perhaps slipping through the "social safety net"—it cannot be plausibly maintained that Mr. Troubled is entitled to have his mortgage payments made *by Ms. Opportunistic.*

Yet, though she does not threaten him, she is attempting to sexually use him. How can this conclusion be reconciled with our overall account of sexually using another person? First of all, I want to suggest that nothing hangs on whether or not we decide to call Ms. Opportunistic's offer "coercive." More important than the label "coercive offer" is an appreciation of the social reality that inclines us to consider the label appropriate. The label most forcefully asserts itself when we reflect on what Mr. Troubled is likely to say after accepting the offer. "I really had no choice." "I didn't want to accept her offer but what could I do? I have my children to think about." Both Mr. Troubled and Ms. Starlet (in our previous case) *reluctantly* consented to sexual interaction, but I think it can be agreed that Ms. Starlet had a choice in a way that Mr. Troubled did not. Mr. Troubled's choice was *severely constrained by his needs,* whereas Ms. Starlet's was not. As for Ms. Opportunistic, it seems that we might describe her approach as in some sense exploiting or taking advantage of Mr. Troubled's desperate situation. It is not so much, as we would say in the case of threats, that she coerces him or his consent, but rather that she achieves her aim of winning consent by taking advantage of the fact that he is already "under coercion," that is, his choice is severely constrained by his need. If we choose to describe what has taken place as a "coercive offer," we should remember that Mr. Troubled is "coerced" (constrained) by his own need or perhaps by preexisting factors in his situation rather than by Ms. Opportunistic or her offer.

Since it is not quite right to say that Ms. Opportunistic is attempting to coerce Mr. Troubled, even if we are prepared to embrace the label "coercive offer," we cannot simply say, as we would say in the case of threats, that she is attempting to sexually use him *via coercion.* The proper account of the way in which Ms. Opportunistic attempts to sexually use Mr. Troubled is somewhat different. Let us say simply that she attempts to sexually use him *by taking advantage of his desperate situation.* The sense behind this distinctive way of sexually using someone is that a person's choice situation can sometimes be subject to such severe prior constraints that the possibility of *voluntary* consent to sexual interaction is precluded. A advances an offer calculated to gain B's reluctant consent to sexual interaction by confronting B, who has no apparent way of alleviating a genuine need, with an opportunity to do so, but makes this opportunity contingent upon consent to sexual interaction. In such a case, should we not say simply that B's need, when coupled with a lack of viable alternatives, results in B being incapable of *voluntarily* accepting A's offer? Thus A, in making an offer which B "cannot refuse," although not coercing B, nevertheless does intentionally act in a way that violates the requirement that B's sexual interaction with A be based upon B's voluntary informed consent. Thus A sexually uses B.

The central claim of this paper is that A sexually uses B if and only if A intentionally acts in a way that violates the requirement that B's sexual interaction with A be based on B's voluntary informed consent. Clearly, deception and coercion are important mechanisms whereby sexual using takes place. But consideration of case 8 has led us to the identification of yet another mechanism. In summary, then, limiting attention to cases of sexual interaction with a fully competent adult partner, A can sexually use B not only (1) by deceiving B or (2) by coercing B but also (3) by taking advantage of B's desperate situation.

NOTES

1 I follow here an account of coercion developed by Michael D. Bayles in "A Concept of Coercion," in J. Roland Pennock and John W. Chapman, eds., *Coercion: Nomos XIV* (Chicago: Aldine-Atherton, 1972), pp. 16–29.

2 Statutory rape, sexual relations with a person under the legal age of consent, can also be construed as the sexual using of another person. In contrast to forcible rape, however, statutory rape need not involve coercion. The victim of statutory rape may freely "consent" to sexual interaction but, at least in the eyes of the law, is deemed incompetent to consent.

3 A man wrestles a woman to the ground. She is the victim of occurrent coercion. He threatens to beat her unless she submits to his sexual demands. Now she becomes the victim of dispositional coercion.

4 My account of this distinction largely derives from Robert Nozick, "Coercion," in Sidney Morgenbesser, Patrick Suppes, and Morton White, eds., *Philosophy, Science, and Method* (New York: St. Martin's Press, 1969), pp. 440–472, and from Michael D. Bayles, "Coercive Offers and Public Benefits," *The Personalist* 55, no. 2 (Spring 1974), 139–144.

5 The National Advisory Council on Women's Educational Programs, *Sexual Harassment: A Report on the Sexual Harassment of Students* (August 1980), p. 12.

6 Virginia Held, "Coercion and Coercive Offers," in *Coercion: Nomos XIV*, p. 58.

7 *Ibid.,* pp. 61, 62.

QUESTIONS

1 Is there a morally relevant sense of *sexually* using another person that is not captured by reference to the notion of voluntary informed consent?

2 What is promiscuity? Is promiscuity immoral?

3 Is prostitution immoral?

Morality and Human Sexuality

Vincent C. Punzo

Vincent C. Punzo is professor of philosophy at St. Louis University. His published articles include "Reason in Morals" and "Natural Law Ethics: Immediate or Mediated Naturalism." Punzo is also the author of *Reflective Naturalism: An Introduction to Moral Philosophy* (1969), from which this selection is excerpted.

Punzo begins by arguing that there is a morally significant difference between sexual intercourse and other types of human activity. Then, emphasizing the historical aspect of the human self, he constructs an argument against premarital sexual intercourse. Marriage, in his view, is constituted by a mutual and total commitment. Apart from this framework of commitment, he argues, sexual unions are "morally deficient because they lack existential integrity." Although Punzo is essentially a proponent of conventional sexual morality, he understands marriage in such a way that he does not condemn "preceremonial" intercourse. He insists that the commitment constitutive of marriage can exist prior to and apart from any legal or ceremonial formalities.

If one sees man's moral task as being simply that of not harming anyone, that is if one sees this task in purely negative terms, he will certainly not accept the argument to be presented in the following section. However, if one accepts the notion of the morality of aspiration, if one accepts the view that man's moral task involves the positive attempt to live up to what is best in man, to give reality to what he sees to be the perfection of himself as a human subject, the argument may be acceptable.

SEXUALITY AND THE HUMAN SUBJECT

[Prior discussion] has left us with the question as to whether sexual intercourse is a type of activity that is similar to choosing a dinner from a menu. This question is of utmost significance in that one's view of the morality of premarital intercourse seems to depend on the significance that one gives to the sexual encounter in human life. Those such as [John] Wilson and [Eustace] Chesser who see nothing immoral about the premarital character of sexual intercourse seem to see sexual intercourse as being no different from myriad of other purely aesthetic matters. This point is seen in Chesser's questioning of the reason for demanding permanence in the relationship of sexual partners when we do not see such permanence as being important to other human relationships.[1] It is also seen in his asking why we raise a moral issue about premarital coition when two people may engage in it, with the resulting social and psychological consequences being no different than if they had gone to a movie.[2]

   Wilson most explicitly makes a case for the view that sexual intercourse does not differ significantly from other human activities. He holds that people think that there is a logical difference between the question "Will you engage in sexual intercourse with me?" and the question, "Will you play tennis with me?" only because they are influenced by the acquisitive character of contemporary society.[3] Granted that the two questions may be identical from the purely formal perspective of logic, the ethician must move beyond this perspective to a consideration of their content. Men and women find themselves involved in many different relationships: for example, as buyer-seller, employer-employee, teacher-student, lawyer-client, and partners or competitors in certain games such as tennis or bridge. Is there any morally significant difference between these relationships and sexual intercourse? We cannot examine all the possible relationships into which a man and woman can enter, but we will consider the employer-employee relationship in order to get some perspective on the distinctive character of the sexual relationship.

A man pays a woman to act as his secretary. What rights does he have over her in such a situation? The woman agrees to work a certain number of hours during the day taking dictation, typing letters, filing reports, arranging appointments and flight schedules, and greeting clients and competitors. In short, we can say that the man has rights to certain of the woman's services or skills. The use of the word "services" may lead some to conclude that this relationship is not significantly different from the relationship between a prostitute and her client in that the prostitute also offers her "services."

It is true that we sometimes speak euphemistically of a prostitute offering her services to a man for a sum of money, but if we are serious about our quest for the difference between the sexual encounter and other types of human relationships, it is necessary to drop euphemisms and face the issue directly. The man and woman who engage in sexual intercourse are giving their bodies, the most intimate physical expression of themselves, over to the other. Unlike the man who plays tennis with a woman, the man who has sexual relations with her has literally entered her. A man and woman engaging in sexual intercourse have united themselves as intimately and as totally as is physically possible for two human beings. Their union is not simply a union of organs, but is as intimate and as total a physical union of two selves as is possible of achievement. Granted the character of this union, it seems strange to imply that there is no need for a man and a woman to give any more thought to the question of whether they should engage in sexual intercourse than to the question of whether they should play tennis.

In opposition to Wilson, I think that it is the acquisitive character of our society that has blinded us to the distinction between the two activities. Wilson's and Chesser's positions seem to imply that exactly the same moral considerations ought to apply to a situation in which a housewife is bartering with a butcher for a few pounds of pork chops and the situation in which two human beings are deciding whether sexual intercourse ought to be an ingredient of their relationship. So long as the butcher does not put his thumb on the scale in the weighing process, so long as he is truthful in stating that the meat is actually pork, so long as the woman pays the proper amount with the proper currency, the trade is perfectly moral. Reflecting on sexual intercourse from the same sort of economic perspective, one can say that so long as the sexual partners are truthful in reporting their freedom from contagious venereal diseases and so long as they are truthful in reporting that they are interested in the activity for the mere pleasure of it or to try out their sexual techniques, there is nothing immoral about such activity. That in the one case pork chops are being exchanged for money whereas in the other the decision concerns the most complete and intimate merging of one's self with another makes no difference to the moral evaluation of the respective cases.

It is not surprising that such a reductionistic outlook should pervade our thinking on sexual matters, since in our society sexuality is used to sell everything from shave cream to underarm deodorants, to soap, to mouthwash, to cigarettes, and to automobiles. Sexuality has come to play so large a role in our commercial lives that it is not surprising that our sexuality should itself come to be treated as a commodity governed by the same moral rules that govern any other economic transaction.

Once sexuality is taken out of this commercial framework, once the character of the sexual encounter is faced directly and squarely, we will come to see that Doctor Mary Calderone has brought out the type of questions that ought to be asked by those contemplating the introduction of sexual intercourse into their relationships: "How many times, and how casually, are you willing to invest a portion of your total self, and to be the custodian of a like investment from the other person, without the sureness of knowing that these investments are being made for keeps?"[4] These questions come out of the recognition that the sexual encounter is a definitive experience, one in which the physical intimacy and merging involves also a merging of the nonphysical dimensions of the partners. With these questions, man moves beyond the negative concern with avoiding his or another's physical and psychological harm to the question of what he is making of himself and what he is contributing to the existential formation of his partner as a human subject.

If we are to make a start toward responding to Calderone's questions we must cease talking about human selfhood in abstraction. The human self is an historical as well as a physical being. He is a being who is capable of making at least a portion of his past an object of his consciousness and thus is able to make this past play a conscious role in his present and in his looking toward the future. He is also a being who looks to the future, who faces tomorrow with plans, ideals, hopes, and fears. The very being of a human self involves his past and his movement toward the future. Moreover, the human self is not completely shut off in his own past and future. Men and women are capable of consciously and purposively uniting themselves in a common career and venture. They can commit themselves to sharing the future with another, sharing it in all its aspects—in its fortunes and misfortunes, in its times of happiness and times of tragedy. Within the lives of those who have so committed themselves to each other, sexual intercourse is a way of asserting and confirming the fullness and totality of their mutual commitment.

Unlike those who have made such a commitment and who come together in the sexual act in the fullness of their selfhood, those who engage in premarital sexual unions and who have made no such commitment act as though they can amputate their bodily existence and the most intimate physical expression of their selfhood from their existence as historical beings. Granting that there may be honesty on the verbal level in that two people engaging in premarital intercourse openly state that they are interested only in the pleasure of the activity, the fact remains that such unions are morally deficient because they lack existential integrity in that there is a total merging and union on a physical level, on the one hand, and a conscious decision not to unite any other dimension of themselves, on the other hand. Their sexual union thus involves a "depersonalization" of their bodily existence, an attempt to cut off the most intimate physical expression of their respective selves from their very selfhood. The mutual agreement of premarital sex partners is an agreement to merge with the other not as a self, but as a body which one takes unto oneself, which one possesses in a most intimate and total fashion for one's own pleasure or designs, allowing the other to treat oneself in the same way. It may be true that no physical or psychological harm may result from such unions, but such partners have failed to existentially incorporate human sexuality, which is at the very least the most intimate physical expression of the human self, into the character of this selfhood.

In so far as premarital sexual unions separate the intimate and total physical union that is sexual intercourse from any commitment to the self in his historicity, human sexuality, and consequently the human body, have been fashioned into external things or objects to be handed over totally to someone else, whenever one feels that he can get possession of another's body, which he can use for his own purposes.[5] The human body has thus been treated no differently from the pork chops spoken of previously or from any other object or commodity, which human beings exchange and haggle over in their day-to-day transactions. One hesitates to use the word that might be used to capture the moral value that has been sacrificed in premarital unions because in our day the word has taken on a completely negative meaning at best, and, at worst, it has become a word used by "sophisticates" to mock or deride certain attitudes toward human sexuality. However, because the word "chastity" has been thus abused is no reason to leave it in the hands of those who have misrepresented the human value to which it gives expression.

The chaste person has often been described as one intent on denying his sexuality. The value of chastity as conceived in this section is in direct opposition to this description. It is the unchaste person who is separating himself from his sexuality, who is willing to exchange human bodies as one would exchange money for tickets to a baseball game—honestly and with no commitment of self to self. Against this alienation of one's sexuality from one's self, an alienation that makes ones' sexuality an object, which is to be given to another in exchange for his objectified sexuality, chastity affirms the integrity of the self in his bodily and historical existence. The sexuality of man is seen as an integral part of his subjectivity. Hence, the chaste man rejects depersonalized sexual relations as a reduction of man in his most intimate physical being to the status of an object or pure instrument for another. He asserts that man is a subject and end in himself, not in some trans-temporal, nonphysical world, but in the historical-physical world in which he carries on his moral task and where he finds his fellow man. He will not freely make of himself in his bodily existence a thing to be handed over to another's possession, nor will he ask that another treat his own body in this way. The total physical intimacy of sexual intercourse will be an expression of total union with the other self on all levels of their beings. Seen from this perspective, chastity is one aspect of man's attempt to attain existential integrity, to accept his body as a dimension of his total personality.

In concluding this section, it should be noted that I have tried to make a case against the morality of premarital sexual intercourse even in those cases in which the partners are completely honest with each other. There is reason to question whether the complete honesty, to which those who see nothing immoral in such unions refer, is as a matter of fact actually found very often among premarital sex partners. We may well have been dealing with textbook cases which present these unions in their best light. One may be pardoned for wondering whether sexual intercourse often occurs under the following conditions: "Hello, my name is Josiah. I am interested in having a sexual experience with you. I can assure you that I am good at it and that I have no communicable disease. If it sounds good to you and if you have taken the proper contraceptive precautions, we might have a go at it. Of course, I want to make it clear to you that I am interested only in the sexual experience and that I have no intention of making any long-range commitment to you." If those, who defend the morality of premarital sexual unions so long as they are honestly entered into, think that I have misrepresented what they mean by honesty, then they must specify what they mean by an honest premarital union. . . .

MARRIAGE AS A TOTAL HUMAN COMMITMENT

The preceding argument against the morality of premarital sexual unions was not based on the view that the moral character of marriage rests on a legal certificate or on a legal or religious ceremony. The argument was not directed against "preceremonial" intercourse, but against premarital intercourse. Morally speaking, a man and woman are married when they make the mutual and total commitment to share the problems and prospects of their historical existence in the world. . . .

. . . A total commitment to another means a commitment to him in his historical existence. Such a commitment is not simply a matter of words or of feelings, however strong. It involves a full existential sharing on the part of two beings of the burdens, opportunities, and challenges of their historical existence.

Granted the importance that the character of their commitment to each other plays in determining the moral quality of a couple's sexual encounter, it is clear that there may be nothing immoral in the behavior of couples who engage in sexual intercourse before participating in the marriage ceremony. For example, it is foolish to say that two people who are totally committed to each other and who have made all the arrangements to live this commitment are immoral if they engage in sexual intercourse the night before the marriage ceremony. Admittedly this position can be abused by those who have made a purely verbal commitment, a commitment, which will be carried out in some vague and ill-defined future. At some time or other, they will unite their two lives totally by setting up house together and by actually undertaking the task of meeting the economic, social, legal, medical responsibilities that are involved in living this commitment. Apart from the reference to a vague and amorphous future time when they will share the full responsibility for each other, their commitment presently realizes itself in going to dances, sharing a box of popcorn at

Saturday night movies, and sharing their bodies whenever they can do so without taking too great a risk of having the girl become pregnant.

Having acknowledged that the position advanced in this section can be abused by those who would use the word "commitment" to rationalize what is an interest only in the body of the other person, it must be pointed out that neither the ethician nor any other human being can tell two people whether they actually have made the commitment that is marriage or are mistaking a "warm glow" for such a commitment. There comes a time when this issue falls out of the area of moral philosophy and into the area of practical wisdom. . . .

The characterization of marriage as a total commitment between two human beings may lead some to conclude that the marriage ceremony is a wholly superfluous affair. It must be admitted that people may be morally married without having engaged in a marriage ceremony. However, to conclude from this point that the ceremony is totally meaningless is to lose sight of the social character of human beings. The couple contemplating marriage do not exist in a vacuum, although there may be times when they think they do. Their existences reach out beyond their union to include other human beings. By making their commitment a matter of public record, by solemnly expressing it before the law and in the presence of their respective families and friends and, if they are religious people, in the presence of God and one of his ministers, they sink the roots of their commitment more deeply and extensively in the world in which they live, thus taking steps to provide for the future growth of their commitment to each other. The public expression of this commitment makes it more fully and more explicitly a part of a couple's lives and of the world in which they live. . . .

NOTES

1 Eustace Chesser, *Unmarried Love* (New York: Pocket Books, 1965), p. 29.
2 *Ibid.,* pp. 35–36, see also p. 66.
3 John Wilson, *Logic and Sexual Morality* (Baltimore, Md.: Penguin Books, 1965). See footnote 1, p. 67.
4 Mary Steichen Calderone, "The Case for Chastity," *Sex in America,* ed. by Henry Anatole Grunwald (New York: Bantam Books, 1964), p. 147.
5 The psychoanalyst Rollo May makes an excellent point in calling attention to the tendency in contemporary society to exploit the human body as if it were only a machine. Rollo May, "The New Puritanism," *Sex in America,* pp. 161–164.

QUESTIONS

1 Could the idea of existential integrity be developed in such a way as to provide a justification for the sex with love approach instead of conventional sexual morality?
2 Punzo says that no one is capable of telling "two people whether they actually have made the commitment that is marriage or are mistaking a 'warm glow' for such a commitment." What factors should a couple consider in attempting to resolve this question?

Gay Basics: Some Questions, Facts, and Values

Richard D. Mohr

Richard D. Mohr is professor of philosophy at the University of Illinois, Urbana. His published work on ancient Greek philosophy includes "A Platonic Happiness" and "Plato on Time and Eternity." He has also published several articles on issues associated with gay liberation and is the author of *Gays/Justice: A Study of Ethics, Society, and Law* (1988).

Mohr advances a set of closely related claims regarding homosexuality. His principal claims include the following: (1) Gays are subject to very extensive (and unjustified) discrimination in American society. (2) There is no credible basis for the moral condemnation of homosexuality. (3) In particular, the attempt to base the moral condemnation of homosexuality on considerations of "unnaturalness" cannot be sustained. (4) Sexual orientation is not typically a matter of choice but rather a matter of "discovery." (5) The social acceptance of gays would have beneficial consequences not only for gays but for all of society.

WHO ARE GAYS ANYWAY?

A recent Gallup poll found that only one in five Americans reports having a gay or lesbian acquaintance.[1] This finding is extraordinary given the number of practicing homosexuals in America. Alfred Kinsey's 1948 study of the sex lives of 12,000 white males shocked the nation: 37 percent had at least one homosexual experience to orgasm in their adult lives; an additional 13 percent had homosexual fantasies to orgasm; 4 percent were exclusively homosexual in their practices; another 5 percent had virtually no heterosexual experience; and nearly 20 percent had at least as many homosexual as heterosexual experiences.[2]

Two out of five men one passes on the street have had orgasmic sex with men. Every second family in the country has a member who is essentially homosexual and many more people regularly have homosexual experiences. Who are homosexuals? They are your friends, your minister, your teacher, your bank teller, your doctor, your mail carrier, your officemate, your roommate, your congressional representative, your sibling, parent, and spouse. They are everywhere, virtually all ordinary, virtually all unknown.

Several important consequences follow. First, the country is profoundly ignorant of the actual experience of gay people. Second, social attitudes and practices that are harmful to gays have a much greater overall harmful impact on society than is usually realized. Third, most gay people live in hiding—in the closet—making the "coming out" experience the central fixture of gay consciousness and invisibility the chief characteristic of the gay community. . . .

ARE GAYS DISCRIMINATED AGAINST? DOES IT MATTER?

. . . Gays are subject to widespread discrimination in employment—the very means by which one puts bread on one's table and one of the chief means by which individuals identify themselves to themselves and achieve personal dignity. Governments are leading offenders here. They do a lot of discriminating themselves, require that others do it (e.g., government contractors), and set precedents favoring discrimination in the private sector. The federal government explicitly discriminates against gays in the armed forces, the CIA, FBI, National Security Agency, and the state department. The federal government refuses to give security clearances to gays and so forces the country's considerable private sector military and aerospace contractors to fire known gay employees. State and local governments regularly fire gay teachers, policemen, firemen, social workers, and anyone who has contact with the public. Further, through licensing laws states officially bar gays from a vast array of occupations and professions—everything from doctors, lawyers, accountants, and nurses to hairdressers, morticians, and used car dealers. The American Civil Liberties Union's handbook *The Rights of Gay People* lists 307 such prohibited occupations.[3]

Gays are subject to discrimination in a wide variety of other ways, including private-sector employment, public accommodations, housing, immigration and naturalization, insurance of all types, custody and adoption, and zoning regulations that bar "singles" or "nonrelated" couples. All of these discriminations affect central components of a meaningful life; some even reach to the means by which life itself is sustained. In half the states, where gay sex is illegal, the central role of sex to meaningful life is officially denied to gays.

All these sorts of discriminations also affect the ability of people to have significant intimate relations. It is difficult for people to live together as couples without having their sexual orientation perceived in the public realm and so becoming targets for discrimination. Illegality, discrimination, and the absorption by gays of society's hatred of them all interact to impede or block altogether the ability of gays and lesbians to create and maintain significant personal relations with loved ones. So every facet of life is affected by discrimination. Only the most compelling reasons could justify it.

BUT AREN'T THEY IMMORAL?

Many people think society's treatment of gays is justified because they think gays are extremely immoral. To evaluate this claim, different senses of "moral" must be distinguished. Sometimes by "morality" is meant the overall beliefs affecting behavior in a society—its mores, norms, and customs. On this understanding, gays certainly are not moral: lots of people hate them and social customs are designed to register widespread disapproval of gays. The problem here is that this sense of morality is merely a *descriptive* one. On this understanding *every* society has a morality—even Nazi society, which had racism and mob rule as central features of its "morality," understood in this sense. What is needed in order to use the notion of morality to praise or condemn behavior is a sense of morality that is *prescriptive* or *normative*—a sense of morality whereby, for instance, the descriptive morality of the Nazis is found wanting.

As the Nazi example makes clear, that something is descriptively moral is nowhere near enough to make it normatively moral. A lot of people in a society saying something is good, even over eons, does not make it so. Our rejection of the long history of socially approved and state-enforced slavery is another good example of this principle at work. Slavery would be wrong even if nearly everyone liked it. So consistency and fairness require that we abandon the belief that gays are immoral simply because most people dislike or disapprove of gays or gay acts, or even because gay sex acts are illegal.

Furthermore, recent historical and anthropological research has shown that opinion about gays has been by no means universally negative. Historically, it has varied widely even within the larger part of the Christian era and even within the church itself.[4] There are even societies—current ones—where homosexuality is not only tolerated but a universal compulsory part of social maturation.[5] Within the last thirty years, American society has undergone a grand turnabout from deeply ingrained, near total condemnation to near total acceptance on two emotionally charged "moral" or "family" issues: contraception and divorce. Society holds its current descriptive morality of gays not because it has to, but because it chooses to.

If popular opinion and custom are not enough to ground moral condemnation of homosexuality, perhaps religion can. Such argument proceeds along two lines. One claims that the condemnation is a direct revelation of God, usually through the Bible; the other claims to be able to detect condemnation in God's plan as manifested in nature.

One of the more remarkable discoveries of recent gay research is that the Bible may not be as univocal in its condemnation of homosexuality as has been usually believed.[6] Christ never mentions homosexuality. Recent interpreters of the Old Testament have pointed out that the story of Lot at Sodom is probably intended to condemn inhospitality rather than homosexuality. Further, some of the Old Testament condemnations of homosexuality seem simply to be ways of tarring those of the Israelites' opponents who happened to accept homosexual practices when the Israelites themselves did not. If so, the condemnation is merely a quirk of history and rhetoric rather than a moral precept.

What does seem clear is that those who regularly cite the Bible to condemn an activity like homosexuality do so by reading it selectively. Do ministers who cite what they take to be condemnations of homosexuality in Leviticus maintain in their lives all the hygienic and dietary laws of Leviticus? If they cite the story of Lot at Sodom to condemn homosexuality, do they also cite the story of Lot in the cave to praise incestuous rape? It seems then not that the Bible is being used to ground condemnations of homosexuality as much as society's dislike of homosexuality is being used to interpret the Bible.[7]

Even if a consistent portrait of condemnation could be gleaned from the Bible, what social significance should it be given? One of the guiding principles of society, enshrined in the Constitution as a check against the government, is that decisions affecting social policy are not made on religious grounds. If the real ground of the alleged immorality invoked by governments to discriminate against gays is religious (as it has explicitly been even in some recent court cases involving teachers and guardians), then one of the major commitments of our nation is violated.

BUT AREN'T THEY UNNATURAL?

The most noteworthy feature of the accusation of something being unnatural (where a moral rather than an advertising point is being made) is that the plaint is so infrequently made. One used to hear the charge leveled against abortion, but that has pretty much faded as anti-abortionists have come to lay all their chips on the hope that people will come to view abortion as murder. Incest used to be considered unnatural but discourse now usually assimilates it to the moral machinery of rape and violated trust. The charge comes up now in ordinary discourse only against homosexuality. This suggests that the charge is highly idiosyncratic and has little, if any, explanatory force. It fails to put homosexuality in a class with anything else so that one can learn by comparison with clear cases of the class just exactly what it is that is allegedly wrong with it.

Though the accusation of unnaturalness looks whimsical, in actual ordinary discourse when applied to homosexuality, it is usually delivered with venom aforethought. It carries a high emotional charge, usually expressing disgust and evincing queasiness. Probably it is nothing but an emotional charge. For people get equally disgusted and queasy at all sorts of things that are perfectly natural—to be expected in nature apart from artifice—and that could hardly be fit subjects for moral condemnation. Two typical examples in current American culture are some people's responses to mothers' suckling in public and to women who do not shave body hair. When people have strong emotional reactions, as they do in these cases, without being able to give good reasons for them, we think of them not as operating morally, but rather as being obsessed and manic. So the feelings of disgust that some people have to gays will hardly ground a charge of immorality. People fling the term "unnatural" against gays in the same breath and with the same force as when they call gays "sick" and "gross." When they do this, they give every appearance of being neurotically fearful and incapable of reasoned discourse.

When "nature" is taken in *technical* rather than ordinary usages, it looks like the notion also will not ground a charge of homosexual immorality. When unnatural means "by artifice" or "made by humans," it need only be pointed out that virtually everything that is good about life is unnatural in this sense, that the chief feature that distinguishes people from other animals is their very ability to make over the world to meet their needs and desires, and that their well-being depends upon these departures from nature. On this understanding of human nature and the natural, homosexuality is perfectly unobjectionable.

Another technical sense of natural is that something is natural and so, good, if it fulfills some function in nature. Homosexuality on this view is unnatural because it allegedly violates the function of genitals, which is to produce babies. One problem with this view is that lots of bodily parts have lots of functions and just because some one activity can be fulfilled by only one organ (say, the mouth for eating) this activity does not condemn other functions of the organ to immorality (say, the mouth for talking, licking stamps, blowing bubbles, or having sex). So the possible use of the genitals to produce children does not, without more, condemn the use of the genitals for other purposes, say, achieving ecstasy and intimacy.

The functional view of nature will only provide a morally condemnatory sense to the unnatural if a thing which might have many uses has but one proper function to the exclusion of other possible functions. But whether this is so cannot be established simply by looking at the thing. For what is seen is all its possible functions. The notion of function seemed like it might ground moral authority, but instead it turns out that moral authority is needed to define proper function. Some people try to fill in this moral authority by appeal to the "design" or "order" of an organ, saying, for instance, that the genitals are designed for the purpose of procreation. But these people cheat intellectually if they do not make explicit *who* the designer and orderer is. If it is God, we are back to square one—holding others accountable for religious beliefs.

Further, ordinary moral attitudes about childbearing will not provide the needed supplement which in conjunction with the natural function view of bodily parts would produce a positive obligation to use the genitals for procreation. Society's attitude toward a childless couple is that of pity not censure—even if the couple could have children. The pity may be an unsympathetic one, that is, not registering a course one would choose *for oneself,* but this does not make it a course one would *require* of others. The couple who discovers they cannot have children are viewed not as having thereby had a debt canceled, but rather as having to forgo some of the richness of life, just as a quadriplegic is viewed not as absolved from some moral obligation to hop, skip, and jump, but as missing some of the richness of life. Consistency requires then that, at most, gays who do not or cannot have children are to be pitied rather than condemned. What *is* immoral is the willful preventing of people from achieving the richness of life. Immorality in this regard lies with those social customs, regulations, and statutes that prevent lesbians and gay men from establishing blood or adoptive families, not with gays themselves.

Sometimes people attempt to establish authority for a moral obligation to use bodily parts in a certain fashion simply by claiming that moral laws are natural laws and vice versa. On this account, inanimate objects and plants are good in that they follow natural laws by necessity, animals by instinct, and persons by a rational will. People are special in that they must first discover the laws that govern them. Now, even if one believes the view—dubious in the post-Newtonian, post-Darwinian world—that natural laws in the usual sense ($E = mc^2$, for instance) have some moral content, it is not at all clear how one is to discover the laws in nature that apply to people.

On the one hand, if one looks to people themselves for a model—and looks hard enough—one finds amazing variety, including homosexuality as a social ideal (upper-class fifth-century Athens) and even as socially mandatory (Melanesia today). When one looks to people, one is simply unable to strip away the layers of social custom, history, and taboo in order to see what's really there to any degree more specific than that people are the creatures that make over their world and are capable of abstract thought. That this is so should raise doubts that neutral principles are to be found in human nature that will condemn homosexuality.

On the other hand, if one looks to nature apart from people for models, the possibilities are staggering. There are fish that change gender over their lifetimes: should we "follow nature" and be operative transsexuals? Orangutans, genetically our next of kin, live completely solitary lives without social organization of any kind: ought we to "follow nature" and be hermits? There are many species where only two members per generation reproduce: should we be bees? The search in nature for people's purpose, far from finding sure models for action, is likely to leave one morally rudderless.

BUT AREN'T GAYS WILLFULLY THE WAY THEY ARE?

It is generally conceded that if sexual orientation is something over which an individual—for whatever reason—has virtually no control, then discrimination against gays is especially deplorable, as it is against racial and ethnic classes, because it holds people accountable without regard for anything they themselves have done. And to hold a person accountable for that over which the person has no control is a central form of prejudice.

Attempts to answer the question whether or not sexual orientation is something that is reasonably thought to be within one's own control usually appeal simply to various claims of the biological or "mental" sciences. But the ensuing debate over genes, hormones, twins, early childhood development, and the like, is as unnecessary as it is currently inconclusive.[8] All that is needed to answer the question is to look at the actual experience of gays in current society and it becomes fairly clear that sexual orientation is not likely a matter of choice. For coming to have a homosexual identity simply does not have the same sort of structure that decision making has.

On the one hand, the "choice" of the gender of a sexual partner does not seem to express a trivial desire that might be as easily well fulfilled by a simple substitution of the desired object. Picking the gender of a sex partner is decidedly dissimilar, that is, to such activities as picking a flavor of ice cream. If an ice-cream parlor is out of one's flavor, one simply picks another. And if people were persecuted, threatened with jail terms, shattered careers, loss of family and housing, and the like, for eating, say, rocky road ice cream, no one would ever eat it; everyone would pick another easily available flavor. That gay people abide in being gay even in the face of persecution shows that being gay is not a matter of easy choice.

On the other hand, even if establishing a sexual orientation is not like making a relatively trivial choice, perhaps it is nevertheless relevantly like making the central and serious life choices by which individuals try to establish themselves as being of some type. Again, if one examines gay experience, this seems not to be the case. For one never sees anyone setting out to become a homosexual, in the way one does see people setting out to become doctors, lawyers, and bricklayers. One does not find "gays-to-be" picking some end—"At some point in the future, I want to become a homosexual"—and then setting about planning and acquiring the ways and means to that end, in the way one does see people deciding that they want to become lawyers, and then sees them plan what courses to take and what sort of temperaments, habits, and skills to develop in order to become lawyers. Typically gays-to-be simply find themselves having homosexual encounters and yet at least initially resisting quite strongly the identification of being homosexual. Such a person even very likely resists having such encounters, but ends up having them anyway. Only with time, luck, and great personal effort, but sometimes never, does the person gradually come to accept her or his orientation, to view it as a given material condition of life, coming as materials do with certain capacities and limitations. The person begins to act in accordance with his or her orientation and its capacities, seeing its actualization as a requisite for an integrated personality and as a central component of personal well-being. As a result, the experience of coming out to oneself has for gays the basic structure of a discovery, not the structure of a choice. And far from signaling immorality, coming out to others affords one of the few remaining opportunities in ever more bureaucratic, mechanistic, and socialistic societies to manifest courage.

HOW WOULD SOCIETY AT LARGE BE CHANGED IF GAYS WERE SOCIALLY ACCEPTED?

Suggestions to change social policy with regard to gays are invariably met with claims that to do so would invite the destruction of civilization itself: after all, isn't that what did Rome in? Actually Rome's decay paralleled not the flourishing of homosexuality but its repression under the later Christianized emperors.[9] Predictions of American civilization's imminent demise have been as premature as they have been frequent. Civilization has shown itself rather resilient here, in large part because of the country's traditional commitments to a respect for privacy, to individual liberties, and especially to people minding their own business. These all give society an open texture and the flexibility to try out things to see what works. And because of this one now need not speculate about what changes reforms in gay social policy might bring to society at large. For many reforms have already been tried.

Half the states have decriminalized homosexual acts. Can you guess which of the following states still have sodomy laws: Wisconsin, Minnesota; New Mexico, Arizona; Vermont, New Hampshire; Nebraska, Kansas. One from each pair does and one does not have sodomy laws. And yet one would be hard pressed to point out any substantial difference between the members of each pair. (If you're interested, it is the second of each pair with them.) Empirical studies have shown that there is no increase in other crimes in states that have decriminalized.[10] Further, sodomy laws are virtually never enforced. They remain on the books not to "protect society" but to insult gays, and for that reason need to be removed.

Neither has the passage of legislation barring discrimination against gays ushered in the end of civilization. Some 50 countries and municipalities, including some of the country's largest cities (like Los Angeles and Boston), have passed such statutes and among the states and colonies Wisconsin and the District of Columbia have model protective codes. Again, no more brimstone has fallen in these places than elsewhere. Staunchly anti-gay cities, like Miami and Houston, have not been spared the AIDS crisis.

Berkeley, California, has even passed domestic partner legislation giving gay couples the same rights to city benefits as married couples, and yet Berkeley has not become more weird than it already was.

Seemingly hysterical predictions that the American family would collapse if such reforms would pass proved false, just as the same dire predictions that the availability of divorce would lessen the ideal and desirability of marriage proved completely unfounded. Indeed if current discriminations, which drive gays into hiding and into anonymous relations, were lifted, far from seeing gays raze American families, one would see gays forming them.

Virtually all gays express a desire to have a permanent lover. Many would like to raise or foster children—perhaps those alarming numbers of gay kids who have been beaten up and thrown out of their "families" for being gay. But currently society makes gay coupling very difficult. A life of hiding is a pressure-cooker existence not easily shared with another. Members of non-gay couples are here asked to imagine what it would take to erase every trace of their own sexual orientation for even just a week.

Even against oppressive odds, gays have shown an amazing tendency to nest. And those gay couples who have survived the odds show that the structure of more usual couplings is not a matter of destiny but of personal responsibility. The so-called basic unit of society turns out not to be a unique immutable atom, but can adopt different parts, be adapted to different needs, and even be improved. Gays might even have a thing or two to teach others about division of labor, the relation of sensuality and intimacy, and stages of development in such relations.

If discrimination ceased, gay men and lesbians would enter the mainstream of the human community openly and with self-respect. The energies that the typical gay person wastes in the anxiety of leading a day-to-day existence of systematic disguise would be released for use in personal flourishing. From this release would be generated the many spinoff benefits that accrue to a society when its individual members thrive.

Society would be richer for acknowledging another aspect of human richness and diversity. Families with gay members would develop relations based on truth and trust rather than lies and fear. And the heterosexual majority would be better off for knowing that they are no longer trampling their gay friends and neighbors.

Finally and perhaps paradoxically, in extending to gays the rights and benefits it has reserved for its dominant culture, America would confirm its deeply held vision of itself as a morally progressing nation, a nation itself advancing and serving as a beacon for others—especially with regard to human rights. The words with which our national pledge ends—"with liberty and justice for all"—are not a description of the present but a call for the future. Ours is a nation given to a prophetic political rhetoric which acknowledges that morality is not arbitrary and that justice is not merely the expression of the current collective will. It is this vision that led the black civil rights movement to its successes. Those congressmen who opposed that movement and its centerpiece, the 1964 Civil Rights Act, on obscurantist grounds, but who lived long enough and were noble enough, came in time to express their heartfelt regret and shame at what they had done. It is to be hoped and someday to be expected that those who now grasp at anything to oppose the extension of that which is best about America to gays will one day feel the same.

NOTES

1 "Public Fears—And Sympathies," *Newsweek,* August 12, 1985, p. 23.
2 Alfred C. Kinsey, *Sexual Behavior in the Human Male* (Philadelphia: Saunders, 1948), pp. 650–651. On the somewhat lower incidences of lesbianism, see Alfred C. Kinsey, *Sexual Behavior in the Human Female* (Philadelphia: Saunders, 1953), pp. 472–475.
3 E. Carrington Boggan, *The Rights of Gay People: The Basic ACLU Guide to a Gay Person's Rights* (New York: Avon, 1975), pp. 211–235.
4 John Boswell, *Christianity, Social Tolerance and Homosexuality: Gay People in Western Europe from the Beginning of the Christian Era to the Fourteenth Century* (Chicago: University of Chicago Press, 1980).
5 See Gilbert Herdt, *Guardians of the Flute: Idioms of Masculinity* (New York: McGraw-Hill, 1981), pp. 232–239, 284–288; and see generally Gilbert Herdt, ed., *Ritualized Homosexuality in Melanesia* (Berkeley: University of California Press, 1984). For another eye-opener, see Walter L. Williams, *The Spirit and the Flesh: Sexual Diversity in American Indian Culture* (Boston: Beacon, 1986).
6 See especially Boswell, *Christianity,* ch. 4.
7 For Old Testament condemnations of homosexual acts, see Leviticus 18:22, 21:3. For hygienic and dietary codes, see, for example, Leviticus 15:19–27 (on the uncleanliness of women) and Leviticus 11:1–47 (on not eating rabbits, pigs, bats, finless water creatures, legless creeping creatures, etc.). For Lot at Sodom, see Genesis 19:1–25. For Lot in the cave, see Genesis 19:30–38.
8 The preponderance of the scientific evidence supports the view that homosexuality is either genetically determined or a permanent result of early childhood development. See the Kinsey Institute's study by Alan Bell, Martin Weinberg, and Sue Hammersmith, *Sexual Preference: Its Development in Men and Women* (Bloomington: Indiana University Press, 1981); Frederick Whitam and Robin Mathy, *Male Homosexuality in Four Societies* (New York: Praeger, 1986), ch. 7.
9 See Boswell, *Christianity,* ch. 3.
10 See Gilbert Geis, "Reported Consequences of Decriminalization of Consensual Adult Homosexuality in Seven American States," *Journal of Homosexuality* 1, no. 4 (1976): 419–426; Ken Sinclair and Michael Ross, "Consequences of Decriminalization of Homosexuality: A Study of Two Australian States," *Journal of Homosexuality* 12, no. 1 (1985): 119–127.

QUESTIONS

1 Is homosexual behavior unnatural? Is it immoral?
2 Is Mohr correct in maintaining that sexual orientation is more a matter of "discovery" than it is a matter of "choice"? Is there any relevant difference in this regard between lesbians and gay males?
3 On balance, would societal acceptance of gays have detrimental or beneficial consequences for society?

Majority Opinion in *Bowers v. Hardwick*

Justice Byron R. White

Byron R. White, associate justice of the United States Supreme Court, is a graduate of Yale Law School. In private practice until 1960, he served as United States deputy attorney general (1961–1962) and was appointed to the Supreme Court in 1962.

In this case, a male homosexual (Hardwick) challenged the constitutionality of the Georgia sodomy statute. The Federal District Court sided with Bowers (the Attorney General of Georgia) and dismissed Hardwick's suit "for failure to state a claim." The Court of Appeals reversed the decision of the District Court, but the United States Supreme Court agreed with the District Court and reversed the judgment of the Court of Appeals.

Justice White, writing the majority opinion in a five-to-four decision, argues against the view that the Constitution confers upon homosexuals a fundamental right to engage in sodomy. He also rejects (1) the view that consensual sodomy is constitutionally protected so long as it occurs in the privacy of the home and (2) the view that majority sentiments about the immorality of sodomy provide an inadequate basis for sodomy statutes.

In August 1982, respondent Hardwick (hereafter respondent) was charged with violating the Georgia statute criminalizing sodomy[1] by committing that act with another adult male in the bedroom of respondent's home. After a preliminary hearing, the District Attorney decided not to present the matter to the grand jury unless further evidence developed.

Respondent then brought suit in the Federal District Court, challenging the constitutionality of the statute insofar as it criminalized consensual sodomy. He asserted that he was a practicing homosexual, that the Georgia sodomy statute, as administered by the defendants, placed him in imminent danger of arrest, and that the statute for several reasons violates the Federal Constitution. The District Court granted the defendants' motion to dismiss for failure to state a claim. . . .

A divided panel of the Court of Appeals for the Eleventh Circuit reversed. . . . The court went on to hold that the Georgia statute violated respondent's fundamental rights because his homosexual activity is a private and intimate association that is beyond the reach of state regulation by reason of the Ninth Amendment and the Due Process Clause of the Fourteenth Amendment. The case was remanded for trial, at which, to prevail, the State would have to prove that the statute is supported by a compelling interest and is the most narrowly drawn means of achieving that end.

. . . We agree with petitioner that the Court of Appeals erred, and hence reverse its judgment.

This case does not require a judgment on whether laws against sodomy between consenting adults in general, or between homosexuals in particular, are wise or de-

United States Supreme Court. 478 U.S. 186 (1986).

sirable. It raises no question about the right or propriety of state legislative decisions to repeal their laws that criminalize homosexual sodomy, or of state-court decisions invalidating those laws on state constitutional grounds. The issue presented is whether the Federal Constitution confers a fundamental right upon homosexuals to engage in sodomy and hence invalidates the laws of the many States that still make such conduct illegal and have done so for a very long time. The case also calls for some judgment about the limits of the Court's role in carrying out its constitutional mandate.

We first register our disagreement with the Court of Appeals and with respondent that the Court's prior cases have construed the Constitution to confer a right of privacy that extends to homosexual sodomy and for all intents and purposes have decided this case. . . . [These cases have been] described as dealing with child rearing and education; with family relationships; with procreation; with marriage; with contraception; and with abortion. [The cases dealing with contraception and abortion] were interpreted as construing the Due Process Clause of the Fourteenth Amendment to confer a fundamental individual right to decide whether or not to beget or bear a child.

Accepting the decisions in these cases and the above description of them, we think it evident that none of the rights announced in those cases bears any resemblance to the claimed constitutional right of homosexuals to engage in acts of sodomy that is asserted in this case. No connection between family, marriage, or procreation on the one hand and homosexual activity on the other has been demonstrated, either by the Court of Appeals or by respondent. Moreover, any claim that these cases nevertheless stand for the proposition that any kind of private sexual conduct between consenting adults is constitutionally insulated from state proscription is unsupportable. . . .

Precedent aside, however, respondent would have us announce, as the Court of Appeals did, a fundamental right to engage in homosexual sodomy. This we are quite unwilling to do. It is true that despite the language of the Due Process Clauses of the Fifth and Fourteenth Amendments, which appears to focus only on the processes by which life, liberty, or property is taken, the cases are legion in which those Clauses have been interpreted to have substantive content, subsuming rights that to a great extent are immune from federal or state regulation or proscription. Among such cases are those recognizing rights that have little or no textual support in the constitutional language. . . .

Striving to assure itself and the public that announcing rights not readily identifiable in the Constitution's text involves much more than the imposition of the Justices' own choice of values on the States and the Federal Government, the Court has sought to identify the nature of the rights qualifying for heightened judicial protection. In *Palko* v. *Connecticut* (1937), it was said that this category includes those fundamental liberties that are "implicit in the concept of ordered liberty," such that "neither liberty nor justice would exist if [they] were sacrificed." A different description of fundamental liberties appeared in *Moore* v. *East Cleveland* (1977), where they are characterized as those liberties that are "deeply rooted in this Nation's history and tradition."

It is obvious to us that neither of these formulations would extend a fundamental right to homosexuals to engage in acts of consensual sodomy. Proscriptions against that conduct have ancient roots. Sodomy was a criminal offense at common law and was forbidden by the laws of the original 13 States when they ratified the Bill of Rights. In 1868, when the Fourteenth Amendment was ratified, all but 5 of the 37 States in the Union had criminal sodomy laws. In fact, until 1961, all 50 States outlawed sodomy, and today, 24 States and the District of Columbia continue to provide criminal penalties for sodomy performed in private and between consenting adults. Against this background, to claim that a right to engage in such conduct is "deeply rooted in this Nation's history and tradition" or "implicit in the concept of ordered liberty" is, at best, facetious.

Nor are we inclined to take a more expansive view of our authority to discover new fundamental rights imbedded in the Due Process Clause. The Court is most vulnerable and comes nearest to illegitimacy when it deals with judge-made constitutional law having little or no cognizable roots in the language or design of the Constitution. . . .

Respondent, however, asserts that the result should be different where the homosexual conduct occurs in the privacy of the home. He relies on *Stanley* v. *Georgia* (1969), where the Court held that the First Amendment prevents conviction for possessing and reading obscene material in the privacy of one's home: "If the First Amendment means anything, it means that a State has no business telling a man, sitting alone in his house, what books he may read or what films he may watch."

Stanley did protect conduct that would not have been protected outside the home, and it partially prevented the enforcement of state obscenity laws; but the decision was firmly grounded in the First Amendment. The right pressed upon us here has no similar support in the text of the Constitution, and it does not qualify for recognition under the prevailing principles for construing the Fourteenth Amendment. Its limits are also difficult to discern. Plainly enough, otherwise illegal conduct is not always immunized whenever it occurs in the home. Victimless crimes, such as the possession and use of illegal drugs, do not escape the law where they are committed at home. *Stanley* itself recognized that its holding offered no protection for the possession in the home of drugs, firearms, or stolen goods. And if respondent's submission is limited to the voluntary sexual conduct between consenting adults, it would be difficult, except by fiat, to limit the claimed right to homosexual conduct while leaving exposed to prosecution adultery, incest, and other sexual crimes even though they are committed in the home. We are unwilling to start down that road.

Even if the conduct at issue here is not a fundamental right, respondent asserts that there must be a rational basis for the law and that there is none in this case other than the presumed belief of a majority of the electorate in Georgia that homosexual sodomy is immoral and unacceptable. This is said to be an inadequate rationale to support the law. The law, however, is constantly based on notions of morality, and if all laws representing essentially moral choices are to be invalidated under the Due Process Clause, the courts will be very busy indeed. Even respondent makes no such claim, but insists that majority sentiments about the morality of homosexuality should be declared inadequate. We do not agree, and are unpersuaded that the sodomy laws of some 25 States should be invalidated on this basis.

Accordingly, the judgment of the Court of Appeals is *Reversed.*

NOTES

1 Georgia Code Ann. § 16–6–2 (1984) provides, in pertinent part, as follows:
"(a) A person commits the offense of sodomy when he performs or submits to any sexual act involving the sex organs of one person and the mouth or anus of another. . . .
"(b) A person convicted of the offense of sodomy shall be punished by imprisonment for not less than one nor more than 20 years. . . ."

QUESTIONS

1 Concerned with the constitutionality of the Georgia sodomy statute, Justice White writes, "This case does not require a judgment on whether laws against sodomy between consenting adults in general, or between homosexuals in particular, are wise or desirable." As a matter of social policy, are such laws well advised?
2 Opponents of the decriminalization of (homosexual) sodomy sometimes argue as follows: It is necessary that homosexual behavior, even between consenting adults in private, be considered a criminal offense; toleration of homosexual behavior would lead to long-term consequences disastrous for society. Is this a sound argument?

Dissenting Opinion in *Bowers v. Hardwick*

Justice Harry A. Blackmun

A biographical sketch of Justice Harry A. Blackmun is found on page 39.

Writing in dissent, Justice Blackmun argues that the Georgia sodomy statute constitutes an impermissible restriction on the right to privacy. He admonishes the Court majority for failing to recognize that all individuals have a fundamental interest in choosing for themselves how to conduct their intimate relationships. Justice Blackmun also critiques and rejects the justifications put forth by Georgia in defense of its sodomy statute. In particular, he rejects the view that the moral convictions of society provide a sufficient warrant for sodomy statutes.

This case is no more about "a fundamental right to engage in homosexual sodomy," as the Court purports to declare, than *Stanley* v. *Georgia* (1969) was about a fundamental right to watch obscene movies, or *Katz* v. *United States* (1967) was about a fundamental right to place interstate bets from a telephone booth. Rather, this case is

United States Supreme Court. 478 U.S. 186 (1986).

about "the most comprehensive of rights and the right most valued by civilized men," namely, "the right to be let alone."

The statute at issue, Ga. Code Ann. § 16–6–2 (1984), denies individuals the right to decide for themselves whether to engage in particular forms of private, consensual sexual activity. The Court concludes that § 16–6–2 is valid essentially because "the laws of . . . many States . . . still make such conduct illegal and have done so for a very long time." But the fact that the moral judgments expressed by statutes like § 16–6–2 may be " 'natural and familiar . . . ought not to conclude our judgment upon the question whether statutes embodying them conflict with the Constitution of the United States.' " Like Justice Holmes, I believe that "[i]t is revolting to have no better reason for a rule of law than that so it was laid down in the time of Henry IV. It is still more revolting if the grounds upon which it was laid down have vanished long since, and the rule simply persists from blind imitation of the past." I believe we must analyze respondent Hardwick's claim in the light of the values that underlie the constitutional right to privacy. If that right means anything, it means that, before Georgia can prosecute its citizens for making choices about the most intimate aspects of their lives, it must do more than assert that the choice they have made is an " 'abominable crime not fit to be named among Christians.' "

I

. . . A fair reading of the statute and of the complaint clearly reveals that the majority has distorted the question this case presents.

. . . The Court's almost obsessive focus on homosexual activity is particularly hard to justify in light of the broad language Georgia has used. . . . Georgia has provided that "[a] person commits the offense of sodomy when he performs or submits to any sexual act involving the sex organs of one person and the mouth or anus of another." The sex or status of the persons who engage in the act is irrelevant as a matter of state law. . . . Michael Hardwick's standing may rest in significant part on Georgia's apparent willingness to enforce against homosexuals a law it seems not to have any desire to enforce against heterosexuals. But his claim that § 16–6–2 involves an unconstitutional intrusion into his privacy and his right of intimate association does not depend in any way on his sexual orientation. . . .

. . . I believe that Hardwick has stated a cognizable claim that § 16–6–2 interferes with constitutionally protected interests in privacy and freedom of intimate association. . . . The Court's cramped reading of the issue before it makes for a short opinion, but it does little to make for a persuasive one.

II

"Our cases long have recognized that the Constitution embodies a promise that a certain private sphere of individual liberty will be kept largely beyond the reach of government." In construing the right to privacy, the Court has proceeded along two somewhat distinct, albeit complementary, lines. First, it has recognized a privacy interest with reference to certain *decisions* that are properly for the individual to make.

Second, it has recognized a privacy interest with reference to certain *places* without regard for the particular activities in which the individuals who occupy them are engaged. The case before us implicates both the decisional and the spatial aspects of the right to privacy.

A

The Court concludes today that none of our prior cases dealing with various decisions that individuals are entitled to make free of governmental interference "bears any resemblance to the claimed constitutional right of homosexuals to engage in acts of sodomy that is asserted in this case." While it is true that these cases may be characterized by their connection to protection of the family, the Court's conclusion that they extend no further than this boundary ignores the warning . . . against "clos[ing] our eyes to the basic reasons why certain rights associated with the family have been accorded shelter under the Fourteenth Amendment's Due Process Clause." We protect those rights not because they contribute, in some direct and material way, to the general public welfare, but because they form so central a part of an individual's life. "[T]he concept of privacy embodies the 'moral fact that a person belongs to himself and not others nor to society as a whole.' " And so we protect the decision whether to marry precisely because marriage "is an association that promotes a way of life, not causes; a harmony in living, not political faiths; a bilateral loyalty, not commercial or social projects." We protect the decision whether to have a child because parenthood alters so dramatically an individual's self-definition, not because of demographic considerations or the Bible's command to be fruitful and multiply. And we protect the family because it contributes so powerfully to the happiness of individuals, not because of a preference for stereotypical households. The Court [has] recognized . . . that the "ability independently to define one's identity that is central to any concept of liberty" cannot truly be exercised in a vacuum; we all depend on the "emotional enrichment from close ties with others."

Only the most willful blindness could obscure the fact that sexual intimacy is "a sensitive, key relationship of human existence, central to family life, community welfare, and the development of human personality." The fact that individuals define themselves in a significant way through their intimate sexual relationships with others suggests, in a Nation as diverse as ours, that there may be many "right" ways of conducting those relationships, and that much of the richness of a relationship will come from the freedom an individual has to *choose* the form and nature of these intensely personal bonds.

In a variety of circumstances we have recognized that a necessary corollary of giving individuals freedom to choose how to conduct their lives is acceptance of the fact that different individuals will make different choices. For example, in holding that the clearly important state interest in public education should give way to a competing claim by the Amish to the effect that extended formal schooling threatened their way of life, the Court declared: "There can be no assumption that today's majority is 'right' and the Amish and others like them are 'wrong.' A way of life that is odd or even erratic but interferes with no rights or interests of others is not to be condemned because it is different." The Court claims that its decision today merely refuses to recognize a fundamental right to engage in homosexual sodomy; what the Court really has refused to recognize is the fundamental interest all individuals have in controlling the nature of their intimate associations with others.

B

The behavior for which Hardwick faces prosecution occurred in his own home, a place to which the Fourth Amendment attaches special significance. The Court's treatment of this aspect of the case is symptomatic of its overall refusal to consider the broad principles that have informed our treatment of privacy in specific cases. Just as the right to privacy is more than the mere aggregation of a number of entitlements to engage in specific behavior, so too, protecting the physical integrity of the home is more than merely a means of protecting specific activities that often take place there. Even when our understanding of the contours of the right to privacy depends on "reference to a 'place,'" the essence of a Fourth Amendment violation is 'not the breaking of [a person's] doors, and the rummaging of his drawers,' but rather is 'the invasion of his indefeasible right of personal security, personal liberty and private property.' "

The Court's interpretation of the pivotal case of *Stanley* v. *Georgia* (1969) is entirely unconvincing. *Stanley* held that Georgia's undoubted power to punish the public distribution of constitutionally unprotected, obscene material did not permit the State to punish the private possession of such material. According to the majority here, *Stanley* relied entirely on the First Amendment, and thus, it is claimed, sheds no light on cases not involving printed materials. But that is not what *Stanley* said. Rather, the *Stanley* Court anchored its holding in the Fourth Amendment's special protection for the individual in his home. . . .

. . . *Stanley* rested as much on the Court's understanding of the Fourth Amendment as it did on the First. . . . "The right of the people to be secure in their . . . houses," expressly guaranteed by the Fourth Amendment, is perhaps the most "textual" of the various constitutional provisions that inform our understanding of the right to privacy, and thus I cannot agree with the Court's statement that "[t]he right pressed upon us here has no . . . support in the text of the Constitution." Indeed, the right of an individual to conduct intimate relationships in the intimacy of his or her own home seems to me to be the heart of the Constitution's protection of privacy.

III

The Court's failure to comprehend the magnitude of the liberty interests at stake in this case leads it to slight the question whether petitioner, on behalf of the State, has justified Georgia's infringement on these interests. I believe that neither of the two general justifications for § 16–6–2 that petitioner has advanced warrants dismissing respondent's challenge for failure to state a claim.

First, petitioner asserts that the acts made criminal by the statute may have serious adverse consequences for "the general public health and welfare," such as spreading communicable diseases or fostering other criminal activity. Inasmuch as this case was dismissed by the District Court on the pleadings, it is not surprising that the record before us is barren of any evidence to support petitioner's claim. In light of the state of the record, I see no justification for the Court's attempt to equate the private, consensual sexual activity at issue here with the "possession in the home of drugs, firearms, or stolen goods," to which *Stanley* refused to extend its protection. None of the behavior so mentioned in *Stanley* can properly be viewed as "[v]ictimless": drugs and weapons are inherently dangerous, and for property to be "stolen," someone must have been wrongfully deprived of it. Nothing in the record before the Court provides any justification for finding the activity forbidden by § 16–6–2 to be physically dangerous, either to the persons engaged in it or to others.

The core of petitioner's defense of § 16–6–2, however, is that respondent and others who engage in the conduct prohibited by § 16–6–2 interfere with Georgia's exercise of the " 'right of the Nation and of the States to maintain a decent society.' " Essentially, petitioner argues, and the Court agrees, that the fact that the acts described in § 16–6–2 "for hundreds of years, if not thousands, have been uniformly condemned as immoral" is a sufficient reason to permit a State to ban them today.

I cannot agree that either the length of time a majority has held its convictions or the passions with which it defends them can withdraw legislation from this Court's scrutiny. As Justice Jackson wrote so eloquently, . . . "we apply the limitations of the Constitution with no fear that freedom to be intellectually and spiritually diverse or even contrary will disintegrate the social organization. . . . [F]reedom to differ is not limited to things that do not matter much. That would be a mere shadow of freedom. The test of its substance is the right to differ as to things that touch the heart of the existing order." It is precisely because the issue raised by this case touches the heart of what makes individuals what they are that we should be especially sensitive to the rights of those whose choices upset the majority.

The assertion that "traditional Judeo-Christian values proscribe" the conduct involved cannot provide an adequate justification for § 16–6–2. That certain, but by no means all, religious groups condemn the behavior at issue gives the State no license to impose their judgments on the entire citizenry. The legitimacy of secular legislation depends instead on whether the State can advance some justification for its law beyond its conformity to religious doctrine. Thus, far from buttressing his case, petitioner's invocation of Leviticus, Romans, St. Thomas Aquinas, and sodomy's heretical status during the Middle Ages undermines his suggestion that § 16–6–2 represents a legitimate use of secular coercive power. A State can no more punish private behavior because of religious intolerance than it can punish such behavior because of racial animus. "The Constitution cannot control such prejudices, but neither can it tolerate them. Private biases may be outside the reach of the law, but the law cannot, directly or indirectly, give them effect." No matter how uncomfortable a certain group may make the majority of this Court, we have held that "[m]ere public intolerance or animosity cannot constitutionally justify the deprivation of a person's physical liberty."

Nor can § 16–6–2 be justified as a "morally neutral" exercise of Georgia's power to "protect the public environment." Certainly, some private behavior can affect the fabric of society as a whole. Reasonable people may differ about whether particular sexual acts are moral or immoral, but "we have ample evidence for believing that people will not abandon morality, will not think any better of murder, cruelty and dishonesty, merely because some private sexual practice which they abominate is not punished by the law." Petitioner and the Court fail to see the difference between laws that protect public sensibilities and those that enforce private morality. Statutes banning public sexual activity are entirely consistent with protecting the individual's liberty interest in decisions concerning sexual relations: the same recognition that those decisions are intensely private which justifies protecting them from governmental interference can justify protecting individuals from unwilling exposure to the sexual activities of others. But the mere fact that intimate behavior may be punished when it takes place in public cannot dictate how States can regulate intimate behavior that occurs in intimate places.

This case involves no real interference with the rights of others, for the mere knowledge that other individuals do not adhere to one's value system cannot be a legally cognizable interest, let alone an interest that can justify invading the houses, hearts, and minds of citizens who choose to live their lives differently.

IV

It took but three years for the Court to see the error in its analysis in *Minersville School District* v. *Gobitis* (1940) and to recognize that the threat to national cohesion posed by a refusal to salute the flag was vastly outweighed by the threat to those same values posed by compelling such a salute. I can only hope that here, too, the Court soon will reconsider its analysis and conclude that depriving individuals of the right to choose for themselves how to conduct their intimate relationships poses a far greater threat to the values most deeply rooted in our Nation's history than tolerance of nonconformity could ever do. Because I think the Court today betrays those values, I dissent.

QUESTIONS

1 As a matter of social policy, would a state be well advised to decriminalize *all* sexual behavior between consenting adults in private?

2 On balance, are sodomy statutes a help or a hindrance in the war on AIDS? Do they effectively deter high-risk sexual behaviors? Do they significantly interfere with—via the fear of criminal liability—the effectiveness of research efforts and safe-sex educational campaigns?

SUGGESTED ADDITIONAL READINGS FOR CHAPTER 5

BAKER, ROBERT, and FREDERICK ELLISTON: *Philosophy and Sex,* New Revised Edition. Buffalo, N.Y.: Prometheus, 1984. This anthology contains a number of articles relevant to the topic of sexual morality.

BARNHART, J. E., and MARY ANN BARNHART: "Marital Faithfulness and Unfaithfulness." *Journal of Social Philosophy,* vol. 4, April 1973, pp. 10–15. The Barnharts argue that we should recognize the legitimacy of different marriage styles, including a marriage style that incorporates extramarital sex.

BEAUCHAMP, DAN E.: "Morality and the Health of the Body Politic." *Hastings Center Report,* vol. 16, December 1986, special supplement, pp. 30–36. Beauchamp argues that society's efforts to deal with the AIDS crisis are undermined by the existence of sodomy statutes and other forms of societal discrimination against gays.

BELLIOTTI, RAYMOND A.: "A Philosophical Analysis of Sexual Ethics." *Journal of Social Philosophy,* vol. 10, September 1979, pp. 8–11. Belliotti contends that sexual interactions have a contractual basis and argues that they are morally objectionable if and only if they involve (1) deception, (2) promise breaking, or (3) exploitation, that is, treating another *merely* as a means to one's own ends.

CAMERON, PAUL: "A Case Against Homosexuality." *Human Life Review,* vol. 4, Summer 1978, pp. 17–49. As a psychologist, Cameron introduces empirical data about homosexuality. He contends that homosexuality is an undesirable life-style and argues against the liberalization of social policy (regarding homosexuality).

LEISER, BURTON M.: *Liberty, Justice and Morals,* 3d ed. New York: Macmillan, 1986. Chapter 2 of this book deals with homosexuality. In the course of constructing a case against criminal sanctions, Leiser analyzes the arguments commonly made in support of the condemnation of homosexual behavior.

PIERCE, CHRISTINE: "AIDS and *Bowers v. Hardwick.*" *Journal of Social Philosophy,* vol. 20, Winter 1989, pp. 21–32. Pierce contends that natural law arguments have aggravated the AIDS crisis by leading to both bad science and bad law. She presents an extensive critique of the Supreme Court's holding in *Bowers v. Hardwick.*

TAYLOR, RICHARD: *Having Love Affairs.* Buffalo, N.Y., Prometheus, 1982. Taylor rejects the idea that adultery is immoral. He also emphasizes the values served by love affairs and defends their moral legitimacy.

VANNOY, RUSSELL: *Sex Without Love: A Philosophical Exploration.* Buffalo, N.Y.: Prometheus, 1980. Vannoy defends sex without love: "I conclude, therefore, that on the whole, sex with a humanistic non-lover is far preferable to sex with an erotic lover." Both Chapter 1, "Sex with Love vs. Sex without Love" (pp. 7–29), and Chapter 4, "Types of Sexual Philosophy: A Summary" (pp. 118–127), are especially relevant to the topic of sexual morality.

WASSERSTROM, RICHARD: "Is Adultery Immoral?" In Richard Wasserstrom, ed., *Today's Moral Problems,* 3d ed. New York: Macmillan, 1985. This helpful article investigates the various arguments that can plausibly be made in support of the claim that adultery is immoral. Wasserstrom's analysis is especially valuable in focusing attention on the presuppositions of such arguments.

WHITELEY, C. H., and W. N. WHITELEY: *Sex and Morals.* New York: Basic, 1967. This book as a whole is useful, but Chapter 5, on "Unfruitful Sex," is especially germane. In this chapter, the Whiteleys examine the morality of masturbation, homosexual behavior, and other types of sexual activity that cut off the possibility of procreation.

CHAPTER 6

Pornography and Censorship

Is the censorship of pornography ethically justified? More specifically, let us pose the central issue of this chapter as follows: Is a government justified in limiting the access of *consenting adults* to pornographic materials? In their most common form, censorship laws seek to limit the access of consenting adults to pornographic materials by prohibiting their distribution, sale, or exhibition. However, it is also possible for censorship laws to prohibit the production of pornography or even its possession.

COMMISSION REPORTS

In 1967, the Congress of the United States, labeling the traffic in obscene and pornographic materials "a matter of national concern," established the Commission on Obscenity and Pornography. This advisory commission, whose members were appointed by President Lyndon Johnson in January 1968, was charged with initiating a thorough study of obscenity and pornography and, on the basis of such a study, submitting recommendations for the regulation of obscene and pornographic materials. In September 1970 the Commission transmitted its final report to the President and the Congress. Its fundamental recommendation was that all legislation prohibiting the sale, exhibition, or distribution of sexual materials to *consenting adults* be repealed. However, the Commission recommended the continuation of legislation intended to protect nonconsenting adults from being confronted with sexually explicit material through public displays and unsolicited mailings. It also recommended the continuation of legislation prohibiting the commercial distribution of certain sexual material to juveniles. The Commission based its fundamental recommendation largely, though not exclusively, on its central factual finding: There is no evidence to support the contention that exposure to explicit sexual materials plays a significant role in the causation of either social harms (via antisocial behavior) or individual harms (such as severe emotional disturbance).

The report of the Commission on Obscenity and Pornography was unwelcome in many quarters. To begin with, only twelve of the Commission's eighteen members voted in support of its fundamental recommendation. In fact, the report itself features a substantial minority report that questions the factual findings as well as the recommendations of the Commission. President Richard Nixon contended that the report was completely unsatisfactory. Many members of Congress were also displeased, and there was a substantial public outcry that the conclusions of the Commission were "morally bankrupt." As a result, there was no significant movement to implement its fundamental recommendation.

In Spring 1985, responsive to a request by President Ronald Reagan, Attorney General Edwin Meese III named an eleven-member commission to *reexamine* the problem of pornography in American society. The Attorney General's Commission on Pornography submitted its final report in July 1986. With regard to the issue of the harmfulness of pornography, some of the factual findings of this second commission (which we will call "the 1986 Commission") stand in stark contrast to the central factual finding of the earlier commission (which we will call "the 1970 Commission"). The 1986 Commission, employing the word "pornography" to refer to material that is "predominantly sexually explicit and intended primarily for the purpose of sexual arousal," thought it important to distinguish among (1) violent pornography, (2) nonviolent but degrading pornography, and (3) nonviolent and nondegrading pornography. The Commission concluded that both category (1) and category (2) materials, but *not* category (3) materials, bear a causal relationship to undesirable attitudinal changes and acts of sexual violence. The thinking of the Commission on these matters is exhibited in an excerpt from the *Final Report* that is reprinted in this chapter.

The 1970 Commission, convinced of the essential harmlessness of pornography, embraced an explicit anticensorship stance. In contrast, the 1986 Commission was fundamentally procensorship and endorsed (and in fact called for vigorous enforcement of) already existing laws that criminalize the sale, distribution, or exhibition of *legally obscene* pornographic materials. The relevant standard of legal obscenity—a category that does not enjoy First Amendment protection—was first enunciated by the Supreme Court in *Miller v. California* (1973). In accordance with "the Miller standard," material is legally obscene if three conditions are satisfied:

(a) . . . "the average person, applying contemporary community standards," would find that the work, taken as a whole, appeals to the prurient interest; (b) . . . the work depicts or describes, in a patently offensive way, sexual conduct specifically defined by the applicable state law; and (c) . . . the work, taken as a whole, lacks serious literary, artistic, political, or scientific value.[1]

The 1986 Commission also called special attention to the problem of child pornography. Since the production of child pornography typically entails the sexual abuse of children, the Commission pointed out that there is a distinctive and compelling rationale for laws that prohibit the production, as well as the sale, exhibition, or distribution, of child pornography.

---

[1]United States Supreme Court. 413 U.S. 15, 24.

LIBERTY-LIMITING PRINCIPLES

Laws limiting the access of consenting adults to pornographic materials, like all prohibitive laws, inevitably involve limitation of individual liberty. Accordingly, one way of approaching our central question is to take notice of the kinds of grounds that may be advanced to justify the limitation of individual liberty. Four suggested liberty-limiting principles are especially noteworthy:[2]

1 The harm principle—Individual liberty is justifiably limited to prevent *harm to others.*

2 The principle of legal paternalism—Individual liberty is justifiably limited to prevent *harm to self.*

3 The principle of legal moralism—Individual liberty is justifiably limited to prevent *immoral behavior.*

4 The offense principle—Individual liberty is justifiably limited to prevent *offense to others.*

The *harm principle* is the most widely accepted liberty-limiting principle. Few will dispute that the law is within its proper bounds when it restricts actions whereby one person causes harm to others. (The category of *harm to others* is understood as encompassing not only personal injury but also damage to the general welfare of society.) What remains a lively source of debate is whether any, or all, of the other suggested principles are legitimate liberty-limiting principles. According to John Stuart Mill (1806–1873), only the harm principle is a legitimate liberty-limiting principle. A short excerpt from his famous essay *On Liberty* appears in this chapter. Though Mill need not be read as unsympathetic to the offense principle, he clearly and vigorously rejects both the principle of legal paternalism and the principle of legal moralism.

According to the *principle of legal paternalism,* the law may justifiably be invoked to prevent self-harm, and thus "to protect individuals from themselves." Supporters of this principle think that the law rightfully serves much as a benevolent parent who limits his or her child's liberty in order to save the child from harm. Some, of course, often in the spirit of Mill, hotly contest the legitimacy of the principle of legal paternalism. It is said, for example, that government does not have the right to meddle in the private life of its citizens. Though there is little doubt that there are presently numerous paternalistic features in our legal system, their justifiability remains a disputed issue. The widespread law that requires motorcyclists to wear protective headgear is one apparent example of a paternalistic law.

According to the *principle of legal moralism,* the law may justifiably be invoked to prevent immoral behavior or, as it is often expressed, to "enforce morals." Such things as kidnapping, murder, and fraud are undoubtedly immoral, but there would seem to be no need to appeal to the principle of legal moralism to justify laws against them. An appeal to the harm principle already provides a widely accepted independent justification. As a result, the principle of legal moralism usually comes

---

[2]Joel Feinberg's discussion of such principles served as a guide for the formulations adopted here. *Social Philosophy* (Englewood Cliffs, N.J.: Prentice-Hall, 1973), chap. 2.

to the fore only when so-called victimless crimes are under discussion. Is it justifiable to legislate against homosexual relations, gambling, and smoking marijuana simply on the grounds that such activities are thought to be morally unacceptable? There are many such laws, and presumably they are intended to enforce conventional morality, but some people continue to call for their repeal on the grounds that the principle of legal moralism is an unacceptable liberty-limiting principle. To accept the principle of legal moralism, in Mill's words, is tantamount to permitting a "tyranny of the majority."

According to the *offense principle,* the law may justifiably be invoked to prevent "offensive" behavior in public. "Offensive" behavior is understood as behavior that causes shame, embarrassment, discomfort, etc., to be experienced by onlookers. The offense principle, unlike the other principles discussed above, is not ordinarily advanced to justify laws that would limit the access of *consenting* adults to pornographic materials. The offense principle, however, is sometimes advanced to justify laws that protect *nonconsenting* adults from "offensive" displays of pornography.

THE CASE FOR CENSORSHIP

Arguments in support of laws that would limit the access of consenting adults to pornographic materials can conveniently be organized by the liberty-limiting principles on which they are based.

1 Arguments Based on the Harm Principle

It is frequently asserted that exposure to pornography is a significant causal factor in sex-related crimes such as rape. Defenders of this thesis sometimes argue for their claim by citing examples of persons exposed to pornographic material who subsequently commit sex-related crimes. Such examples, however, fail to establish that the crime, which *follows* exposure to pornography, is a *causal result* of exposure to pornography. Indeed, the 1970 Commission reported that there is no evidence to support such a causal connection. On the other hand, the 1986 Commission surveyed the available evidence and reported the existence of a causal connection between exposure to certain kinds of pornography (namely, *violent* pornography and *degrading* pornography) and acts of sexual violence. All of these matters continue to be hotly debated. However, since the harm principle is a widely accepted liberty-limiting principle, a formidable argument for censorship emerges to the extent that a causal connection between the use of pornography (or certain kinds of pornography) and antisocial behavior can be established.

A second line of argument based on the harm principle emphasizes the alleged disastrous effects of the widespread exposure to pornography on the overall welfare of society. It is said, for example, that society will become obsessed with impersonal expressions of sexuality, that love will disappear, and that children entering such a society will be psychologically deprived. It has even been suggested that unlimited access to pornographic materials might eventually culminate in the total decay of order and civilization. "What is at stake is civilization and humanity, nothing less."[3] According to a closely related line of thought, pornography functions to break down the feelings of shame associated with sex and thereby represents a serious threat to democracy.

> To live together requires rules and a governing of the passions, and those who are without shame will be unruly and unreliable; having lost the ability to restrain themselves by observing the rules they collectively give themselves, they will have to be ruled by others. Tyranny is the natural and inevitable mode of government for the shameless and the self-indulgent who have carried liberty beyond any restraint.[4]

In the face of harm-principle arguments to the effect that widespread exposure to pornography will (in the long run) produce dire consequences for society, two responses are commonly made: (1) The anticipated dire effects will not in fact occur. (2) The anticipated effects are so speculative as not to constitute a "clear and present danger."

2 Arguments Based on the Principle of Legal Paternalism

It is often said that those exposed to pornography will be harmed by such exposure. They will, it is thought, develop or reinforce emotional problems; they will render themselves incapable of love and other human relationships necessary for a happy and satisfying life. In a more abstract and possibly rhetorical version of this argument, it is alleged that frequent exposure to pornography "depersonalizes" or "dehumanizes," and presumably such effects are at least in a broad sense harmful to the individual. Arguments based on the principle of legal paternalism are answered in two ways: (1) The alleged self-harm does not occur. (2) Regardless of the truth or falsity of the claim of self-harm, the principle of legal paternalism is not an acceptable liberty-limiting principle.

3 Arguments Based on the Principle of Legal Moralism

It is frequently claimed that there is a widespread consensus to the effect that pornography is morally repugnant. Inasmuch as the principle of legal moralism seems to allow a community to enforce its moral convictions, it follows that the access of consenting adults to pornographic materials may rightfully be restricted. Arguments thus based on the principle of legal moralism are answered in two ways: (1) The alleged consensus of moral opinion is nonexistent. (2) Regardless of the truth or falsity of the claim of an existing moral consensus, the principle of legal moralism is not an acceptable liberty-limiting principle.

The morality of pornography is an important ethical issue in its own right. To some extent, of course, one's moral assessment of pornography will be a function of

---

[3]Irving Kristol, "Pornography, Obscenity, and the Case for Censorship," *The New York Times Magazine,* March 28, 1971, p. 113.

[4]Walter Berns, "Pornography vs. Democracy: The Case for Censorship," *Public Interest,* vol. 22, Winter 1971, p. 13.

one's views on sexual morality in general. In one of this chapter's selections, Charles H. Keating, Jr., argues on rather traditional grounds that pornography is clearly immoral. Because Keating takes his view to be the consensus view of society, and because he explicitly endorses the principle of legal moralism, he is a vigorous proponent of censorship.

THE CASE AGAINST CENSORSHIP

The overall case against laws limiting the access of consenting adults to pornographic materials usually takes the following direction: The principle of legal paternalism is an unacceptable liberty-limiting principle; the government has no business meddling in the private affairs of its citizens since such meddling is likely to produce more harm than it prevents. The principle of legal moralism is also an unacceptable liberty-limiting principle; to enforce the moral views of the majority is, in effect, to allow a "tyranny of the majority." A government can rightfully legislate against the private activity of consenting adults only on the grounds that such activity is *harmful to others.* At the present time, however, it has not been established that the access of consenting adults to pornographic materials presents a "clear and present danger." Thus censorship, especially in view of the administrative nightmares it is likely to generate and the very real possibility that the power of the censor will be abused, is clearly unwarranted.

It is sometimes further argued by opponents of censorship that pornography is in fact beneficial to those exposed to it and to society as a whole. Here it is said, for example, that exposure to pornography can aid normal sexual development, that it can invigorate sexual relationships, and that it can provide a socially harmless release from sexual tension. Such considerations are developed by G. L. Simons in one of the readings in this chapter.

FEMINISM AND PORNOGRAPHY

In recent years, an important new critique of pornography has arisen from a feminist point of view. In contrast to more traditional critics of pornography, feminists do not ordinarily object to the sexual explicitness that is found in pornography. Rather, their concern is rooted in the fact that pornography typically portrays *women* in a degrading and dehumanizing way. Related to this central concern is a distinction that feminists ordinarily draw between *pornography* (which is morally and socially problematic) and mere *erotica* (which is not).

In one of this chapter's selections, Helen E. Longino defines pornography as "material that explicitly represents or describes degrading and abusive sexual behavior so as to endorse and/or recommend the behavior as described." Because pornography is *injurious* to women in a number of related ways, she maintains, its production and distribution are justifiably subject to control. In essence, then, Longino presents a procensorship argument based on the harm principle. However, not all feminists advocate the censorship of pornography. In another of this chapter's selections, Mark R. Wicclair vigorously defends an anticensorship stance within the framework of feminism. He emphasizes the values associated with the principle of freedom of expression and calls attention to the detrimental side effects of censorship. He also maintains, against the procensorship feminist, that the connection between pornography and harm to women is too speculative to warrant incurring the social costs of censorship.

Thomas A. Mappes

Majority Opinion in *Paris Adult Theatre I v. Slaton*

Justice Warren Burger

Warren Burger served as chief justice of the United States Supreme Court from 1969 to 1987. Admitted to the Minnesota bar in 1931, he then spent a number of years in private practice, while simultaneously serving on the faculty of the Mitchell College of Law in St. Paul. He also served as assistant attorney general (1953–1956) and as judge of the United States Court of Appeals, District of Columbia Circuit (1956–1969).

The state of Georgia sought an injunction against the showing of two films—*It All Comes Out in the End* and *Magic Mirror*—by the Paris Adult Theatres I and II (Atlanta). The state claimed that the films were obscene under the relevant Georgia standards. The trial court refused to grant the injunction, holding that the showing of the films could be prohibited only if it were proved that they were shown to minors or nonconsenting adults. The Supreme Court of Georgia reversed the decision of the trial court, and the Supreme Court of the United States upheld the reversal, though by a mere five-to-four majority.

In Chief Justice Burger's majority opinion, he argues that there are legitimate state interests at stake in the state regulation of consenting adults' access to obscene material. According to Chief Justice Burger, such interests include the maintenance of a decent society, the tone of commerce in large cities, and "possibly" the public safety. Chief Justice Burger acknowledges that there is no conclusive proof of a connection between obscene material and antisocial behavior, but he nevertheless considers the belief in such a connection to be a reasonable one. In arguing that state regulation of obscene material is constitutionally acceptable, he emphasizes two points: (1) State regulation of obscene material in no way violates the constitutionally protected right to privacy. (2) State regulation of obscene material is not tantamount to restricting the communication of ideas and thus does not violate the First Amendment.

We categorically disapprove the theory, apparently adopted by the trial judge, that obscene, pornographic films acquire constitutional immunity from state regulation simply because they are exhibited for consenting adults only. This holding was prop-

United States Supreme Court. 413 U.S. 49 (1973).

erly rejected by the Georgia Supreme Court. Although we have often pointedly recognized the high importance of the state interest in regulating the exposure of obscene materials to juveniles and unconsenting adults, this Court has never declared these to be the only legitimate state interests permitting regulation of obscene material. The States have a long-recognized legitimate interest in regulating the use of obscene material in local commerce and in all places of public accommodation, as long as these regulations do not run afoul of specific constitutional prohibitions. "In an unbroken series of cases extending over a long stretch of this Court's history, it has been accepted as a postulate that 'the primary requirements of decency may be enforced against obscene publications.' "

In particular, we hold that there are legitimate state interests at stake in stemming the tide of commercialized obscenity, even assuming it is feasible to enforce effective safeguards against exposure to juveniles and to the passerby. Rights and interests "other than those of the advocates are involved." These include the interest of the public in the quality of life and the total community environment, the tone of commerce in the great city centers, and, possibly, the public safety itself. The Hill-Link Minority Report of the Commission on Obscenity and Pornography indicates that there is at least an arguable correlation between obscene material and crime. Quite apart from sex crimes, however, there remains one problem of large proportions aptly described by Professor Bickel:

> It concerns the tone of the society, the mode, or to use terms that have perhaps greater currency, the style and quality of life, now and in the future. A man may be entitled to read an obscene book in his room, or expose himself indecently there. . . . We should protect his privacy. But if he demands a right to obtain the books and pictures he wants in the market and to foregather in public places—discreet, if you will, but accessible to all—with others who share his tastes, *then to grant him his right is to affect the world about the rest of us, and to impinge on other privacies.* Even supposing that each of us can, if he wishes, effectively avert the eye and stop the ear (which, in truth, we cannot), what is commonly read and seen and heard and done intrudes upon us all, want it or not.[1] [Emphasis supplied.]

As Chief Justice Warren stated there is a "right of the Nation and of the States to maintain a decent society. . . ."

But, it is argued, there is no scientific data which conclusively demonstrates that exposure to obscene materials adversely affects men and women or their society. It is urged on behalf of the petitioner that, absent such a demonstration, any kind of state regulation is "impermissible." We reject this argument. It is not for us to resolve empirical uncertainties underlying state legislation, save in the exceptional case where that legislation plainly impinges upon rights protected by the Constitution itself. Mr. Justice Brennan, speaking for the Court in *Ginsberg v. New York (1968),* said "We do not demand of legislatures 'scientifically certain criteria of legislation.' " Although there is no conclusive proof of a connection between antisocial behavior and obscene material, the legislature of Georgia could quite reasonably determine that such a connection does or might exist. . . .

If we accept the unprovable assumption that a complete education requires the reading of certain books, and the well nigh universal belief that good books, plays, and art lift the spirit, improve the mind, enrich the human personality and develop character, can we then say that a state legislature may not act on the corollary assumption that commerce in obscene books, or public exhibitions focused on obscene conduct, have a tendency to exert a corrupting and debasing impact leading to antisocial behavior? "Many of these effects may be intangible and indistinct, but they are nonetheless real." Mr. Justice Cardozo said that all laws in Western civilization are "guided by a robust common sense. . . ." The sum of experience, including that of the past two decades, affords an ample basis for legislatures to conclude that a sensitive, key relationship of human existence, central to family life, community welfare, and the development of human personality, can be debased and distorted by crass commercial exploitation of sex. Nothing in the Constitution prohibits a State from reaching such a conclusion and acting on it legislatively simply because there is no conclusive evidence or empirical data.

It is argued that individual "free will" must govern, even in activities beyond the protection of the First Amendment and other constitutional guarantees of privacy, and that Government cannot legitimately impede an individual's desire to see or acquire obscene plays, movies, and books. We do indeed base our society on certain assumptions that people have the capacity for free choice. Most exercises of individual free choice—those in politics, religion, and expression of ideas—are explicitly protected by the Constitution. Totally unlimited play for free will, however, is not allowed in ours or any other society. We have just noted, for example, that neither the First Amendment nor "free will" precludes States from having "blue sky" laws to regulate what sellers of securities may write or publish about their wares. Such laws are to protect the weak, the uninformed, the unsuspecting, and the gullible from the exercise of their own volition. Nor do modern societies leave disposal of garbage and sewage up to the individual "free will," but impose regulation to protect both public health and the appearance of public places. States are told by some that they must await a "laissez faire" market solution to the obscenity-pornography problem, paradoxically "by people who have never otherwise had a kind word to say for laissez-faire," particularly in solving urban, commercial, and environmental pollution problems.

The States, of course, may follow such a "laissez faire" policy and drop all controls on commercialized obscenity, if that is what they prefer, just as they can ignore consumer protection in the market place, but nothing in the Constitution *compels* the States to do so with regard to matters falling within state jurisdiction. . . .

It is asserted, however, that standards for evaluating state commercial regulations are inapposite in the present context, as state regulation of access by consenting adults to obscene material violates the constitutionally protected right to privacy enjoyed by petitioners' customers. Even assuming that petitioners have vicarious standing to assert potential customers' rights, it is unavailing to compare a theatre, open to the public for a fee, with the private home of *Stanley v. Georgia* (1969) and the marital bedroom of *Griswold v. Connecticut* (1965). This Court, has, on numerous occasions, refused to hold that commercial ventures such as a motion-picture house are "private" for the purpose of civil rights litigation and civil rights statutes. The Civil Rights Act of 1964 specifically defines motion-picture houses and theatres as places of "public accommodation" covered by the Act as operations affecting commerce.

Our prior decisions recognizing a right to privacy guaranteed by the Fourteenth Amendment included "only those personal rights that can be deemed 'fundamental' or 'implicit in the concept of ordered liberty.' " This privacy right encompasses and protects the personal intimacies of the home, the family, marriage, motherhood, procreation, and child rearing. Nothing, however, in this Court's decisions intimates that there is any "fundamental" privacy right "implicit in the concept of ordered liberty" to watch obscene movies in places of public accommodation.

If obscene material unprotected by the First Amendment in itself carried with it a "penumbra" of constitutionally protected privacy, this Court would not have found it necessary to decide *Stanley* on the narrow basis of the "privacy of the home," which was hardly more than a reaffirmation that "a man's home is his castle." Moreover, we have declined to equate the privacy of the home relied on in *Stanley* with a "zone" of "privacy" that follows a distributor or a consumer of obscene materials wherever he goes. The idea of a "privacy" right and a place of public accommodation are, in this context, mutually exclusive. Conduct or depictions of conduct that the state police power can prohibit on a public street does not become automatically protected by the Constitution merely because the conduct is moved to a bar or a "live" theatre stage, any more than a "live" performance of a man and woman locked in a sexual embrace at high noon in Times Square is protected by the Constitution because they simultaneously engage in a valid political dialogue.

It is also argued that the State has no legitimate interest in "control [of] the moral content of a person's thoughts," and we need not quarrel with this. But we reject the claim that the State of Georgia is here attempting to control the minds or thoughts of those who patronize theatres. Preventing unlimited display or distribution of obscene material, which by definition lacks any serious literary, artistic, political, or scientific value as communication, is distinct from a control of reason and the intellect. Where communication of ideas, protected by the First Amendment, is not involved, nor the particular privacy of the home protected by *Stanley,* nor any of the other "areas or zones" of constitutionally protected privacy, the mere fact that, as a consequence, some human "utterances" or "thoughts" may be incidentally affected does not bar the State from acting to protect legitimate state interests. The fantasies of a drug addict are his own and beyond the reach of government, but government regulation of drug sales is not prohibited by the Constitution.

Finally, petitioners argue that conduct which directly involves "consenting adults" only has, for that sole reason, a special claim to constitutional protection. Our Constitution establishes a broad range of conditions on the exercise of power by the states, but for us to say that our Constitution incorporates the proposition that conduct involving consenting adults only is always beyond state regulation, that is a step we are unable to take. Commercial exploitation of depictions, descriptions, or exhibitions of obscene conduct on commercial premises open to the adult public falls within a State's broad power to regulate commerce and protect the public environment. The issue in this context goes beyond whether someone, or even the majority, considers the conduct depicted as "wrong" or "sinful." The States have the power to make a morally neutral judgment that public exhibition of obscene material, or commerce in such material, has a tendency to injure the community as a whole, to endanger the public safety, or to jeopardize in Chief Justice Warren's words, the States' "right . . . to maintain a decent society."

To summarize, we have today reaffirmed the basic holding of *Roth v. United States* (1957) that obscene material has no protection under the First Amendment. We have directed our holdings, not at thoughts or speech, but at depiction and description of specifically defined sexual conduct that States may regulate within limits designed to prevent infringement of First Amendment rights. We have also reaffirmed the holdings of *United States v. Reidel* (1971) and *United States v. Thirty-Seven Photographs* (1971) that commerce in obscene material is unprotected by any constitutional doctrine of privacy. In this case we hold that the States have a legitimate interest in regulating commerce in obscene material and in regulating exhibition of obscene material in places of public accommodation, including so-called "adult" theatres from which minors are excluded. In light of these holdings, nothing precludes the State of Georgia from the regulation of the allegedly obscene materials exhibited in Paris Adult Theatre I or II, provided that the applicable Georgia law, as written or authoritatively interpreted by the Georgia courts, meets the First Amendment standards set forth in *Miller v. California* (1973). . . .

NOTES

1 The Public Interest 25, 25–26 (Winter, 1971).

QUESTIONS

1 To what extent, if at all, does the opinion of Chief Justice Burger reveal a commitment to the principle of legal moralism and/or the principle of legal paternalism?
2 Chief Justice Burger contends that state regulation of obscene material is not tantamount to restricting the communication of ideas and thus does not violate the First Amendment. Is this a defensible position?

Dissenting Opinion in *Paris Adult Theatre I v. Slaton*

Justice William Brennan

William Brennan, associate justice of the United States Supreme Court, is a graduate of the Harvard University Law School. He maintained a private law practice in Newark, New Jersey, until 1949. He then served as superior court judge (1949–1950), appellate division judge (1950–1952), and justice of the Supreme Court of New Jersey (1952–1956). Justice Brennan was appointed to the United States Supreme Court in 1956.

United States Supreme Court. 413 U.S. 49 (1973).

Justice Brennan acknowledges that there may be a class of material—obscene material—that in itself is not protected by the First Amendment guarantee of free speech. He argues, however, that it is impossible to specifically define "obscenity," and, as a result, that state efforts to totally suppress obscene material inevitably lead to the erosion of protected speech, thus infringing on the First Amendment. Likewise, he contends, such state efforts inevitably infringe on the Fourteenth Amendment and generate "costly institutional harms." He analyzes the interests of the state in suppressing obscene material and concludes that such interests are not sufficient to "justify the substantial damage to constitutional rights and to this nation's judicial machinery."

Our experience since *Roth v. United States* (1957) requires us not only to abandon the effort to pick out obscene materials on a case-by-case basis, but also to reconsider a fundamental postulate of *Roth:* that there exists a definable class of sexually oriented expression that may be totally suppressed by the Federal and State Governments. Assuming that such a class of expression does in fact exist, I am forced to conclude that the concept of "obscenity" cannot be defined with sufficient specificity and clarity to provide fair notice to persons who create and distribute sexually oriented materials, to prevent substantial erosion of protected speech as a by-product of the attempt to suppress unprotected speech, and to avoid very costly institutional harms. Given these inevitable side-effects of state efforts to suppress what is assumed to be *unprotected* speech, we must scrutinize with care the state interest that is asserted to justify the suppression. For in the absence of some very substantial interest in suppressing such speech, we can hardly condone the ill-effects that seem to flow inevitably from the effort. . . .

Because we assumed—incorrectly, as experience has proven—that obscenity could be separated from other sexually oriented expression without significant costs either to the First Amendment or to the judicial machinery charged with the task of safeguarding First Amendment freedoms, we had no occasion in *Roth* to probe the asserted state interest in curtailing unprotected, sexually oriented speech. Yet as we have increasingly come to appreciate the vagueness of the concept of obscenity, we have begun to recognize and articulate the state interests at stake. Significantly, in *Redrup v. New York* (1967), where we set aside findings of obscenity with regard to three sets of material, we pointed out that

> [i]n none of the cases was there a claim that the statute in question reflected a specific and limited state concern for juveniles. In none was there any suggestion of an assault upon individual privacy by publication in a manner so obtrusive as to make it impossible for an unwilling individual to avoid exposure to it. And in none was there evidence of the sort of 'pandering' which the Court found significant in *Ginzburg v. United States* (1966).

The opinions in *Redrup* and *Stanley v. Georgia* (1969) reflected our emerging view that the state interests in protecting children and in protecting unconsenting adults may stand on a different footing from the other asserted state interests. . . .

But whatever the strength of the state interests in protecting juveniles and unconsenting adults from exposure to sexually oriented materials, those interests cannot be asserted in defense of the holding of the Georgia Supreme Court in this case. That court assumed for the purposes of its decision that the films in issue were exhibited only to persons over the age of 21 who viewed them willingly and with prior knowledge of the nature of their contents. And on that assumption the state court held that the films could still be suppressed. The justification for the suppression must be found, therefore, in some independent interest in regulating the reading and viewing habits of consenting adults.

At the outset it should be noted that virtually all of the interests that might be asserted in defense of suppression, laying aside the special interests associated with distribution to juveniles and unconsenting adults, were also posited in *Stanley v. Georgia* where we held that the State could not make the "mere private possession of obscene material a crime." That decision presages the conclusions I reach here today.

In *Stanley* we pointed out that "[t]here appears to be little empirical basis for" the assertion that "exposure to obscene materials may lead to deviant sexual behavior or crimes of sexual violence." In any event, we added that "if the State is only concerned about printed or filmed materials inducing antisocial conduct, we believe that in the context of private consumption of ideas and information we should adhere to the view that '[a]mong free men, the deterrents ordinarily to be applied to prevent crime are education and punishment for violations of the law. . . .' "

Moreover, in *Stanley* we rejected as "wholly inconsistent with the philosophy of the First Amendment," the notion that there is a legitimate state concern in the "control [of] the moral content of a person's thoughts," and we held that a State "cannot constitutionally premise legislation on the desirability of controlling a person's private thoughts." That is not to say, of course, that a State must remain utterly indifferent to—and take no action bearing on—the morality of the community. The traditional description of state police power does embrace the regulation of morals as well as the health, safety, and general welfare of the citizenry. And much legislation—compulsory public education laws, civil rights laws, even the abolition of capital punishment—are grounded at least in part on a concern with the morality of the community. But the State's interest in regulating morality by suppressing obscenity, while often asserted, remains essentially unfocused and ill-defined. And, since the attempt to curtail unprotected speech necessarily spills over into the area of protected speech, the effort to serve this speculative interest through the suppression of obscene material must tread heavily on rights protected by the First Amendment.

In *Roe v. Wade* (1973), we held constitutionally invalid a state abortion law, even though we were aware of

> the sensitive and emotional nature of the abortion controversy, of the vigorous opposing views, even among physicians, and of the deep and seemingly absolute convictions that the subject inspires. One's philosophy, one's experiences, one's exposure to the raw edges of human existence, one's religious training, one's attitudes toward life and family and their values, and the moral standards one establishes and seeks to observe, are all likely to influence and to color one's thinking and conclusions about abortion.

Like the proscription of abortions, the effort to suppress obscenity is predicated on unprovable, although strongly held, assumptions about human behavior, morality, sex, and religion. The existence of these assumptions cannot validate a statute that substantially undermines the guarantees of the First Amendment, any more than the existence of similar assumptions on the issue of abortion can validate a statute that infringes the constitutionally protected privacy interests of a pregnant woman.

If, as the Court today assumes, "a state legislature may . . . act on the . . . assumption that . . . commerce in obscene books, or public exhibitions focused on obscene conduct, have a tendency to exert a corrupting and debasing impact leading to antisocial behavior," then it is hard to see how state-ordered regimentation of our minds can ever be forestalled. For if a State may, in an effort to maintain or create a particular moral tone, prescribe what its citizens cannot read or cannot see, then it would seem to follow that in pursuit of that same objective a State could decree that its citizens must read certain books or must view certain films. However laudable its goal—and that is obviously a question on which reasonable minds may differ—the State cannot proceed by means that violate the Constitution. . . .

Recognizing these principles, we have held that so-called thematic obscenity—obscenity which might persuade the viewer or reader to engage in "obscene" conduct—is not outside the protection of the First Amendment:

> It is contended that the State's action was justified because the motion picture attractively portrays a relationship which is contrary to the moral standards, the religious precepts, and the legal code of its citizenry. This argument misconceives what it is that the Constitution protects. Its guarantee is not confined to the expression of ideas that are conventional or shared by a majority. It protects advocacy of the opinion that adultery may sometimes be proper, no less than advocacy of socialism or the single tax. And in the realm of ideas it protects expression which is eloquent no less than that which is unconvincing. *Kingsley Int'l Pictures Corp. v. Regents* (1959).

Even a legitimate, sharply focused state concern for the morality of the community cannot, in other words, justify an assault on the protections of the First Amendment. Where the state interest in regulation of morality is vague and ill-defined, interference with the guarantees of the First Amendment is even more difficult to justify.

In short, while I cannot say that the interests of the State—apart from the question of juveniles and unconsenting adults—are trivial or nonexistent, I am compelled to conclude that these interests cannot justify the substantial damage to constitutional rights and to this Nation's judicial machinery that inevitably results from state efforts to bar the distribution even of unprotected material to consenting adults. I would hold, therefore, that at least in the absence of distribution to juveniles or obtrusive exposure to unconsenting adults, the First and Fourteenth Amendments prohibit the state and federal governments from attempting wholly to suppress sexually oriented materials on the basis of their allegedly "obscene" contents. Nothing in this approach precludes those governments from taking action to serve what may be strong and legitimate interests through regulation of the manner of distribution of sexually oriented material.

QUESTIONS

1 Is it impossible, as Justice Brennan believes, to specifically define "obscenity," or can a workable definition be advanced and defended?
2 Is "substantial damage to constitutional rights and to this nation's judicial machinery" the inevitable outcome of state efforts to suppress obscene material?
3 To what extent, if at all, does the opinion of Justice Brennan reveal a commitment to the principle of legal moralism?

The Harm Principle

John Stuart Mill

John Stuart Mill (1806–1873) is known primarily as an advocate of utilitarianism. Unlike most contemporary philosophers, Mill was not an academician. He had a successful career with the British East India Company and served one term as a Member of Parliament. Mill's most important works include *Utilitarianism, On Liberty,* and the feminist classic, *The Subjection of Women.*

In this excerpt from his classic work *On Liberty* (1859), Mill contends that society is warranted in restricting individual liberty only if an action is harmful to others, never because an action in one way or another is harmful to the person who performs the action. He clearly rejects both the principle of legal paternalism and the principle of legal moralism. Mill argues on utilitarian grounds for an exclusive adherence to the harm principle, holding that society will be better off by tolerating all expressions of individual liberty that involve no harm to others, rather than by "compelling each to live as seems good to the rest." While alluding to offenses against decency, he makes it clear that certain actions may be exclusively "self-harming" when done in private and yet, when done in public, may constitute an offense against others.

The object of this Essay is to assert one very simple principle, as entitled to govern absolutely the dealings of society with the individual in the way of compulsion and control, whether the means used be physical force in the form of legal penalties, or the moral coercion of public opinion. That principle is, that the sole end for which mankind are warranted, individually or collectively, in interfering with the liberty of action of any of their number, is self-protection. That the only purpose for which power can be rightfully exercised over any member of a civilized community, against his will, is to prevent harm to others. His own good, either physical or moral, is not a sufficient warrant. He cannot rightfully be compelled to do or forbear because it will be better for him to do so, because it will make him happier, because, in the opinions of others, to do so would be wise, or even right. These are good reasons

Reprinted from the original edition of *On Liberty* (London, 1859).

for remonstrating with him, or reasoning with him, or persuading him, or entreating him, but not for compelling him, or visiting him with any evil in case he do otherwise. To justify that, the conduct from which it is desired to deter him, must be calculated to produce evil to some one else. The only part of the conduct of any one, for which he is amenable to society, is that which concerns others. In the part which merely concerns himself, his independence is, of right, absolute. Over himself, over his own body and mind, the individual is sovereign.

It is, perhaps, hardly necessary to say that this doctrine is meant to apply only to human beings in the maturity of their faculties. We are not speaking of children, or of young persons below the age which the law may fix as that of manhood and womanhood. Those who are still in a state to require being taken care of by others, must be protected against their own actions as well as against external injury. . . .

There is a sphere of action in which society, as distinguished from the individual, has, if any, only an indirect interest; comprehending all that portion of a person's life and conduct which affects only himself, or if it also affects others, only with their free, voluntary, and undeceived consent and participation. When I say only himself, I mean directly, and in the first instance: for whatever affects himself, may affect others *through* himself; and the objection which may be grounded on this contingency, will receive consideration in the sequel. This, then, is the appropriate region of human liberty. It comprises, first, the inward domain of consciousness; demanding liberty of conscience, in the most comprehensive sense; liberty of thought and feeling; absolute freedom of opinion and sentiment on all subjects, practical or speculative, scientific, moral, or theological. The liberty of expressing and publishing opinions may seem to fall under a different principle, since it belongs to that part of the conduct of an individual which concerns other people; but, being almost of as much importance as the liberty of thought itself, and resting in great part on the same reasons, is practically inseparable from it. Secondly, the principle requires liberty of tastes and pursuits; of framing the plan of our life to suit our own character; of doing as we like, subject to such consequences as may follow; without impediment from our fellow-creatures, so long as what we do does not harm them, even though they should think our conduct foolish, perverse, or wrong. Thirdly, from this liberty of each individual, follows the liberty, within the same limits, of combination among individuals; freedom to unite, for any purpose not involving harm to others: the persons combining being supposed to be of full age, and not forced or deceived.

No society in which these liberties are not, on the whole, respected, is free, whatever may be its form of government; and none is completely free in which they do not exist absolute and unqualified. The only freedom which deserves the name, is that of pursuing our own good in our own way, so long as we do not attempt to deprive others of theirs, or impede their efforts to obtain it. Each is the proper guardian of his own health, whether bodily, or mental and spiritual. Mankind are greater gainers by suffering each other to live as seems good to themselves, than by compelling each to live as seems good to the rest. . . .

Again, there are many acts which, being directly injurious only to the agents themselves, ought not to be legally interdicted, but which, if done publicly, are a violation of good manners, and coming thus within the category of offences against others, may rightfully be prohibited. Of this kind are offences against decency; on which it is unnecessary to dwell, the rather as they are only connected indirectly with our subject, the objection to publicity being equally strong in the case of many actions not in themselves condemnable, nor supposed to be so. . . .

QUESTIONS

1 Would Mill find permissible laws restricting the access of consenting adults to pornography? Would Mill find permissible laws restricting the access of minors to pornography? Would Mill find permissible laws prohibiting pornographic billboards? Explain.

2 Is it true, as Mill claims, that "Mankind are greater gainers by suffering each other to live as seems good to themselves, than by compelling each to live as seems good to the rest?"

3 Are those who are exposed to pornography themselves harmed by such exposure? If so, is the fact of self-harm sufficient to justify laws that limit the access of consenting adults to pornographic materials?

Pornography and the Public Morality

Charles H. Keating, Jr.

Charles H. Keating, Jr., is a lawyer and businessman whose name is now associated with problems in the savings and loan industry. In 1956, he founded Citizens for Decent Literature, Inc. Keating, who served as a member of the (1970) Commission on Obscenity and Pornography, vigorously dissented from the findings of the majority. This short selection is taken from his extensive dissenting statement.

Keating characterizes pornography as a form of prostitution; it provides sexual pleasure for a price. In his view, which he identifies as "the traditional Judeo-Christian ethic," any form of impersonal sexual activity is debasing, a violation of human dignity. The use of pornography is immoral, he contends, because it involves the pursuit of pleasure for its own sake, thereby excluding "the higher purposes and values to which pleasure is attached." In vivid contrast to John Stuart Mill, Keating explicitly endorses the principle of legal moralism. Even if it were admitted that access to pornographic material plays no significant role in the causation of social or individual harms, he insists, antipornography laws are justified. In his view, the need to protect the public morality is not only the historical reason for antipornography laws but also a sufficient justification for them.

. . . I cannot undertake consideration of the subject of pornography without commenting on its underlying philosophical and moral basis.

Reprinted from the "Statement of Charles H. Keating, Jr.," in *The Report of the Commission on Obscenity and Pornography* (Washington, D.C.: Government Printing Office, 1970).

For those who believe in God, in His absolute supremacy as the Creator and Law-giver of life, in the dignity and destiny which He has conferred upon the human person, in the moral code that governs sexual activity—for those who believe in these "things," no argument against pornography should be necessary.

Though the meaning of pornography is generally understood, reference is seldom made to the root meaning of the term itself. This seems important to me. The Greeks had a word for it, for many "its." And the Greek word for pornography is highly significant. It comes from two Greek words, in fact: "prostitute" and "write." So, the dictionary defines pornography as "originally a description of prostitutes and their trade."

Pornography is not merely associated in this historical sense with prostitution, but it is actually a form of prostitution because it advertises and advocates "sex for sale," pleasure for a price.

The use of sexual powers is intimately bound up with both love and life, not merely with the momentary satisfaction of desire. Only a person is capable of love, but any of the lower forms of animal life can experience pleasure as a mere sense reaction. A person is much more than a body, and any form of sexual activity which is impersonal, which uses the body alone for pleasure, violates the integrity of the person and thereby reduces him to the level of an irrational and irresponsible animal.

The traditional Judeo-Christian ethic does not condemn pleasure as an evil in itself; it does condemn the pursuit of pleasure for its own sake, as an end rather than a means, deliberately excluding the higher purposes and values to which pleasure is attached. Everybody knows that the appetite for food makes the necessity of eating more palatable, more pleasurable. To eat to live is rational, sound procedure; to live to eat is an abuse of a basically good thing. The same is true of the sex drive. It serves the individual and the common good of the human race, only when it is creative, productive, when it ministers to love and life. When, however, it serves only itself, it becomes a perversion, actually an antisocial force disruptive and eventually destructive of all love and life. Every word by which the organs of sex are designated bears out this statement: genital, generative, reproductive, procreative. Love is always fruitful of lasting good; mere pleasure is of its nature transitory, barren, the only residue likely to be unhappy, remorseful memories. This thought could be amplified and graphically illustrated.

Those who speak in defense of sexual morality are accused of making sex "dirty." It's the other way around. The defenders of pornography are guilty of degrading sex. Marcel Proust, French novelist *(Sodom and Gomorrah),* described the effect of his early reading of erotica upon himself: "Oh stream of hell that undermined my adolescence." Literature is a better reflection of life than is scientific opinion; and I am certain that the testimony of men like Proust could be multiplied if someone took the time to assemble the sources.

No, the state cannot legislate virtue, cannot make moral goodness by merely enacting law; but the state can and does legislate against vices which publicly jeopardize the virtue of people who might prefer to remain virtuous. If it is not the proper function of law to offer citizens such protection, then what is it? . . .

EFFECTS OF PORNOGRAPHY

We should begin by saying the law is clear. The law founded in reason and common sense recognizes obscenity as intrinsically evil and does not demand the "clear and present danger" test so ardently advocated by [Commission on Obscenity and Pornography] Chairman Lockhart and the American Civil Liberties Union. The law, rather, proscribes pornography on the basis of the public good—protecting public health and welfare, public decency, and morality, a condition absolutely essential to the well-being of the nation. . . .

One can consult all the experts he chooses, can write reports, make studies, etc., but the fact that obscenity corrupts lies within the common sense, the reason, and the logic of every man. . . .

If man is affected by his environment, by circumstances of his life, by reading, by instruction, by anything, he is then certainly affected by pornography. The mere nature of pornography makes it impossible for pornography to effect good. Therefore, it must necessarily effect evil. Sexual immorality, more than any other causative factor, historically speaking, is the root cause of the demise of all great nations and all great peoples. (Ref. Toynbee: Moral decay from within destroyed most of the world's great civilizations.) . . .

The Commission majority bases their recommended repeal of all federal and state laws that "prohibit consensual distribution of sexual material to adults" on the statement that "extensive empirical investigation, both by the Commission and by others, provides no evidence that exposure to or use of explicit sexual materials play a significant role in the causation of social or individual harms such as crime, delinquency, sexual or nonsexual deviancy or severe emotional disturbances."

While it is a fact that a significant percentage of nationally recognized psychiatric authorities and many law enforcement officials at all levels of jurisdiction would disagree with that statement, the important point I want to make here is that the reasons for obscenity laws are *not* contained in the statement. Obscenity laws have existed historically in recognition of the need to protect the *public morality*. . . .

I submit that never in the history of modern civilization have we seen more obvious evidence of a decline in public morality than we see today. Venereal disease is at epidemic proportions and literally out of control in many large urban centers—despite medicine. Illegitimacy statistics are skyrocketing—despite the pill and other contraceptive devices—and despite the relatively easy access to abortion. Both of these social statistics reflect a promiscuous attitude toward sex which is no doubt contributed to by many factors—but certainly one factor has to be the deluge of pornography which is screaming at young people from records, motion picture screens, newsstands, the United States mail and their peer groups.

To say that pornography has no effect is patently ridiculous. I submit that if pornography does *not* affect a person—that person has a problem. Pornography is intended to arouse the sexual appetite—one of the most volatile appetites of human nature. Once that appetite is aroused, it will seek satisfaction—and the satisfaction sought—without proper moral restraints—is often reflected in the social statistics discussed above. . . .

In addition to the social problems of venereal disease and illegitimacy, it is also of the very nature of obscenity to degrade sex and distort the role that sex plays in a normal life. There is no way to measure the terrible effects that pornography has had and is having on marital infidelity that is reflected in divorce statistics, abortions, suicide and other social problems that further reflect the decline in public morality. . . .

QUESTIONS

1 Is pornography immoral?
2 Is there a widespread consensus in American society to the effect that pornography is morally repugnant? If so, is the existence of such a consensus sufficient to justify laws that limit the access of consenting adults to pornographic materials?
3 Is the principle of legal moralism an acceptable liberty-limiting principle?

Is Pornography Beneficial?

G. L. Simons

G. L. Simons, an Englishman, is an author who has written extensively on various aspects of human sexuality. His books include *A History of Sex* (1970), *A Place for Pleasure, The History of the Brothel* (1975), and *Pornography without Prejudice* (1972), from which this selection is excerpted.

Emphasizing that individual liberty is justifiably limited only when there is clear evidence that an activity produces significant harm, Simons constructs a case against censorship. In a more positive vein, he actively defends easy access to pornography. In the first place, he argues, pornography provides pleasure without producing significant harms; moreover, pornography is socially beneficial. Simons cites evidence in support of the view that pornography can aid normal sexual development. He also contends that pornography can provide "sex by proxy" for lonely and deprived people. Finally, he contends, with regard to an especially important aspect of sex by proxy, it is at least plausible to think that the availability of pornography provides release for sexual desires that might otherwise be released through socially harmful behavior.

It is not sufficient, for the objectors' case, that they demonstrate that some harm has flowed from pornography. It would be extremely difficult to show that pornography had *never* had unfortunate consequences, but we should not make too much of this. Harm has flowed from religion, patriotism, alcohol and cigarettes without this fact impelling people to demand abolition. The harm, if established, has to be weighed against a variety of considerations before a decision can be reached as to the propriety of certain laws. Of the British Obscenity Laws the Arts Council Report comments[1] that "the harm would need to be both indisputable and very dire indeed before it could be judged to outweigh the evils and anomalies inherent in the Acts we have been asked to examine."

The onus therefore is upon the anti-pornographers to demonstrate not only that harm is caused by certain types of sexual material but that the harm is considerable: if the first is difficult the second is necessarily more so, and the attempts to date have not been impressive. It is even possible to argue that easily available pornography has a number of benefits. Many people will be familiar with the *catharsis* argument whereby pornography is said to cut down on delinquency by providing would-be criminals with substitute satisfactions. This is considered later but we mention it here to indicate that access to pornography may be socially beneficial in certain instances, and that where this is possible the requirement for anti-pornographers to *justify* their objections must be stressed.

The general conclusion[2] of the U.S. Commission was that no adequate proof had been provided that pornography was harmful to individual or society—"if a case is to be made out against 'pornography' [in 1970] it will have to be made on grounds other than demonstrated effects of a damaging personal or social nature." . . .

The heresy (to some ears) that pornography is harmless is compounded by the even greater impiety that it may be beneficial. Some of us are managing to adjust to the notion that pornography is unlikely to bring down the world in moral ruin, but the idea that it may actually do good is altogether another thing. When we read of Professor Emeritus E. T. Rasmussen, a pioneer of psychological studies in Denmark, and a government adviser, saying that there is a possibility "that pornography can be beneficial," many of us are likely to have *mixed* reactions, to say the least. In fact this thesis can be argued in a number of ways.

The simplest approach is to remark that people enjoy it. This can be seen to be true whether we rely on personal testimony or the most respectable index of all in capitalist society—"preparedness to pay." The appeal that pornography has for many people is hardly in dispute, and in a more sober social climate that would be justification enough. Today we are not quite puritan enough to deny that *pleasure* has a worthwhile place in human life: not many of us object to our food being tasty or our clothes being attractive. It was not always like this. In sterner times it was *de rigueur* to prepare food without spices and to wear the plainest clothes. The cult of puritanism reached its apotheosis in the most fanatical asceticism, where it was fashionable for holy men to wander off into a convenient desert and neglect the body to the point of cultivating its lice as "pearls of God." In such a bizarre philosophy pleasure was not only condemned in its sexual manifestations but in all areas where the body could conceivably take satisfaction. These days we are able to countenance pleasure in most fields but in many instances still the case for *sexual* pleasure has to be argued.

Pleasure is not of course its own justification. If it clearly leads to serious malaise, early death, or the *dis*pleasure of others, then there is something to be said against it.

But the serious consequences have to be demonstrated: it is not enough to condemn certain forms of pleasurable experience on the grounds of *possible* ill effect. With such an approach *any* human activity could be censured and freedom would have no place. In short, if something is pleasurable and its bad effects are small or nonexistent then it is to be encouraged: opposition to such a creed should be recognized as an unwholesome antipathy to human potential. Pleasure is a good except where it is harmful (and where the harmfulness is *significant*). . . .

That pornography is enjoyable to many people is the first of the arguments in its favour. In any other field this would be argument enough. It is certainly sufficient to justify many activities that have—unlike a taste for pornography—demonstrably harmful consequences. Only in a sexually neurotic society could a tool for heightening sexual enjoyment be regarded as reprehensible and such as to warrant suppression by law. The position is well summarized[3] in the *first* of the Arts Council's twelve reasons for advocating the repeal of the Obscenity Publications Acts:

> "It is not for the State to prohibit private citizens from choosing what they may or may not enjoy in literature or art unless there were incontrovertible evidence that the result would be injurious to society. There is no such evidence."

A further point is that availability of pornography may *aid,* rather than frustrate normal sexual development. Thus in 1966, for example, the New Jersey Committee for the Right to Read presented the findings of a survey conducted among nearly a thousand psychiatrists and psychologists of that state. Amongst the various personal statements included was the view that "sexually stimulating materials" might help particular people develop a normal sex drive.[4] In similar spirit, Dr. John Money writes[5] that pornography "may encourage normal sexual development and broadmindedness," a view that may not sound well to the anti-pornographers. And even in circumstances where possible dangers of pornography are pointed out conceivable good effects are sometimes acknowledged. In a paper issued[6] by the Danish Forensic Medicine Council it is pointed out that neurotic and sexually shy people may, by reading pornographic descriptions of normal sexual activity, be freed from some of their apprehension regarding sex and may thereby attain a freer and less frustrated attitude to the sexual side of life. . . .

One argument in favour of pornography is that it can serve as a substitute for actual sexual activity involving another person or other people. This argument has two parts, relating as it does to (1) people who fantasize over *socially acceptable* modes of sexual involvement, and (2) people who fantasize over types of sexual activity that would be regarded as illegal or at least immoral. The first type relates to lonely and deprived people who for one reason or another have been unable to form "normal" sexual contacts with other people; the second type are instances of the much quoted *catharsis* argument.

One writer notes[7] that pornography can serve as a substitute for both the knowledge of which some people have been deprived and the pleasure in sexual experience which they have not enjoyed. One can well imagine men or women too inhibited to secure sexual satisfaction with other adults and where explicit sexual material can alleviate some of their misery. It is facile to remark that such people should seek psychiatric assistance or even "make an effort": the factors that prevent the forming of effective sexual liaisons are just as likely to inhibit any efforts to seek medical or other assistance. Pornography provides *sex by proxy,* and in such usage it can have a clear justification.

It is also possible to imagine circumstances in which men or women—for reasons of illness, travel or bereavement—are unable to seek sexual satisfaction with spouse or other loved one. Pornography can help here too. Again it is easy to suggest that a person abstain from sexual experience, or, if having *permanently* lost a spouse, seek out another partner. Needless to say such advice is often quite impractical—and the alternative to pornography may be prostitution or adultery. Montagu notes that pornography can serve the same purpose as "dirty jokes," allowing a person to discharge harmlessly repressed and unsatisfied sexual desires.

In this spirit, Mercier (1970) is quoted by the U.S. Commission:

". . . it is in periods of sexual deprivation—to which the young and the old are far more subject than those in their prime—that males, at any rate, are likely to reap psychological benefit from pornography."

And also Kenneth Tynan (1970):

"For men on long journeys, geographically cut off from wives and mistresses, pornography can act as a portable memory, a welcome shortcut to remembered bliss, relieving tension without involving disloyalty."

It is difficult to see how anyone could object to the use of pornography in such circumstances, other than on the grounds of a morbid anti-sexuality.

The *catharsis argument* has long been put forward to suggest that availability of pornography will neutralize "aberrant" sexual tendencies and so reduce the incidence of sex crime or clearly immoral behaviour in related fields. (Before evidence is put forward for this thesis it is worth remarking that it should not be necessary to demonstrate a *reduction* in sex crime to justify repeal of the Obscenity Laws. It should be quite sufficient to show that an *increase* in crime will not ensue following repeal. We may even argue that a small increase may be tolerable if other benefits from easy access to pornography could be shown: but it is no part of the present argument to put this latter contention.)

Many psychiatrists and psychologists have favoured the catharsis argument. Chesser, for instance, sees[8] pornography as a form of voyeurism in which—as with sadomasochistic material—the desire to hurt is satisfied passively. If this is so and the analogy can be extended we have only to look at the character of the voyeur—generally furtive and clandestine—to realize that we have little to fear from the pornography addict. Where consumers are preoccupied with fantasy there is little danger to the rest of us. Karpman (1959), quoted by the U.S. Commission, notes that people reading "salacious literature" are less likely to become sexual offenders than those who do not since the reading often neutralizes "aberrant sexual interests." Similarly the Kronhausens have argued that "these 'unholy' instruments" may be a safety-valve for the sexual deviate and potential sex offender. And Cairns, Paul and Wishner (1962) have remarked that *obscene materials* provide a way of releasing strong sexual urges without doing harm to others.

It is easy to see the plausibility of this argument. The popularity of all forms of sexual literature—from the superficial, *sexless*, sentimentality of the popular women's magazine to the clearest "hard-core" porn—has demonstrated over the ages the perennial appetite that people have for fantasy. To an extent, a great extent with many single people and frustrated married ones, the fantasy constitutes an important part of the sex-life. The experience may be vicarious and sterile but it self-evidently fills a need for many individuals. If literature, as a *symbol* of reality, can so involve human sensitivities it is highly likely that when the sensitivities are *distorted* for one reason or another the same sublimatory function can occur: the "perverted" or potentially criminal mentality can gain satisfaction, as does the lonely unfortunate, in *sex by proxy*. If we wanted to force the potential sex criminal onto the streets in search of a human victim perhaps we would do well to deny him his sublimatory substitutes: deny him fantasy and he will be forced to go after the real thing. . . .

The importance of this possibility should be fully faced. If a causal connection *does* exist between availability of pornographic material and a *reduction* in the amount of sex crime—and the evidence is wholly consistent with this possibility rather than its converse—then people who deliberately restrict pornography by supporting repressive legislation are prime architects of sexual offences against the individual. The anti-pornographers would do well to note that their anxieties may be driving them into a position the exact opposite of the one they explicitly maintain—their commitment to reduce the amount of sexual delinquency in society.

The most that the anti-pornographers can argue is that at present the evidence is inconclusive. . . . But if the inconclusive character of the data is once admitted then the case for repressive legislation falls at once. For in a *free* society, or one supposedly aiming after freedom, social phenomena are, like individuals, innocent until proven guilty—and an activity will be permitted unless there is clear evidence of its harmful consequences. This point was well put—in the specific connection with pornography—by Bertrand Russell, talking[9] when he was well over 90 to Rupert Crawshay-Williams.

After noting how people beg the question of causation in instances such as the Moors murders (where the murders and the reading of de Sade *may* have a common cause), Russell ("Bertie") said that on the whole he disapproved of sadistic pornography being available. But when Crawshay-Williams put the catharsis view, that such material might provide a harmless release for individuals who otherwise may be dangerous, Russell said at once—"Oh, well, if that's true, then I don't see that there is anything against sadistic pornography. In fact it should be encouraged. . . ." When it was stressed that there was no preponderating evidence either way Russell argued that we should fall back on an overriding principle—"in this case the principle of free speech."

Thus in the absence of evidence of harm we should be permissive. Any other view is totalitarian. . . .

If human enjoyment *per se* is not to be condemned then it is not too rash to say that we *know* pornography does good. We can easily produce our witnesses to testify to experiencing pleasure. If in the face of this—and no other favourable argument— we are unable to demonstrate a countervailing harm, then the case for easy availability of pornography is unassailable. If, in such circumstances, we find some people unconvinced it is futile to seek out further empirical data. Once we commit ourselves to the notion that the evil nature of something is axiomatic we tacitly concede that evidence is largely irrelevant to our position. If pornography never fails to fill us with predictable loathing then statistics on crime, or measured statements by careful specialists, will not be useful: our reactions will stay the same. But in this event we would do well to reflect on what our emotions tell us of our own mentality. . . .

NOTES

1 *The Obscenity Laws,* André Deutsch, 1969, p. 33.
2 *The Report of the Commission on Obscenity and Pornography,* Part Three, II, Bantam Books, 1970, p. 169.
3 *The Obscenity Laws,* André Deutsch, 1969, p. 35.
4 Quoted by Isadore Rubin, "What Should Parents Do About Pornography?" *Sex in the Adolescent Years,* Fontana, 1969, p. 202.
5 John Money, contribution to "Is Pornography Harmful to Young Children?" *Sex in the Childhood Years,* Fontana, 1971, p. 181–5.
6 Paper from the Danish Forensic Medicine Council to The Danish Penal Code Council, published in The Penal Code Council Report on Penalty for Pornography, Report No. 435, Copenhagen, 1966, pp. 78–80, and as appendix to *The Obscenity Laws,* pp. 120–4.
7 Ashley Montagu, "Is Pornography Harmful to Young Children?" *Sex in the Childhood Years,* Fontana, 1971, p. 182.
8 Eustace Chesser, *The Human Aspects of Sexual Deviation,* Arrow Books, 1971, p. 39.
9 Rupert Crawshay-Williams, *Russell Remembered,* Oxford University Press, 1970, p. 144.

QUESTIONS

1 Is pornography of genuine benefit to society?
2 Consider the following claim: Seeking access to pornographic materials is not in a person's own best interest because the immediate pleasure that pornography provides is far outweighed by its detrimental impact on the person in the long run. Is this a defensible position?
3 If the access of consenting adults to pornographic materials were left totally unregulated, what would be the long-term impact on the general welfare? Would the results, on balance, be desirable or undesirable?

The Question of Harm

Attorney General's Commission on Pornography

The Attorney General's Commission on Pornography was formed by Attorney General Edwin Meese III in the Spring of 1985. This eleven-member group was chaired by Henry E. Hudson, who was at that time commonwealth attorney in Arlington County, Virginia. This selection is excerpted from the Commission's final report, which was submitted in July 1986.

In considering the question whether pornography is harmful, the 1986 Commission distinguishes among (1) violent pornography, (2) nonviolent but degrading pornography, and (3) nonviolent and nondegrading pornography. On its interpretation of the evidence, material in category (1) bears a causal relationship to undesirable attitudinal changes and to acts of sexual violence. The Commission also asserts that these same effects are causally connected with category (2) material. On the other hand, the Commission concludes that category (3) material does not bear a causal relationship to acts of sexual violence. In a brief reference to the category of child pornography, the Commission emphasizes the way in which the production of child pornography entails child abuse.

MATTERS OF METHOD

. . . The analysis of the hypothesis that pornography causes harm must start with the identification of hypothesized harms, proceed to the determination of whether those hypothesized harms are indeed harmful, and then conclude with the examination of whether a causal link exists between the material and the harm. When the conse-quences of exposure to sexually explicit material are not harmful, or when there is no causal relationship between exposure to sexually explicit material and some harmful consequence, then we cannot say that the sexually explicit material is harm-ful. But if sexually explicit material of some variety is causally related to, or in-creases the incidence of, some behavior that *is* harmful, then it is safe to conclude that the material is harmful. . . .

The Problem of Multiple Causation

The world is complex, and most consequences are "caused" by numerous factors. Are highway deaths caused by failure to wear seat belts, failure of the automobile companies to install airbags, failure of the government to require automobile compa-nies to install airbags, alcohol, judicial leniency towards drunk drivers, speeding, and so on and on? Is heart disease caused by cigarette smoking, obesity, stress, or excess animal fat in our diets? As with most other questions of this type, the answers can only be "all of the above," and so too with the problem of pornography. We have concluded, for example, that some forms of sexually explicit material bear a causal relationship both to sexual violence and to sex discrimination, but we are hardly so

Reprinted from *Final Report* (Washington, D.C.: United States Department of Justice, July 1986).

naive as to suppose that were these forms of pornography to disappear the problems of sex discrimination and sexual violence would come to an end.

If this is so, then what does it mean to identify a causal relationship? It means that the evidence supports the conclusion that if there were none of the material being tested, then the incidence of the consequences would be less. We live in a world of multiple causation, and to identify a factor as a *cause* in such a world means only that if this factor were eliminated while everything else stayed the same then the problem would at least be lessened. In most cases it is impossible to say any more than this, although to say this is to say quite a great deal. But when we identify something as a cause, we do not deny that there are other causes, and we do not deny that some of these other causes might bear an even *greater* causal connection than does some form of pornography. That is, it may be, for example, and there is some evidence that points in this direction, that certain magazines focusing on guns, martial arts, and related topics bear a closer causal relationship to sexual violence than do some magazines that are, in a term we will explain shortly, "degrading." If this is true, then the amount of sexual violence would be reduced more by eliminating the weaponry magazines and keeping the degrading magazines than it would be reduced by eliminating the degrading magazines and keeping the weaponry magazines. . . .

OUR CONCLUSIONS ABOUT HARM

We present in the following sections our conclusions regarding the harms we have investigated with respect to the various subdividing categories we have found most useful. . . .

Sexually Violent Material

The category of material on which most of the evidence has focused is the category of material featuring actual or unmistakably simulated or unmistakably threatened violence presented in sexually explicit fashion with a predominant focus on the sexually explicit violence. Increasingly, the most prevalent forms of pornography, as well as an increasingly prevalent body of less sexually explicit material, fit this description. Some of this material involves sado-masochistic themes, with the standard accoutrements of the genre, including whips, chains, devices of torture, and so on. But another theme of some of this material is not sado-masochistic, but involves instead the recurrent theme of a man making some sort of sexual advance to a woman, being rebuffed, and then raping the woman or in some other way violently forcing himself on the woman. In almost all of this material, whether in magazine or motion picture form, the woman eventually becomes aroused and ecstatic about the initially forced sexual activity, and usually is portrayed as begging for more. There is also a large body of material, more "mainstream" in its availability, that portrays sexual activity or sexually suggestive nudity coupled with extreme violence, such as disfigurement or murder. The so-called "slasher" films fit this description, as does some material, both in films and in magazines, that is less or more sexually explicit than the prototypical "slasher" film.

It is with respect to material of this variety that the scientific findings and ultimate conclusions of the 1970 Commission are least reliable for today, precisely because material of this variety was largely absent from that Commission's inquiries. It is not, however, absent from the contemporary world, and it is hardly surprising that conclusions about this material differ from conclusions about material not including violent themes.

When clinical and experimental research has focused particularly on sexually violent material, the conclusions have been virtually unanimous. In both clinical and experimental settings, exposure to sexually violent materials has indicated an increase in the likelihood of aggression. More specifically, the research, which is described in much detail later in this Report, shows a causal relationship between exposure to material of this type and aggressive behavior towards women.

Finding a link between aggressive behavior towards women and sexual violence, whether lawful or unlawful, requires assumptions not found exclusively in the experimental evidence. We see no reason, however, not to make these assumptions. The assumption that increased aggressive behavior towards women is causally related, for an aggregate population, to increased sexual violence is significantly supported by the clinical evidence, as well as by much of the less scientific evidence. They are also to all of us assumptions that are plainly justified by our own common sense. This is not to say that all people with heightened levels of aggression will commit acts of sexual violence. But it is to say that over a sufficiently large number of cases we are confident in asserting that an increase in aggressive behavior directed at women will cause an increase in the level of sexual violence directed at women.

Thus we reach our conclusions by combining the results of the research with highly justifiable assumptions about the generalizability of more limited research results. Since the clinical and experimental evidence supports the conclusion that there is a causal relationship between exposure to sexually violent materials and an increase in aggressive behavior directed towards women, and since we believe that an increase in aggressive behavior towards women will in a population increase the incidence of sexual violence in that population, we have reached the conclusion, unanimously and confidently, that the available evidence strongly supports the hypothesis that substantial exposure to sexually violent materials as described here bears a causal relationship to antisocial acts of sexual violence and, for some subgroups, possibly to unlawful acts of sexual violence.

Although we rely for this conclusion on significant scientific empirical evidence, we feel it worthwhile to note the underlying logic of the conclusion. The evidence says simply that the images that people are exposed to bears a causal relationship to their behavior. This is hardly surprising. What would be surprising would be to find otherwise, and we have not so found. We have not, of course, found that the images people are exposed to are a greater cause of sexual violence than all or even many other possible causes the investigation of which has been beyond our mandate. Nevertheless, it would be strange indeed if graphic representations of a form of behavior, especially in a form that almost exclusively portrays such behavior as desirable, did not have at least some effect on patterns of behavior.

Sexual violence is not the only negative effect reported in the research to result from substantial exposure to sexually violent materials. The evidence is also strongly supportive of significant attitudinal changes on the part of those with substantial exposure to violent pornography. These attitudinal changes are numerous. Victims of rape and other forms of sexual violence are likely to be perceived by people so exposed as more responsible for the assault, as having suffered less injury, and as having been less degraded as a result of the experience. Similarly, people with a substantial exposure to violent pornography are likely to see the rapist or other sexual offender as less responsible for the act and as deserving of less stringent punishment.

These attitudinal changes have been shown experimentally to include a larger range of attitudes than those just discussed. The evidence also strongly supports the conclusion that substantial exposure to violent sexually explicit material leads to a greater acceptance of the "rape myth" in its broader sense—that women enjoy being coerced into sexual activity, that they enjoy being physically hurt in sexual context, and that as a result a man who forces himself on a woman sexually is in fact merely acceding to the "real" wishes of the woman, regardless of the extent to which she seems to be resisting. The myth is that a woman who says "no" really means "yes," and that men are justified in acting on the assumption that the "no" answer is indeed the "yes" answer. We have little trouble concluding that this attitude is both pervasive and profoundly harmful, and that any stimulus reinforcing or increasing the incidence of this attitude is for that reason alone properly designated as harmful.

. . . All of the harms discussed here, including acceptance of the legitimacy of sexual violence against women but not limited to it, are more pronounced when the sexually violent materials depict the woman as experiencing arousal, orgasm, or other form of enjoyment as the ultimate result of the sexual assault. This theme, unfortunately very common in the materials we have examined, is likely to be the major, albeit not the only, component of what it is in the materials in this category that causes the consequences that have been identified. . . .

Nonviolent Materials Depicting Degradation, Domination, Subordination, or Humiliation

. . . It appears that effects similar to, although not as extensive as that involved with violent material, can be identified with respect to . . . degrading material, but that these effects are likely absent when neither degradation nor violence is present.

An enormous amount of the most sexually explicit material available, as well as much of the material that is somewhat less sexually explicit, is material that we would characterize as "degrading," the term we use to encompass the undeniably linked characteristics of degradation, domination, subordination, and humiliation. The degradation we refer to is degradation of people, most often women, and here we are referring to material that, although not violent, depicts people, usually women, as existing solely for the sexual satisfaction of others, usually men, or that depicts people, usually women, in decidedly subordinate roles in their sexual relations with others, or that depicts people engaged in sexual practices that would to most people be considered humiliating. Indeed, forms of degradation represent the largely predominant proportion of commercially available pornography.

With respect to material of this variety, our conclusions are substantially similar to those with respect to violent material, although we make them with somewhat less assumption than was the case with respect to violent material. The evidence, scientific and otherwise, is more tentative, but supports the conclusion that the material we describe as degrading bears some causal relationship to the attitudinal changes we have previously identified. That is, substantial exposure to material of this variety is likely to increase the extent to which those exposed will view rape or other forms of sexual violence as less serious than they otherwise would have, will view the victims of rape and other forms of sexual violence as significantly more responsible, and will view the offenders as significantly less responsible. We also conclude that the evidence supports the conclusion that substantial exposure to material of this type will increase acceptance of the proposition that women like to be forced into sexual practices, and, once again, that the woman who says "no" really means "yes."

. . . We believe we are justified in drawing the following conclusions: Over a large enough sample of population that believes that many women like to be raped, that believes that sexual violence or sexual coercion is often desired or appropriate, and that believes that sex offenders are less responsible for their acts, will commit more acts of sexual violence or sexual coercion than would a population holding these beliefs to a lesser extent.

. . . Thus, we conclude that substantial exposure to materials of this type bears some causal relationship to the level of sexual violence, sexual coercion, or unwanted sexual aggression in the population so exposed.

We need mention as well that our focus on these more violent or more coercive forms of actual subordination of women should not diminish what we take to be a necessarily incorporated conclusion: Substantial exposure to materials of this type bears some causal relationship to the incidence of various nonviolent forms of discrimination against or subordination of women in our society. To the extent that these materials create or reinforce the view that women's function is disproportionately to satisfy the sexual needs of men, then the materials will have pervasive effects on the treatment of women in society far beyond the incidence of identifiable acts of rape or other sexual violence. We obviously cannot here explore fully all the forms in which women are discriminated against in contemporary society. Nor can we explore all of the causes of that discrimination against women. But we feel confident in concluding that the view of women as available for sexual domination is one cause of that discrimination, and we feel confident as well in concluding that degrading material bears a causal relationship to the view that women ought to subordinate their own desires and beings to the sexual satisfaction of men. . . .

Non-Violent and Non-Degrading Materials

Our most controversial category has been the category of sexually explicit materials that are not violent and are not degrading as we have used that term. They are materials in which the participants appear to be fully willing participants occupying substantially equal roles in a setting devoid of actual or apparent violence or pain. This category is in fact quite small in terms of currently available materials. There is some, to be sure, and the amount may increase as the division between the degrading and the non-degrading becomes more accepted, but we are convinced that only a small amount of currently available highly sexually explicit material is neither violent nor degrading. We thus talk about a small category, but one that should not be ignored.

We have disagreed substantially about the effects of such materials, and that should come as no surprise. We are dealing in this category with "pure" sex, as to which there are widely divergent views in this society. That we have disagreed among ourselves does little more than reflect the extent to which we are representative of the population as a whole. In light of that disagreement, it is perhaps more appropriate to explain the various views rather than indicate a unanimity that does not exist, within this Commission or within society, or attempt the preposterous task of saying that some fundamental view about the role of sexuality and portrayals of sexuality was accepted or defeated by such-and-such vote. We do not wish to give easy answers to hard questions, and thus feel better with describing the diversity of opinion rather than suppressing part of it.

In examining the material in this category, we have not had the benefit of extensive evidence. Research has only recently begun to distinguish the non-violent but degrading from material that is neither violent nor degrading, and we have all relied on a combination of interpretation of existing studies that may not have drawn the same divisions, studies that did draw these distinctions, clinical evidence, interpretation of victim testimony, and our own perceptions of the effect of images on human behavior. Although the social science evidence is far from conclusive, we are, on the current state of the evidence, persuaded that material of this type does not bear a causal relationship to rape and other acts of sexual violence. . . .

That there does not appear from the social science evidence to be a causal link with sexual violence, however, does not answer the question of whether such materials might not themselves simply for some other reason constitute a harm in themselves, or bear a causal link to consequences other than sexual violence but still taken to be harmful. And it is here that we and society at large have the greatest differences in opinion.

One issue relates to materials that, although undoubtedly consensual and equal, depict sexual practices frequently condemned in this and other societies. In addition, level of societal condemnation varies for different activities; some activities are condemned by some people, but not by others. We have discovered that to some significant extent the assessment of the harmfulness of materials depicting such activities correlates directly with the assessment of the harmfulness of the activities themselves. Intuitively and not experimentally, we can hypothesize that materials portraying such an activity will either help to legitimize or will bear some causal relationship to that activity itself. With respect to these materials, therefore, it appears that a conclusion about the harmfulness of these materials turns on a conclusion about the harmfulness of the activity itself. As to this, we are unable to agree with respect to many of these activities. Our differences reflect differences now extant in society at large, and actively debated, and we can hardly resolve them here.

A larger issue is the very question of promiscuity. Even to the extent that the behavior depicted is not inherently condemned by some or any of us, the manner of presentation almost necessarily suggests that the activities are taking place outside of the context of marriage, love, commitment, or even affection. Again, it is far from implausible to hypothesize that materials depicting sexual activity without marriage, love, commitment, or affection bear some causal relationship to sexual activity without marriage, love, commitment, or affection. There are undoubtedly many causes for what used to be called the "sexual revolution," but it is absurd to suppose that depictions or descriptions of uncommitted sexuality were not among them. Thus, once again our disagreements reflect disagreements in society at large, although not to as great an extent. Although there are many members of this society who can and have made affirmative cases for uncommitted sexuality, none of us believes it to be a good thing. A number of us, however, believe that the level of commitment in sexuality is a matter of choice among those who voluntarily engage in the activity. Others of us believe that uncommitted sexual activity is wrong for the individuals involved and harmful to society to the extent of its prevalence. Our view of the ultimate harmfulness of much of this material, therefore, is reflective of our individual views about the extent to whether sexual commitment is purely a matter of individual choice. . . .

THE SPECIAL HORROR OF CHILD PORNOGRAPHY

What is commonly referred to as "child pornography" is not so much a form of pornography as it is a form of sexual exploitation of children. The distinguishing characteristic of child pornography, as generally understood, is that actual children are photographed while engaged in some form of sexual activity, either with adults or with other children. To understand the very idea of child pornography requires understanding the way in which real children, whether actually identified or not, are photographed, and understanding the way in which the use of real children in photographs creates a special harm largely independent of the kinds of concerns often expressed with respect to sexually explicit materials involving only adults.

Thus, the necessary focus of an inquiry into child pornography must be on the process by which children, from as young as one week up to the age of majority, are induced to engage in sexual activity of one sort or another, and the process by which children are photographed while engaging in that activity. The inevitably permanent record of that sexual activity created by a photograph is rather plainly a harm to the children photographed. But even if the photograph were never again seen, the very activity involved in creating the photograph is itself an act of sexual exploitation of children, and thus the issues related to the sexual abuse of children and those related to child pornography are inextricably linked. Child pornography necessarily includes the sexual abuse of a real child, and there can be no understanding of the special problem of child pornography until there is understanding of the special way in which child pornography *is* child abuse. . . .

QUESTIONS

1 Is it possible to provide a workable definition of "degrading pornography" or is this concept hopelessly subjective?

2 Which of the following, if any, would you endorse: (1) the censorship of violent pornography; (2) the censorship of nonviolent but degrading pornography; (3) the censorship of nonviolent and nondegrading pornography?

3 In *Ohio v. Osborne* (1990), the Supreme Court ruled that it is constitutional for states to prohibit by law even the private *possession* of child pornography. In view of the special evil of child pornography, would you endorse such a law?

Pornography, Oppression, and Freedom: A Closer Look

Helen E. Longino

Helen E. Longino is associate professor of philosophy at Mills College. Her published articles include "Evidence and Hypothesis," "Scientific Objectivity and the Logics of Science," and "Can There Be a Feminist Science?" Longino is the coeditor of *Competition: A Feminist Taboo?* (1987).

Longino constructs a case against pornography from a feminist point of view. She begins by defining pornography in such a way as to distinguish it from both erotica and moral realism; pornography is "material that explicitly represents or describes degrading and abusive sexual behavior so as to endorse and/or recommend the behavior as described." In Longino's view, pornography is immoral not because it is sexually explicit but because it typically portrays women in a degrading and dehumanizing way. She explicitly identifies a number of related ways in which pornography is injurious to women. Because of pornography's injurious character, she concludes, its production and distribution are justifiably subject to control.

I INTRODUCTION

The much-touted sexual revolution of the 1960's and 1970's not only freed various modes of sexual behavior from the constraints of social disapproval, but also made possible a flood of pornographic material. According to figures provided by WAVPM (Women Against Violence in Pornography and Media), the number of pornographic magazines available at newsstands has grown from zero in 1953 to forty in 1977, while sales of pornographic films in Los Angeles alone have grown from $15 million in 1969 to $85 million in 1976.[1]

Traditionally, pornography was condemned as immoral because it presented sexually explicit material in a manner designed to appeal to "prurient interests" or a

"morbid" interest in nudity and sexuality, material which furthermore lacked any re-
deeming social value and which exceeded "customary limits of candor." While these
phrases, taken from a definition of "obscenity" proposed in the 1954 American Law
Institute's *Model Penal Code,*[2] require some criteria of application to eliminate
vagueness, it seems that what is objectionable is the explicit description or representation of bodily parts or sexual behavior for the purpose of inducing sexual stimulation or pleasure on the part of the reader or viewer. This kind of objection is part of
a sexual ethic that subordinates sex to procreation and condemns all sexual interactions outside of legitimated marriage. It is this code which was the primary target of
the sexual revolutionaries in the 1960's, and which has given way in many areas to
more open standards of sexual behavior.

One of the beneficial results of the sexual revolution has been a growing acceptance of the distinction between questions of sexual mores and questions of morality.
This distinction underlies the old slogan, "Make love, not war," and takes harm to
others as the defining characteristic of immorality. What is immoral is behavior
which causes injury to or violation of another person or people. Such injury may be
physical or it may be psychological. To cause pain to another, to lie to another, to
hinder another in the exercise of her or his rights, to exploit another, to degrade another, to misrepresent and slander another are instances of immoral behavior. Masturbation or engaging voluntarily in sexual intercourse with another consenting adult
of the same or the other sex, as long as neither injury nor violation of either individual or another is involved, are not immoral. Some sexual behavior is morally objectionable, but not because of its sexual character. Thus, adultery is immoral not because it involves sexual intercourse with someone to whom one is not legally married, but because it involves breaking a promise (of sexual and emotional fidelity to
one's spouse). Sadistic, abusive, or forced sex is immoral because it injures and violates another.

The detachment of sexual chastity from moral virtue implies that we cannot condemn forms of sexual behavior merely because they strike us as distasteful or sub-
versive of the Protestant work ethic, or because they depart from standards of behavior we have individually adopted. It has thus seemed to imply that no matter how
offensive we might find pornography, we must tolerate it in the name of freedom
from illegitimate repression. I wish to argue that this is not so, that pornography is
immoral because it is harmful to people.

II WHAT IS PORNOGRAPHY?

I define pornography as *verbal or pictorial explicit representations of sexual behavior that,* in the words of the Commission on Obscenity and Pornography, *have as a
distinguishing characteristic "the degrading and demeaning portrayal of the role
and status of the human female. . . as a mere sexual object to be exploited and manipulated sexually."*[3] In pornographic books, magazines, and films, women are represented as passive and as slavishly dependent upon men. The role of female characters is limited to the provision of sexual services to men. To the extent that wom-
en's sexual pleasure is represented at all, it is subordinated to that of men and is

never an end in itself as is the sexual pleasure of men. What pleases women is the use of their bodies to satisfy male desires. While the sexual objectification of women is common to all pornography, women are the recipients of even worse treatment in violent pornography, in which women characters are killed, tortured, gang-raped, mutilated, bound, and otherwise abused, as a means of providing sexual stimulation or pleasure to the male characters. It is this development which has attracted the attention of feminists and been the stimulus to an analysis of pornography in general.[4]

Not all sexually explicit material is pornography, nor is all material which contains representations of sexual abuse and degradation pornography.

A representation of a sexual encounter between adult persons which is characterized by mutual respect is, once we have disentangled sexuality and morality, not morally objectionable. Such a representation would be one in which the desires and experiences of each participant were regarded by the other participants as having a validity and a subjective importance equal to those of the individual's own desire and experiences. In such an encounter, each participant acknowledges the other participant's basic human dignity and personhood. Similarly, a representation of a nude human body (in whole or in part) in such a manner that the person shown maintains self-respect—e.g., is not portrayed in a degrading position—would not be morally objectionable. The educational films of the National Sex Forum, as well as a certain amount of erotic literature and art, fall into this category. While some erotic materials are beyond the standards of modesty held by some individuals, they are not for this reason immoral.

A representation of a sexual encounter which is not characterized by mutual respect, in which at least one of the parties is treated in a manner beneath her or his dignity as a human being, is no longer simple erotica. That a representation is of degrading behavior does not in itself, however, make it pornographic. Whether or not it is pornographic is a function of contextual features. Books and films may contain descriptions or representations of a rape in order to explore the consequences of such an assault upon its victim. What is being shown is abusive or degrading behavior which attempts to deny the humanity and dignity of the person assaulted, yet the context surrounding the representation, through its exploration of the consequences of the act, acknowledges and reaffirms her dignity. Such books and films, far from being pornographic, are (or can be) highly moral, and fall into the category of moral realism.

What makes a work a work of pornography, then, is not simply its representation of degrading and abusive sexual encounters, but its implicit, if not explicit, approval and recommendation of sexual behavior that is immoral, i.e., that physically or psychologically violates the personhood of one of the participants. Pornography, then, is verbal or pictorial material which represents or describes sexual behavior that is degrading or abusive to one or more of the participants *in such a way as to endorse the degradation.* The participants so treated in virtually all heterosexual pornography are women or children, so heterosexual pornography is, as a matter of fact, material which endorses sexual behavior that is degrading and/or abusive to women and children. As I use the term "sexual behavior," this includes sexual encounters between persons, behavior which produces sexual stimulation or pleasure for one of the participants, and behavior which is preparatory to or invites sexual activity. Behavior that is degrading or abusive includes physical harm or abuse, and physical or psychological coercion. In addition, behavior which ignores or devalues the real interests, desires, and experiences of one or more participants in any way is degrading. Finally, that a person has chosen or consented to be harmed, abused, or subjected to coercion does not alter the degrading character of such behavior.

Pornography communicates its endorsement of the behavior it represents by various features of the pornographic context: the degradation of the female characters is represented as providing pleasure to the participant males and, even worse, to the participant females, and there is no suggestion that this sort of treatment of others is inappropriate to their status as human beings. These two features are together sufficient to constitute endorsement of the represented behavior. The contextual features which make material pornographic are intrinsic to the material. In addition to these, extrinsic features, such as the purpose for which the material is presented—i.e., the sexual arousal/pleasure/satisfaction of its (mostly) male consumers—or an accompanying text, may reinforce or make explicit the endorsement. Representations which in and of themselves do not show or endorse degrading behavior may be put into a pornographic context by juxtaposition with others that are degrading, or by a text which invites or recommends degrading behavior toward the subject represented. In such a case the whole complex—the series of representations or representations with text—is pornographic.

The distinction I have sketched is one that applies most clearly to sequential material—a verbal or pictorial (filmed) story—which represents an action and provides a temporal context for it. In showing the before and after, a narrator or film-maker has plenty of opportunity to acknowledge the dignity of the person violated or clearly to refuse to do so. It is somewhat more difficult to apply the distinction to single still representations. The contextual features cited above, however, are clearly present in still photographs or pictures that glamorize degradation and sexual violence. Phonograph album covers and advertisements offer some prime examples of such glamorization. Their representations of women in chains (the Ohio Players), or bound by ropes and black and blue (the Rolling Stones) are considered high-quality commercial "art" and glossily prettify the violence they represent. Since the standard function of prettification and glamorization is the communication of desirability, these albums and ads are communicating the desirability of violence against women. Representations of women bound or chained, particularly those of women bound in such a way as to make their breasts, or genital or anal areas vulnerable to any passerby, endorse the scene they represent by the absence of any indication that this treatment of women is in any way inappropriate.

To summarize: Pornography is not just the explicit representation or description of sexual behavior, nor even the explicit representation or description of sexual behavior which is degrading and/or abusive to women. Rather, it is material that explicitly represents or describes degrading and abusive sexual behavior so as to endorse and/or recommend the behavior as described. The contextual features, moreover, which communicate such endorsement are intrinsic to the material; that is, they are features whose removal or alteration would change the representation or description.

This account of pornography is underlined by the etymology and original meaning of the word "pornography." *The Oxford English Dictionary* defines pornography as "Description of the life, manners, etc. of prostitutes and their patrons [from πόρνη (porne) meaning "harlot" and γράφειν (graphein) meaning "to write"]; hence the expression or suggestion of obscene or unchaste subjects in literature or art."[5]

Let us consider the first part of the definition for a moment. In the transactions between prostitutes and their clients, prostitutes are paid, directly or indirectly, for the use of their bodies by the client for sexual pleasure.[6] Traditionally males have obtained from female prostitutes what they could not or did not wish to get from their wives or women friends, who, because of the character of their relation to the male, must be accorded some measure of human respect. While there are limits to what treatment is seen as appropriate toward women as wives or women friends, the prostitute as prostitute exists to provide sexual pleasure to males. The female characters of contemporary pornography also exist to provide pleasure to males, but in the pornographic context no pretense is made to regard them as parties to a contractual arrangement. Rather, the anonymity of these characters makes each one Everywoman, thus suggesting not only that all women are appropriate subjects for the enactment of the most bizarre and demeaning male sexual fantasies, but also that this is their primary purpose. The recent escalation of violence in pornography—the presentation of scenes of bondage, rape, and torture of women for the sexual stimulation of the male characters or male viewers—while shocking in itself, is from this point of view merely a more vicious extension of a genre whose success depends on treating women in a manner beneath their dignity as human beings.

III PORNOGRAPHY: LIES AND VIOLENCE AGAINST WOMEN

What is wrong with pornography, then, is its degrading and dehumanizing portrayal of women (and *not* its sexual content). Pornography, by its very nature, requires that women be subordinate to men and mere instruments for the fulfillment of male fantasies. To accomplish this, pornography must lie. Pornography lies when it says that our sexual life is or ought to be subordinate to the service of men, that our pleasure consists in pleasing men and not ourselves, that we are depraved, that we are fit subjects for rape, bondage, torture, and murder. Pornography lies explicitly about women's sexuality, and through such lies fosters more lies about our humanity, our dignity, and our personhood.

Moreover, since nothing is alleged to justify the treatment of the female characters of pornography save their womanhood, pornography depicts all women as fit objects of violence by virtue of their sex alone. Because it is simply being female that, in the pornographic vision, justifies being violated, the lies of pornography are lies about all women. Each work of pornography is on its own libelous and defamatory, yet gains power through being reinforced by every other pornographic work. The sheer number of pornographic productions expands the moral issue to include not only assessing the morality or immorality of individual works, but also the meaning and force of the mass production of pornography.

The pornographic view of women is thoroughly entrenched in a booming portion of the publishing, film, and recording industries, reaching and affecting not only all who look to such sources for sexual stimulation, but also those of us who are forced into an awareness of it as we peruse magazines at newsstands and record albums in record stores, as we check the entertainment sections of city newspapers, or even as we approach a counter to pay for groceries. It is not necessary to spend a great deal of time reading or viewing pornographic material to absorb its male-centered definition of women. No longer confined within plain brown wrappers, it jumps out from billboards that proclaim "Live X-rated Girls!" or "Angels in Pain" or "Hot and Wild," and from magazine covers displaying a woman's genital area being spread open to the viewer by her own fingers.[7] Thus, even men who do not frequent pornographic shops and movie houses are supported in the sexist objectification of women by their environment. Women, too, are crippled by internalizing as self-images those that are presented to us by pornographers. Isolated from one another and with no source of support for an alternative view of female sexuality, we may not always find the strength to resist a message that dominates the common cultural media.

The entrenchment of pornography in our culture also gives it a significance quite beyond its explicit sexual messages. To suggest, as pornography does, that the primary purpose of women is to provide sexual pleasure to men is to deny that women are independently human or have a status equal to that of men. It is, moreover, to deny our equality at one of the most intimate levels of human experience. This denial is especially powerful in a hierarchical, class society such as ours, in which individuals feel good about themselves by feeling superior to others. Men in our society have a vested interest in maintaining their belief in the inferiority of the female sex, so that no matter how oppressed and exploited by the society in which they live and work, they can feel that they are at least superior to someone or some category of individuals—a woman or women. Pornography, by presenting women as wanton, depraved, and made for the sexual use of men, caters directly to that interest.[8] The very intimate nature of sexuality which makes pornography so corrosive also protects it from explicit public discussion. The consequent lack of any explicit social disavowal of the pornographic image of women enables this image to continue fostering sexist attitudes even as the society publicly proclaims its (as yet timid) commitment to sexual equality.

In addition to finding a connection between the pornographic view of women and the denial to us of our full human rights, women are beginning to connect the consumption of pornography with commiting rape and other acts of sexual violence against women. Contrary to the findings of the Commission on Obscenity and Pornography a growing body of research is documenting (1) a correlation between exposure to representations of violence and the committing of violent acts generally, and (2) a correlation between exposure to pornographic materials and the committing of sexually abusive or violent acts against women.[9] While more study is needed to establish precisely what the causal relations are, clearly so-called hard-core pornography is not innocent.

From "snuff" films and miserable magazines in pornographic stores to *Hustler,* to phonograph album covers and advertisements, to *Vogue,* pornography has come to occupy its own niche in the communications and entertainment media and to acquire a quasi-institutional character (signaled by the use of diminutives such as "porn" or "porno" to refer to pornographic material, as though such familiar naming could take the hurt out). Its acceptance by the mass media, whatever the motivation, means a cultural endorsement of its message. As much as the materials themselves, the social tolerance of these degrading and distorted images of women in such quantities is harmful to us, since it indicates a general willingness to see women in ways incompatible with our fundamental human dignity and thus to justify treating us in those ways.[10] The tolerance of pornographic representations of the rape, bondage, and torture of women helps to create and maintain a climate more tolerant of the actual physical abuse of women.[11] The tendency on the part of the legal system to view the victim of a rape as responsible for the crime against her is but one manifestation of this.

In sum, pornography is injurious to women in at least three distinct ways:

1 Pornography, especially violent pornography, is implicated in the committing of crimes of violence against women.

2 Pornography is the vehicle for the dissemination of a deep and vicious lie about women. It is defamatory and libelous.

3 The diffusion of such a distorted view of women's nature in our society as it exists today supports sexist (i.e., male-centered) attitudes, and thus reinforces the oppression and exploitation of women.

Society's tolerance of pornography, especially pornography on the contemporary massive scale, reinforces each of these modes of injury: By not disavowing the lie, it supports the male-centered myth that women are inferior and subordinate creatures. Thus, it contributes to the maintenance of a climate tolerant of both psychological and physical violence against women. . . .

CONCLUSION

I have defined pornography in such a way as to distinguish it from erotica and from moral realism, and have argued that it is defamatory and libelous toward women, that it condones crimes against women, and that it invites tolerance of the social, economic, and cultural oppression of women. The production and distribution of pornographic material is thus a social and moral wrong. Contrasting both the current volume of pornographic production and its growing infiltration of the communications media with the status of women in this culture makes clear the necessity for its control. . . .

Appeals for action against pornography are sometimes brushed aside with the claim that such action is a diversion from the primary task of feminists—the elimination of sexism and of sexual inequality. This approach focuses on the enjoyment rather than the manufacture of pornography, and sees it as merely a product of sexism which will disappear when the latter has been overcome and the sexes are socially and economically equal. Pornography cannot be separated from sexism in this way: Sexism is not just a set of attitudes regarding the inferiority of women but the behaviors and social and economic rules that manifest such attitudes. Both the manufacture and distribution of pornography and the enjoyment of it are instances of sexist behavior. The enjoyment of pornography on the part of individuals will presumably decline as such individuals begin to accord women their status as fully human. A cultural climate which tolerates the degrading representation of women is not a climate which facilitates the development of respect for women. Furthermore, the demand for pornography is stimulated not just by the sexism of individuals but by the pornography industry itself. Thus, both as a social phenomenon and in its effect on individuals, pornography, far from being a mere product, nourishes sexism. The campaign against it is an essential component of women's struggle for legal, economic, and social equality, one which requires the support of all feminists.[12]

NOTES

1 *Women Against Violence in Pornography and Media Newspage,* Vol. II, No. 5, June 1978; and Judith Reisman in *Women Against Violence in Pornography and Media Proposal.*

2 American Law Institute *Model Penal Code,* sec. 251.4.

3 *Report of the Commission on Obscenity and Pornography* (New York: Bantam Books, 1970), p. 239. The Commission, of course, concluded that the demeaning content of pornography did not adversely affect male attitudes toward women.

4 Among recent feminist discussions are Diana Russell, "Pornography: A Feminist Perspective" and Susan Griffin, "On Pornography," *Chrysalis,* Vol. I, No. 4, 1978; and Ann Garry, "Pornography and Respect for Women," *Social Theory and Practice,* Vol. 4, Spring 1978, pp. 395–421.

5 *The Oxford English Dictionary,* Compact Edition (London: Oxford University Press, 1971), p. 2242.

6 In talking of prostitution here, I refer to the concept of, rather than the reality of, prostitution. The same is true of my remarks about relationships between women and their husbands or men friends.

7 This was a full-color magazine cover seen in a rack at the check-out counter of a corner delicatessen.

8 Pornography thus becomes another tool of capitalism. One feature of some contemporary pornography—the use of Black and Asian women in both still photographs and films—exploits the racism as well as the sexism of its white consumers. For a discussion of the interplay between racism and sexism under capitalism as it relates to violent crimes against women, see Angela Y. Davis, "Rape, Racism, and the Capitalist Setting," *The Black Scholar,* Vol. 9, No. 7, April 1978.

9 Urie Bronfenbrenner, *Two Worlds of Childhood* (New York: Russell Sage Foundation, 1970); H. J. Eysenck and D.K.B. Nias, *Sex, Violence and the Media* (New York: St. Martin's Press, 1978); and Michael Goldstein, Harold Kant, and John Hartman, *Pornography and Sexual Deviance* (Berkeley: University of California Press, 1973); and the papers by Diana Russell, Pauline Bart, and Irene Diamond included in [Laura Lederer, ed., *Take Back the Night* (New York: William Morrow, 1980)].

10 This tolerance has a linguistic parallel in the growing acceptance and use of nonhuman nouns such as "chick," "bird," "filly," "fox," "doll," "babe," "skirt," etc., to refer to women, and of verbs of harm such as "fuck," "screw," "bang," to refer to sexual inter-

course. See Robert Baker and Frederick Elliston, " 'Pricks' and 'Chicks': A Plea for Persons." *Philosophy and Sex* (Buffalo, N.Y.: Prometheus Books, 1975).

11 This is supported by the fact that in Denmark the number of rapes committed has increased while the number of rapes reported to the authorities has decreased over the past twelve years. See *WAVPM Newspage,* Vol. II, No. 5, June, 1978, quoting M. Harry, "Denmark Today—The Causes and Effects of Sexual Liberty" (paper presented to The Responsible Society, London, England, 1976). See also Eysenck and Nias, *Sex, Violence and the Media* (New York: St. Martin's Press, 1978), pp. 120–124.

12 Many women helped me to develop and crystallize the ideas presented in this paper. I would especially like to thank Michele Farrell, Laura Lederer, Pamela Miller, and Dianne Romain for their comments in conversation and on the first written draft. Portions of this material were presented orally to members of the Society for Women in Philosophy and to participants in the workshops on "What Is Pornography?" at the Conference on Feminist Perspectives on Pornography, San Francisco, November 17, 18, and 19, 1978. Their discussion was invaluable in helping me to see problems and to clarify the ideas presented here.

QUESTIONS

1 Do you accept Longino's suggested definition of pornography? Is there a better definition?
2 Emphasizing the injurious impact of pornography on women, Longino concludes that "its control is necessary." What specific controls on the production and distribution of pornography would you endorse?

Feminism, Pornography, and Censorship

Mark R. Wicclair

Mark R. Wicclair is professor of philosophy at West Virginia University and associate at the Center for Medical Ethics, University of Pittsburgh. He is the author of *Ethics and the Elderly* (forthcoming). His published articles include "Preferential Treatment and Desert," "Human Rights and Intervention," and "Is Prostitution Morally Wrong?"

Wicclair operates with the definition of pornography suggested by Longino. He argues, however, that censorship of pornography is not a legitimate means to achieve the aims of feminism, nor even the most effective means. In his view, there is a strong presumption against censorship; this presumption is based on the principle of freedom of expression as well as the likely negative side effects of censorship. In rejecting the argument that censorship of pornography is a legitimate means of preventing harm to women, he claims that the connection between pornography and harm to women is too speculative to warrant incurring the costs of censorship. In addition to emphasizing the costs of censorship, Wicclair warns against overestimating its expected benefits. He concludes by presenting the procensorship feminist with a series of difficulties.

It is sometimes claimed that pornography is objectionable because it violates conventional standards of sexual morality. Although feminists tend to agree that pornography is objectionable, they reject this particular argument against it.[1] This argument is unacceptable to feminists because it is associated with an oppressive Puritanical sexual ethic that inhibits the sexual fulfillment of all people, but especially women. In order to understand why feminists find pornography objectionable, one has to keep in mind that they do not equate the terms "pornographic" and "sexually explicit." Rather, sexually explicit material is said to be "pornographic" only if it depicts and condones the exploitation, dehumanization, subordination, abuse, or denigration of women. By definition, then, all pornography is sexist and misogynistic. Some pornographic material has the additional feature of depicting and condoning acts of *violence* against women (e.g., rape, brutality, torture, sadism). Thus there is a world of difference between harmless "erotica" and pornography. Whereas erotica depicts sexual activity in a manner which is designed to produce sexual arousal and is therefore likely to be objectionable only to those who subscribe to a Puritanical sexual ethic, pornography is "material that explicitly represents or describes degrading and abusive sexual behavior so as to endorse and/or recommend the behavior as described."[2]

Despite the general agreement among feminists that pornography, understood in the way just described, is objectionable, they are sharply divided over the question of its *censorship.* Whereas some feminists find pornography to be so objectionable that they call for its censorship, others oppose this proposal.[3] I will argue that anyone who supports the aims of feminism and who seeks the liberation of all people should reject the censorship of pornography.[4]

When discussing censorship, it is important to keep in mind that there are very strong reasons to be wary of its use. In our society, the importance of the principle of freedom of expression—an anticensorship principle—is widely recognized. The ability to speak one's mind and to express ideas and feelings without the threat of legal penalties or government control is rightly perceived as an essential feature of a truly free society. Moreover, an environment that tolerates the expression of differing views about politics, art, lifestyles, etc., encourages progress and aids in the search for truth and justice. In addition to the many important values associated with the principle of freedom of expression, it is also necessary to consider likely negative side effects of censorship. There is a serious risk that once any censorship is allowed, the power to censor will, over time, expand in unintended and undesirable directions (the "slippery slope"). This is not mere speculation, for such an expansion of the power to censor is to be expected in view of the fact that it is extremely difficult, if not impossible, to formulate unequivocal and unambiguous criteria of censorship. Then, too, the power to censor can all too easily be abused or misused. Even though it may arise in a genuine effort to promote the general welfare and to protect certain rights, officials and groups might use the power to censor as a means to advance their own interests and values and to suppress the rights, interests, and values of others. Thus, given the value of freedom of expression and the many dangers associated with censorship, there is a strong *prima facie* case against censorship. In other words, advocates of censorship have the burden of showing that there are sufficiently strong overriding reasons which would justify it in a specific area.

Like racist and antisemitic material, sexist and misogynistic films, books, and magazines surely deserve condemnation. But censorship is another matter. In view of the strength of the case against censorship in general, it is unwise to advocate it merely to prevent depicting morally objectionable practices in a favorable light. Fortunately, proponents of the censorship of pornography tend to recognize this, for they usually base their call for censorship on a claim about the *effects* of pornography. Pornography, it is held, is *injurious* or *harmful* to women because it fosters the objectionable practices that it depicts. Pornography generally is said to promote the exploitation, humiliation, denigration, subordination, etc., of women; and pornography that depicts acts of violence against women is said to cause murder, rape, assault, and other acts of violence. On the basis of the "harm principle"—a widely accepted principle that allows us to restrict someone's freedom in order to prevent harm to others—it would appear to be justified to override the principle of freedom of expression and to restrict the freedom of would-be producers, distributors, sellers, exhibitors, and consumers of pornography. In short it seems that censorship of pornography is a legitimate means of preventing harm to women.

However, there are a number of problems associated with this attempt to justify censorship. To begin with, it is essential to recognize the important difference between words and images, on the one hand, and actions, on the other hand. A would-be rapist poses a *direct* threat to his intended victim, and by stopping him, we prevent an act of violence. But if there is a connection between the depiction of a rape—even one which appears to condone it—and someone's committing an act of violence against a woman, the connection is relatively *indirect;* and stopping the production, distribution, sale, and exhibition of depictions of rape does not directly restrict the freedom of would-be rapists to commit acts of violence against women. In recognition of the important difference between restricting words and images and preventing harmful behavior, exceptions to the principle of freedom of expression are generally thought to be justified only if words or images present a "clear and present danger" of harm or injury. Thus, to cite a standard example, it is justified to stop someone from falsely shouting "Fire!" in a crowded theater, for this exclamation is likely to cause a panic that would result in serious injury and even death.

It is doubtful that pornography satisfies the "clear and present danger" condition. For there does not seem to be conclusive evidence that establishes its *causal* significance. Most studies are limited to violent pornography. And even though some of these studies do suggest a *temporary* impact on *attitudes* (e.g., those who view violent pornography may be more likely to express the view that women seek and "enjoy" violence), this does not show that viewing violent pornography causes violent *behavior.* Moreover, there is some evidence suggesting that the effect on attitudes is only temporary and that it can be effectively counteracted by additional information.[5]

But even if there is no conclusive evidence that pornography causes harm, is it not reasonable to "play it safe," and does this not require censorship? Unfortunately, the situation is not as simple as this question appears to suggest. For one thing, it is sometimes claimed that exposure to pornography has a "cathartic" effect and that it therefore produces a net *reduction* in harm to women. This claim is based upon two assumptions, neither of which has been proven to be false: (1) Men who are not already violence-prone are more likely to be "turned off" than to be "turned on" by depictions of rape, brutality, dismemberment, etc. (2) For men in the latter category, exposure to pornography can function as a substitute for actually causing harm. It is also necessary to recall that there are significant values associated with the principle of freedom of expression, and that a failure to observe it involves a number of serious dangers. Since censorship has costs which are substantial and not merely speculative, the more speculative the connection between pornography and harm to women, the less basis there is for incurring the costs associated with censorship.

Just as it is easy to overlook the negative side of censorship, it is also common to overplay its positive effects. Surely it would be foolish to think that outlawing antisemitism in sexually explicit material would have halted the slaughter of Jews in Hitler Germany or that prohibiting racism in sexually explicit material would reduce the suffering of Blacks in South Africa. Similarly, in view of the violent nature of American society generally and the degree to which sexism persists to this day, it is unlikely that censorship of pornography by itself would produce any significant improvement in the condition of women in the United States. Fortunately, there are other, more effective and direct means of eliminating sexism than by censoring pornography. Passage and strict enforcement of the Equal Rights Amendment, electing feminists to local, state, and national political office, achieving genuine economic justice for women, and securing their reproductive freedom will do considerably more to foster the genuine liberation of women in the United States than will the censorship of pornography. With respect to rape and other acts of violence, it has often been noted that American society is extremely violent, and, sadly, there are no magic solutions to the problems of rape and violence. But the magnitude of the problem suggests that censoring pornography only addresses a symptom and not the underlying disease. Although there is still much dispute about the causes of violence generally and rape in particular, it is unlikely that there will be a serious reduction in acts of violence against women until there are rather drastic changes in the socioeconomic environment and in the criminal justice system.

Those who remain concerned about the possible contribution of pornography to violence and sexism should keep in mind that it can be "neutralized" in ways that avoid the dangers of censorship. One important alternative to government censorship is to help people understand why pornography is objectionable and why it and its message should be rejected. This can be accomplished by means of educational campaigns, discussions of pornography on radio and television and at public forums, letter writing, and educational picketing. In addition, attempts might be made to prevent or restrict the production, distribution, display, sale, and consumption of pornographic material by means of organized pickets, boycotts, and the like. Such direct measures by private citizens raise some troubling questions, but the dangers and risks which they pose are considerably less than those associated with government censorship.

There are several other reasons for questioning the view that the sexist and misogynistic nature of pornography justifies its censorship. Some of the more important of these include the following:

1 Although pornography depicts some practices that are both morally objectionable and illegal (e.g., rape, assault, torture), many of the practices depicted are morally repugnant *but do not break any law.* Thus, for example, our legal system does not explicitly prohibit men from treating women in a degrading or humiliating manner; and with some exceptions, it is not a crime to treat women exclusively as sex objects or to use them exclusively as means and not ends. But is it not odd to recommend making illegal the production, distribution, sale, and exhibition of materials that depict practices that are not themselves illegal?

2 It is essential that laws be clearly formulated and that vagueness be avoided. Vague laws can have a "chilling effect" on unobjectionable activities, and they tend to undermine the fair and effective enforcement of the law by giving police, prosecutors, and judges too much discretionary power. But those who call for the censorship of pornography on the grounds that it is sexist and misogynistic fail to recognize the difficulty of formulating laws which would have an acceptable degree of clarity and specificity. Proponents of censorship use terms like "degrading," "humiliating," "debasing," "exploitative," and "subordination of women." But these terms are far from unambiguous. In fact, they are highly subjective in the sense that different people have different criteria for deciding when something is degrading, humiliating, etc. For example, someone might think that the depiction of an unmarried female or a lesbian couple having and enjoying sex is "demeaning" or "debasing." Thus, in order to prevent censorship from being applied in unintended and undesirable ways, it is necessary to offer clear and unambiguous operational criteria for terms like "demeaning," "humiliating," etc. But the feasibility of articulating generally acceptable criteria of this sort remains highly doubtful.

3 Sexually explicit material that depicts violence against women or that depicts sexist practices is said to be subject to censorship only if it *condones* the objectionable practices. Thus, for example, news films, documentaries, and works which take a critical stance toward those practices are not to be censored. But it is exceedingly difficult in many cases to determine the "point of view" of films, books, photographs, etc.[6] If scholars who have advanced degrees in film, literature, and art can come to no general consensus about the "meaning" or "message" of certain works, is it plausible to think that prosecutors, judges, and juries are likely to fare any better?

4 Why call for the censorship of sexist and misogynistic books, magazines, films, and photographs only if they include an explicit depiction of *sexual activity?* There is no conclusive evidence showing that material that includes a depiction of sexual activity has a greater causal impact on attitudes and behavior.[7] Moreover, it will not do to claim that such material is not worthy of protection under the principle of freedom of expression. Surely, many works which include explicit depictions of sex are not totally devoid of significant and challenging ideas. Consequently, advocates of censorship are faced with a dilemma: Either they can call for the censorship of *all* material that contains objectionable images of women; or they can call for censorship only in the case of sexually explicit materials of that nature. If the first alternative is chosen, then given the pervasiveness of objectionable portrayals of women in art, literature, and the mass media, very little would be immune from censorship. But in view of the strong *prima facie* case against censorship, this seems unacceptable. On the other hand, if the second alternative is chosen, this invites the suspicion that the restriction to sexual material is based upon the very same Puritanical sexual ethic which feminists rightly tend to reject. I am not suggesting that feminists who call for censorship wish to champion sexual oppression. But it is noteworthy that many conservatives who generally do not support the aims of feminism align themselves with feminists who advocate censoring pornography.

5 Why call for censorship of materials only if they depict violence or other objectionable practices in relation to *women?* Wouldn't consistency require censoring *all* violence and material that portrays *anyone* in a derogatory light? But this is clearly unacceptable. For so much of our culture is permeated with images of violence and morally distasteful treatment of people that it is hard to think of many films, television programs, books, or magazines which would be totally immune from censorship. Censorship would be the rule rather than an exception, and such pervasive censorship is incompatible with a truly free society. It also won't do to limit censorship to members of historically oppressed groups (e.g., women, Blacks, Jews). First, it is very unlikely that such "preferential censorship" would be accepted by the majority for too long. Sooner or later others would object and/or press for protection too. Second, in view of the significant costs of censorship, even if it were limited to the protection of historically oppressed groups, it would not be justified unless there were a demonstrable "clear and present danger;" and this remains doubtful. But what about the view that only pornography should be subject to censorship because *women need special protection?* This position is also unacceptable. For since men are victimized by acts of racism, antisemitism, and violence, and since there is no evidence to prove that depictions of objectionable practices have a greater effect on behavior in pornographic material than they do in nonpornographic material, this position seems to be based on the sexist assumption that women need greater protection than men because they are "naturally" more fragile and vulnerable.

I have tried to show that censorship of pornography is neither the most effective nor a legitimate means to achieve the aims of feminism. Much pornographic material is morally repugnant, but there are less costly ways to express one's moral outrage and to attempt to "neutralize" pornography than by censorship. Moreover, pornography is only a relatively minor manifestation of the sexist practices and institutions that still pervade our society. Hence, the genuine liberation of women—and men—is best served by directly attacking those oppressive practices and institutions. It may be easier to identify and attack pornography—and to win some battles—but the payoff would be slight, and the negative side effects would be substantial.

NOTES

1 Just as the civil rights movement in the United States in the 1950's and 1960's included many people who were not black, so one does not have to be a woman to be a feminist. As I am using the term, a feminist is any person who supports the fundamental goal of feminism: the liberation of women.

2 Helen E. Longino, "Pornography, Oppression, and Freedom: A Closer Look," in Laura Lederer, ed., *Take Back the Night* (New York: William Morrow and Company, Inc., 1980), p. 44. Longino also stipulates that the sexual activities depicted in pornography are degrading or abusive *to women.*

3 In response to the generally pro-censorship Women Against Violence in Pornography and Media, other feminists have organized the Feminist Anti-Censorship Taskforce.

4 Until recently, advocates of censorship have pressed for laws which prohibit or restrict the production, distribution, sale, and exhibition of pornographic material. However, pro-censorship feminists have hit upon a new strategy: Ordinances which stipulate that pornography is *sex discrimination,* enabling women to file sex discrimination lawsuits against producers, distributors, sellers, and exhibitors of pornography. Most of the criticisms of censorship which I discuss in this paper apply to both strategies.

5 For a discussion of research on the effects of pornography, see Edward Donnerstein and Neil Malamuth, eds., *Pornography and Sexual Aggression* (New York: Academic Press, 1984).

6 An informative illustration of how a film can resist unambiguous classification as either progressive or retrograde from a feminist perspective is provided in Lucy Fischer and Marcia Landy, *"The Eyes of Laura Mars:* A Binocular Critique," *Screen,* Vol. 23, Nos. 3–4 (September–October 1982).

7 In fact some researchers claim that the impact of depictions of violence is *greater* in material which is *not* pornographic. See, for example, the contribution of Edward Donnerstein and Daniel Linz to a section on pornography, "Pornography: Love or Death?" in *Film Comment,* vol. 20, No. 6 (December 1984), pp. 34–35.

QUESTIONS

1 Does the easy availability of pornography pose a "clear and present danger" to women?

2 Considering the aims of feminism, are feminists well advised to endorse the censorship of pornography?

SUGGESTED ADDITIONAL READINGS FOR CHAPTER 6

BERGER, FRED R.: *Freedom of Expression.* Belmont, Calif.: Wadsworth, 1980. This anthology, which addresses a number of issues related to freedom of expression, includes two notable selections relevant to the problem of pornography and censorship. The first selection, "The Moral Theory of Free Speech and Obscenity Law" (pp. 99–127), is by David A. J. Richards. The second selection, "Women Fight Back" (pp. 128–133), is an excerpt from Susan Brownmiller's *Against Our Will: Men, Women and Rape* (1975).

COPP, DAVID, and SUSAN WENDELL: *Pornography and Censorship.* Buffalo, N.Y.: Prometheus, 1983. Part I of this anthology contains a number of excellent philosophical essays. Part II contains essays by social scientists on the question of whether the wide availability of pornography has harmful consequences. Part III contains judicial essays.

DeCEW, JUDITH WAGNER: "Violent Pornography: Censorship, Morality and Social Alternatives." *Journal of Applied Philosophy,* vol. 1, March 1984, pp. 79–93. DeCew discusses the morality of violent pornography. She does not endorse its censorship but finds other suggested social responses also to be unsatisfactory.

DEVLIN, PATRICK: *The Enforcement of Morals.* New York: Oxford University Press, 1965. Lord Devlin, a prominent English judge, is the foremost contemporary spokesperson for the legitimacy of the principle of legal moralism. This short book contains seven of his essays.

DYAL, ROBERT: "Is Pornography Good for You?" *Southwestern Journal of Philosophy,* vol. 7, Fall 1976, pp. 95–118. Dyal argues that pornographic materials ought not to be subject to censorship. He also encourages individuals to loosen "autonomous controls" so as "to explore the aesthetic possibilities, cultural dimensions, and existential depths opened up by pornography."

FEINBERG, JOEL: *Social Philosophy.* Englewood Cliffs, N.J.: Prentice-Hall, 1973. Chapters 2 and 3 of this book provide a very helpful discussion of liberty-limiting principles.

HILL, JUDITH M.: "Pornography and Degradation." *Hypatia,* vol. 2, Summer 1987, pp. 39–54. Hill analyzes the concept of degradation and argues that the pornography industry degrades all women by perpetuating derogatory myths about womankind.

HOLBROOK, DAVID, ed.: *The Case against Pornography.* New York: Library Press, 1973. In this anthology, Holbrook has collected nearly thirty selections, all of which develop (from various points of view) the case against pornography.

LEDERER, LAURA, ed.: *Take Back the Night: Women on Pornography.* New York: Morrow, 1980. This anthology provides an overall indictment of pornography from a feminist point of view.

LEISER, BURTON M.: *Liberty, Justice and Morals,* 3d ed. New York: Macmillan, 1986. Part I of this book features a broad-based discussion of the enforcement of morals. Chapter 1 critiques the views of Lord Devlin. Chapter 5 deals with freedom of expression and censorship.

SOBLE, ALAN: "Pornography: Defamation and the Endorsement of Degradation." *Social Theory and Practice,* vol. 11, Spring 1985, pp. 61–87. Soble critiques and rejects two arguments commonly made by feminists (e.g., Longino) against pornography. He finds deficient both (1) the argument that pornography defames women and (2) the argument that pornography endorses the degradation of women.

CHAPTER 7

Discrimination
and Preferential
Treatment

Prior to the 1960s and 1970s, blatant racial discrimination was a fact of life for many minorities, especially blacks. The majority of blacks were in the lowest economic strata of American society due to various factors, including discrimination in housing, inferior education, and outright denial of access to most nonmenial positions as well as to union membership. Women, too, were blatantly discriminated against in many ways. Sexual discrimination was commonplace in the economic sphere, for example, and women's earning power was much less than that of men. Today the earnings gap between men and women is still very wide. While men predominate in the best-paying jobs, women, in disproportionate numbers, are clustered in the lowest-paying ones. In respect to blacks and other minorities, statistics show that whites predominate in the most desirable occupations while blacks and other minorities predominate in the least desirable and worst-paying ones.

There is widespread agreement today that the hiring and education practices of the past, which routinely disadvantaged women and blacks, as well as other minorities, were morally wrong. There is also widespread agreement about why this racial and sexual discrimination was wrong. However, there is widespread disagreement about the correct answers to the following sorts of questions. To what extent is sexual and racial discrimination an ongoing reality that continues to deny women, blacks, and other minority groups equal opportunities in education and employment? Does society owe a debt to groups whose members have been systematically denied equality of opportunity in the past? Must it rectify the wrongs resulting from past discrimination? Since equality of opportunity for all members of society is a worthy social goal, what social policies are most likely to eradicate the ongoing racial and sexual inequalities that work against this goal? This chapter focuses primarily on consideration of these sorts of questions.

THE WRONGNESS OF RACIAL AND SEXUAL DISCRIMINATION

Why are actions and practices that deny people various opportunities simply on the basis of their race or sex morally wrong? The usual answer is that such actions and practices violate the *principle of equality*. According to this principle, equals should be treated equally and unequals should be treated unequally, in proportion to their differences. This is sometimes called the "formal principle of justice." But what constitutes equality or inequality? In what ways must two individuals be alike before we can claim that they should receive the same treatment? In what ways must two individuals differ before we can claim that they should be accorded unequal treatment?

The usual way of answering these questions is to say that the differences between them must be *relevant* to the treatment in question. When a particular kind of employment is at issue, for example, it would seem that what is relevant is having the appropriate abilities, competencies, or skills. If Joe Smith and John Doe both apply for a job as lifeguard, a difference in their ethnic background seems to have no bearing on which of them should get the job. But if Joe is a nonswimmer and John an Olympic swimming champion, that difference between them is relevant to the hiring decision. On this line of reasoning, sex may be relevant when what is at issue is maternity leave. But it is not relevant when a choice is made between competing accountants, although mathematical ability is relevant. A qualified woman accountant who is not hired to fill an accounting position simply because of her sex is treated unjustly—she is denied an employment opportunity on the basis of a characteristic unrelated to the task in hand. When this happens, the principle of equality is clearly violated.

The discussion so far has focused on that part of the principle of equality that states that equals should be treated equally. But some unequal treatment is also in keeping with the principle of equality. Young children cannot be given the same rights and responsibilities as adults, for example. A five-year-old cannot be expected to take on responsibilities such as voting or signing binding contracts. This kind of unequal treatment of young children and adults is consistent with the principle of equality, since young children differ from adults in relevant respects. They are incapable of exercising the rational capacities needed to assume certain responsibilities.

To sum up, both institutional practices that treat equals equally and those that treat unequals unequally, in proportion to their differences, are morally correct according to the principle of equality. But when individuals are treated unequally on the basis of irrelevant characteristics, the principle of equality is clearly violated.

It is widely agreed that the racial and sexual discrimination practiced in the past was obviously unjust insofar as it involved gross violations of the principle of equality. For the same reason, it is also widely agreed that ongoing discrimination against minorities and women (unequal treatment on the basis of irrelevant grounds) is wrong—although, as Mary Rowe points out in this chapter, current discrimination is sometimes so subtle that it is not recognized as such by the discriminator. It also seems undeniable that past discrimination is to a large extent responsible for many of the racial and sexual inequalities existing today. Especially crucial to the perpetuation of racial and sexual inequalities are the existing economic and educational disadvantages that have resulted from past discrimination, as well as other factors resulting from this discrimination, such as the dearth of appropriate role models. What is a matter of great dispute, however, can be expressed in the following question: What obligations, if any, does society have to undo some of the self-perpetuating wrongs caused by past discrimination or to compensate women, blacks, and other minorities for burdens and injustices suffered due to sexism and racism? Much of the contemporary controversy centers on certain hiring, promotion, and admission policies adopted by businesses and educational institutions, largely in response to government affirmative-action requirements. To understand this controversy, it is useful to look briefly at the ways in which the call for affirmative action has been understood and reflected in hiring, promotion, and admission policies.

AFFIRMATIVE ACTION

Employers have responded to calls for affirmative action in various ways. Some have adopted practices of *passive nondiscrimination* that simply require all decisions about hiring and promotion to disregard race and sex. Note that passive nondiscrimination involves no compensation for past injustices. Nor does it help to undo the ongoing effects of past discrimination. The limitations of this approach are readily apparent, moreover, when we realize the extent to which seniority systems perpetuate old discriminatory patterns. Other employers have adopted measures that more accurately fall under the heading "affirmative" action. Some of these measures involve no more than making every effort to find women and minority applicants and to ensure that employment and promotion opportunities are highly visible. Here the pool of women and minority applicants may be enlarged, but they receive no preference when decisions are made about hiring and promotion. Other employers committed to affirmative action have attempted to go further by giving preference to women and minority applicants. The programs involved, often called "preferential treatment" programs, are the focal point of the moral debate about affirmative-action programs. Preferential treatment programs are of two types. The first type involves hard quotas or specific numerical goals. Such preferential treatment programs specify some set number or proportion of women and minority applicants who must be hired or promoted. The second type involves neither a hard quota nor a specific numerical goal, but nevertheless does require the preferential treatment of women and minority applicants.

Institutions of higher learning, such as law and medical schools, have also attempted to establish affirmative-action admissions policies, including preferential treatment programs. Some of these programs have led to landmark lawsuits. A preferential treatment program at the University of Washington Law School, for example, led to the well-known *DeFunis v. Odegaard* case.[1] Another program, at the University of California at Davis Medical School, resulted in the *University of California v. Bakke* case presented in this chapter. The *DeFunis* case illustrates some of the

---

[1] *DeFunis v. Odegaard,* 82 Wash. 2d 11 (1973).

moral perplexities raised by preferential treatment programs as well as the kind of reasoning that is sometimes advanced in their defense.

In the DeFunis case, Marco DeFunis, a nonminority applicant, was denied admission to the University of Washington Law School's first-year law class in 1971. He filed a suit claiming that the Law School's Admissions Committee had treated him unfairly insofar as it had discriminated against him on the basis of race. Preferential treatment that year was accorded to blacks, American Indians, Chicanos, and Filipinos. The Law School had 150 available spaces in its first-year law class. There were 1,601 applicants. In order to enroll 150 students, 275 applicants were offered acceptances. Among the 275 who were accepted there were 37 minority applicants. Of these 37, 18 actually enrolled. The Law School Admission Test (LSAT) scores and Projected Grade Point Averages (PGAs) of almost all these minority applicants were lower than those of some of the rejected nonminority applicants, who were denied admission simply because their PGAs and LSAT scores fell below a certain level. Minority applicants, however, whose scores fell even below the level of some rejected nonminority applicants were evaluated on the basis of other criteria and then admitted to the school.

The Supreme Court of the State of Washington ruled against DeFunis and argued as follows: (1) Racial classifications are not unconstitutional in themselves. A state university can take race and ethnic background into account when considering applicants. (2) If there is a compelling state interest that can be served only through the use of racial classifications, such use is acceptable. (3) The shortage of minority attorneys, and, therefore, also minority prosecutors, judges, and public officials, constitutes an undeniably compelling state interest. Although the case was appealed to the United States Supreme Court, the Court did not hand down a ruling. Since DeFunis had been attending the Law School while the case was making its way through the courts and was then in his last year, the case was declared moot. The first university preferential treatment case decided by the United States Supreme Court was the Bakke case, mentioned above. The Court ruled in favor of Bakke, declaring Davis's hard quota approach constitutionally unacceptable. The Court also ruled, however, that admissions policies can take race into account when evaluating individual applicants.

THE MORAL JUSTIFIABILITY OF PREFERENTIAL TREATMENT

In this chapter, our primary concern is not with the legal and constitutional issues raised by cases such as *DeFunis* and *Bakke* but with the *moral justifiability* of the sorts of preferential treatment programs that gave rise to these cases. One attempt to justify preferential treatment is primarily *backward-looking* insofar as it is based in the claim that *compensation* is due to groups whose members have been unjustly discriminated against in the past. This approach appeals to the *principle of compensatory justice,* which states that whenever an injustice has been committed, just compensation or reparation must be made to the injured parties. The principle of compensatory justice is implicitly invoked, for example, when the claim is made that American Indians must be compensated for the past unjust deprivation of tribal land

and water rights due to government exploitation. On this line of reasoning, preferential treatment programs that favor women, blacks, or other minorities are seen as compensatory in nature. Since their purpose is to make reparations for past injustices, these programs are morally justified by appeal to the principle of compensatory justice.

Many objections are raised against the compensatory approach. One objection appeals to the principle of equality. As noted above, the principle of equality is violated whenever individuals are denied equal treatment simply on the basis of generally irrelevant characteristics such as sex or race. This is what seems to have happened to DeFunis and Bakke. They were not accorded the same treatment as members of the favored minority groups. The unequal treatment given Bakke and DeFunis is sometimes called "reverse discrimination." This label is used to describe actions or practices that discriminate against an individual or group, on the basis of some normally irrelevant characteristic, *because* preference is being given to members of previously discriminated against groups. In keeping with our earlier account of the principle of equality, reverse discrimination certainly appears to be morally wrong. In one of the readings in this chapter, Lisa H. Newton implicitly appeals to the principle of equality in her criticisms of the compensatory approach to the justification of reverse discrimination. Strict justice, she maintains, precludes the use of any criteria other than merit or qualification when hiring and admissions decisions are made. Not everyone who rejects a compensatory justification of preferential treatment policies would maintain that members of groups wronged by racial and sexual discrimination do not deserve some sort of compensation. What those who reject this approach do maintain, however, is that preferential treatment in schooling and employment is a morally unacceptable means of providing that compensation because it violates the very principle of equality that is the basis of the claim that racial and sexual discrimination is morally wrong.

Other major objections to the compensatory approach include the following. First, individuals receiving preferential treatment may not themselves have actually suffered any unjust treatment. Second, individuals who lose out because others receive preferential treatment may themselves have been severely disadvantaged economically and socially. Third, if compensatory justice requires preferential treatment for *individuals who have been treated unjustly in the past,* then race or sex is irrelevant. What is relevant is past unjust treatment, and individuals who have been treated unjustly belong to both sexes and to many different ethnic and racial groups.

Still another line of attack against the compensatory approach utilizes an infinite regress argument: Suppose we are required to give preference today to individuals belonging to groups that were discriminated against in the past in order to compensate them for past inequality of treatment. Will we be required to give compensatory preferential treatment in the future to members of groups denied equality of treatment by today's compensatory programs? And what about the compensation due to those treated unequally by those future programs?

Not everyone who defends preferential treatment adopts a compensatory stance. Many defenders utilize a consequentialist approach. One consequentialist line of argument is advanced and briefly discussed by Edwin C. Hettinger in this chapter.

Hettinger questions an important presumption underlying many of the attacks on preferential treatment programs—the presumption that only those characteristics directly related to job performance are relevant in hiring and admission decisions. He argues, in contrast, that the underlying purpose of a preferential treatment policy may render the race or sex of applicants a morally relevant characteristic. Take, for example, a specific preferential admissions policy whose purpose is to provide more role models for members of previously discriminated against groups in order to bring about a more sexually and racially egalitarian society. In light of this purpose, the sex or race of the applicants is a relevant characteristic. Thus admissions decisions made in accordance with this preferential treatment policy would not violate the principle of equality because that principle requires only that differential treatment not be based on irrelevant characteristics.

In contrast to compensatory approaches, which are backward-looking, consequentialist defenses of preferential treatment can be seen as both backward- and forward-looking. They can be seen as backward-looking because they identify past wrongs and argue for policies intended to rectify the ongoing effects of past injustices. They are forward-looking, however, insofar as they argue for preferential treatment as a necessary means to the achievement of a morally desirable social goal—a more egalitarian society free of racism and sexism. Hettinger's reasoning in this chapter exemplifies this consequentialist approach. In his view, if affirmative-action practices help to eliminate the grave injustice of sexual and racial inequality, and thereby contribute to the achievement of a more egalitarian society, the social good achieved will far outweigh the relatively minor injustices resulting from reverse discrimination. Clearly, such consequentialist reasoning avoids some of the difficulties raised for the compensatory approach. On the consequentialist approach, for example, the question of whether or not a particular black woman who benefits from a preferential hiring decision was herself the direct victim of past discrimination becomes irrelevant. She is not being treated preferentially in order to compensate her for some specific wrong that she herself has suffered. Rather, the justification for the preferential treatment policy by which she benefits is its instrumental role in undoing the effects of past discrimination and bringing about a more egalitarian society.

Defenders of preferential treatment who depend on consequentialist arguments must pay special attention to *factual* issues. They must attempt to answer the following kinds of questions. Will preferential treatment programs in fact result in greater sexual and racial equality? Are preferential treatment programs necessary to prevent ongoing sexual and racial discrimination? Is discrimination, albeit often subtle, still so pervasive in our society that mandatory quota systems are required to eliminate continued discrimination against women and minorities? Will preferential treatment programs eventually result in greater equality of opportunity for everyone in society regardless of race or sex? A challenge to the consequentialist defense of preferential treatment is expressed, for example, in Charles Murray's article in this chapter. Murray argues that preferential treatment policies favoring blacks are not functioning to eliminate racism. On the contrary, they are responsible for what he describes as a new form of racism. Derek Bok in this chapter challenges Murray's contentions and discusses some of the good results of the preferential policies adopted by universities such as Harvard. In another reading in this chapter, Lawrence Blum raises wider questions about the measures required to achieve genuine equality of opportunity for everyone in society, regardless of race, sex, or economic or social background.

Jane S. Zembaty

Barriers to Equality: The Power of Subtle Discrimination to Maintain Unequal Opportunity

Mary Rowe

Mary Rowe serves as special assistant to the president and as ombudsman at the Massachusetts Institute of Technology. She is also adjunct professor at the Sloan School of Management. Rowe's published articles include "Go Find Yourself a Mentor," "Moving Up: Role Models, Mentors, and the Patron System," and "Dealing with Sexual Harassment."

On Rowe's view, *subtle* discrimination is a major factor working against women, minorities, and others who obviously "differ" from the people making decisions in matters such as hiring and promotion. Rowe describes a wide variety of what she calls "discriminatory microinequities." She asks the reader to think about how the situations she describes function to maintain the "glass ceiling and walls" that keep women and minorities from reaching the top of traditionally Anglo, male institutions.

INTRODUCTION

In recent years there has been much discussion of the glass ceiling, the invisible barrier that keeps women and African Americans, Latinos and other minorities, from going to the top of traditionally "Anglo," male institutions. There is also an emergent discussion about whether Caucasians (as well as blacks and women), can make it to the top in companies run by Asians. Glass *walls* are equally impenetrable; glass walls keep women and minorities barred from certain occupations within society and within institutions; it is easy for each of us to observe occupational segregation in our own places of work.

There are of course several reasons for the glass barriers. For example, an important difficulty for women is the need for family supports, like adequate leaves and child care. It is the hypothesis of this article that subtle discrimination also contributes much to the glass barriers; it is the practical (not necessarily conscious) manifestation of the fact that senior managers want to choose people like themselves to succeed them. I believe that subtle discrimination is now, in most workplaces, the principal scaffolding for segregation in the United States, the framework for discrim-

Reprinted with permission of the author and Plenum Publishing Corporation from *Employee Responsibilities and Rights Journal,* vol. 3 (1990), pp. 153–163.

ination against everyone who is obviously "different" from the person making decisions about whatever is the matter at hand.

Most major U.S. institutions have long since begun to address major manifestations of prejudice. In many companies, a major act of discrimination that could immediately be proven would immediately be rectified, if brought to the attention of senior management. However, subtle barriers maintain their strength, by for example, not inviting African Americans to strategy meetings, leaving women home from field trips, blaming problems on the person who is obviously different, expecting failure from the person of difference. As we enter the 1990s, a decade in which it is expected that only about one in ten of all new entrants into the U.S. labor force will be an Anglo white male, diversity will be the most important aspect of the U.S. labor force, and the glass barriers will become even more critical.

There has been much discussion of whether discrimination works by keeping minority people out, or by affecting the minority person so that he or she behaves in an unacceptable or unproductive fashion. Blame the aggressor? Or blame the victim? This paper suggests that discrimination maintains itself in a wide variety of ways, working within the dominant culture and within the person discriminated against. The mechanism functions through a wide variety of "micro" events, or in the terms of this paper, microinequities.

The analysis is drawn from seventeen years as ombudsman to MIT and as a consultant to companies in North America. All the quotations that follow are real. Nearly all are from 1989. Although some will find the examples banal and trivial, for the persons who were the objects of each example these sentences were full of pain. Indeed, this is the point of the article.

WHAT ARE MICROINEQUITIES? WHY LOOK AT THEM?

It will become obvious, from the discussion that follows, that each person is his or her own expert on what constitutes a microinequity in any given instance. Discriminatory microinequities are tiny, damaging characteristics of an environment, as these characteristics affect a person not indigenous to that environment. They are distinguished by the fact that for all practical purposes one cannot do anything about them; one cannot take them to court or file a grievance. They are actions which are unjust toward individuals, when reasonable people would agree the particular treatment of the individual occurs only because of a group characteristic unrelated to creativity and work performance (for example, sex, race, religion, age, or country of origin). ("*You cannot send her to represent us in that negotiation; most of their top people are European. She will be treated politely but she won't be taken seriously.*". . . . "*Would the Senator's staff be convinced by a black lobbyist?*")

These are the situations where a minority person is not introduced; when mail is addressed to a male rather than a female technical manager, because it is presumed that he is technically more competent. These are the comments about physical appearance (*"You make me think about tepees and tomahawks."*) in talking with a Native American colleague. These are the presumptions, uncountered by Anglo male superiors, that a Latina cannot negotiate the contract in Japan; or that it is professionally acceptable to show sex films at a professional conference *("It's OK. We warned the ladies about the porn flicks, so if they want to, they can stay away from the evening meetings.")*. This is the hand on the knee from a senior vice-president at the banquet table; these are the disrespectful comments to an African-American member of the board *("Martin Luther King Day is just a foolish and costly gesture to yet another special interest group.")*. These are the two-sided stereotypes about technical ability *("Hey, Paul Wu, you made a mistake in math! How come? I thought you guys never made a mistake!". . . . "We hired an Hispanic engineer and he was incompetent; never again.")*. This is the supercompetent, white American who will never make it to the top of a Japanese company, though he was brought up in Japan, is bilingual, and can "pass" on the telephone.

There is a useful literature about where these phenomena come from, why people overlook or fear or put down those whom they perceive to be "not like us." In studies of racism Dr. Chester Pierce calls many of these microevents, "microaggressions."[1] Jean-Paul Sartre has written about these phenomena as the expectations of anti-Semites about what it means to be a Jew.[2] One may think of subtle discrimination as a projection of our negative feelings about ourselves, or as a scapegoating process, supported by myths and by selective perception which supports the myths. This article is about the *effects* of subtle discrimination and how it works.

Microinequities are fiendishly efficient in perpetuating unequal opportunity, because they are in the air we breathe, in the books we read, in the television we all watch, and because we cannot change the personal characteristic that leads to the inequity. Microinequities are woven into all the threads of our work life and of U.S. education. They are "micro," not at all in the sense of trivial, but in the sense of miniature. I write about these events, in this paper, with a focus on racism and sexism. However, the same points may be made with respect to nationality, religion, age, handicap, sexual orientation, and many other dimensions of diversity, especially as the U.S. internationalizes and becomes more heterogeneous.

HOW DO THE MINUTIAE OF DISCRIMINATION MAINTAIN THE GLASS BARRIERS?

I know of no systematic, scientific study of "microinequities," but one can suggest many hypotheses as to why such behavior may do damage. I personally do believe these inequities cause serious damage; I believe they are the major explanation for glass barriers. I will therefore set forth my hypotheses. *I believe that microinequities exert their influence both by walling out the "different" person, and by making the person of difference less effective:*

• Microinequities sometimes cause damage because they predispose a manager to even worse behavior. Thus "seeing through" an "invisible" African-American, or paying no attention to support staff women, may make them feel like part of the furniture. This habit may also lead to underpaying minorities and women, because the senior person has little idea what the "invisible people" actually contribute. It may also lead to overlooking someone who might be the best-qualified person for promotion. Every experienced manager has seen examples where a senior person will start recruiting from outside, while not "seeing" the woman in front of him who has been a significant contributor, and who could be promoted *("What really hurt was that then I was expected to train him to do the job.")*.

• In addition to the above, some microinequities cause extended damage, because at the time they occur they are preventing *better* behavior from occurring. If an executive assistant is unreasonably overloaded with routine or personal work for a supervisor, she may be prevented from doing the kind of creative work that would have prepared her for promotion *("I would like to be taking on the accounting, but he just sees me as the person who bought his wife's Christmas presents so skillfully.")*.

• Microinequities may also have a negative Pygmalion quality. That is, the expectation of poor performance, or the lack of expectation of good performance, may do damage because managers and students and employees have a strong tendency to do what is expected of them. The Asian-American who is expected to be docile may later be thought not to be sufficiently assertive *("He just called me in whenever he needed error-free, technical work on no notice and with no back talk. I would stay up all night. At the end of the year my evaluation said I didn't speak up enough.")*.

• Microinequities cause damage in part because they are a kind of "punishment" which cannot be predicted, in any functional sense; microinequities are *irrational*. That is, by and large, they occur in the context of merit, and of striving for excellence, but do not have anything to *do* with excellence or merit. This is, of course, by definition what makes them "inequities"; that the punishment occurs in the context of work but *without relevance to performance ("It was the damndest thing; he got off the phone from talking with his daughter, and he blew up at me (the only woman in the group) about a budget proposal that I did not have anything at all to do with!")*. It is therefore important to look at such phenomena in the context of what we know from behavior modification theory. As an intermittent, unpredictable, "negative reinforcement," microinequities have peculiar power as a negative learning tool (unpredictable, intermittent reinforcement being a powerful type of reinforcement). Moreover, because one cannot change the provocation for negative reinforcement (for example, one's race or gender), one inevitably feels some helplessness.

• Microinequities are often difficult to detect or be sure about *("I can't put my finger exactly on it. But white institutions are just cold.")*. This means for one thing that it is hard for the subject to take effective action *("Tell me, how can I fight a wisp of fog?")*. It also means that frequent targets of inequities, like Latinos, Native Americans, Asian-Americans, African-Americans, and women, may constantly range through emotions, from legitimate anger (which may or may not have a constructive outlet), to paranoia. The constant experience of being uncertain, about whether one was "left out" or put down, inevitably leads to some displaced and misplaced anger *("I spend my day going through changes.")*. Any misplaced anger itself is a problem, because it may in turn offend innocent (or not innocent) bystanders. Uncertainty may also lead to ignoring *real* insults in such a way that they persist.

• Microinequities are also often not *intentional* in any conscious or even unconscious way, even when objective observers would agree that they exist—that an injury really took place. This is another reason they are hard for a victim to respond to (*"I know that no one meant for me to feel out of place. But I could not stand the belly dancers at the dinner. I hated the annual sales meeting after that."*). We are all socialized to believe that *intent* to injure is an important part of injury, and it is certainly critical to our actually dealing with injuries at the hands of others. Faced with a microaggression, the victim may not be certain of the motives of the aggressor, and may be unwilling to engage in hostility where no injury was intended. Under conditions of uncertainty about motives, most victims are sometimes in the position of either not getting angry when they should (which reinforces the aggression and may weaken the victim's professional image and self-image) or of protesting sometimes when no injury was *consciously* intended even though it actually occurred. The latter situation is occasionally salutary for all concerned, especially if the aggressor reacts by acknowledging that an injury took place. But sometimes the aggressor is totally unaware of aggressing, even though observers would agree that injury took place. The aggressor may then respond to protest with bewilderment, frustration, humiliation, anger, or feelings of betrayal. Or, what is worse, the aggressor may then undermine the minority person who challenged him (*"He said that my joke was racist. Do you think he is really on the team?"*).

• Microaggressions and inequities grow in infinite variety. It is hard to stay ahead of the proliferation of types, let alone the number, of petty injuries. For this reason minorities and women may find themselves being too alert for some new kind of insult, because of past frustration. And every experienced manager is familiar with apparently inappropriate anger from someone who was probably responding to "the last war" and not the present one (*"I blew it. It was one too many. He just asked who could possibly have done this brilliant work. I did not realize it was a compliment. I felt totally insulted and blew up; I cannot believe I did that."*).

• Microinequities also cause damage in part because they take up time and energy. Sorting out what is happening, and then dealing with one's pain and anger, take work (*"The worst thing, after she was so mean, was not being able to concentrate; I could not seem to think straight that whole week."*). Moreover, studies show that extra time is also required of many minorities and women to help deal with the pain caused by microinequities suffered by *other* minorities and women, because people of difference turn to each other for advice and solace (*"I get calls from people almost every night, about what happened to them that day."*).

• Communications between genders and among different ethnic groups are sometimes more difficult than between persons who are alike. It is also harder to make sound judgments about persons of difference. Microinequities worsen difficult communications, and difficult communications also increase subtle discrimination. It is obvious that none of us knows what it was like to be brought up as a member of the other sex or of a different race. And the forms of racism and sexism are so specific that each group is isolated from the other's experience, and therefore may not intuitively understand the pain of others. Thus, small inequities can add to the fact that cross-group communications are already slower and more difficult; and that cross-group judgments are harder to make well. For example, a white supervisor may find it hard to evaluate the leadership abilities of a person of color—and then, through prejudice, also fail to give constructive criticism and adequate feedback *("Nobody ever criticized my work or made any suggestions. They just never promoted me.")*. This sometimes happens quite consciously when a white male supervisor is afraid to mention a performance problem *("She seems so* touchy!*")*. The lack of communication and subtle discrimination then feed off each other and may lead to a downward spiral *("If she weren't black, she would have been fired long ago, but nobody has ever said a thing to her.")*. It is becoming increasingly common not only to find this difficulty between minorities and nonminorities, but also *between* minority groups. For example, Asian-Americans and African-Americans may have difficulty making and then expressing appropriate judgments about each other's work, because of strong differences in cultural background exacerbated by subtle discrimination.

• Microaggressions seem petty, in a world where available redress may often seem heavy-handed or too clumsy a tool. This is a problem even for those who appear to have some power. Formal grievances, going to court, and appeal to the CEO are heavy weapons; using them is often thought to carry high cost. The perceived lack of *appropriate* modes of redress therefore helps to perpetuate microaggressions. This is especially true where the aggrieved person does not want to lose privacy or professional image. What can an African-American vice-president do, if someone he is negotiating with sneers in private? What can a female plant manager do, if the boss stares directly at her bosom whenever they are alone? Until the person of difference learns how to handle these events effectively (which takes work), the apparent lack of redress is, at best, frustrating *("I am a first-rate engineer. I do* not *want to be known as a 'harassment case'; I do not see that there is anything I can do about his touching me.")*.

DO MICROAGGRESSIONS DO MORE HARM TO MINORITIES AND WOMEN THAN TO WHITE MEN?

Don't micro problems just "happen to everyone" *("Haven't you just been describing the general inhumanities of large organizations?")*? Is this really discrimination *("I harass everybody, Mary. I don't discriminate.")*? This question sometimes arises when an employer has done an employee attitude survey on racism or sexism without a white male control group; white males may protest *("We also get treated terribly. We just don't complain about it; we get on with the job.")*. Let me raise here hypotheses as to why microproblems may be worse for minorities and women than for the "average" white male. (I do not mean to say that male Caucasians are impervious to mean behavior.) Some of the hypotheses as to why microinequities may do more damage to minorities and women are, of course, analogous to the hypotheses as to why they do damage at all.

• "General" harassment often takes a specifically sexist form when applied to women, a racist form when applied to African-Americans, and so on. Instead of saying to some average white male, *"Your work on this project has been inexcusably sloppy, you blinking idiot; you'll never make it that way!,"* the remark may come out, *"My God, you think no better than my wife; why don't you go home and have babies!,"*, or, *"We will never be able to make up for the generations of Southern schools that produced you!"* The harassment of African-Americans piles up in allusions to race, the harassment of women as allusions to sex roles and sex, instead of being randomly applied, or appropriately focused on work. Like the dripping of water, random drops may do little damage; endless drops in one place can have profound effects (*"I got A's in college, and here I am losing all self-esteem; I feel as if I can't do anything right."*). This is especially important where the "micro" problem is sexualized behavior, and where the object of the aggression was sexually abused in childhood (or saw someone like themselves sexually abused). Thus the estimated 20%–35% of women and 5%–15% of men who were sexually abused in childhood may be especially vulnerable to even quite minor sexualizations in the workplace (*"I know this sounds crazy, but I feel as if I had been raped."*).

• Many minorities and women were socialized to respond disproportionately swiftly to disapproval. Parents often teach their daughters to cooperate rather than to compete with men. Some African-American parents teach their children to be sensitive and cautious about anger and criticism from white males. And I find it is sometimes difficult to persuade Asians and Asian-Americans to resist harassment that whites and other U.S. minorities will no longer put up with. Conversely one can find many white males who were explicitly socialized to expect hard knocks, to compete ferociously and openly, even (or especially) when injured, and to have a very high pain threshold. It would be hard to prove that either kind of socialization is "right" or "wrong" in absolute terms, but it is easy to see how these cultural paths run afoul of each other. If a white male supervisor shouts angrily for five minutes at a young woman, she may not wholly "recover" from the attack for weeks or months (*"I never asked him a question again. I avoided him whenever I could until I got out of there."*). Later, in a discussion with the supervisor, one may hear that he's completely forgotten his "random grouchiness," or thought it was trivial. Thus, behavior that might be trivial or survivable for the average white male may be quite destructive to others, in a manner that has nothing directly to do with the work at hand.

• Microinequities are more often reported where more powerful people have offended less powerful people. (I think no one knows whether they originate more in this direction than in the reverse. Perhaps power is corrupting; perhaps aggressive underdogs are always eliminated over time or, more likely, more powerful people ignore or are not so easily injured by microinsults from below. Perhaps the generally higher pay and status of the more powerful gives adequate recompense.) It is generally the less powerful who have most difficulties in coping with inequities, since less powerful people by definition have less influence. It is especially difficult to stop an aggressor who is a supervisor (*"What do you mean, did I speak up when he insulted me? Are you kidding? He's my boss!"*). Disproportionate numbers of less powerful people are minority and female; these groups are therefore statistically more vulnerable to microinequities.

• In a traditionally white male atmosphere it is much harder to get certain kinds of microinequities to stop, because the slights are culturally so "normal" that they simply are not noticed. Many whites are acutely uncomfortable around persons of color; they ignore them or fail to look at and address them—but do not notice that they are doing so. Sexy calenders on walls; "humorous" surveys and cartoons about sex; "humorous" mimicry of the handicapped and of other races; ethnic and sexist jokes; and the use of sex in ads, announcements, and in computer hacking, are so ubiquitous that many whites and many men literally do not notice them *("I complained about some extremely offensive girlie calendars in the machine shop. He said, 'What calendars?' He did not even see them!").*

• Traditionally white male environments may even reinforce certain kinds of discriminatory behavior that are perceived as actively enjoyable, like the aggressive and humiliating recounting of sex and ethnic jokes, or AIDS or handicap jokes *("You should see Chris. Chris does a spaz routine, dragging his leg on the street. It'll really crack you up.").* This reinforcement may directly interfere with the pursuit of excellence. *("The recruiting team got a reference that said: 'She is not very creative. Of course you can hire her if you want, but if I were looking for someone new in the lab, I'd rather have her body than her mind.' Can you believe it? They did not return the reference; they said, 'Let's hire her!' ")*

• There is a more acute role-modeling problem for persons of difference, because of their constantly witnessing microinequities against others like themselves. That is, disproportionately more Latinos, African-Americans, and women see people "like them" put down or ignored or ill-served by their superiors and elders *("After what happened to Carlos, I just gave up.").* This point may be clearer when one remembers that in most work environments, the principal (if unintended) same-sex and same-race role models, for persons of color and women, are clerical workers and hourly workers, and these are the groups most frequently reporting microinequities. This inadvertent, damaging role-modeling is even stronger because nearly all minorities and women are continuously being taken to be holding the lower level jobs traditionally held by minorities and women, even if they are managers *("I am constantly being taken to be a file clerk,"* says an African-American woman engineer. *"I constantly feel a struggle to develop my own self-image, but it is not affirmed by most of the world around me, as it is for my majority male colleagues.").*

• It is often harder for minorities and women to find mentors to help them deal with microinequities. There are so few senior minorities and women in most organizations that junior members of the community cannot, on the average, find the same amount of high-status, same-race, same-sex mentorship that white males can find. Frequently the higher-status women and minorities try to compensate by spending extra time as same-sex, same-race mentors. It is, however, almost inevitable that the burden of dealing with microinequities falls on senior people who are already somewhat disproportionately drained of energy by caring for others. This is of course an especially powerful support to glass barriers *("I went to see a brother in upper management, and told him what had happened to me. He just stood looking out of the window, clenching his fists.").*

• There is another reason why it is sometimes hard to find an appropriate mentor when a woman and/or minority person is offended by a microproblem. If one goes to a white male, he may or may not understand. If one goes to a friend of the same race and sex, he or she may be just wonderful in helping one to deal with it, or may not be helpful at all. *("I told her he put his hands under my blouse. She asked me if I were wearing a slinky black blouse that day.").* That is, listeners of the same sex and race may be so discouraged and bitter, or so full of denial, that they are worse than useless.

In sum, I believe that it is often more difficult for minorities and women to find adequate help in dealing with racism and sexism, than for majority men to deal with "general inhumanities." I believe many minority and women managers, students, and employees have a disproportionate need for supportive white male mentorship, and are disproportionately injured when an advisor or teacher or supervisor assigned to them is just generally unfriendly. Let us take a hypothetical example, Awilda Hernandez, who is a management trainee in a Midwest bank. She has a need for support, if only because she will inevitably live through many microinequities. She needs someone to advise her about advancement in an Anglo male environment, because it is foreign to her. The support that she gets from back home is not likely to be professional support. She is, in other words, less well supported by the general society and may be less well supported by her family than if she were a white male. If her supervisor turns out to be generally inattentive, grouchy, or cold *("What do you mean, am I a mentor? Cream rises to the top; mentorship is a bloody waste of my time."),* she has been deprived of a mentor in circumstances where she, more than others, needed a mentor. The situation will be compounded if she is afraid to ask for a new advisor or does not know how to find substitute help.

This paper has suggested many reasons why the problems of microinequities for minorities and women go beyond the general inhumanities of large organizations. The point may be clearer if you will imagine (this is a real example) being a solo, young, white, male, child-care worker in a large, conservative, inner-city daycare system. The "general harassment" might include sincere questions and snide comments on your sexuality. Other white males might find you odd. Women might distrust your skills *("Wait, Jim, let me show you how to do that.")* or your interest in children *("Are you married?").* You might *be* in fact inept, in some ways, your first year. You might be very sensitive to just run-of-the-mill anger from your cross-sex, perhaps cross-race, supervisor. You might find the constant assumption that women-are-better to be very oppressive—the ads, the jokes, the pictures of women and children on the walls, the many fathers deprived of custody. You might have no one like yourself to turn to. You might get to hate always being asked to fix things *("I was constantly being asked why I wanted to be there, as if I might molest the children, or drop a baby.").*

I believe that discriminatory behavior itself causes pain, and also may constitute for minorities and women a situation they cannot control, evade, or ameliorate (or, as we have said, they may see it that way). Continued experience of destructive situations that cannot be improved can start unhappy cycles of behavior ranging from declining self-esteem (which makes one feel still less efficacious in changing the environment) to withdrawal, resignation, poor work, fantasies of violence, and so on *("I struggled for days to deal with my anger at what he said; I will never forget that bastard as long as I live. If I ever find myself in a position to do him in, you can bet I will do my best.").* At the very least it either takes a lot of energy to deal with an environment perceived as hostile, or it takes lots of energy to maintain one's level of denial of difficulties.

In my own environment, as in all others in the U.S., I believe microinequities cause stress. Over the years there have been occasional, unpublished studies at the Massachusetts Institute of Technology about the performance of men and women, for example the in-house surveys of "sex-blind" admissions. These studies typically show that women and men do randomly as well as each other. However, women also regularly report high stress levels and lower self-esteem, for example, in a study of the academic environment for male and female graduate students (Committee on Women Student Interests, 1987, unpublished). Small departmental studies report pain from microinequities (e.g., Barriers to Equality, 1984, unpublished). Persons of color also report pain from microinequities (Racial Climate Report, 1988, unpublished).

ARE MICROINEQUITIES EVER USEFUL?

Occasionally one will find someone who believes that hardship is good for people; creativity requires incessant pain; harassment inspires excellence *("My parents were immigrants; I made it through—so can everyone else.")*.

It is hard to respond to these ideas because individual situations vary so much. The speaker who remembers having survived terrible hurdles may also have had exceptional health and energy, or a wonderfully supportive parent or uncle or religion, or extended family—or may be the only person of his or her type ever to have survived that background—or may have come through "successful," but terribly scarred.

I think most of us believe that challenge is good (in the right doses), that creativity requires intense concentration and effort, and that excellence itself, and high expectations, inspire excellence. But most people believe that intermittent positive reinforcement—the carrot—is more powerful than the stick. I personally do not believe our world to be so devoid of sticks that we need more of them. And there seem to me to be enough good reasons to believe that microinequities cause *damage* that we should try to ameliorate them. The Law of Parsimony would suggest that it is simplest to assume that human ability is randomly distributed *("We could double the numbers of excellent managers and scientists in the U.S., if we knew how to provide real equal opportunity for minorities and women.")*. Is this not a sufficient incentive for us to try to undo damage that occurs? Is it not more reasonable to assume that people survive in spite of damage rather than because of it?

NOTES

1 Pierce, C. (1970). Offensive mechanisms. In Barbour, F. (Ed.), *The Black 70's*. Boston: Sargent.

2 Sartre, J. P. (1965). *Anti-Semite and Jew*. New York: Schocken Books.

QUESTIONS

1 To what extent is subtle discrimination a reality in our society?

2 What policies should business adopt to ensure true equality of opportunity?

Bakke and Davis: Justice, American Style

Lisa H. Newton

Lisa H. Newton is professor of philosophy at Fairfield University and adjunct professor of philosophy at Sacred Heart University. Newton is the author of *Ethics in America: Study Guide* (1989). Her published articles include "Surrogate Motherhood and the Limits of Rational Ethics" and "Applied Ethics: Premises and Promises of the Discipline."

In this short essay, which first appeared as the nation awaited the decision of the Supreme Court in the Bakke case, Newton focuses on the quota system employed at the University of California at Davis Medical School. She attacks all preferential treatment programs as morally indefensible for the following reasons (the first set appeals to justice; the second set, to consequences): (1) Those candidates who unjustly "lose out" because they do not belong to the preferred group are expected to make "reparations" for "wrongs" they did not commit; strict justice requires that the merit system be strictly applied. (2) The bad effects of quota systems will far outweigh any "social goods" produced.

The use of the special minority quota or "goal" to achieve a desirable racial mix in certain professions might appear to be an attractive solution to the problem of justice posed by generations of racial discrimination.[1] Ultimately, however, the quota solution fails. It puts an intolerable burden of injustice on a system strained by too much of that in the past, and prolongs the terrible stereotypes of inferiority into the indefinite future. It is a serious error to urge this course on the American people.

The quota system, as employed by the University of California's medical school at Davis or any similar institution, is unjust, for all the same reasons that the discrimination it attempts to reverse is unjust.[2] It diminishes the opportunities of some candidates for a social purpose that has nothing to do with them, to make "reparation" for acts they never committed. And "they" are no homogeneous "majority": as Swedish-Americans, Irish-Americans, Americans of Polish or Jewish or Italian descent, they can claim a past history of the same irrational discrimination, poverty and cultural deprivation that now plagues Blacks and Spanish-speaking individuals. In simple justice, all applicants (except, of course, the minority of WASPs!) should have access to a "track" specially constructed for their group, if any do. And none should. The salvation of every minority in America has been strict justice, the merit

Reprinted with permission of the author and the publisher from *National Forum (The Phi Kappa Phi Journal)*, vol. LVIII, no. 1 (Winter 1978), pp. 22–23.

system strictly applied; the Davis quota system is nothing but a suspension of justice in favor of the most recent minorities, and is flatly unfair to all the others.

The quota system is generally defended by suggesting that a little bit of injustice is far outweighed by the great social good which will follow from it; the argument envisions a fully integrated society where all discrimination will be abolished. Such a result hardly seems likely. Much more likely, if ethnic quotas are legitimated by the Court in the Bakke Case, all the other ethnic minorities will promptly organize to secure special tracks of their own, including minorities which have never previously organized at all. In these days, the advantage of a medical education is sufficiently attractive to make the effort worthwhile. As elsewhere, grave political penalties will be inflicted on legislatures and institutions that attempt to ignore these interest groups. I give Davis, and every other desirable school in the country, one decade from a Supreme Court decision favorable to quotas, to collapse under the sheer administrative weight of the hundreds of special admissions tracks and quotas it will have to maintain.

But the worst effect of the quota system is on the minorities supposedly favored by it. In the past, Blacks were socially stereotyped as less intelligent than whites because disproportionately few Blacks could get into medical school; the stereotype was the result of the very racial discrimination that it attempted to justify. Under any minority quota system, ironically, that stereotype would be tragically reinforced. From the day the Court blesses the two-track system of admissions at Davis, the word is out that Black physicians, or those of Spanish or Asian derivation, are less qualified, just a little less qualified, than their "White-Anglo" counterparts, for they did not have to meet as strict a test for admission to medical school. And that judgment will apply, as the quota applies, on the basis of race alone, for we will have no way of knowing which Blacks, Spanish or Asians were admitted in a medical school's regular competition and which were admitted on the "special minority" track. The opportunity to bury their unfavorable ethnic stereotypes by clean and public success in strictly fair competition, an opportunity that our older ethnic groups seized enthusiastically, will be denied to these "special minorities" for yet another century.

In short, there are no gains, for American society or for groups previously disadvantaged by it, in quota systems that attempt reparation by reverse discrimination. The larger moral question of whether we should set aside strict justice for some larger social gain, does not have to be taken up in a case like this one, where procedural injustice produces only substantive harm for all concerned. Blacks, Hispanic and other minority groups which are presently economically disadvantaged will see real progress when, and only when, the American economy expands to make room for more higher status employment for all groups. The economy is not improved in the least by special tracks and quotas for special groups; on the contrary, it is burdened by the enormous weight of the nonproductive administrative procedure required to implement them. No social purpose will be served, and no justice done, by the establishment of such procedural monsters; we should hope that the Supreme Court will see its way clear to abolishing them once and for all.

NOTES

1 See, for example, *The New York Times* editorial, "Reparation, American Style," June 19, 1977.
2 See my "Reverse Discrimination as Unjustified," *Ethics* 83:308 (July, 1973).

QUESTIONS

1 Can you specify criteria for determining that a group had been sufficiently discriminated against in the past to warrant preferential treatment in the present?
2 If there were no affirmative-action programs, do you believe that the *merit system would be strictly applied* in all hiring, promotions, and school admissions in the United States? If not, would injustice be rampant in hiring, etc.?

Opinion in *University of California v. Bakke*

Justice Lewis F. Powell, Jr.

A biographical sketch of Justice Lewis F. Powell, Jr., is found on p. 154.

Allen Bakke, a white male, applied for admission to the University of California at Davis Medical School. The school, which had a hard quota preferential treatment admissions policy favoring minority students, had set aside 16 of its 100 places in the first-year class for those students. Admission was denied to Bakke, but it was granted to minority students whose college grade-point averages (GPAs) and scores on the Medical College Admission Test (MCAT) were much lower than Bakke's. The trial court ruled that Bakke was a victim of *invidious* racial discrimination, and the Supreme Court of the State of California upheld that decision. The justices of the United States Supreme Court were divided four-to-four on the major issues in the case, with Justice Powell providing the decisive vote. Justice Powell sided with Chief Justice Warren E. Burger, Justice Potter Stewart, Justice William H. Rehnquist, and Justice John Paul Stevens in holding that the admissions program which resulted in Bakke's rejection was unlawful. With them he ruled that Bakke must be admitted to the medical school. But Justice Powell sided with Justice William J. Brennan, Justice Byron R. White, Justice Thurgood Marshall, and Justice Harry A. Blackmun in holding that colleges and universities *can* consider race as a factor in the admissions process.

In this excerpt from Justice Powell's opinion, the Court rejects "quotas" or "goals" drawn on the basis of race or ethnic status and holds that such quotas are not legitimated *simply* by their benign purposes. Justice Powell examines the purported purposes of the special admissions program at Davis to see if the program's racial classification is constitutionally permissible. In its previous rulings the Court had held that in "order to justify the use of a suspect classification a State must show that its purpose or interest is both constitutionally permissible and

United States Supreme Court, 438 U.S. 265 (1978).

substantial, and that its use of the classification is 'necessary . . . to the accomplishment' of its purpose or the safeguarding of its interest." Justice Powell maintains that the Davis program is not constitutionally permissible; but he concludes that other admissions programs, such as Harvard's, which take race into account but treat each applicant as an individual in the admissions process, are constitutionally acceptable.

I

Over the past 30 years, this Court has embarked upon the crucial mission of interpreting the Equal Protection Clause with the view of assuring to all persons "the protection of equal laws," in a Nation confronting a legacy of slavery and racial discrimination. Because the landmark decisions in this area arose in response to the continued exclusion of Negroes from the mainstream of American society, they could be characterized as involving discrimination by the "majority" white race against the Negro minority. But they need not be read as depending upon that characterization for their results. It suffices to say that "[o]ver the years, this Court has consistently repudiated '[d]istinctions between citizens solely because of their ancestry' as being 'odious to a free people whose institutions are founded upon the doctrine of equality.' "

Petitioner urges us to adopt for the first time a more restrictive view of the Equal Protection Clause and hold that discrimination against members of the white "majority" cannot be suspect if its purpose can be characterized as "benign." The clock of our liberties, however, cannot be turned back to 1868. It is far too late to argue that the guarantee of equal protection to *all* persons permits the recognition of special wards entitled to a degree of protection greater than that accorded others. "The Fourteenth Amendment is not directed solely against discrimination due to a 'two-class theory'—that is, based upon differences between 'white' and Negro." . . .

II

We have held that in "order to justify the use of a suspect classification, a State must show that its purpose or interest is both constitutionally permissible and substantial, and that its use of the classification is 'necessary . . . to the accomplishment' of its purpose or the safeguarding of its interest." The special admissions program purports to serve the purposes of: (i) "reducing the historic deficit of traditionally disfavored minorities in medical schools and in the medical profession"; (ii) countering the effects of societal discrimination; (iii) increasing the number of physicians who will practice in communities currently underserved; and (iv) obtaining the educational benefits that flow from an ethnically diverse student body. It is necessary to decide which, if any, of these purposes is substantial enough to support the use of a suspect classification.

A

If petitioner's purpose is to assure within its student body some specified percentage of a particular group merely because of its race or ethnic origin, such a preferential purpose must be rejected not as insubstantial but as facially invalid. Preferring members of any one group for no reason other than race or ethnic origin is discrimination for its own sake. This the Constitution forbids.

B

The State certainly has a legitimate and substantial interest in ameliorating, or eliminating where feasible, the disabling effects of identified discrimination. The line of school desegregation cases, commencing with *Brown v. Board of Education* (1954) attests to the importance of this state goal and the commitment of the judiciary to affirm all lawful means toward its attainment. In the school cases, the States were required by court order to redress the wrongs worked by specific instances of racial discrimination. That goal was far more focused than the remedying of the effects of "societal discrimination," an amorphous concept of injury that may be ageless in its reach into the past.

We have never approved a classification that aids persons perceived as members of relatively victimized groups at the expense of other innocent individuals in the absence of judicial, legislative, or administrative findings of constitutional or statutory violations. After such findings have been made, the governmental interest in preferring members of the injured groups at the expense of others is substantial, since the legal rights of the victims must be vindicated. In such a case, the extent of the injury and the consequent remedy will have been judicially, legislatively, or administratively defined. Also, the remedial action usually remains subject to continuing oversight to assure that it will work the least harm possible to other innocent persons competing for the benefit. Without such findings of constitutional or statutory violations, it cannot be said that the government has any greater interest in helping one individual than in refraining from harming another. Thus, the government has no compelling justification for inflicting such harm.

Petitioner does not purport to have made, and is in no position to make, such findings. Its broad mission is education, not the formulation of any legislative policy or the adjudication of particular claims of illegality. . . . [I]solated segments of our vast governmental structures are not competent to make those decisions, at least in the absence of legislative mandates and legislatively determined criteria. Before relying upon these sorts of findings in establishing a racial classification, a governmental body must have the authority and capability to establish, in the record, that the classification is responsive to identified discrimination. Lacking this capability, petitioner has not carried its burden of justification on this issue.

Hence, the purpose of helping certain groups whom the faculty of the Davis Medical School perceived as victims of "societal discrimination" does not justify a classification that imposes disadvantages upon persons like respondent, who bear no responsibility for whatever harm the beneficiaries of the special admissions program are thought to have suffered. To hold otherwise would be to convert a remedy heretofore reserved for violations of legal rights into a privilege that all institutions throughout the Nation could grant at their pleasure to whatever groups are perceived as victims of societal discrimination. That is a step we have never approved.

C

Petitioner identifies, as another purpose of its program, improving the delivery of health-care services to communities currently underserved. It may be assumed that in some situations a State's interest in facilitating the health care of its citizens is sufficiently compelling to support the use of a suspect classification. But there is virtually no evidence in the record indicating that petitioner's special admissions program is either needed or geared to promote that goal. The court below addressed this failure of proof:

> "The University concedes it cannot assure that minority doctors who entered under the program, all of whom expressed an 'interest' in practicing in a disadvantaged community, will actually do so. It may be correct to assume that some of them will carry out this intention, and that it is more likely they will practice in minority communities than the average white doctor. Nevertheless, there are more precise and reliable ways to identify applicants who are genuinely interested in the medical problems of minorities than by race. An applicant of whatever race who has demonstrated his concern for disadvantaged minorities in the past and who declares that practice in such a community is his primary professional goal would be more likely to contribute to alleviation of the medical shortage than one who is chosen entirely on the basis of race and disadvantage. In short, there is no empirical data to demonstrate that any one race is more selflessly socially oriented or by contrast that another is more selfishly acquisitive."

Petitioner simply has not carried its burden of demonstrating that it must prefer members of particular ethnic groups over all other individuals in order to promote better health-care delivery to deprived citizens. Indeed, petitioner has not shown that its preferential classification is likely to have any significant effect on the problem.

D

The fourth goal asserted by petitioner is the attainment of a diverse student body. This clearly is a constitutionally permissible goal for an institution of higher education. Academic freedom, though not a specifically enumerated constitutional right, long has been viewed as a special concern of the First Amendment. The freedom of a university to make its own judgments as to education includes the selection of its student body.

Ethnic diversity, however, is only one element in a range of factors a university properly may consider in attaining the goal of a heterogeneous student body. Although a university must have wide discretion in making the sensitive judgments as to who should be admitted, constitutional limitations protecting individual rights may not be disregarded. Respondent urges—and the courts below have held—that petitioner's dual admissions program is a racial classification that impermissibly infringes his rights under the Fourteenth Amendment. As the interest of diversity is compelling in the context of a university's admissions program, the question remains whether the program's racial classification is necessary to promote this interest.

III

A

It may be assumed that the reservation of a specified number of seats in each class for individuals from the preferred ethnic groups would contribute to the attainment of considerable ethnic diversity in the student body. But petitioner's argument that this is the only effective means of serving the interest of diversity is seriously flawed. In a most fundamental sense the argument misconceives the nature of the state interest that would justify consideration of race or ethnic background. It is not an interest in simple ethnic diversity, in which a specified percentage of the student body is in effect guaranteed to be members of selected ethnic groups, with the remaining percentage an undifferentiated aggregation of students. The diversity that furthers a compelling state interest encompasses a far broader array of qualifications and characteristics of which racial or ethnic origin is but a single though important element. Petitioner's special admissions program, focused *solely* on ethnic diversity, would hinder rather than further attainment of genuine diversity.

Nor would the state interest in genuine diversity be served by expanding petitioner's two-track system into a multitrack program with a prescribed number of seats set aside for each identifiable category of applicants. Indeed, it is inconceivable that a university would thus pursue the logic of petitioner's two-track program to the illogical end of insulating each category of applicants with certain desired qualifications from competition with all other applicants.

The experience of other university admissions programs, which take race into account in achieving the educational diversity valued by the First Amendment, demonstrates that the assignment of a fixed number of places to a minority group is not a necessary means toward that end. An illuminating example is found in the Harvard College program:

> "In recent years Harvard College has expanded the concept of diversity to include students from disadvantaged economic, racial and ethnic groups. Harvard College now recruits not only Californians or Louisianans but also blacks and Chicanos and other minority students. . . .
>
> "In practice, this new definition of diversity has meant that race has been a factor in some admission decisions. When the Committee on Admissions reviews the large middle group of applicants who are 'admissible' and deemed capable of doing good work in their courses, the race of an applicant may tip the balance in his favor just as geographic origin or a life spent on a farm may tip the balance in other candidates' cases. A farm boy from

Idaho can bring something to Harvard College that a Bostonian cannot offer. Similarly, a black student can usually bring something that a white person cannot offer. . . .

"In Harvard college admissions the Committee has not set target-quotas for the number of blacks, or of musicians, football players, physicists or Californians to be admitted in a given year. . . . But that awareness [of the necessity of including more than a token number of black students] does not mean that the Committee sets a minimum number of blacks or of people from west of the Mississippi who are to be admitted. It means only that in choosing among thousands of applicants who are not only 'admissible' academically but have other strong qualities, the Committee, with a number of criteria in mind, pays some attention to distribution among many types and categories of students."

In such an admissions program, race or ethnic background may be deemed a "plus" in a particular applicant's file, yet it does not insulate the individual from comparison with all other candidates for the available seats. The file of a particular black applicant may be examined for his potential contribution to diversity without the factor of race being decisive when compared, for example, with that of an applicant identified as an Italian-American if the latter is thought to exhibit qualities more likely to promote beneficial educational pluralism. Such qualities could include exceptional personal talents, unique work or service experience, leadership potential, maturity, demonstrated compassion, a history of overcoming disadvantage, ability to communicate with the poor, or other qualifications deemed important. In short, an admissions program operated in this way is flexible enough to consider all pertinent elements of diversity in light of the particular qualifications of each applicant, and to place them on the same footing for consideration, although not necessarily according them the same weight. Indeed, the weight attributed to a particular quality may vary from year to year depending upon the "mix" both of the student body and the applicants for the incoming class.

This kind of program treats each applicant as an individual in the admissions process. The applicant who loses out on the last available seat to another candidate receiving a "plus" on the basis of ethnic background will not have been foreclosed from all consideration for that seat simply because he was not the right color or had the wrong surname. It would mean only that his combined qualifications, which may have included similar nonobjective factors, did not outweigh those of the other applicant. His qualifications would have been weighed fairly and competitively, and he would have no basis to complain of unequal treatment under the Fourteenth Amendment.

It has been suggested that an admissions program which considers race only as one factor is simply a subtle and more sophisticated—but no less effective—means of according racial preference than the Davis program. A facial intent to discriminate, however, is evident in petitioner's preference program and not denied in this case. No such facial infirmity exists in an admissions program where race or ethnic background is simply one element—to be weighed fairly against other elements—in the selection process. "A boundary line," as Mr. Justice Frankfurter remarked in another connection, "is none the worse for being narrow." And a court would not assume that a university, professing to employ a facially nondiscriminatory admissions policy, would operate it as a cover for the functional equivalent of a quota system. In short, good faith would be presumed in the absence of a showing to the contrary in the manner permitted by our cases.

B

In summary, it is evident that the Davis special admissions program involves the use of an explicit racial classification never before countenanced by this Court. It tells applicants who are not Negro, Asian, or Chicano that they are totally excluded from a specific percentage of the seats in an entering class. No matter how strong their qualifications, quantitative and extracurricular, including their own potential for contribution to educational diversity, they are never afforded the chance to compete with applicants from the preferred groups for the special admissions seats. At the same time, the preferred applicants have the opportunity to compete for every seat in the class.

The fatal flaw in petitioner's preferential program is its disregard of individual rights as guaranteed by the Fourteenth Amendment. Such rights are not absolute. But when a State's distribution of benefits or imposition of burdens hinges on ancestry or the color of a person's skin or ancestry, that individual is entitled to a demonstration that the challenged classification is necessary to promote a substantial state interest. Petitioner has failed to carry this burden. For this reason, that portion of the California court's judgment holding petitioner's special admissions program invalid under the Fourteenth Amendment must be affirmed.

C

In enjoining petitioner from ever considering the race of any applicant, however, the courts below failed to recognize that the State has a substantial interest that legitimately may be served by a properly devised admissions program involving the competitive consideration of race and ethnic origin. For this reason, so much of the California court's judgment as enjoins petitioner from any consideration of the race of any applicant must be reversed.

QUESTIONS

1 Are there any morally good reasons for having two sets of criteria for judging applicants to institutions of higher learning?
2 Can you suggest any criteria that should be used to distinguish morally acceptable racial classifications from invidious and pernicious ones?

What Is Wrong with Reverse Discrimination?

Edwin C. Hettinger

Edwin C. Hettinger, assistant professor of philosophy at the College of Charleston, specializes in political philosophy, environmental philosophy, and ethics. His published articles include "The Responsible Use of Animals in Biomedical Research" and "Justifying Intellectual Property."

Hettinger adopts a consequentialist approach to the justification of reverse discrimination. He defends affirmative-action practices that are committed to the hiring and admission of slightly less well qualified women or blacks rather than slightly more qualified white males. In Hettinger's view, such reverse discrimination is justified insofar as its ultimate goal is the eradication of sexual and/or racial inequality. Hettinger discusses and evaluates various objections to reverse discrimination and identifies the following two objections as morally troubling: (1) When reverse discrimination takes place, people are judged on the basis of involuntary characteristics—characteristics over which they have no control. (2) Job-seeking white males who are subject to reverse discrimination are not compensated for the sacrifices they make in bearing a disproportionate share of the costs of achieving an egalitarian society. In Hettinger's view, the problems pinpointed by these two objections are relatively minor, however, when weighed against the serious injustice of racial and sexual inequality.

Many people think it obvious that reverse discrimination is unjust. Calling affirmative action reverse discrimination itself suggests this. This discussion evaluates numerous reasons given for this alleged injustice. Most of these accounts of what is wrong with reverse discrimination are found to be deficient. The explanations for why reverse discrimination is morally troubling show only that it is unjust in a relatively weak sense. This result has an important consequence for the wider issue of the moral justifiability of affirmative action. If social policies which involve minor injustice are permissible (and perhaps required) when they are required in order to overcome much greater injustice, then the mild injustice of reverse discrimination is easily overridden by its contribution to the important social goal of dismantling our sexual and racial caste system.

By 'reverse discrimination' or 'affirmative action' I shall mean hiring or admitting a slightly less well qualified woman or black, rather than a slightly more qualified white male, for the purpose of helping to eradicate sexual and/or racial inequality, or for the purpose of compensating women and blacks for the burdens and injustices they have suffered due to past and ongoing sexism and racism. There are weaker forms of affirmative action, such as giving preference to minority candidates only when qualifications are equal, or providing special educational opportunities for

Reprinted with permission of the author from *Business & Professional Ethics Journal,* vol. 6 (Fall 1987), pp. 39–51.

youths in disadvantaged groups. This paper seeks to defend the more controversial sort of reverse discrimination defined above. I begin by considering several spurious objections to reverse discrimination. In the second part, I identify the ways in which this policy is morally troubling and then assess the significance of these negative features.

SPURIOUS OBJECTIONS

1 Reverse Discrimination as Equivalent to Racism and Sexism

In a discussion on national television, George Will, the conservative news analyst and political philosopher, articulated the most common objection to reverse discrimination. It is unjust, he said, because it is discrimination on the basis of race or sex. Reverse discrimination against white males is the same evil as traditional discrimination against women and blacks. The only difference is that in this case it is the white male who is being discriminated against. Thus if traditional racism and sexism are wrong and unjust, so is reverse discrimination, and for the very same reasons.

But reverse discrimination is not at all like traditional sexism and racism. The motives and intentions behind it are completely different, as are its consequences. Consider some of the motives underlying traditional racial discrimination. Blacks were not hired or allowed into schools because it was felt that contact with them was degrading, and sullied whites. These policies were based on contempt and loathing for blacks, on a feeling that blacks were suitable only for subservient positions and that they should never have positions of authority over whites. Slightly better qualified white males are not being turned down under affirmative action for any of these reasons. No defenders or practitioners of affirmative action (and no significant segment of the general public) think that contact with white males is degrading or sullying, that white males are contemptible and loathsome, or that white males—by their nature—should be subservient to blacks or women.

The consequences of these two policies differ radically as well. Affirmative action does not stigmatize white males; it does not perpetuate unfortunate stereotypes about white males; it is not part of a pattern of discrimination that makes being a white male incredibly burdensome. Nor does it add to a particular group's "already overabundant supply" of power, authority, wealth, and opportunity, as does traditional racial and sexual discrimination. On the contrary, it results in a more egalitarian distribution of these social and economic benefits. If the motives and consequences of reverse discrimination and of traditional racism and sexism are completely different, in what sense could they be morally equivalent acts? If acts are to be individuated (for moral purposes) by including the motives, intentions, and consequences in their description, then clearly these two acts are not identical.

It might be argued that although the motives and consequences are different, the act itself is the same: reverse discrimination is discrimination on the basis of race and sex, and this is wrong in itself independently of its motives or consequences. But discriminating (i.e., making distinctions in how one treats people) on the basis of race or sex is not always wrong, nor is it necessarily unjust. It is not wrong, for example, to discriminate against one's own sex when choosing a spouse. Nor is racial or sexual discrimination in hiring necessarily wrong. This is shown by Peter Singer's example in which a director of a play about ghetto conditions in New York City refuses to consider any white applicants for the actors because she wants the play to be authentic.[1] If I am looking for a representative of the black community, or doing a study about blacks and disease, it is perfectly legitimate to discriminate against all whites. Their whiteness makes them unsuitable for my (legitimate) purposes. Similarly, if I am hiring a wet-nurse, or a person to patrol the women's change rooms in my department store, discriminating against males is perfectly legitimate.

These examples show that racial and sexual discrimination are not wrong in themselves. This is not to say that they are never wrong; most often they clearly are. Whether or not they are wrong, however, depends on the purposes, consequences, and context of such discrimination.

2   Race and Sex as Morally Arbitrary and Irrelevant Characteristics

A typical reason given for the alleged injustice of all racial and sexual discrimination (including affirmative action) is that it is morally arbitrary to consider race or sex when hiring, since these characteristics are not relevant to the decision. But the above examples show that not all uses of race or sex as a criterion in hiring decisions are morally arbitrary or irrelevant. Similarly, when an affirmative action officer takes into account race and sex, use of these characteristics is not morally irrelevant or arbitrary. Since affirmative action aims to help end racial and sexual inequality by providing black and female role models for minorities (and non-minorities), the race and sex of the job candidates are clearly relevant to the decision. There is nothing arbitrary about the affirmative action officer focusing on race and sex. Hence, if reverse discrimination is wrong, it is not wrong for the reason that it uses morally irrelevant and arbitrary characteristics to distinguish between applicants.

3   Reverse Discrimination as Unjustified Stereotyping

It might be argued that reverse discrimination involves judging people by alleged average characteristics of a class to which they belong, instead of judging them on the basis of their individual characteristics, and that such judging on the basis of stereotypes is unjust. But the defense of affirmative action suggested in this paper does not rely on stereotyping. When an employer hires a slightly less well qualified woman or black over a slightly more qualified white male for the purpose of helping to overcome sexual and racial inequality, she judges the applicants on the basis of their individual characteristics. She uses this person's sex or skin color as a mechanism to help achieve the goals of affirmative action. Individual characteristics of the white male (his skin color and sex) prevent him from serving one of the legitimate goals of employment policies, and he is turned down on this basis.

Notice that the objection does have some force against those who defend reverse discrimination on the grounds of compensatory justice. An affirmative action policy whose purpose is to compensate women and blacks for past and current injustices judges that women and blacks on the average are owed greater compensation than are white males. Although this is true, opponents of affirmative action argue that some white males have been more severely and unfairly disadvantaged than some women and blacks. A poor white male from Appalachia may have suffered greater undeserved disadvantages than the upper-middle class woman or black with whom he competes. Although there is a high correlation between being female (or being black) and being especially owed compensation for unfair disadvantages suffered, the correlation is not universal.

Thus defending affirmative action on the grounds of compensatory justice may lead to unjust treatment of white males in individual cases. Despite the fact that certain white males are owed greater compensation than are some women or blacks, it is the latter that receive compensation. This is the result of judging candidates for jobs on the basis of the average characteristics of their class, rather than on the basis of their individual characteristics. Thus compensatory justice defenses of reverse discrimination may involve potentially problematic stereotyping. But this is not the defense of affirmative action considered here.

4   Failing to Hire the Most Qualified Person Is Unjust

One of the major reasons people think reverse discrimination is unjust is because they think that the most qualified person should get the job. But why should the most qualified person be hired?

A   Efficiency   One obvious answer to this question is that one should hire the most qualified person because doing so promotes efficiency. If job qualifications are positively correlated with job performance, then the more qualified person will tend to do a better job. Although it is not always true that there is such a correlation, in general there is, and hence this point is well taken. There are short term efficiency costs of reverse discrimination as defined here.

Note that a weaker version of affirmative action has no such efficiency costs. If one hires a black or woman over a white male only in cases where qualifications are roughly equal, job performance will not be affected. Furthermore, efficiency costs will be a function of the qualifications gap between the black or woman hired, and the white male rejected: the larger the gap, the greater the efficiency costs. The existence of efficiency costs is also a function of the type of work performed. Many of the jobs in our society are ones which any normal person can do (e.g., assembly line worker, janitor, truck driver, etc.). Affirmative action hiring for these positions is unlikely to have significant efficiency costs (assuming whoever is hired is willing to work hard). In general, professional positions are the ones in which people's performance levels will vary significantly, and hence these are the jobs in which reverse discrimination could have significant efficiency costs.

While concern for efficiency gives us a reason for hiring the most qualified person, it in no way explains the alleged injustice suffered by the white male who is passed over due to reverse discrimination. If the affirmative action employer is treating the white male unjustly, it is not because the hiring policy is inefficient. Failing to maximize efficiency does not generally involve acting unjustly. For instance, a person who carries one bag of groceries at a time, rather than two, is acting inefficiently, though not unjustly.

It is arguable that the manager of a business who fails to hire the most qualified person (and thereby sacrifices some efficiency) treats the owners of the company unjustly, for their profits may suffer, and this violates one conception of the manager's fiduciary responsibility to the shareholders. Perhaps the administrator of a hospital who hires a slightly less well qualified black doctor (for the purposes of affirmative action) treats the future patients at that hospital unjustly, for doing so may reduce the level of health care they receive (and it is arguable that they have a legitimate expectation to receive the best health care possible for the money they spend). But neither of these examples of inefficiency leading to injustice concern the white male "victim" of affirmative action, and it is precisely this person who the opponents of reverse discrimination claim is being unfairly treated.

To many people, that a policy is inefficient is a sufficient reason for condemning it. This is especially true in the competitive and profit oriented world of business. However, profit maximization is not the only legitimate goal of business hiring policies (or other business decisions). Businesses have responsibilities to help heal society's ills, especially those (like racism and sexism) which they in large part helped to create and perpetuate. Unless one takes the implausible position that business' only legitimate goal is profit maximization, the efficiency costs of affirmative action are not an automatic reason for rejecting it. And as we have noted, affirmative action's efficiency costs are of no help in substantiating and explaining its alleged injustice to white males.

B The Most Qualified Person Has a Right to the Job One could argue that the most qualified person for the job has a right to be hired in virtue of superior qualifications. On this view, reverse discrimination violates the better qualified white male's right to be hired for the job. But the most qualified applicant holds no such right. If you are the best painter in town, and a person hires her brother to paint her house, instead of you, your rights have not been violated. People do not have rights to be hired for particular jobs (though I think a plausible case can be made for the claim that there is a fundamental human right to employment). If anyone has a right in this matter, it is the employer. This is not to say, of course, that the employer cannot do wrong in her hiring decision; she obviously can. If she hires a white because she loathes blacks, she does wrong. The point is that her wrong does not consist in violating the right some candidate has to her job (though this would violate other rights of the candidate).

C The Most Qualified Person Deserves the Job It could be argued that the most qualified person should get the job because she deserves it in virtue of her superior qualifications. But the assumption that the person most qualified for a job is the one who most deserves it is problematic. Very often people do not deserve their qualifications, and hence they do not deserve anything on the basis of those qualifications. A person's qualifications are a function of at least the following factors: (a) innate abilities, (b) home environment, (c) socio-economic class of parents, (d) quality of the schools attended, (e) luck, and (f) effort or perseverance. A person is only responsible for the last factor on this list, and hence one only deserves one's qualifications to the extent that they are a function of effort.

It is undoubtedly often the case that a person who is less well qualified for a job is more deserving of the job (because she worked harder to achieve those lower qualifications) than is someone with superior qualifications. This is frequently true of women and blacks in the job market: they worked harder to overcome disadvantages most (or all) white males never faced. Hence, affirmative action policies which permit the hiring of slightly less well qualified candidates may often be more in line with considerations of desert than are the standard meritocratic procedures.

The point is not that affirmative action is defensible because it helps insure that more deserving candidates get jobs. Nor is it that desert should be the only or even the most important consideration in hiring decisions. The claim is simply that hiring the most qualified person for a job need not (and quite often does not) involve hiring the most deserving candidate. Hence the intuition that morality requires one to hire the most qualified people cannot be justified on the grounds that these people deserve to be hired.

D   The Most Qualified Person Is Entitled to the Job   One might think that although the most qualified person neither deserves the job nor has a right to the job, still this person is entitled to the job. By 'entitlement' in this context, I mean a natural and legitimate expectation based on a type of social promise. Society has implicitly encouraged the belief that the most qualified candidate will get the job. Society has set up a competition and the prize is a job which is awarded to those applying with the best qualifications. Society thus reneges on an implicit promise it has made to its members when it allows reverse discrimination to occur. It is dashing legitimate expectations it has encouraged. It is violating the very rules of a game it created.

Furthermore, the argument goes, by allowing reverse discrimination, society is breaking an explicit promise (contained in the Civil Rights Act of 1964) that it will not allow race or sex to be used against one of its citizens. Title VII of that Act prohibits discrimination in employment on the basis of race or sex (as well as color, religion, or national origin).

In response to this argument, it should first be noted that the above interpretation of the Civil Rights Act is misleading. In fact, the Supreme Court has interpreted the Act as allowing race and sex to be considered in hiring or admission decisions.[2] More importantly, since affirmative action has been an explicit national policy for the last twenty years (and has been supported in numerous court cases), it is implausible to argue that society has promised its members that it will not allow race or sex to outweigh superior qualifications in hiring decisions. In addition, the objection takes a naive and utopian view of actual hiring decisions. It presents a picture of our society as a pure meritocracy in which hiring decisions are based solely on qualifications. The only exception it sees to these meritocratic procedures is the unfortunate policy of affirmative action. But this picture is dramatically distorted. Elected government officials, political appointees, business managers, and many others clearly do not have their positions solely or even mostly because of their qualifications. Given the widespread acceptance in our society of procedures which are far from meritocratic, claiming that the most qualified person has a socially endorsed entitlement to the job is not believable.

5   Undermining Equal Opportunity for White Males

It has been claimed that the right of white males to an equal chance of employment is violated by affirmative action. Reverse discrimination, it is said, undermines equality of opportunity for white males.

If equality of opportunity requires a social environment in which everyone at birth has roughly the same chance of succeeding through the use of his or her natural talents, then it could well be argued that given the social, cultural, and educational disadvantages placed on women and blacks, preferential treatment of these groups brings us closer to equality of opportunity. White males are full members of the community in a way in which women and blacks are not, and this advantage is diminished by affirmative action. Affirmative action takes away the greater than equal opportunity white males generally have, and thus it brings us closer to a situation in which all members of society have an equal chance of succeeding through the use of their talents.

It should be noted that the goal of affirmative action is to bring about a society in which there is equality of opportunity for women and blacks without preferential treatment of these groups. It is not the purpose of the sort of affirmative action defended here to disadvantage white males in order to take away the advantage a sexist and racist society gives to them. But noticing that this occurs is sufficient to dispel the illusion that affirmative action undermines the equality of opportunity for white males.

LEGITIMATE OBJECTIONS

The following two considerations explain what is morally troubling about reverse discrimination.

1   Judging on the Basis of Involuntary Characteristics

In cases of reverse discrimination, white males are passed over on the basis of membership in a group they were born into. When an affirmative action employer hires a slightly less well qualified black (or woman), rather than a more highly qualified white male, skin color (or sex) is being used as one criterion for determining who gets a very important benefit. Making distinctions in how one treats people on the basis of characteristics they cannot help having (such as skin color or sex) is morally problematic because it reduces individual autonomy. Discriminating between people on the basis of features they can do something about is preferable, since it gives them some control over how others act towards them. They can develop the characteristics others use to give them favorable treatment and avoid those characteristics others use as grounds for unfavorable treatment.

For example, if employers refuse to hire you because you are a member of the American Nazi Party, and if you do not like the fact that you are having a hard time finding a job, you can choose to leave the party. However, if a white male is having trouble finding employment because slightly less well qualified women and blacks are being given jobs to meet affirmative action requirements, there is nothing he can do about this disadvantage, and his autonomy is curtailed.

Discriminating between people on the basis of their involuntary characteristics is morally undesirable, and thus reverse discrimination is also morally undesirable. Of course, that something is morally undesirable does not show that it is unjust, nor that it is morally unjustifiable.

How morally troubling is it to judge people on the basis of involuntary characteristics? Notice that our society frequently uses these sorts of features to distinguish between people. Height and good looks are characteristics one cannot do much about, and yet basketball players and models are ordinarily chosen and rejected on the basis of precisely these features. To a large extent our intelligence is also a feature beyond our control, and yet intelligence is clearly one of the major characteristics our society uses to determine what happens to people.

Of course there are good reasons why we distinguish between people on the basis of these sorts of involuntary characteristics. Given the goals of basketball teams, model agencies, and employers in general, hiring the taller, better looking, or more intelligent person (respectively) makes good sense. It promotes efficiency, since all these people are likely to do a better job. Hiring policies based on these involuntary characteristics serve the legitimate purposes of these businesses (e.g., profit and serving the public), and hence they may be morally justified despite their tendency to reduce the control people have over their own lives.

This argument applies to reverse discrimination as well. The purpose of affirmative action is to help eradicate racial and sexual injustice. If affirmative action policies help bring about this goal, then they can be morally justified despite their tendency to reduce the control white males have over their lives.

In one respect this sort of consequentialist argument is more forceful in the case of affirmative action. Rather than merely promoting the goal of efficiency (which is the justification for businesses hiring naturally brighter, taller, or more attractive individuals), affirmative action promotes the nonutilitarian goal of an egalitarian society. In general, promoting a consideration of justice (such as equality) is more important than is promoting efficiency or utility. Thus in terms of the importance of the objective, this consequentialist argument is stronger in the case of affirmative action. If one can justify reducing individual autonomy on the grounds that it promotes efficiency, one can certainly do so on the grounds that it reduces the injustice of racial and sexual inequality.

2   Burdening White Males without Compensation

Perhaps the strongest moral intuition concerning the wrongness of reverse discrimination is that it is unfair to job seeking white males. It is unfair because they have been given an undeserved disadvantage in the competition for employment; they have been handicapped because of something that is not their fault. Why should white males be made to pay for the sins of others?

It would be a mistake to argue for reverse discrimination on the grounds that white males deserve to be burdened and that therefore we should hire women and blacks even when white males are better qualified. Young white males who are now entering the job market are not more responsible for the evils of racial and sexual inequality than are other members of society. Thus, reverse discrimination is not properly viewed as punishment administered to white males.

The justification for affirmative action supported here claims that bringing about sexual and racial equality necessitates sacrifice on the part of white males who seek employment. An important step in bringing about the desired egalitarian society involves speeding up the process by which women and blacks get into positions of power and authority. This requires that white males find it harder to achieve these same positions. But this is not punishment for deeds done.

Thomas Nagel's helpful analogy is state condemnation of property under the right of eminent domain for the purpose of building a highway. Forcing some in the community to move in order that the community as a whole may benefit is unfair. Why should these individuals suffer rather than others? The answer is: Because they happen to live in a place where it is important to build a road. A similar response should be given to the white male who objects to reverse discrimination with the same "Why me?" question. The answer is: Because job seeking white males happen to be in the way of an important road leading to the desired egalitarian society. Job-seeking white males are being made to bear the brunt of the burden of affirmative action because of accidental considerations, just as are homeowners whose property is condemned in order to build a highway.[3]

This analogy is extremely illuminating and helpful in explaining the nature of reverse discrimination. There is, however, an important dissimilarity that Nagel does not mention. In cases of property condemnation, compensation is paid to the owner. Affirmative action policies, however, do not compensate white males for shouldering this burden of moving toward the desired egalitarian society. So affirmative action is unfair to job seeking white males because they are forced to bear an unduly large share of the burden of achieving racial and sexual equality without being compensated for this sacrifice. Since we have singled out job seeking white males from the larger pool of white males who should also help achieve this goal, it seems that some compensation from the latter to the former is appropriate.

This is a serious objection to affirmative action policies only if the uncompensated burden is substantial. Usually it is not. Most white male "victims" of affirmative action easily find employment. It is highly unlikely that the same white male will repeatedly fail to get hired because of affirmative action. The burdens of affirmative action should be spread as evenly as possible among all the job seeking white males. Furthermore, the burden job seeking white males face—of finding it somewhat more difficult to get employment—is inconsequential when compared to the burdens ongoing discrimination places on women and blacks. Forcing job seeking white males to bear an extra burden is acceptable because this is a necessary step toward achieving a much greater reduction in the unfair burdens our society places on women and blacks. If affirmative action is a necessary mechanism for a timely dismantlement of our racial and sexual caste system, the extra burdens it places on job seeking white males are justified.

Still the question remains: Why isn't compensation paid? When members of society who do not deserve extra burdens are singled out to sacrifice for an important community goal, society owes them compensation. This objection loses some of its force when one realizes that society continually places undeserved burdens on its members without compensating them. For instance, the burden of seeking efficiency is placed on the shoulders of the least naturally talented and intelligent. That one is born less intelligent (or otherwise less talented) does not mean that one deserves to have reduced employment opportunities, and yet our society's meritocratic hiring procedures make it much harder for less naturally talented members to find meaningful employment. These people are not compensated for their sacrifices either.

Of course, pointing out that there are other examples of an allegedly problematic social policy does not justify that policy. Nonetheless, if this analogy is sound, failing to compensate job-seeking white males for the sacrifices placed on them by reverse discrimination is not without precedent. Furthermore, it is no more morally troublesome than is failing to compensate less talented members of society for their undeserved sacrifice of employment opportunities for the sake of efficiency.

CONCLUSION

This article has shown the difficulties in pinpointing what is morally troubling about reverse discrimination. The most commonly heard objections to reverse discrimination fail to make their case. Reverse discrimination is not morally equivalent to traditional racism and sexism since its goals and consequences are entirely different, and the act of treating people differently on the basis of race or sex is not necessarily morally wrong. The race and sex of the candidates are not morally irrelevant in all hiring decisions, and affirmative action hiring is an example where discriminating on the basis of race or sex is not morally arbitrary. Furthermore, affirmative action can be defended on grounds that do not involve stereotyping. Though affirmative action hiring of less well qualified applicants can lead to short run inefficiency, failing to hire the most qualified applicant does not violate this person's rights, entitlements, or deserts. Additionally, affirmative action hiring does not generally undermine equal opportunity for white males.

Reverse discrimination is morally troublesome in that it judges people on the basis of involuntary characteristics and thus reduces the control they have over their lives. It also places a larger than fair share of the burden of achieving an egalitarian society on the shoulders of job seeking white males without compensating them for this sacrifice. But these problems are relatively minor when compared to the grave injustice of racial and sexual inequality, and they are easily outweighed if affirmative action helps alleviate this far greater injustice.

NOTES

I thank Cheshire Calhoun, Beverly Diamond, John Dickerson, Jasper Hunt, Glenn Lesses, Richard Nunan, and Martin Perlmutter for helpful comments.

1 Peter Singer, "Is Racial Discrimination Arbitrary?" *Philosophia,* vol. 8 (November 1978), pp. 185–203.
2 See Justice William Brennan's majority opinion in United Steel Workers and Kaiser Aluminum v. Weber, United States Supreme Court, *443 U.S. 193* (1979). See also Justice Lewis Powell's majority opinion in the University of California v. Bakke, United States Supreme Court, *438 U.S. 265* (1978).
3 Thomas Nagel, "A Defense of Affirmative Action" in *Ethical Theory and Business,* 2nd edition, ed. Tom Beauchamp and Norman Bowie (Englewood Cliffs, NJ: Prentice-Hall, 1983), p. 484.

QUESTIONS

1 Are there morally significant differences between reverse discrimination and traditional racism and sexism?
2 Do consequentialist considerations justify preferential treatment policies? Explain your reasoning.

Affirmative Racism

Charles Murray

Charles Murray is senior research fellow at the Manhattan Institute for Policy Research. He is the author of *Losing Ground: American Social Policy 1950–1980* (1986) and *In Pursuit of Happiness and Good Government* (1988).

On Murray's view, preferential treatment admissions and hiring practices have fostered a new form of racism and thus have worked against the interests of blacks. He claims that preferential treatment has had the following two undesirable outcomes: (1) it has demoralized blacks by forcing them to compete at levels beyond their abilities and (2) it has encouraged a new form of racism—one that tacitly assumes that blacks are, at least temporarily, inferior to whites. Murray sees this new racism as perpetuating the race-based inequality it is supposed to eliminate.

Reprinted with permission from *The New Republic,* December 31, 1984.

A few years ago, I got into an argument with a lawyer friend who is a partner in a New York firm. I was being the conservative, arguing that preferential treatment of blacks was immoral; he was being the liberal, urging that it was the only way to bring blacks to full equality. In the middle of all this he abruptly said, "But you know, let's face it. We must have hired at least ten blacks in the last few years, and none of them has really worked out." He then returned to his case for still stronger affirmative action, while I wondered what it had been like for those ten blacks. And if he could make a remark like that so casually, what remarks would he be able to make some years down the road, if by that time it had been fifty blacks who hadn't "really worked out"?

My friend's comment was an outcropping of a new racism that is emerging to take its place alongside the old. It grows out of preferential treatment for blacks, and it is not just the much-publicized reactions, for example, of the white policemen or firemen who are passed over for promotion because of an affirmative action court order. The new racism that is potentially most damaging is located among the white elites—educated, affluent, and occupying the positions in education, business, and government from which this country is run. It currently focuses on blacks; whether it will eventually extend to include Hispanics and other minorities remains to be seen.

The new racists do not think blacks are inferior. They are typically longtime supporters of civil rights. But they exhibit the classic behavioral symptom of racism: they treat blacks differently from whites, because of their race. The results can be as concretely bad and unjust as any that the old racism produces. Sometimes the effect is that blacks are refused an education they otherwise could have gotten. Sometimes blacks are shunted into dead-end jobs. Always, blacks are denied the right to compete as equals.

The new racists also exhibit another characteristic of racism: they *think* about blacks differently from the way they think about whites. Their global view of blacks and civil rights is impeccable. Blacks must be enabled to achieve full equality. They are still unequal, through no fault of their own (it is the fault of racism, it is the fault of inadequate opportunity, it is the legacy of history). But the new racists' local view is that the blacks they run across professionally are not, on the average, up to the white standard. Among the new racists, lawyers have gotten used to the idea that the brief a black colleague turns in will be a little less well-rehearsed and argued than the one they would have done. Businessmen expect that a black colleague will not read a balance sheet as subtly as they do. Teachers expect black students to wind up toward the bottom of the class.

The new racists also tend to think of blacks as a commodity. The office must have a sufficient supply of blacks, who must be treated with special delicacy. The personnel problems this creates are more difficult than most because whites barely admit to themselves what's going on.

What follows is a foray into very poorly mapped territory. . . . The cases I present are composites constructed from my own observations and taken from first-hand accounts. All are based on real events and real people, stripped of their particularities. But the individual cases are not intended as evidence, because I cannot tell you how often they happen. They have not been the kind of thing that social scientists or journalists have wanted to count. I am writing this because so many people, both white and black, to whom I tell such stories know immediately what I am talking about. It is apparent that a problem exists. How significant is it? What follows is as much an attempt to elicit evidence as to present it.

As in so many of the crusades of the 1960s, the nation began with a good idea. It was called "affirmative action," initiated by Lyndon Johnson through Executive Order 11246 in September 1965. It was an attractive label and a natural corrective to past racism: actively seek out black candidates for jobs, college, or promotions, without treating them differently in the actual decision to hire, admit, or promote. The term originally evoked both the letter and the spirit of the order.

Then, gradually, affirmative action came to mean something quite different. In 1970 a federal court established the legitimacy of quotas as a means of implementing Johnson's executive order. In 1971 the Supreme Court ruled that an employer could not use minimum credentials as a prerequisite for hiring if the credentials acted as a "built-in headwind" for minority groups—even when there was no discriminatory intent and even when the hiring procedures were "fair in form." In 1972 the Equal Employment Opportunity Commission acquired broad, independent enforcement powers.

Thus by the early 1970s it had become generally recognized that a good-faith effort to recruit qualified blacks was not enough—especially if one's school depended on federal grants or one's business depended on federal contracts. Even for businesses and schools not directly dependent on the government, the simplest way to withstand an accusation of violating Title VII of the Civil Rights Act of 1964 was to make sure not that they had not just interviewed enough minority candidates, but that they had actually hired or admitted enough of them. Employers and admissions committees arrived at a rule of thumb: if the blacks who are available happen to be the best candidates, fine; if not, the best available black candidates will be given some sort of edge in the selection process. Sometimes the edge will be small; sometimes it will be predetermined that a black candidate is essential, and the edge will be very large.

Perhaps the first crucial place where the edge applies is in admission to college. Consider the cases of the following three students: John, William, and Carol, 17 years old and applying to college, are all equal on paper. Each has a score of 520 in the mathematics section of the Scholastic Aptitude Test, which puts them in the top third—at the 67th percentile—of all students who took the test. (Figures are based on 1983 data.)

John is white. A score of 520 gets him into the state university. Against the advice of his high school counselor, he applies to a prestigious school, Ivy U. where his application is rejected in the first cut—its average white applicant has math scores in the high 600s.

William is black, from a middle-class family who sent him to good schools. His score of 520 puts him at the 95th percentile of all blacks who took the test. William's high school counselor points out that he could probably get into Ivy U. William applies and is admitted—Ivy U. uses separate standards for admission of whites and blacks, and William is among the top blacks who applied.

Carol is black, educated at an inner-city school, and her score of 520 represents an extraordinary achievement in the face of terrible schooling. An alumnus of Ivy U. who regularly looks for promising inner-city candidates finds her, recruits her, and sends her off with a full scholarship to Ivy U.

When American universities embarked on policies of preferential admissions by race, they had the Carols in mind. They had good reason to be optimistic that preferential treatment would work—for many years, the best universities had been weighting the test scores of applicants from small-town public schools when they were compared against those of applicants from the top private schools, and had been giving special breaks to students from distant states to ensure geographic distribution. The differences in preparation tended to even out after the first year or so. Blacks were being brought into a longstanding and successful tradition of preferential treatment.

In the case of blacks, however, preferential treatment ran up against a large black-white gap in academic performance combined with ambitious goals for proportional representation. This gap has been the hardest for whites to confront. But though it is not necessary or even plausible to believe that such differences are innate, it is necessary to recognize openly that the differences exist. By pretending they don't, we begin the process whereby both the real differences and the racial factor are exaggerated. . . .

Take the situation of William—a slightly above-average student who, because he is black, gets into a highly competitive school. William studies very hard during the first year. He nonetheless gets mediocre grades. He has a choice. He can continue to study hard and continue to get mediocre grades, and be seen by his classmates as a black who cannot do very well. Or he can explicitly refuse to engage in the academic game. He decides to opt out, and his performance gets worse as time goes on. He emerges from college with a poor education and is further behind the whites than he was as a freshman.

If large numbers of other black students at the institution are in the same situation as William, the result can be group pressure not to compete academically. (At Harvard, it is said, the current term among black students for a black who studies like a white is "incognegro.") The response is not hard to understand. If one subpopulation of students is conspicuously behind another population and is visibly identifiable, then the population that is behind must come up with a good excuse for doing poorly. "Not wanting to do better" is as good as any.

But there is another crucial reason why blacks might not close the gap with whites during college: they are not taught as well as whites are. Racist teachers impeding the progress of students? Perhaps, but most college faculty members I know tend to bend over backward to be "fair" to black students—and that may be the problem. I suggest that inferior instruction is more likely to be a manifestation of the new racism than the old.

Consider the case of Carol, with outstanding abilities but deprived of decent prior schooling: she struggles the first year, but she gets by. Her academic skills still show the aftereffects of her inferior preparation. Her instructors diplomatically point out the more flagrant mistakes, but they ignore minor lapses, and never push her in the aggressive way they push white students who have her intellectual capacity. Some of them are being patronizing (she is doing quite well, considering). Others are being prudent: teachers who criticize black students can find themselves being called racists in the classroom, in the campus newspaper, or in complaints to the administration.

The same process continues in graduate school. Indeed, because there are even fewer blacks in graduate schools than in undergraduate schools, the pressure to get black students through to the degree, no matter what, can be still greater. But apart from differences in preparation and ability that have accumulated by the end of schooling, the process whereby we foster the appearance of black inferiority continues. Let's assume that William did not give up during college. He goes to business school, where he gets his Masters degree. He signs up for interviews with the corporate recruiters. There are 100 persons in his class, and William is ranked near the middle. But of the 5 blacks in his class, he ranks first (remember that he was at the 95th percentile of blacks taking the Scholastic Aptitude Test). He is hired on his first interview by his first-choice company, which also attracted the very best of the white students. He is hired alongside 5 of the top-ranking white members of the class.

William's situation as one of 5 blacks in a class of 100 illustrates the proportions that prevail in business schools, and business schools are by no means one of the more extreme examples. The pool of black candidates for any given profession is a small fraction of the white pool. This works out to a 20-to-1 edge in business; it is even greater in most of the other professions. The result, when many hiring institutions are competing, is that a major gap between the abilities of new black and white employees in any given workplace is highly likely. Everyone needs to hire a few blacks, and the edge that "being black" confers in the hiring decision warps the sequence of hiring in such a way that a scarce resource (the blacks with a given set of qualifications) is exhausted at an artificially high rate, producing a widening gap in comparison with the remaining whites from which an employer can choose.

The more aggressively affirmative action is enforced, the greater the imbalance. In general, the first companies to hire can pursue strategies that minimize or even eliminate the difference in ability between the new black and white employees. IBM and Park Avenue law firms can do very well, just as Harvard does quite well in attracting the top black students. But the more effectively they pursue these strategies, the more quickly they strip the population of the best black candidates.

To this point I have been discussing problems that are more or less driven by realities we have very little hope of manipulating in the short term except by discarding the laws regarding preferential treatment. People do differ in acquiring abilities. Currently, acquired abilities in the white and black populations are distributed differently. Schools and firms do form a rough hierarchy when they draw from these distributions. The results follow ineluctably. The dangers they represent are not a matter of statistical probabilities, but of day-to-day human reactions we see around us.

The damage caused by these mechanistic forces should be much less in the world of work than in the schools, however. Schools deal in a relatively narrow domain of skills, and "talent" tends to be assigned specific meanings and specific measures. Workplaces deal in highly complex sets of skills, and "talent" consists of all sorts of combinations of qualities. A successful career depends in large part upon finding jobs that elicit and develop one's strengths.

At this point the young black professional must sidestep a new series of traps laid by whites who need to be ostentatiously nonracist. Let's say that William goes to work for the XYZ Corporation, where he is assigned with another management trainee (white) to a department where much of the time is spent preparing proposals for government contracts. The white trainee is assigned a variety of scut work—proofreading drafts, calculating the costs of minor items in the bid, making photocopies, taking notes at conferences. William gets more dignified work. He is assigned portions of the draft to write (which are later rewritten by more experienced staff), sits in on planning sessions, and even goes to Washington as a highly visible part of the team to present the bid. As time goes on, the white trainee learns a great deal about how the company operates, and is seen as a go-getting young member of the team. William is perceived to be a bright enough fellow, but not much of a detail man and not really much of a self-starter.

Even if a black is hired under terms that put him on a par with his white peers, the subtler forms of differential treatment work against him. Particularly for any corporation that does business with the government, the new employee has a specific, immediate value purely because he is black. There are a variety of requirements to be met and rituals to be observed for which a black face is helpful. These have very little to do with the long-term career interests of the new employee; on the contrary, they often lead to a dead end as head of the minority-relations section of the personnel department.

Added to this is another problem that has nothing to do with the government. When the old racism was at fault (as it often still is), the newly hired black employee was excluded from the socialization process because the whites did not want him to become part of the group. When the new racism is at fault, it is because many whites are embarrassed to treat black employees as badly as they are willing to treat whites. Hence another reason that whites get on-the-job training that blacks do not: much of the early training of an employee is intertwined with menial assignments and mild hazing. Blacks who are put through these routines often see themselves as racially abused (and when a black is involved, old-racist responses may well have crept in). But even if the black is not unhappy about the process, the whites are afraid that he is, and so protect him from it. There are many variations, all having the same effect: the black is denied an apprenticeship that the white has no way of escaping. Without serving the apprenticeship, there is no way of becoming part of the team.

Carol suffers a slightly different fate. She and a white woman are hired as reporters by a major newspaper. They both work hard, but after a few months there is no denying it: neither one of them can write. The white woman is let go. Carol is kept on, because the paper cannot afford to have any fewer blacks than it already has. She is kept busy with reportorial work, even though they have to work around the writing problem. She is told not to worry—there's lots more to being a journalist than writing.

It is the mascot syndrome. A white performing at a comparable level would be fired. The black is kept on, perhaps to avoid complications with the Equal Employment Opportunity Commission (it can be very expensive to fire a black), perhaps out of a more diffuse wish not to appear discriminatory. Everybody pretends that nothing is wrong—but the black's career is at a dead end. The irony, of course, is that the white who gets fired and has to try something else has been forced into accepting a chance of making a success in some other line of work whereas the black is seduced into *not* taking the same chance.

Sometimes differential treatment takes an even more pernicious form: the conspiracy to promote a problem out of existence. As part of keeping Carol busy, the newspaper gives her some administrative responsibilities. They do not amount to much. But she has an impressive title on a prominent newspaper and she is black—a potent combination. She gets an offer from a lesser paper in another part of the country to take a senior editorial post. Her current employer is happy to be rid of an awkward situation and sends along glowing references. She gets a job that she is unequipped to handle—only this time, she is in a highly visible position, and within a few weeks the deficiencies that were covered up at the old job have become the subject of jokes all over the office. Most of the jokes are openly racist.

It is important to pause and remember who Carol is: an extremely bright young woman, not (in other circumstances) a likely object of condescension. But being bright is no protection. Whites can usually count on the market to help us recognize egregious career mistakes and to prevent us from being promoted too far from a career line that fits our strengths, and too far above our level of readiness. One of the most prevalent characteristics of white differential treatment of blacks has been to exempt blacks from these market considerations, substituting for them a market premium attached to race.

The most obvious consequence of preferential treatment is that every black professional, no matter how able, is tainted. Every black who is hired by a white-run organization that hires blacks preferentially has to put up with the knowledge that many of his coworkers believe he was hired because of his race; and he has to put up with the suspicion in his own mind that they might be right.

Whites are curiously reluctant to consider this a real problem—it is an abstraction, I am told, much less important than the problem that blacks face in getting a job in the first place. But black professionals talk about it, and they tell stories of mental breakdowns; of people who had to leave the job altogether; of long-term professional paralysis. What white would want to be put in such a situation? Of course it would be a constant humiliation to be resented by some of your coworkers and condescended to by others. Of course it would affect your perceptions of yourself and your self-confidence. No system that produces such side effects—as preferential treatment *must* do—can be defended unless it is producing some extremely important benefits.

And that brings us to the decisive question. If the alternative were no job at all, as it was for so many blacks for so long, the resentment and condescension are part of the price of getting blacks into the positions they deserve. But is that the alternative today? If the institutions of this country were left to their own devices now, to what extent would they refuse to admit, hire, and promote people because they were black? To what extent are American institutions kept from being racist by the government's intervention?

It is another one of those questions that are seldom investigated aggressively, and I have no evidence. Let me suggest a hypothesis that bears looking into: that the signal event in the struggle for black equality during the last thirty years, the one with real impact, was not the Civil Rights Act of 1964 or Executive Order 11246 or any other governmental act. It was the civil rights movement itself. It raised to a pitch of acute and lasting discomfort the racial consciousness of the generations of white Americans who are now running the country. I will not argue that the old racism is dead at any level of society. I will argue, however, that in the typical corporation or in the typical admissions office, there is an abiding desire to be not-racist. This need not be construed as brotherly love. Guilt will do as well. But the civil rights movement did its job. I suggest that the laws and the court decisions and the continuing intellectual respectability behind preferential treatment are not holding many doors open to qualified blacks that would otherwise be closed.

Suppose for a moment that I am right. Suppose that, for practical purposes, racism would not get in the way of blacks if preferential treatment were abandoned. How, in my most optimistic view, would the world look different?

There would be fewer blacks at Harvard and Yale; but they would all be fully competitive with the whites who were there. White students at the state university would encounter a cross-section of blacks who span the full range of ability, including the top levels, just as whites do. College remedial courses would no longer be disproportionately black. Whites rejected by the school they wanted would quit assuming they were kept out because a less-qualified black was admitted in their place. Blacks in big corporations would no longer be shunted off to personnel-relations positions, but would be left on the mainline tracks toward becoming comptrollers and sales managers and chief executive officers. Whites would quit assuming that black colleagues had been hired because they were black. Blacks would quit worrying that they had been hired because they were black.

Would blacks still lag behind? As a population, yes, for a time, and the nation should be mounting a far more effective program to improve elementary and secondary education for blacks than it has mounted in the last few decades. But in years past virtually every ethnic group in America has at one time or another lagged behind as a population, and has eventually caught up. In the process of catching up, the ones who breached the barriers were evidence of the success of that group. Now blacks who breach the barriers tend to be seen as evidence of the inferiority of that group.

And that is the evil of preferential treatment. It perpetuates an impression of inferiority. The system segments whites and blacks who come in contact with each other so as to maximize the likelihood that whites have the advantage in experience and ability. The system then encourages both whites and blacks to behave in ways that create self-fulfilling prophecies even when no real differences exist.

It is here that the new racism links up with the old. The old racism has always openly held that blacks are permanently less competent than whites. The new racism tacitly accepts that, in the course of overcoming the legacy of the old racism, blacks are temporarily less competent than whites. It is an extremely fine distinction. As time goes on, fine distinctions tend to be lost. Preferential treatment is providing persuasive evidence for the old racists, and we can already hear it *sotto voce:* "We gave you your chance, we let you educate them and push them into jobs they couldn't have gotten on their own and coddle them every way you could. And see: they still aren't as good as whites, and you are beginning to admit it yourselves." Sooner or later this message is going to be heard by a white elite that needs to excuse its failure to achieve black equality.

The only happy aspect of the new racism is that the corrective—to get rid of the policies encouraging preferential treatment—is so natural. Deliberate preferential treatment by race has sat as uneasily with America's equal-opportunity ideal during the post-1965 period as it did during the days of legalized segregation. We had to construct tortuous rationalizations when we permitted blacks to be kept on the back of the bus—and the rationalizations to justify sending blacks to the head of the line have been just as tortuous. Both kinds of rationalization say that sometimes it is all right to treat people of different races in different ways. For years, we have instinctively sensed this was wrong in principle but intellectualized our support for it as an expedient. I submit that our instincts were right. There is no such thing as good racial discrimination.

QUESTIONS

1 Are Murray's examples sufficient to support his view that preferential treatment practices should be abandoned because they are a roadblock to the abolition of race-based inequality?
2 Do Murray's examples lend support to the following claim? If we are to become a sexually and racially egalitarian society, what must be eliminated are the sort of subtle discriminations discussed by Rowe in this chapter.

The Case for Racial Preferences: Admitting Success

Derek Bok

Derek Bok is president of Harvard University. He is the author of *Beyond the Ivory Tower: Social Responsibilities of the Modern University* (1982) and *Higher Learning* (1986).

Bok attacks Charles Murray's reasoning and conclusions. First, he challenges Murray's contentions about the effects of preferential treatment programs on black and white attitudes. Second, he argues that historical evidence counts against Murray's contention that the best way to resolve the problems resulting from the past unjust treatment of blacks is to simply treat all applicants equally in admissions and hiring. Third, he points out some of the hoped for long-term results of preferential admissions policies.

Reprinted with permission from *The New Republic,* February 4, 1985.

For 15 years, colleges and universities have sought to increase educational opportunities for minority students by admitting blacks (as well as Hispanics and Native Americans) with SAT scores lower than those of white applicants. Charles Murray criticizes this policy and accuses higher education of helping to foster a new racism. In his view, preferential admissions practices, and affirmative action programs by employers, only demoralize blacks by forcing them to compete beyond their abilities while fostering stereotypes among whites that blacks really are inferior.

Murray offers a simple solution to this problem. Treat all applicants equally in admissions (and hiring), and allow them to make their way without any discrimination or preference on grounds of race. The immediate consequence, he admits, will be a severe drop in the number of black students, especially at more selective colleges and universities. Eventually, however, blacks will participate fully and successfully in American life just as other initially disadvantaged ethnic groups have done.

Murray's arguments are not new. Even so, they may gain a wider following at a time when the nation seems to be reassessing many of its priorities and practices. University administrators need to take the criticisms seriously rather than ignore them in the hope that they will disappear.

Murray mentions only the disappointments and failures of preferential admissions without recognizing its many successes. Since his conclusions are subjective and not based on data, it is also hard to know what to make of his assertions about the effects of preferential admissions on white and black attitudes. For what it's worth, his impressions do not accord with the anonymous survey results at the one institution I know. In a Harvard poll of 1,200 undergraduates conducted in 1978, many students said they suspected that "others" might question the ability of blacks. But less than five percent of black undergraduates felt they had moderate to severe doubts about their own academic ability, and over 75 percent reported no doubts whatsoever. Almost 60 percent of white undergraduates believed that they had no such doubts about blacks, and barely 10 percent indicated moderate or severe doubts.

Historical evidence also cuts against Murray's proposals. In 1965 most colleges and universities outside the South were following the policy that Murray advocates now; they neither discriminated against black applicants nor gave them any preference. And what were the results? A full century after the Civil War, only two percent of the nation's doctors and under two percent of the lawyers were black. Although *Brown* v. *Board of Education* had been decided more than a decade earlier, the proportions of black students preparing for the major professions were still abysmally low. Only slightly more than one percent of the nation's law students were black, and a mere handful of blacks attended the predominantly white graduate schools of medicine and business. Little or no progress had been made in raising these proportions over the preceding generation.

Murray professes a desire to help blacks by warding off a new racism hardly less vicious than the old. If so, he should explain in detail just how his policies would work and why they would fare any better now than they did prior to 1965. It is surely not enough merely to draw an analogy to the experience of other ethnic groups with backgrounds and problems that differ markedly from the legacy of slavery and discrimination that black people have had to overcome. Years of experience with this model yielded little or no progress for blacks and engendered prejudices and resentments just as severe as any that have accompanied affirmative action.

Murray may respond that 1985 is not 1965, and that blacks would now apply and be admitted to universities in much larger numbers than they were 20 years ago. If this is his argument, he should recognize that the very policies he deplores played a major role in encouraging more blacks to seek a college and professional education after 1965. Since he is ultimately concerned with the feelings, attitudes, and stereotypes that result from current admissions practices, he should also explain how universities could suddenly (by his own figures) reduce black enrollments to 1.5 percent or less in scores of selective colleges and professional schools without a devastating effect on the morale and aspirations of blacks—not to mention a strengthening of racial stereotypes on the part of many whites.

I do not mean to overlook the resentments that can arise on the part of whites who feel unjustly excluded from the school of their choice. These disappointments are real, although I wonder why there are not similar resentments against other groups of favored applicants, such as athletes and alumni offspring. I also do not condone everything that has been done in the name of preferential admissions. Some schools have undoubtedly reached too far by admitting blacks with all but insurmountable academic handicaps. Some black students have failed to apply themselves sufficiently, and others have been too quick to reject efforts to help them academically as racist and insulting. Many universities have not been persistent or imaginative enough in developing special ways of assisting blacks and others needing help to overcome deficiencies in their academic backgrounds.

Notwithstanding these defects, most universities have had clear reasons for seeking to admit black students in significant numbers—better reasons, I believe, than those Murray advances to oppose preferential admissions. In the first place, admissions officers do not feel that high scores on SATs and other standardized tests confer a moral entitlement to admission, since such tests are only modestly correlated with subsequent academic success and give no reliable indication of achievement in later life. Instead, they believe that it is educationally enriching for blacks and whites, and important for the country as a whole, for students of all races to live and study together. Academic officials also feel that blacks will have unusual opportunities to contribute to our society in the coming generation and that higher education can play a useful role by helping them to make the most of these possibilities. Finally, educators believe that the growing numbers of black doctors, lawyers, businessmen, and other professionals will serve as examples to encourage more black youths to set higher educational and career goals for themselves.

In adopting these policies, universities have taken the long view. Academic achievement and persistence depend in some significant part on the parents' education, income, and occupation. A promising long-term strategy for helping overcome the racial handicaps of the past is to do what we can to increase the number of blacks with an education, income, and occupational background that will not only serve their own interests, but also help to instill higher educational aspirations and achievement in their children. The hoped-for results may not be fully realized for several decades, and there will be plenty of disappointments along the way. But no one should ever have supposed that we could solve in a single generation problems that were the bitter fruit of so many years of oppression and discrimination.

In the end, the vital question is not whether preferential admission is a success after 15 years, but whether it has made more progress toward overcoming the legacy of discrimination than other strategies that universities might have pursued. On that crucial point, Murray is not convincing. The policies he advances did not work in the past, and he offers no arguments and advances no data to suggest why they would work today. Instead, he gives us his pessimistic impressions of the current situation and compares them unfavorably with his hope of what might occur in some distant, unspecified future if we but followed his prescription. In the face of such arguments, universities should stick by their conviction that a judicious concern for race in admitting students will eventually help to lift the arbitrary burdens that have hampered blacks in striving to achieve their goals in our society.

QUESTIONS

1 Does Bok effectively rebut Murray's central claims?
2 In our society today, how important is a family's economic and educational status to the educational and economic accomplishments of their children?

Opportunity and Equality of Opportunity

Lawrence A. Blum

Lawrence A. Blum is professor of philosophy at the University of Massachusetts. He specializes in social philosophy, political philosophy, and ethics. Blum is the coauthor of *A Truer Liberty: Simone Weil and Marxism* (1989) and the author of *Friendship, Altruism and Morality* (1980), "Compassion," and "Moral Exemplars: Reflections on Schindler, The Tracmes, and Others."

Blum focuses on the notion of competitive opportunity—the opportunity to compete with others for a valued but scarce goal. He argues that equal competitive opportunity does not exist in our society and speculates about how this inequality might be corrected. Blum concludes by arguing that although equality of competitive opportunity does not exist in our society and can never fully exist, it is a worthy social goal.

The idea of "opportunity" is central to the American creed. Americans have traditionally thought of their country as providing opportunity for all—the opportunity to

Reprinted with permission from *Public Affairs Quarterly,* vol. 2 (October 1988), pp. 1–13.

better oneself, to make something of oneself, to get ahead. The individual must take advantage of the opportunity, but the opportunity itself is there. . . .

I OPPORTUNITY AND COMPETITIVE OPPORTUNITY

As it has been understood historically, the notion of "opportunity" presumes some desirable goal and involves the idea that this goal can be achieved or attained by one's own efforts. Work, land, a decent living, a small business requiring little capital to begin: these were the goals for which, historically, opportunities were cherished and sought. Central to this notion of opportunity is that the achieving of this desirable good by the individual is not dependent on his or her social standing, noble birth, or connections. An opportunity is something available if only one takes advantage of it.

This notion of "opportunity" still resonates profoundly in the American consciousness; but the reality to which it once corresponded is increasingly disappearing. Once, as long as one had a reasonable amount of ability, it was possible to open a shop, get some land, or start a small business primarily through one's own efforts. Now large corporations dominate economic life. To start a small business or open a professional practice takes more capital than most Americans can muster. The picture of the individual making his or her way in the world purely on his or her own effort, gumption, and ability has become increasingly obsolete in a world where making a living involves fitting into and striving to advance in large, complex organizations whose nature is determined by political and economic decisions far from the control of the individual.

The new reality of "opportunity" is of the *opportunity to compete with others* for a limited number of desirable positions in society. One has to make application and be considered along with others, many of whom will not be chosen; it is the organization which decides who will get the position—not the individual. What *is* available to the individual, largely independent of connections, birth, race, sex, is only the opportunity to enter this competition. . . .

Let us call the opportunity to compete with others for a valued but scarce goal "competitive opportunity." By and large it is only competitive opportunity, rather than opportunity in its original, "land of opportunity" sense, that is broadly available in our society. Yet by continuing to speak simply of "opportunity," and thus carrying the older associations of the term with it, people are led to think that something is available to them which really is not. If I think of my competing with 100 others for a position in medical school purely as an opportunity to be secured by my own efforts and perseverance, but then I am not admitted, I may tend to think that it is simply my fault that I did not get in, that there is something wrong with me. But this is not necessarily so; it may be that I could readily have done the medical school course and been a competent doctor; there simply were not enough places in the medical schools. So, in contrast to the original notion of "opportunity," when one merely has "*competitive* opportunity" the failure to gain the desired good is no longer something purely in one's own control.

II EQUAL COMPETITIVE OPPORTUNITY AND MERITOCRACY

Although "competitive opportunity" is a much diminished notion of "opportunity," it is still important in its own right as a notion of opportunity suited to our own current realities; we must therefore examine it as well.

The idea of competitive opportunity links up with a view of society called "meritocracy." According to this view, among the aspirants competing for a particular position of responsibility in society, the person with the greatest *ability* to fill that position is the one who is, or should be, chosen, and who therefore is to receive the greater rewards attaching to that position. Selection based on ability alone is central to meritocracy. People's final place in society should have to do only with their abilities and efforts, not with their race, sex, class background, family, and other accidents of birth over which they had no control. If some factor other than ability determines who fills responsible positions in society, not only is this unfair to the individual but it is bad for the society as well, since the most able person will not have been chosen for the job. So an organization or society is meritocratic, and in that sense both fair and efficient, if it embodies "equal competitive opportunity" (or, as it is usually called, "equal opportunity"), that is, if positions within the society are determined only by ability and not by irrelevant factors.

We can illustrate the notion of equal competitive opportunity with the example of physical disability. Imagine a blind college student hoping to go on to law school. At the college in question there are no special provisions for blind persons—no braille markings, no readers for blind students, no attempt of the professors to facilitate the learning of blind students (e.g. by always saying out loud everything they write on the board). On the other hand, the blind student is not prevented from doing the best she can. She is not excluded from taking any classes or participating in any activities.

Can it be claimed that this student has an equal opportunity with everyone else to do well in college and compete for a slot in law school? After all nothing prevents her from striving to achieve a grade point average necessary to get into law school. If she wishes to hire a tutor to help her she can do so. Perhaps she does have a harder time of it than the sighted students; but still she has as much opportunity as anyone else; or so it might be claimed.

Yet this claim is not true; the blind student's opportunities are *not* equal to those of the other students. Compared to them, everything is made more difficult for her. It is not only her *abilities* but her *blindness* which affects how well she is able to gain the qualifications for law school. It would only be *equal* opportunity if the college facilitated the blind student's having no more difficulty than sighted students in availing herself of the resources of the college. What is true of the blind student in the situation described is that she has *some* (competitive) opportunity—but not that she has *equal* (competitive) opportunity.

Why is this? It is because the notion of equal (competitive) opportunity involves something like a race. The race is fair—each contestant has "equal opportunity"—if each one starts from the same place, so that the winner is the person with the most ability, effort, stamina, and the like. The race is *not* fair if *not* everyone starts at the same starting line. Analogously, the blind student's performance in college must depend only on her academic abilities, and not on her physical disability; if it depended on the latter it would be as if she were beginning behind the starting line. For her to have equal opportunity, the college must provide support services for her.

Providing equal opportunity for all students, including handicapped ones, thus requires unequal expenditure. The blind student needs to be provided, at the college's expense, with a reader or tutor not provided to everyone else. Nevertheless this is not advantaging the blind student at the expense of the others, but only bringing her to the same starting point. The blind student should not pay for her own reader, since this requires from her an expense which the other students do not have to bear in order to reach the same point (namely to read the material for classes). In the absence of the supplementary expenses the blind student has only *some* but *unequal* (competitive) opportunity. But a pure meritocracy requires not only some opportunity but equal opportunity.

III   THE REALITY OF COMPETITIVE OPPORTUNITY

This is the theory of meritocracy and equal competitive opportunity. But is it the reality? In particular, do people in our society *actually* gain valued positions and rewards solely on the basis of their abilities? Are the successful ones always those with the greatest ability, independent of background, race, sex, connections, and the like? Is there really *equal* competitive opportunity, or only *some but unequal* competitive opportunity?

It is evident that equal competitive opportunity does not in fact exist in our country, for many reasons. In many areas women and minorities are at a disadvantage even if they are fully qualified for a position. Sometimes the reason is outright racism or sexism on the part of those choosing people for positions—the white males doing most of the hiring may just prefer other white males rather than minorities or women. Often the discrimination is more subtle. Women and minorities are simply not perceived to be qualified even when they actually *are* qualified. A qualified woman is seen, perhaps entirely unwittingly, as "aggressive," a black as "uppity." The law may not sanction this discrimination; but it exists nevertheless.

This sort of racism and sexism is now generally acknowledged, and some efforts—gathered under the general rubric of "affirmative action"—have been made to correct for it, though such efforts have diminished in recent years and the Reagan administration has mounted a strong attack (though an only partially successful one) on them. One aspect of affirmative action does itself involve at least a short-term denial of competitive equality of opportunity. More qualified white males are sometimes turned down in favor of less qualified blacks or women (or both). This development is, however, weaker, especially in recent years, than the public perception of it, especially among white males. Moreover, this so-called "reverse discrimination" is certainly a much less powerful and widespread phenomenon than the original sexism and racism which occasioned it in the first place. And, finally, it may be that this inequality of competitive opportunity in the present is the best method for achieving true equality of competitive opportunity in the future, at least with regard to sex and race.

The controversy over affirmative action programs has actually served to cover over the deeper significance of the notion of "equal (competitive) opportunity." *Both* sides in the controversy have tended to see their position as expressing "equal opportunity," and the impression has been given that the notion of equal opportunity primarily concerns whether sex and race are to be taken into account in determining who gets jobs and places in professional schools.

But equal (competitive) opportunity is a much more general and significant idea than this, and discrimination on the basis of sex and race is by no means the only form of its denial. Persons can fail to be judged purely on ability because they have not gone to certain colleges or professional schools, because they do not know the right people, because they do not present themselves in a certain way. And, again, sometimes this sort of discrimination takes place without either those doing the discriminating or those being discriminated against realizing it. It can be quite subtle. Often these denials of equal opportunity have a lot to do with class background, as well as race or sex, or with a combination of these. For example a typical study showed that of two children with the same native abilities, the one born into the top socio-economic tenth is twelve times more likely to complete college than the one born into the bottom tenth.[1]

So our society certainly does not at this point provide equality of competitive opportunity. And yet the distance from true equality of competitive opportunity is even greater than we have mentioned so far. For we have been discussing only the situation of people with the "best" qualifications or ability failing to gain the position they seek, because of discrimination. But often there is not equal opportunity to acquire the qualifications relevant to a job in the first place. Discrimination at an earlier stage in a person's history can deny someone the equal opportunity to *acquire* qualifications. Suppose there are two candidates for a position in a medical school. Joan has had to work forty hours a week to support herself during college. While she has done relatively well, her financial and work situation have cut into her capacity to do as well as her abilities might allow for. Ted is not pressed by the same economic necessities and is able to attain higher grades than Joan, even though they each have (let us assume) roughly equal natural ability.

Let us assume that in admitting candidates to medical school, the actual qualifications of Joan and Ted are acknowledged and judged accurately, and that there is none of the sex, class, or race discrimination mentioned above. In this sense Joan and Ted have equal competitive opportunity—each is judged on qualifications alone. Yet in another sense do we not feel that full equality of competitive opportunity has not been provided? For while Joan has had *some* opportunity to acquire the qualifications for medical school, this opportunity has not really been *equal* to that of Ted. She has been disadvantaged in the *acquiring of qualifications* by her economic class position.

The idea of equal competitive opportunity within meritocracy really depends on selecting people according to *ability* and not simply *qualifications*. For it is the actual ability to carry out the responsibilities of the position (engineer, manager) which should be the basis of selection for the position. Of course it is often not practical to disregard qualifications in favor of judging ability directly (nor is the distinction between these always an easy, or even possible, one to draw). But this is precisely why it is so important to remove obstacles to people's having the equal access to acquiring the qualifications which are consonant with their abilities. Given the practicalities—that qualifications rather than ability are the usual criteria of selection—any denial of this equal access is a significant injustice in regard to equal competitive opportunity.

IV CORRECTING FOR UNEQUAL COMPETITIVE OPPORTUNITY

In these ways "equal competitive opportunity," like the original "opportunity for all," is a myth, not a reality, in our society. And yet even if we acknowledge that this is so, it is important to look at the resources that our system has for correction of this situation. Perhaps in time changes in attitude and practices could, with proper effort, erase the sources of discrimination which deny equal competitive opportunity. Bias and discrimination, it could be said, are distortions within the overall system; they can be corrected for within the system.

In order to evaluate this possibility, we must have a clearer picture of what it would be like for equality of competitive opportunity actually to exist. Let us take the crucial area of schools, which are rightly seen as an important underpinning of whatever degree of competitive opportunity actually exists. Schools are seen as the great equalizer; students from diverse backgrounds can equally develop their particular abilities in school. If schooling works properly in a democratic society it can provide the "same starting point" from which each can go on to compete against the others for the desirable positions in society.

Clearly some schools are in fact much better than other schools; and equally clearly a student emerging from a better school has an advantage, everything else being equal, over one emerging from a worse one. This is partly because better schools provide a better education. But it is also because if the better school also has a reputation for being better, then its students will be *thought* to be better educated to an even greater degree than they actually *are* better educated. And this will give them an advantage in being admitted for example to colleges, or to getting a job. Even if the student from Harvard has really done no better than the student from State University, the former will, in general, have an advantage over the latter, just because she *is* from Harvard. Despite the initial disadvantage, the graduate of the less excellent or prestigious college may end up doing as well as the Harvard graduate, but the point is that her chance of doing so is less than the latter's, and this is precisely what it means to say that she has less than equal opportunity.

Thus for truly equal competitive opportunity it would be necessary to eliminate, or at least greatly reduce, such strong differences in quality between schools; all schools would have to be (roughly) equally capable of developing pupils' abilities. (There would have to be "leveling up" rather than "leveling down.") There are many elements which make one school superior to another; but one contributory factor is certainly financial. Thus one necessary (though by no means sufficient) part of creating equality of competitive opportunity would be to provide some rough equality in the financial resources available to different schools. Students going to school in poorer areas, such as Charlestown or Roxbury, would have comparable educational resources to students in wealthier areas, like Wellesley or Weston. (These are all communities in the Boston area.) To do this would of course be quite a radical change from our current form of financing education, in which communities fund their schools according to their own quite divergent financial resources. But true equality of competitive opportunity would seem to require this.

Other changes in schools would probably also be necessary. If private schools existed in a meritocracy they would have to be prevented from becoming a stratum of schools distinctly superior to the public ones; otherwise people who could afford private schools would have too much advantage over those who could not. (The system would have to be more like the California higher education system than the Massachusetts one.) The quality of the public schools would have to be made to keep pace with the privates (if the latter became, for a time, superior) to prevent the snowball effect of advantage breeding greater advantage. (This is not to deny that there may be other reasons—such as tolerance for innovation and variety—in favor of retaining private schools.)

Another way in which the provision of genuine equality of competitive opportunity would require quite radical changes concerns equal opportunity between men and women. As long as women are regarded as having a greater responsibility than men for the day-to-day running of the household and for the care of their family, there can not be *equal* competitive opportunity between men and women. For such responsibility makes it much more difficult to sustain a demanding full-time job; makes it somewhat less likely that a woman will exert the effort to acquire the necessary qualifications; makes it more likely that she will be discouraged by others (especially her husband) from attempting to secure a full-time demanding job. It seems that equal competitive opportunity in the world of work would require virtual equality between men and women in their responsibilities regarding home and family. The provision of equal competitive opportunity between men and women would require a radical shift in the current sexual division of labor and the organization of the family.

The examples of school and of male/female inequality suggest that inequalities in competitive opportunity are not merely distortions within the American system, but are rather quite deeply rooted in that system itself. They could not be corrected merely by eliminating biased attitudes of individuals, for they are embodied in structural aspects of that system. It would not be enough for teachers to not favor middle class over working class children in their classroom, or for employers to regard male and female applicants in a gender-blind way; for the inequality is rooted in the superiority of the middle class school itself and in the gender-biased structure of domestic responsibilities.

To say that the inequalities are structural does not by itself mean that we should not try as much as possible to *reduce* these departures from equality of competitive opportunity by working to change those biased and stereotyped attitudes as much as possible. But it does mean that equality of competitive opportunity can not be brought about without radical and structural changes in our system.

V   CAN COMPETITIVE OPPORTUNITIES EVER BE EQUAL?

And yet there is an even deeper problem with the idea of equality of competitive opportunity than those just discussed. This is a problem with the very idea that opportunity which is *competitive* could ever also be *equal*. For equality of competitive opportunity involves the equal opportunity to become unequal. The goal for which one wants opportunity is a position on a ladder, or hierarchy—a position (e.g. doctor, executive) in which one's financial and status rewards are higher than those of positions below oneself on that scale (e.g. sales clerk, machine operator). This is the whole point of the competitive nature of equality of (competitive) opportunity, as expressed in the analogy of the "race"—each individual should have an equal chance to beat the other person.

But there is a problem of carrying this inequality of rewards into an equality of (competitive) opportunity for the next generation. Imagine a hypothetical society with true equal competitive opportunity, in which there is no discrimination due to race, sex, family background, connections, and the like. How about the next generation, the children of the persons in this hypothetical society? True equality of competitive opportunity would mean that despite the inequalities in their parents' life situations, the children would compete on an equal basis (on ability and effort alone). However, out of love for their children, or from a consciousness of family status, or for other reasons, the advantaged people from the first generation would naturally try to pass on the advantages of their positions to their children. This would result in the children from more successful families having competitive advantages over those from less successful families in the younger generation's competition for positions in society.

The high-status parents would attempt to assure better education for their children, using their superior financial resources and influence to do so. They would have a better understanding of the characteristics, both of mind and of personality, which make for success in the society; and they would be able to be more successful in passing this knowledge and these characteristics on to their children. Through living in this world of the professionals and executives, these children would gain a greater understanding than children of the waitresses and machine operators of what that world demands and how to behave within it. They would make "contacts" which, no matter how meritocratic a society is, inevitably play some part in "getting ahead." They would try to shape the rules of the competition to favor their own children's success.

Remember that we are not here imagining our own actual society, in which the inequalities of opportunity are much greater, but a hypothetical society of equal competitive opportunity. In such a society the factors which lead to inequality in the opportunities of the children would, in contrast to our own society, be mitigated by mechanisms of equal opportunity present (by hypothesis) in the larger society—equal schools, fair assessment of ability, and the like. Schools, for example, would to some extent "even out" the inequalities in family advantages. But the advantages of children of the successful would still remain substantial, undermining any claim of the society to represent true equality of (competitive) opportunity.

For the second generation and every subsequent one in our hypothetical society there would be only unequal competitive opportunity. Moreover, as each generation became more accustomed to these inequalities, influencing their expectations and aspirations, the inequalities would become progressively more solid and rigid, constituting a substantial counterweight against the forces promoting true equality of competitive opportunity in the outer society.

It seems then that "equality of competitive opportunity" is essentially impossible; it could not be achieved past one generation. For the equality at the starting point is undercut by the inequality at the end point. The only way in which this contradiction could be resolved, it seems, is by giving every child an environment which was independent of his or her family's actual position in the reward structure of the meritocratic society. Only then could one be sure of preventing a child's being advantaged, or disadvantaged, by the accident of his or her birth. . . .

In summary, then, our society still holds an image of itself as providing "opportunity for all"—an image of individuals choosing, pursuing, and reaching goals by their own effort alone. Such an image is largely historically obsolete (and for a large number of citizens and slaves was never true in any case), as our complex bureaucratic and industrial society has rendered such pure individualism largely a thing of the past.

More recently the meritocratic ideal of "equality of competitive opportunity" has arisen to preserve some notion of opportunity in changed conditions. We have seen that this notion represents a substantial come-down from the original "opportunity for all"—a pale imitation of that grand inspiring ideal which animates American creed and ideology.

To add insult to injury, we have also seen that equality of competitive opportunity itself is not a reality in our country; at best we have *inequality* of competitive opportunity. Finally we have seen that this inequality is no superficial element in the system under which we live; rather it is built into its very fabric. Even if equality of competitive opportunity could be achieved at the starting point, it could not last past one generation, for the inequalities which result from the competition would necessarily render unequal the opportunities in the next generation.

Though equality of competitive opportunity does not exist and can never fully exist, it is nevertheless a worthy social goal. Making our schools more equal; making the situation of men and women more equal in the home and at work; reducing the degree to which people who make a lot of money can thereby pass advantages on to their offspring who have done nothing to earn them; making the rewards for different jobs much less grossly unequal than they are now; trying to rid individuals and institutions of biased attitudes and practices—all these are important tasks, even if they cannot achieve complete equality of (competitive) opportunity.

Such goals are often resisted on the grounds that they seem to restrict the ability of those with money to do what they want with that money—to buy superior education, connections, opportunities for their children. Such a concern can not simply be dismissed without much further exploration beyond the scope of my discussion here; like equality of opportunity, this kind of freedom too has deep roots in our country's public philosophy. Nevertheless it is difficult to see how the unrestricted freedom to dispose of one's financial resources could itself be as fundamental a principle as that of equal opportunity. Furthermore, what seems a restraint on freedom is often relative to one's options and to what one is accustomed to. Because we are used to gross differences in quality among schools in different locales, many persons with money feel it an outrageous constraint not to be able to send their children to the "best" schools. But if schools were themselves more equal in (high) quality, there would not be such an imperative to buy one's children's way into the best ones. If people were used to a society, such as Denmark and Sweden, more closely approaching equality of competitive opportunity than does our own, its institutions would be experienced as involving less of a restraint on freedom than they do to people in our society.[2]. . .

NOTES

1 For this and comparable statistics, see Richard de Lone, *Small Futures: Children, Inequality, and the Limits of Liberal Reform* (New York: Harcourt, Brace, Jovanovich, 1979), pp. 209 ff.

2 This paper was written in connection with a course on "Equality" at the University of Massachusetts at Boston. I would like to thank the many students in that course over the years whose responses to earlier drafts have so shaped the paper. I would also like to thank Tony Skillen, Richard Norman, and Judy Smith for comments on an earlier draft.

QUESTIONS

1 If individuals do not have an equal opportunity to develop their abilities, can it correctly be said that they have an equal opportunity to compete for some position when the hiring decision is made on the basis of *developed abilities?*

2 What sorts of changes would have to be made in our educational institutions in order to promote greater equality of competitive opportunity?

SUGGESTED ADDITIONAL READINGS FOR CHAPTER 7

BEAUCHAMP, TOM L.: "The Justification of Reverse Discrimination." In William T. Blackstone and Robert Heslep, eds., *Social Justice and Preferential Treatment.* Athens: University of Georgia Press, 1976. Beauchamp offers a utilitarian argument in favor of policies productive of reverse discrimination in hiring. He proffers "factual evidence" to support his claim that such policies are a necessary means to achieve a morally desirable end—the demise of the continued discrimination against women and blacks.

COHEN, MARSHALL, THOMAS NAGEL, and THOMAS SCANLON, eds.: *Equality and Preferential Treatment.* Princeton, N.J.: Princeton University Press, 1977. This is an excellent collection of articles which, with one exception, originally appeared in different volumes of *Philosophy and Public Affairs.* The authors include Thomas Nagel, George Sher, Ronald Dworkin, Owen M. Fiss, Alan H. Goldman, Judith Jarvis Thomson, and Robert Simon. Ronald Dworkin's article, which was not originally published in *Philosophy and Public Affairs,* is especially interesting insofar as Dworkin compares and contrasts the issues raised by two important legal decisions—the first dealing with a 1945 admittance policy which denied a black man admittance to the University of Texas Law School, the second with a 1971 admissions policy which worked to keep a white male (DeFunis) out of the University of Washington Law School.

GROSS, BARRY R., ed.: *Reverse Discrimination.* Buffalo, N.Y.: Prometheus, 1977. This anthology includes some well-known articles on the topic, including those of Sidney Hook, Lisa H. Newton, Bernard Boxhill, and Alan H. Goldman. The large collection of articles is organized into three sections, labeled "Facts and Polemics," "The Law," and "Value."

HELD, VIRGINIA: "Reasonable Progress and Self-Respect." *The Monist,* vol. 57, January 1973, pp. 12–27. Held focuses on two questions: How long is it reasonable to expect the victims of past discrimination to wait for a redress of their wrongs? What reasonable rate of progress would not involve a loss of self-respect?

KATZNER, LOUIS: "Is the Favoring of Women and Blacks in Employment and Educational Opportunities Justified?" In Joel Feinberg and Hyman Gross, eds., *Philosophy of Law.* Encino, Calif.: Dickenson, 1975, pp. 291–296. Katzner's argument for the justification of reverse discrimination is based on the claim that the obligation to compensate for past wrongs justifies present policies productive of reverse discrimination.

SHER, GEORGE: "Reverse Discrimination, the Future, and the Past." *Ethics,* vol. 90, October 1979, pp. 81–87. Sher analyzes and criticizes some of the "forward-looking arguments" made to support preferential treatment programs.

THALBERG, IRVING: "Justification of Institutional Racism." *Philosophical Forum* (Boston), vol. 3, Winter 1972, pp. 243–264. Thalberg criticizes the arguments of those who oppose the kinds of changes which, on his view, are necessary to equalize the economic and political status of blacks.

WARREN, MARY ANNE: "Secondary Sexism and Quota Hiring." *Philosophy and Public Affairs,* vol. 6, 1977, pp. 240–261. Warren argues that there exist certain discriminatory practices that although not explicitly based on sex, *de facto* discriminate against women. To counter this ongoing discrimination, she contends, minimum numerical quotas for the hiring and promotion of women are necessary.

WASSERSTROM, RICHARD: "A Defense of Programs of Preferential Treatment." *National Forum, The Phi Kappa Phi Journal,* vol. LVIII, no. 1, Winter 1978, pp. 15–18. Wasserstrom primarily attacks two arguments against preferential treatment programs.

CHAPTER 8

Economic Justice
and Welfare

Should everyone in an affluent society be guaranteed a minimum income? Should people be required to work for that income even if they do not want to work? Should they even be required to work at menial jobs they dislike? Is it morally correct to tax the income of those who work to provide incomes for those who do not? Questions such as these fall in the domain of economic justice. Answering them requires theorizing about what constitutes an economically just society. And this in turn involves us in questions about the part that a just government ought to play in the economic sphere and about the justifiable limits of government interference with individual liberty.

AN ECONOMICALLY JUST SOCIETY

In a short story called "The Babylon Lottery," Jorge Luis Borges describes a society in which all societal benefits and obligations are distributed solely on the basis of a periodic lottery. Simply as the result of chance, an individual may be a slave at one period, an influential government official the following period, and a person sentenced to jail the third one. When the temporary social and economic status of the individual is determined, no account is taken of the actual contribution the individual has made to society during a preceding period or of the individual's merit, effort, or need.[1] Such a situation strikes us as capricious. We are accustomed to think that there are some valid principles according to which a society's economic goods are distributed, even if we disagree about what principles ought to be operative in an economically just society. In the United States, for example, certain forms of government assistance such as Aid to Families with Dependent Children (AFDC) are sometimes said to be distributed on the basis of need; promotions in government offices and business firms are supposedly awarded on the basis of merit and achievement; and the high incomes of physicians and lawyers are assumed to be due them on the basis of either the contribution they make to society or the effort they exert in preparing for their professions.

---

[1]Jorge Luis Borges, "The Babylon Lottery," in *Ficciones* (New York: Grove Press, 1956).

Whether, and to what extent, merit and achievement, need, effort, or productive contribution ought to be taken into account in the distribution of society's benefits are basic questions of economic justice. In responding to these questions, philosophers propose and defend various principles of economic justice. According to their proposals, the wealth of society ought to be distributed on the basis of one or more of the following sorts of principles.

1 To each individual an equal share
2 To each individual according to that individual's needs
3 To each individual according to that individual's ability, merit, or achievement
4 To each individual according to that individual's effort
5 To each individual according to that individual's actual productive contribution

We will briefly discuss the second principle since it is especially relevant to the readings in the chapter.

If distribution is to be made on the basis of needs, it is necessary to determine just what "needs" are to be considered. Are we to consider only essential or basic needs, such as the needs for food, clothing, shelter, and health care? Or are we to consider other human needs as well, such as the needs for aesthetic satisfaction and intellectual stimulation? Whether the principle of need is accepted as the sole determinant of a just economic distribution within the society or as only one of those determinants, we need to select some way of ranking needs. If, on the one hand, the principle of need is the sole determinant of economic justice, we must first determine which needs take precedence—which needs must be satisfied before the satisfaction of other less important needs is even considered. Then, if our society has the means to meet not only these basic needs but other less essential ones, we should find some way of ranking the latter. (For example, does an artist's need for subsidy take precedence over a scientist's need to satisfy his or her intellectual curiosity about the existence of life on Mars?) If, on the other hand, the principle of need is to be taken as only one of the determinants of economic justice, we ought to determine which needs must be satisfied before some other principle can be used as the basis for distributing the rest of society's wealth.

Note that if either or both of the first two principles are held to be the determinants of economic justice, the individual's own efforts, achievements, abilities, or productive contribution to society are not taken into account in determining that individual's benefits. When the claim is made, for example, that each family in a society ought to be guaranteed a minimum yearly income, the moral justification for this claim is often given either in terms of the principle of need or in terms of the conjunction of that principle and the principle of equal sharing: All human beings, just because they are human beings, are entitled to equal treatment in some important respects; they are entitled, for example, to have at least their most basic needs met by the society to which they belong.

Philosophers, economists, and others vehemently disagree about whether the principle of need (or the principle of need in conjunction with the principle of equal sharing) is a morally acceptable principle of economic justice. Their disagreements stem in large measure from their different conceptions of the moral ideal around which the institutions of any just society ought to be organized. To understand three of the major positions on the relation between need and economic justice, it is necessary to understand the part played by certain moral ideals in theories about (1) the morally correct role of the government in economic activity and (2) the justifiable limits of government interference with individual liberty.

LIBERTY, EQUALITY, NEED, AND GOVERNMENT INTERFERENCE

Two moral ideals, liberty and equality, are of key importance in conceptions of justice in general, and economic justice in particular. A *libertarian* or *individualist* conception of justice (sometimes labeled the "classic liberal" view) holds *liberty* to be the ultimate moral ideal. A *socialist* conception of justice takes *social equality* to be the ultimate ideal; and a *liberal* conception of justice tries to combine both equality and liberty into one ultimate moral ideal.

The Libertarian Conception of Justice

For the libertarian, a society is just when individual liberty is maximized. To understand the libertarian position on liberty, it is necessary to see that liberty is not synonymous with freedom. Freedom is the broader category; liberty is one aspect of freedom. If freedom is understood as the overall absence of constraint, liberty can be understood as the absence of a specific kind of constraint—*coercion,* the forceful and deliberate interference by human beings in the affairs of other human beings. Coercion can take two forms—either the direct use of physical force or the threat of harm, backed up by enforcement power. An example will illustrate why liberty is not synonymous with freedom. In some countries, citizens need a government permit to live and work in certain cities. Thus their freedom, more specifically their liberty, to go to live and work in those cities is restricted by coercion, the threat of harm should they disobey the rules. In the United States, citizens do not need such permits. There are no laws that threaten them with harm should they choose to move to New York City or Los Angeles. But not everyone who wants to do so is free to go to live and work in either city. All kinds of constraints may prevent it. Individuals may not have the money for transportation, for example, and this lack may limit their freedom to do what they wish to do. The jobs they are capable of doing may not be available and this lack, too, may prevent them from moving to the city of their choice. So individual freedom may be limited in many different ways. It is important to see that when libertarians advocate the maximization of liberty, they are not concerned with maximizing freedom in general. Their focus is on minimizing coercion, especially on minimizing the coercive interferences of governments.

On a libertarian view, individuals have certain *moral rights* to life, liberty, and property that any just society must recognize and respect. These rights are sometimes described as *warnings against interference:* If A has a right to X, no one should prevent A from pursuing X or deprive A of X, since A is entitled to it. According to a libertarian, the sole function of the government is to protect the individual's life, liberty, and property against force and fraud. Everything else in society is a matter of individual responsibility, decision, and action. Providing for the welfare of those who cannot or will not provide for themselves is not a morally justifiable function of government. To make such provisions, the government would have to take from some against their will in order to give to others. This is perceived as an unjustifiable coercive limitation on individual liberty. Individuals own their own bodies (or lives) and, therefore, the labor they exert. It follows, for the libertarian, that individuals have the right to whatever income or wealth their labor can earn in a free marketplace. Taxing some to give to others is analogous to robbery. John Hospers, who defends a libertarian position in this chapter, argues that laws requiring people to help one another (e.g., via welfare payments) rob Peter to pay Paul.

The Socialist Conception of Justice

A direct challenge to libertarians comes from those who defend a socialist conception of justice. Although there are many varieties of socialism, one common element in socialist thought is a commitment to social equality and to government or collective measures furthering that equality. These measures include the collective ownership of productive property. Since social equality is the ultimate ideal, limitations on individual liberty that are necessary to promote equality are seen as justified. Socialists attack libertarian views on the primacy of liberty, in at least three ways. *First,* they offer defenses of their ideal of social equality. These take various forms and will not concern us here. *Second,* they point out the meaninglessness of libertarian rights to those who lack adequate food, shelter, health care, etc. For those who lack the money to buy the food and health care needed to sustain life, the libertarian right to life is an empty sham. The rights of liberty, such as the right to freedom of speech, are a joke to those who cannot exercise them because of economic considerations. *Third,* some defenders of socialism argue that most people will have much more freedom in a socialist system than in a libertarian one because they will have more control over their economic lives. The freedom that the socialist wants to maximize, however, requires a society in which individuals have the greatest possible range of choices and not simply one in which government interference is minimal. Defenders of socialism may use the word "liberty" in discussing the freedom that they believe a socialist system will maximize, but it is important to recognize the difference between the way they use "liberty" and the notion of liberty explicated above. Thus where libertarians stress liberty, understood as freedom from coercion, especially from government interference, socialists stress freedom from want. Where libertarians stress *negative* rights (rights not to be interfered with), socialists stress *positive rights* —rights *to* food, health care, productive work, etc. Where libertarians criticize socialism for the limitations it imposes on liberty, socialists criticize libertarianism for allowing gross inequalities among those who are "equally human."

The Liberal Conception of Justice

Like the socialist, the liberal rejects the libertarian conception of justice since that conception does not include what liberals perceive as a fundamental moral concern. Any purported conception of justice that does not require those who have more than enough to help those in need is morally unacceptable to liberals. Henry Shue's reasoning in an article in this chapter is in line with liberal thinking. He argues that all human beings have a basic right to minimal economic security. In his view this is a positive right that must be socially guaranteed. Socialists and liberals also agree in recognizing the extent to which economic constraints in an industrial society effectively limit the exercise of libertarian rights by those lacking economic power. Unlike many socialists, however, liberals consider some of the libertarian's negative rights extremely important and advocate social institutions that do two important things—ensure certain basic liberties for all (e.g., freedom of speech) and yet provide for the economic needs of the disadvantaged members of society. Liberals also differ from socialists insofar as they do not advocate the communal ownership of the means of production. Nor do liberals oppose all social and economic inequalities. Liberals disagree among themselves, however, concerning both the morally acceptable extent of such inequalities and their correct justification. A utilitarian committed to a liberal position might hold that inequalities are justified to the extent that allowing them maximizes the total amount of good in a society. If, for example, increased productivity depends on giving workers a significantly higher income than that given to those collecting welfare,[2] and if such incentive-stimulated productivity increases the total amount of good in a society, then the inequalities between the assembly-line worker and the welfare recipient would be justified for the utilitarian. A different approach, argued for by John Rawls,[3] maintains that only those inequalities of social goods are justified that will contribute to raising the position of the *least*-advantaged groups in the society. Here the concern is not with the total amount of good in a society but with the good of the least advantaged. In this view, income inequalities necessary for productivity gains are justified only if the productivity gains function to benefit those in the lowest economic strata.

Libertarianism, Liberalism, and Welfare

Some of the practical ramifications of the libertarian and liberal conceptions of justice are brought out in Trudy Govier's article in this chapter. Govier is concerned with the question, "Should the needy have a legal right to welfare benefits?" Working from a liberal point of view, Govier criticizes the libertarian (individualist) posi-

---

[2]Just what constitutes *welfare* or a welfare program is a matter of dispute. Many would include a number of very different programs under this heading, e.g., unemployment benefits paid out of a fund supported by a mandatory payroll tax paid by employers, social security benefits paid out of a fund supported by a mandatory payroll tax on both employers and employees, Medicaid programs paid out of state and federal funds, and AFDC paid out of state and federal funds. Usually, when what is at issue is a contrast between the incomes of workers and welfare recipients, the welfare in question includes such payments as AFDC, food stamps, and Medicaid.

[3]John Rawls, *A Theory of Justice* (Cambridge, Mass: Harvard University Press, 1971).

tion on welfare. Her arguments for a legal right to welfare are based on both utilitarian and justice considerations. On Govier's analysis, the morally appropriate approach to welfare is what she calls the *permissive* approach. The permissive approach holds that in societies with sufficient resources, the right to welfare should be unconditional. On this view, the right to receive benefits should not depend on one's attitude or behavior—on one's willingness to work, for example—but simply on need. Proponents of what are called *workfare programs* challenge this approach. Workfare programs, described and defended by Peter Germanis in this chapter, require employable recipients to work for their welfare benefits. In another reading in this chapter, Mary Hawkesworth attacks workfare programs and the justifications commonly advanced in their support.

Jane S. Zembaty

What Libertarianism Is

John Hospers

John Hospers is professor of philosophy at the University of Southern California and past editor of *Pacific Philosophical Quarterly*. His books include *Human Conduct: Problems of Ethics* (1972), *Libertarianism: A Political Philosophy for Tomorrow* (1971), *Understanding the Arts* (1982), and *An Introduction to Philosophical Analysis* (3d ed., 1988).

Hospers defends two ideas central to libertarianism: (1) Individuals own their own lives. They, therefore, have the right to act as they choose unless their actions interfere with the liberty of others to act as they choose; (2) The only appropriate function of government is to protect human rights, understood as negative rights (i.e., rights of noninterference).

The political philosophy that is called libertarianism (from the Latin *libertas,* liberty) is the doctrine that every person is the owner of his own life, and that no one is the owner of anyone else's life; and that consequently every human being has the right to act in accordance with his own choices, unless those actions infringe on the equal liberty of other human beings to act in accordance with *their* choices.

There are several other ways of stating the same libertarian thesis:

1 *No one is anyone else's master, and no one is anyone else's slave.* Since I am the one to decide how my life is to be conducted, just as you decide about yours, I have no right (even if I had the power) to make you my slave and be your master, nor have you the right to become the master by enslaving me. Slavery is *forced* servitude, and since no one owns the life of anyone else, no one has the right to enslave

Reprinted with permission of Nelson-Hall Inc., Publishers from Tibor R. Machan, ed., *The Libertarian Alternative* (1974).

another. Political theories past and present have traditionally been concerned with who should be the master (usually the king, the dictator, or government bureaucracy) and who should be the slaves, and what the extent of the slavery should be. Libertarianism holds that no one has the right to use force to enslave the life of another, or any portion or aspect of that life.

2 *Other men's lives are not yours to dispose of.* I enjoy seeing operas; but operas are expensive to produce. Opera-lovers often say, "The state (or the city, etc.) should subsidize opera, so that we can all see it. Also it would be for people's betterment, cultural benefit, etc." But what they are advocating is nothing more or less than legalized plunder. They can't pay for the productions themselves, and yet they want to see opera, which involves a large number of people and their labor; so what they are saying in effect is, "Get the money through legalized force. Take a little bit more out of every worker's paycheck every week to pay for the operas we want to see." But I have no right to take by force from the workers' pockets to pay for what I want.

Perhaps it would be better if he *did* go to see opera—then I should try to convince him to go voluntarily. But to take the money from him forcibly, because in my opinion it would be good for *him,* is still seizure of his earnings, which is plunder.

Besides, if I have the right to force him to help pay for my pet projects, hasn't he equally the right to force me to help pay for his? Perhaps he in turn wants the government to subsidize rock-and-roll, or his new car, or a house in the country? If I have the right to milk him, why hasn't he the right to milk me? If I can be a moral cannibal, why can't he too?

We should beware of the inventors of utopias. They would remake the world according to their vision—with the lives and fruits of the labor of *other* human beings. Is it someone's utopian vision that others should build pyramids to beautify the landscape? Very well, then other men should provide the labor; and if he is in a position of political power, and he can't get men to do it voluntarily, then he must *compel* them to "cooperate"—i.e. he must enslave them.

A hundred men might gain great pleasure from beating up or killing just one insignificant human being; but other men's lives are not theirs to dispose of. "In order to achieve the worthy goals of the next five-year-plan, we must forcibly collectivize the peasants . . ."; but other men's lives are not theirs to dispose of. Do you want to occupy, rent-free, the mansion that another man has worked for twenty years to buy? But other men's lives are not yours to dispose of. Do you want operas so badly that everyone is forced to work harder to pay for their subsidization through taxes? But other men's lives are not yours to dispose of. Do you want to have free medical care at the expense of other people, whether they wish to provide it or not? But this would require them to work longer for you whether they want to or not, and other men's lives are not yours to dispose of.

> *The freedom to engage in any type of enterprise, to produce, to own and control property, to buy and sell on the free market, is derived from the rights to life, liberty, and property . . . which are stated in the Declaration of Independence . . . [but] when a government guarantees a "right" to an education or parity on farm products or a guaranteed annual income, it is staking a claim on the property of one group of citizens for the sake of another group. In short, it is violating one of the fundamental rights it was instituted to protect.*[1]

3 *No human being should be a nonvoluntary mortgage on the life of another.* I cannot claim your life, your work, or the products of your effort as mine. The fruit of one man's labor should not be fair game for every freeloader who comes along and demands it as his own. The orchard that has been carefully grown, nurtured, and harvested by its owner should not be ripe for the plucking for any bypasser who has a yen for the ripe fruit. The wealth that some men have produced should not be fair game for looting by government, to be used for whatever purposes its representatives determine, no matter what their motives in so doing may be. The theft of your money by a robber is not justified by the fact that he used it to help his injured mother.

It will already be evident that libertarian doctrine is embedded in a view of the rights of man. Each human being has the right to live his life as he chooses, compatibly with the equal right of all other human beings to live their lives as they choose.

All man's rights are implicit in the above statement. Each man has the right to life: any attempt by others to take it away from him, or even to injure him, violates this right, through the use of coercion against him. Each man has the right to liberty: to conduct his life in accordance with the alternatives open to him without coercive action by others. And every man has the right to property: to work to sustain his life (and the lives of whichever others he chooses to sustain, such as his family) and to retain the fruits of his labor.

People often defend the rights of life and liberty but denigrate property rights, and yet the right to property is as basic as the other two; indeed, without property rights no other rights are possible. Depriving you of property is depriving you of the means by which you live.

> . . . *All that which an individual possesses by right (including his life and property) are morally his to use, dispose of and even destroy, as he sees fit. If I own my life, then it follows that I am free to associate with whom I please and not to associate with whom I please. If I own my knowledge and services, it follows that I may ask any compensation I wish for providing them for another, or I may abstain from providing them at all, if I so choose. If I own my house, it follows that I may decorate it as I please and live in it with whom I please. If I control my own business, it follows that I may charge what I please for my products or services, hire whom I please and not hire whom I please. All that which I own in fact, I may dispose of as I choose to in reality. For anyone to attempt to limit my freedom to do so is to violate my rights.*
>
> *Where do my rights end? Where yours begin. I may do anything I wish with my own life, liberty and property without your consent; but I may do nothing with your life, liberty and property without your consent. If we recognize the principle of man's rights, it follows that the individual is sovereign of the domain of his own life and property, and is sovereign of no other domain. To attempt to interfere forcibly with another's use, disposal or destruction of his own property is to initiate force against him and to violate his rights.*

I have no right to decide how *you* should spend your time or your money. I can make that decision for myself, but not for you, my neighbor. I may deplore your choice of life-style, and I may talk with you about it provided you are willing to listen to me. But I have no right to use force to change it. Nor have I the right to decide how you should spend the money you have earned. I may appeal to you to give it to the Red Cross, and you may prefer to go to prizefights. But that is your decision, and however much I may chafe about it I do not have the right to interfere forcibly with it, for example by robbing you in order to use the money in accordance with *my* choices. (If I have the right to rob you, have you also the right to rob me?)

When I claim a right, I carve out a niche, as it were, in my life, saying in effect, "This activity I must be able to perform without interference from others. For you and everyone else, this is off limits." And so I put up a "no trespassing" sign, which marks off the area of my right. Each individual's right is his "no trespassing" sign in relation to me and others. I may not encroach upon his domain any more than he upon mine, without my consent. Every right entails a duty, true—but the duty is only that of *forbearance*—that is, of *refraining* from violating the other person's right. If you have a right to life, I have no right to take your life; if you have a right to the products of your labor (property), I have no right to take it from you without your consent. The non-violation of these rights will not guarantee you protection against natural catastrophes such as floods and earthquakes, but it will protect you against the aggressive activities *of other men.* And rights, after all, have to do with one's relations to other human beings, not with one's relations to physical nature.

Nor were these rights created by government; governments—some governments, obviously not all—*recognize* and *protect* the rights that individuals already have. Governments regularly forbid homicide and theft; and, at a more advanced stage, protect individuals against such things as libel and breach of contract. . . .

Government is the most dangerous institution known to man. Throughout history it has violated the rights of men more than any individual or group of individuals could do: it has killed people, enslaved them, sent them to forced labor and concentration camps, and regularly robbed and pillaged them of the fruits of their expended labor. Unlike individual criminals, government has the power to arrest and try; unlike individual criminals, it can surround and encompass a person totally, dominating every aspect of one's life, so that one has no recourse from it but to leave the country (and in totalitarian nations even that is prohibited). Government throughout history has a much sorrier record than any individual, even that of a ruthless mass murderer. The signs we see on bumper stickers are chillingly accurate: "Beware: the Government is Armed and Dangerous."

The only proper role of government, according to libertarians, is that of the protector of the citizen against aggression by other individuals. The government, of course, should never initiate aggression; its proper role is as the embodiment of the *retaliatory* use of force against anyone who initiates its use.

If each individual had constantly to defend himself against possible aggressors, he would have to spend a considerable portion of his life in target practice, karate exercises, and other means of self-defenses, and even so he would probably be helpless against groups of individuals who might try to kill, maim, or rob him. He would have little time for cultivating those qualities which are essential to civilized life, nor would improvements in science, medicine, and the arts be likely to occur. The function of government is to take this responsibility off his shoulders: the government undertakes to defend him against aggressors and to punish them if they attack him. When the government is effective in doing this, it enables the citizen to go about his business unmolested and without constant fear for his life. To do this, of course, government must have physical power—the police, to protect the citizen from aggression within its borders, and the armed forces, to protect him from aggressors outside. Beyond that, the government should not intrude upon his life, either to run his business, or adjust his daily activities, or prescribe his personal moral code.

Government, then, undertakes to be the individual's protector; but historically governments have gone far beyond this function. Since they already have the physical power, they have not hesitated to use it for purposes far beyond that which was entrusted to them in the first place. Undertaking initially to protect its citizens against aggression, it has often itself become an aggressor—a far greater aggressor, indeed, than the criminals against whom it was supposed to protect its citizens. Governments have done what no private citizens can do: arrest and imprison individuals without a trial and send them to slave labor camps. Government must have power in order to be effective—and yet the very means by which alone it can be effective make it vulnerable to the abuse of power, leading to managing the lives of individuals and even inflicting terror upon them.

What then should be the function of government? In a word, the *protection of human rights.*

1 *The right to life:* libertarians support all such legislation as will protect human beings against the use of force by others, for example, laws against killing, attempted killing, maiming, beating, and all kinds of physical violence.

2 *The right to liberty:* there should be no laws compromising in any way freedom of speech, of the press, and of peaceable assembly. There should be no censorship of ideas, books, films, or of anything else by government.

3 *The right to property:* libertarians support legislation that protects the property rights of individuals against confiscation, nationalization, eminent domain, robbery, trespass, fraud and misrepresentation, patent and copyright, libel and slander.

Someone has violently assaulted you. Should he be legally liable? Of course. He has violated one of your rights. He has knowingly injured you, and since he has initiated aggression against you he should be made to expiate.

Someone has negligently left his bicycle on the sidewalk where you trip over it in the dark and injure yourself. He didn't do it intentionally; he didn't mean you any harm. Should he be legally liable? Of course; he has, however unwittingly, injured you, and since the injury is caused by him and you are the victim, he should pay.

Someone across the street is unemployed. Should you be taxed extra to pay for his expenses? Not at all. You have not injured him, you are not responsible for the fact that he is unemployed (unless you are a senator or bureaucrat who agitated for further curtailing of business, which legislation passed, with the result that your neighbor was laid off by the curtailed business). You may voluntarily wish to help him out, or better still, try to get him a job to put him on his feet again; but since you have initiated no aggressive act against him, and neither purposely nor accidentally injured him in any way, you should not be legally penalized for the fact of his unemployment. (Actually, it is just such penalties that increase unemployment.)

One man, A, works hard for years and finally earns a high salary as a professional man. A second man, B, prefers not to work at all, and to spend wastefully what money he has (through inheritance), so that after a year or two he has nothing left. At the end of this time he has a long siege of illness and lots of medical bills to pay. He demands that the bills be paid by the government—that is, by the taxpayers of the land, including Mr. A.

But of course B has no such right. He chose to lead his life in a certain way—that was his voluntary decision. One consequence of that choice is that he must depend on charity in case of later need. Mr. A chose not to live that way. (And if everyone lived like Mr. B, on whom would he depend in case of later need?) Each has a right to live in the way he pleases, but each must live with the consequences of his own decision (which, as always, fall primarily on himself). He cannot, in time of need, claim A's beneficence as his right. . . .

Laws may be classified into three types: (1) laws protecting individuals against themselves, such as laws against fornication and other sexual behavior, alcohol, and drugs; (2) laws protecting individuals against aggressions by other individuals, such as laws against murder, robbery, and fraud; (3) laws requiring people to help one another; for example, all laws which rob Peter to pay Paul, such as welfare.

Libertarians reject the first class of laws totally. Behavior which harms no one else is strictly the individual's own affair. Thus, there should be no laws against becoming intoxicated, since whether or not to become intoxicated is the individual's own decision; but there should be laws against driving while intoxicated, since the drunken driver is a threat to every other motorist on the highway (drunken driving falls into type 2). Similarly, there should be no laws against drugs (except the prohibition of sale of drugs to minors) as long as the taking of these drugs poses no threat to anyone else. Drug addiction is a psychological problem to which no present solution exists. Most of the social harm caused by addicts, other than to themselves, is the result of thefts which they perform in order to continue their habit—and then the *legal* crime is the theft, not the addiction. The actual cost of heroin is about ten cents a shot; if it were legalized, the enormous traffic in illegal sale and purchase of it would stop, as well as the accompanying proselytization to get new addicts (to make more money for the pusher) and the thefts performed by addicts who often require eighty dollars a day just to keep up the habit. Addiction would not stop, but the crimes would: it is estimated that 75 percent of the burglaries in New York City today are performed by addicts, and all these crimes would be wiped out at one stroke through the legalization of drugs. (Only when the taking of drugs could be shown to constitute a threat to *others,* should it be prohibited by law. It is only laws protecting people against *themselves* that libertarians oppose.)

Laws should be limited to the second class only: aggression by individuals against other individuals. These are laws whose function is to protect human beings against encroachment by others; and this, as we have seen, is (according to libertarianism) the sole function of government.

Libertarians also reject the third class of laws totally: no one should be forced by law to help others, not even to tell them the time of day if requested, and certainly not to give them a portion of one's weekly paycheck. Governments, in the guise of humanitarianism, have given to some by taking from others (charging a "handling fee" in the process, which, because of the government's waste and inefficiency, sometimes is several hundred percent). And in so doing they have decreased incentive, violated the rights of individuals, and lowered the standard of living of almost everyone.

All such laws constitute what libertarians call *moral cannibalism.* A cannibal in the physical sense is a person who lives off the flesh of other human beings. A *moral* cannibal is one who believes he has a right to live off the "spirit" of other human beings—who believes that he has a moral claim on the productive capacity, time, and effort expended by others.

It has become fashionable to claim virtually everything that one needs or desires as one's *right.* Thus, many people claim that they have a right to a job, the right to free medical care, to free food and clothing, to a decent home, and so on. Now if one asks, apart from any specific context, whether it would be desirable if everyone had these things, one might well say yes. But there is a gimmick attached to each of them: *At whose expense?* Jobs, medical care, education, and so on, don't grow on trees. These are goods and services *produced only by men.* Who, then, is to provide them, and under what conditions?

If you have a right to a job, who is to supply it? Must an employer supply it even if he doesn't want to hire you? What if you are unemployable, or incurably lazy? (If you say "the government must supply it," does that mean that a job must be created for you which no employer needs done, and that you must be kept in it regardless of how much or little you work?) If the employer is forced to supply it at his expense even if he doesn't need you, then isn't *he* being enslaved to that extent? What ever happened to *his* right to conduct his life and his affairs in accordance with his choices?

If you have a right to free medical care, then, since medical care doesn't exist in nature as wild apples do, some people will have to supply it to you for free: that is, they will have to spend their time and money and energy taking care of you whether they want to or not. What ever happened to *their* right to conduct their lives as they see fit? Or do you have a right to violate theirs? Can there be a right to violate rights?

All those who demand this or that as a "free service" are consciously or unconsciously evading the fact that there is in reality no such thing as free services. All man-made goods and services are the result of human expenditure of time and effort. There is no such thing as "something for nothing" in this world. If you demand something free, you are demanding that other men give their time and effort to you without compensation. If they voluntarily choose to do this, there is no problem; but if you demand that they be *forced* to do it, you are interfering with their right not to do it if they so choose. "Swimming in this pool ought to be free!" says the indignant passerby. What he means is that others should build a pool, others should provide the materials, and still others should run it and keep it in functioning order, so that *he* can use it without fee. But what right has he to the expenditure of *their* time and effort? To expect something "for free" is to expect it *to be paid for by others* whether they choose to or not.

Many questions, particularly about economic matters, will be generated by the libertarian account of human rights and the role of government. Should government have no role in assisting the needy, in providing social security, in legislating minimum wages, in fixing prices and putting a ceiling on rents, in curbing monopolies, in erecting tariffs, in guaranteeing jobs, in managing the money supply? To these and all similar questions the libertarian answers with an unequivocal no.

"But then you'd let people go hungry!" comes the rejoinder. This, the libertarian insists, is precisely what would not happen; with the restrictions removed, the economy would flourish as never before. With the controls taken off business, existing enterprises would expand and new ones would spring into existence satisfying more and more consumer needs; millions more people would be gainfully employed instead of subsisting on welfare, and all kinds of research and production, released from the stranglehold of government, would proliferate, fulfilling man's needs and desires as never before. It has always been so whenever government has permitted men to be free traders on a free market. But *why* this is so, and how the free market is the best solution to all problems relating to the material aspect of man's life, is another and far longer story. . . .

NOTES

1 William W. Bayes, "What Is Property?" *The Freeman,* July 1970, p. 348.

QUESTIONS

1 Some libertarians argue that from a moral standpoint there is no difference between the actions of an ordinary thief and those of a government when it seizes money from some in order to support others. They assume that if the former are wrong, then so are the latter. Are they correct?
2 Do you agree that the government should have no role in assisting the needy? What reasons can you advance to defend your answer?

A Basic Right to Subsistence

Henry Shue

Henry Shue is professor of philosophy and director of the Program on Ethics/Public Life at Cornell University. He specializes in social philosophy. Shue is the author of *Basic Rights: Subsistence, Affluence, and U.S. Foreign Policy* (1980), from which this selection is excerpted, and the editor of *Nuclear Deterrence and Moral Restraint* (1989). His published articles include "Mediating Duties," "Transnational Transgressions," and "Morality of Offense Determines Morality of Defense."

In contrast to Hospers, Shue argues that human beings have at least some positive rights—those that he describes as basic rights. A "basic right" is one whose recognition is necessary for the enjoyment of all other rights. In advancing a case for the existence of a basic right to subsistence, Shue begins by discussing security rights in order to identify the fundamental assumptions that support the usual judgment that security rights are basic rights. On Shue's analysis, the reasons that establish security rights as basic rights also support the claim that human beings have a basic right to subsistence.

One of the chief purposes of morality in general, and certainly of conceptions of rights, and of basic rights above all, is . . . to provide some minimal protection against utter helplessness to those too weak to protect themselves. Basic rights are a shield for the defenseless against at least some of the more devastating and more common of life's threats, which include, as we shall see, loss of security and loss of subsistence. Basic rights are a restraint upon economic and political forces that would otherwise be too strong to be resisted. They are social guarantees against actual and threatened deprivations of at least some basic needs. Basic rights are an attempt to give to the powerless a veto over some of the forces that would otherwise harm them the most.

It is not surprising that what is in an important respect the essentially negative goal of preventing or alleviating helplessness is a central purpose of something as important as conceptions of basic rights. For everyone healthy adulthood is bordered on each side by helplessness, and it is vulnerable to interruption by helplessness, temporary or permanent, at any time. . . . Nor is it surprising that although the goal is negative, the duties correlative to rights . . . include positive actions. The infant and the aged do not need to be assaulted in order to be deprived of health, life, or the capacity to enjoy active rights. The classic liberal's [i.e., libertarian's] main prescription for the good life—do not interfere with thy neighbor—is the only poison they need. To be helpless they need only to be left alone. . . .

Basic rights, then, are everyone's minimum reasonable demands upon the rest of humanity. They are the rational basis for justified demands the denial of which no self-respecting person can reasonably be expected to accept. Why should anything be so important? The reason is that rights are basic in the sense used here only if enjoyment of them is essential to the enjoyment of all other rights. This is what is distinctive about a basic right. When a right is genuinely basic, any attempt to enjoy any other right by sacrificing the basic right would be quite literally self-defeating, cutting the ground from beneath itself. Therefore, if a right is basic, other, non-basic rights may be sacrificed, if necessary, in order to secure the basic right. But the protection of a basic right may not be sacrificed in order to secure the enjoyment of a non-basic right. It may not be sacrificed because it cannot be sacrificed successfully. If the right sacrificed is indeed basic, then no right for which it might be sacrificed can actually be enjoyed in the absence of the basic right. The sacrifice would have proven self-defeating.

In practice, what this priority for basic rights usually means is that basic rights need to be established securely before other rights can be secured. The point is that people should be able to *enjoy,* or *exercise,* their other rights. The point is simple but vital. It is not merely that people should "have" their other rights in some merely legalistic or otherwise abstract sense compatible with being unable to make any use of the substance of the right. For example, if people have rights to free association, they ought not merely to "have" the rights to free association but also to enjoy their free association itself. Their freedom of association ought to be provided for by the relevant social institutions. This distinction between merely having a right and actually enjoying a right may seem a fine point, but it turns out later to be critical. . . .

SECURITY RIGHTS

Our first project will be to see why people have a basic right to physical security—a right that is basic not to be subjected to murder, torture, mayhem, rape, or assault. The purpose in raising the questions why there are rights to physical security and why they are basic is not that very many people would seriously doubt either that there are rights to physical security or that they are basic. Although it is not unusual in practice for members of at least one ethnic group in a society to be physically insecure—to be, for example, much more likely than other people to be beaten by the police if arrested—few, if any, people would be prepared to defend in principle the contention that anyone lacks a basic right to physical security. Nevertheless, it can be valuable to formulate explicitly the presuppositions of even one's most firmly held beliefs, especially because these presuppositions may turn out to be general principles that will provide guidance in other areas where convictions are less firm. Precisely because we have no real doubt that rights to physical security are basic, it can be useful to see why we may properly think so.

If we had to justify our belief that people have a basic right to physical security to someone who challenged this fundamental conviction, we could in fact give a strong argument that shows that if there are any rights (basic or not basic) at all, there are basic rights to physical security:

• No one can fully enjoy any right that is supposedly protected by society if someone can credibly threaten him or her with murder, rape, beating, etc., when he or she tries to enjoy the alleged right. Such threats to physical security are among the most serious and—in much of the world—the most widespread hindrances to the enjoyment of any right. If any right is to be exercised except at great risk, physical security must be protected. In the absence of physical security people are unable to use any other rights that society may be said to be protecting without being liable to encounter many of the worst dangers they would encounter if society were not protecting the rights.

• A right to full physical security belongs, then, among the basic rights—not because the enjoyment of it would be more satisfying to someone who was also enjoying a full range of other rights, but because its absence would leave available extremely effective means for others, including the government, to interfere with or prevent the actual exercise of any other rights that were supposedly protected. Regardless of whether the enjoyment of physical security is also desirable for its own sake, it is desirable as part of the enjoyment of every other right. No rights other than a right to physical security can in fact be enjoyed if a right to physical security is not protected. Being physically secure is a necessary condition for the exercise of any other right, and guaranteeing physical security must be part of guaranteeing anything else as a right.

A person could, of course, always try to enjoy some other right even if no social provision were made to protect his or her physical safety during attempts to exercise the right. Suppose there is a right to peaceful assembly but it is not unusual for peaceful assemblies to be broken up and some of the participants beaten. Whether any given assembly is actually broken up depends largely on whether anyone else (in or out of government) is sufficiently opposed to it to bother to arrange an attack. People could still try to assemble, and they might sometimes assemble safely. But it would obviously be misleading to say that they are protected in their right to assemble if they are as vulnerable as ever to one of the most serious and general threats to enjoyment of the right, namely physical violence by other people. If they are as helpless against physical threats with the right "protected" as they would have been without the supposed protection, society is not actually protecting their exercise of the right to assembly.

So anyone who is entitled to anything as a right must be entitled to physical security as a basic right so that threats to his or her physical security cannot be used to thwart the enjoyment of the other right. This argument has two critical premises. The first is that everyone is entitled to enjoy something as a right.[1] The second, which further explains the first, is that everyone is entitled to the removal of the most serious and general conditions that would prevent or severely interfere with the exercise of whatever rights the person has. I take this second premise to be part of what is meant in saying that everyone is entitled to enjoy something as a right. . . . Since this argument applies to everyone, it establishes a right that is universal.

SUBSISTENCE RIGHTS

The main reason for discussing security rights, which are not very controversial, was to make explicit the basic assumptions that support the usual judgment that security rights are basic rights. Now that we have available an argument that supports them, we are in a position to consider whether matters other than physical security should, according to the same argument, also be basic rights. It will emerge that subsistence, or minimal economic security, which is more controversial than physical security, can also be shown to be as well justified for treatment as a basic right as physical security is—and for the same reasons.

By minimal economic security, or subsistence, I mean unpolluted air, unpolluted water, adequate food, adequate clothing, adequate shelter, and minimal preventive public health care. Many complications about exactly how to specify the boundaries of what is necessary for subsistence would be interesting to explore. But the basic idea is to have available for consumption what is needed for a decent chance at a reasonably healthy and active life of more or less normal length, barring tragic interventions. This central idea is clear enough to work with, even though disputes can occur over exactly where to draw its outer boundaries. A right to subsistence would not mean, at one extreme, that every baby born with a need for open-heart surgery has a right to have it, but it also would not count as adequate food a diet that produces a life expectancy of 35 years of fever-laden, parasite-ridden listlessness.

By a "right to subsistence" I shall always mean a right to at least subsistence. People may or may not have economic rights that go beyond subsistence rights, and I do not want to prejudge that question here. But people may have rights to subsistence even if they do not have any strict rights to economic well-being extending beyond subsistence. Subsistence rights and broader economic rights are separate questions, and I want to focus here on subsistence.

I also do not want to prejudge the issue of whether healthy adults are entitled to be provided with subsistence *only* if they cannot provide subsistence for themselves. . . . By a "right to subsistence," then, I shall mean a right to subsistence that includes the provision of subsistence at least to those who cannot provide for themselves. I do not assume that no one else is also entitled to receive subsistence—I simply do not discuss cases of healthy adults who could support themselves but refuse to do so. If there is a right to subsistence in the sense discussed here, at least the people who cannot provide for themselves, including the children, are entitled to receive at least subsistence. Nothing follows one way or the other about anyone else. . . .

The same considerations that support the conclusion that physical security is a basic right support the conclusion that subsistence is a basic right. Since the argument is now familiar, it can be given fairly briefly.

It is quite obvious why, if we still assume that there are some rights that society ought to protect and still mean by this the removal of the most serious and general hindrances to the actual enjoyment of the rights, subsistence ought to be protected as a basic right:

- No one can fully, if at all, enjoy any right that is supposedly protected by society if he or she lacks the essentials for a reasonably healthy and active life. Deficiencies in the means of subsistence can be just as fatal, incapacitating, or painful as violations of physical security. The resulting damage or death can at least as decisively prevent the enjoyment of any right as can the effects of security violations. Any form of malnutrition, or fever due to exposure, that causes severe and irreversible brain damage, for example, can effectively prevent the exercise of any right requiring clear thought and may, like brain injuries caused by assault, profoundly disturb personality. And, obviously, any fatal deficiencies end all possibility of the enjoyment of rights as firmly as an arbitrary execution.

- Indeed, prevention of deficiencies in the essentials for survival is, if anything, more basic than prevention of violations of physical security. People who lack protection against violations of their physical security can, if they are free, fight back against their attackers or flee, but people who lack essentials, such as food, because of forces beyond their control, often can do nothing and are on their own utterly helpless.

The scope of subsistence rights must not be taken to be broader than it is. In particular, this step of the argument does not make the following absurd claim: since death and serious illness prevent or interfere with the enjoyment of rights, everyone has a basic right not to be allowed to die or to be seriously ill. Many causes of death and illness are outside the control of society, and many deaths and illnesses are the result of very particular conjunctions of circumstances that general social policies cannot control. But it is not impractical to expect some level of social organization to protect the minimal cleanliness of air and water and to oversee the adequate production, or import, and the proper distribution of minimal food, clothing, shelter, and elementary health care. It is not impractical, in short, to expect effective management, when necessary, of the supplies of the essentials of life. So the argument is: when death and serious illness could be prevented by different social policies regarding the essentials of life, the protection of any human right involves avoidance of fatal or debilitating deficiencies in these essential commodities. And this means fulfilling subsistence rights as basic rights. This is society's business because the problems are serious and general. This is a basic right because failure to deal with it would hinder the enjoyment of all other rights.

Thus, the same considerations that establish that security rights are basic for everyone also support the conclusion that subsistence rights are basic for everyone. It is not being claimed or assumed that security and subsistence are parallel in all, or even very many, respects. The only parallel being relied upon is that guarantees of security and guarantees of subsistence are equally essential to providing for the actual exercise of any other rights. As long as security and subsistence are parallel in this respect, the argument applies equally to both cases, and other respects in which security and subsistence are not parallel are irrelevant. . . .

It would be misleading to construe security or subsistence—or the substance of any other basic right—merely as "means" to the enjoyment of all other rights. The enjoyment of security and subsistence is an essential part of the enjoyment of all other rights. Part of what it means to enjoy any other right is to be able to exercise that right without, as a consequence, suffering the actual or threatened loss of one's physical security or one's subsistence. And part of what it means to be able to enjoy any other right is not to be prevented from exercising it by lack of security or of subsistence. To claim to guarantee people a right that they are in fact unable to exercise is fraudulent, like furnishing people with meal tickets but providing no food. . . .

Why, then, according to the argument so far, are security and subsistence basic rights? Each is essential to a normal healthy life. Because the actual deprivation of either can be so very serious—potentially incapacitating, crippling, or fatal—even the threatened deprivation of either can be a powerful weapon against anyone whose security or subsistence is not in fact socially guaranteed. People who cannot provide for their own security and subsistence and who lack social guarantees for both are very weak, and possibly helpless, against any individual or institution in a position to deprive them of anything else they value by means of threatening their security or subsistence. A fundamental purpose of acknowledging any basic rights at all is to prevent, or to eliminate, insofar as possible the degree of vulnerability that leaves people at the mercy of others. Social guarantees of security and subsistence would go a long way toward accomplishing this purpose.

Security and subsistence are basic rights, then, because of the roles they play in both the enjoyment and the protection of all other rights. Other rights could not be enjoyed in the absence of security or subsistence, even if the other rights were somehow miraculously protected in such a situation. And other rights could in any case not be protected if security or subsistence could credibly be threatened. The enjoyment of the other rights requires a certain degree of physical integrity, which is temporarily undermined, or eliminated, by deprivations of security or of subsistence. Someone who has suffered exposure or a beating is incapable of enjoying the substances of other rights, although only temporarily, provided he or she receives good enough care to recover the use of all essential faculties.

But as our earlier discussion of helplessness made clear, either the actual or the credibly threatened loss of security or subsistence leaves a person vulnerable to any other deprivations the source of the threat has in mind. Without security or subsistence one is helpless, and consequently one may also be helpless to protect whatever can be protected only at the risk of security or subsistence. Therefore, security and subsistence must be socially guaranteed, if any rights are to be enjoyed. This makes them basic rights. . . .

NOTES

1 At considerable risk of encouraging unflattering comparisons I might as well note myself that in its general structure the argument here has the same form as the argument in H.L.A. Hart's classic, "Are There Any Natural Rights?" *Philosophical Review,* 64:2 (April 1955), pp. 175–191. That is, Hart can be summarized as maintaining: if there are any rights, there are rights to liberty. I am saying: if there are any rights, there are rights to security—and to subsistence. The finer structures of the arguments are of course quite different.

QUESTIONS

1 In an affluent society such as ours, do all individuals who are unable to support themselves have a *moral* right to welfare assistance?

2 How would Shue respond to Hospers' contention that the only proper role of government is to protect the citizens against aggression by other individuals?

Majority Opinion in *Wyman v. James*

Justice Harry A. Blackmun

A biographical sketch of Justice Harry A. Blackmun is found on p. 39.

This case centers on the question, "Can a beneficiary of the AFDC program refuse a home visit by a caseworker without risking the termination of benefits?" One such beneficiary, Barbara James, refused such a visit. When notified that refusal meant the termination of benefits, she brought a suit against the commissioner of the New York department of social services (Wyman) and others. James argued that a caseworker's visit constitutes a search and thereby violates Fourth and Fourteenth Amendment rights. (The Fourth Amendment asserts "the right of the people to be secure in their persons, houses, papers, and effects." The Fourteenth Amendment prohibits states from depriving any person of life, liberty, or property "without due process of law.") The District Court of New York ruled in favor of James. The case was appealed to the United States Supreme Court, which reversed the lower court's decision.

In ruling against James, the Court held that the home visitation in question is a *reasonable* administrative tool and does not violate any Fourth or Fourteenth Amendment rights. In presenting the factors which make it a reasonable tool, Justice Blackmun draws an analogy between AFDC payments and the dispensation of purely private charity. He stresses the public interest (1) in seeing that the money is utilized as those who supply the funds intend it to be and (2) in assisting and rehabilitating the beneficiary.

I

Plaintiff Barbara James is the mother of a son, Maurice, who was born in May 1967. They reside in New York City. Mrs. James first applied for AFDC assistance shortly before Maurice's birth. A caseworker made a visit to her apartment at that time without objection. The assistance was authorized.

Two years later, on May 8, 1969, a caseworker wrote Mrs. James that she would visit her home on May 14. Upon receipt of this advice, Mrs. James telephoned the worker that, although she was willing to supply information "reasonable and relevant" to her need for public assistance, any discussion was not to take place at her home. The worker told Mrs. James that she was required by law to visit in her home and that refusal to permit the visit would result in the termination of assistance. Permission was still denied.

On May 13 the City Department of Social Services sent Mrs. James a notice of intent to discontinue assistance because of the visitation refusal. The notice advised the beneficiary of her right to a hearing before a review officer. The hearing was requested and was held on May 27. Mrs. James appeared with an attorney at that hearing. They continued to refuse permission for a worker to visit the James home,

United States Supreme Court. 400 U.S. 309 (1971).

but again expressed willingness to cooperate and to permit visits elsewhere. The review officer ruled that the refusal was a proper ground for the termination of assistance. His written decision stated:

> "The home visit which Mrs. James refuses to permit is for the purpose of determining if there are any changes in her situation that might affect her eligibility to continue to receive Public Assistance, or that might affect the amount of such assistance, and to see if there are any social services which the Department of Social Services can provide to the family."

A notice of termination was issued on June 2.

Thereupon, without seeking a hearing at the state level, Mrs. James, individually and on behalf of Maurice, and purporting to act on behalf of all other persons similarly situated, instituted the present civil rights suit. She alleged the denial of rights guaranteed to her under the First, Third, Fourth, Fifth, Sixth, Ninth, Tenth, and Fourteenth Amendments, and under Subchapters IV and XVI of the Social Security Act and regulations issued thereunder. She further alleged that she and her son have no income, resources, or support other than the benefits received under the AFDC program. . . .

II

When a case involves a home and some type of official intrusion into that home, as this case appears to do, an immediate and natural reaction is one of concern about Fourth Amendment rights and the protection which that Amendment is intended to afford. Its emphasis indeed is upon one of the most precious aspects of personal security in the home: "The right of the people to be secure in their persons, houses, papers, and effects. . . ." This Court has characterized that right as "basic to a free society." And over the years the Court consistently has been most protective of the privacy of the dwelling. . . .

III

This natural and quite proper protective attitude, however, is not a factor in this case, for the seemingly obvious and simple reason that we are not concerned here with any search by the New York social service agency in the Fourth Amendment meaning of that term. It is true that the governing statute and regulations appear to make mandatory the initial home visit and the subsequent periodic "contacts" (which may include home visits) for the inception and continuance of aid. It is also true that the caseworker's posture in the home visit is perhaps, in a sense, both rehabilitative and investigative. But this latter aspect, we think, is given too broad a character and far more emphasis than it deserves if it is equated with a search in the traditional criminal law context. We note, too, that the visitation in itself is not forced or compelled, and that the beneficiary's denial of permission is not a criminal act. If consent to the visitation is withheld, no visitation takes place. The aid then never begins or merely ceases, as the case may be. There is no entry of the home and there is no search.

IV

If however, we were to assume that a caseworker's home visit, before or subsequent to the beneficiary's initial qualification for benefits, somehow (perhaps because the average beneficiary might feel she is in no position to refuse consent to the visit), and despite its interview nature, does possess some of the characteristics of a search in the traditional sense, we nevertheless conclude that the visit does not fall within the Fourth Amendment's proscription. This is because it does not descend to the level of unreasonableness. It is unreasonableness which is the Fourth Amendment's standard. . . .

There are a number of factors that compel us to conclude that the home visit proposed for Mrs. James is not unreasonable:

1 The public's interest in this particular segment of the area of assistance to the unfortunate is protection and aid for the dependent child whose family requires such aid for that child. The focus is on the *child* and, further, it is on the child who is *dependent.* There is no more worthy object of the public's concern. The dependent child's needs are paramount, and only with hesitancy would we relegate those needs, in the scale of comparative values, to a position secondary to what the mother claims as her rights.

2 The agency, with tax funds provided from federal as well as from state sources, is fulfilling a public trust. The State, working through its qualified welfare agency, has appropriate and paramount interest and concern in seeing and assuring that the intended and proper objects of that tax-produced assistance are the ones who benefit from the aid it dispenses. Surely it is not unreasonable, in the Fourth Amendment sense or in any other sense of that term, that the State have at its command a gentle means, of limited extent and of practical and considerate application, of achieving that assurance.

3 One who dispenses purely private charity naturally has an interest in and expects to know how his charitable funds are utilized and put to work. The public, when it is the provider, rightly expects the same. It might well expect more, because of the trust aspect of public funds, and the recipient, as well as the caseworker, has not only an interest but an obligation.

4 The emphasis of the New York statutes and regulations is upon the home, upon "close contact" with the beneficiary, upon restoring the aid recipient "to a condition of self-support," and upon the relief of his distress. The federal emphasis is no different. It is upon "assistance and rehabilitation," upon maintaining and strengthening family life, and upon "maximum self-support and personal independence consistent with the maintenance of continuing parental care and protection. . . ." It requires cooperation from the state agency upon specified standards and in specified ways. . . .

5 The means employed by the New York agency are significant. Mrs. James received written notice several days in advance of the intended home visit.[1] . . .

6 Mrs. James, in fact, on this record presents no specific complaint of any unreasonable intrusion of her home. . . . She alleges only, in general and nonspecific terms, that on previous visits and, on information and belief, on visitation at the home of other aid recipients, "questions concerning personal relationships, beliefs and behavior are raised and pressed which are unnecessary for a determination of continuing eligibility.". . . What Mrs. James appears to want from the agency that provides her and her infant son with the necessities for life is the right to receive those necessities upon her own informational terms, to utilize the Fourth Amendment as a wedge for imposing those terms, and to avoid questions of any kind. . . .

V

Our holding today does not mean, of course, that a termination of benefits upon refusal of a home visit is to be upheld against constitutional challenge under all conceivable circumstances. The early morning mass raid upon homes of welfare recipients is not unknown. But that is not this case. Facts of that kind present another case for another day.

We therefore conclude that the home visitation as structured by the New York statutes and regulations is a reasonable administrative tool; that it serves a valid and proper administrative purpose for the dispensation of the AFDC program; that it is not an unwarranted invasion of personal privacy; and that it violates no right guaranteed by the Fourth Amendment. . . .

NOTES

1 It is true that the record contains 12 affidavits, all essentially identical, of aid recipients (other than Mrs. James) which recite that a caseworker "most often" comes without notice; that when he does, the plans the recipient had for that time cannot be carried out; that the visit is "very embarrassing to me if the caseworker comes when I have company"; and that the caseworker "sometimes asks very personal questions" in front of children.

QUESTIONS

1 Justice Blackmun sees private dispensation of charity as analogous to government dispensation of welfare monies. Is this a good analogy? Explain.
2 Are people like Barbara James expected to sacrifice certain important political rights for economic reasons? If yes, is this morally acceptable?

Dissenting Opinion in *Wyman v. James*

Justice William O. Douglas

William O. Douglas (1898–1980), who received his law degree from the Yale University Law School and taught law for a number of years, served as associate justice of the United States Supreme Court from 1939 to 1975. Justice Douglas is the author of many books, including *The Right of the People* (1958), *The Anatomy of Liberty* (1963), and *The Court Years: The Autobiography of William O. Douglas* (1980).

United States Supreme Court. 400 U.S. 309 (1971).

Justice Douglas asks whether "the government by force of its largesse has the power to 'buy up rights' guaranteed by the Constitution." Citing various forms of government payments, Douglas sees it as inconsistent that the recipients of some of these payments are not subjected to "searches without warrant," but that the recipients of AFDC are. He criticizes the view that the latter kind of aid is equivalent to charity and that its recipients are rightfully subject to policing activities which deny them their constitutional rights.

We are living in a society where one of the most important forms of property is government largesse which some call the "new property." The payrolls of government are but one aspect of that "new property." Defense contracts, highway contracts, and the other multifarious forms of contracts are another part. So are subsidies to air, rail, and other carriers. So are disbursements by government for scientific research. So are TV and radio licenses to use the air space which of course is part of the public domain. Our concern here is not with those subsidies but with grants that directly or indirectly implicate the *home life* of the recipients.

In 1969 roughly 127 billion dollars were spent by the federal, state, and local governments on "social welfare." To farmers alone almost four billion dollars were paid, in part for not growing certain crops. Almost 129,000 farmers received $5,000 or more, their total benefits exceeding $1,450,000,000. Those payments were in some instances very large, a few running a million or more a year. But the majority were payments under $5,000 each.

Yet almost every beneficiary whether rich or poor, rural or urban, has a "house"—one of the places protected by the Fourth Amendment against "unreasonable searches and seizures." The question in this case is whether receipt of largesse from the government makes the *home* of the beneficiary subject to access by an inspector of the agency of oversight, even though the beneficiary objects to the intrusion and even though the Fourth Amendment's procedure for access to one's *house* or *home* is not followed. The penalty here is not, of course, invasion of the privacy of Barbara James, only her loss of federal or state largesse. That, however, is merely rephrasing the problem. Whatever the semantics, the central question is whether the government by force of its largesse has the power to "buy up" rights guaranteed by the Constitution. But for the assertion of her constitutional right, Barbara James in this case would have received the welfare benefit. . . .

. . . In See v. *City of Seattle* (1967) we [decided] that the "businessman, like the occupant of a residence, has a constitutional right to go about his business free from unreasonable official entries upon his private commercial property." There is not the slightest hint in *See* that the Government could condition a business license on the "consent" of the licensee to the administrative searches we held violated the Fourth Amendment. It is a strange jurisprudence indeed which safeguards the businessman at his place of work from warrantless searches but will not do the same for a mother in her *home*.

Is a search of her home without a warrant made "reasonable" merely because she is dependent on government largesse?

Judge Skelly Wright has stated the problem succinctly:

"Welfare has long been considered the equivalent of charity and its recipients have been subjected to all kinds of dehumanizing experiences in the government's effort to police its welfare payments. In fact, over half a billion dollars are expended annually for administration and policing in connection with the Aid to Families with Dependent Children program. Why such large sums are necessary for administration and policing has never been adequately explained. No such sums are spent policing the government subsidies granted to farmers, airlines, steamship companies, and junk mail dealers, to name but a few. The truth is that in this subsidy area society has simply adopted a double standard, one for aid to business and the farmer and a different one for welfare." Poverty, Minorities, and Respect For Law, 1970 Duke L. J. 425, 437–438.

If the welfare recipient was not Barbara James but a prominent, affluent cotton or wheat farmer receiving benefit payments for not growing crops, would not the approach be different? Welfare in aid of dependent children, like social security and unemployment benefits, has an aura of suspicion. There doubtless are frauds in every sector of public welfare whether the recipient be a Barbara James or someone who is prominent or influential. But constitutional rights—here the privacy of the *home*—are obviously not dependent on the poverty or on the affluence of the beneficiary. It is the precincts of the *home* that the Fourth Amendment protects; and their privacy is as important to the lowly as to the mighty. . . .

I would place the same restrictions on inspectors entering the *homes* of welfare beneficiaries as are on inspectors entering the *homes* of those on the payroll of government, or the *homes* of those who contract with the government, or the *homes* of those who work for those having government contracts. The values of the *home* protected by the Fourth Amendment are not peculiar to capitalism as we have known it; they are equally relevant to the new form of socialism which we are entering. Moreover, as the numbers of functionaries and inspectors multiply, the need for protection of the individual becomes indeed more essential if the values of a free society are to remain. . . .

QUESTIONS

1 At the beginning of his opinion, Justice Douglas lists various subsidy programs as examples of government largesse. Are the programs he lists analogous to the welfare program under which Barbara James received funds? What are the similarities? What are the differences?

2 Is it morally correct for those who receive what is traditionally called "welfare" (e.g., AFDC) to be subjected to attempts to "reform" their lives and to checkups by government caseworkers?

The Right to Eat and the Duty to Work

Trudy Govier

Trudy Govier is a philosopher who has taught at Trent University, Ontario. Her areas of specialization are moral philosophy and logic. Govier's articles include "What Should We Do About Future People?," "Nuclear Illusions and Individual Obligations," and "Thoughts From Under the Nuclear Umbrella."

Govier focuses on issues arising out of the question, "Should the needy have a legal right to welfare benefits?" She first examines three positions that could be adopted in response: (1) the individualist (libertarian) position; (2) the permissive position; and (3) the puritan position. She proceeds to evaluate the three positions' policies regarding welfare on the basis of both utilitarian considerations and considerations of social justice. Govier concludes that permissivism is superior from both standpoints.

Although the topic of welfare is not one with which philosophers have often concerned themselves, it is a topic which gives rise to many complex and fascinating questions—some in the area of political philosophy, some in the area of ethics, and some of a more practical kind. The variety of issues related to the subject of welfare makes it particularly necessary to be clear just which issue one is examining in a discussion of welfare. In a recent book on the subject, Nicholas Rescher asks:

> In what respects and to what extent is society, working through the instrumentality of the state, responsible for the welfare of its members? What demands for the promotion of his welfare can an individual reasonably make upon his society? These are questions to which no answer can be given in terms of some a *priori* approach with reference to universal ultimates. Whatever answer can appropriately be given will depend, in the final analysis, on what the society decides it should be.[1]

Rescher raises this question only to avoid it. His response to his own question is that a society has all and only those responsibilities for its members that it thinks it has. Although this claim is trivially true as regards legal responsibilities, it is inadequate from a moral perspective. If one imagines the case of an affluent society which leaves the blind, the disabled, and the needy to die of starvation, the incompleteness of Rescher's account becomes obvious. In this imagined case one is naturally led to raise the question as to whether those in power ought to supply those in need with the necessities of life. Though the needy have no legal right to welfare benefits of any kind, one might very well say that they ought to have such a right. It is this claim which I propose to discuss here.[2]

I shall approach this issue by examining three positions which may be adopted in response to it. These are:

Reprinted with permission of the publisher from *Philosophy of the Social Sciences,* vol. 5 (1975), pp. 125–143.

1 *The Individualist Position:* Even in an affluent society, one ought not to have any legal right to state-supplied welfare benefits.

2 *The Permissive Position:* In a society with sufficient resources, one ought to have an unconditional legal right to receive state supplied welfare benefits. (That is, one's right to receive such benefits ought not to depend on one's behaviour; it should be guaranteed.)

3 *The Puritan Position:* In a society with sufficient resources one ought to have a legal right to state-supplied welfare benefits; this right ought to be conditional, however, on one's willingness to work.

But before we examine these positions, some preliminary clarification must be attempted. . . .

Welfare systems are state-supported systems which supply benefits, usually in the form of cash income, to those who are in need. Welfare systems thus exist in the sort of social context where there is some private ownership of property. If no one owned anything individually (except possibly his own body), and all goods were considered to be the joint property of everyone, then this type of welfare system could not exist. A state might take on the responsibility for the welfare of its citizens, but it could not meet this responsibility by distributing a level of cash income which such citizens would spend to purchase the goods essential for life. The welfare systems which exist in the western world do exist against the background of extensive private ownership of property. It is in this context that I propose to discuss moral questions about having a right to welfare benefits. By setting out my questions in this way, I do not intend to endorse the institution of private property, but only to discuss questions which many people find real and difficult in the context of the social organization which they actually do experience. The present analysis of welfare is intended to apply to societies which *(a)* have the institution of private property, if not for means of production, at least for some basic good; and *(b)* possess sufficient resources so that it is at least possible for every member of the society to be supplied with the necessities of life.

1 The Individualist View

It might be maintained that a person in need has no legitimate moral claim on those around him and that the hypothetical inattentive society which left its blind citizens to beg or starve cannot rightly be censured for doing so. This view, which is dramatically at odds with most of contemporary social thinking, lives on in the writings of Ayn Rand and her followers.[3] The Individualist sets a high value on uncoerced personal choice. He sees each person as a responsible agent who is able to make his own decisions and to plan his own life. He insists that with the freedom to make decisions goes responsibility for the consequences of those decisions. A person has every right, for example, to spend ten years of his life studying Sanskrit—but if, as a result of this choice, he is unemployable, he ought not to expect others to labour on his behalf. No one has a proper claim on the labour of another, or on the income ensuing from that labour, unless he can repay the labourer in a way acceptable to that labourer himself. Government welfare schemes provide benefits from funds gained largely by taxing earned income. One cannot "opt out" of such schemes. To the Individualist, this means that a person is forced to work part of his time for others.

Suppose that a man works forty hours and earns two hundred dollars. Under modern-day taxation, it may well be that he can spend only two-thirds of that money as he chooses. The rest is taken by government and goes to support programmes which the working individual may not himself endorse. The beneficiaries of such programmes—those beneficiaries who do not work themselves—are as though they have slaves working for them. Backed by the force which government authorities can command, they are able to exist on the earnings of others. Those who support them do not do so voluntarily, out of charity; they do so on government command.

> Someone across the street is unemployed. Should you be taxed extra to pay for his expenses? Not at all. You have not injured him, you are not responsible for the fact that he is unemployed (unless you are a senator or bureaucrat who agitated for further curtailing of business which legislation passed, with the result that your neighbour was laid off by the curtailed business). You may voluntarily wish to help him out, or better still, try to get him a job to put him on his feet again; but since you have initiated no aggressive act against him, and neither purposefully nor accidentally injured him in any way, you should not be legally penalized for the fact of his unemployment.[4]

The Individualist need not lack concern for those in need. He may give generously to charity; he might give more generously still, if his whole income were his to use, as he would like it to be. He may also believe that, as a matter of empirical fact, existing government programmes do not actually help the poor. They support a cumbersome bureaucracy and they use financial resources which, if untaxed, might be used by those with initiative to pursue job-creating endeavours. The thrust of the Individualist's position is that each person owns his own body and his own labour; thus each person is taken to have a virtually unconditional right to the income which that labour can earn him in a free market place.[5] For anyone to pre-empt part of a worker's earnings without that worker's voluntary consent is tantamount to robbery. And the fact that the government is the intermediary through which this deed is committed does not change its moral status one iota.

On an Individualist's view, those in need should be cared for by charities or through other schemes to which contributions are voluntary. Many people may wish to insure themselves against unforeseen calamities and they should be free to do so. But there is no justification for non-optional government schemes financed by taxpayers' money. . . .

2 The Permissive View

Directly contrary to the Individualist view of welfare is what I have termed the Permissive view. According to this view, in a society which has sufficient resources so that everyone could be supplied with the necessities of life, every individual ought to be given the legal right to social security, and this right ought not to be conditional in any way upon an individual's behavior. *Ex hypothesi* the society which we are discussing has sufficient goods to provide everyone with food, clothing, shelter and other necessities. Someone who does without these basic goods is scarcely living at all, and a society which takes no steps to change this state of affairs implies by its inaction that the life of such a person is without value. It does not execute him; but it may allow him to die. It does not put him in prison; but it may leave him with a life of lower quality than that of some prison inmates. A society which can rectify these circumstances and does not can justly be accused of imposing upon the needy either death or lifelong deprivation. And those characteristics which make a person needy—whether they be illness, old age, insanity, feeblemindedness, inability to find paid work, or even poor moral character—are insufficient to make him deserve the fate to which an inactive society would in effect condemn him. One would not be executed for inability or failure to find paid work; neither should one be allowed to die for this misfortune or failing.

A person who cannot or does not find his own means of social security does not thereby forfeit his status as a human being. If other human beings, with physical, mental and moral qualities different from his, are regarded as having the right to life and to the means of life, then so too should he be regarded. A society which does not accept the responsibility for supplying such a person with the basic necessities of life is, in effect, endorsing a difference between its members which is without moral justification. . . .

The adoption of a Permissive view of welfare would have significant practical implications. If there were a legal right, unconditional upon behaviour, to a specified level of state-supplied benefits, then state investigation of the prospective welfare recipient could be kept to a minimum. Why he is in need, whether he can work, whether he is willing to work, and what he does while receiving welfare benefits are on this view quite irrelevant to his right to receive those benefits. A welfare recipient is a person who claims from his society that to which he is legally entitled under a morally based welfare scheme. The fact that he makes this claim licenses no special state or societal interference with his behaviour. If the Permissive view of welfare were widely believed, then there would be no social stigma attached to being on welfare. There is such a stigma, and many long-term welfare recipients are considerably demoralized by their dependent status.[6] These facts suggest that the Permissive view of welfare is not widely held in our society.

3 The Puritan View

This view of welfare rather naturally emerges when we consider that no one can have a right to something without someone else's, or some group of other persons', having responsibilities correlative to this right. In the case in which the right in question is a legal right to social security, the correlative responsibilities may be rather extensive. They have been deemed responsibilities of "the state." The state will require resources and funds to meet these responsibilities, and these do not emerge from the sky miraculously, or zip into existence as a consequence of virtually effortless acts of will. They are taken by the state from its citizens, often in the form of taxation on earned income. The funds given to the welfare recipient and many of the goods which he purchases with these funds are produced by other members of society, many of whom give a considerable portion of their time and their energy to this end. If a state has the moral responsibility to ensure the social security of its citizens then all the citizens of that state have the responsibility to provide state agencies with the means to carry out their duties. This responsibility, in our present contingent circumstances, seems to generate an obligation to *work*.

A person who works helps to produce the goods which all use in daily living and, when paid, contributes through taxation to government endeavours. The person who does not work, even though able to work, does not make his contribution to social efforts towards obtaining the means of life. He is not entitled to a share of the goods produced by others if he chooses not to take part in their labours. Unless he can show that there is a moral justification for his not making the sacrifice of time and energy which others make, he has no legitimate claim to welfare benefits. If he is disabled or unable to obtain work, he cannot work; hence he has no need to justify his failure to work. But if he does choose not to work, he would have to justify his choice by saying "others should sacrifice their time and energy for me; I have no need to sacrifice time and energy for them." This principle, a version of what Rawls refers to as a free-rider's principle, simply will not stand up to criticism.[7] To deliberately avoid working and benefit from the labours of others is morally indefensible.

Within a welfare system erected on these principles, the right to welfare is conditional upon one's satisfactorily accounting for his failure to obtain the necessities of life by his own efforts. Someone who is severely disabled mentally or physically, or who for some other reason cannot work, is morally entitled to receive welfare benefits. Someone who chooses not to work is not. The Puritan view of welfare is a kind of compromise between the Individualist view and the Permissive view. . . .

The Puritan view of welfare, based as it is on the inter-relation between welfare and work, provides a rationale for two connected principles which those establishing welfare schemes in Canada and in the United States seem to endorse. First of all, those on welfare should never receive a higher income than the working poor. Secondly, a welfare scheme should, in some way or other, incorporate incentives to work. These principles, which presuppose that it is better to work than not to work, emerge rather naturally from the contingency which is at the basis of the Puritan view: the goods essential for social security are products of the labour of some members of society. If we wish to have a continued supply of such goods, we must encourage those who work to produce them. . . .

APPRAISAL OF POLICIES: SOCIAL CONSEQUENCES AND SOCIAL JUSTICE

In approaching the appraisal of prospective welfare policies under these two aspects I am, of course, making some assumptions about the moral appraisal of suggested social policies. Although these cannot possibly be justified here, it may be helpful to articulate them, at least in a rough way.

Appraisal of social policies is in part teleological. To the extent that a policy, P, increases the total human welfare more than does an alternative policy, P', P is a better social policy than P'. Or, if P leaves the total human welfare as it is, while P' diminishes it, then to that extent, P is a better social policy than P'. Even this skeletal formulation of the teleological aspect of appraisal reveals why appraisal cannot be entirely teleological. We consider total consequences—effects upon the total of "human well-being" in a society. But this total is a summation of consequences on different individuals. It includes no judgements as to how far we allow one individual's well-being to decrease while another's increases, under the same policy. Judgements relating to the latter problems are judgements about social justice.

In appraising social policies we have to weigh up considerations of total well-being against considerations of justice. Just how this is to be done, precisely, I would not pretend to know. However, the absence of precise methods does not mean that we should relinquish attempts at appraisal: some problems are already with us, and thought which is necessarily tentative and imprecise is still preferable to no thought at all.

1 Consequences of Welfare Schemes

First, let us consider the consequences of the non-scheme advocated by the Individualist. He would have us abolish all non-optional government programmes which have as their goal the improvement of anyone's personal welfare. This rejection extends to health schemes, pension plans and education, as well as to welfare and unemployment insurance. So following the Individualist would lead to very sweeping changes.

The Individualist will claim (as do Hospers and Ayn Rand) that on the whole his non-scheme will bring beneficial consequences. He will admit, as he must, that there are people who would suffer tremendously if welfare and other social security programmes were simply terminated. Some would even die as a result. We cannot assume that spontaneously developing charities would cover every case of dire need. Nevertheless the Individualist wants to point to benefits which would accrue to businessmen and to working people and their families if taxation were drastically cut. It is his claim that consumption would rise, hence production would rise, job opportunities would be extended, and there would be an economic boom, if people could only spend all their earned income as they wished. This boom would benefit both rich and poor.

There are significant omissions which are necessary in order to render the Individualist's optimism plausible. Either workers and businessmen would have insurance of various kinds, or they would be insecure in their prosperity. If they did have insurance to cover health problems, old age and possible job loss, then they would pay for it; hence they would not be spending their whole earned income on consumer goods. Those who run the insurance schemes could, of course, put this money back into the economy—but government schemes already do this. The economic boom under Individualism would not be as loud as originally expected. Furthermore the goal of increased consumption-increased productivity must be questioned from an ecological viewpoint: many necessary materials are available only in limited quantities.

Finally, a word about charity. It is not to be expected that those who are at the mercy of charities will benefit from this state, either materially or psychologically. Those who prosper will be able to choose between giving a great deal to charity and suffering from the very real insecurity and guilt which would accompany the existence of starvation and grim poverty outside their padlocked doors. It is to be hoped that they would opt for the first alternative. But, if they did, this might be every bit as expensive for them as government-supported benefit schemes are now. If they did not give generously to charity, violence might result. However one looks at it, the consequences of Individualism are unlikely to be good.

Welfare schemes operating in Canada today are almost without exception based upon the principles of the Puritan view. To see the consequences of that type of welfare scheme we have only to look at the results of our own welfare programmes. Taxation to support such schemes is high, though not so intolerably so as to have led to widescale resentment among taxpayers. Canadian welfare programmes are attended by complicated and often cumbersome bureaucracy, some of which results from the interlocking of municipal, provincial and federal governments in the administration and financing of welfare programmes. The cost of the programmes is no doubt increased by this bureaucracy; not all the tax money directed to welfare programmes goes to those in need. Puritan welfare schemes do not result in social catastrophe or in significant business stagnation—this much we know, because we already live with such schemes. Their adverse consequences, if any, are felt primarily not by society generally nor by businessmen and the working segment of the public, but rather by recipients of welfare.

Both the Special Senate Committee Report on Poverty and the Real Poverty Report criticize our present system of welfare for its demoralization of recipients, who often must deal with several levels of government and are vulnerable to arbitrary interference on the part of administering officials. Welfare officials have the power to check on welfare recipients and cut off or limit their benefits under a large number of circumstances. The dangers to welfare recipients in terms of anxiety, threats to privacy and loss of dignity are obvious. According to the Senate Report, the single aspect shared by all Canada's welfare systems is "a record of failure and insufficiency, of bureaucratic rigidities that often result in the degradation, humiliation and alienation of recipients."[8] The writers of this report cite many instances of humiliation, leaving the impression that these are too easily found to be "incidental aberrations."[9] Concern that a welfare recipient either be unable to work or be willing to work (if unemployed) can easily turn into concern about how he spends the income supplied him, what his plans for the future are, where he lives, how many children he has. And the rationale underlying the Puritan scheme makes the degradation of welfare recipients a natural consequence of welfare institutions. Work is valued and only he who works is thought to contribute to society. Welfare recipients are regarded as parasites and spongers—so when they are treated as such, this is only what we should have expected. Being on welfare in a society which thinks and acts in this fashion can be psychologically debilitating. Welfare recipients who are demoralized by their downgraded status and relative lack of personal freedom can be expected to be made less capable of self-sufficiency. To the extent that this is so, welfare systems erected on Puritan principles may defeat their own purposes.

In fairness, it must be noted here that bureaucratic checks and controls are not a feature only of Puritan welfare systems. To a limited extent, Permissive systems would have to incorporate them too. Within those systems, welfare benefits would be given only to those whose income was inadequate to meet basic needs. However, there would be no checks on "willingness to work," and there would be no need for welfare workers to evaluate the merits of the daily activities of recipients. If a Permissive guaranteed income system were administered through income tax returns, everyone receiving the basic income and those not needing it paying it back in taxes, then the special status of welfare recipients would fade. They would no longer be singled out as a special group within the population. It is to be expected that living solely on government-supplied benefits would be psychologically easier in that type of situation.

Thus it can be argued that for the recipients of welfare, a Permissive scheme has more advantages than a Puritan one. This is not a very surprising conclusion. The Puritan scheme is relatively disadvantageous to recipients, and Puritans would acknowledge this point; they will argue that the overall consequences of Permissive schemes are negative in that these schemes benefit some at too great a cost to others. (Remember, we are not yet concerned with the *justice* of welfare policies, but solely with their consequences as regards *total* human well-being within the society in question.) The concern which most people have regarding the Permissive scheme relates to its costs and its dangers to the "work ethic." It is commonly thought that people work only because they have to work to survive in a tolerable style. If a guaranteed income scheme were adopted by the government, this incentive to work would disappear. No one would be faced with the choice between a nasty and boring job and starvation. Who would do the nasty and boring jobs then? Many of them are not eliminable and they have to be done somehow, by someone. Puritans fear that a great many people—even some with relatively pleasant jobs—might simply cease to work if they could receive non-stigmatized government money to live on. If this were to happen, the permissive society would simply grind to a halt.

In addressing these anxieties about the consequences of Permissive welfare schemes, we must recall that welfare benefits are set to ensure only that those who do not work have a bearable existence, with an income sufficient for basic needs, and that they have this income regardless of why they fail to work. Welfare benefits will not finance luxury living for a family of five! If jobs are adequately paid so that workers receive more than the minimum welfare income in an earned salary, then there will still be a financial incentive to take jobs. What guaranteed income schemes will do is to raise the salary floor. This change will benefit the many non-unionized workers in service and clerical occupations.

Furthermore it is unlikely that people work solely due to (i) the desire for money and the things it can buy and (ii) belief in the Puritan work ethic. There are many other reasons for working, some of which would persist in a society which had adopted a Permissive welfare system. Most people are happier when their time is structured in some way, when they are active outside their own homes, when they feel themselves part of an endeavour whose purposes transcend their particular ego-istic ones. Women often choose to work outside the home for these reasons as much as for financial ones. With these and other factors operating I cannot see that the adoption of a Permissive welfare scheme would be followed by a level of slothful-ness which would jeopardize human well-being.

Another worry about the Permissive scheme concerns cost. It is difficult to com-ment on this in a general way, since it would vary so much from case to case. Of Canada at the present it has been said that a guaranteed income scheme administered through income tax would cost less than social security payments administered through the present bureaucracies. It is thought that this saving would result from a drastic cut in administrative costs. The matter of the work ethic is also relevant to the question of costs. Within a Puritan framework it is very important to have a high level of employment and there is a tendency to resist any reorganization which re-sults in there being fewer jobs available. Some of these proposed reorganizations would save money; strictly speaking we should count the cost of keeping jobs which are objectively unnecessary as part of the cost of Puritanism regarding welfare.

In summary, we can appraise Individualism, Puritanism and Permissivism with respect to their anticipated consequences, as follows: Individualism is unacceptable; Puritanism is tolerable, but has some undesirable consequences for welfare recipi-ents; Permissivism appears to be the winner. Worries about bad effects which Per-missive welfare schemes might have due to high costs and (alleged) reduced work-incentives appear to be without solid basis.

2   Social Justice under Proposed Welfare Schemes

We must now try to consider the merits of Individualism, Puritanism and Permissiv-ism with regard to their impact on the distribution of the goods necessary for well-being. [Robert] Nozick has argued against the whole conception of a distributive jus-tice on the grounds that it presupposes that goods are like manna from heaven: we simply get them and then have a problem—to whom to give them. According to Nozick we know where things come from and we do not have the problem of to whom to give them. There is not really a problem of distributive justice, for there is no central distributor giving out manna from heaven! It is necessary to counter Nozick on this point since his reaction to the (purported) problems of distributive justice would undercut much of what follows.[10]

There is a level at which Nozick's point is obviously valid. If A discovers a cure for cancer, then it is A and not B or C who is responsible for this discovery. On Nozick's view this is taken to imply that A should reap any monetary profits which are forthcoming; other people will benefit from the cure itself. Now although it can-not be doubted that A is a bright and hardworking person, neither can it be denied that A and his circumstances are the product of many co-operative endeavours: schools and laboratories, for instance. Because this is so, I find Nozick's claim that "we know where things come from" unconvincing at a deeper level. Since achieve-ments like A's presuppose extensive social co-operation, it is morally permissible to regard even the monetary profits accruing from them as shareable by the "owner" and society at large.

Laws support existing income levels in many ways. Governments specify taxation so as to further determine net income. Property ownership is a legal matter. In all these ways people's incomes and possibilities for obtaining income are affected by deliberate state action. It is always possible to raise questions about the moral desirability of actual conventional arrangements. Should university professors earn less than lawyers? More than waitresses? Why? Why not? Anyone who gives an account of distributive justice is trying to specify principles which will make it possible to answer questions such as these, and nothing in Nozick's argument suffices to show that the questions are meaningless or unimportant.

Any human distribution of anything is unjust insofar as differences exist for no good reason. If goods did come like manna from heaven and the Central Distributor gave A ten times more than B, we should want to know why. The skewed distribution might be deemed a just one if A's needs were objectively ten times greater than B's, or if B refused to accept more than his small portion of goods. But if no reason at all could be given for it, or if only an irrelevant reason could be given (e.g., A is blue-eyed and B is not), then it is an unjust distribution. All the views we have expounded concerning welfare permit differences in income level. Some philosophers would say that such differences are never just, although they may be necessary, for historical or utilitarian reasons. Whether or not this is so, it is admittedly very difficult to say just what would constitute a good reason for giving A a higher income than B. Level of need, degree of responsibility, amount of training, unpleasantness of work—all these have been proposed and all have some plausibility. We do not need to tackle all this larger problem in order to consider justice under proposed welfare systems. For we can deal here solely with the question of whether everyone should receive a floor level of income; decisions on this matter are independent of decisions on overall equality or principles of variation among incomes above the floor. The Permissivist contends that all should receive at least the floor income; the Individualist and the Puritan deny this. All would claim justice for their side.

The Individualist attempts to justify extreme variations in income, with some people below the level where they can fulfill their basic needs, with reference to the fact of people's actual accomplishments. This approach to the question is open to the same objections as those which have already been raised against Nozick's non-manna-from-heaven argument, and I shall not repeat them here. Let us move on to the Puritan account. It is because goods emerge from human efforts that the Puritan advances his view of welfare. He stresses the unfairness of a system which would permit some people to take advantage of others. A Permissive welfare system would do this, as it makes no attempt to distinguish between those who choose not to work and those who cannot work. No one should be able to take advantage of another under the auspices of a government institution. The Puritan scheme seeks to eliminate this possibility, and for that reason, Puritans would allege, it is a more just scheme than the Permissive one.

Permissivists can best reply to this contention by acknowledging that any instance of free-riding would be an instance where those working were done an injustice, but by showing that any justice which the Puritan preserves by eliminating free-riding is outweighted by *injustice* perpetrated elsewhere. Consider the children of the Puritan's free-riders. They will suffer greatly for the "sins" of their parents. Within the institution of the family, the Puritan cannot suitably hurt the guilty without cruelly depriving the innocent. There is a sense, too, in which Puritanism does injustice to the many people on welfare who are not free-riders. It perpetuates the opinion that they are non-contributors to society and this doctrine, which is over-simplified if not downright false, has a harmful effect upon welfare recipients.

Social justice is not simply a matter of the distribution of goods, or the income with which goods are to be purchased. It is also a matter of the protection of rights. Western societies claim to give their citizens equal rights in political and legal contexts; they also claim to endorse the larger conception of a right to life. Now it is possible to interpret these rights in a limited and formalistic way, so that the duties correlative to them are minimal. On the limited, or negative, interpretation, to say that A has a right to life is simply to say that others have a duty not to interfere with A's attempts to keep himself alive. This interpretation of the right to life is compatible with Individualism as well as with Puritanism. But it is an inadequate interpretation of the right to life and of other rights. A right to vote is meaningless if one is starving and unable to get to the polls; a right to equality before the law is meaningless if one cannot afford to hire a lawyer. And so on.

Even a Permissive welfare scheme will go only a very small way towards protecting people's rights. It will amount to a meaningful acknowledgement of a right to life, by ensuring income adequate to purchase food, clothing and shelter—at the very least. These minimum necessities are presupposed by all other rights a society may endorse in that their possession is a precondition of being able to exercise these other rights. Because it protects the rights of all within a society better than do Puritanism and Individualism, the Permissive view can rightly claim superiority over the others with regard to justice.

NOTES

1 Nichols Rescher, *Welfare: Social Issues in Philosophical Perspective,* p. 114.

2 One might wish to discuss moral questions concerning welfare in the context of natural rights doctrines. Indeed, Article 22 of the United Nations Declaration of Human Rights states, "Everyone, as a member of society, has the right to social security and is entitled, through national effort and international cooperation and in accordance with the organization and resources of each State, to the economic, social and cultural rights indispensable for his dignity and the free development of his personality." I make no attempt to defend the right to welfare as a natural right. Granting that rights imply responsibilities or duties and that "ought" implies "can," it would only be intelligible to regard the right to social security as a natural right if all states were able to ensure the minimum well-being of their citizens. This is not the case. And a natural right is one which is by definition supposed to belong to all human beings simply in virtue of their status as human beings. The analysis given here in the permissive view is compatible with the claim that all human beings have a *prima facie* natural right to social security. It is not, however, compatible with the claim

that all human beings have a natural right to social security if this right is regarded as one which is so absolute as to be inviolable under any and all conditions.

3 See, for example, Ayn Rand's *Atlas Shrugged, The Virtue of Selfishness,* and *Capitalism: the Unknown Ideal.*

4 John Hospers, *Libertarianism: A Political Philosophy for Tomorrow,* p. 67.

5 I say virtually unconditional, because an Individualist such as John Hospers sees a legitimate moral role for government in preventing the use of force by some citizens against others. Since this is the case, I presume that he would also regard as legitimate such taxation as was necessary to support this function. Presumably that taxation would be seen as consented to by all, on the grounds that all "really want" government protection.

6 Ian Adams, William Cameron, Brian Hill, and Peter Penz, *The Real Poverty Report,* pp. 167–187.

7 See *A Theory of Justice,* pp. 124, 136. Rawls defines the free-rider as one who relies on the principle "everyone is to act justly except for myself, if I choose not to," and says that his position is a version of egoism which is eliminated as a morally acceptable principle by formal constraints. This conclusion regarding the tenability of egoism is one which I accept and which is taken for granted in the present context.

8 *Senate Report on Poverty,* p. 73.

9 The Hamilton Public Welfare Department takes automobile licence plates from recipients, making them available again only to those whose needs meet with the Department's approval. (*Real Poverty Report,* p. 186.) The *Globe and Mail* for 12 January 1974 reported that welfare recipients in the city of Toronto are to be subjected to computerized budgeting. In the summer of 1973, the two young daughters of an Alabama man on welfare were sterilized against their own wishes and without their parents' informed consent. (See *Time,* 23 July 1973.)

10 Robert Nozick, "Distributive Justice," *Philosophy and Public Affairs,* Fall 1973.

QUESTIONS

1 Which of the three approaches to welfare described by Govier (individualist, permissive, puritan) is found in our society?

2 Govier finds the permissive position superior to the others on the basis of both utilitarian and justice considerations. What arguments could an individualist offer to rebut Govier's arguments? What arguments could an advocate of the puritan position offer to counter Govier's?

Workfare: Breaking the Poverty Cycle

Peter G. Germanis

Peter G. Germanis is a policy analyst at the Heritage Foundation, a conservative think tank in Washington, D.C. He is the coauthor of *Understanding Reaganomics* (1982).

Germanis adopts a puritan stance on welfare in his defense of workfare programs—programs that require employable recipients to work for their welfare benefits. In his view, workfare programs serve many purposes. First, community work that would otherwise not get done gets done. Second, participants in these programs develop crucial work habits and have their value as productive members of the work force enhanced by their work experience. Third, workfare programs save money insofar as they deter employable individuals from applying for or staying on welfare.

Expenditures on welfare programs have been rising at an alarming rate over the last two decades. A principal cause of this enormous expansion is the work disincentive created by continual benefit liberalizations. Rather than paving the way for a higher standard of living, however, many of these government programs have tended to foster permanent dependency on welfare by providing benefits of greater value than the income an individual could earn by working. In effect, the American welfare system allows an able-bodied individual to ask himself: "Will I be better off if I work or if I allow myself and my family to become dependent upon the work of other individuals?" A system permitting this question to be posed is a system desperately in need of review and reform.

STILL ON THE DOLE

Encouraging welfare recipients to become self-supporting is supposed to be a major objective of many government programs. Most of these programs provide recipients cash incentives to work their way off the dole. In many cases, however, the result has been that individuals with relatively high incomes continue to receive welfare benefits. . . . Moreover, although these programs may be designed to aid the poor, in the long run they may actually lower their living standard by discouraging them from entering the labor market where they could acquire the job skills that eventually could lift many from poverty's depths.

There is an alternative to the self-defeating, degrading system of the dole which long has characterized the U.S. welfare system. This alternative is widely known as Community Work Experience Programs (CWEP), or more commonly as "workfare," in which employable recipients of public assistance—primarily able-bodied males and mothers of school age children—must perform some public service without pay

Reprinted with permission from The Heritage Foundation *Backgrounder*, no. 195 (July 9, 1982).

in return for their welfare benefits. . . . As such, workfare reflects the American work ethic. Its objective is to promote financial independence by giving people greater incentives to seek out unsubsidized employment. This work requirement is crucial for successful welfare reform because it is the most effective way to offset the work disincentives now created by the welfare system. . . . Several existing job search programs already are cost-effective.

Example: Oregon's Coordinated Job Placement Program. About 10 percent of the applicant pool was kept off the rolls in fiscal 1981 because the applicants had found employment. Oregon's AFDC caseload has declined by 25 percent since the job search program began in August 1980, despite a 40 percent rise in the unemployment rate.

Example: In Kent County, Michigan, the job search demonstration program for unemployed parents cut the caseload by 60 percent. Of that, one-third found jobs before collecting benefits and the remainder either withdrew their applications or were dropped from consideration for refusing to participate.

The program thus tends to discourage those unwilling to work from viewing welfare as an alternative. Other states and localities also report that job search is an effective tool in placing welfare recipients in jobs, even in areas plagued by high unemployment. . . .

BENEFITS OF WORKFARE

There are several inherent advantages to the *quid pro quo* concept of workfare.

I The community receives something in exchange for its assistance. All communities surely have work that needs doing but has been ignored because of budgetary constraints. Admittedly, workfare participants' contributions may be small, but since the welfare grants would be paid whether or not work is performed, the community's gain nevertheless is real. Among the jobs created by workfare in some of the optional CWEP programs are maintenance, custodial, day care and library services and assistance to police and emergency medical personnel. Existing workers are not displaced since workfare project tasks would not otherwise have been performed. . . .

II Participants in the program may find that their attractiveness to potential employers has been enhanced through their exposure to a working environment. Even if the jobs provided give little in the way of training, they introduce work disciplines. Such informal training encourages development of crucial work habits—punctuality, dependability and good working relations with fellow workers. The work experience also gives participants a chance to gain the kind of references, such as a letter of recommendation, which will help them in future job searches. The workfare experience thus may very well enhance the value of participants as productive members of the workforce and ease their transition into unsubsidized employment.

III A workfare program may reduce welfare costs by deterring some persons who should be self-supporting from remaining on the dole. Though not intended as a primary objective, workfare has a "deterrent effect" that eliminates welfare recipients who either refuse to participate or have another source of employment which prevents them from doing so. Establishing a work requirement would give employable recipients an incentive to seek other, more attractive means of support when they realize that their benefits no longer are free. Workfare has proved an effective means of sizeably reducing the fraud and abuse so prevalent in our current system by encouraging the departure of undeserving recipients, thereby reducing the burden on the taxpayer and making more money available for those in genuine need. . . .

One of the most efficiently administered workfare programs is in Cincinnati, which has been part of the General Relief welfare program for over 40 years. Most of the work has little skill content, with heavy emphasis placed on having the participants put in their time. The program appears to have been cost-effective. Notes one evaluation:

> There is a very high initial attrition rate, when people realize they have to work for their benefits. It is sometimes necessary to assign 200 people to get 50 to show up at the work site. The average no show rate may run as high as 60-75 percent. . . . although the deterrent effect and the reduction in the caseload is not an explicit objective, it is an obvious reality.
>
> Although no formal cost/benefit assessments have been made, the amount of GR grant money saved from case closings and the deterrent effect, appear to be far more than the costs of administering the program. On that score alone the program has won general support and agency endorsement. . . .

A second workfare program, and one which very likely will receive a great deal of attention because it is part of the AFDC program, is the Utah Work Experience and Training Program (WEAT). For many years, Utah was the only state with a statewide mandatory work program that included AFDC recipients, although it exempted mothers with children under the age of six. Utah's WEAT program, established in 1974, requires employable recipients to work three days a week and to participate in job search for two days. This approach assures work-site sponsors a stable work schedule. A twelve-week limit on workfare participation ensures that workfare participants do not become permanently dependent on workfare in place of regular employment.

Of those assigned to projects, 27 percent were removed because they failed to perform. Usher West, who heads the Utah program, acknowledges that "WEAT had a general housecleaning effect." In addition, the program also helped many of those assigned work by enhancing their employability. The *Wall Street Journal* reported:

> One of those who benefited is Dennis Wickert, a 42-year-old Marine Corps veteran with a ninth-grade education. A combination of inadequate training and absences caused by problems with bad gums, plus relentless bill collectors, bounced him from the last of several service-station jobs and back onto AFDC several years ago, Mr. Wickert recalls. Indeed, he was feeling like a loser, until the WEAT program assigned him to a neighborhood maintenance crew working out of a local community-action office.
>
> After that "I could walk up to my neighbor and say I earn my welfare money, it's honest," he says with conviction. Mr. Wickert's performance persuaded his employer to hire him as a crew chief. Today he is off AFDC, earning $800 a month plus some extra cash from odd hauling jobs done with his own truck. . . .

Although not all experiences in workfare have met expectations, it does appear that a properly administered program could reduce significantly burgeoning welfare costs while helping many of the poor overcome the "poverty wall" created by America's current welfare and tax systems.

It is quite possible that the recent immigrants to this country who speak no English are better off than many of the poor because the newcomers do not know how to take advantage of the welfare programs. Social analyst Tom Bethell has characterized their plight: "The newcomers are compelled to take those demeaning jobs at the bottom, but they soon work their way up, as immigrants always have in the past, and eventually rise above those on the isolated welfare platform." The purpose of workfare is not to put the poor to work on workfare projects, but to get them into the productive and rewarding labor force by improving the incentives for serious job search.

QUESTIONS

1 Are the workfare programs described by Germanis morally acceptable?
2 Are there good reasons to think that workfare programs will contribute to a solution of the poverty problem in the United States?

Workfare and the Imposition of Discipline

Mary Hawkesworth

Mary Hawkesworth is professor of political science at the University of Louisville in Kentucky. Her research interests include contemporary political philosophy, feminist theory, and social policy. Hawkesworth is the editor of *The Routledge Encyclopaedia of Government and Politics* (1991) and the author of *Beyond Oppression: Feminist Theory and Political Strategy* (1990) and *Theoretical Issues in Policy Analysis* (1988).

Hawkesworth attacks workfare programs and the justifications advanced in their support on two grounds. First she challenges the conception of poverty that is implicit in arguments in defense of workfare. That conception identifies the causes of poverty with the attitudes of the poor, specifically with the failure of those on welfare to identify with the work ethic and to develop appropriate work habits. Second, she focuses on the dual objectives of workfare programs. One of workfare's objectives is to increase the employability of participants by teaching them marketable skills, increasing their self-esteem, and helping them to develop proper work habits and work motivation. Its other objective is to deter those who are able-bodied from applying for or staying on welfare, by requiring them to labor in unattractive jobs. Hawkesworth argues that these two objectives are incompatible.

Reprinted with permission of the author and the publisher from *Social Theory and Practice,* vol. 11 (Summer 1985), pp. 169–173, 177–180.

Workfare, a government program which requires recipients of public assistance to "work off" the value of their benefits through unpaid labor in community service projects, has been hailed as the "welfare reform of the 1980s."[1]. . .

Proponents of workfare have noted that the primary reasons for incorporating a mandatory work requirement in public assistance programs are to "encourage recipient identification with the labor market, provide recipients with a work history and develop the discipline necessary for accepting employment in the regular economy."[2] For this reason, workfare requirements are targeted at the "able-bodied," "employable" poor; exemptions are allowed for those who are physically or mentally unfit for work, for mothers who have children under the age of three and for individuals who are already employed for eighty or more hours per month. Workfare derives its justification from a particular conception of poverty, one which explains the causes of poverty in terms of the attitudes and the psychology of the poor. The problem to be addressed in any successful welfare policy is the mindset of the "professional poor who have adopted welfare as a way of life,"[3] who intentionally waste their skills and talents by willfully refusing to work.

The assumptions underlying this conception of poverty have been developed systematically in an essay published in *The Public Interest.* Claiming that it is impossible to explain the high rates of unemployment among disadvantaged groups "by appealing to lack of jobs, discrimination or other social conditions over which the disadvantaged have no control,"[4] Lawrence Mead suggests that the problem of poverty must be understood in terms of the poor's unwillingness to accept the jobs which are available to them. The underdevelopment of the work ethic is the fundamental problem of the poor. Mead links this pervasive moral problem to 20 years of welfare programs which "merely give things to their recipients . . . [which] support recipients while expecting nothing in return. Specifically, welfare programs contain no effective requirements that recipients work in return for their benefits."[5] In direct contrast to the market which reinforces the work ethic in individuals by relating rewards to individuals' investments of effort and contributions to society, welfare undermines the value of reciprocity by severing the connection between benefits and obligations. To rectify this problem, Mead argues that welfare programs "should try to assure recipients the same balance of rights and obligations that nondependent people face in their daily lives. The needy should be supported, but they should also be expected to work, if employable, to stay in school, if young, to obey the law and so on. This is the only way these programs can support and justify, rather than tacitly undercut, the civic sense their clients need to progress in American society."[6] Workfare must replace welfare in order to ensure the future prosperity of the currently disadvantaged members of society and to facilitate their integration into the mainstream of American life. Acknowledging that the success of workfare requires the exercise of authority, and at times coercion, over welfare recipients, Mead offers a legitimation of the policy consonant with popular concepts in public administration. "Low wage work is no longer a 'private good,' something the individual will seek spontaneously because it benefits him. Rather, it has become a 'public good,' something in which society as a whole has an interest, for reasons of morals or social integration, but which may not serve individual interests. Like other public goods, it now has to be produced using government authority rather than through the dynamic of individual interest operating in the marketplace. Government must now obligate program recipients to work rather than just entice them. What is obligatory cannot simply be offered as a choice—it has to be enforced by sanctions, in this case, loss of the welfare grant."[7]

Once poverty is understood in terms of particular debilitating attitudes held by the poor, workfare as a social policy designed specifically to alter individual attitudes toward work, emerges as an appropriate remedy to the contemporary welfare crisis. Requiring welfare recipients to work on a regular basis will cultivate in them a work "habit" while simultaneously overcoming their fears of not being able to compete in a job market. On-the-job experience in public service projects will increase welfare recipients' feelings of self-worth and self-confidence as they realize they are contributing something of value to their communities. The dependency bred by reliance upon government handouts will be supplanted by a growing sense of self-sufficiency as workfare participants gain a sense of mastery in their job assignments. The gradual accrual of job experience will enhance the marketable skills and hence the employability of workfare participants. Over time the regular exposure to the world of work coupled with the newfound confidence and marketability will facilitate the individual's transition from workfare to permanent paid employment in the private sector. Thus the long-term consequence of workfare will be a reduction in state and federal expenditures for welfare as the total number of recipients is reduced due to job placements. State and federal governments will also realize immediate reductions in their welfare expenditures as those recipients who are unwilling to assume their workfare responsibilities are terminated from the welfare rolls. Workfare also produces an additional residual benefit: reduction in the stigma associated with welfare. As the rolls are purged of welfare "cheats," workfare participants will encounter a new respect as the American public recognizes that the poor "have earned" the benefits which they receive.[8]

Should the success of workfare appear to rest upon excessively optimistic assessments of the effect of unpaid community work experience upon individual attitudes and behavior, proponents of workfare would respond that workfare also possesses a "deterrent" capacity. . . .

Reducing benefits while simultaneously requiring recipients to work off those benefits was intended to deter people from seeing welfare as an alternative to work. The image of welfare as a "pre-paid lifetime vacation plan" would be permanently replaced by a conception of welfare as minimal subsistence support which would be "administered with a sufficient degree of harshness and limitation in benefits that people who could work would be happy to get off and those who did work would stay off."[9] Thus an adequate understanding of workfare must include an awareness of both its positive incentives, the opportunity for the poor to develop work skills and habits, self-esteem and confidence, a basic "marketability"; and its deterrence capabilities, the assignment of individuals to menial jobs without pay as a condition for the receipt of minimal subsistence benefits.

To assess the merits of workfare, it is important to examine the assumptions upon which the program is based, the internal consistency of the program's objectives, and the adequacy of the mechanisms established to achieve the policy's goals. Workfare is premised upon the "pathological" theory of poverty, which explains poverty in terms of the characteristics or "defects" of the poor themselves. In the contemporary United States, this view is associated with a constellation of beliefs about capitalism, the function of the market and the sphere of individual freedom and responsibility. At the center of these beliefs lies the notion that upward social mobility is possible for any individual who possesses determination, energy and talent. Economic success is the market's reward for hard work. But if success is within the reach of any hardworking individual, if individual effort is all that stands between the rich and the poor, then the poor are peculiarly responsible for their own fate. Those who worsen their conditions by willfully refusing to take advantage of the opportunities which the free market affords are morally reprehensible. On this view, "laziness" or unwillingness to work is a form of moral defect for which the poor should be held strictly accountable.

But is the pathological theory an adequate account of poverty? An examination of the demographic characteristics of the poor suggests that the pathological theory is fundamentally flawed. More than two-thirds of the poor in the contemporary United States are unable to work because of age, disability or caretaking responsibilities for preschool age children. Forty-eight percent of the households with pre-transfer incomes below the poverty line are headed by individuals aged 65 or older, another 12% are headed by disabled individuals; 7% are headed by women with children under the age of 6. Of the remaining households below the poverty line, 7.5% are headed by persons who work full-time year round but whose incomes are insufficient to meet family subsistence needs, 20.4% are headed by persons who are employed but not on a full-time basis and 5% are headed by students.[10] Moreover, recent studies of AFDC recipients, the group of the poor most frequently discussed in terms of the pathological theory, indicate that the idea that AFDC household heads don't work or won't work is simply wrong. Seventy percent of AFDC households have at least one earner during the years on welfare: in 40% of these households, it is the head who earns the income; in the remainder, the earnings are those of older children within the household.[11] Furthermore, there is much greater movement between welfare and work than the pathological theory admits. Only a small proportion of households receiving public benefits remain on welfare for long periods of time.[12] The vast majority resort to welfare to upgrade their total income because their earnings from work are inadequate or because their earning capacity has been temporarily undermined due to unemployment.

A number of studies of the attitudes of the poor toward work also challenge the pathological theory's accuracy. "In answer to the question, 'Do the poor want to work?,' research on the orientations of the poor has concluded that yes, the poor do want to work. The work ethic is upheld strongly by AFDC recipients and work plays an important role in their life goals."[13] Indeed, results from the most comprehensive study on the attitudes of the poor towards work "unambiguously indicate that AFDC recipients, regardless of sex, age or race, identify their self-esteem with work as strongly as do the non-poor. . . . Despite their adverse position in society and their past failures in the labor force, these persons clearly upheld the work ethic and voiced strong commitments toward work."[14] In summary then, the pathological theory of poverty which underlies the workfare policy is mistaken. The able-bodied poor share the American commitment to the work ethic and they do work. Their problem is not one of attitude but one of inadequate pay or inadequate employment opportunities. The market economy has not afforded these individuals the mythologized avenues of upward social mobility. And recent research suggests that even in an expanding economy, the market will not provide an escape from poverty for these individuals in the future.

> The evidence from the recent past suggests that economic growth will not raise the earnings of the poor enough to enable many of them to escape poverty without government assistance. The major factor contributing to the reduction of poverty since 1966 seems to have been the growth in government transfers, which offset increases in poverty resulting from demographic changes and high unemployment rates. Economic growth per se seems to have had little effect.[15]

Proponents of workfare have repeatedly emphasized the dual objectives of the program: 1) to increase the employability of the poor by inculcating work habits and work motivation, by teaching marketable skills and by increasing self-esteem; and 2) to use mandatory labor in unattractive jobs to deter the able bodied poor from resorting to welfare. To ask if these two objectives are internally consistent is to ask if they both can be accomplished simultaneously without undermining each other. The first objective of workfare can best be understood in terms of an attempt to "constitute" or create a productive member of the workforce. The constitution of such a worker implies not only the transmission of particular work skills but also the inculcation of a commitment to work sufficiently powerful to serve as a continuing motive to work. Traditionally, the development of such a work commitment has been related either to the intrinsic rewards of the work (the inherently satisfying nature of the activity) or to the extrinsic rewards of the work (the level of pay, prestige, power, or "perks" which the work affords). The work motive of the typical worker is fueled by: 1) the intrinsic value of the work which overrides concern with extrinsic rewards; 2) the extrinsic rewards which offset any negative aspects of the work activity itself; or 3) the optimal situation, in which the intrinsic value of the work is accompanied by favorable extrinsic rewards. The second objective of workfare emphasizes worker "deterrence," requiring welfare recipients as a condition for receipt of minimal subsistence benefits to perform tasks sufficiently onerous that no worker would ever be attracted to the welfare alternative. Now it would appear highly improbable that a job sufficiently onerous to satisfy the worker "deterrence" objective could simultaneously satisfy the worker "constitution" objective. To achieve the desired deterrence effect workfare must minimize the intrinsic value of mandatory job assignments. And the workfare format, unpaid labor in exchange for minimal subsistence benefits, precludes the use of extrinsic rewards to offset the unpleasant aspects of the required labor. What remains in lieu of the intrinsic and extrinsic rewards of work is a program of forced labor operating under the sanction of starvation (forfeiture of benefits). While such a program does serve as a considerable deterrent to employed workers, it is incapable of fostering self-esteem or a positive commitment to work. On the contrary, it is likely to breed hostility and resentment among its involuntary participants. . . .

According to the rhetoric of proponents of workfare, the public service assignments of workfare participants should both serve a useful community purpose and afford opportunities for the development of marketable skills. . . . In practice, the great majority of welfare recipients have been placed in low-level maintenance and clerical positions. "Jobs such as cutting grass, picking up trash, washing dishes, mopping and waxing floors, driving senior citizen vans, moving furniture, assisting the dog catcher and doing general office work are typical."[16] Evaluation studies note that workfare program administrators have made no effort to offer participants jobs which utilize work skills which they already possess, nor have administrators made placements which enable participants to acquire marketable skills. Workfare assignments tend to be in unskilled jobs, precisely the kind of jobs which are prone to elimination during periods of economic recession. Thus, even if performance in these unskilled jobs is considered a form of "skills-training", the acquired "skills" are not marketable because equivalent employment is not readily available in the regular workforce. Pursuit of the "deterrence" objective justifies such unskilled job placements for workfare participants, but these placements are incompatible with the goal of creating an employable worker. Indeed several evaluation studies suggest that placing workfare participants in jobs which require few job skills actually lessens their chances of obtaining employment which affords sufficient income to escape poverty. A workfare participant who succeeds in finding a job in the workforce equivalent to the workfare assignment will earn too little to support a household. The welfare rolls will not be reduced because government transfers will still be required to supplement an inadequate income.

Proponents of workfare have emphasized the importance of work as a mechanism to heighten the self-esteem of the poor. Although the precise relationship between individual experience, social values and self-esteem is not thoroughly understood by existing psychological theories, there are good reasons to challenge any view which postulates the development of self-esteem as an automatic response to work, regardless of the nature of the work or the conditions under which the work is performed. Under the rubrics of workfare, work is mandatory as a condition for the receipt of welfare benefits. Individual participants have no choice in job assignments and no control over the conditions under which they work. In many instances, workfare participants are required to work side by side with individuals who are receiving salaries for performing the same tasks. Evaluation studies indicate that paid employees tend to denigrate workfare participants both for being unable to secure paid employment and for agreeing to "work for nothing."[17] Thus workfare participants must contend with the onus of mandatory menial labor, with complete lack of control over their work lives, with interactions with program administrators who dictate the conditions of their existence, and with co-workers who stigmatize them for complying with a policy over which they have no control. Such an array of forces scarcely can be expected to contribute to the self-esteem of the average individual. Nor should it be expected that these negative forces could be offset by the fact that workfare "makes a contribution to the community." The unattractive nature of workfare assignments (leaf raking, dish washing, and so on), coupled with their involuntary status, tend to undermine any sense of pride associated with performance of a public service. Finally, the sense of being a "victim of an inequitable system" is bound to constrain the development of self-esteem among workfare participants. The individuals who are required to participate in workfare programs know that they are not the only persons who receive economic benefits from the government. They comprise a small fraction of welfare recipients. The dollar value of their subsistence benefits is miniscule in comparison to the value of government benefits accorded to corporations, businesses, farmers, home owners in the form of tax deductions, investment credits, price supports, and direct services. Yet they alone are singled out and required to perform punitive public service to pay back their benefits. Awareness of the fundamental unfairness of this requirement is likely to color workfare participants' assessments of the workfare experience and reactions informed by this sense of victimization are not likely to be consonant with high self-esteem.

The practices associated with the implementation of workfare are conducive to the achievement of the program's deterrent objective: no human being would embrace the opportunity to comply with workfare's punitive provisions; but they are singularly at odds with the more benign objectives emphasized in the rhetoric of program advocates. Workfare does not provide meaningful public service opportunities for the poor; it does not afford training or marketable skills; and it does not contribute to the self-esteem of individuals who already possess a commitment to the work ethic but who stand in desperate need of permanent employment at a decent wage. Moreover, if the pathological theory of the poor is incorrect; if people resort to welfare because the labor market does not provide enough jobs for all who desire them, then the deterrent objective of workfare degenerates into a cruel policy of punishing the poor for fluctuations in the labor market over which they have no control. Based upon an incorrect theory of poverty, workfare cannot reduce the welfare rolls; it simply intensifies the burdens imposed upon the poor as a condition of survival. Evaluation studies indicate that workfare has not generated the predicted savings in welfare expenditures due to reductions in the caseloads.[18] On the contrary, they indicate that the administrative costs associated with workfare registration, screening, job placement, supervision and imposition of sanctions, make the program more expensive than previous welfare policies.[19]

[In sum] I have argued that workfare is a troubled policy. It is founded upon erroneous assumptions concerning the causes of poverty. It embodies incompatible objectives: its goal of constituting employable workers for an advanced industrial economy is undermined by its commitment to serve as a deterrent. And the means adopted to implement workfare are incapable of achieving the program's objectives: the menial labor assigned to participants is incapable of increasing their self-esteem or of equipping them with marketable skills; the deterrent objective cannot be achieved because high unemployment rates and inadequate incomes continue to increase the ranks of the poor; and the high administrative costs of the program increase rather than decrease the cost of the government's welfare expenditures. . . .

NOTES

1 Rep. Paul Findley (R-Ill.), Letter to Members of Congress seeking co-sponsors of his Workfare bill (December 22, 1980).

2 Richard Schweiker, Secretary, United States Department of Health and Human Services, *Testimony Before the Subcommittee on Public Assistance and Unemployment Compensation,* U.S. Congress, House Committee on Ways and Means (97th Congress, March 11, 1981), p. 8.

3 This theme figured prominently in Ronald Reagan's 1970 campaign for Governor of California as well as in his 1980 bid for the Presidency of the United States; cited in Harold Wilensky, *The Welfare State and Equality* (Berkeley: University of California Press, 1975), p. 33.

4 Lawrence Mead, "Social Programs and Social Obligations," *The Public Interest* 69 (1982): 20. . . .

5 Mead, p. 22.

6 Ibid., p. 23.

7 Ibid., p. 28. Mead provides a more detailed discussion of the relationship between authority, coercion and the probable success of workfare programs in "Expectations and Welfare Work: WIN in New York City," *Policy Studies Review* 2 (1983): 648–62.

8 All of these arguments have surfaced during Congressional hearings and debates on workfare. For a helpful summary of these views, see Barbara Linden and Deborah Vincent, *Workfare in Theory and Practice* (Washington, D.C.: National Social Science and Law Center, 1982), pp. 9–10.

9 Nathan Glazer, "The Social Policy of the Reagan Administration: A Review," *The Public Interest* 75 (1984): 85.

10 Sheldon Danziger & Peter Gottschalk, "The Measurement of Poverty: Implications for Anti-Poverty Policy," *American Behavioral Scientist* 26 (1983): 751.

11 Mildred Rein, *Dilemmas of Welfare Policy* (New York: Praeger Pub., 1982), p. 123. It is interesting to note that Rein's study found that in direct contrast to popular stereotypes, black women receiving AFDC worked more often than did white women.

12 Linden & Vincent, p. 12.

13 Berkeley Planning Associates, Inc., *Evaluation Design: Assessment of Work-Welfare Projects* (Washington, D.C.: U.S. Department of Health and Human Services, 1980), p. 95.

14 Ibid., p. 92. The quotation was referring to the landmark study by Leonard Goodwin, *Do the Poor Want to Work? A Socio-Psychological Study of Work Orientations* (Washington, D.C.: The Brookings Institute, 1972). . . .

15 Danziger & Gottschalk, p. 750.

16 Linden & Vincent, p. 33.

17 Linden & Vincent, p. 38.

18 Linda Demkovich, "Workfare—Punishment for Being Poor or An End to the Welfare Stigma," *National Journal* 12 (1981): 1204.

19 Abe Levine, "Administration of Public Welfare in the Case of AFDC," in Lester M. Salamon, ed., *Welfare: The Elusive Consensus* (New York: Praeger, 1978), p. 244.

QUESTIONS

1 Is it possible to design a workfare program that will meet Hawkesworth's objections?

2 Workfare programs have been criticized on the following grounds: workfare participants are

neither paid amounts equivalent to what they would earn as regular employees nor are they given the usual employee benefits such as vacations and sick leave. Thus these programs violate the principle that individuals should be justly remunerated for their work. Do you agree with this criticism?

SUGGESTED ADDITIONAL READINGS FOR CHAPTER 8

ARTHUR, JOHN, and WILLIAM SHAW, eds.: *Justice and Economic Distribution.* Englewood Cliffs, N.J.: Prentice-Hall, 1978. This collection of articles epitomizes the dominant current approach to distributive justice. That approach is highly abstract, pays little attention to practical applications, and is usually restricted to the intranational level. The theories which dominate current discussion are those of John Rawls, Robert Nozick, and utilitarianism. The first part of the book presents selections by Rawls, Nozick, and utilitarians. The second part consists of selections which present positions offered in opposition to the dominant theories.

FRIEDMAN, MILTON: *Capitalism and Freedom.* Chicago: University of Chicago Press, 1962. For Friedman, an economist and libertarian, the ethical principle governing the distribution of income in a free society is "to each according to what he or the instruments he owns produces." He sees economic freedom as a necessary condition for political freedom.

HARRINGTON, MICHAEL: *Socialism.* New York: Saturday Review Press, 1970, 1972. Harrington explores various "socialisms"—positions which he considers antisocialist. He presents his account of socialism as a possible alternative to both communism and the welfare state.

HAYEK, F. A.: *Law, Legislation and Liberty.* Vol. 2, *The Mirage of Social Justice.* Chicago: University of Chicago Press, 1976. Hayek, a libertarian, considers and criticizes the concept of "social justice." On Hayek's view the ideal of social justice (1) has no meaning, (2) is the harmful and dangerous cause of the misdirection of well-meant efforts, and (3) is a remnant of a closed society and incompatible with the individual freedom promised by an open society.

HELD, VIRGINIA, ed.: *Property, Profits, and Economic Justice.* Belmont, Calif.: Wadsworth, 1980. This is an excellent collection of readings centering on questions about our rights and interests in acquiring and holding property and in increasing or limiting profits.

MACHAN, TIBOR R., ed.: *The Libertarian Alternative: Essays in Social and Political Philosophy.* The writers anthologized in this volume represent a wide spectrum of views although they can all be characterized as "individualist" or "libertarian."

NIELSEN, KAI: *Equality and Liberty: A Defense of Radical Egalitarianism.* Totowa, N.J.: Rowman & Littlefield, 1984. Nielsen defends the egalitarian ideal that is at the basis of socialist thinking.

NOZICK, ROBERT: *Anarchy, State, and Utopia.* New York: Basic, 1974. This book has engendered a great deal of discussion among philosophers concerned with distributive justice. Nozick, who endorses the libertarian conception of justice, holds the libertarian ideal to be exemplified by the principle, "from each as he chooses, to each as he is chosen."

RAWLS, JOHN: "Justice as Fairness." *Philosophical Review,* vol. 67, April 1958, pp. 164–194. In this article, Rawls offers a definition of justice in terms of two principles, which he maintains all rational, self-interested persons would agree are in the equal interests of all. He argues (1) that everyone has the right to equal liberty, and (2) that differences of wealth and privilege are justified only if everyone is free to compete for them and if everyone benefits from them.

————: *A Theory of Justice*. Cambridge, Mass.: Harvard University Press, 1971. This is a more developed discussion of the position Rawls presents in the above article. It is a seminal work that has stimulated a great deal of discussion among philosophers.

SHUE, HENRY: *Basic Rights: Subsistence, Affluence, and U.S. Foreign Policy*. Princeton, N.J.: Princeton University Press, 1980. Shue argues that there is at least one small set of economic rights, subsistence rights, that have equal priority with the highest-ranked political rights.

THUROW, LESTER: *The Zero Sum Society*. New York: Basic, 1980. Thurow, a professor of economics and management, analyzes the unprecedented economic predicament presently confronting the United States and discusses various policy prescriptions designed to solve our economic problems. In Thurow's view, the government must be willing to make equity decisions designed to achieve and maintain a just distribution of income.

CHAPTER 9

World Hunger

In the world today, widespread hunger is an undeniable fact. Famines are common-place in Africa and Southeast Asia, and, for many people in very diverse places on the globe, malnutrition is an everyday fact of life. Very few of the victims of famine and malnutrition actually "die of hunger"; but they die of illnesses, such as flu and intestinal problems, which they could have survived if they had not been weakened by hunger. The victims are often very old or very young. Aftereffects for those who survive are often tragic and long-lasting. A large number of children are stunted in growth and suffer incapacitating brain damage as a result of malnutrition. Whole populations are permanently weakened, listless, and lethargic, lacking the energy for any economic advances that might help prevent future famines. From a moral point of view, what should affluent countries (or their people) do to prevent such devastating hunger and malnutrition? What *can* they do? This chapter presents some recent attempts to answer these two inseparable questions. As the readings show, answers concerning the moral *obligations* of more affluent individuals and nations in regard to world hunger are intertwined with answers concerning the *causes of world hunger* and *effective ways of eliminating those causes*.

NEO-MALTHUSIANISM

One answer regarding the causes of world hunger is offered by people labeled "neo-Malthusians." Following Thomas Robert Malthus (1766-1834), they identify the cause as *overpopulation*. For Malthus, unrestricted population growth necessarily outstrips economic growth, especially the growth in food supplies. This, in turn, *necessarily* results in famines. Uncontrolled fertility is the cause of poverty, and poverty is the cause of the miseries of the poor, including starvation. It has been shown that Malthus was wrong in certain respects, since in many countries the economic growth rate, including the growth in food supplies, has far outstripped the population growth rate. But contemporary neo-Malthusians hold that the economic growth rate cannot be sustained. They offer different reasons in support of this view (e.g., political or technical ones), but they all agree that continued economic growth is impossible. Having identified overpopulation as *the cause* of scarcity, neo-Malthusians locate the solution to problems of world hunger in population control. Optimistic neo-Malthusians hold that birth-control measures can eventually succeed in curbing population growth sufficiently to avert future famines. Pessimistic neo-Malthusians hold that serious political and psychological obstacles to planned population-control measures make famines inevitable in some countries. They predict that these famines will in turn effectively curb unmaintainable population growth unless those in more affluent countries intervene. Some pessimistic neo-Malthusians, including Garrett Hardin in this chapter, use their Malthusian analyses of world hunger to support claims about what more affluent individuals and nations *ought* to do regarding the needs of potential famine victims. The expressions "ethics of triage" and "lifeboat ethics" are often applied to the ethical approaches advocated by pessimistic neo-Malthusians.

The expression "method of triage" was first used to describe the French approach to their wounded in the First World War. The wounded were sorted into three categories. Those with the slightest injuries were given quick first aid. Those who could not be helped were simply allowed to die. Those in between received the most intensive medical care. Analogously, applying the method of triage to countries having serious food problems involves classifying them into three groups. The first group consists of countries that will survive even without aid. The second group consists of countries that will survive—given sufficient aid—because they are prepared to do what is necessary to bring their food resources and populations into line. Countries in the second group ought to be given the necessary aid. The third group consists of countries whose problems are insoluble in the long run because they are not willing to adopt the necessary population-control measures. According to the ethics of triage, countries in the third group should receive no help. Thus, the proponents of the ethics of triage argue that the affluent should help only those potential victims of famine and malnutrition who reside in countries which are effectively trying to bring population size into line with the country's food supply.[1]

The argument for the moral correctness of the ethics of triage is a consequentialist one and depends on the correctness of the following factual claim: Economic aid to countries with long-run "insoluble" problems is only a stopgap measure that in the long run will have highly undesirable consequences. Aid to societies in group 3, it is said, may alleviate current suffering, but it will cause more long-term suffering for the members of both the needy and affluent countries. Suffering will increase because economic aid will enable more people to survive and reproduce. If no real attempt is made to control population growth, the ever increasing population will make ever increasing demands on the world food supply. These demands will have a strong adverse effect on the quality of the life led by future members of today's more affluent societies. In time, it will be impossible even for the members of the once affluent countries to survive. If help is withheld from the countries in group 3, however, one of two things will follow. Either the needy countries will instigate measures to limit their populations in keeping with their own resources, or else nature itself through famine and disease will decimate the population to the appropriate level. In effect, those who argue in this way maintain that responsibilities and rights go hand in hand. People in the afflicted societies cause their own problems by hav-

---

[1] See especially Paul and William Paddock, *Famine—1975!* (Boston: Little, Brown, 1968).

ing too many children. They are entitled to have their most basic needs met by more affluent individuals and societies only if they accept a crucial responsibility—the responsibility for limiting their fertility sufficiently so that they do not continue to place an ever growing burden on the world's food resources.

Garrett Hardin's lifeboat-ethics argument echoes some of the major contentions of the ethics of triage. Comparing nations to boats, Hardin maintains that many countries have outstripped their "carrying capacity." He advances a consequentialist argument to support his claim that the affluent *ought not* to help those in the overpopulating countries. In Hardin's view, the long-range effects of food aid will be not only harmful but disastrous for everyone. They will be disastrous for countries whose fertility rates remain uncontrolled by either human planning or nature, since future generations in these countries will suffer massive starvation and profound misery. They will be disastrous for the human species as a whole, since the eventual outcome may be the elimination of the species. Hardin sees no real need to use the method of triage in making decisions about which countries should be given aid. If giving food to *any* overpopulated country does more harm than good, he argues, that food should not be given. For Hardin, "the question of triage does not even arise."[2]

NON-MALTHUSIAN ALTERNATIVES

Criticisms of neo-Malthusians take many forms. Some critics, for example, attack the *moral* claims of pessimistic neo-Malthusians. Rejecting the consequentialist approach to the moral dilemma, they maintain that no matter what the long-term consequences might be, we have an obligation to meet the most basic need of *existing* persons—the need for food. The most prominent attacks against Malthusianism, however, center around rejections of some or all of the Malthusian claims regarding the causes and/or the inevitability of famine and malnutrition in needy, developing countries. The counteranalyses offered reject the neo-Malthusian contention that the necessary economic growth is impossible. On these analyses, economic growth in the developing countries *themselves* is both possible and an essential part of the solution to problems of world hunger. Two major lines of argument emerge in these counteranalyses.

The first counteranalysis focuses on identifying the causes of high fertility rates among the poor in developing countries. Only if we understand why the poor have high rates of reproduction can we help to instigate and support social practices which will tend to end the cycle of poverty, high birth rates, and starvation which neo-Malthusians see as inevitable. Against the pessimistic neo-Malthusians, proponents of this analysis argue that famines and malnutrition are not inevitable. Against the optimistic neo-Malthusians, they argue that planned birth-control practices backed by government policies are not the solution. Ironically, the major factors influencing high fertility rates are identified as hunger and poverty. The Presidential Commission on World Hunger makes the point succinctly:

---

[2] Garrett Hardin, "Carrying Capacity as an Ethical Concept," in George R. Lucas, Jr., and Thomas W. Ogletree, eds., *Lifeboat Ethics* (New York: Harper & Row, 1976), p. 131.

Where hunger and poverty prevail, the population growth rate is more likely to increase than to decrease. Under inequitable social and economic conditions, a poor couple's desire for many children is a response to high infant mortality, the need for extra hands to help earn the family's daily bread, and the hope of support in old age. The key to reducing family size is to improve the social conditions which make large families a reasonable option.[3]

On this analysis, eradicating famine and malnutrition requires social and economic changes in the developing countries themselves, changes which would eliminate some of the gross inequalities of wealth and property in these countries. Without the recommended changes, it is argued, economic growth, including growth in the food supply, will not take place, population growth will not be slowed, and the tragic cycle will be repeated indefinitely.

Some of those who utilize this first approach against neo-Malthusians argue that the practices of members of more affluent nations prevent some of the poorest countries from increasing their own food supply. The identified culprits include multinational agribusinesses based in Western societies. It is charged that these multinationals have shifted the production of luxury items for the Western market from the highly industrialized countries to underdeveloped ones where cheap land and labor are available. As a result, the land in needy, underdeveloped countries is used to produce goods for members of the more affluent countries, while the food that is needed for the home market remains unproduced. In addition, it is argued that the international economic order favors the affluent, industrialized nations and is shaped by their needs. It is the affluent, industrialized societies that largely determine the prices for both the manufactured goods which developing nations must import and the agricultural products that the needy countries export. To the extent that the practices of those in affluent societies work against the potential self-sufficiency and real economic growth of the developing countries, they help create and perpetuate the cycle of poverty, high fertility rates, and hunger. In a reading in this chapter, Robert N. Van Wyk cites examples in support of the view that those in affluent nations are often directly or indirectly responsible for the poverty and hunger in at least some poorer nations.

The second counteranalysis advanced against neo-Malthusian reasoning comes from Marxist-socialists and incorporates some of the elements of the first counteranalysis. Marxist-socialists reject both the contention that overpopulation is the cause of scarcity in the world and the contention that the requisite economic growth is impossible. They identify capitalism as the major cause of worldwide scarcity. Agreeing with the kinds of claims just discussed concerning the negative impact of multinational corporations on the economic growth of developing countries, they see a Marxist-socialist economic system as the only solution to the problem of world hunger.[4]

---

[3] The Presidential Commission on World Hunger, *Overcoming World Hunger: The Challenge Ahead* (1980), p. 26.

[4] See, for example, Howard L. Parsons, "Malthusianism and Socialism" in *Revolutionary World,* special issue, "Self, Global Issues, and Ethics," vols. 21/22 (1977).

WHAT OUGHT WE TO DO?

What responsibilities do we as individuals have toward potential and actual famine victims? As the above discussion shows, our answers may depend on what we take to be a correct analysis of the causes of famine and malnutrition in the world. Van Wyk argues in the following vein, for example. We have obligations to provide aid to those countries for whose poverty and hunger we are at least partly responsible. We have these obligations because morality requires us to compensate others for the harms we do them. If Van Wyk is correct, then we have moral obligations to at least some disadvantaged countries. But we must also raise a more general question, which sets aside the issue of the causes of starvation and malnutrition: Do we have a moral obligation to eliminate starvation and malnutrition among the needy?

In a reading in this chapter, Peter Singer, a utilitarian, argues for such a moral obligation. Utilitarianism holds that an action or practice is morally correct only if it is likely to produce the greatest balance of good over evil, everyone considered. Proceeding in a utilitarian spirit, Singer argues for an obligation to famine victims on the basis of the following principle: "Persons are morally required to prevent something bad from happening if they can do so without sacrificing anything of comparable moral significance." In Singer's view, even a weaker version of this principle is sufficient to establish a moral obligation to aid the victims of severe famines.

In contrast to Singer, some thinkers adopt a nonutilitarian approach when arguing for an obligation to aid those in distress. Van Wyk, for example, argues that if we fail to relieve others' distress by providing them with the necessities of life, our actions are inconsistent with treating them as having any value as ends in themselves. Van Wyk's approach is based on the ethical system developed by Immanuel Kant (1724–1804).

Kant rejects the consequentialist approach to morality embodied in utilitarianism. In Kant's view what is fundamental in morality is respect for persons. Every person by virtue of his or her humanity (i.e., rational nature) has an inherent dignity. All persons, as rational creatures, are entitled to respect. Kant asserts that morality requires us to "act in such a way that you always treat humanity, whether in your own person or in the person of any other, never simply as a means, but always at the same time as an end." Note that Kant does not say that one person (A) cannot use another (B) as a means to her or his (A's) ends. But A cannot use B *merely* as a means. There is nothing morally problematic, for example, in A hiring B to paint A's house when B does so voluntarily and is paid for the work. But if A were to enslave B in order to force B to paint A's house and to perform other services for A, A *would* be using B merely as a means and would be failing to treat B as a person.

From the fundamental principle of respect for persons, Kant maintains, we can derive certain duties, which can be classified as either "perfect" or "imperfect." "Perfect duties" require us to always perform or abstain from certain acts. *There are no legitimate exceptions to perfect duties.* These duties are binding in all circumstances, because certain kinds of action are simply incompatible with respect for persons and, therefore, are strictly impermissible. Kant's examples of perfect duties include the duty not to kill an innocent person and the duty not to lie. Murderers exhibit obvious disrespect for the persons whose lives they are taking. Liars, in misinforming others, violate the respect due to persons as rational creatures, having a fundamental interest in the truth. In both cases, individuals are being treated not as persons with rational interests of their own but merely as a means to the wrongdoers' ends.

In addition to our perfect duties to others, we also have what Kant calls "imperfect duties." Whereas perfect duties require us to strictly abstain from performing those actions that involve using a person merely as a means, imperfect duties have a very different underlying sense. Imperfect duties require the promotion of certain goals such as the happiness or welfare of others. To understand Kant's notion of our imperfect duty to promote the happiness or welfare of others, it is useful to first discuss the notion of beneficence. If one acts in such a way as to further another's happiness or welfare, one acts beneficently. Beneficence can be contrasted with *nonmaleficence,* which is usually understood as the noninfliction of harm on others. Acts which harm others are maleficent acts. Someone who *refrains* from harming another acts in a nonmaleficent fashion. But someone who acts in a more positive way to *contribute to the welfare of another* acts in a beneficent fashion. Beneficence can best be understood as including the following types of activity: (1) preventing evil or harm from befalling someone; (2) removing an evil that is presently afflicting someone; (3) providing benefits ("doing good") for someone.

In Kant's view, perfect duties are owed by all persons to all persons. We can never treat any person merely as a means to our ends. The case is different with imperfect duties. We as individuals are free to choose which *specific* beneficent actions we will perform. The duty of beneficence does not require one to act beneficently every time the opportunity arises. One would violate the duty of beneficence, however, if one failed to incorporate in one's life plans some sort of overall commitment to promote the well-being of others. In other words, individuals are free to choose which beneficent actions they will perform in their efforts to further others' well-being. One person might contribute to the relief of famine while another might contribute to a battered women's center. However, no individual is free to abandon the general goal of furthering the well-being of others.

One commentator on Kant's ethical system has stated the contrast between perfect and imperfect duties in the following way: "We transgress perfect duties by treating any person merely as a means. We transgress imperfect duties by failing to treat a person as an end, even though we do not actively treat him as a means."[5] In arguing from this Kantian perspective, Van Wyk does not maintain that we have perfect duties to all individuals suffering from hunger. Each of us, however, does have a perfect duty to give *at least a fair share* toward seeing that all human beings are treated as ends in themselves.

Jane S. Zembaty

---

[5] H. J. Paton, *The Categorical Imperative: A Study in Kant's Moral Philosophy* (Chicago: University of Chicago Press, 1948), p. 172.

Why Should the United States Be Concerned?

The Presidential Commission on World Hunger

In 1978 President Jimmy Carter appointed a Presidential Commission on World Hunger, chaired by Ambassador Sol Linowitz. It included Dr. Jean Mayer, Dr. Stephen Muller, Dr. Norman Borlaug, David W. Brooks, Harry Chapin, John Denver, Senator Robert Dole, Dr. Walter P. Falcon, Orville Freeman, Representative Benjamin Gilman, Senator Patrick Leahy, Bess Myerson, Representative Richard Nolan, Dr. Howard A. Schneider, Dr. Adele Smith Simmons, Raymond Singletary, Jr., Dr. Eugene L. Stockwell, Dr. Clifford Wharton, Thomas H. Wyman, and Daniel E. Shaughnessy. The Commission was charged with the following tasks: (1) to identify the basic causes of domestic and international hunger and malnutrition; (2) to assess past and present national programs and policies that affect hunger and malnutrition; (3) to review existing studies and research on hunger; (4) to recommend to the President and Congress specific actions to create a coherent national food and hunger policy; and (5) to help implement those recommendations and focus public attention on food and hunger issues. This selection is excerpted from the Commission's final report, *Overcoming World Hunger: The Challenge Ahead.*

The Commission's major recommendation is that the elimination of hunger should be the primary focus of the United States government in its relationship with developing countries. The Commission bases its recommendations on the following reasons: (1) The moral obligation to overcome hunger, based on two universal values—respect for human dignity and social justice; (2) the dependence of national security on the economic well-being of the developing countries; and (3) the dependence of the economic vitality of the United States on a healthy international economy.

The major recommendation of the Presidential Commission on World Hunger is that the United States make the elimination of hunger the primary focus of its relations with the developing world—with all that implies for U.S. policy toward development assistance, trade, foreign investment and foreign affairs. In the Commission's view, there are significant reasons for the United States to place the elimination of hunger at the top of its list of global concerns.

MORAL OBLIGATION AND RESPONSIBILITY

Moral obligation alone would justify giving highest priority to the task of overcoming hunger. Even now, millions of human beings live on the edge of starvation—in conditions of subhuman poverty that, if we think about them at all, must fill us with shame and horror. We see this now most poignantly in famine conditions, but it is a fact of life every day for half a billion people. At least one out of every eight men,

Reprinted from *Overcoming World Hunger: The Challenge Ahead* (Washington, D.C.: Government Printing Office, 1980).

women and children on earth suffers malnutrition severe enough to shorten life, stunt physical growth, and dull mental ability.

Whether one speaks of human rights or basic human needs, the right to food is the most basic of all. Unless that right is first fulfilled, the protection of other human rights becomes a mockery for those who must spend all their energy merely to maintain life itself. The correct moral and ethical position on hunger is beyond debate. The major world religions and philosophical systems share two universal values: respect for human dignity and a sense of social justice. Hunger is the ultimate affront to both. Unless all governments begin now to act upon their rhetorical commitments to ending hunger, the principle that human life is sacred, which forms the very underpinnings of human society, will gradually but relentlessly erode. By concentrating its international efforts on the elimination of hunger, the United States would provide the strongest possible demonstration of its renewed dedication to the cause of human rights.

Moral obligation includes responsibility. In the Commission's view, the United States has a special capability and hence a special responsibility to lead the campaign against world hunger. The United States is by far the most powerful member of the world's increasingly interdependent food system. It harvests more than half the grain that crosses international borders. Its corporations dominate world grain trade. Its grain reserves are the largest on earth. Because of its agricultural productivity, its advanced food technology, and its market power, the United States inevitably exerts a major influence on all aspects of the international food system.

Global interdependence in food means that two straight years of bad harvests in any of the major grain-producing nations of the world could precipitate another global food crisis like the one that occurred in 1972-74. Recurrent crises of this nature could bring widespread famine and political disorder to the developing countries and would severely disrupt a fragile world economy already weakened by energy shortages and rampant inflation. U.S. policies will have a major role in determining whether or not this scenario will be played out.

American policies and resources also hold the key to solving that continuing world food crisis embodied in the swelling ranks of the chronically malnourished. To these hungry millions, it makes no difference whether such policies are made by choice or inertia, by acts of commission or acts of omission. In view of the undeniable influence that this nation's actions will have on world hunger, the Commission urges immediate yet careful long-range planning to assure that U.S. policy truly helps rather than harms the world's hungry people. Delay will only make the same ends more difficult and expensive to accomplish, and will not lift responsibility from the United States.

The Commission does not mean to imply that the United States alone can solve the world hunger problem. All nations, including those of the developing world, must make the conquest of hunger a common cause. However, the Commission is persuaded that unless the United States plays a major role by increasing its own commitment and action toward this goal, no effective and comprehensive global program to combat hunger is likely to be undertaken in the foreseeable future. Moreover, once its own commitment is clear, the United States will be in a particularly strong position to encourage others to do more. The Commission believes that the United States is uniquely situated to influence the fate of millions who do not get enough to eat.

NATIONAL SECURITY

The Commission believes that promoting economic development in general, and overcoming hunger in particular, are tasks far more critical to the U.S. national security than most policymakers acknowledge or even believe. Since the advent of nuclear weapons most Americans have been conditioned to equate national security with the strength of strategic military forces. The Commission considers this prevailing belief to be a simplistic illusion. Armed might represents merely the physical aspect of national security. Military force is ultimately useless in the absence of the global security that only coordinated international progress toward social justice can bring. . . .

ECONOMIC INTEREST

The Commission also finds compelling economic reasons for the United States to focus on the elimination of hunger. The United States can maintain its own economic vitality only within a healthy international economy whose overall strength will increase as each of its component parts becomes more productive, more equitable and more internationally competitive. To sustain a healthy global economy, the purchasing power of today's poor people must rise substantially, in order to set in motion that mutually reinforcing exchange of goods, services and commodities which provides the foundation for viable economic partnership and growth. . . .

[Thus we conclude that there] are compelling moral, economic and national security reasons for the United States Government to make the elimination of hunger the central focus of its relations with the developing world. . . .

QUESTIONS

1 According to the Commission, there are compelling *economic* reasons for the United States to focus on the elimination of hunger in its relations with developing countries. If this is correct, what evidence can be given to support it?
2 It has been said that the United States cannot solve the problem of world hunger; it *is* the problem. What reasons could be offered to support such a contention?

Famine, Affluence, and Morality

Peter Singer

A biographical sketch of Peter Singer is found on p. 88.

Singer expresses concern over the fact that while members of the more affluent
nations spend money on trivia, people in the needier nations are starving. He argues
that it is morally wrong not to prevent suffering whenever one can do so without
sacrificing anything morally significant. Giving aid to the victims of famine can
prevent such suffering. Even if giving requires a drastic reduction in the standard of
living of the members of the more affluent societies, the latter are morally required
to meet at least the basic need for food of people who will otherwise starve to
death.

As I write this, in November 1971, people are dying in East Bengal from lack of
food, shelter, and medical care. The suffering and death that are occurring there now
are not inevitable, not unavoidable in any fatalistic sense of the term. Constant poverty, a cyclone, and a civil war have turned at least nine million people into destitute
refugees; nevertheless, it is not beyond the capacity of the richer nations to give
enough assistance to reduce any further suffering to very small proportions. The decisions and actions of human beings can prevent this kind of suffering. Unfortunately, human beings have not made the necessary decisions. At the individual level,
people have, with very few exceptions, not responded to the situation in any significant way. Generally speaking, people have not given large sums to relief funds; they
have not written to their parliamentary representatives demanding increased government assistance; they have not demonstrated in the streets, held symbolic fasts, or
done anything else directed toward providing the refugees with the means to satisfy
their essential needs. At the government level, no government has given the sort of
massive aid that would enable the refugees to survive for more than a few days. Britain, for instance, has given rather more than most countries. It has, to date, given
£14,750,000. For comparative purposes, Britain's share of the nonrecoverable development costs of the Anglo-French Concorde project is already in excess of
£275,000,000, and on present estimates will reach £440,000,000. The implication is
that the British government values a supersonic transport more than thirty times as
highly as it values the lives of the nine million refugees. Australia is another country
which, on a per capita basis, is well up in the "aid to Bengal" table. Australia's aid,
however, amounts to less than one-twelfth of the cost of Sydney's new opera house.
The total amount given, from all sources, now stands at about £65,000,000. The estimated cost of keeping the refugees alive for one year is £464,000,000. Most of the
refugees have now been in the camps for more than six months. The World Bank has

Peter Singer, "Famine, Affluence, and Morality," *Philosophy & Public Affairs,* 1, no. 3 (Spring 1972).
Copyright © 1972 by Princeton University Press. Reprinted by permission.

said that India needs a minimum of £300,000,000 in assistance from other countries before the end of the year. It seems obvious that assistance on this scale will not be forthcoming. India will be forced to choose between letting the refugees starve or diverting funds from her own development program, which will mean that more of her own people will starve in the future.[1]

These are the essential facts about the present situation in Bengal. So far as it concerns us here, there is nothing unique about this situation except its magnitude. The Bengal emergency is just the latest and most acute of a series of major emergencies in various parts of the world, arising both from natural and from man-made causes. There are also many parts of the world in which people die from malnutrition and lack of food independent of any special emergency. I take Bengal as my example only because it is the present concern, and because the size of the problem has ensured that it has been given adequate publicity. Neither individuals nor governments can claim to be unaware of what is happening there.

What are the moral implications of a situation like this? In what follows, I shall argue that the way people in relatively affluent countries react to a situation like that in Bengal cannot be justified; indeed, the whole way we look at moral issues—our moral conceptual scheme—needs to be altered, and with it, the way of life that has come to be taken for granted in our society.

In arguing for this conclusion I will not, of course, claim to be morally neutral. I shall, however, try to argue for the moral position that I take, so that anyone who accepts certain assumptions, to be made explicit, will, I hope, accept my conclusion.

I begin with the assumption that suffering and death from lack of food, shelter, and medical care are bad. I think most people will agree about this, although one may reach the same view by different routes. I shall not argue for this view. People can hold all sorts of eccentric positions, and perhaps from some of them it would not follow that death by starvation is in itself bad. It is difficult, perhaps impossible, to refute such positions, and so for brevity I will henceforth take this assumption as accepted. Those who disagree need read no further.

My next point is this: if it is in our power to prevent something bad from happening, without thereby sacrificing anything of comparable moral importance, we ought, morally, to do it. By "without sacrificing anything of comparable moral importance" I mean without causing anything else comparably bad to happen, or doing something that is wrong in itself, or failing to promote some moral good, comparable in significance to the bad thing that we can prevent. This principle seems almost as uncontroversial as the last one. It requires us only to prevent what is bad, and not to promote what is good, and it requires this of us only when we can do it without sacrificing anything that is, from the moral point of view, comparably important. I could even, as far as the application of my argument to the Bengal emergency is concerned, qualify the point so as to make it: if it is in our power to prevent something very bad from happening, without thereby sacrificing anything morally significant, we ought, morally, to do it. An application of this principle would be as follows: if I am walking past a shallow pond and see a child drowning in it, I ought to wade in and pull the child out. This will mean getting my clothes muddy, but this is insignificant, while the death of the child would presumably be a very bad thing.

The uncontroversial appearance of the principle just stated is deceptive. If it were acted upon, even in its qualified form, our lives, our society, and our world would be fundamentally changed. For the principle takes, firstly, no account of proximity or distance. It makes no moral difference whether the person I can help is a neighbor's child ten yards from me or a Bengali whose name I shall never know, ten thousand miles away. Secondly, the principle makes no distinction between cases in which I am the only person who could possibly do anything and cases in which I am just one among millions in the same position.

I do not think I need to say much in defense of the refusal to take proximity and distance into account. The fact that a person is physically near to us, so that we have personal contact with him, may make it more likely that we *shall* assist him, but this does not show that we *ought* to help him rather than another who happens to be further away. If we accept any principle of impartiality, universalizability, equality, or whatever, we cannot discriminate against someone merely because he is far away from us (or we are far away from him). Admittedly, it is possible that we are in a better position to judge what needs to be done to help a person near to us than one far away, and perhaps also to provide the assistance we judge to be necessary. If this were the case, it would be a reason for helping those near to us first. This may once have been a justification for being more concerned with the poor in one's own town than with famine victims in India. Unfortunately for those who like to keep their moral responsibilities limited, instant communication and swift transportation have changed the situation. From the moral point of view, the development of the world into a "global village" has made an important, though still unrecognized, difference to our moral situation. Expert observers and supervisors, sent out by famine relief organizations or permanently stationed in famine-prone areas, can direct our aid to a refugee in Bengal almost as effectively as we could get it to someone in our own block. There would seem, therefore, to be no possible justification for discriminating on geographical grounds.

There may be a greater need to defend the second implication of my principle—that the fact that there are millions of other people in the same position, in respect to the Bengali refugees, as I am, does not make the situation significantly different from a situation in which I am the only person who can prevent something very bad from occurring. Again, of course, I admit that there is a psychological difference between the cases; one feels less guilty about doing nothing if one can point to others, similarly placed, who have also done nothing. Yet this can make no real difference to our moral obligations. Should I consider that I am less obliged to pull the drowning child out of the pond if on looking around I see other people, no further away than I am, who have also noticed the child but are doing nothing? One has only to ask this question to see the absurdity of the view that numbers lessen obligation. It is a view that is an ideal excuse for inactivity; unfortunately most of the major evils—poverty, overpopulation, pollution—are problems in which everyone is almost equally involved.

The view that numbers do make a difference can be made plausible if stated in this way: if everyone in circumstances like mine gave £5 to the Bengal Relief Fund, there would be enough to provide food, shelter, and medical care for the refugees;

there is no reason why I should give more than anyone else in the same circumstances as I am; therefore I have no obligation to give more than £5. Each premise in this argument is true, and the argument looks sound. It may convince us, unless we notice that it is based on a hypothetical premise, although the conclusion is not stated hypothetically. The argument would be sound if the conclusion were: if everyone in circumstances like mine were to give £5, I would have no obligation to give more than £5. If the conclusion were so stated, however, it would be obvious that the argument has no bearing on a situation in which it is not the case that everyone else gives £5. This, of course, is the actual situation. It is more or less certain that not everyone in circumstances like mine will give £5. So there will not be enough to provide the needed food, shelter, and medical care. Therefore by giving more than £5 I will prevent more suffering than I would if I gave just £5.

It might be thought that this argument has an absurd consequence. Since the situation appears to be that very few people are likely to give substantial amounts, it follows that I and everyone else in similar circumstances ought to give as much as possible, that is, at least up to the point at which by giving more one would begin to cause serious suffering for oneself and one's dependents—perhaps even beyond this point to the point of marginal utility, at which by giving more one would cause oneself and one's dependents as much suffering as one would prevent in Bengal. If everyone does this, however, there will be more than can be used for the benefit of the refugees, and some of the sacrifice will have been unnecessary. Thus, if everyone does what he ought to do, the result will not be as good as it would be if everyone did a little less than he ought to do, or if only some do all that they ought to do.

The paradox here arises only if we assume that the actions in question—sending money to the relief funds—are performed more or less simultaneously, and are also unexpected. For if it is to be expected that everyone is going to contribute something, then clearly each is not obliged to give as much as he would have been obliged to had others not been giving too. And if everyone is not acting more or less simultaneously, then those giving later will know how much more is needed, and will have no obligation to give more than is necessary to reach this amount. To say this is not to deny the principle that people in the same circumstances have the same obligations, but to point out that the fact that others have given, or may be expected to give, is a relevant circumstance: those giving after it has become known that many others are giving and those giving before are not in the same circumstances. So the seemingly absurd consequence of the principle I have put forward can occur only if people are in error about the actual circumstances—that is, if they think they are giving when others are not, but in fact they are giving when others are. The result of everyone doing what he really ought to do cannot be worse than the result of everyone doing less than he ought to do, although the result of everyone doing what he reasonably believes he ought to do could be.

If my argument so far has been sound, neither our distance from a preventable evil nor the number of other people who, in respect to that evil, are in the same situation as we are, lessens our obligation to mitigate or prevent that evil. I shall therefore take as established the principle I asserted earlier. As I have already said, I need to assert it only in its qualified form: if it is in our power to prevent something very bad from happening, without thereby sacrificing anything else morally significant, we ought, morally, to do it.

The outcome of this argument is that our traditional moral categories are upset. The traditional distinction between duty and charity cannot be drawn, or at least, not in the place we normally draw it. Giving money to the Bengal Relief Fund is regarded as an act of charity in our society. The bodies which collect money are known as "charities." These organizations see themselves in this way—if you send them a check, you will be thanked for your "generosity." Because giving money is regarded as an act of charity, it is not thought that there is anything wrong with not giving. The charitable man may be praised, but the man who is not charitable is not condemned. People do not feel in any way ashamed or guilty about spending money on new clothes or a new car instead of giving it to famine relief. (Indeed, the alternative does not occur to them.) This way of looking at the matter cannot be justified. When we buy new clothes not to keep ourselves warm but to look "well-dressed" we are not providing for any important need. We would not be sacrificing anything significant if we were to continue to wear our old clothes, and give the money to famine relief. By doing so, we would be preventing another person from starving. It follows from what I have said earlier that we ought to give money away, rather than spend it on clothes which we do not need to keep us warm. To do so is not charitable, or generous. Nor is it the kind of act which philosophers and theologians have called "supererogatory"—an act which it would be good to do, but not wrong not to do. On the contrary, we ought to give the money away, and it is wrong not to do so.

I am not maintaining that there are no acts which are charitable, or that there are no acts which it would be good to do but not wrong not to do. It may be possible to redraw the distinction between duty and charity in some other place. All I am arguing here is that the present way of drawing the distinction, which makes it an act of charity for a man living at the level of affluence which most people in the "developed nations" enjoy to give money to save someone else from starvation, cannot be supported. It is beyond the scope of my argument to consider whether the distinction should be redrawn or abolished altogether. There would be many other possible ways of drawing the distinction—for instance, one might decide that it is good to make other people as happy as possible, but not wrong not to do so.

Despite the limited nature of the revision in our moral conceptual scheme which I am proposing, the revision would, given the extent of both affluence and famine in the world today, have radical implications. These implications may lead to further objections, distinct from those I have already considered. I shall discuss two of these.

One objection to the position I have taken might be simply that it is too drastic a revision of our moral scheme. People do not ordinarily judge in the way I have suggested they should. Most people reserve their moral condemnation for those who violate some moral norm, such as the norm against taking another person's property. They do not condemn those who indulge in luxury instead of giving to famine relief. But given that I did not set out to present a morally neutral description of the way people make moral judgments, the way people do in fact judge has nothing to do with the validity of my conclusion. My conclusion follows from the principle which I advanced earlier, and unless that principle is rejected, or the arguments shown to be unsound, I think the conclusion must stand, however strange it appears. . . .

The second objection to my attack on the present distinction between duty and charity is one which has from time to time been made against utilitarianism. It follows from some forms of utilitarian theory that we all ought, morally, to be working full time to increase the balance of happiness over misery. The position I have taken here would not lead to this conclusion in all circumstances, for if there were no bad occurrences that we could prevent without sacrificing something of comparable moral importance, my argument would have no application. Given the present conditions in many parts of the world, however, it does follow from my argument that we ought, morally, to be working full time to relieve great suffering of the sort that occurs as a result of famine or other disasters. Of course, mitigating circumstances can be adduced—for instance, that if we wear ourselves out through overwork, we shall be less effective than we would otherwise have been. Nevertheless, when all considerations of this sort have been taken into account, the conclusion remains: we ought to be preventing as much suffering as we can without sacrificing something else of comparable moral importance. This conclusion is one which we may be reluctant to face. I cannot see, though, why it should be regarded as a criticism of the position for which I have argued, rather than a criticism of our ordinary standards of behavior. Since most people are self-interested to some degree, very few of us are likely to do everything that we ought to do. It would, however, hardly be honest to take this as evidence that it is not the case that we ought to do it. . . .

The conclusion reached earlier [raises] the question of just how much we all ought to be giving away. One possibility, which has already been mentioned, is that we ought to give until we reach the level of marginal utility—that is, the level at which, by giving more, I would cause as much suffering to myself or my dependents as I would relieve by my gift. This would mean, of course, that one would reduce oneself to very near the material circumstances of a Bengali refugee. It will be recalled that earlier I put forward both a strong and a moderate version of the principle of preventing bad occurrences. The strong version, which required us to prevent bad things from happening unless in doing so we would be sacrificing something of a comparable moral significance, does seem to require reducing ourselves to the level of marginal utility. I should also say that the strong version seems to me to be the correct one. I proposed the more moderate version—that we should prevent bad occurrences unless, to do so, we had to sacrifice something morally significant—only in order to show that even on this surely undeniable principle a great change in our way of life is required. On the more moderate principle, it may not follow that we ought to reduce ourselves to the level of marginal utility, for one might hold that to reduce oneself and one's family to this level is to cause something significantly bad to happen. Whether this is so I shall not discuss, since, as I have said, I can see no good reason for holding the moderate version of the principle rather than the strong version. Even if we accepted the principle only in its moderate form, however, it should be clear that we would have to give away enough to ensure that the consumer society, dependent as it is on people spending on trivia rather than giving to famine relief, would slow down and perhaps disappear entirely. There are several reasons why this would be desirable in itself. The value and necessity of economic growth are now being questioned not only by conservationists, but by economists as well.[2] There is no doubt, too, that the consumer society has had a distorting effect on the goals and purposes of its members. Yet looking at the matter purely from the point of view of overseas aid, there must be a limit to the extent to which we should deliberately slow down our economy; for it might be the case that if we gave away, say, forty percent of our Gross National Product, we would slow down the economy so much that in absolute terms we would be giving less than if we gave twenty-five percent of the much larger GNP that we would have if we limited our contribution to this smaller percentage.

I mention this only as an indication of the sort of factor that one would have to take into account in working out an ideal. Since Western societies generally consider one percent of the GNP an acceptable level for overseas aid, the matter is entirely academic. Nor does it affect the question of how much an individual should give in a society in which very few are giving substantial amounts.

It is sometimes said, though less often now than it used to be, that philosophers have no special role to play in public affairs, since most public issues depend primarily on an assessment of facts. On questions of fact, it is said, philosophers as such have no special expertise, and so it has been possible to engage in philosophy without committing oneself to any position on major public issues. No doubt there are some issues of social policy and foreign policy about which it can truly be said that a really expert assessment of the facts is required before taking sides or acting, but the issue of famine is surely not one of these. The facts about the existence of suffering are beyond dispute. Nor, I think, is it disputed that we can do something about it, either through orthodox methods of famine relief or through population control or both. This is therefore an issue on which philosophers are competent to take a position. The issue is one which faces everyone who has more money than he needs to support himself and his dependents, or who is in a position to take some sort of political action. These categories must include practically every teacher and student of philosophy in the universities of the Western world. If philosophy is to deal with matters that are relevant to both teachers and students, this is an issue that philosophers should discuss.

Discussion, though, is not enough. What is the point of relating philosophy to public (and personal) affairs if we do not take our conclusions seriously? In this instance, taking our conclusion seriously means acting upon it. The philosopher will not find it any easier than anyone else to alter his attitudes and way of life to the extent that, if I am right, is involved in doing everything that we ought to be doing. At the very least, though, one can make a start. The philosopher who does so will have to sacrifice some of the benefits of the consumer society, but he can find compensation in the satisfaction of a way of life in which theory and practice, if not yet in harmony, are at least coming together.

NOTES

1 There was also a third possibility: that India would go to war to enable the refugees to return to their lands. Since I wrote this paper, India has taken this way out. The situation is no longer that described above, but this does not affect my argument, as the next paragraph indicates.

2 See, for instance, John Kenneth Galbraith, *The New Industrial State* (Boston, 1967); and E. J. Mishan, *The Costs of Economic Growth* (London, 1967).

QUESTIONS

1 Think about the following claim: Contributing to famine relief is not a moral obligation which we must perform if we are to act in a morally correct way, but an act of charity which we may or may not perform. Can you offer any arguments to defend it?

2 Singer says, "We ought to be preventing as much suffering as we can without sacrificing something else of comparable moral importance." What moral considerations would outweigh the obligation Singer claims we have to aid famine victims?

Living on a Lifeboat

Garrett Hardin

Garrett Hardin is professor of biology at the University of California at Santa Barbara. He is the author of many books, including *Population, Evolution, and Birth Control* (1969), *Exploring New Ethics for Survival* (1972), *The Limits of Altruism: An Ecologist's View of Survival* (1977), and *Promethean Ethics: Living with Death, Competition, and Triage* (1980).

Using the metaphor of a lifeboat, Hardin argues that the time may have come to refuse aid in the form of food to needy countries which do not accept the responsibility for limiting their population growth. He maintains that adherence to the principle "From each according to his ability; to each according to his need" will have strong adverse effects. Bolstered by our aid, needy countries will continue their irresponsible policies in regard to food production and population growth. Furthermore, the food we supply will enable these populations to continue to increase. This in the long run will jeopardize the survival of the human species.

No generation has viewed the problem of the survival of the human species as seriously as we have. Inevitably, we have entered this world of concern through the door of metaphor. Environmentalists have emphasized the image of the earth as a spaceship—Spaceship Earth. Kenneth Boulding (1966) is the principal architect of this

Reprinted, with permission, from the October 1974 issue of *BioScience,* © American Institute of Biological Sciences.

metaphor. It is time, he says, that we replace the wasteful "cowboy economy" of the past with the frugal "spaceship economy" required for continued survival in the limited world we now see ours to be. The metaphor is notably useful in justifying pollution control measures.

Unfortunately, the image of a spaceship is also used to promote measures that are suicidal. One of these is a generous immigration policy, which is only a particular instance of a class of policies that are in error because they lead to the tragedy of the commons (Hardin 1968). These suicidal policies are attractive because they mesh with what we unthinkingly take to be the ideals of "the best people." What is missing in the idealistic view is an insistence that rights and responsibilities must go together. The "generous" attitude of all too many people results in asserting inalienable rights while ignoring or denying matching responsibilities.

For the metaphor of a spaceship to be correct the aggregate of people on board would have to be under unitary sovereign control (Ophuls 1974). A true ship always has a captain. It is conceivable that a ship could be run by a committee. But it could not possibly survive if its course were determined by bickering tribes that claimed rights without responsibilities.

What about Spaceship Earth? It certainly has no captain, and no executive committee. The United Nations is a toothless tiger, because the signatories of its charter wanted it that way. The spaceship metaphor is used only to justify spaceship demands on common resources without acknowledging corresponding spaceship responsibilities.

An understandable fear of decisive action leads people to embrace "incrementalism"—moving toward reform in tiny stages. As we shall see, this strategy is counterproductive in the area discussed here if it means accepting rights before responsibilities. Where human survival is at stake, the acceptance of responsibilities is a precondition to the acceptance of rights, if the two cannot be introduced simultaneously.

LIFEBOAT ETHICS

Before taking up certain substantive issues let us look at an alternative metaphor, that of a lifeboat. In developing some relevant examples the following numerical values are assumed. Approximately two-thirds of the world is desperately poor, and only one-third is comparatively rich. The people in poor countries have an average per capita GNP (Gross National Product) of about $200 per year; the rich, of about $3,000. (For the United States it is nearly $5,000 per year.) Metaphorically, each rich nation amounts to a lifeboat full of comparatively rich people. The poor of the world are in other, much more crowded lifeboats. Continuously, so to speak, the poor fall out of their lifeboats and swim for a while in the water outside, hoping to be admitted to a rich lifeboat, or in some other way to benefit from the "goodies" on board. What should the passengers on a rich lifeboat do? This is the central problem of "the ethics of a lifeboat."

First we must acknowledge that each lifeboat is effectively limited in capacity. The land of every nation has a limited carrying capacity. The exact limit is a matter for argument, but the energy crunch is convincing more people every day that we have already exceeded the carrying capacity of the land. We have been living on "capital"—stored petroleum and coal—and soon we must live on income alone.

Let us look at only one lifeboat—ours. The ethical problem is the same for all, and is as follows. Here we sit, say 50 people in a lifeboat. To be generous, let us assume our boat has a capacity of 10 more, making 60. (This, however, is to violate the engineering principle of the "safety factor." A new plant disease or a bad change in the weather may decimate our population if we don't preserve some excess capacity as a safety factor.)

The 50 of us in the lifeboat see 100 others swimming in the water outside, asking for admission to the boat, or for handouts. How shall we respond to their calls? There are several possibilities.

One. We may be tempted to try to live by the Christian ideal of being "our brother's keeper," or by the Marxian ideal (Marx 1875) of "from each according to his abilities, to each according to his needs." Since the needs of all are the same, we take all the needy into our boat, making a total of 150 in a boat with a capacity of 60. The boat is swamped, and everyone drowns. Complete justice, complete catastrophe.

Two. Since the boat has an unused excess capacity of 10, we admit just 10 more to it. This has the disadvantage of getting rid of the safety factor, for which action we will sooner or later pay dearly. Moreover, *which* 10 do we let in? "First come, first served?" The best 10? The neediest 10? How do we *discriminate?* And what do we say to the 90 who are excluded?

Three. Admit no more to the boat and preserve the small safety factor. Survival of the people in the lifeboat is then possible (though we shall have to be on our guard against boarding parties).

The last solution is abhorrent to many people. It is unjust, they say. Let us grant that it is.

"I feel guilty about my good luck," say some. The reply to this is simple: *Get out and yield your place to others.* Such a selfless action might satisfy the conscience of those who are addicted to guilt but it would not change the ethics of the lifeboat. The needy person to whom a guilt-addict yields his place will not himself feel guilty about his sudden good luck. (If he did he would not climb aboard.) The net result of conscience-stricken people relinquishing their unjustly held positions is the elimination of their kind of conscience from the lifeboat. The lifeboat, as it were, purifies itself of guilt. The ethics of the lifeboat persist, unchanged by such momentary aberrations.

This then is the basic metaphor within which we must work out our solutions. Let us enrich the image step by step with substantive additions from the real world.

REPRODUCTION

The harsh characteristics of lifeboat ethics are heightened by reproduction, particularly by reproductive differences. The people inside the lifeboats of the wealthy nations are doubling in numbers every 87 years; those outside are doubling every 35 years, on the average. And the relative difference in prosperity is becoming greater.

Let us, for a while, think primarily of the U.S. lifeboat. As of 1973 the United

States had a population of 210 million people, who were increasing by 0.8% per year, that is, doubling in number every 87 years.

Although the citizens of rich nations are outnumbered two to one by the poor, let us imagine an equal number of poor people outside our lifeboat—a mere 210 million poor people reproducing at a quite different rate. If we imagine these to be the combined populations of Colombia, Venezuela, Ecuador, Morocco, Thailand, Pakistan, and the Philippines, the average rate of increase of the people "outside" is 3.3% per year. The doubling time of this population is 21 years.

Suppose that all these countries, and the United States, agreed to live by the Marxian ideal, "to each according to his needs," the ideal of most Christians as well. Needs, of course, are determined by population size, which is affected by reproduction. Every nation regards its rate of reproduction as a sovereign right. If our lifeboat were big enough in the beginning it might be possible to live *for a while* by Christian-Marxian ideals. *Might.*

Initially, in the model given, the ratio of non-Americans to Americans would be one to one. But consider what the ratio would be 87 years later. By this time Americans would have doubled to a population of 420 million. The other group (doubling every 21 years) would now have swollen to 3,540 million. Each American would have more than eight people to share with. How could the lifeboat possibly keep afloat?

All this involves extrapolation of current trends into the future, and is consequently suspect. Trends may change. Granted: but the change will not necessarily be favorable. If—as seems likely—the rate of population increase falls faster in the ethnic group presently inside the lifeboat than it does among those now outside, the future will turn out to be even worse than mathematics predicts, and sharing will be even more suicidal.

RUIN IN THE COMMONS

The fundamental error of the sharing ethics is that it leads to the tragedy of the commons. Under a system of private property the man (or group of men) who own property recognize their responsibility to care for it, for if they don't they will eventually suffer. A farmer, for instance, if he is intelligent, will allow no more cattle in a pasture than its carrying capacity justifies. If he overloads the pasture, weeds take over, erosion sets in, and the owner loses in the long run.

But if a pasture is run as a commons open to all, the right of each to use it is not matched by an operational responsibility to take care of it. It is no use asking independent herdsmen in a commons to act responsibly, for they dare not. The considerate herdsman who refrains from overloading the commons suffers more than a selfish one who says his needs are greater. (As Leo Durocher says, "Nice guys finish last.") Christian-Marxian idealism is counterproductive. That it *sounds* nice is no excuse. With distribution systems, as with individual morality, good intentions are no substitute for good performance.

A social system is stable only if it is insensitive to errors. To the Christian-Marxian idealist a selfish person is a sort of "error." Prosperity in the system of the commons cannot survive errors. If *everyone* would only restrain himself, all would be well; but it takes *only one less than everyone* to ruin a system of voluntary restraint. In a crowded world of less than perfect human beings—and we will never know any other—mutual ruin is inevitable in the commons. This is the core of the tragedy of the commons. . . .

WORLD FOOD BANKS

In the international arena we have recently heard a proposal to create a new commons, namely an international depository of food reserves to which nations will contribute according to their abilities, and from which nations may draw according to their needs. Nobel laureate Norman Borlaug has lent the prestige of his name to this proposal.

A world food bank appeals powerfully to our humanitarian impulses. We remember John Donne's celebrated line, "Any man's death diminishes me." But before we rush out to see for whom the bell tolls let us recognize where the greatest political push for international granaries comes from, lest we be disillusioned later. Our experience with Public Law 480 clearly reveals the answer. This was the law that moved billions of dollars worth of U.S. grain to food-short, population-long countries during the past two decades. When P.L. 480 first came into being, a headline in the business magazine *Forbes* (Paddock 1970) revealed the power behind it: "Feeding the World's Hungry Millions: How it will mean billions for U.S. business."

And indeed it did. In the years 1960 to 1970 a total of $7.9 billion was spent on the "Food for Peace" program, as P.L. 480 was called. During the years of 1948 to 1970 an additional $49.9 billion were extracted from American taxpayers to pay for other economic aid programs, some of which went for food and food-producing machinery. (This figure does *not* include military aid.) That P.L. 480 was a give-away program was concealed. Recipient countries went through the motions of paying for P.L. 480 food—with IOU's. In December 1973 the charade was brought to an end as far as India was concerned when the United States "forgave" India's $3.2 billion debt (Anonymous 1974). Public announcement of the cancellation of the debt was delayed for two months: one wonders why. . . .

What happens if some organizations budget for emergencies and others do not? If each organization is solely responsible for its own well-being, poorly managed ones will suffer. But they should be able to learn from experience. They have a chance to mend their ways and learn to budget for infrequent but certain emergencies. The weather, for instance, always varies and periodic crop failures are certain. A wise and competent government saves out of the production of the good years in anticipation of bad years that are sure to come. This is not a new idea. The Bible tells us that Joseph taught this policy to Pharaoh in Egypt more than 2,000 years ago. Yet it is literally true that the vast majority of the governments of the world today have no such policy. They lack either the wisdom or the competence, or both. Far more difficult than the transfer of wealth from one country to another is the transfer of wisdom between sovereign powers or between generations.

"But it isn't their fault! How can we blame the poor people who are caught in an emergency? Why must we punish them?" The concepts of blame and punishment are irrelevant. The question is, what are the operational consequences of establishing a world food bank? If it is open to every country every time a need develops, slovenly rulers will not be motivated to take Joseph's advice. Why should they? Others will bail them out whenever they are in trouble.

Some countries will make deposits in the world food bank and others will withdraw from it: there will be almost no overlap. Calling such a depository-transfer unit a "bank" is stretching the metaphor of *bank* beyond its elastic limits. The proposers, of course, never call attention to the metaphorical nature of the word they use.

THE RATCHET EFFECT

An "international food bank" is really, then, not a true bank but a disguised oneway transfer device for moving wealth from rich countries to poor. In the absence of such a bank, in a world inhabited by individually responsible sovereign nations, the population of each nation would repeatedly go through a cycle of the sort shown in Figure 1. P_2 is greater than P_1, either in absolute numbers or because a deterioration of the food supply has removed the safety factor and produced a dangerously low ratio of resources to population. P_2 may be said to represent a state of overpopulation, which becomes obvious upon the appearance of an "accident," e.g., a crop failure. If the "emergency" is not met by outside help, the population drops back to the "normal" level—the "carrying capacity" of the environment—or even below. In the absence of population control by a sovereign, sooner or later the population grows to P_2 again and the cycle repeats. The long-term population curve (Hardin 1966) is an irregularly fluctuating one, equilibrating more or less about the carrying capacity.

A demographic cycle of this sort obviously involves great suffering in the restrictive phase, but such a cycle is normal to any independent country with inadequate population control. The third century theologian Tertullian (Hardin 1969) expressed what must have been the recognition of many wise men when he wrote: "The scourges of pestilence, famine, wars, and earthquakes have come to be regarded as a blessing to overcrowded nations, since they serve to prune away the luxuriant growth of the human race."

Only under a strong and farsighted sovereign—which theoretically could be the people themselves, democratically organized—can a population equilibrate at some

Fig. 1

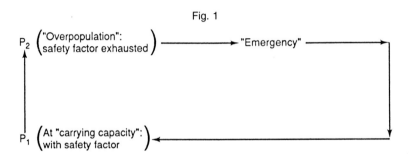

set point below the carrying capacity, thus avoiding the pains normally caused by periodic and unavoidable disasters. For this happy state to be achieved it is necessary that those in power be able to contemplate with equanimity the "waste" of surplus food in times of bountiful harvests. It is essential that those in power resist the temptation to convert extra food into extra babies. On the public relations level it is necessary that the phrase "surplus food" be replaced by "safety factor."

But wise sovereigns seem not to exist in the poor world today. The most anguishing problems are created by poor countries that are governed by rulers insufficiently wise and powerful. If such countries can draw on a world food bank in times of "emergency," the population *cycle* of Figure 1 will be replaced by the population *escalator* of Figure 2. The input of food from a food bank acts as the pawl of a ratchet, preventing the population from retracing its steps to a lower level. Reproduction pushes the population upward, inputs from the world bank prevent its moving downward. Population size escalates, as does the absolute magnitude of "accidents" and "emergencies." The process is brought to an end only by the total collapse of the whole system, producing a catastrophe of scarcely imaginable proportions.

Such are the implications of the well-meant sharing of food in a world of irresponsible reproduction. . . .

To be generous with one's own possessions is one thing; to be generous with posterity's is quite another. This, I think, is the point that must be gotten across to those who would, from a commendable love of distributive justice, institute a ruinous system of the commons. . . .

If the argument of this essay is correct, so long as there is no true world government to control reproduction everywhere it is impossible to survive in dignity if we are to be guided by Spaceship ethics. Without a world government that is sovereign in reproductive matters mankind lives, in fact, on a number of sovereign lifeboats.

Fig. 2

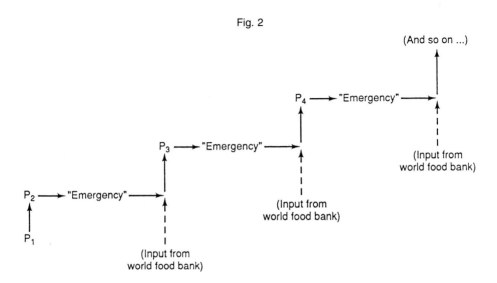

For the foreseeable future survival demands that we govern our actions by the ethics of a lifeboat. Posterity will be ill served if we do not.

REFERENCES

1 Anonymous. 1974. *Wall Street Journal* 19 Feb.
2 Boulding, K. 1966. The economics of the coming spaceship earth. In H. Jarrett, ed. *Environmental Quality in a Growing Economy.* Johns Hopkins Press, Baltimore.
3 Hardin, G. 1966. Chap. 9 in *Biology: Its Principles and Implications,* 2nd ed. Freeman, San Francisco.
4 ———. 1968. The tragedy of the commons. *Science* 162: 1243–1248.
5 ———. 1969. Page 18 in *Population, Evolution, and Birth Control,* 2nd ed. Freeman, San Francisco.
6 Marx, K. 1875. *Critique of the Gotha program.* Page 388 in R. C. Tucker, ed. *The Marx-Engels Reader,* Norton, N.Y., 1972.
7 Ophuls, W. 1974. The scarcity society. *Harpers* 248 (1487): 47–52.
8 Paddock, W. C. 1970. How green is the green revolution? *Bioscience* 20:897–902.

QUESTIONS

1 What evidence is available to support the claim that the resources of the world will not be able to save all the poor countries? If it cannot be conclusively proved that all the poor countries cannot be saved, can a moral justification be given for refusing to aid famine victims in all those countries?

2 Suppose that it is highly unlikely that all the nations in the world can be saved. Which would be the better moral choice: (1) to deliberately cut off aid to those least likely to survive in order to ensure the survival of the others or (2) to continue our aid despite our awareness of the consequences which will probably follow?

Perspectives on World Hunger and the Extent of Our Positive Duties

Robert N. Van Wyk

Robert N. Van Wyk is associate professor of philosophy at the University of Pittsburgh, Johnstown. He specializes in ethics, philosophy of religion, and social philosophy. Van Wyk's published articles include "Autonomy Theses Revisited" and "Liberalism, Religion, and Politics."

Van Wyk criticizes both Singer's and Hardin's positions regarding the morally appropriate response to world hunger. Against Hardin, he points out some of the problems with the lifeboat metaphor. Van Wyk's primary focus, however, is on moral theory. He rejects the utilitarian approach presupposed by both Hardin and

Reprinted with permission from *Public Affairs Quarterly,* vol. 2 (April 1988), pp. 75–90.

Singer and develops a Kantian approach to the issue. On Van Wyk's analysis, individuals have the following duties: (1) duties of reparation to some of the poor of the world for past harms committed against them; these duties result from the violation of our duty not to harm others; (2) duties to do our fair share to help those in distress; these duties are based on the fundamental moral requirement that we treat others as having value as ends in themselves; and (3) a duty to exert upward pressure on the prevailing idea of a fair share; this duty involves putting pressure on our government to ensure that its policies protect the vulnerable. Van Wyk concludes with some "Kantian" reflection on qualifications and limitations to the above duties.

I INTRODUCTION TO THE ISSUE

A moral problem that faces institutions—especially governments, as well as individuals, is the question of the extent of the duty to prevent harm to other people, and/or benefit them. This is not an academic problem but one that stares us in the face through the eyes of starving and malnourished people, and in particular, children. . . . What duties do individuals have to help?

II UTILITARIAN/CONSEQUENTIALIST APPROACHES

A The Views of Peter Singer and Garrett Hardin

According to some moral theories the very fact of widespread hunger imposes a duty on each person to do whatever he or she is capable of doing to accomplish whatever is necessary to see to it that all people have enough to eat. Peter Singer, a utilitarian, writes:

> I begin with the assumption that suffering and death from lack of food, shelter, and medical care are bad . . . My next point is this: if it is in our power to prevent something bad from happening without thereby sacrificing anything of comparable moral importance, we ought, morally, to do it.[1]

Does this mean that governments of prosperous countries ought to call upon their citizens to sacrifice enough of the luxuries of life to pay taxes that will be used to see to it that everyone in the world has the basic necessities of life? Suppose that governments do not do this. Suppose I give a considerable amount to famine relief but the need remains great because many others have not given. Is this case parallel to the following one to which Singer compares it? I have saved the life of one drowning person. There is still another person who needs to be saved. Other people could have saved the second person while I was saving the first but no one did. Even though I have saved one, and even though other people have failed in their duty to try to save the other, it would seem reasonable to claim that I have a duty to try to do so. Would I similarly have a duty to keep on giving more to aid the hungry regardless of the personal sacrifice involved? Many objections raised against giving sacrificially have to do with whether certain kinds of assistance really do much good. But such objections do not really affect the question of how much one should sacrifice to help others, but only have to do with the best way of using what is given (for example, for food assistance, development assistance, family planning, encouraging political change, supporting education, and so on). But if we reach the conclusion that we have a duty to do all we can, just as in the case of the drowning people, we are faced with the problem that James Fishkin has written about, of being overwhelmed with obligations in a way that expands the area of moral duty to the point of obliterating both the area of the morally indifferent and the area of the morally supererogatory.[2]

There are, however, other considerations. What are the long range consequences of keeping people alive? 'Neo-malthusians" and "crisis environmentalists" argue that population growth is outstripping food production and also leading both to the depletion of the world's natural resources and the pollution of the environment, so that the more people who are saved the more misery there will be in the long run. Garrett Hardin compares rich nations to lifeboats and the poor of the world to drowning people trying to get into the lifeboats. To allow them in would be to risk sinking the lifeboats and so to risk bringing disaster on everyone. The high rate of population growth among the poor nations insures that even if there is enough room at the moment, eventually the lifeboats will be swamped.[3] The lifeboat ethic is an application of what Hardin calls the logic of the commons. If a pasture is held as common property each herdsman is tempted to overgraze it for the sake of short-term profits. Even the individual who wants to preserve the land for the future has no reason to stop as long as there are others who will continue to overgraze it. Similarly, if we regard the food production of the world as a "commons" to which everyone is entitled we undermine any incentive among the poor of the world to increase production and limit population growth. The increasing population will continually reduce the amount available for each individual while at the same time increasing pollution and putting other strains on the environment.[4] So Hardin writes that "for posterity's sake we should never send food to any population that is beyond the realistic carrying capacity of its land."[5] This view that certain countries should be left to have "massive diebacks of population,"[6] while others should perhaps be helped, has been called "triage."

B Questions about These Approaches

One way of responding to Hardin's argument is to raise questions about the choice of metaphors and their applicability.[7] Why speak of lifeboats rather than of luxury liners? Why should the Asian or African people be compared to the "sheep" who are the greatest threat to the commons when the average American uses up thirty times the amount of the earth's resources as does the average Asian or African, and when the developed nations import more protein from the developing nations than they export to them? How are the lifeboat metaphors applicable when apart from special famine conditions almost every country in the world has the resources necessary to feed its people if they were used primarily for that purpose?

The focus here, however, will be on moral theory. In spite of their very different conclusions, Singer and Hardin both presuppose a utilitarian position that says that what we ought to do depends completely on the anticipated consequences of our choices. A defender of Singer might say that all Hardin's observations do is to impose on all people a duty to redouble their efforts to find and support solutions that avoid both short range hunger and long range disaster. But that answer only increases the problem of overload that Fishkin is concerned with.

III HUNGER, RESPECT FOR PERSONS AND NEGATIVE DUTIES

Many philosophers, especially those emphasizing the stringency of negative duties, subscribe to Kant's principle of respect for persons, whether or not they are supporters of Kant's moral philosophy taken as a whole. Robert Nozick uses the principle of respect for persons to defend absolute duties to do no harm while at the same time denying the existence of any duties to benefit others.[8] Kant himself, however, maintained that we have imperfect duties to help others. One might still claim that government may not collect taxes for the sake of aiding others, since one ought not to force people (taxpayers) to fulfill imperfect duties when doing so violates the perfect duty to respect the right of citizens to use their resources as they themselves choose to do so. Kant himself did not reach such a conclusion,[9] but Nozick does, arguing that since "individuals are ends and not merely means; they may not be sacrificed, or used for the achieving of other ends without their consent."[10]

Nozick's views can be attacked at many points. Even if they were correct, however, it would not follow that governments would have no right to tax citizens to aid people in distress. This is because individuals, corporations (to which individuals are related as stockholders and employees), and governments would still have duties not to harm, and thus also duties to take corrective action in response to past harms. So wealthy countries and their citizens could still have many responsibilities of compensatory justice with respect to the world's poor. Some countries face poverty because their economies are heavily dependent on a single export material or crop (for example, copper in Chile), the prices of which are subject to great fluctuations. If the original situation, or the subsequent fluctuations, were brought about by policies of wealthy nations or their corporations, then suffering does not just happen but is caused by the actions of people in developed nations. If corporations can strangle economies of developing nations and choose to do so if they do not get special tax advantages, or unfairly advantageous contracts, then poverty and hunger are harms caused by the decisions of the wealthy. If, furthermore, government officials are bribed to keep taxes down, as was done in Honduras by the banana companies, then poverty is directly caused by human actions. If a developed nation overthrows the government of a poor nation which tries to correct some past injustice (as was done when the C.I.A. helped overthrow the democratically elected government of Guatamala in 1954 in order to protect the interests of the United Fruit Company), then poverty is a harm caused by human actions. The decisions of the Soviet Union to import large amounts of grain from the United States during the Nixon administration led to a dramatic and unexpected rise in the price of grain on the world market, which in turn caused hunger. Americans' use of energy at twice the rate of Western Europeans must raise energy prices for the poor. Dramatic price increases by oil exporting nations no doubt meant that people went without petroleum-based fertilizers, or energy to transport food or pump water for irrigation, and so led to additional people dying of hunger. When petroleum prices fall the poverty of people in some oil-exporting countries is aggravated because of the difficulty their governments have financing their debts—debts which were acquired partially due to the encouragement of the banks in the wealthy countries.

What duties do the wealthy countries have to the poor and hungry of the world? The first duty is not to harm them. While seldom are the hungry intentionally killed, they are often killed in the same way that someone is killed by a reckless driver who just does not take into consideration what his actions might do to other vulnerable human beings, and there is no doubt that reckless drivers are to be held accountable for what they do. In some cases it may be morally justifiable to endanger the lives of people in order to work toward some desirable goal, as it may be morally justifiable to risk people's lives in order to rush a critically ill person to the hospital. But a person who is speeding for good reason, or who benefits from that speeding, is not thereby relieved of responsibility for someone who is thereby injured, for otherwise the endangered or harmed would be treated only as means to the ends of others. Similarly, those who make or benefit from economic and political decisions are not relieved of responsibility for those who are thereby harmed or endangered. So even if we were to accept the view that no individual or government has any duty to aid those in distress simply because they are in distress, there would still be few people of more than adequate means in the real world who would not have an obligation to aid those in need. As Onora Nell writes:

> Only if we knew that we were not part of any system of activities causing unjustifiable deaths could we have no duties to support policies which seek to avoid such deaths. Modern economic causal chains are so complex that it is likely that only those who are economically isolated and self-sufficient could know that they are part of no such system of activities.[11]

With respect to compensating those who have been harmed we do not have to be part of the causal chain that causes harm in order to have an obligation to those who still bear the effects of past harm. If A stole B's money yesterday and gave the money to C today, C obviously has a duty to return it. While in some cases mentioned above decisions were made by companies, individuals and governments still were beneficiaries of such decisions through lower prices and increased tax revenue. Furthermore, it would not make any difference if A stole B's money before C was born. Consider the following case:

> Bengal (today's Bangledesh and the West Bengal state of India), the first territory the British conquered in Asia, was a prosperous province with highly developed centers of manufacturing and trade, and an economy as advanced as any prior to the industrial revolution. The British reduced Bengal to poverty through plunder, heavy land taxes and trade restrictions that barred competitive Indian goods from England, but gave British goods free entry into India. India's late Prime Minister Nehru commented bitterly, "Bengal can take pride in the fact that she helped greatly in giving birth to the Industrial Revolution in England."[12]

Those who benefited from the Industrial Revolution in England, including those alive today, would still have duties to aid Bengal, just as those who inherited a fortune partially based on stolen money have a duty to return what was stolen, with interest, even though they themselves are in no way guilty of the theft. So it is with most citizens of the industrialized West with respect to the poor of some parts of the world. However, in the light of the complexity of both the causal chains of harm and the causal chains of benefit, we are again faced with a great deal of uncertainty as to the allocation of responsibility for correcting for past injustices.[13]

IV HUNGER, POSITIVE DUTIES, AND THE IDEA OF A FAIR SHARE

So there is no doubt that a Kantian ethic would include duties of reparation for harms done to people in the past and that this would be a basis of obligations to aid many of the underdeveloped countries in the world today, even though it would be difficult to specify the extent of obligation. But is there a duty to help those in severe need even if the causes of the need are not due to any past injustice or are unknown, as may also be true about parts of the world today? Kant does not always treat duties to aid others as fully binding, but whether or not, as one Kantian argues, "it is impermissible not to promote the well-being of others,"[14] it can be argued that it is impermissible not to relieve others in distress and provide them with the basic necessities of life, for this is to fail to treat them as having any value as ends in themselves. To put it another way, failing to help is to violate subsistence rights, and, as Henry Shue argues, whatever sorts of reasons can be given in favor of regarding human beings as having security rights can also be given in favor of regarding them as having subsistence rights.[15] Or, to put it another way, it is to fail to take into account the vulnerability of the world's poor toward the affluent (taken collectively), and it is the vulnerability of people to others (individually or collectively) that is the foundation of most (or all) of both our positive and negative duties to others.[16]

To what extent do individuals and nations have a duty to relieve those in distress? Is there a middle way between Singer and Nozick? Perhaps the following line of reasoning would provide a guideline. An estimate can be made of what resources would be needed to feed the hungry, bring about political and economic change, promote development, limit population growth, and to do whatever is necessary to see that all people have a minimally decent standard of living (or that their basic rights are met). Some formula based on ability to help could determine what a fair share would be for each citizen of a developed country to contribute to the needs of those in distress in that country and to that country's share of helping the people of other nations. To the extent that nations adopt this procedure and make it part of their tax structure a person could fulfill the duty of doing her share by paying her taxes. The ideal would be for nations to do this so that the responsibilities would be carried out and the burden would be distributed fairly. To the extent that nations have not done this (and it is unlikely that any have) what duties do citizens have to contribute through private or religious agencies? Henry Shue correctly observes that "How much sacrifice can reasonably be expected from one person for the sake of another, even for the sake of honoring the other's rights, is one of the most fundamental questions in morality."[17] Nozick, as we have seen, answers with "None." Many answer with "Some" without going on to give a more precise answer. In the absence of adequate government action each individual could still make some sort of estimate of what a fair share would be and give that amount (or what remains of that amount after taking into consideration that part of her taxes that are used for appropriate purposes) through private or religious agencies. I am claiming that it is a strict duty or duty of perfect obligation for an individual to give at least her fair share, according to some plausible formula, toward seeing that all human beings are treated as ends in themselves, which involves seeing that they have the basic necessities of life in so far as that can depend on the actions of others. This conclusion can also be supported by a generalization argument. If everyone contributed at least a fair share the subsistence rights of human beings would cease to be violated (since that would be one of the criteria for deciding on a fair share). There is a problem about the applicability of generalization arguments where the efforts of one individual accomplishes nothing if most other people do not also do their fair share. (It is, for example, probably pointless to be the only person who refrains from taking a short cut across the grass; the grass will not grow.) In such cases the failure of some to fulfill their duties may relieve others of theirs. The duty to contribute to the cause of combatting hunger, however, is not of this sort, since one individual's contributions still accomplish some good whether or not other people are giving their fair share.

On the other hand there is the problem of whether the failure of some people to fulfill their duties increases the duties of others. If many are not giving a fair share, does the individual who is already giving a fair share have a duty to give more? The example of the two drowning people suggests that the individual who has done his fair share does have a duty to do more. But there is a major difference between the two cases. Saving people from drowning, in so far as the chances of losing one's own life are not great, is something that takes a minimal amount of time out of the rescuer's life and does not threaten his ability to live a life of pursuing goals he sets for himself. A similar duty to keep on giving of one's resources, even after one has done his fair share, would threaten to eclipse everything else a person might choose to do with his life, for example, develop his talents, raise a family, send his children to college, and so on, so that that person would become nothing but a means to meeting the needs of others. The idea of a strict duty to do at least one's fair share seems to avoid the problem of overload (unless the total need is overwhelming) and draws a line at a plausible point somewhere between doing nothing and sacrificing one's whole life to the cause of relieving the distress of others. This approach does make one's duty to those in need agent-specific, since one's duty does depend on one's past history, on what sacrifices one has already made, but it is not clear to me why this is a defect. Of course a person might choose to make the rescuing of those in distress her special vocation, and it may be noble for her to do so, but to claim that if the needs of others are great enough she has a duty to surrender any choice about the direction of her own life is to claim that a person has a duty to be purely the means to meeting the needs of others, and so in fact a duty to love others not as oneself, but instead of oneself. On the other hand, not to recognize a duty to give a fair share is to indicate that one believes either that it is not important that the needs of those in distress should be met (perhaps because they do not have subsistence rights) or that others should do more than their fair share.[18] It might be said that the first is at least a sin against compassion (if not also against justice) and the second is a sin against fairness or justice. In either case one is treating the ends and purposes of others as having less validity than one's own, or, from another point of view, one is not loving others as oneself.

V CONSIDERATIONS BEYOND A FAIR SHARE

If redistribution of wealth were in fact the major need of the most vulnerable in the world, and if in fact government foreign aid programs could be modified so that they could be trusted to meet that need, then, in agreement with Shue and Goodin, I would claim that for the sake of fairness both to those in need and those willing to help, it would be better if everyone did his or her fair share and it would be legitimate to coerce people through the tax system to do so.[19] In the absence of such taxation and in the absence of any official calculation of such a share, individuals generally do not have the information on which to assess their own fair share, and if they did they would probably tend to underestimate it. What most people tend to think of as their fair share depends much less on any informed calculation than on what they think their neighbors, fellow citizens, or fellow church members, are contributing,[20] consoling themselves with the thought that it cannot really be their duty to do more than others. But since most people who do something probably tend to think that they are doing more with respect to their resources than others, the idea of a duty to do a fair share is in danger of succumbing to a downward pressure to require less and less. If the vulnerable are to be protected, then perhaps doing one's fair share to meet their needs is not the only duty. Rather there must also be a duty to put upward pressure on the prevailing idea of a fair share. This can be done only by those who do considerably more than what is perceived of as a fair share, and often more than an actual fair share. This is embodied in Christian ethics in the ideal of being a light to witness to a higher and more demanding way of life and in the ideal of being the salt of the earth that preserves it from decay, perhaps primarily the decay brought about by downward pressure on prevailing standards. Probably a secular counterpart to these ideals would be accepted by others.

There are doubts about whether redistribution of wealth is the major need, as opposed to various changes in policies, including trade policies. There are also grave doubts concerning the degree to which government aid in the past has really benefited the most vulnerable and about its prospects of doing so in the future. That raises the possibility that the major duty individuals have is that of exerting pressure on government to make sure that policies do protect the vulnerable. (In American society people are not quick to recognize this as a moral duty. Churches have much more success in getting their members to contribute to "One Great Hour of Sharing" and "Hunger Fund" offerings than they do in getting them to write letters to their Senators and Congressmen about hunger issues.) Donald Regan writes that our duty is "to cooperate with whoever else is cooperating, in the production of the best consequences possible given the behaviour of non-cooperators."[21] There is an organization, Bread for the World, which analyzes policy, supports legislation on hunger issues, and conducts coordinated letter-writing drives through its members and its affiliated churches. Those who would write letters to their representatives in conjunction with such an effort would be acting in accordance with Regan's principle. But the principle does not say how much time, effort, and money an individual has a duty to devote to cooperating with others to bring it about that governments act in ways that protect the vulnerable.[22] Giving one's fair share to help those in need accomplishes some good whether or not others are cooperating by doing their share. In the matter of influencing legislation an insufficient number of people doing their fair share (with respect to all who might participate in the effort) may accomplish nothing. Does the failure of enough others to do their fair share release one from one's duty to work for change (as it may release one from the duty not to walk on the grass)? If so, the vulnerable are left without protection. Or does such a failure impose a duty on others to do as much as possible (as in the case of saving drowning people), so that we could again be faced with the problem of overload? In this case, however, one sort of fair share is so minimal there is no problem in doing much more. If an individual wrote at least one letter a year to her Senators and Congressman on one piece of legislation critical to meeting the needs of the hungry in the world, that individual would on this matter be doing perhaps 50 times a fair share, in that letters from two percent of the electorate would be regarded by those legislators as an overwhelming mandate on the issue. But an individual could write many such letters a year, and encourage others to do likewise, without sacrificing anything significant. Perhaps there is no precise answer to the question of just how much more money or effort than prevailing standards require one "ought" to devote to the cause here being considered, since this may be a matter of living up to an ideal rather than fulfilling a perfect duty to a specific individual, or a perfect duty of doing a fair share. Even in the absence of any way of determining what a fair share might be one can attempt to live by this ideal by doing significantly more than the society as a whole generally thinks is required.

Furthermore, may not some people have an agent-specific duty to do more than a fair share (perhaps much more) about some specific matter because of their peculiar awareness of the problem, knowledge of what needs to be done, and sensitivity to it? Religious people might say that all people have a duty to ask themselves whether they may have been "called" to a special vocation of taking on this cause, with the assurance that some people are called to this vocation and all people are called to some such vocation(s). In addition, a religious ethic generally emphasizes the faithfulness of one's witness more than the extent of one's accomplishments, and so may succeed in sustaining an individual's efforts to bring about change when the prospects of succeeding seem slight. Perhaps some would argue for secular equivalents to these emphases.

VI POSTSCRIPT: ADDITIONAL KANTIAN REFLECTIONS ON DUTIES TO OTHERS

There are still a number of things to be taken into consideration. Kant says that a person should "not push the expenditure of his means in beneficence . . . to the point where he would finally need the beneficence of others."[23] That could be regarded as treating others as a means to one's own end of trying to achieve some kind of sainthood. Secondly, help should not be given in a manner or to an extent that reduces the ability of the person (or group) that is helped to be self-reliant and self-determining. It is doubtful whether the wealthy have ever given too much help to the poor, but they have sometimes (perhaps frequently) given in a manner which made the recipients more dependent in the long run, for example, in a way that reduced the incentives of local farmers to increase production. Thirdly, according to Kant, every effort must be made to "carefully avoid any appearance of intending to obligate the other person, lest he (the giver) not render a true benefit, inasmuch as by his act he expresses that he wants to lay an obligation upon the receiver."[24] Presumably nations such as the United States can and do give aid for ulterior purposes, such as to get rid of agricultural surpluses, help farm prices, gain political influence, or to stimulate markets and/or a favorable climate of investment for U.S. companies, but then citizens of these nations ought not congratulate themselves on their generosity (as Americans often do). Such acts are not acts of beneficence and from Kant's point of view they have no moral worth since they are not done for the sake of duty, nor are they done from other motives that might be regarded as being other than morally neutral.

Fourthly, there are conditions under which it could be argued that a wealthy country has the right to refuse to give aid, other than emergency disaster aid, if it is not something that is owed as reparations. Suppose that achieving the goal of advancing the self-sufficiency and self-determination of a nation depends in part on the receiving nation's own effort to make necessary changes such as redistributing land, bringing population growth under control, and so on. It could be argued that if the receiving nation fails to make a good-faith effort to bring about these changes, and if it then asks for additional aid, the developed country may legitimately claim that it is being used, and its people are being used, solely as means to the ends of the underdeveloped country or its people. The major problem with using this line of argument is that the people who are facing hunger may have little to say about the decisions of their government. That problem, however, does not prevent the aid-giving country from legitimately making demands for reform in advance, from doing what it can to see to it that they are carried out, and from threatening sanctions other than those that would increase the deprivation of hungry people.[25] Perhaps it has seldom, if ever, happened that a developed nation has given enough non-military aid to an underdeveloped nation to be in a position to dictate what steps the receiving nation should take to improve the ability of its people to be self-sufficient; or perhaps it has been in the interest of the political strategy, military effort, or business investment of the developed nations not to demand that specific remedial steps be taken on the part of the receiving country; but it would seem to be legitimate to make such demands.

NOTES

1 Peter Singer, "Famine, Affluence, and Morality," *Philosophy and Public Affairs,* vol. 1 (1972), p. 231.

2 James Fishkin, *The Limits of Obligation* (New Haven: Yale University Press, 1982), especially chapters 1–7, 9 and 18.

3 Garrett Hardin, "Lifeboat Ethics: "The Case Against Helping the Poor," *Psychology Today,* vol. 8 (1974), pp. 38–43, 123–126.

4 Garrett Hardin, "The Tragedy of the Commons," *Science,* vol. 102 (1968), pp. 1243–1248.

5 Garrett Hardin, "Carrying Capacity as an Ethical Concept," in George R. Lucas and Thomas W. Ogletree (eds.), *Lifeboat Ethics: The Moral Dilemmas of World Hunger,* (New York: Harper and Row, 1976), p. 131.

6 Part of the title of an article by Garrett Hardin, "Another Face of Bioethics: The Case for Massive 'Diebacks' of Population," *Modern Medicine,* vol. 65 (March 1, 1975).

7 Paul Verghese, "Muddled Metaphors," in Lucas and Ogletree, *op. cit.,* p. 152.

8 Robert Nozick, *Anarchy, State, and Utopia* (New York: Basic Books, Inc., 1974), pp. 30–35.

9 Immanuel Kant, *The Metaphysical Elements of Justice* (Part 1 of the *Metaphysics of Morals*), tr. by John Ladd (Indianapolis: Bobbs-Merrill Co., 1965), p. 93 (326).

10 Nozick, *op. cit.,* p. 31.

11 Onora Nell, "Lifeboat Earth," *Philosophy and Public Affairs,* vol. 4 (1975), p. 286.

12 Arthur Simon, *Bread for the World,* (New York: Paulist Press, 1975), p. 41.

13 For some of these problems see Goodin, *Protecting the Vulnerable* (Chicago: University of Chicago Press, 1986), pp. 159–160.

14 Alan Donagan, *Theory of Morality* (Chicago: University of Chicago Press, 1977), p. 85.

15 Henry Shue, *Basic Rights* (Princeton: Princeton University Press, 1980), Chapters 1 & 2.

16 This is the thesis of Goodin's book *(op. cit.)* with which I am in general agreement.

17 Shue, *op. cit.,* p. 114.

18 See also Goodin, *op. cit.,* p. 165.

19 *Ibid.,* p. 164; Shue, *op. cit.,* p. 118.

20 See Singer, "Famine, Affluence, and Morality," *op. cit.,* p. 30.

21 Donald Regan, *Utilitarianism and Cooperation* (Oxford: Clarendon Press, 1980), p. 124; also cited by Goodin as expressing his own view (*op. cit.,* p. 164).

22 For some suggestions concerning such ways, see Frances Moore Lappé and Joseph Collins, *World Hunger: 10 Myths,* (San Francisco: Institute for Food and Development Policy, 4th ed., 1982), pp. 49–50.

23 *Metaphysical Principles of Virtue, op. cit.,* p. 118 (454).

24 *Ibid.* (453).

25 See Shue, *Basic Rights,* Part III, "Policy Implications," *op. cit.,* pp. 155–174.

QUESTIONS

1 If affluent nations and their citizens are at least in part causally responsible for hunger and famine in poorer countries, do the former have an obligation to help the latter in order to compensate them for past, or perhaps even ongoing, harms?

2 If morality requires us to treat other humans as ends in themselves, does it necessarily follow that we are required to meet the subsistence needs of those who are unable to meet their own needs?

SUGGESTED ADDITIONAL READINGS FOR CHAPTER 9

AIKEN, WILLIAM, and HUGH LAFOLLETTE, eds.: *World Hunger and Moral Obligation.* Englewood Cliffs, N.J.: Prentice-Hall, 1977. With the exception of Joseph Fletcher, a theologian, and Garrett Hardin, a biologist, all the authors in this collection are philosophers. The writers examine various issues raised by the central question, "What moral responsibility do affluent nations (or the people in them) have to the starving masses?" The article by Peter Singer which is reprinted in this chapter is also reprinted in this volume and is followed by a postscript in which Singer (1) presents some later thoughts on the topic and (2) responds to some critics.

BROWN, PETER G., and HENRY SHUE, eds.: *Food Policy.* New York: Free Press, 1977. This book is designed to provide a foundation for a reflective appraisal of questions about the moral obligation of the agriculturally affluent in regard to world hunger. The articles, which were all written specifically for this volume, are divided into four sections: (1) "Needs and Obligations," (2) "Responsibilities in the Public Sector," (3) "Responsibilities in the Private Sector," and (4) "Reducing Dependence."

EBERSTADT, NICK: "Myths of the Food Crisis." *New York Review of Books,* February 19, 1976, pp. 32–37. Eberstadt attacks the myths about world hunger which distort our perception of the problems and lead to the pessimism exemplified by Garrett Hardin.

GUSSOW, JOAN DYE: *The Feeding Web: Issues in Nutritional Ecology.* Palo Alto, Calif.: Bull, 1978. Gussow, a nutritionist, provides a collection of readings accompanied by her interpretations of those readings. She is concerned with "what the facts about the present state of the world" imply for "living human organisms completely dependent on complex foodstuffs for survival." The readings examine the biological, technical, social, scientific, and commercial matrices in which the production, purchasing, and consumption of food are embedded.

LAPPÉ, FRANCES MOORE, and JOSEPH COLLINS: *World Hunger: Twelve Myths.* New York: Grove, 1986. Lappé and Collins criticize both some of the common beliefs about the causes of world hunger and some present approaches to its alleviation.

LUCAS, GEORGE R., JR., and THOMAS OGLETREE, eds.: *Lifeboat Ethics.* New York: Harper & Row, 1976. Most of the articles in this anthology appeared initially in *Soundings.* The articles are written by ethicists (many of whom are theologians) and scientists and grew out of concerns stemming from the advocacy of triage as a methodological response to world hunger.

LUPER-FOY, STEVEN, ed.: *Problems of International Justice.* Boulder, Colo., and London: Westview, 1988. Part One of this book is devoted to the topic of world resources and distributive justice. It includes articles on the general issue of international distributive justice and on the specific issue of the obligation to help the needy.

MURDOCH, WILLIAM W., and ALLAN OATEN: "Population and Food: Metaphors and the Reality." *Bioscience,* September 9, 1975, pp. 561–567. Murdoch and Oaten criticize Garrett Hardin's lifeboat, commons, and ratchet metaphors and bring out various factors, other than food supply, that affect population growth.

RACHELS, JAMES: "Killing and Starving to Death." *Philosophy,* vol. 54, April 1979, pp. 159–171. Rachels, attacking the view that killing is worse than letting die, argues that letting die is just as bad as killing. For Rachels our duty not to let people die from starvation is as strong as our duty not to kill them.

WATTS, MICHAEL: *Silent Violence: Food, Famine & Peasantry in Northern Nigeria.* Berkeley: University of California Press, 1983. Watts, whose discipline is geography, looks at the current food crisis in Africa from a historical perspective. He traces the varying character of food systems among Hausa peasants in northern Nigeria, examining the relationship among food crises, climate, and society.

WOGAMAN, J. PHILIP, ed.: *The Population Crisis and Moral Responsibility*. Washington, D.C.: Public Affairs Press, 1973. This anthology emphasizes theological perspectives but contains articles by ethicists and population experts as well. The various articles are collected in four separate sections: (1) the moral basis of policy objectives, (2) the moral responsibility of government, (3) moral analysis of policy proposals, and (4) moral responsibility of religious communities.

CHAPTER 10

Animals

Human beings are responsible for a great deal of animal suffering. We use animals in experiments, raise and slaughter animals for food, and hunt and kill animals, sometimes merely for sport. Our treatment of animals raises numerous moral questions, some of which are discussed in this chapter.

SPECIESISM AND THE MORAL STATUS OF ANIMALS

In a now well-known book, *Animal Liberation,* Peter Singer forcefully calls attention to the suffering that human beings routinely inflict on nonhuman animals. In order to satisfy human desires for meat, we raise animals in such a way that their short lives are dominated by pain and suffering. In order to obtain information, purportedly for the benefit of humans, we devise experimental projects that involve the infliction of intense pain on animals. Our experimentation on animals and our meat-eating habits are paradigm examples, for Singer, of morally unacceptable practices in regard to animals. Because Singer finds human beings so willing to subordinate important animal interests (e.g., an interest in avoiding suffering) to much less important human interests, he charges the human community with *speciesism.* In an excerpt from *Animal Liberation* reprinted in this chapter, Singer defines speciesism as a "prejudice or attitude of bias toward the interests of members of one's own species and against those of members of other species." Singer uses the term "speciesism" in order to emphasize the similarities between sexist and racist practices on the one hand, and our treatment of animals on the other. (The wrongness of racism and sexism is discussed in the introduction to Chapter 7.) In Singer's view, it is just as wrong to discriminate against animals because of their species as it is to discriminate against women because of their sex and blacks because of their race.

Singer's arguments, in effect, attribute moral status to animals. An entity has moral status if it is due moral consideration in its own right and not simply because of its relations to other beings. Some philosophers have argued that animals have no moral status. In their view, any obligations we have regarding animals are based on the interests or rights of human beings. If we have an obligation not to mistreat dogs, for example, it may be because the mistreatment of dogs causes suffering to human beings, many of whom sympathetically identify with the suffering of animals.

Singer, in contrast, appeals directly to animal interests in condemning much of our current use of animals. Like L. W. Sumner in Chapter 1, Singer, in effect, holds that sentience is the relevant criterion in determining whether some entity has moral status. Sentience can be described as the capacity to have conscious experiences such as pleasure and pain. *All* sentient beings, Singer maintains, have interests, including an interest in avoiding pain and suffering. A fundamental principle of morality—*the principle of equal consideration of interests*—requires us to give equal consideration to the interests of all beings affected by our decisions. Animals, like human beings, are sentient beings with an interest in avoiding pain and suffering. Hence, we violate a fundamental principle of morality when we make decisions about the use of animals in experiments if we consider only human interests and fail to give equal consideration to the interests that animals have in avoiding suffering.

Whereas Singer focuses on animal *interests* as he advances a utilitarian line of reasoning, Tom Regan in this chapter focuses on animal *rights* as he advances a Kantian attack on speciesism. (Utilitarian and Kantian ethical reasoning are discussed in the introduction to Chapter 9.) On Regan's analysis, animals, like humans, are bearers of rights because animals, like humans, have inherent value. To have inherent value, Regan maintains, an entity must be a conscious creature whose welfare is valuable or important to it, so that its having value is not dependent on its usefulness to others. Since animals are creatures of this sort, they have rights that must be respected. Regan rejects the view that animals, while having some inherent value, have less inherent value than human beings. In his view, all entities that have inherent value have it equally, and have an equal right to be treated with respect. Any attempt to specify a difference (e.g., rationality) between human beings and animals that would purport to justify the attribution of lesser inherent value to the latter would require us to attribute a lesser degree of inherent value to some "nonparadigm" human beings (e.g., the severely brain-damaged) if we are to be consistent in our moral reasoning. The same problem is faced, Regan maintains, by those who attempt to specify some criterion that rights holders must possess (e.g., the capacity for autonomy) that would exclude animals from the class of entities having rights.

Regan's claim that animals have rights is attacked by Carl Cohen in this chapter. Cohen's position rests on his conception of rights as claims or potential claims within a community of moral agents. Moral agency presupposes a capacity for free moral judgment and for exercising and responding to moral claims. To be a moral agent, one must have a capacity to understand the rules of duty that govern all members of the human community and to act in accordance with these rules. Only human beings have the relevant capacities. Hence, for Cohen, only human beings have moral rights. Cohen rejects Regan's contention that any criterion that might be used to exclude all animals from the class of entities having rights would also require us to exclude nonparadigm humans. In Cohen's view, although animals cannot have rights because they lack the relevant capacities, nonparadigm humans who also lack the relevant capacities (e.g., the severely mentally retarded) do have rights. In his view, such nonparadigmatic humans are still the bearers of rights because they belong to a species whose members are normally capable of moral reasoning. Cohen does not deny that animals have some sort of moral status. He grants that we do have some obligations *to* animals, including an obligation not to cause them needless suffering. In contrast to Singer, however, Cohen maintains that it is wrong to give animal and human interests equal consideration. Whatever moral status animals have because of their sentience, it is significantly less than that of human beings.

The question of possible differences in the moral status of human beings and animals is addressed by Mary Anne Warren in this chapter's final reading. A distinction made in the introduction to Chapter 1 between full moral status and partial moral status is useful here. Entities have full moral status if they have the same rights as paradigmatic (i.e., normal adult) human beings. They have partial moral status if their rights are lesser in some sense than those of paradigmatic humans. In comparing and contrasting human and animal rights, Warren effectively ascribes partial moral status to animals. According to her analysis, animal and human rights differ in respect to both their content and their strength (i.e., in the strength of the reasons required to override them). Warren holds that sentience is the basis for at least some rights. Thus she rejects Cohen's conception of rights. Warren argues, however, that moral agency (moral autonomy), as well as other differences between humans and animals, may be a basis for attributing stronger rights to human beings than to animals. In respect to nonparadigmatic humans, Warren advances reasons to support the claim that we can consistently grant them the same rights as those of paradigm humans while attributing only lesser rights to animals.

VEGETARIANISM

Is the human interest in eating meat sufficiently important to justify our practice of raising and slaughtering animals? Intertwined with this question is the issue of a vegetarian diet. Advocates of vegetarianism offer diverse arguments to support their position. Some advocate a vegetarian diet simply because they believe it to be superior in terms of health benefits. If a vegetarian diet does offer special health advantages (a controversial claim), then each individual, as a matter of personal prudence, would be well advised to adopt it. Apart from this *prudential argument,* many vegetarians advance *moral arguments* in defense of their diet. One common moral argument, closely related to the considerations developed in Chapter 9, is based on the fact that hunger, malnutrition, and starvation seriously threaten many people in our world. It is morally indefensible, the argument goes, to waste desperately needed protein by feeding our grain to animals whom we then eat. Eight pounds of protein in the form of grain are necessary on the average to produce one pound of protein in the form of meat. Since this process is so inefficient, we are morally obliged to adopt a vegetarian diet so that our protein resources in the form of grain can be shared with those who desperately need help. Though this particular moral argument is not without force, it would seem that it does not establish a need for a completely vegetarian diet. It may well be that world hunger could effectively be alleviated if people in affluent countries simply consumed *less meat.*

The most important moral arguments advanced in defense of a vegetarian diet are those that take account of the impact of meat production on the animals themselves. Three lines of argument in this category may be distinguished. (1) Though it is not necessarily wrong to kill animals for food (assuming the killing is relatively pain-less), it is morally indefensible to subject them to the cruelty of "factory farming." Since the meat available in our society is produced in just this way, we are morally obliged not to eat it. (2) It is morally wrong to kill animals for food, however pain-less the killing; animals, like human beings, have a right to life. Regan's Kantian approach in this chapter exemplifies this second line of reasoning. (3) It is morally wrong to kill animals for food, however painless the killing, on utilitarian grounds. Bart Gruzalski in this chapter advances this third line of reasoning. Gruzalski asserts, in the spirit of classical act utilitarianism, that "an action is right if it is the best bet a person has to avoid producing painful consequences and to bring about pleasurable or happy consequences." On Gruzalski's utilitarian analysis, raising and slaughtering animals for their flesh cannot be justified. Even if we raise animals humanely, we will on balance produce more painful consequences than if we adopt a policy of veg-etarianism. Among the good consequences resulting from vegetarianism, Gruzalski includes the sorts of considerations discussed above regarding the alleviation of star-vation in the world.

ANIMAL EXPERIMENTATION

The use of animals in scientific experimentation intended to benefit human beings raises its own set of troubling questions. Is there any need to use animals in experi-mentation intended to benefit human beings? If there is a genuine need, can this pro-vide a moral justification for the resulting pain, or even death, of animals? It is pos-sible to distinguish four major lines of reasoning on the morality of animal experi-mentation. (1) Animal experimentation is never justified because using animals in this way is inconsistent with treating them with the respect due to entities having inherent worth. Entities of this sort cannot be used merely as things for others' ben-efit. Just as the use of human beings in experiments without their informed consent violates their right to be treated with the respect due those with inherent value, so, too, does the use of animals in experiments conducted in order to benefit humans. This first line of reasoning is in keeping with Regan's position. (2) Animal experi-mentation is justified only in those cases where we would be willing to conduct the same experiments on brain-damaged human subjects. This is Singer's claim. The un-derlying reasoning here may be expressed as follows: There may be relevant differ-ences between "normal, adult" humans and animals that would justify our using the latter, but not the former in some experiments—those that might be essential to save human lives or prevent great suffering. However, animals and certain nonparadigm humans do not differ in relevant respects. Hence we are justified in using the former in experiments only where we are justified in using the latter. (3) Given sufficiently important human interests, the presumption against using animals as experimental subjects may be overridden. Although animals because of their sentience have rights that have to be taken into account, serious human interests can override them. The rights of nonparadigm humans cannot be overridden on the same grounds, however, since their rights are grounded not only in sentience but in other considerations. Warren's article exemplifies this third line of argument. (4) Animal experimentation for the benefit of humans is justifiable simply by appeal to human rights and interests. However, although animals do not have rights, not every experiment using animals is morally acceptable. If the same results could be achieved by using alternative methods (e.g., computer simulation), for example, then it would be morally wrong to conduct an experiment that inflicts needless suffering on animals. Cohen accepts this fourth position. He states, however, that it would be a mistake to think that alternative techniques could shortly replace most of the present experimentation using live animals as subjects.

Jane S. Zembaty

All Animals Are Equal

Peter Singer

A biographical sketch of Peter Singer is found on p. 88.

Singer rejects speciesism, which he defines as a prejudice or attitude of bias in favor of the interests of members of one's own species and against those of members of other species. In his view, speciesism is analogous to racism and sexism. Just as we have a moral obligation to give equal consideration to the interests of all human beings, regardless of sex or skin color, so, too, we have a moral obligation to give equal consideration to the interests of animals. Insofar as animals, like humans, have the capacity to suffer, they have an interest in not suffering. Not to take that interest into account is speciesist and immoral. Singer attacks our current practice of using animals in experiments that frequently inflict tremendous suffering, often for very trivial reasons. As a guiding principle for determining when an experiment using animals might be morally justifiable, Singer suggests that an experiment is justifiable only if it is so important that the use of brain-damaged humans would also be justifiable.

"Animal Liberation" may sound more like a parody of other liberation movements than a serious objective. The idea of "The Rights of Animals" actually was once used to parody the case for women's rights. When Mary Wollstonecraft, a forerunner of today's feminists, published her *Vindication of the Rights of Woman* in 1792, her views were widely regarded as absurd, and before long an anonymous publication appeared entitled *A Vindication of the Rights of Brutes.* The author of this satirical work (now known to have been Thomas Taylor, a distinguished Cambridge philosopher) tried to refute Mary Wollstonecraft's arguments by showing that they could be carried one stage further. If the argument for equality was sound when applied to women, why should it not be applied to dogs, cats, and horses? The reasoning

Reprinted with permission of the author from *Animal Liberation,* New York Review, second edition (1990), pp. 1–9, 36–37, 40, 81–83, 85–86.

seemed to hold for these "brutes" too; yet to hold that brutes had rights was manifestly absurd. Therefore the reasoning by which this conclusion had been reached must be unsound, and if unsound when applied to brutes, it must also be unsound when applied to women, since the very same arguments had been used in each case.

In order to explain the basis of the case for the equality of animals, it will be helpful to start with an examination of the case for the equality of women. Let us assume that we wish to defend the case for women's rights against the attack by Thomas Taylor. How should we reply?

One way in which we might reply is by saying that the case for equality between men and women cannot validly be extended to nonhuman animals. Women have a right to vote, for instance, because they are just as capable of making rational decisions about the future as men are; dogs, on the other hand, are incapable of understanding the significance of voting, so they cannot have the right to vote. There are many other obvious ways in which men and women resemble each other closely, while humans and animals differ greatly. So, it might be said, men and women are similar beings and should have similar rights, while humans and nonhumans are different and should not have equal rights.

The reasoning behind this reply to Taylor's analogy is correct up to a point, but it does not go far enough. There are obviously important differences between humans and other animals, and these differences must give rise to some differences in the rights that each have. Recognizing this evident fact, however, is no barrier to the case for extending the basic principle of equality to nonhuman animals. The differences that exist between men and women are equally undeniable, and the supporters of Women's Liberation are aware that these differences may give rise to different rights. Many feminists hold that women have the right to an abortion on request. It does not follow that since these same feminists are campaigning for equality between men and women they must support the right of men to have abortions too. Since a man cannot have an abortion, it is meaningless to talk of his right to have one. Since dogs can't vote, it is meaningless to talk of their right to vote. There is no reason why either Women's Liberation or Animal Liberation should get involved in such nonsense. The extension of the basic principle of equality from one group to another does not imply that we must treat both groups in exactly the same way, or grant exactly the same rights to both groups. Whether we should do so will depend on the nature of the members of the two groups. The basic principle of equality does not require equal or identical *treatment;* it requires equal consideration. Equal consideration for different beings may lead to different treatment and different rights.

So there is a different way of replying to Taylor's attempt to parody the case for women's rights, a way that does not deny the obvious differences between human beings and nonhumans but goes more deeply into the question of equality and concludes by finding nothing absurd in the idea that the basic principle of equality applies to so-called brutes. At this point such a conclusion may appear odd; but if we examine more deeply the basis on which our opposition to discrimination on grounds of race or sex ultimately rests, we will see that we would be on shaky ground if we were to demand equality for blacks, women, and other groups of oppressed humans while denying equal consideration to nonhumans. To make this clear we need to see, first, exactly why racism and sexism are wrong. When we say that all human beings, whatever their race, creed, or sex, are equal, what is it that we are asserting? Those who wish to defend hierarchical, inegalitarian societies have often pointed out that by whatever test we choose it simply is not true that all humans are equal. Like it or not we must face the fact that humans come in different shapes and sizes; they come with different moral capacities, different intellectual abilities, different amounts of benevolent feeling and sensitivity to the needs of others, different abilities to communicate effectively, and different capacities to experience pleasure and pain. In short, if the demand for equality were based on the actual equality of all human beings, we would have to stop demanding equality.

Still, one might cling to the view that the demand for equality among human beings is based on the actual equality of the different races and sexes. Although, it may be said, humans differ as individuals, there are no differences between the races and sexes as such. From the mere fact that a person is black or a woman we cannot infer anything about that person's intellectual or moral capacities. This, it may be said, is why racism and sexism are wrong. The white racist claims that whites are superior to blacks, but this is false; although there are differences among individuals, some blacks are superior to some whites in all of the capacities and abilities that could conceivably be relevant. The opponent of sexism would say the same: a person's sex is no guide to his or her abilities, and this is why it is unjustifiable to discriminate on the basis of sex.

The existence of individual variations that cut across the lines of race or sex, however, provides us with no defense at all against a more sophisticated opponent of equality, one who proposes that, say, the interests of all those with IQ scores below 100 be given less consideration than the interests of those with ratings over 100. Perhaps those scoring below the mark would, in this society, be made the slaves of those scoring higher. Would a hierarchical society of this sort really be so much better than one based on race or sex? I think not. But if we tie the moral principle of equality to the factual equality of the different races or sexes, taken as a whole, our opposition to racism and sexism does not provide us with any basis for objecting to this kind of inegalitarianism.

There is a second important reason why we ought not to base our opposition to racism and sexism on any kind of factual equality, even the limited kind that asserts that variations in capacities and abilities are spread evenly among the different races and between the sexes: we can have no absolute guarantee that these capacities and abilities really are distributed evenly, without regard to race or sex, among human beings. So far as actual abilities are concerned there do seem to be certain measurable differences both among races and between sexes. These differences do not, of course, appear in every case, but only when averages are taken. More important still, we do not yet know how many of these differences are really due to the different genetic endowments of the different races and sexes, and how many are due to poor schools, poor housing, and other factors that are the result of past and continuing discrimination. Perhaps all of the important differences will eventually prove to be environmental rather than genetic. Anyone opposed to racism and sexism will certainly hope that this will be so, for it will make the task of ending discrimination a lot easier; nevertheless, it would be dangerous to rest the case against racism and sexism on the belief that all significant differences are environmental in origin. The opponent of, say, racism who takes this line will be unable to avoid conceding that if differences in ability did after all prove to have some genetic connection with race, racism would in some way be defensible.

Fortunately there is no need to pin the case for equality to one particular outcome of a scientific investigation. The appropriate response to those who claim to have found evidence of genetically based differences in ability among the races or between the sexes is not to stick to the belief that the genetic explanation must be wrong, whatever evidence to the contrary may turn up; instead we should make it quite clear that the claim to equality does not depend on intelligence, moral capacity, physical strength, or similar matters of fact. Equality is a moral idea, not an assertion of fact. There is no logically compelling reason for assuming that a factual difference in ability between two people justifies any difference in the amount of consideration we give to their needs and interests. *The principle of the equality of human beings is not a description of an alleged actual equality among humans: it is a prescription of how we should treat human beings.*

Jeremy Bentham, the founder of the reforming utilitarian school of moral philosophy, incorporated the essential basis of moral equality into his system of ethics by means of the formula: "Each to count for one and none for more than one." In other words, the interests of every being affected by an action are to be taken into account and given the same weight as the like interests of any other being. A later utilitarian, Henry Sidgwick, put the point in this way: "The good of any one individual is of no more importance, from the point of view (if I may say so) of the Universe, than the good of any other." More recently the leading figures in contemporary moral philosophy have shown a great deal of agreement in specifying as a fundamental presupposition of their moral theories some similar requirement that works to give everyone's interests equal consideration—although these writers generally cannot agree on how this requirement is best formulated.[1]

It is an implication of this principle of equality that our concern for others and our readiness to consider their interests ought not to depend on what they are like or on what abilities they may possess. Precisely what our concern or consideration requires us to do may vary according to the characteristics of those affected by what we do: concern for the well-being of children growing up in America would require that we teach them to read; concern for the well-being of pigs may require no more than that we leave them with other pigs in a place where there is adequate food and room to run freely. But the basic element—the taking into account of the interests of the being, whatever those interests may be—must, according to the principle of equality, be extended to all beings, black or white, masculine or feminine, human or nonhuman.

Thomas Jefferson, who was responsible for writing the principle of the equality of men into the American Declaration of Independence, saw this point. It led him to oppose slavery even though he was unable to free himself fully from his slaveholding background. He wrote in a letter to the author of a book that emphasized the notable intellectual achievements of Negroes in order to refute the then common view that they had limited intellectual capacities:

Be assured that no person living wishes more sincerely than I do, to see a complete refutation of the doubts I myself have entertained and expressed on the grade of understanding allotted to them by nature, and to find that they are on a par with ourselves . . . but whatever be their degree of talent it is no measure of their rights. Because Sir Isaac Newton was superior to others in understanding, he was not therefore lord of the property or persons of others.[2]

Similarly, when in the 1850s the call for women's rights was raised in the United States, a remarkable black feminist named Sojourner Truth made the same point in more robust terms at a feminist convention:

They talk about this thing in the head; what do they call it? ["Intellect," whispered someone nearby.] That's it. What's that got to do with women's rights or Negroes' rights? If my cup won't hold but a pint and yours holds a quart, wouldn't you be mean not to let me have my little half-measure full?[3]

It is on this basis that the case against racism and the case against sexism must both ultimately rest; and it is in accordance with this principle that the attitude that we may call "speciesism," by analogy with racism, must also be condemned. Speciesism—the word is not an attractive one, but I can think of no better term—is a prejudice or attitude of bias in favor of the interests of members of one's own species and against those of members of other species. It should be obvious that the fundamental objections to racism and sexism made by Thomas Jefferson and Sojourner Truth apply equally to speciesism. If possessing a higher degree of intelligence does not entitle one human to use another for his or her own ends, how can it entitle humans to exploit nonhumans for the same purpose?[4]

Many philosophers and other writers have proposed the principle of equal consideration of interests, in some form or other, as a basic moral principle; but not many of them have recognized that this principle applies to members of other species as well as to our own. Jeremy Bentham was one of the few who did realize this. In a forward-looking passage written at a time when black slaves had been freed by the French but in the British dominions were still being treated in the way we now treat animals, Bentham wrote:

The day *may* come when the rest of the animal creation may acquire those rights which never could have been withholden from them but by the hand of tyranny. The French have already discovered that the blackness of the skin is no reason why a human being should be abandoned without redress to the caprice of a tormentor. It may one day come to be recognized that the number of the legs, the villosity of the skin, or the termination of the *os sacrum* are reasons equally insufficient for abandoning a sensitive being to the same fate. What else is it that should trace the insuperable line? Is it the faculty of reason, or perhaps the faculty of discourse? But a full-grown horse or dog is beyond comparison a more rational, as well as a more conversable animal, than an infant of a day or a week or even a month, old. But suppose they were otherwise, what would it avail? The question is not, Can they *reason?* nor Can they *talk?* but, Can they *suffer?*[5]

In this passage Bentham points to the capacity for suffering as the vital characteristic that gives a being the right to equal consideration. The capacity for suffering—or more strictly, for suffering and/or enjoyment or happiness—is not just another characteristic like the capacity for language or higher mathematics. Bentham is not saying that those who try to mark "the insuperable line" that determines whether the interests of a being should be considered happen to have chosen the wrong characteristic. By saying that we must consider the interests of all beings with the capacity for suffering or enjoyment Bentham does not arbitrarily exclude from consideration any interests at all—as those who draw the line with reference to the possession of reason or language do. The capacity for suffering and enjoyment is *a prerequisite for having interests at all,* a condition that must be satisfied before we can speak of interests in a meaningful way. It would be nonsense to say that it was not in the interests of a stone to be kicked along the road by a schoolboy. A stone does not have interests because it cannot suffer. Nothing that we can do to it could possibly make any difference to its welfare. The capacity for suffering and enjoyment is, however, not only necessary, but also sufficient for us to say that a being has interests—at an absolute minimum, an interest in not suffering. A mouse, for example, does have an interest in not being kicked along the road, because it will suffer if it is.

Although Bentham speaks of "rights" in the passage I have quoted, the argument is really about equality rather than about rights. Indeed, in a different passage, Bentham famously described "natural rights" as "nonsense" and "natural and imprescriptable rights" as "nonsense upon stilts." He talked of moral rights as a shorthand way of referring to protections that people and animals morally ought to have; but the real weight of the moral argument does not rest on the assertion of the existence of the right, for this in turn has to be justified on the basis of the possibilities for suffering and happiness. In this way we can argue for equality for animals without getting embroiled in philosophical controversies about the ultimate nature of rights.

In misguided attempts to refute the arguments of this book, some philosophers have gone to much trouble developing arguments to show that animals do not have rights.[6] They have claimed that to have rights a being must be autonomous, or must be a member of a community, or must have the ability to respect the rights of others, or must possess a sense of justice. These claims are irrelevant to the case for Animal Liberation. The language of rights is a convenient political shorthand. It is even more valuable in the era of thirty-second TV news clips than it was in Bentham's day; but in the argument for a radical change in our attitude to animals, it is in no way necessary.

If a being suffers there can be no moral justification for refusing to take that suffering into consideration. No matter what the nature of the being, the principle of equality requires that its suffering be counted equally with the like suffering—insofar as rough comparisons can be made—of any other being. If a being is not capable of suffering, or of experiencing enjoyment or happiness, there is nothing to be taken into account. So the limit of sentience (using the term as a convenient if not strictly accurate shorthand for the capacity to suffer and/or experience enjoyment) is the only defensible boundary of concern for the interests of others. To mark this boundary by some other characteristic like intelligence or rationality would be to mark it in an arbitrary manner. Why not choose some other characteristic, like skin color?

Racists violate the principle of equality by giving greater weight to the interests of members of their own race when there is a clash between their interests and the interests of those of another race. Sexists violate the principle of equality by favoring the interests of their own sex. Similarly, speciesists allow the interests of their own species to override the greater interests of members of other species. The pattern is identical in each case.

ANIMALS AND RESEARCH

Most human beings are speciesists. . . . Ordinary human beings—not a few exceptionally cruel or heartless humans, but the overwhelming majority of humans—take an active part in, acquiesce in, and allow their taxes to pay for practices that require the sacrifice of the most important interests of members of other species in order to promote the most trivial interests of our own species. . . .

The practice of experimenting on nonhuman animals as it exists today throughout the world reveals the consequences of speciesism. Many experiments inflict severe pain without the remotest prospect of significant benefits for human beings or any other animals. Such experiments are not isolated instances, but part of a major industry. In Britain, where experimenters are required to report the number of "scientific procedures" performed on animals, official government figures show that 3.5 million scientific procedures were performed on animals in 1988.[7] In the United States there are no figures of comparable accuracy. Under the Animal Welfare Act, the U.S. secretary of agriculture publishes a report listing the number of animals used by facilities registered with it, but this is incomplete in many ways. It does not include rats, mice, birds, reptiles, frogs, or domestic farm animals used for experimental purposes; it does not include animals used in secondary schools; and it does not include experiments performed by facilities that do not transport animals interstate or receive grants or contracts from the federal government.

In 1986 the U.S. Congress Office of Technology Assessment (OTA) published a report entitled "Alternatives to Animal Use in Research, Testing and Education." The OTA researchers attempted to determine the number of animals used in experimentation in the U.S. and reported that "estimates of the animals used in the United States each year range from 10 million to upwards of 100 million." They concluded that the estimates were unreliable but their best guess was "at least 17 million to 22 million."[8]

This is an extremely conservative estimate. In testimony before Congress in 1966, the Laboratory Animal Breeders Association estimated that the number of mice, rats, guinea pigs, hamsters, and rabbits used for experimental purposes in 1965 was around 60 million.[9] In 1984 Dr. Andrew Rowan of Tufts University School of Veterinary Medicine estimated that approximately 71 million animals are used each year. In 1985 Rowan revised his estimates to distinguish between the number of animals produced, acquired, and actually used. This yielded an estimate of between 25 and 35 million animals used in experiments each year.[10] (This figure omits animals who die in shipping or are killed before the experiment begins.) A stock market analysis of just one major supplier of animals to laboratories, the Charles River Breeding Laboratory, stated that this company alone produced 22 million laboratory animals annually.[11]

The 1988 report issued by the Department of Agriculture listed 140,471 dogs, 42,271 cats, 51,641 primates, 431,457 guinea pigs, 331,945 hamsters, 459,254 rabbits, and 178,249 "wild animals": a total of 1,635,288 used in experimentation. Remember that this report does not bother to count rats and mice, and covers at most an estimated 10 percent of the total number of animals used. Of the nearly 1.6 million animals reported by the Department of Agriculture to have been used for experimental purposes, over 90,000 are reported to have experienced "unrelieved pain or distress." Again, this is probably at most 10 percent of the total number of animals suffering unrelieved pain and distress—and if experimenters are less concerned about causing unrelieved pain to rats and mice than they are to dogs, cats, and primates, it could be an even smaller proportion.

Other developed nations all use large numbers of animals. In Japan, for example, a very incomplete survey published in 1988 produced a total in excess of eight million.[12] . . .

Among the tens of millions of experiments performed, only a few can possibly be regarded as contributing to important medical research. Huge numbers of animals are used in university departments such as forestry and psychology; many more are used for commercial purposes, to test new cosmetics, shampoos, food coloring agents, and other inessential items. All this can happen only because of our prejudice against taking seriously the suffering of a being who is not a member of our own species. Typically, defenders of experiments on animals do not deny that animals suffer. They cannot deny the animals' suffering, because they need to stress the similarities between humans and other animals in order to claim that their experiments may have some relevance for human purposes. The experimenter who forces rats to choose between starvation and electric shock to see if they develop ulcers (which they do) does so because the rat has a nervous system very similar to a human being's, and presumably feels an electric shock in a similar way.

There has been opposition to experimenting on animals for a long time. This opposition has made little headway because experimenters, backed by commercial firms that profit by supplying laboratory animals and equipment, have been able to convince legislators and the public that opposition comes from uninformed fanatics who consider the interests of animals more important than the interests of human beings. But to be opposed to what is going on now it is not necessary to insist that all animal experiments stop immediately. All we need to say is that experiments serving no direct and urgent purpose should stop immediately, and in the remaining fields of research, we should whenever possible, seek to replace experiments that involve animals with alternative methods that do not. . . . .

When are experiments on animals justifiable? Upon learning of the nature of many of the experiments carried out, some people react by saying that all experiments on animals should be prohibited immediately. But if we make our demands as absolute as this, the experimenters have a ready reply: Would we be prepared to let thousands of humans die if they could be saved by a single experiment on a single animal?

This question is, of course, purely hypothetical. There has never been and never could be a single experiment that saved thousands of lives. The way to reply to this hypothetical question is to pose another: Would the experimenters be prepared to carry out their experiment on a human orphan under six months old if that were the only way to save thousands of lives?

If the experimenters would not be prepared to use a human infant then their readiness to use nonhuman animals reveals an unjustifiable form of discrimination on the basis of species, since adult apes, monkeys, dogs, cats, rats, and other animals are more aware of what is happening to them, more self-directing, and, so far as we can tell, at least as sensitive to pain as a human infant. (I have specified that the human infant be an orphan, to avoid the complications of the feelings of parents. Specifying the case in this way is, if anything, overgenerous to those defending the use of nonhuman animals in experiments, since mammals intended for experimental use are usually separated from their mothers at an early age, when the separation causes distress for both mother and young.)

So far as we know, human infants possess no morally relevant characteristic to a higher degree than adult nonhuman animals, unless we are to count the infants' potential as a characteristic that makes it wrong to experiment on them. Whether this characteristic should count is controversial—if we count it, we shall have to condemn abortion along with experiments on infants, since the potential of the infant and the fetus is the same. To avoid the complexities of this issue, however, we can alter our original question a little and assume that the infant is one with irreversible brain damage so severe as to rule out any mental development beyond the level of a six-month-old infant. There are, unfortunately, many such human beings, locked away in special wards throughout the country, some of them long since abandoned by their parents and other relatives, and, sadly, sometimes unloved by anyone else. Despite their mental deficiencies, the anatomy and physiology of these infants are in nearly all respects identical with those of normal humans. If, therefore, we were to force-feed them with large quantities of floor polish or drip concentrated solutions of cosmetics into their eyes [as has been done in experiments using animals], we would have a much more reliable indication of the safety of these products for humans than we now get by attempting to extrapolate the results of tests on a variety of other species. . . .

So whenever experimenters claim that their experiments are important enough to justify the use of animals, we should ask them whether they would be prepared to use a brain-damaged human being at a similar mental level to the animals they are planning to use. I cannot imagine that anyone would seriously propose carrying out the experiments described in this chapter on brain-damaged human beings. Occasionally it has become known that medical experiments have been performed on human beings without their consent; one case did concern institutionalized intellectually disabled children, who were given hepatitis. When such harmful experiments on human beings become known, they usually lead to an outcry against the experimenters, and rightly so. They are, very often, a further example of the arrogance of the research worker who justifies everything on the grounds of increasing knowledge. But if the experimenter claims that the experiment is important enough to justify inflicting suffering on animals, why is it not important enough to justify inflicting suffering on humans at the same mental level? What difference is there between the two? Only that one is a member of our species and the other is not? But to appeal to that difference is to reveal a bias no more defensible than racism or any other form of arbitrary discrimination. . . .

We have still not answered the question of when an experiment might be justifiable. It will not do to say "Never!" Putting morality in such black-and-white terms is appealing, because it eliminates the need to think about particular cases; but in extreme circumstances, such absolutist answers always break down. Torturing a human being is almost always wrong, but it is not absolutely wrong. If torture were the only way in which we could discover the location of a nuclear bomb hidden in a New York City basement and timed to go off within the hour, then torture would be justifiable. Similarly, if a single experiment could cure a disease like leukemia, that experiment would be justifiable. But in actual life the benefits are always more remote, and more often than not they are nonexistent. So how do we decide when an experiment is justifiable?

We have seen that experimenters reveal a bias in favor of their own species whenever they carry out experiments on nonhumans for purposes that they would not think justified them in using human beings, even brain-damaged ones. This principle gives us a guide toward an answer to our question. Since a speciesist bias, like a racist bias, is unjustifiable, an experiment cannot be justifiable unless the experiment is so important that the use of a brain-damaged human would also be justifiable.

This is not an absolutist principle. I do not believe that it could never be justifiable to experiment on a brain-damaged human. If it really were possible to save several lives by an experiment that would take just one life, and there were no other way those lives could be saved, it would be right to do the experiment. But this would be an extremely rare case. Admittedly, as with any dividing line, there would be a gray area where it was difficult to decide if an experiment could be justified. But we need not get distracted by such considerations now. . . . We are in the midst of an emergency in which appalling suffering is being inflicted on millions of animals for purposes that on any impartial view are obviously inadequate to justify the suffering. When we have ceased to carry out all those experiments, then there will be time enough to discuss what to do about the remaining ones which are claimed to be essential to save lives or prevent greater suffering. . . .

NOTES

1 For Bentham's moral philosophy, see his *Introduction to the Principles of Morals and Legislation,* and for Sidgwick's see *The Methods of Ethics,* 1907 (the passage is quoted from the seventh edition; reprint, London: Macmillan, 1963), p. 382. As examples of leading contemporary moral philosophers who incorporate a requirement of equal consideration of interests, see R. M. Hare, *Freedom and Reason* (New York: Oxford University Press, 1963), and John Rawls, *A Theory of Justice* (Cambridge: Harvard University Press, Belknap Press, 1972). For a brief account of the essential agreement on this issue between these and other positions, see R. M. Hare, "Rules of War and Moral Reasoning," *Philosophy and Public Affairs* 1 (2) (1972).

2 Letter to Henry Gregoire, February 25, 1809.

3 Reminiscences by Francis D. Gage, from Susan B. Anthony, *The History of Woman Suffrage,* vol. 1; the passage is to be found in the extract in Leslie Tanner, ed., *Voices From Women's Liberation* (New York: Signet, 1970).

4 I owe the term "speciesism" to Richard Ryder. It has become accepted in general use since the first edition of this book, and now appears in *The Oxford English Dictionary,* second edition (Oxford: Clarendon Press, 1989).

5 *Introduction to the Principles of Morals and Legislation,* chapter 17.

6 See M. Levin, "Animal Rights Evaluated," *Humanist* 37:14–15 (July/August 1977); M. A. Fox, "Animal Liberation: A Critique," *Ethics* 88: 134–138 (1978); C. Perry and G. E. Jones, "On Animal Rights," *International Journal of Applied Philosophy* 1: 39–57 (1982).

7 *Statistics of Scientific Procedures on Living Animals, Great Britain, 1988,* Command Paper 743 (London: Her Majesty's Stationery Office, 1989).

8 U.S. Congress Office of Technology Assessment, *Alternatives to Animal Use in Research, Testing and Education* (Washington, D.C.: Government Printing Office, 1986), p. 64.

9 Hearings before the Subcommittee on Livestock and Feed Grains of the Committee on Agriculture, U.S. House of Representatives, 1966, p. 63.

10 See A. Rowan, *Of Mice, Models and Men* (Albany: State University of New York Press, 1984), p. 71; his later revision is in a personal communication to the Office of Technology Assessment; see *Alternatives to Animal Use in Research, Testing and Education,* p. 56.

11 OTA, *Alternatives to Animal Use in Research, Testing and Education,* p. 56.

12 *Experimental Animals* 37: 105 (1988).

QUESTIONS

1 Is speciesism analogous to sexism and racism? Why or why not?

2 Has Singer advanced convincing reasons in support of the following claim: An experiment using animals cannot be justifiable unless the experiment is so important that the use of a brain-damaged human would also be justifiable.

The Case against Raising and Killing Animals for Food

Bart Gruzalski

Bart Gruzalski, associate professor of philosophy at Northeastern University, Boston, specializes in ethics, medical ethics, and oriental philosophy. He is coeditor of *Value Conflicts in Health Care Delivery* (1982) and the author of "When to Keep Patients Alive against Their Wishes," "Two Accounts of Our Obligations to Respect Persons," and "Parfit's Impact on Utilitarianism."

Gruzalski presents a brief utilitarian argument against raising and killing animals for food and discusses the following two objections. (1) If we raise animals humanely, the result of our raising animals for food is an increased amount of

Reprinted with permission of Humana Press from *Ethics and Animals* (1983), edited by Harlan B. Miller and William H. Williams, pp. 251–255, 257–260.

pleasure in the world. (2) Since animals ultimately must die anyway and thus experience whatever anguish dying involves, a change in our eating practices will not eliminate this suffering. The suffering that animals will avoid if they are not raised for food is that caused by confinement. If, however, we balance animal frustration due to confinement against the frustration of human beings who cannot satisfy their preference for meat, both eating and not eating meat result in a similar amount of pleasure and frustration. In responding to these objections, Gruzalski argues that when other foreseeable bad consequences of raising animals for food are taken into account along with the suffering caused to animals, utilitarians cannot justify the eating of animal flesh.

The important ethical view that one ought to live in such a way that one contributes as little as possible to the total amount of suffering in the world and as much as possible to the world's total happiness is called utilitarianism. In this paper I develop the classical utilitarian argument against raising and killing animals for food. I then examine this position in light of [two] arguments which have recently been raised to show that utilitarianism permits this use of animals. Throughout the paper I refer to nonhuman animals as animals, and to human animals as humans. Although such usage suggests an elitism that might offend some humans, the substantive arguments in the paper are better expressed if we follow ordinary usage, however unenlightened it may be.

THE UTILITARIAN ARGUMENT AGAINST RAISING AND SLAUGHTERING ANIMALS FOR FOOD

According to the classical utilitarianism of John Stuart Mill, actions are right insofar as they tend to produce the greatest happiness for the greatest number. For our purposes it will be helpful to interpret this general slogan as a specific principle regarding the foreseeable consequences of individual actions. In so doing we want to be responsive to the fact that most acts have several mutually exclusive foreseeable consequences that are of different values (e.g., rolling a die has six foreseeable consequences and we may value some more than others). One way to take these different contingencies into account is to assign a number to each foreseeable consequence to represent its desirability (or lack thereof). If we multiply the desirability of a foreseeable consequence by its probability and then sum these products of the likelihood and the desirability of each of the foreseeable consequences, we have the *expected desirability* of doing the action, which, roughly, tells us the odds that the action will produce consequences of a certain value. According to classical act utilitarianism so interpreted, an action is right if it is the best bet a person has to avoid producing painful consequences and to bring about pleasurable or happy consequences (more technically: if its expected desirability is no less than the expected desirability of any alternative). In applying this view we will be using the standard conception of consequences: an event is a consequence of an action only if there is some other action the agent could have performed that would have prevented the occurrence of the event in question. For example, my glass being full of water is a consequence of my holding it under the tap, since had I placed the glass on the counter, an alternative I could have performed, it would still be empty.

From the utilitarian viewpoint there are strong reasons for thinking that raising and slaughtering animals for food is wrong. When we raise animals they suffer because of confinement, transportation, and slaughter-related activities in ways they would not suffer were we not raising them for food. These actions are therefore wrong on utilitarian grounds unless there are other consequences which outweigh these sufferings inflicted on animals. Of course, there are other consequences of these acts besides the pain the animals experience. The most obvious of these consequences is that the animals become tasty morsels of food. But it is doubtful whether the enjoyment of those who are eating these animals can overcome the pain of captivity and slaughter. Does a family at a Kentucky Fried Chicken experience such pleasure from eating chicken that this pleasure overcomes the frustration, pain, and terror which the chicken had to undergo in order to wind up on a cole slaw garnished paper plate?

The plausibility of a utilitarian justification of raising animals for food is even weaker than the previous rhetorical question suggests. In order that the practice of raising and slaughtering animals for their flesh be justified, the animal's pain must not only be *outweighed* by the omnivore's pleasure, but *there can be no alternative act that would foreseeably result in a better balance of pleasure over pain.* Since eating plants is one alternative, and since this alternative produces the pleasures of taste and health without inflicting pain on animals, it follows that, if one is interested in contributing to the total amount of happiness in the world and not contributing to any unnecessary suffering, then one ought not to raise, slaughter, or eat animals, for by doing any of these actions one contributes to a kind of suffering that is unnecessary. Although the above argument may seem sound, some philosophers have raised objections to it while accepting the utilitarian point of view. In the following sections I shall examine two utilitarian defenses of using animals for food.

OBJECTION ONE: RAISING ANIMALS BENEVOLENTLY

According to the first utilitarian defense of raising and slaughtering animals, the use of animals for food can be justified on utilitarian grounds even if we take into account only the pleasures and pains of the animals involved. James Cargile states this defense of a carnivorous animal husbandry as follows:

> Every year I buy several pigs from a neighboring hog farm and raise them to slaughter for food. They are given lots of room and food, everything a pig could want for a good life but a short one. It would be nice if they could have longer lives. But I believe that their good, short lives are better than no life at all . . . These animals are getting the best deal people are willing to give them, and I do not see the vegetarians as giving them even that much.[1]

Cargile concludes that he has done "more for the happiness of pigs than most vegetarians."

In his book *Animal Liberation,* Peter Singer claims that the argument Cargile raises, which I refer to as the animal husbandry argument,

. . . could be refuted merely by pointing out that life for an animal in a modern factory farm is so devoid of any pleasure that this kind of existence is *in no sense a benefit* to the animal.[2]

Cargile does not overlook this important and ethically relevant consideration. He agrees that we should stop "cruel animal raisers." His, however, is not a cruel form of animal husbandry. If we raise animals in such a way that their lives are *more* of a pleasure than a burden, as Cargile does, then Cargile can claim that we do what will increase the amount of happiness in the world and so what is right on utilitarian grounds.

The animal husbandry argument rests on an assortment of claims:

(1) The pleasures of the animals we raise would not occur if we did not raise them.

(2) The pleasures of these animals increase the total amount of happiness in the world.

(3) The burdens of these animals are outweighed by their pleasures (and, if not, then that sort of animal husbandry is immoral).

(4) There is no alternative policy that would increase the foreseeable amount of happiness in the world.

It is reasonable for us to assume that (1), (2), and (3) are true. Importantly and realistically, (3) assumes that the animals raised for consumption suffer from their confinement and slaughter. But the core of the argument is that there is no alternative to a humane animal husbandry that would foreseeably produce more pleasure. The alternative in question is vegetarianism. What can be shown is that vegetarianism produces more foreseeable pleasure *on the whole* and that, not unsurprisingly, the animal husbandry argument does not provide a utilitarian justification of raising animals for food.

If we adopted the vegetarian alternative and stopped raising marketable animals we would need to farm much less land to feed the same number of people we feed by raising such animals for food, since plants yield about ten times more protein per acre than meat. Hence, if our concern is to feed the same number of people we now feed and produce as much animal pleasure as possible, there is an alternative available that would accomplish this better than raising any animals for food. The alternative is to allow 90 percent of the resources currently used to raise livestock to be idle. These resources—lands lying fallow, empty barns—which previously supported market-bound animals, would then support other sorts of animals: chipmunks, rabbits, snakes, deer, and similarly unmarketable animals whose numbers are currently restricted by our practices of animal husbandry. These other animals would use the resources we currently direct to the animals we butcher for market, and these other animals would experience the sort of pleasures experienced by Cargile's cattle and pigs without suffering from restricted movement and slaughter. Animals in the wild do not have to experience the frustrations and anxiety of confinement or the terror of waiting passively "in line" to be killed. Although it is true that by failing to raise pigs or chickens, we fail to produce *pig* pleasures and *chicken* pleasures, there is no reason to think that the pleasures of these animals are not on an even par with *chipmunk* pleasures, *rabbit* pleasures, *prairie dog* pleasures, and *snake* pleasures. This observation defeats the central idea behind the animal husbandry argument, the idea that the total amount of animal pleasure is best increased if we raise livestock, something we will not do unless we subsequently slaughter these animals for food.

The policy of allowing 90 percent of the resources we currently use to support livestock to lie idle may, however, be undesirable from a utilitarian point of view. Many of the peoples of the world are suffering and dying from protein deficiencies. In the United States during 1968, we fed to livestock (excluding dairy cows) 20 million tons of plant protein that could have been consumed by humans. Although the livestock provided 2 million tons of protein, the 18 million tons of protein "wasted" by this process would have removed 90 percent of the yearly world protein deficit. Thus, a more humane use of our farming resources would eliminate a great deal of human suffering without imposing any additional suffering on market-bound animals. It is generally thought that a policy of reducing the suffering of beings that do and will exist independently of our choice is a more efficient way of maximizing happiness than a policy that involves the creation of additional beings. If this is true, then using the resources we currently expend on livestock to feed starving peoples would be the policy justified on utilitarian grounds.

More likely than not, a move toward vegetarianism would involve a mix of both policies. The result would be the alleviation of human starvation as well as an increase in the number of wild animals. What is central to this criticism of the animal husbandry argument is that each of these alternative policies increases pleasure and decreases suffering without imposing any additional suffering on animals. . . .

OBJECTION TWO: THE SIGNIFICANCE OF HUMAN PREFERENCES GIVEN THAT ANIMALS DIE ANYWAY

One may think that I have overestimated the amount of animal suffering that results from our use of animals as food. Whether we raise animals or not, animals must die and experience whatever anguish is involved in dying. Hence, whatever animal suffering is generally associated with the death of an animal cannot be considered a result of our raising animals for food. This reduction in the amount of suffering attributable to our animal husbandry is significant, for the main source of suffering that remains is the suffering caused by the frustrations of confinement. Since this is a frustration of animal preferences, and since not eating meat is a frustration of human preferences, there seems to be no significant difference in terms of total pleasure between satisfying the animal preference for less confinement and satisfying the human preference for the taste of meat. Hence, it may seem that we cannot condemn eating meat on utilitarian grounds, for both eating meat and its alternative lead to a similar amount of pleasure and frustration.

A chief source of animal suffering is the animal frustration caused by various sorts of restrictions. Domestic animals, in order to be profitably raised at all, must be somewhat restricted. The restrictions will be on movement (do Cargile's pigs forage through the Blue Ridge Mountains?), on social intercourse (in packs of ten or twenty?), and diet (eating acorns?). Although domestic animals are selectively bred, it is reasonable to believe with the experts that

> . . . the natural, instinctive urges and behavioral patterns . . . appropriate to the high degree of social organization as found in the ancestral wild species . . . have been little, if at all, bred out in the process of domestication.[3]

Where there are animals being raised, even humanely, it is noncontroversial that there will be a good deal of frustration even under the care of humane animal husbanders. The issue is how much of such frustration is justified by the pleasure of eating meat. Would the frustration experienced by a young boy locked in a room be outweighed by the pleasure of a parent derived from watching an "adult" TV show? If that comparison cannot *clearly* be made out in favor of the satisfaction of the parent's preference, it becomes hard to imagine anyone reasonably claiming that satisfying the preference to eat meat outweighs the many months of animal frustration caused by space, diet, and socialization restrictions.

But there are two additional factors which make this allegedly utilitarian defense of eating flesh implausible. The first focuses on the kind and numbers of deaths domestic animals undergo to satisfy the meat eater's taste for flesh. The second raises the issue of whether the pleasures of taste that "justify" raising animals for food are not, in the final analysis, *trivial when compared with the animal suffering required to satisfy these tastes.*

Even in those slaughterhouses in which the animals are killed as painlessly as possible, the animal hears, sees, and smells the slaughter and becomes terrified. In terror, in an unfamiliar environment, the animal, physically healthy, is prodded along. At that point, in these "humane" slaughterhouses, the animal is stunned by a captive-bolt pistol or an electric current before being killed painlessly. In smaller settings these stunning devices are too expensive and, in addition, skill at killing quickly is not as practiced. One would expect that the small farmer who clubs, slices, or shoots his animals must not infrequently confront an injured, squealing animal that by now is utterly terrified and even harder to kill.

Everything we have learned about animals suggests that in terms of experiencing terror, pain, grief, anxiety and stress these sentient beings are relevantly similar to humans. It is reasonable to believe that our knowledge of the quality of human dying will also tell us something about the dying process of other animals. For humans, the most horrible deaths involve terror. When this factor is not present, and especially when the process of dying is not unexpected for the dying person, dying can be peaceful. From this minimal observation about human dying and the observation that domestic animals are typically slaughtered in circumstances that are unfamiliar and terrifying for the animals, it follows that the experience of being slaughtered is no worse for these animals than the worst deaths experienced in the wild and significantly worse than the deaths of wild animals that die from disease or old age in familiar and unterrifying surroundings. In addition, because the life of an adult animal raised for food is much shorter than the life of a similar animal in the wild, there will be more dyings per total adult population among these animals than among wild animals of similar species. Hence, both in quantity and quality of deaths, rearing animals for food produces a great deal of death-related anguish and terror that is directly a consequence of humans using them for food.

These are some of the foreseeable disutilities that are a consequence even of a "humane" animal husbandry. In order to justify our producing this foreseeable animal suffering, we must ask whether it is plausible to believe that these foreseeable bad consequences are outweighed by the foreseeable pleasures of eating meat. But we must first clarify this question for, as stated, it suggests that whatever pleasures we derive from eating meat are to be compared with whatever sufferings animals experience solely as a result of farming practices. But that is not an accurate interpretation of this crucial question. Rather, we are *only* interested in *the amount of pleasure that would occur were we to eat meat and that would not occur were we to eat tasty vegetable dishes instead.* That is the amount of pleasure which is a consequence of our eating meat (as opposed to eating in general). Since much of the world's population finds that vegetarian meals can be delightfully tasty, there is good reason for thinking that the pleasures many people derive from eating meat can be completely replaced with pleasures from eating vegetables. Hence, the pleasures to be derived from the eating of meat are so minimal as to be insignificant. It follows that any defense of flesh-eating along the above lines is totally unacceptable for the utilitarian. . . .[4]

NOTES

1 James Cargile, "Comments on 'The Priority of Human Interests,' " p. 249 in *Ethics and Animals,* H. Miller and W. Williams (eds.) (Clifton, NJ: Humana Press, 1983).

2 Singer, P. *Animal Liberation* (New York: Random House, 1975) p. 241. Those unfamiliar with how animals are turned into meat will find Chapter Three of Singer's book enlightening.

3 W. H. Thorpe in the Brambell Report (1965), quoted in Singer, 1975, p. 135.

4 I am indebted to Henry West for encouraging me to write the hedonistic act utilitarian's account of our duties toward animals; to William DeAngelis, Michael Lipton, Stephen Nathanson, and others who commented on an earlier version I read at a colloquium for the Department of Philosophy and Religion, Northeastern University, December, 1979; and to the editors of Humana Press for many helpful suggestions. I am also grateful to Sharon B. Young for her many helpful comments on earlier versions of this paper as well as for sharing with me her active exploration of vegetarian cuisine. Finally, I am pleased to thank Barbara Jones and Walter Knoppel for initially introducing me to vegetarianism in an intelligent, effective, and tasty manner.

QUESTIONS

1 Has Gruzalski given satisfactory responses to the two objections advanced against his utilitarian argument, which condemns the raising and killing of animals for food?

2 Are we morally obliged to adopt a vegetarian diet?

The Case for Animal Rights

Tom Regan

Tom Regan is professor of philosophy at North Carolina State University, Raleigh. Specializing in ethics, he has written extensively on animal rights and environmental issues. Regan is the author of *The Case for Animal Rights* (1984), editor of *Earthbound: New Introductory Essays in Environmental Ethics* (1984), and coeditor, with Peter Singer, of *Animal Rights and Human Obligations* (2d ed., 1989).

Like Singer, Regan attacks speciesism. In his view, animals, like humans, have rights which are violated when they are not treated with the respect due to beings who have inherent value. Regan maintains not only that animals, like humans, have inherent value but also that all beings that have inherent value have it equally. In his view, any attempt to specify some characteristic such as intelligence as a basis for attributing a lesser degree of inherent value to animals must be rejected since consistency in our moral reasoning would require us to attribute a lesser degree of inherent value to some human beings. Regan concludes by calling for the abolition of all scientific experiments using animals and the dissolution of all commercial animal agriculture.

I regard myself as an advocate of animal rights—as a part of the animal rights movement. That movement, as I conceive it, is committed to a number of goals, including:

- the total abolition of the use of animals in science;
- the total dissolution of commercial animal agriculture;
- the total elimination of commercial and sport hunting and trapping.

There are, I know, people who profess to believe in animal rights but do not avow these goals. Factory farming, they say, is wrong—it violates animals' rights—but traditional animal agriculture is all right. Toxicity tests of cosmetics on animals violate their rights, but important medical research—cancer research, for example—does not. The clubbing of baby seals is abhorrent, but not the harvesting of adult seals. I used to think I understood this reasoning. Not any more. You don't change unjust institutions by tidying them up.

What's wrong—fundamentally wrong—with the way animals are treated isn't the details that vary from case to case. It's the whole system. The forlornness of the veal calf is pathetic, heart wrenching; the pulsing pain of the chimp with electrodes planted deep in her brain is repulsive; the slow, tortuous death of the racoon caught in the leg-hold trap is agonizing. But what is wrong isn't the pain, isn't the suffering, isn't the deprivation. These compound what's wrong. Sometimes—often—they make it much, much worse. But they are not the fundamental wrong.

The fundamental wrong is the system that allows us to view animals as *our re-*

Reprinted with permission of Basil Blackwell, Inc. from *In Defense of Animals* (1985), edited by Peter Singer, pp. 13–15, 21–25.

sources, here for *us*—to be eaten, or surgically manipulated, or exploited for sport or money. Once we accept this view of animals—as our resources—the rest is as predictable as it is regrettable. Why worry about their loneliness, their pain, their death? Since animals exist for us, to benefit us in one way or another, what harms them really doesn't matter—or matters only if it starts to bother us, makes us feel a trifle uneasy when we eat our veal escalope, for example. So, yes, let us get veal calves out of solitary confinement, give them more space, a little straw, a few companions. But let us keep our veal escalope.

But a little straw, more space and a few companions won't eliminate—won't even touch—the basic wrong that attaches to our viewing and treating these animals as our resources. A veal calf killed to be eaten after living in close confinement is viewed and treated in this way: but so, too, is another who is raised (as they say) 'more humanely'. To right the wrong of our treatment of farm animals requires more than making rearing methods 'more humane'; it requires the total dissolution of commercial animal agriculture.

How we do this, whether we do it or, as in the case of animals in science, whether and how we abolish their use—these are to a large extent political questions. People must change their beliefs before they change their habits. Enough people, especially those elected to public office, must believe in change—must want it—before we will have laws that protect the rights of animals. This process of change is very complicated, very demanding, very exhausting, calling for the efforts of many hands in education, publicity, political organization and activity, down to the licking of envelopes and stamps. As a trained and practising philosopher, the sort of contribution I can make is limited but, I like to think, important. The currency of philosophy is ideas—their meaning and rational foundation—not the nuts and bolts of the legislative process, say, or the mechanics of community organization. That's what I have been exploring over the past ten years or so in my essays and talks and, most recently, in my book, *The Case for Animal Rights.* I believe the major conclusions I reach in the book are true because they are supported by the weight of the best arguments. I believe the idea of animal rights has reason, not just emotion, on its side.

In the space I have at my disposal here I can only sketch, in the barest outline, some of the main features of the book. Its main themes—and we should not be surprised by this—involve asking and answering deep, foundational moral questions about what morality is, how it should be understood and what is the best moral theory, all considered. I hope I can convey something of the shape I think this theory takes. . . .

What to do? Where to begin? . . . Suppose we consider that you and I, for example, do have value as individuals—what we'll call *inherent value.* To say we have such value is to say that we are something more than, something different from, mere receptacles. Moreover, to ensure that we do not pave the way for such injustices as slavery or sexual discrimination, we must believe that all who have inherent value have it equally, regardless of their sex, race, religion, birthplace and so on. Similarly to be discarded as irrelevant are one's talents or skills, intelligence and wealth, personality or pathology, whether one is loved and admired or despised and loathed. The genius and the retarded child, the prince and the pauper, the brain surgeon and the fruit vendor, Mother Teresa and the most unscrupulous used-car sales-man—all have inherent value, all possess it equally, and all have an equal right to be treated with respect, to be treated in ways that do not reduce them to the status of things, as if they existed as resources for others. My value as an individual is inde-pendent of my usefulness to you. Yours is not dependent on your usefulness to me. For either of us to treat the other in ways that fail to show respect for the other's independent value is to act immorally, to violate the individual's rights.

Some of the rational virtues of this view—what I call the rights view—should be evident. . . . For example, the rights view *in principle* denies the moral tolerability of any and all forms of racial, sexual or social discrimination; and . . . this view *in principle* denies that we can justify good results by using evil means that violate an individual's rights—denies, for example, that it could be moral to kill my Aunt Bea to harvest beneficial consequences for others. That would be to sanction the disre-spectful treatment of the individual in the name of the social good, something the rights view will not—categorically will not—ever allow.

The rights view, I believe, is rationally the most satisfactory moral theory. It sur-passes all other theories in the degree to which it illuminates and explains the foun-dation of our duties to one another—the domain of human morality. On this score it has the best reasons, the best arguments, on its side. Of course, if it were possible to show that only human beings are included within its scope, then a person like my-self, who believes in animal rights, would be obliged to look elsewhere.

But attempts to limit its scope to humans only can be shown to be rationally de-fective. Animals, it is true, lack many of the abilities humans possess. They can't read, do higher mathematics, build a bookcase or make *baba ghanoush.* Neither can many human beings, however, and yet we don't (and shouldn't) say that they (these humans) therefore have less inherent value, less of a right to be treated with respect, than do others. It is the *similarities* between those human beings who most clearly, most non-controversially have such value (the people reading this, for example), not our differences, that matter most. And the really crucial, the basic similarity is sim-ply this: we are each of us the experiencing subject of a life, a conscious creature having an individual welfare that has importance to us whatever our usefulness to others. We want and prefer things, believe and feel things, recall and expect things. And all these dimensions of our life, including our pleasure and pain, our enjoyment and suffering, our satisfaction and frustration, our continued existence or our un-timely death—all make a difference to the quality of our life as lived, as experi-enced, by us as individuals. As the same is true of those animals that concern us (the ones that are eaten and trapped, for example), they too must be viewed as the expe-riencing subjects of a life, with inherent value of their own.

Some there are who resist the idea that animals have inherent value. 'Only hu-mans have such value,' they profess. How might this narrow view be defended? Shall we say that only humans have the requisite intelligence, or autonomy, or rea-son? But there are many, many humans who fail to meet these standards and yet are reasonably viewed as having value above and beyond their usefulness to others. Shall we claim that only humans belong to the right species, the species *Homo sapi-ens?* But this is blatant speciesism. Will it be said, then, that all—and only—humans have immortal souls? Then our opponents have their work cut out for them. I am myself not ill-disposed to the proposition that there are immortal souls. Personally, I profoundly hope I have one. But I would not want to rest my position on a controversial ethical issue on the even more controversial question about who or what has an immortal soul. That is to dig one's hole deeper, not to climb out. Rationally, it is better to resolve moral issues without making more controversial assumptions than are needed. The question of who has inherent value is such a question, one that is resolved more rationally without the introduction of the idea of immortal souls than by its use.

Well, perhaps some will say that animals have some inherent value, only less than we have. Once again, however, attempts to defend this view can be shown to lack rational justification. What could be the basis of our having more inherent value than animals? Their lack of reason, or autonomy, or intellect? Only if we are willing to make the same judgement in the case of humans who are similarly deficient. But it is not true that such humans—the retarded child, for example, or the mentally deranged—have less inherent value than you or I. Neither, then, can we rationally sustain the view that animals like them in being the experiencing subjects of a life have less inherent value. *All* who have inherent value have it *equally,* whether they be human animals or not.

Inherent value, then, belongs equally to those who are the experiencing subjects of a life. Whether it belongs to others—to rocks and rivers, trees and glaciers, for example—we do not know and may never know. But neither do we need to know, if we are to make the case for animal rights. We do not need to know, for example, how many people are eligible to vote in the next presidential election before we can know whether I am. Similarly, we do not need to know how many individuals have inherent value before we can know that some do. When it comes to the case for animal rights, then, what we need to know is whether the animals that, in our culture, are routinely eaten, hunted and used in our laboratories, for example, are like us in being subjects of a life. And we do know this. We do know that many—literally, billions and billions—of these animals are the subjects of a life in the sense explained and so have inherent value if we do. And since, in order to arrive at the best theory of our duties to one another, we must recognize our equal inherent value as individuals, reason—not sentiment, not emotion—reason compels us to recognize the equal inherent value of these animals and, with this, their equal right to be treated with respect.

That, *very* roughly, is the shape and feel of the case for animal rights. Most of the details of the supporting argument are missing. They are to be found in the book to which I alluded earlier. Here, the details go begging, and I must, in closing, limit myself to [one] final point. . . .

Having set out the broad outlines of the rights view, I can now say why its implications for farming and science, among other fields, are both clear and uncompromising. In the case of the use of animals in science, the rights view is categorically abolitionist. Lab animals are not our tasters; we are not their kings. Because these animals are treated routinely, systematically as if their value were reducible to their usefulness to others, they are routinely, systematically treated with a lack of respect, and thus are their rights routinely, systematically violated. This is just as true when they are used in trivial, duplicative, unnecessary or unwise research as it is when they are used in studies that hold out real promise of human benefits. We can't justify harming or killing a human being (my Aunt Bea, for example) just for these sorts of reason. Neither can we do so even in the case of so lowly a creature as a laboratory rat. It is not just refinement or reduction that is called for, not just larger, cleaner cages, not just more generous use of anaesthetic or the elimination of multiple surgery, not just tidying up the system. It is complete replacement. The best we can do when it comes to using animals in science is—not to use them. That is where our duty lies, according to the rights view.

As for commercial animal agriculture, the rights view takes a similar abolitionist position. The fundamental moral wrong here is not that animals are kept in stressful close confinement or in isolation, or that their pain and suffering, their needs and preferences are ignored or discounted. All these *are* wrong, of course, but they are not the fundamental wrong. They are symptoms and effects of the deeper, systematic wrong that allows these animals to be viewed and treated as lacking independent value, as resources for us—as, indeed, a renewable resource. Giving farm animals more space, more natural environments, more companions does not right the fundamental wrong, any more than giving lab animals more anaesthesia or bigger, cleaner cages would right the fundamental wrong in their case. Nothing less than the total dissolution of commercial animal agriculture will do this, just as, for similar reasons I won't develop at length here, morality requires nothing less than the total elimination of hunting and trapping for commercial and sporting ends. The rights view's implications, then, as I have said, are clear and uncompromising. . . .

QUESTIONS

1 Do all sentient beings have the same inherent value? Why or why not?

2 Is it always wrong to use animals in experiments intended to benefit human beings?

The Case for the Use of Animals in Biomedical Research

Carl Cohen

Carl Cohen is professor of philosophy at the University of Michigan at Ann Arbor. He specializes in social and political philosophy. Cohen is the editor of *Communism, Fascism, and Democracy* (1972) and *Democracy* (1971) and the author of *Four Systems* (1982). His numerous published articles include "Free Speech and Political Extremism: How Nasty Are We Free to Be?".

Reprinted with permission from *The New England Journal of Medicine,* vol. 315 (October 2, 1986), pp. 865–870.

Cohen, identifying himself as a speciesist, attacks both Singer and Regan and defends the use of animals in biomedical research. Against Regan, Cohen argues that animals have no rights, since they lack the capacities for free moral judgment and for exercising or responding to moral claims. Against Singer, he maintains that speciesism is not analogous to racism and sexism and that all sentient beings do not have equal moral standing. Furthermore, Cohen argues, we have an obligation to enlarge the use of animals in research in the interest of protecting potential human subjects. In his view, although we do have obligations to animals, they have no rights against us on which research can infringe.

Using animals as research subjects in medical investigations is widely condemned on two grounds: first, because it wrongly violates the *rights* of animals,[1] and second, because it wrongly imposes on sentient creatures much avoidable *suffering.*[2] Neither of these arguments is sound. The first relies on a mistaken understanding of rights; the second relies on a mistaken calculation of consequences. Both deserve definitive dismissal.

WHY ANIMALS HAVE NO RIGHTS

A right, properly understood, is a claim, or potential claim, that one party may exercise against another. The target against whom such a claim may be registered can be a single person, a group, a community, or (perhaps) all humankind. The content of rights claims also varies greatly: repayment of loans, nondiscrimination by employers, noninterference by the state, and so on. To comprehend any genuine right fully, therefore, we must know *who* holds the right, *against whom* it is held, and *to what* it is a right.

Alternative sources of rights add complexity. Some rights are grounded in constitution and law (e.g., the right of an accused to trial by jury); some rights are moral but give no legal claims (e.g., my right to your keeping the promise you gave me); and some rights (e.g., against theft or assault) are rooted both in morals and in law.

The differing targets, contents, and sources of rights, and their inevitable conflict, together weave a tangled web. Notwithstanding all such complications, this much is clear about rights in general: they are in every case claims, or potential claims, within a community of moral agents. Rights arise, and can be intelligibly defended, only among beings who actually do, or can, make moral claims against one another. Whatever else rights may be, therefore, they are necessarily human; their possessors are persons, human beings.

The attributes of human beings from which this moral capability arises have been described variously by philosophers, both ancient and modern: the inner consciousness of a free will (Saint Augustine[3]); the grasp, by human reason, of the binding character of moral law (Saint Thomas[4]); the self-conscious participation of human beings in an objective ethical order (Hegel[5]); human membership in an organic moral community (Bradley[6]); the development of the human self through the consciousness of other moral selves (Mead[7]); and the underivative, intuitive cognition of the rightness of an action (Prichard[8]). Most influential has been Immanuel Kant's emphasis on the universal human possession of a uniquely moral will and the autonomy its use entails.[9] Humans confront choices that are purely moral; humans—but certainly not dogs or mice—lay down moral laws, for others and for themselves. Human beings are self-legislative, morally *auto-nomous*.

Animals (that is, nonhuman animals, the ordinary sense of that word) lack this capacity for free moral judgment. They are not beings of a kind capable of exercising or responding to moral claims. Animals therefore have no rights, and they can have none. This is the core of the argument about the alleged rights of animals. The holders of rights must have the capacity to comprehend rules of duty, governing all including themselves. In applying such rules, the holders of rights must recognize possible conflicts between what is in their own interest and what is just. Only in a community of beings capable of self-restricting moral judgments can the concept of a right be correctly invoked.

Humans have such moral capacities. They are in this sense self-legislative, are members of communities governed by moral rules, and do possess rights. Animals do not have such moral capacities. They are not morally self-legislative, cannot possibly be members of a truly moral community, and therefore cannot possess rights. In conducting research on animal subjects, therefore, we do not violate their rights, because they have none to violate.

To animate life, even in its simplest forms, we give a certain natural reverence. But the possession of rights presupposes a moral status not attained by the vast majority of living things. We must not infer, therefore, that a live being has, simply in being alive, a "right" to its life. The assertion that all animals, only because they are alive and have interests, also possess the "right to life"[10] is an abuse of that phrase, and wholly without warrant.

It does not follow from this, however, that we are morally free to do anything we please to animals. Certainly not. In our dealings with animals, as in our dealings with other human beings, we have obligations that do not arise from claims against us based on rights. Rights entail obligations, but many of the things one ought to do are in no way tied to another's entitlement. Rights and obligations are not reciprocals of one another, and it is a serious mistake to suppose that they are.

Illustrations are helpful. Obligations may arise from internal commitments made: physicians have obligations to their patients not grounded merely in their patients' rights. Teachers have such obligations to their students, shepherds to their dogs, and cowboys to their horses. Obligations may arise from differences of status: adults owe special care when playing with young children, and children owe special care when playing with young pets. Obligations may arise from special relationships: the payment of my son's college tuition is something to which he may have no right, although it may be my obligation to bear the burden if I reasonably can; my dog has no right to daily exercise and veterinary care, but I do have the obligation to provide these things for her. Obligations may arise from particular acts or circumstances: one may be obliged to another for a special kindness done, or obliged to put an animal out of its misery in view of its condition—although neither the human benefactor nor the dying animal may have had a claim of right.

Plainly, the grounds of our obligations to humans and to animals are manifold and cannot be formulated simply. Some hold that there is a general obligation to do no gratuitous harm to sentient creatures (the principle of nonmaleficence); some hold that there is a general obligation to do good to sentient creatures when that is reasonably within one's power (the principle of beneficence). In our dealings with animals, few will deny that we are at least obliged to act humanely—that is, to treat them with the decency and concern that we owe, as sensitive human beings, to other sentient creatures. To treat animals humanely, however, is not to treat them as humans or as the holders of rights.

A common objection, which deserves a response, may be paraphrased as follows:

> If having rights requires being able to make moral claims, to grasp and apply moral laws, then many humans—the brain-damaged, the comatose, the senile—who plainly lack those capacities must be without rights. But that is absurd. This proves [the critic concludes] that rights do not depend on the presence of moral capacities.[1, 10]

This objection fails; it mistakenly treats an essential feature of humanity as though it were a screen for sorting humans. The capacity for moral judgment that distinguishes humans from animals is not a test to be administered to human beings one by one. Persons who are unable, because of some disability, to perform the full moral functions natural to human beings are certainly not for that reason ejected from the moral community. The issue is one of kind. Humans are of such a kind that they may be the subject of experiments only with their voluntary consent. The choices they make freely must be respected. Animals are of such a kind that it is impossible for them, in principle, to give or withhold voluntary consent or to make a moral choice. What humans retain when disabled, animals have never had.

A second objection, also often made, may be paraphrased as follows:

> Capacities will not succeed in distinguishing humans from the other animals. Animals also reason; animals also communicate with one another; animals also care passionately for their young; animals also exhibit desires and preferences.[11,12] Features of moral relevance—rationality, interdependence, and love—are not exhibited uniquely by human beings. Therefore [this critic concludes], there can be no solid moral distinction between humans and other animals.[10]

This criticism misses the central point. It is not the ability to communicate or to reason, or dependence on one another, or care for the young, or the exhibition of preference, or any such behavior that marks the critical divide. Analogies between human families and those of monkeys, or between human communities and those of wolves, and the like, are entirely beside the point. Patterns of conduct are not at issue. Animals do indeed exhibit remarkable behavior at times. Conditioning, fear, instinct, and intelligence all contribute to species survival. Membership in a community of moral agents nevertheless remains impossible for them. Actors subject to moral judgment must be capable of grasping the generality of an ethical premise in a practical syllogism. Humans act immorally often enough, but only they—never wolves or monkeys—can discern, by applying some moral rule to the facts of a case, that a given act ought or ought not to be performed. The moral restraints imposed by humans on themselves are thus highly abstract and are often in conflict with the self-interest of the agent. Communal behavior among animals, even when most intelligent and most endearing, does not approach autonomous morality in this fundamental sense.

Genuinely moral acts have an internal as well as an external dimension. Thus, in law, an act can be criminal only when the guilty deed, the actus reus, is done with a guilty mind, mens rea. No animal can ever commit a crime; bringing animals to criminal trial is the mark of primitive ignorance. The claims of moral right are similarly inapplicable to them. Does a lion have a right to eat a baby zebra? Does a baby zebra have a right not to be eaten? Such questions, mistakenly invoking the concept of right where it does not belong, do not make good sense. Those who condemn biomedical research because it violates "animal rights" commit the same blunder.

IN DEFENSE OF "SPECIESISM"

Abandoning reliance on animal rights, some critics resort instead to animal sentience—their feelings of pain and distress. We ought to desist from the imposition of pain insofar as we can. Since all or nearly all experimentation on animals does impose pain and could be readily forgone, say these critics, it should be stopped. The ends sought may be worthy, but those ends do not justify imposing agonies on humans, and by animals the agonies are felt no less. The laboratory use of animals (these critics conclude) must therefore be ended—or at least very sharply curtailed.

Argument of this variety is essentially utilitarian, often expressly so[13]; it is based on the calculation of the net product, in pains and pleasures, resulting from experiments on animals. Jeremy Bentham, comparing horses and dogs with other sentient creatures, is thus commonly quoted: "The question is not, Can they reason? nor Can they talk? but, Can they suffer?"[14]

Animals certainly can suffer and surely ought not to be made to suffer needlessly. But in inferring, from these uncontroversial premises, that biomedical research causing animal distress is largely (or wholly) wrong, the critic commits two serious errors.

The first error is the assumption, often explicitly defended, that all sentient animals have equal moral standing. Between a dog and a human being, according to this view, there is no moral difference; hence the pains suffered by dogs must be weighed no differently from the pains suffered by humans. To deny such equality, according to this critic, is to give unjust preference to one species over another; it is "speciesism." The most influential statement of this moral equality of species was made by Peter Singer:

> The racist violates the principle of equality by giving greater weight to the interests of members of his own race when there is a clash between their interests and the interests of those of another race. The sexist violates the principle of equality by favoring the interests of his own sex. Similarly the speciesist allows the interests of his own species to override the greater interests of members of other species. The pattern is identical in each case.[2]

This argument is worse than unsound; it is atrocious. It draws an offensive moral conclusion from a deliberately devised verbal parallelism that is utterly specious. Racism has no rational ground whatever. Differing degrees of respect or concern for humans for no other reason than that they are members of different races is an injustice totally without foundation in the nature of the races themselves. Racists, even if acting on the basis of mistaken factual beliefs, do grave moral wrong precisely because there is no morally relevant distinction among the races. The supposition of such differences has led to outright horror. The same is true of the sexes, neither sex being entitled by right to greater respect or concern than the other. No dispute here.

Between species of animate life, however—between (for example) humans on the one hand and cats or rats on the other—the morally relevant differences are enormous, and almost universally appreciated. Humans engage in moral reflection; humans are morally autonomous; humans are members of moral communities, recognizing just claims against their own interest. Human beings do have rights; theirs is a moral status very different from that of cats or rats.

I am a speciesist. Speciesism is not merely plausible; it is essential for right conduct, because those who will not make the morally relevant distinctions among species are almost certain, in consequence, to misapprehend their true obligations. The analogy between speciesism and racism is insidious. Every sensitive moral judgment requires that the differing natures of the beings to whom obligations are owed be considered. If all forms of animate life—or vertebrate animal life?—must be treated equally, and if therefore in evaluating a research program the pains of a rodent count equally with the pains of a human, we are forced to conclude (1) that neither humans nor rodents possess rights, or (2) that rodents possess all the rights that humans possess. Both alternatives are absurd. Yet one or the other must be swallowed if the moral equality of all species is to be defended.

Humans owe to other humans a degree of moral regard that cannot be owed to animals. Some humans take on the obligation to support and heal others, both humans and animals, as a principal duty in their lives; the fulfillment of that duty may require the sacrifice of many animals. If biomedical investigators abandon the effective pursuit of their professional objectives because they are convinced that they may not do to animals what the service of humans requires, they will fail, objectively, to do their duty. Refusing to recognize the moral differences among species is a sure path to calamity. (The largest animal rights group in the country is People for the Ethical Treatment of Animals; its codirector, Ingrid Newkirk, calls research using animal subjects "fascism" and "supremacism." "Animal liberationists do not separate out the *human* animal," she says, "so there is no rational basis for saying that a human being has special rights. A rat is a pig is a dog is a boy. They're all mammals."[15])

Those who claim to base their objection to the use of animals in biomedical research on their reckoning of the net pleasures and pains produced make a second error, equally grave. Even if it were true—as it is surely not—that the pains of all animate beings must be counted equally, a cogent utilitarian calculation requires that we weigh all the consequences of the use, and of the nonuse, of animals in laboratory research. Critics relying (however mistakenly) on animal rights may claim to ignore the beneficial results of such research, rights being trump cards to which interest and advantage must give way. But an argument that is explicitly framed in terms of interest and benefit for all over the long run must attend also to the disadvantageous consequences of not using animals in research, and to all the achievements attained and attainable only through their use. The sum of the benefits of their use is utterly beyond quantification. The elimination of horrible disease, the increase of longevity, the avoidance of great pain, the saving of lives, and the improvement of the quality of lives (for humans and for animals) achieved through research using animals is so incalculably great that the argument of these critics, systematically pursued, establishes not their conclusion but its reverse: to refrain from using animals in biomedical research is, on utilitarian grounds, morally wrong.

When balancing the pleasures and pains resulting from the use of animals in research, we must not fail to place on the scales the terrible pains that would have resulted, would be suffered now, and would long continue had animals not been used. Every disease eliminated, every vaccine developed, every method of pain relief devised, every surgical procedure invented, every prosthetic device implanted—indeed, virtually every modern medical therapy is due, in part or in whole, to experimentation using animals. Nor may we ignore, in the balancing process, the predictable gains in human (and animal) well-being that are probably achievable in the future but that will not be achieved if the decision is made now to desist from such research or to curtail it.

Medical investigators are seldom insensitive to the distress their work may cause animal subjects. Opponents of research using animals are frequently insensitive to the cruelty of the results of the restrictions they would impose.[2] Untold numbers of human beings—real persons, although not now identifiable—would suffer grievously as the consequence of this well-meaning but shortsighted tenderness. If the morally relevant differences between humans and animals are borne in mind, and if all relevant considerations are weighed, the calculation of long-term consequences must give overwhelming support for biomedical research using animals.

CONCLUDING REMARKS

Substitution

The humane treatment of animals requires that we desist from experimenting on them if we can accomplish the same result using alternative methods—in vitro experimentation, computer simulation, or others. Critics of some experiments using animals rightly make this point.

It would be a serious error to suppose, however, that alternative techniques could soon be used in most research now using live animal subjects. No other methods now on the horizon—or perhaps ever to be available—can fully replace the testing of a drug, a procedure, or a vaccine, in live organisms. The flood of new medical possibilities being opened by the successes of recombinant DNA technology will turn to a trickle if testing on live animals is forbidden. When initial trials entail great risks, there may be no forward movement whatever without the use of live animal subjects. In seeking knowledge that may prove critical in later clinical applications, the unavailability of animals for inquiry may spell complete stymie. In the United States, federal regulations require the testing of new drugs and other products on animals, for efficacy and safety, before human beings are exposed to them.[16,17] We would not want it otherwise.

Every advance in medicine—every new drug, new operation, new therapy of any kind—must sooner or later be tried on a living being for the first time. That trial, controlled or uncontrolled, will be an experiment. The subject of that experiment, if it is not an animal, will be a human being. Prohibiting the use of live animals in biomedical research, therefore, or sharply restricting it, must result either in the blockage of much valuable research or in the replacement of animal subjects with human subjects. These are the consequences—unacceptable to most reasonable persons—of not using animals in research.

Reduction

Should we not at least reduce the use of animals in biomedical research? No, we should increase it, to avoid when feasible the use of humans as experimental subjects. Medical investigations putting human subjects at some risk are numerous and greatly varied. The risks run in such experiments are usually unavoidable, and (thanks to earlier experiments on animals) most such risks are minimal or moderate. But some experimental risks are substantial.

When an experimental protocol that entails substantial risk to humans comes before an institutional review board, what response is appropriate? The investigation, we may suppose, is promising and deserves support, so long as its human subjects are protected against unnecessary dangers. May not the investigators be fairly asked, Have you done all that you can to eliminate risk to humans by the extensive testing of that drug, that procedure, or that device on animals? To achieve maximal safety for humans we are right to require thorough experimentation on animal subjects before humans are involved.

Opportunities to increase human safety in this way are commonly missed; trials in which risks may be shifted from humans to animals are often not devised, sometimes not even considered. Why? For the investigator, the use of animals as subjects is often more expensive, in money and time, than the use of human subjects. Access to suitable human subjects is often quick and convenient, whereas access to appropriate animal subjects may be awkward, costly, and burdened with red tape. Physician-investigators have often had more experience working with human beings and know precisely where the needed pool of subjects is to be found and how they may be enlisted. Animals, and the procedures for their use, are often less familiar to these investigators. Moreover, the use of animals in place of humans is now more likely to be the target of zealous protests from without. The upshot is that humans are sometimes subjected to risks that animals could have borne, and should have borne, in their place. To maximize the protection of human subjects, I conclude, the wide and imaginative use of live animal subjects should be encouraged rather than discouraged. This enlargement in the use of animals is our obligation.

Consistency

Finally, inconsistency between the profession and the practice of many who oppose research using animals deserves comment. This frankly ad hominem observation aims chiefly to show that a coherent position rejecting the use of animals in medical research imposes costs so high as to be intolerable even to the critics themselves.

One cannot coherently object to the killing of animals in biomedical investigations while continuing to eat them. Anesthetics and thoughtful animal husbandry render the level of actual animal distress in the laboratory generally lower than that in the abattoir. So long as death and discomfort do not substantially differ in the two contexts, the consistent objector must not only refrain from all eating of animals but also protest as vehemently against others eating them as against others experimenting on them. No less vigorously must the critic object to the wearing of animal hides in coats and shoes, to employment in any industrial enterprise that uses animal parts, and to any commercial development that will cause death or distress to animals.

Killing animals to meet human needs for food, clothing, and shelter is judged entirely reasonable by most persons. The ubiquity of these uses and the virtual universality of moral support for them confront the opponent of research using animals with an inescapable difficulty. How can the many common uses of animals be judged morally worthy, while their use in scientific investigation is judged unworthy?

The number of animals used in research is but the tiniest fraction of the total used to satisfy assorted human appetites. That these appetites, often base and satisfiable in other ways, morally justify the far larger consumption of animals, whereas the quest for improved human health and understanding cannot justify the far smaller, is wholly implausible. Aside from the numbers of animals involved, the distinction in terms of worthiness of use, drawn with regard to any single animal, is not defensible. A given sheep is surely not more justifiably used to put lamb chops on the supermarket counter than to serve in testing a new contraceptive or a new prosthetic device. The needless killing of animals is wrong; if the common killing of them for our food or convenience is right, the less common but more humane uses of animals in the service of medical science are certainly not less right.

Scrupulous vegetarianism, in matters of food, clothing, shelter, commerce, and recreation, and in all other spheres, is the only fully coherent position the critic may adopt. At great human cost, the lives of fish and crustaceans must also be protected, with equal vigor, if speciesism has been forsworn. A very few consistent critics adopt this position. It is the reductio ad absurdum of the rejection of moral distinctions between animals and human beings.

Opposition to the use of animals in research is based on arguments of two different kinds—those relying on the alleged rights of animals and those relying on the consequences for animals. I have argued that arguments of both kinds must fail. We surely do have obligations to animals, but they have, and can have, no rights against us on which research can infringe. In calculating the consequences of animal research, we must weigh all the long-term benefits of the results achieved—to animals and to humans—and in that calculation we must not assume the moral equality of all animate species.

REFERENCES

1 Regan T. The case for animal rights. Berkeley, Calif.: University of California Press, 1983.

2 Singer P. Animal liberation. New York: Avon Books, 1977.

3 St. Augustine. Confessions. Book Seven. 397 A.D. New York: Pocketbooks, 1957:104–26.

4 St. Thomas Aquinas. Summa theologica. 1273 A.D. Philosophic texts. New York: Oxford University Press, 1960:353–66.

5 Hegel GWF. Philosophy of right. 1821. London: Oxford University Press, 1952:105–10.

6 Bradley FH. Why should I be moral? 1876. In: Melden AI, ed. Ethical theories. New York: Prentice-Hall, 1950:345–59.

7 Mead GH. The genesis of the self and social control. 1925. In: Reck AJ, ed. Selected writings. Indianapolis: Bobbs-Merrill, 1964:264–93.

8 Prichard HA. Does moral philosophy rest on a mistake? 1912. In: Cellars W, Hospers J, eds. Readings in ethical theory. New York: Appleton-Century-Crofts, 1952:149–63.

9 Kant I. Fundamental principles of the metaphysic of morals. 1785. New York: Liberal Arts Press, 1949.

10 Rollin BE. Animal rights and human morality. New York: Prometheus Books, 1981.

11 Hoff C. Immoral and moral uses of animals. N Engl J Med 1980; 302:115–8.

12 Jamieson D. Killing persons and other beings. In: Miller HB, Williams WH, eds. Ethics and animals. Clifton, N.J.: Humana Press, 1983:135–46.

13 Singer P. Ten years of animal liberation. New York Review of Books. 1985; 31:46–52.

14 Bentham J. Introduction to the principles of morals and legislation. London: Athlone Press, 1970.

15 McCabe K. Who will live, who will die? Washingtonian Magazine. August 1986:115.

16 U.S. Code of Federal Regulations, Title 21, Sect. 505(i). Food, drug, and cosmetic regulations.

17 U.S. Code of Federal Regulations, Title 16, Sect. 1500.40–2. Consumer product regulations.

QUESTIONS

1 Is speciesism a morally defensible position?

2 Do animals have rights?

Human and Animal Rights Compared

Mary Anne Warren

A biographical sketch of Mary Anne Warren is found on p. 9.

Along with Singer, Gruzalski, and Regan, Warren ascribes moral status to animals. In her view, animals, as sentient beings, do have rights. Her major concern, however, is with bringing out the *differences* between the rights of animals and

Reprinted with permission of the author from *Environmental Philosophy: A Collection of Readings* (Penn State University Press, 1983), edited by Robert Elliot and Arran Gare, pp. 112, 115–123.

those of human beings and with providing a justification for those differences. On Warren's account, the rights of animals and humans differ in respect to both their *content* and their *strength*—that is, in the strength of the reasons that are necessary to override them. Two reasons support the view that these differences are not arbitrary. (1) Human desires and interests are more extensive than those of animals, calling for differences in both the extent and strength of human rights. (2) The human capacity for moral autonomy, while not a necessary condition for having rights, can provide a reason for according somewhat stronger rights to human beings than to animals. Warren concludes by discussing the case of nonparadigm humans, who may not have a capacity for moral autonomy, and yet, unlike animals, have the *same* basic moral rights as paradigm humans, according to her analysis. She does not assert that animals and nonparadigm humans differ in their intrinsic value. Rather, both have intrinsic value and possess certain rights by virtue of their sentience. However, Warren argues, there are additional reasons, such as the value that nonparadigm humans have for paradigm humans, for ascribing stronger rights to nonparadigm humans than to animals.

None of the animal liberationists have thus far provided a clear explanation of how and why the moral status of (most) animals differs from that of (most) human beings; and this is a point which must be clarified if their position is to be made fully persuasive. That there is such a difference seems to follow from some very strong moral intuitions which most of us share. A man who shoots squirrels for sport may or may not be acting reprehensibly; but it is difficult to believe that his actions should be placed in *exactly* the same moral category as those of a man who shoots women, or black children, for sport. So too it is doubtful that the Japanese fishermen who slaughtered dolphins because the latter were thought to be depleting the local fish populations were acting quite *as* wrongly as if they had slaughtered an equal number of their human neighbours for the same reason. . . . There are two dimensions in which we may find differences between the rights of human beings and those of animals. The first involves the *content* of those rights, while the second involves their strength; that is, the strength of the reasons which are required to override them.

Consider, for instance, the right to liberty. The *human* right to liberty precludes imprisonment without due process of law, even if the prison is spacious and the conditions of confinement cause no obvious physical suffering. But it is not so obviously wrong to imprison animals, especially when the area to which they are confined provides a fair approximation of the conditions of their natural habitat, and a reasonable opportunity to pursue the satisfactions natural to their kind. Such conditions, which often result in an increased lifespan, and which may exist in wildlife sanctuaries or even well-designed zoos, need not frustrate the needs or interests of animals in any significant way, and thus do not clearly violate their rights. Similarly treated human beings, on the other hand (e.g., native peoples confined to prison-like reservations), do tend to suffer from their loss of freedom. Human dignity and the fulfillment of the sorts of plans, hopes and desires which appear (thus far) to be uniquely human, require a more extensive freedom of movement than is the case with at least many nonhuman animals. Furthermore, there are aspects of human freedom, such as freedom of thought, freedom of speech and freedom of political association, which simply do not apply in the case of animals.

Thus, it seems that the human right to freedom is more extensive; that is, it precludes a wider range of specific ways of treating human beings than does the corresponding right on the part of animals. The argument cuts both ways, of course. *Some* animals, for example, great whales and migratory birds, may require at least as much physical freedom as do human beings if they are to pursue the satisfactions natural to their kind, and this fact provides a moral argument against keeping such creatures imprisoned. And even chickens may suffer from the extreme and unnatural confinement to which they are subjected on modern "factory farms". Yet it seems unnecessary to claim for *most* animals a right to a freedom quite as broad as that which we claim for ourselves.

Similar points may be made with respect to the right to life. Animals, it may be argued, lack the cognitive equipment to value their lives in the way that human beings do. Ruth Cigman argues that animals have *no* right to life because death is no misfortune for them.[1] In her view, the death of an animal is not a misfortune, because animals have no desires which are *categorical;* that is which do not "merely presuppose being alive (like the desire to eat when one is hungry), but rather answer the question whether one wants to remain alive".[2] In other words, animals appear to lack the sorts of long-range hopes, plans, ambitions and the like, which give human beings such a powerful interest in continued life. Animals, it seems, take life as it comes and do not specifically desire that it go on. True, squirrels store nuts for the winter and deer run from wolves; but these may be seen as instinctive or conditioned responses to present circumstances, rather than evidence that they value life as such.

These reflections probably help to explain why the death of a sparrow seems less tragic than that of a human being. Human lives, one might say, have greater intrinsic value, because they are worth more *to their possessors.* But this does not demonstrate that no nonhuman animal has *any* right to life. Premature death may be a less *severe* misfortune for sentient nonhuman animals than for human beings, but it is a misfortune nevertheless. In the first place, it is a misfortune in that it deprives them of whatever pleasures the future might have held for them, regardless of whether or not they ever *consciously anticipated* those pleasures. The fact that they are not here afterwards, to *experience* their loss, no more shows that they have not lost anything than it does in the case of humans. In the second place, it is (possibly) a misfortune in that it frustrates whatever future-oriented desires animals *may* have, unbeknownst to us. Even now, in an age in which apes have been taught to use simplified human languages and attempts have been made to communicate with dolphins and whales, we still know very little about the operation of nonhuman minds. We know much too little to assume that nonhuman animals never consciously pursue relatively distant future goals. To the extent that they do, the question of whether such desires provide them with *reasons for living* or merely *presuppose* continued life, has no satisfactory answer, since they cannot contemplate these alternatives—or, if they can, we have no way of knowing what their conclusions are. All we know is that the more intelligent and psychologically complex an animal is, the more *likely* it is that it possesses specifically future-oriented desires, which would be frustrated even by *painless* death.

For these reasons, it is premature to conclude from the apparent intellectual inferiority of nonhuman animals that they have no right to life. A more plausible conclusion is that animals do have a right to life but that it is generally somewhat weaker than that of human beings. It is, perhaps, weak enough to enable us to justify killing animals when we have no other ways of achieving such vital goals as feeding or clothing ourselves, or obtaining knowledge which is necessary to save human lives. Weakening their right to life in this way does not render meaningless the assertion that they have such a right. For the point remains that *some* serious justification for the killing of sentient nonhuman animals is always necessary; they may not be killed merely to provide amusement or minor gains in convenience.

If animals' rights to liberty and life are somewhat weaker than those of human beings, may we say the same about their right to *happiness;* that is, their right not to be made to suffer needlessly or to be deprived of the pleasures natural to their kind? If so, it is not immediately clear why. There is little reason to suppose that pain or suffering are any less unpleasant for the higher animals (at least) than they are for us. Our large brains *may* cause us to experience pain more intensely than do most animals, and *probably* cause us to suffer more from the anticipation or remembrance of pain. These facts might tend to suggest that pain is, on the whole, a worse experience for us than for them. But it may also be argued that pain may be *worse* in some respects for nonhuman animals, who are presumably less able to distract themselves from it by thinking of something else, or to comfort themselves with the knowledge that it is temporary. Brigid Brophy points out that "pain is likely to fill the sheep's whole capacity for experience in a way it seldom does in us, whose intellect and imagination can create breaks for us in the immediacy of our sensations."[3]

The net result of such contrasting considerations is that we cannot possibly claim to know whether pain is, on the whole, worse for us than for animals, or whether their pleasures are any more or any less intense than ours. Thus, while we may justify assigning them a somewhat weaker right to life or liberty, on the grounds that they desire these goods less intensely than we do, we cannot discount their rights to freedom from needlessly inflicted pain or unnatural frustration on the same basis. There may, however, be *other* reasons for regarding all of the moral rights of animals as somewhat less stringent than the corresponding human rights.

A number of philosophers who deny that animals have moral rights point to the fact that nonhuman animals evidently lack the capacity for moral autonomy. Moral autonomy is the ability to act as a moral agent; that is, to act on the basis of an understanding of, and adherence to, moral rules or principles. H.J. McCloskey, for example, holds that "it is the capacity for moral autonomy . . . that is basic to the possibility of possessing a right".[4] McCloskey argues that it is inappropriate to ascribe moral rights to any entity which is not a moral agent, or *potentially* a moral agent, because a right is essentially an entitlement granted to a moral agent, licensing him or her to *act* in certain ways and to *demand* that other moral agents refrain from interference. For this reason, he says, "Where there is no possibility of [morally autonomous] action, potentially or actually . . . and where the being is not a member of a kind which is normally capable of [such] action, we withhold talk of rights."[5]

If moral autonomy—or being *potentially* autonomous, or a member of a kind which is *normally* capable of autonomy—is a necessary condition for having moral rights, then probably no nonhuman animal can qualify. For moral autonomy requires such probably uniquely human traits as "the capacity to be critically self-aware, manipulate concepts, use a sophisticated language, reflect, plan, deliberate, choose, and accept responsibility for acting".[6]

But why, we must ask, should the capacity for autonomy be regarded as a precondition for possessing moral rights? Autonomy is clearly crucial for the *exercise* of many human moral or legal rights, such as the right to vote or to run for public office. It is less clearly relevant, however, to the more basic human rights, such as the right to life or to freedom from unnecessary suffering. The fact that animals, like many human beings, cannot *demand* their moral rights (at least not in the words of any conventional human language) seems irrelevant. For, as Joel Feinberg points out, the interests of non-morally autonomous human beings may be defended by others, for example, in legal proceedings; and it is not clear why the interests of animals might not be represented in a similar fashion.[7]

It is implausible, therefore, to conclude that because animals lack moral autonomy they should be accorded *no moral rights whatsoever.* Nevertheless, it may be argued that the moral autonomy of (most) human beings provides a second reason, in addition to their more extensive interests and desires, for according somewhat *stronger* moral rights to human beings. The fundamental insight behind contractualist theories of morality is that, for morally autonomous beings such as ourselves, there is enormous mutual advantage in the adoption of a moral system designed to protect each of us from the harms that might otherwise be visited upon us by others. Each of us ought to accept and promote such a system because, to the extent that others also accept it, we will all be safer from attack by our fellows, more likely to receive assistance when we need it, and freer to engage in individual as well as cooperative endeavours of all kinds.

Thus, it is the possibility of *reciprocity* which motivates moral agents to extend *full and equal* moral rights, in the first instance, only to other moral agents. I respect your rights to life, liberty and the pursuit of happiness in part because you are a sentient being, whose interests have intrinsic moral significance. But I respect them as *fully equal to my own* because I hope and expect that you will do the same for me. Animals, insofar as they lack the degree of rationality necessary for moral autonomy, cannot agree to respect our interests as equal in moral importance to their own, and neither do they expect or demand such respect from us. Of course, domestic animals may expect to be fed, etc. But they do not, and cannot, expect to be treated as moral equals, for they do not understand that moral concept or what it implies. Consequently, it is neither pragmatically feasible nor morally obligatory to extend to them the same *full and equal* rights which we extend to human beings.

Is this a speciesist conclusion? Defenders of a more extreme animal-rights position may point out that this argument, from the lack of moral autonomy, has exactly the same form as that which has been used for thousands of years to rationalize denying equal moral rights to women and members of "inferior" races. Aristotle, for example, argued that women and slaves are naturally subordinate beings, because they lack the capacity for moral autonomy and self-direction;[8] and contemporary versions of this argument, used to support racist or sexist conclusions, are easy to find. Are we simply repeating Aristotle's mistake, in a different context?

The reply to this objection is very simple: animals, unlike women and slaves, really *are* incapable of moral autonomy, at least to the best of our knowledge. Aristotle certainly *ought* to have known that women and slaves are capable of morally autonomous action; their capacity to use moral language alone ought to have alerted him to this likelihood. If comparable evidence exists that (some) nonhuman animals are moral agents we have not yet found it. The fact that some apes (and, possibly, some **cetaceans**) are capable of learning radically simplified human languages, the terms of which refer primarily to objects and events in their immediate environment, in no way demonstrates that they can understand abstract moral concepts, rules or principles, or use this understanding to regulate their own behaviour.

On the other hand, this argument implies that if we *do* discover that certain nonhuman animals are capable of moral autonomy (which is certainly not impossible), then we ought to extend full and equal moral rights to those animals. Furthermore, if we someday encounter extraterrestrial beings, or build robots, **androids** or supercomputers which function as self-aware moral agents, then we must extend full and equal moral rights to these as well. Being a member of the human species is not a necessary condition for the possession of full "human" rights. Whether it is nevertheless a *sufficient* condition is the question to which we now turn.

THE MORAL RIGHTS OF NONPARADIGM HUMANS

If we are justified in ascribing somewhat different, and also somewhat stronger, moral rights to human beings than to sentient but non-morally autonomous animals, then what are we to say of the rights of human beings who happen not to be capable of moral autonomy, perhaps not even potentially? Both Singer and Regan have argued that if any of the superior intellectual capacities of normal and mature human beings are used to support a distinction between the moral status of *typical,* or paradigm, human beings, and that of animals, then consistency will require us to place certain "nonparadigm" humans, such as infants, small children and the severely retarded or incurably brain damaged, in the same inferior moral category.[9] Such a result is, of course, highly counterintuitive.

Fortunately, no such conclusion follows from the autonomy argument. There are many reasons for extending strong moral rights to nonparadigm humans; reasons which do not apply to most nonhuman animals. Infants and small children are granted strong moral rights in part because of their *potential* autonomy. But *potential* autonomy, as I have argued elsewhere,[10] is not in itself a sufficient reason for the ascription of full moral rights; if it were, then not only human foetuses (from conception onwards) but even ununited human sperm-egg pairs would have to be regarded as entities with a right to life the equivalent of our own—thus making not only abortion, but any intentional failure to procreate, the moral equivalent of murder. Those who do not find this extreme conclusion acceptable must appeal to reasons other than the *potential* moral autonomy of infants and small children to explain the strength of the latter's moral rights.

One reason for assigning strong moral rights to infants and children is that they possess not just *potential* but *partial* autonomy, and it is not clear how much of it they have at any given moment. The fact that, unlike baby chimpanzees, they are already learning the things which will enable them to *become* morally autonomous, makes it likely that their minds have more subtleties than their speech (or the lack of it) proclaims. Another reason is simply that most of us tend to place a very high value on the lives and well-being of infants. Perhaps we are to some degree "programmed" by nature to love and protect them; perhaps our reasons are somewhat egocentric; or perhaps we value them for their potential. Whatever the explanation, the fact that we do feel this way about them is in itself a valid reason for extending to them stronger moral and legal protections than we extend to nonhuman animals, even those which may have just as well or better-developed psychological capacities. A third, and perhaps the most important, reason is that if we did *not* extend strong moral rights to infants, far too few of them would ever *become* responsible, morally autonomous adults; too many would be treated "like animals" (i.e., in ways that it is generally wrong to treat even animals), and would consequently become socially crippled, antisocial or just very unhappy people. If any part of our moral code is to remain intact, it seems that infants and small children *must* be protected and cared for.

Analogous arguments explain why strong moral rights should also be accorded to other nonparadigm humans. The severely retarded or incurably senile, for instance, may have no potential for moral autonomy, but there are apt to be friends, relatives or other people who care what happens to them. Like children, such individuals may have more mental capacities than are readily apparent. Like children, they are more apt to achieve, or return to moral autonomy if they are valued and well cared for. Furthermore, any one of us may someday become mentally incapacitated to one degree or another, and we would all have reason to be anxious about our own futures if such incapacitation were made the basis for denying strong moral rights.

There are, then, sound reasons for assigning strong moral rights even to human beings who lack the mental capacities which justify the general distinction between human and animal rights. Their rights are based not only on the value which they themselves place upon their lives and well-being, but also on the value which other human beings place upon them.

But is this a valid basis for the assignment of moral rights?. . . Regan argues that we cannot justify the ascription of stronger rights to nonparadigm humans than to nonhuman animals in the way suggested, because "what underlies the ascription of rights to any given X is that X has value independently of anyone's valuing X".[11] After all, we do not speak of expensive paintings or gemstones as having rights, although many people value them and have good reasons for wanting them protected.

There is, however, a crucial difference between a rare painting and a severely retarded or senile human being; the latter not only has (or may have) value for other human beings but *also* has his or her own needs and interests. It may be this which leads us to say that such individuals have intrinsic value. The sentience of nonparadigm humans, like that of sentient nonhuman animals, gives them a place in the sphere of rights holders. So long as the moral rights of all sentient beings are given due recognition, there should be no objection to providing some of them with *additional* protections, on the basis of our interests as well as their own. Some philosophers speak of such additional protections, which are accorded to X on the basis of interests other than X's own, as *conferred* rights, in contrast to *natural* rights, which are entirely based upon the properties of X itself. But such "conferred" rights are not necessarily any weaker or less binding upon moral agents than are "natural" rights. Infants, and most other nonparadigm humans have the *same* basic moral rights that the rest of us do, even though the reasons for ascribing those rights are somewhat different in the two cases. . . .

NOTES

1 Ruth Cigman, "Death, Misfortune, and Species Inequality", *Philosophy and Public Affairs* 10, no. 1 (Winter 1981): p. 48.

2 Ibid., pp. 57–58. The concept of a categorical desire is introduced by Bernard Williams, "The Makropoulous Case", in his *Problems of the Self* (Cambridge: Cambridge University Press), 1973.

3 Brigid Brophy, "In Pursuit of a Fantasy," in *Animals, Men and Morals,* ed. Stanley and Rosalind Godlovitch (New York: Taplinger Publishing Co., 1972), p. 129.

4 H. J. McCloskey, "Moral Rights and Animals", *Inquiry* 22, nos. 1–2 (1979): 31.

5 Ibid., p. 29.

6 Michael Fox, "Animal Liberation: A Critique", *Ethics* 88, no. 2 (January 1978): 111.

7 Joel Feinberg, "The Rights of Animals and Unborn Generations," in *Philosophy and Environmental Crisis,* ed. William T. Blackstone (Athens, Ga.: University of Georgia Press), 1974, pp. 46–47.

8 Aristotle, *Politics* I. 1254, 1260, and 1264.

9 Peter Singer, *Animal Liberation: A New Ethics for Our Treatment of Animals* (New York: Avon, 1975), pp. 75–76; Tom Regan, "One Argument Concerning Animal Rights," *Inquiry* 22, nos. 1–2 (1979): 189–217.

10 Mary Anne Warren, "Do Potential People Have Moral Rights?", *Canadian Journal of Philosophy* 7, no. 2 (June 1977): 275–89.

11 Regan, "One Argument Concerning Animal Rights", p. 189.

QUESTIONS

1 Is Warren correct in making the following claim: If we someday encounter extraterrestrial beings, or build robots, androids, or supercomputers which function as self-aware moral agents, then we must extend full and equal moral rights to these.

2 What human needs, if any, are sufficiently important to warrant the infliction of pain and suffering on animals?

SUGGESTED ADDITIONAL READINGS FOR CHAPTER 10

DOMBROWSKI, DANIEL A.: *The Philosophy of Vegetarianism.* Amherst: University of Massachusetts Press, 1984. This book provides an interesting historical background for contemporary philosophical discussions of vegetarianism. Its critical examination focuses primarily on ancient Greek sources, from the early poetic tradition of Hesiod and Homer down to the neoplatonists in the Christian era.

FEINBERG, JOEL: "The Rights of Animals and Unborn Generations." In William Blackstone, ed., *Philosophy and Environmental Crisis.* Athens: University of Georgia Press, 1974. On Feinberg's analysis of the concept of a right, only those beings who are capable of having interests can meaningfully be said to have rights. Individual animals are such beings.

FREY, R. G.: *Interests and Rights: The Case against Animals.* Oxford: Clarendon, 1980. In Frey's view, animals do not have interests, and thus they do not have moral rights. Accordingly, he contends, arguments for vegetarianism that are based on the claim that animals have moral rights are unsound.

MILLER, HARLAN B., and WILLIAM H. WILLIAMS, eds.: *Ethics and Animals.* Clifton, N.J.: Humana, 1983. This collection of articles focuses on the morality of human treatment of nonhuman animals. Among the topics covered are animal rights to life, killing animals for food, hunting, and animal experimentation.

REGAN, TOM: *The Case for Animal Rights.* Berkeley, Calif.: University of California Press, 1983. Regan argues that animals have a basic moral right to respectful treatment. He derives the following conclusions: (1) vegetarianism is obligatory; (2) hunting and trapping are wrong; (3) the use of animals in science is impermissible.

———, and PETER SINGER, eds.: *Animal Rights and Human Obligations,* 2d ed. Englewood Cliffs, N.J.: Prentice-Hall, 1989. This very useful anthology begins with a section on animals in the history of Western thought. Some of the other sections are "Animal Rights," "Killing and the Value of Life," "The Treatment of Farm Animals," and "The Treatment of Animals in Science."

ROLLIN, BERNARD E.: *Animal Rights and Human Morality.* Buffalo, N.Y.: Prometheus, 1981. Rollin suggests an overall account of the rights of animals. He also provides an extensive discussion of both animals as research subjects and animals as pets.

SECHZER, JERI A.: *The Role of Animals in Biomedical Research.* New York: The New York Academy of Sciences, 1983. This issue of the *Annals of the New York Academy of Sciences* (vol. 406) contains papers, discussions, and summaries on a wide range of topics dealing with animal experimentation. Topics include the methodologies employed as well as some of the relevant ethical and public policy issues.

SINGER, PETER: *Animal Liberation,* 2d ed. New York: New York Review, 1990. Singer advances a vigorous critique of our present attitudes toward animals and our dealings with them. He also provides a wealth of relevant factual material.

TANNENBAUM, JERROLD, and ANDREW N. ROWAN: "Rethinking the Morality of Animal Research." *Hastings Center Report,* vol. 15, October 1985, pp. 32–43. The authors argue that we need a clearer understanding of the ethical issues involved in animal research to provide the groundwork for public policy. Their article discusses some of these issues.

CHAPTER 11

The Environment

Much of our traditional thinking about morality is *anthropocentric*—it assumes that moral obligation is essentially a function of *human* interests. Increasingly, however, anthropocentric approaches to morality are being challenged. Many thinkers concerned with our moral obligations with respect to the environment, like many of those concerned with our obligations with respect to animals, question whether an anthropocentric ethic can provide an adequate basis for all our moral obligations, including environmental ones. This chapter focuses on our moral obligations with respect to the environment and the appropriate moral foundation for those obligations.

THE BASIS FOR OUR MORAL OBLIGATIONS REGARDING THE ENVIRONMENT

We are becoming increasingly aware of the extent to which human activities pollute and destroy the natural environment. Many people would agree that much of this pollution and destruction is morally wrong. Philosophers and other writers who are concerned with environmental issues disagree, however, about *why* it is morally wrong, for example, to pollute the environment, destroy wilderness areas, or contribute to the destruction of species. What is the basis of our moral obligations regarding the natural environment? It is possible to distinguish three fundamentally different types of approaches taken in response to this question: (1) anthropocentric approaches, (2) sentientist approaches, and (3) biocentric or ecocentric approaches.

Anthropocentric Approaches

On an anthropocentric approach, human interests determine what obligations human beings have regarding the environment. It seems clear, for example, that we can appeal to human interests in order to ground a prima facie duty not to pollute the environment (i.e., a duty not to pollute unless there are overriding moral considerations). Human welfare, in fact human life, crucially depends on such necessities as breathable air, drinkable water, and eatable food. Thus, in the absence of overriding moral considerations, pollution is morally unacceptable precisely because it is damaging to the public welfare. On an alternative construal, still using an anthropocentric approach, the prima facie duty not to pollute may be understood as based on a basic human right, the right to a livable environment. Thus we can assert, with some confidence, that there is a prima facie duty not to pollute. We are left, however, with the problem of weighing the collective human interest in a nonpolluted environment against competing human interests, often economic in nature.

The following schematic example illustrates some of the complexities that confront us when environmental and economic interests clash. An industrial plant, representing a (small, large, massive) financial investment, producing a product that is (unessential, very desirable, essential) to society, and providing a (small, large, enormous) number of jobs, pollutes the environment in a (minor, substantial, major) way. In which of these several cases is the continued operation of the plant morally unacceptable? Certainly the general public interest in the quality of the environment must be recognized. But what about the economic interests of owners, employees, and potential customers? In sum, how is the collective human interest in a nonpolluted environment to be equitably weighed against competing economic interests? At this point, many people tend to appeal to the kind of cost-benefit analyses that characterize utilitarian thinking. William F. Baxter, who defends an anthropocentric ethical stance in this chapter, adopts this cost-benefit approach in arguing for "optimal pollution"—pollution whose harms are outweighed by various human interests, including economic and aesthetic ones.

An anthropocentric moral stance can be taken on other environmental issues as well. For example, it can be argued that the preservation of wilderness serves numerous human interests, including scientific, athletic, and recreational ones. Thus these interests can be viewed as the basis for our obligation to preserve wilderness areas. In one of the readings in this chapter, William Godfrey-Smith presents an anthropocentric case for an obligation to preserve wilderness, although his own ethical approach is nonanthropocentric.

Sentientist Approaches

On a *sentientist* approach, the interests of sentient beings determine our obligations regarding the environment. All sentient beings are seen as having an *inherent* (intrinsic) value and not merely an instrumental value. As the distinction between inherent and instrumental value is usually drawn, some things are valuable as a *means* to some valued end; thus their value is instrumental. Other things are valuable in themselves and thus are said to have inherent or intrinsic value. (Singer in Chapter 10 takes a sentientist approach insofar as he uses sentience as the criterion for determining what sorts of things are entitled to an equal consideration of their interests.) Since sentient beings include human beings, it can be argued on a sentientist approach just as on an anthropocentric one, that, for example, mountains, forests, and snail darters should be preserved because of their aesthetic value to human beings. But insofar as nonhuman animals are also sentient beings, a sentientist would insist that animal interests must also be considered when determining our environmental obligations. Bernard Rollins's reasoning in this chapter illustrates sentientist thinking. Rollins maintains that we might have a moral obligation to preserve some natural habitat that is of no value to human beings if its destruction would harm some nonhuman animals.

Biocentric (Ecocentric) Approaches

In recent years various writers have argued for an even more radical revision of our traditional approaches to morality than that proposed by sentientists. In fact, sentientism is sometimes criticized as analogous to racism and speciesism insofar as all three involve giving unjustified preference to one's own "kind." John Rodman, who coined the term "sentientism," criticizes the sentientist approach as follows:

> The rest of nature is left in a state of thinghood, having no intrinsic worth, acquiring instrumental value only as resources for the well-being of an elite of sentient beings. Homocentrist rationalism has widened out into a kind of zoocentrist sentientism. . . . If it would seem arbitrary to a visitor from Mars to find one species claiming a monopoly of intrinsic value by virtue of its allegedly exclusive possession of reason, free will, soul, or some other occult quality, would it not seem almost as arbitrary to find that same species claiming a monopoly of intrinsic value for itself and those species most resembling it . . . by virtue of their common and allegedly exclusive possession of sentience?[1]

Although the thinking of those who argue for a revolutionary environmental ethic differs in many respects, a common thread can be identified: moral consideration must be extended to all of nature. Aldo Leopold (1887–1948), whose essay "The Land Ethic" has encouraged others to work at developing a truly new environmental ethic, writes:

> The land ethic simply enlarges the boundaries of the community to include soils, waters, plants, and animals, or collectively the land. . . . In short, a land ethic changes the role of *Homo sapiens* from conqueror of the land-community to plain member and citizen of it. It implies respect for his fellow-members, and also respect for the community as such. . . . A thing is right when it tends to preserve the integrity, stability, and beauty of the biotic community. It is wrong when it tends otherwise.[2]

This more radical approach to our moral obligations in respect to the environment is sometimes said to involve a *biotic* view ("biotic" means "relating to life"), and is, therefore, called *biocentric*. Proponents of a biocentric ethic consider all life to be inherently valuable—and understand "life" in such a broad sense that it includes even things that biologists classify as nonliving, such as rivers, landscapes, ecosystems, and "the living earth." Since biocentric approaches attach moral standing to ecosystems, they are sometimes labeled "ecocentric." (An "ecosystem" can be defined as a unit made up of a community of living things taken in conjunction with the nonliving factors of its environment.)

Proponents of a biocentric approach to our environmental obligations sometimes distinguish between *shallow ecology* and *deep ecology*. Whereas biocentrists identify

---

[1]John Rodman, "The Liberation of Nature?" *Inquiry,* vol. 20 (1977), p. 91.
[2]Aldo Leopold, "The Land Ethic," in *A Sand County Almanac* (New York: Oxford University Press, 1966), pp. 219, 220, 240.

their views with deep ecology, they identify anthropocentric approaches with shallow ecology. Shallow ecology is concerned with making a case for human moral obligations not to pollute or destroy the environment, but grounds its moral reasoning in human interests and concerns. Deep ecologists see shallow ecologists as focusing primarily on economic interests in developing a case for environmental obligations. But as Baxter's reasoning in this chapter shows, the anthropocentric approach does not preclude concern with wider human interests. At any rate, deep ecology, in contrast to shallow ecology, takes a more radical approach and rejects both anthropocentric and sentientist approaches to environmental obligations. It calls for a radical, fundamental revision in our attitude toward the natural world. Two proponents of deep ecology incorporate the following statements in their platform of the deep ecology movement:

> The flourishing of human and non-human life on Earth has intrinsic value. The value of non-human life forms is independent of the usefulness these may have for narrow human purposes. . . . Richness and diversity of life forms are values in themselves and contribute to the flourishing of human and non-human life on Earth. . . . Humans have no right to reduce this richness and diversity except to satisfy vital needs.[3]

Both Peter Wenz and Godfrey-Smith represent the deep ecology perspective in this chapter. Although Godfrey-Smith discusses an anthropocentric, instrumental justification for the duty to preserve wilderness, he himself maintains that the instrumentalist approach is insufficient to provide a satisfactory rationale for our moral obligations in respect to the environment. In his view, although the environment has substantial instrumental value, it has intrinsic value as well. In a similar vein, Wenz argues that we have a prima facie obligation to protect ecosystems, irrespective of all possible advantage to human beings.

CRITICISMS OF DEEP ECOLOGY

Biocentric approaches have not gone uncriticized. Three of the articles in this chapter incorporate such criticisms. Rollin argues, for example, that no useful purpose is served by attributing inherent value to nonsentient beings. In his view, moral obligations to sentient beings can adequately account for our moral obligations regarding the environment without raising the difficulties posed for those who attribute noninstrumental value to nonsentient natural objects, such as rivers, and quasi-abstract entities, such as species. Lily-Marlene Russow's criticisms are aimed primarily at those, including deep ecologists, who try to argue for a duty to protect species rather than simply individual members of species. The most wide-ranging critique of deep ecology, however, is offered by Ramachandra Guha, who, arguing from a Third World perspective, criticizes American radical environmentalism. Guha rejects the anthropocentric-biocentric distinction that he identifies with American deep ecology.

---

[3]Arne Naess, *Ecology, Community and Lifestyle* (New York: Cambridge University Press, 1989), p. 29. These statements are part of a platform of the deep ecology movement formulated in 1984 by two biocentrists—Arne Naess and George Sessions.

He maintains that the distinction is of little use in helping us to understand the dynamics of environmental degradation. Guha argues for what he considers a much more radical approach to environmental issues—an approach that he sees as exemplified in countries such as Germany and India. This approach emphasizes the need to change the ecological and sociopolitical basis of the consumerism and militarism that, on his view, are responsible for so much of the destruction of the environment. Thus, Guha's approach is "radical" in a different way than are biocentric approaches. Biocentric approaches are radical insofar as they call for a revolutionary revision of our fundamental moral categories. Guha's approach is politically radical, however, insofar as it calls for a rethinking of some of our fundamental sociopolitical institutions.

Jane S. Zembaty

People or Penguins: The Case for Optimal Pollution

William F. Baxter

William F. Baxter is William Benjamin Scott and Luna M. Scott Professor of Law at Stanford University. From 1981 to 1983 he served as assistant attorney general in charge of the antitrust division of the United States Department of Justice. Baxter is the author of *People or Penguins: The Case for Optimal Pollution* (1974), from which this piece is excerpted. He is coeditor of *Retail Banking in the Electronic Age: The Law and Economics of Electronic Fund Transfer* (1977).

Baxter adopts an anthropocentric approach to environmental trade-offs. He states four general goals that, on his view, should serve as criteria for evaluating solutions to environmental problems. Baxter defends his anthropocentric approach and briefly discusses the kinds of trade-offs involved when interests in controlling pollution must be weighed against competing interests, including economic ones.

I start with the modest proposition that, in dealing with pollution, or indeed with any problem, it is helpful to know what one is attempting to accomplish. Agreement on how and whether to pursue a particular objective, such as pollution control, is not possible unless some more general objective has been identified and stated with reasonable precision. We talk loosely of having clean air and clean water, of preserving our wilderness areas, and so forth. But none of these is a sufficiently general objective: each is more accurately viewed as a means rather than as an end.

With regard to clean air, for example, one may ask, "how clean?" and "what does clean mean?" It is even reasonable to ask, "why have clean air?" Each of these ques-

Reprinted with permission of Columbia University Press from William F. Baxter, *People or Penguins: The Case for Optimal Pollution* (1974), pp. 1–13.

tions is an implicit demand that a more general community goal be stated—a goal sufficiently general in its scope and enjoying sufficiently general assent among the community of actors that such "why" questions no longer seem admissible with respect to that goal.

If, for example, one states as a goal the proposition that "every person should be free to do whatever he wishes in contexts where his actions do not interfere with the interests of other human beings," the speaker is unlikely to be met with a response of "why." The goal may be criticized as uncertain in its implications or difficult to implement, but it is so basic a tenet of our civilization—it reflects a cultural value so broadly shared, at least in the abstract—that the question "why" is seen as impertinent or imponderable or both.

I do not mean to suggest that everyone would agree with the "spheres of freedom" objective just stated. Still less do I mean to suggest that a society could subscribe to four or five such general objectives that would be adequate in their coverage to serve as testing criteria by which all other disagreements might be measured. One difficulty in the attempt to construct such a list is that each new goal added will conflict, in certain applications, with each prior goal listed; and thus each goal serves as a limited qualification on prior goals.

Without any expectation of obtaining unanimous consent to them, let me set forth four goals that I generally use as ultimate testing criteria in attempting to frame solutions to problems of human organization. My position regarding pollution stems from these four criteria. If the criteria appeal to you and any part of what appears hereafter does not, our disagreement will have a helpful focus: which of us is correct, analytically, in supposing that his position on pollution would better serve these general goals. If the criteria do not seem acceptable to you, then it is to be expected that our more particular judgments will differ, and the task will then be yours to identify the basic set of criteria upon which your particular judgments rest.

My criteria are as follows:

1 The spheres of freedom criterion stated above.

2 Waste is a bad thing. The dominant feature of human existence is scarcity—our available resources, our aggregate labors, and our skill in employing both have always been, and will continue for some time to be, inadequate to yield to every man all the tangible and intangible satisfactions he would like to have. Hence, none of those resources, or labors, or skills, should be wasted—that is, employed so as to yield less than they might yield in human satisfactions.

3 Every human being should be regarded as an end rather than as a means to be used for the betterment of another. Each should be afforded dignity and regarded as having an absolute claim to an evenhanded application of such rules as the community may adopt for its governance.

4 Both the incentive and the opportunity to improve his share of satisfactions should be preserved to every individual. Preservation of incentive is dictated by the "no-waste" criterion and enjoins against the continuous, totally egalitarian redistribution of satisfactions, or wealth; but subject to that constraint, everyone should receive, by continuous redistribution if necessary, some minimal share of aggregate wealth so as to avoid a level of privation from which the opportunity to improve his situation becomes illusory.

The relationship of these highly general goals to the more specific environmental issues at hand may not be readily apparent, and I am not yet ready to demonstrate their pervasive implications. But let me give one indication of their implications. Recently scientists have informed us that use of DDT in food production is causing damage to the penguin population. For the present purposes let us accept that assertion as an indisputable scientific fact. The scientific fact is often asserted as if the correct implication—that we must stop agricultural use of DDT—followed from the mere statement of the fact of penguin damage. But plainly it does not follow if my criteria are employed.

My criteria are oriented to people, not penguins. Damage to penguins, or sugar pines, or geological marvels is, without more, simply irrelevant. One must go further, by my criteria, and say: Penguins are important because people enjoy seeing them walk about rocks; and furthermore, the well-being of people would be less impaired by halting use of DDT than by giving up penguins. In short, my observations about environmental problems will be people-oriented, as are my criteria. I have no interest in preserving penguins for their own sake.

It may be said by way of objection to this position, that it is very selfish of people to act as if each person represented one unit of importance and nothing else was of any importance. It is undeniably selfish. Nevertheless I think it is the only tenable starting place for analysis for several reasons. First, no other position corresponds to the way most people really think and act—i.e., corresponds to reality.

Second, this attitude does not portend any massive destruction of nonhuman flora and fauna, for people depend on them in many obvious ways, and they will be preserved because and to the degree that humans do depend on them.

Third, what is good for humans is, in many respects, good for penguins and pine trees—clean air for example. So that humans are, in these respects, surrogates for plant and animal life.

Fourth, I do not know how we could administer any other system. Our decisions are either private or collective. Insofar as Mr. Jones is free to act privately, he may give such preferences as he wishes to other forms of life: he may feed birds in winter and do with less himself, and he may even decline to resist an advancing polar bear on the ground that the bear's appetite is more important than those portions of himself that the bear may choose to eat. In short my basic premise does not rule out private altruism to competing life-forms. It does rule out, however, Mr. Jones' inclination to feed Mr. Smith to the bear, however hungry the bear, however despicable Mr. Smith.

Insofar as we act collectively on the other hand, only humans can be afforded an opportunity to participate in the collective decisions. Penguins cannot vote now and are unlikely subjects for the franchise—pine trees more unlikely still. Again each individual is free to cast his vote so as to benefit sugar pines if that is his inclination. But many of the more extreme assertions that one hears from some conservationists amount to tacit assertions that they are specially appointed representatives of sugar pines, and hence that their preferences should be weighted more heavily than the preferences of other humans who do not enjoy equal rapport with "nature." The simplistic assertion that agricultural use of DDT must stop at once because it is harmful to penguins is of that type.

Fifth, if polar bears or pine trees or penguins, like men, are to be regarded as ends rather than means, if they are to count in our calculus of social organization, someone must tell me how much each one counts, and someone must tell me how these life-forms are to be permitted to express their preferences, for I do not know either answer. If the answer is that certain people are to hold their proxies, then I want to know how those proxy-holders are to be selected: self-appointment does not seem workable to me.

Sixth, and by way of summary of all the foregoing, let me point out that the set of environmental issues under discussion—although they raise very complex technical questions of how to achieve any objective—ultimately raise a normative question: what *ought* we to do. Questions of *ought* are unique to the human mind and world— they are meaningless as applied to a nonhuman situation.

I reject the proposition that we *ought* to respect the "balance of nature" or to "preserve the environment" unless the reason for doing so, express or implied, is the benefit of man.

I reject the idea that there is a "right" or "morally correct" state of nature to which we should return. The word "nature" has no normative connotation. Was it "right" or "wrong" for the earth's crust to heave in contortion and create mountains and seas? Was it "right" for the first amphibian to crawl up out of the primordial ooze? Was it "wrong" for plants to reproduce themselves and alter the atmospheric composition in favor of oxygen? For animals to alter the atmosphere in favor of carbon dioxide both by breathing oxygen and eating plants? No answers can be given to these questions because they are meaningless questions.

All this may seem obvious to the point of being tedious, but much of the present controversy over environment and pollution rests on tacit normative assumptions about just such nonnormative phenomena: that it is "wrong" to impair penguins with DDT, but not to slaughter cattle for prime rib roasts. That it is wrong to kill stands of sugar pines with industrial fumes, but not to cut sugar pines and build housing for the poor. Every man is entitled to his own preferred definition of Walden Pond, but there is no definition that has any moral superiority over another, except by reference to the selfish needs of the human race.

From the fact that there is no normative definition of the natural state, it follows that there is no normative definition of clean air or pure water—hence no definition of polluted air—or of pollution—except by reference to the needs of man. The "right" composition of the atmosphere is one which has some dust in it and some lead in it and some hydrogen sulfide in it—just those amounts that attend a sensibly organized society thoughtfully and knowledgeably pursuing the greatest possible satisfaction for its human members.

The first and most fundamental step toward solution of our environmental problems is a clear recognition that our objective is not pure air or water but rather some optimal state of pollution. That step immediately suggests the question: How do we define and attain the level of pollution that will yield the maximum possible amount of human satisfaction?

Low levels of pollution contribute to human satisfaction but so do food and shelter and education and music. To attain ever lower levels of pollution, we must pay the cost of having less of these other things. I contrast that view of the cost of pollution control with the more popular statement that pollution control will "cost" very large numbers of dollars. The popular statement is true in some senses, false in others; sorting out the true and false senses is of some importance. The first step in that sorting process is to achieve a clear understanding of the difference between dollars and resources. Resources are the wealth of our nation; dollars are merely claim checks upon those resources. Resources are of vital importance; dollars are comparatively trivial.

Four categories of resources are sufficient for our purposes: At any given time a nation, or a planet if you prefer, has a stock of labor, of technological skill, of capital goods, and of natural resources (such as mineral deposits, timber, water, land, etc.). These resources can be used in various combinations to yield goods and services of all kinds—in some limited quantity. The quantity will be larger if they are combined efficiently, smaller if combined inefficiently. But in either event the resource stock is limited, the goods and services that they can be made to yield are limited; even the most efficient use of them will yield less than our population, in the aggregate, would like to have.

If one considers building a new dam, it is appropriate to say that it will be costly in the sense that it will require x hours of labor, y tons of steel and concrete, and z amount of capital goods. If these resources are devoted to the dam, then they cannot be used to build hospitals, fishing rods, schools, or electric can openers. That is the meaningful sense in which the dam is costly.

Quite apart from the very important question of how wisely we can combine our resources to produce goods and services, is the very different question of how they get distributed—who gets how many goods? Dollars constitute the claim checks which are distributed among people and which control their share of national output. Dollars are nearly valueless pieces of paper except to the extent that they do represent claim checks to some fraction of the output of goods and services. Viewed as claim checks, all the dollars outstanding during any period of time are worth, in the aggregate, the goods and services that are available to be claimed with them during that period—neither more nor less.

It is far easier to increase the supply of dollars than to increase the production of goods and services—printing dollars is easy. But printing more dollars doesn't help because each dollar then simply becomes a claim to fewer goods, i.e., becomes worth less.

The point is this: many people fall into error upon hearing the statement that the decision to build a dam, or to clean up a river, will cost $X million. It is regrettably easy to say: "It's only money. This is a wealthy country, and we have lots of money." But you cannot build a dam or clean a river with $X million—unless you also have a match, you can't even make a fire. One builds a dam or cleans a river by diverting labor and steel and trucks and factories from making one kind of goods to making another. The cost in dollars is merely a shorthand way of describing the extent of the diversion necessary. If we build a dam for $X million, then we must recognize that we will have $X million less housing and food and medical care and electric can openers as a result.

Similarly, the costs of controlling pollution are best expressed in terms of the other goods we will have to give up to do the job. This is not to say the job should not be done. Badly as we need more housing, more medical care, and more can openers, and more symphony orchestras, we could do with somewhat less of them, in my judgment at least, in exchange for somewhat cleaner air and rivers. But that is the nature of the trade-off, and analysis of the problem is advanced if that unpleasant reality is kept in mind. Once the trade-off relationship is clearly perceived, it is possible to state in a very general way what the optimal level of pollution is. I would state it as follows:

People enjoy watching penguins. They enjoy relatively clean air and smog-free vistas. Their health is improved by relatively clean water and air. Each of these benefits is a type of good or service. As a society we would be well advised to give up one washing machine if the resources that would have gone into that washing machine can yield greater human satisfaction when diverted into pollution control. We should give up one hospital if the resources thereby freed would yield more human satisfaction when devoted to elimination of noise in our cities. And so on, trade-off by trade-off, we should divert our productive capacities from the production of existing goods and services to the production of a cleaner, quieter, more pastoral nation up to—and no further than—the point at which we value more highly the next washing machine or hospital that we would have to do without than we value the next unit of environmental improvement that the diverted resources would create.

Now this proposition seems to me unassailable but so general and abstract as to be unhelpful—at least unadministerable in the form stated. It assumes we can measure in some way the incremental units of human satisfaction yielded by very different types of goods. . . . But I insist that the proposition stated describes the result for which we should be striving—and again, that it is always useful to know what your target is even if your weapons are too crude to score a bull's eye.

QUESTIONS

1 Does the life of a penguin have value only if humans value it?

2 Is human benefit the only morally relevant criterion in determining our obligations in regard to the rest of the natural world?

The Value of Wilderness

William Godfrey-Smith

William Godfrey-Smith is an Australian philosopher whose major philosophical interests include environmental philosophy and the metaphysics of time. These interests are reflected in such articles as "The Rights of Non-Humans and Intrinsic Values," "Beginning and Ceasing to Exist," and "Special Relativity and the Present."

Godfrey-Smith investigates the kinds of justification that might come into play in making a case for the preservation of wilderness. He begins by calling attention to a characteristic assumption of Western moral thought: "Value can be ascribed to the nonhuman world only insofar as it is good for the sake of the well-being of human beings." In the light of this "decidedly anthropocentric bias," he contends, only *instrumental* justifications for preserving wilderness are deemed acceptable. Though Godfrey-Smith maintains that a powerful case for the preservation of wilderness can be founded on its instrumental value (i.e., its value for humankind), he believes that we must develop an ecologically based morality which recognizes natural systems as possessing their own intrinsic value. In the spirit of Aldo Leopold, Godfrey-Smith argues that the boundaries of the moral community should be extended. In his view, we must learn to extend moral consideration to "items treated heretofore as matters of expediency."

Wilderness is the raw material out of which man has hammered the artifact called civilization.

Aldo Leopold
A Sand County Almanac (New York: Oxford University Press, 1949), p. 188.

The framework which I examine is the framework of *Western* attitudes toward our natural environment, and wilderness in particular. The philosophical task to which I shall address myself is an exploration of attitudes toward wilderness, especially the sorts of justification to which we might legitimately appeal for the preservation of wilderness: what grounds can we advance in support of the claim that wilderness is something which we should *value?*

There are two different ways of appraising something as valuable. It may be that the thing in question is good or valuable *for the sake* of something which we hold to be valuable. In this case the thing is not considered to be good in itself; value in this sense is ascribed in virtue of the thing's being a *means* to some valued end, and not as an *end in itself.* Such values are standardly designated *instrumental* values. Not everything which we hold to be good or valuable can be good for the sake of something else: our values must ultimately be *grounded* in something which is held to be good or valuable in itself. Such things are said to be *intrinsically* valuable. As a mat-

Reprinted, as a shortened version prepared by the author, from "The Value of Wilderness," *Environmental Ethics,* vol. 1 (Winter 1979), pp. 309–319. Copyright © by William Godfrey-Smith.

ter of historical fact, those things which have been held to be instrinsically valuable, within our Western traditions of thought, have nearly always been taken to be states or conditions of *persons,* e.g., happiness, pleasure, knowledge, or self-realization, to name but a few.

It follows from this that a very central assumption of Western moral thought is that value can be ascribed to the nonhuman world only insofar as it is good for the sake of the well-being of human beings.[1] Our entire attitude toward the natural environment, therefore, has a decidedly anthropocentric bias, and this fact is reflected in the sorts of justification which are standardly provided for the preservation of the natural environment.

A number of thinkers, however, are becoming increasingly persuaded that our anthropocentric morality is in fact inadequate to provide a satisfactory basis for a moral philosophy of ecological obligation. It is for this reason that we hear not infrequently the claim that we need a "new morality." A new moral framework—that is, a network of recognized obligations and duties—is not, however, something that can be casually conjured up in order to satisfy some vaguely felt need. The task of developing a sound biologically based moral philosophy, a philosophy which is not anthropocentrically based, and which provides a satisfactory justification for ecological obligation and concern, is, I think, one of the most urgent tasks confronting moral philosophers at the present. It will entail a radical reworking of accepted attitudes—attitudes which we currently accept as "self-evident"—and this is not something which can emerge suddenly. Indeed, I think the seminal work remains largely to be done.

In the absence of a comprehensive and convincing ecologically based morality we naturally fall back on *instrumental* justifications for concern for our natural surroundings, and for preserving wilderness areas and animal species. We can, I think, detect at least four main lines of instrumental justification for the preservation of wilderness. By *wilderness* I understand any reasonably large tract of the Earth, together with its plant and animal communities, which is substantially unmodified by humans and in particular by human technology. The natural contrast to *wilderness* and *nature* is an *artificial* or *domesticated* environment. The fact that there are borderline cases which are difficult to classify does not, of course, vitiate this distinction.

The first attitude toward wilderness espoused by conservationists to which I wish to draw attention is what I shall call the "cathedral" view. This is the view that wilderness areas provide a vital opportunity for spiritual revival, moral regeneration, and aesthetic delight. The enjoyment of wilderness is often compared in this respect with religious or mystical experience. Preservation of magnificent wilderness areas for those who subscribe to this view is essential for human well-being, and its destruction is conceived as something akin to an act of vandalism, perhaps comparable to—some may regard it as more serious than[2]—the destruction of a magnificent and moving human edifice, such as the Parthenon, the Taj Mahal, or the Palace of Versailles.

Insofar as the "cathedral" view holds that value derives solely from human satisfactions gained from its contemplation it is clearly an instrumentalist attitude. It does, however, frequently approach an *intrinsic value* attitude, insofar as the feeling arises that there is importance in the fact that it is there to be contemplated, whether or not anyone actually takes advantage of this fact. Suppose for example, that some wilderness was so precariously balanced that *any* human intervention or contact would inevitably bring about its destruction. Those who maintained that the area should, nevertheless, be preserved, unexperienced and unenjoyed, would certainly be ascribing to it an intrinsic value.

The "cathedral" view with respect to wilderness in fact is a fairly recent innovation in Western thought. The predominant Graeco-Christian attitude, which generally speaking was the predominant Western attitude prior to eighteenth- and nineteenth-century romanticism, had been to view wilderness as threatening or alarming, an attitude still reflected in the figurative uses of the expression *wilderness,* clearly connoting a degenerate state to be avoided. Christianity, in general, has enjoined "the transformation of wilderness, those dreaded haunts of demons, the ancient nature-gods, into farm and pasture,"[3] that is, to a domesticated environment.

The second instrumental justification of the value of wilderness is what we might call the "laboratory" argument. This is the argument that wilderness areas provide vital subject matter for scientific inquiry which provides us with an understanding of the intricate interdependencies of biological systems, their modes of change and development, their energy cycles, and the source of their stabilities. If we are to understand our own biological dependencies, we require natural systems as a norm, to inform us of the biological laws which we transgress at our peril.

The third instrumentalist justification is the "silo" argument which points out that one excellent reason for preserving reasonable areas of the natural environment intact is that we thereby preserve a stockpile of genetic diversity, which it is certainly prudent to maintain as a backup in case something should suddenly go wrong with the simplified biological systems which, in general, constitute agriculture. Further, there is the related point that there is no way of anticipating our future needs, or the undiscovered applications of apparently useless plants, which might turn out to be, for example, the source of some pharmacologically valuable drug—a cure, say, for leukemia. This might be called, perhaps, the "rare herb" argument, and it provides another persuasive instrumental justification for the preservation of wilderness.

The final instrumental justification which I think should be mentioned is the "gymnasium" argument, which regards the preservation of wilderness as important for athletic or recreational activities.

An obvious problem which arises from these instrumental arguments is that the various activities which they seek to justify are not always possible to reconcile with one another. The interests of the wilderness lover who subscribes to the "cathedral" view are not always reconcilable with those of the ordinary vacationist. Still more obvious is the conflict between the recreational use of wilderness and the interests of the miner, the farmer, and the timber merchant.

The conflict of interest which we encounter here is one which it is natural to try and settle through the economic calculus of cost-benefit considerations. So long as the worth of natural systems is believed to depend entirely on instrumental values, it is natural to suppose that we can sort out the conflict of interests within an objective frame of reference, by estimating the human satisfactions to be gained from the preservation of wilderness, and by weighing these against the satisfactions which are to be gained from those activities which may lead to its substantial modification, domestication, and possibly even, destruction.

Many thinkers are liable to encounter here a feeling of resistance to the suggestion that we can apply purely economic considerations to settle such conflicts of interest. The assumption behind economic patterns of thought, which underlie policy formulation and planning, is that the values which we attach to natural systems and to productive activities are commensurable; and this is an assumption which may be called into question. It is not simply a question of the difficulty of quantifying what value should be attached to the preservation of the natural environment. The feeling is more that economic considerations are simply out of place. This feeling is one which is often too lightly dismissed by tough-minded economists as being obscurely mystical or superstitious; but it is a view worth examining. What it amounts to, I suggest, is the belief that there is something *morally* objectionable in the destruction of natural systems, or at least in their wholesale elimination, and this is precisely the belief that natural systems, or economically "useless" species, do possess an *intrinsic* value. That is, it is an attempt to articulate the rejection of the anthropocentric view that all value, ultimately, resides in *human* interest and concerns.

A feeling persists that cost-benefit analyses tend to overlook important values. One consideration which tends to be discounted from policy deliberations is that which concerns *economically* unimportant species of animals or plants. A familiar subterfuge which we frequently encounter is the attempt to invest such species with spurious economic value, as illustrated in the rare herb argument. A typical example of this, cited by Leopold, is the reaction of ornithologists to the threatened disappearance of certain species of songbirds: they at once came forward with some distinctly shaky evidence that they played an essential role in the control of insects.[4] The dominance of economic modes of thinking is again obvious: the evidence has to be economic in order to be acceptable. This exemplifies the way in which we turn to instrumentalist justifications for the maintenance of biotic diversity.

The alternative to such instrumentalist justifications, the alternative which Leopold advocated with great insight and eloquence, is to widen the boundary of the moral community to include animals, plants, the soil, or collectively *the land*.[5] This involves a radical shift in our conception of nature, so that land is recognized not simply as property, to be dealt with or disposed of as a matter of expediency: land in Leopold's view is not a commodity which belongs to us, but a community to which we belong. This change in conception is far-reaching and profound. It involves a shift in our metaphysical conception of nature—that is, a change in what sort of thing we take our natural surroundings to *be*.

The predominant Western conception of the natural world is largely a legacy of the philosophy of Descartes. This philosophy has alienated man from the natural world through its sharp ontological division between conscious minds and mechanically arranged substances which, for Descartes, constitute the rest of nature. An adequate environmental ethic must, *inter alia,* replace the world-view which emerges from Cartesian metaphysics.

This will involve a shift from the piecemeal reductive conception of natural items, to a *holistic* or systemic view in which we come to appreciate the symbiotic interdependencies of the natural world. On the holistic or total-field view, organisms—including man—are conceived as nodes in a biotic web of intrinsically related parts.[6] That is, our understanding of biological organisms requires more than just an understanding of their structure and properties; we also have to attend seriously to their interrelations. Holistic or systemic thinking does not deny that organisms are complex physicochemical systems, but it affirms that the methods employed in establishing the high-level functional relationships expressed by physical laws are often of very limited importance in understanding the nature of biological systems.

The holistic conception of the natural world contains, I think, the possibility of extending the idea of community beyond human society. And in this way biological wisdom does, I think, carry implications for ethics. Just as Copernicus showed us that man does not occupy the physical center of the universe, Darwin and his successors have shown us that man occupies no *biologically* privileged position. We still have to assimilate the implications which this biological knowledge has for morality.

Can we regard man and the natural environment as constituting a community in any morally significant sense? Passmore, in particular, has claimed that this extended sense of community is entirely spurious.[7] Leopold, on the other hand, found the biological extension of community entirely natural.[8] If we regard a community as a collection of individuals who engage in cooperative behavior, Leopold's extension seems to me entirely legitimate. An ethic is no more than a code of conduct designed to ensure cooperative behavior among the members of a community. Such cooperative behavior is required to underpin the health of the community, in this biologically extended sense, *health* being understood as the biological capacity for self-renewal,[9] and *ill-health* as the degeneration or loss of this capacity.

Man, of course, cannot be placed on "all fours" with his biologically fellow creatures in all respects. In particular, man is the only creature who can act as a full-fledged moral agent, i.e., an individual capable of exercising reflective rational choice on the basis of principles. What distinguishes man from his fellow creatures is not the capacity to *act,* but the fact that his actions are, to a great extent, free from programming. This capacity to modify our own behavior is closely bound up with the capacity to acquire knowledge of the natural world, a capacity which has enabled us, to an unprecedented extent, to manipulate the environment, and—especially in the recent past—to alter it rapidly, violently, and globally. Our hope must be that the capacity for knowledge, which has made ecologically hazardous activities possible, will lead to a more profound understanding of the delicate biological interdependencies which some of these actions now threaten, and thereby generate the wisdom for restraint.

To those who are skeptical of the possibility of extending moral principles, in the manner of Leopold, to include items treated heretofore as matters of expediency, it can be pointed out that extensions have, to a limited extent, already taken place. One clear—if partial—instance, is in the treatment of animals. It is now generally accepted, and this is a comparatively recent innovation,[10] that we have at least a *prima facie* obligation not to treat animals cruelly or sadistically. And this certainly constitutes a shift in moral attitudes. If—as seems to be the case—cruelty to animals is accepted as intrinsically wrong, then there *is* at least one instance in which it is *not* a matter of moral indifference how we behave toward the nonhuman world.

More familiar perhaps are the moral revolutions which have occurred within the specific domain of human society—witness the progressive elimination of the "right" to racial, class, and sex exploitation. Each of these shifts involves the acceptance, on the part of some individuals, of new obligations, rights, and values which, to a previous generation, would have been considered unthinkable.[11] The essential step in recognizing an enlarged community involves coming to see, feel, and understand what was previously perceived as alien and apart: it is the evolution of the capacity of *empathy*.

We can, however, provide—and it is important that we can provide—an answer to the question: "What is the *use* of wilderness?" We certainly ought to preserve and protect wilderness areas as gymnasiums, as laboratories, as stockpiles of genetic diversity, and as cathedrals. Each of these reasons provides a powerful and sufficient instrumental justification for their preservation. But note how the very posing of this question about the *utility* of wilderness reflects an anthropocentric system of values. From a genuinely ecocentric point of view the question "What is the *use* of wilderness?" would be as absurd as the question "What is the *use* of happiness?"

The philosophical task is to try to provide adequate justification, or at least clear the way, for a scheme of values according to which concern and sympathy for our environment is immediate and natural, and the desirability of protecting and preserving wilderness self-evident. When once controversial propositions become platitudes, the philosophical task will have been successful.

I will conclude, nevertheless, on a deflationary note. It seems to me (at least much of the time) that the shift in attitudes which I think is required for promoting genuinely harmonious relations with nature is too drastic, too "unthinkable," to be very persuasive for most people. If this is so, then it will be more expedient to justify the preservation of wilderness in terms of instrumentalist considerations; and I have argued that there *are* powerful arguments for preservation which can be derived from the purely anthropocentric considerations of human self-interest. I hope, however, that there will be some who feel that such anthropocentric considerations are not wholly satisfying, i.e., that they do not really do justice to our intuitions. But at a time when *human* rights are being treated in some quarters with a great deal of skepticism it is perhaps unrealistic to expect the rights of nonhumans to receive sympathetic attention. Perhaps, though, we should not be too abashed by this: extensions in ethics have seldom followed the path of political expediency.

NOTES

1 Other cultures have certainly included the idea that nature should be valued for its own sake in their moral codes, e.g., the American Indians, the Chinese, and the Australian Aborigines.

2 We can after all *replace* human artifacts such as buildings with something closely similar, but the destruction of a wilderness or a biological species is irreversible.

3 John Passmore, *Man's Responsibility for Nature* (London. Duckworth, 1974; New York: Charles Scribner's Sons, 1974), p. 17; cf. chap. 5.

4 Aldo Leopold, "The Land Ethic," in *Sand County Almanac,* p. 210.

5 Cf. Aldo Leopold, "The Conservation Ethic," *Journal of Forestry* 31 (1933): 634–43, and "The Land Ethic," *Sand County Almanac.*

6 Cf. Arne Naess, "The Shallow and the Deep, Long-Range Ecology Movement," *Inquiry* 16 (1973): 95–100.

7 Passmore, *Man's Responsibility for Nature,* chap. 6; "Attitudes to Nature," in R. S. Peters, ed., *Nature and Conduct* (London: Macmillan, 1975), p. 262.

8 Leopold, "The Land Ethic."

9 *Ibid.,* p. 221.

10 Cf. Passmore, "The Treatment of Animals," *Journal of the History of Ideas* 36 (1975): 195–218.

11 Cf. Christopher D. Stone, "Should Trees Have Standing? Toward Legal Rights for Natural Objects," *Southern California Law Review* 45 (1972): 450–501.

QUESTIONS

1 Does wilderness have only instrumental value?

2 Is it true, as Godfrey-Smith maintains, that our anthropocentric morality is "inadequate to provide a satisfactory basis for a moral philosophy of ecological obligations"?

Environmental Ethics

Bernard E. Rollin

Bernard E. Rollin is professor of philosophy and director of bioethical planning at Colorado State University. His specializations are bioethics and theory of meaning. Rollin is the author of *Animal Rights and Human Morality* (1981) and *The Unheeded Cry* (1989).

In contrast to Baxter's anthropocentric approach as well as Godfrey-Smith's biocentric approach, Rollin adopts a sentientist approach to environmental issues. He contends that because humans and other animals are sentient beings who can be harmed, they have intrinsic value and moral rights. Rivers, forests, species, and ecosystems, in contrast, have only instrumental value since they are not sentient beings and thus cannot be harmed, except in a metaphorical sense. Nonetheless, Rollin maintains, once we recognize the intrinsic value of *all* sentient beings, we can develop a rich environmental ethic based on the interests of human beings and other animals.

The past two decades have witnessed a major revolutionary thrust in social moral awareness, one virtually unknown in mainstream Western ethical thinking, although

Reprinted with permission of Westview Press from *Problems of International Justice* (1988), edited by Steven Luper-Foy, pp. 125–131.

not unrecognized in other cultural traditions; for example, the Navajo, whose descriptive language for nature and animals is suffused with ethical nuances; the Australian Aboriginal people; and the ancient Persians. This thrust is the recognition that nonhuman entities enjoy some moral status as objects of moral concern and deliberation. Although the investigation of the moral status of nonhuman entities has sometimes been subsumed under the global rubric of environmental ethics, such a blanket term does not do adequate justice to the substantial conceptual differences of its components.

THE MORAL STATUS OF NONHUMAN THINGS

As a bare minimum, environmental ethics comprises two fundamentally divergent concerns—namely, concern with individual nonhuman animals as direct objects of moral concern and concern with species, ecosystems, environments, wilderness areas, forests, the biosphere, and other nonsentient natural or even abstract objects as direct objects of moral concern. Usually, although with a number of major exceptions,[1] those who give primacy to animals have tended to deny the moral significance of environments and species as direct objects of moral concern, whereas those who give moral primacy to enviro-ecological concerns tend to deny or at least downplay the moral significance of individual animals.[2] Significant though these differences are, they should not cloud the dramatic nature of this common attempt to break out of a moral tradition that finds loci of value only in human beings and, derivatively, in human institutions.

Because of the revolutionary nature of these attempts, they also remain somewhat undeveloped and embryonic. . . .

The most plausible strategy in attempting to revise traditional moral theory and practice is to show that the seeds of the new moral notions or extensions of old moral notions are, in fact, already implicit in the old moral machinery developed to deal with other issues. Only when such avenues are exhausted will it make sense to recommend major rebuilding of the machinery, rather than putting it to new uses. The classic examples of such extensions are obviously found in the extension of the moral/legal machinery of Western democracies to cover traditionally disenfranchised groups such as women and minorities. The relatively smooth flow of such applications owes much of its smoothness to the plausibility of a simple argument of the form:

> Our extant moral principles ought to cover all humans.
> Women are humans.
> ∴ Our extant moral principles ought to cover women.

On the other hand, conceptually radical departures from tradition do not lend themselves to such simple rational reconstruction. Thus, for example, the principle of *favoring* members of traditionally disenfranchised groups at the expense of innocent members of nondisenfranchised groups for the sake of rectifying historically based injustice is viewed as much more morally problematic and ambivalent than simply according rights to these groups. Thus, it would be difficult to construct a simple syllogism in defense of this practice that would garner universal acquiescence with the ease of the one indicated previously.

Thus, one needs to distinguish between moral revolutionary thrusts that are ostensibly paradoxical to common sense and practice because they have been ignored in a wholesale fashion, yet are in fact logical extensions of common morality, and those revolutionary thrusts that are genuinely paradoxical to previous moral thinking and practice because they are not implicit therein. Being genuinely paradoxical does not invalidate a new moral thrust—it does, however, place upon its proponents a substantially greater burden of proof. Those philosophers, like myself, who have argued for a recognition of the moral status of individual animals and the rights and legal status that derive therefrom, have attempted to place ourselves in the first category. We recognize that a society that kills and eats billions of animals, kills millions more in research, and disposes of millions more for relatively frivolous reasons and that relies economically on animal exploitation as a mainstay of social wealth, considers talk of elevating the moral status of animals as impossible and paradoxical. But this does not mean that such an elevation does not follow unrecognized from moral principles we all hold. Indeed, the abolition of slavery or the liberation of women appeared similarly paradoxical and economically impossible, yet gradually both were perceived as morally necessary, in part because both were implicit, albeit unrecognized, in previously acknowledged assumptions.[3]

My own argument for elevating the status of animals has been a relatively straightforward deduction of unnoticed implications of traditional morality. I have tried to show that no morally relevant grounds for excluding animals from the full application of our moral machinery will stand up to rational scrutiny. Traditional claims that rely on notions such as animals have no souls, are inferior to humans in power or intelligence or evolutionary status, are not moral agents, are not rational, are not possessed of free will, are not capable of language, are not bound by social contract to humans, and so forth, do not serve as justifiable reasons for excluding animals and their interests from the moral arena.

By the same token, morally relevant similarities exist between us and them in the case of the "higher" animals. Animals can suffer, as Jeremy Bentham said; they have interests; what we do to them matters to them; they can feel pain, fear, anxiety, loneliness, pleasure, boredom, and so on. Indeed, the simplicity and power of the argument calling attention to such morally relevant similarities has led Cartesians from Descartes to modern physiologists with a vested interest against attributing moral status to animals to declare that animals are machines with no morally relevant modes of awareness, a point often addressed today against moral claims such as mine. In fact, such claims have become a mainstay of what I have elsewhere called the "common sense of science." Thus, one who argues for an augmented moral status for animals finds it necessary to establish philosophically and scientifically what common sense takes for granted—namely, that animals *are* conscious.[4] Most people whose common sense is intact are not Cartesians and can see that moral talk cannot be withheld from animals and our treatment of them.

In my own work, appealing again to common moral practice, I have stressed our society's quasi-moral, quasi-legal notion of rights as a reflection of our commitment to the moral primacy of the individual, rather than the state. Rights protect what are hypothesized as the fundamental interests of human beings from cavalier encroachment by the common good—such interests as speech, assembly, belief, property, privacy, freedom from torture, and so forth. But those animals who are conscious also have fundamental interests arising out of *their* biologically given natures (or *teloi*), the infringement upon which matters greatly to them, and the fulfillment of which is central to their lives. Hence, I deduce the notion of animal rights from our common moral theory and practice and attempt to show that conceptually, at least, it is a deduction from the moral framework of the status quo rather than a major revision therein. Moral concern for individual animals follows from the hitherto ignored presence of morally relevant characteristics, primarily sentience, in animals. As a result, I am comfortable in attributing what Immanuel Kant called "intrinsic value," not merely use value, to animals if we attribute it to people.[5]

The task is far more formidable for those who attempt to make nonsentient natural objects, such as rivers and mountains, or, worse, quasi-abstract entities, such as species and ecosystems, into direct objects of moral concern. Interestingly enough, in direct opposition to the case of animals, such moves appear prima facie plausible to common morality, which has long expressed concern for the value and preservation of some natural objects, while condoning wholesale exploitation of others. In the same way, common practice often showed extreme concern for certain favored kinds of animals, while systematically exploiting others. Thus, many people in the United States strongly oppose scientific research on dogs and cats, but are totally unconcerned about such use of rodents or swine. What is superficially plausible, however, quite unlike the case of animals, turns out to be deeply paradoxical given the machinery of traditional morality.

Many leading environmental ethicists have attempted to do for nonsentient natural objects and abstract objects the same sort of thing I have tried to do for animals—namely, attempted to elevate their status to direct objects of intrinsic value, ends in themselves, which are morally valuable not only because of their relations and utility to sentient beings, but in and of themselves.[6] To my knowledge, none of these theorists has attempted to claim, as I do for animals, that the locus of such value lies in the fact that what we do to these entities matters to them. No one has argued that we can harm rivers, species, or ecosystems in ways that matter to them.

Wherein, then, do these theorists locate the intrinsic value of these entities? This is not at all clear in the writings, but seems to come down to one of the following doubtful moves:

1 Going from the fact that environmental factors are absolutely essential to the well-being or survival of beings that are loci of intrinsic value to the conclusion that environmental factors therefore enjoy a similar or even higher moral status. Such a move is clearly fallacious. Just because I cannot survive without insulin, and I am an object of intrinsic value, it does not follow that insulin is, too. In fact, the insulin is a paradigmatic example of instrumental value.

2 Going from the fact that the environment "creates" all sentient creatures to the fact that its welfare is more important than theirs. This is really a variation on (1) and succumbs to the same sort of criticism, namely, that this reasoning represents a genetic fallacy. The cause of something valuable need not itself be valuable and certainly not necessarily more valuable than its effect—its value must be established independently of its result. The Holocaust may have caused the state of Israel; that does not make the Holocaust more valuable than the state of Israel.

3 Confusing aesthetic or instrumental value for sentient creatures, notably humans, with intrinsic value and underestimating aesthetic value as a category. We shall return to this shortly, for I suspect it is the root confusion in those attempting to give nonsentient nature intrinsic value.

4 Substituting rhetoric for logic at crucial points in the discussions and using a poetic rhetoric (descriptions of natural objects in terms such as "grandeur," "majesty," "novelty," "variety") as an unexplained basis for according them "intrinsic value."

5 Going from the metaphor that infringement on natural objects "matters" to them in the sense that disturbance evokes an adjustment by their self-regulating properties, to the erroneous conclusion that such self-regulation, being analogous to conscious coping in animals, entitles them to direct moral status.

In short, traditional morality and its theory do not offer a viable way to raise the moral status of nonsentient natural objects and abstract objects so that they are direct objects of moral concern on a par with or even higher than sentient creatures. Ordinary morality and moral concern take as their focus the effects of actions on beings who can be helped and harmed, in ways that matter to them, either directly or by implication. If it is immoral to wreck someone's property, it is because it is someone's; if it is immoral to promote the extinction of species, it is because such extinction causes aesthetic or practical harm to humans or to animals or because a species is, in the final analysis, a group of harmable individuals.

There is nothing, of course, to stop environmental ethicists from making a recommendation for a substantial revision of common and traditional morality. But such recommendations are likely to be dismissed or whittled away by a moral version of Occam's razor: Why grant animals rights and acknowledge in animals intrinsic value? Because they are conscious and what we do to them matters to them? Why grant rocks, or trees, or species, or ecosystems rights? Because these objects have great aesthetic value, or are essential to us, or are basic for survival? But these are paradigmatic examples of *instrumental* value. A conceptual confusion for a noble purpose is still a conceptual confusion.

There is nothing to be gained by attempting to elevate the moral status of nonsentient natural objects to that of sentient ones. One can develop a rich environmental ethic by locating the value of nonsentient natural objects in their relation to sentient ones. One can argue for the preservation of habitats because their destruction harms animals; one can argue for preserving ecosystems on the grounds of unforeseen pernicious consequences resulting from their destruction, a claim for which much empirical evidence exists. One can argue for the preservation of animal species as the sum of a group of individuals who would be harmed by its extinction. One can argue for preserving mountains, snail darters, streams, and cockroaches on aesthetic grounds. Too many philosophers forget the moral power of aesthetic claims and tend to see aesthetic reasons as a weak basis for preserving natural objects. Yet the moral imperative not to destroy unique aesthetic objects and even nonunique ones is an onerous one that is well ingrained into common practice—witness the worldwide establishment of national parks, preserves, forests, and wildlife areas.

Rather than attempting to transcend all views of natural objects as instrumental by grafting onto nature a mystical intrinsic value that can be buttressed only by poetic rhetoric, it would be far better to nurture public appreciation of subtle instrumental value, especially aesthetic value. People can learn to appreciate the unique beauty of a desert, or of a fragile ecosystem, or even of a noxious creature like a tick, when they understand the complexity and history therein and can read the story each life form contains. I am reminded of a colleague in parasitology who is loath to destroy worms he has studied upon completing his research because he has aesthetically learned to value their complexity of structure, function, and evolutionary history and role.

It is important to note that the attribution of value to nonsentient natural objects as a relational property arising out of their significance (recognized or not) for sentient beings does not denigrate the value of natural objects. Indeed, this attribution does not even imply that the interests or desires of individual sentient beings always trump concern for nonsentient ones. Our legal system has, for example, valuable and irreplaceable property laws that forbid owners of aesthetic objects, say a collection of Vincent Van Gogh paintings, to destroy them at will, say by adding them to one's funeral pyre. To be sure, this restriction on people's right to dispose of their own property arises out of a recognition of the value of these objects to other humans, but this is surely quite sensible. How else would one justify such a restriction? Nor, as we said earlier, need one limit the value of natural objects to their relationship to humans. Philosophically, one could, for example, sensibly (and commonsensically) argue for preservation of acreage from the golf-course developer because failure to do so would mean the destruction of thousands of sentient creatures' habitats—a major infringement of their interests—while building the golf course would fulfill the rarefied and inessential interests of a few.

Thus, in my view, one would accord moral concern to natural objects in a variety of ways, depending on the sort of object being considered. Moral status for individual animals would arise from their sentience. Moral status of species and their protection from humans would arise from the fact that a species is a collection of morally relevant individuals; moral status also would arise from the fact that humans have an aesthetic concern in not letting a unique and irreplaceable aesthetic object (or group of objects) disappear forever from our *Umwelt* (environment). Concern for wilderness areas, mountains, deserts, and so on would arise from their survival value for sentient animals as well as from their aesthetic value for humans. (Some writers have suggested that this aesthetic value is so great as to be essential to human mental/physical health, a point perfectly compatible with my position.[7]

Nothing in what I have said as yet tells us how to weigh conflicting interests, whether between humans and other sentient creatures or between human desires and environmental protection. How does one weigh the aesthetic concern of those who oppose blasting away part of a cliff against the pragmatic concern of those who wish to build on a cliffside? But the problem of weighing is equally thorny in traditional ethics—witness lifeboat questions or questions concerning the allocation of scarce medical resources. Nor does the intrinsic value approach help in adjudicating such issues. How does one weigh the alleged intrinsic value of a cliffside against the interests of the (intrinsic-value-bearing) homebuilders?

Furthermore, the intrinsic value view can lead to results that are repugnant to common sense and ordinary moral consciousness. Thus, for example, it follows from what has been suggested by one intrinsic value theorist that if a migratory herd of plentiful elk were passing through an area containing an endangered species of moss, it would be not only permissible but obligatory to kill the elk in order to protect the moss because in one case we would lose a species, in another "merely" individuals.[8] In my view, such a case has a less paradoxical resolution. Destruction of the moss does not matter to the moss, whereas elk presumably care about living or being injured. Therefore, one would give prima facie priority to the elk. This might presumably be trumped if, for example, the moss were a substratum from which was extracted an ingredient necessary to stop a raging, lethal epidemic in humans or animals. But such cases—and indeed most cases of conflicting interests—must be decided on the actual occasion. These cases are decided by a careful examination of the facts of the situation. Thus, our suggestion of a basis for environmental ethics does not qualitatively change the situation from that of current ethical deliberation, whereas granting intrinsic value to natural objects would leave us with a "whole new ball game"—and one where we do not know the rules.

In sum, then, the question of environmental ethics . . . must be analyzed into two discrete components. First are those questions that pertain to direct objects of moral concern—nonhuman animals whose sentience we have good reason to suspect—and that require the application of traditional moral notions to a hitherto ignored domain of moral objects. Second are those questions pertaining to natural objects or abstract natural objects. Although it is nonsensical to attribute intrinsic or direct moral value to these objects, they nonetheless must become (and are indeed becoming) central to our social moral deliberations. This centrality derives from our increasing recognition of the far-reaching and sometimes subtle instrumental value these objects have for humans and animals. Knowing that contamination of remote desert areas by pollutants can destroy unique panoplies of fragile beauty, or that dumping wastes into the ocean can destroy a potential source of antibiotics, or that building a pipeline can have undreamed-of harmful effects goes a long way toward making us think twice about these activities—a far longer way than endowing them with quasi-mystical rhetorical status subject to (and begging for) positivistic torpedoing. . . .

NOTES

1 See the chapters in Tom Regan, *All That Dwell Therein* (Berkeley: University of California Press, 1982).

2 See Aldo Leopold, *A Sand County Almanac* (Oxford: Oxford University Press, 1949); J. Baird Callicott, "Animal Liberation: A Triangular Affair," *Environmental Ethics* 2 (1980):311–338; Holmes Rolston III, *Philosophy Gone Wild* (Buffalo, N.Y.: Prometheus Books, 1986).

3 See the discussions of this point in Peter Singer, *Animal Liberation* (New York: New York Review of Books, 1975); and B. Rollin, *Animal Rights and Human Morality* (Buffalo, N.Y.: Prometheus Books, 1981).

4 See my "Animal Pain," in M. Fox and L. Mickley (eds.), *Advances in Animal Welfare Science 1985* (The Hague; Martinus Nijhoff, 1985); and my "Animal Consciousness and Scientific Change," *New Ideas in Psychology* 4, no. 2 (1986):141–152, as well as the replies to the latter by P. K. Feyerabend, H. Rachlin, and T. Leahey in the same issue, p. 153. See also my *Animal Consciousness, Animal Pain, and Scientific Change* (tentative title) (Oxford: Oxford University Press, forthcoming).

5 See my *Animal Rights,* Part I.

6 See the works mentioned in footnotes 1 and 2.

7 This point is made with great rhetorical force in Edward Abbey, *Desert Solitaire* (New York: Ballantine Books, 1971).

8 See Holmes Rolston, "Duties to Endangered Species," *Philosophy Gone Wild.*

QUESTIONS

1 Is Rollin correct in holding that only sentient beings have intrinsic value?

2 Do you agree that once we recognize the subtle instrumental value of ecosystems, forests, etc., we will have a very strong foundation for revising those human activities that damage or destroy nonsentient natural objects?

Ecology and Morality

Peter S. Wenz

Peter S. Wenz is professor of philosophy at Sangamon State University. He specializes in ethics and philosophy of law. Wenz is the author of *Environmental Justice* (1988), "Concentric Circle Pluralism: A Response to Rolston," and "Treating Animals Naturally."

In the first part of this selection, Wenz, a deep ecologist, briefly characterizes healthy ecosystems. In the second, he presents two cases intended to test readers' moral intuitions. These cases are calculated to show that our current morality includes prima facie obligations toward ecosystems that depend on neither the interests of human beings nor those of other sentient beings.

In the first section of this article I characterize good or healthy ecosystems. In the second I argue that we have a *prima facie* obligation to protect such ecosystems irrespective of all possible advantage to human beings.

Reprinted with permission of Humana Press from *Ethics and Animals* (1983), edited by Harlan B. Miller and William H. Williams, pp. 185–191.

GOOD ECOSYSTEMS

An ecosystem is what Aldo Leopold referred to as a "biotic pyramid." He describes it this way (1970, p. 252):

> Plants absorb energy from the sun. This energy flows through a circuit called the biota, which may be represented by a pyramid consisting of layers. The bottom layer is the soil. A plant layer rests on the soil, an insect layer on the plants, a bird and rodent layer on the insects, and so on up through various animal groups to the apex layer, which consists of the large carnivores.
>
> Proceeding upward, each successive layer decreases in numerical abundance. Thus, for every carnivore there are hundreds of his prey, thousands of their prey, millions of insects, uncountable plants.
>
> The lines of dependency for food and other services are called food chains. Thus soil-oak-deer-Indian is a chain that has now largely converted to soil-corn-cow-farmer. Each species, including ourselves, is a link in many chains. The deer eats a hundred plants other than oak, and the cow a hundred plants other than corn. Both, then, are links in a hundred chains. The pyramid is a tangle of chains so complex as to seem disorderly, yet the stability of the system proves it to be a highly organized structure.[1]

It is so highly organized that Leopold and others write of it, at times, as if it were a single organism which could be in various stages of health or disease (p. 274):

> Paleontology offers abundant evidence that wilderness maintained itself for immensely long periods; that its component species were rarely lost, neither did they get out of hand; that weather and water built soil as fast or faster than it was carried away. Wilderness, then, assumes unexpected importance as a laboratory for the study of land-health.

By contrast,

> When soil loses fertility, or washes away faster than it forms, and when water systems exhibit abnormal floods and shortages, the land is sick (p. 272).
>
> The disappearance of plant and animal species without visible cause, despite efforts to protect them, and the irruption of others as pests despite efforts to control them, must, in the absence of simpler explanations, be regarded as symptoms of sickness in the land organism (pp. 272–273).

In general, a healthy ecosystem consists of a great diversity of flora and fauna, as "the trend of evolution is to elaborate and diversify the biota" (p. 253). This flora and fauna is in a relatively stable balance, evolving slowly rather than changing rapidly, because its diversity enables it to respond to change in a flexible manner that retains the system's integrity. In all of these respects a healthy ecosystem is very much like a healthy plant or animal.

A description of one small part of one ecosystem will conclude this account of the nature of ecosystems. It is Leopold's description of a river's sand bar in August (1970, p. 55):

> The work begins with a broad ribbon of silt brushed thinly on the sand of a reddening shore. As this dries slowly in the sun, goldfinches bathe in its pools, and deer, herons, killdeers, raccoons, and turtles cover it with a lacework of tracks. There is no telling, at this stage, whether anything further will happen.

But when I see the silt ribbon turning green with Eleocharis,* I watch closely thereafter, for this is the sign that the river is in a painting mood. Almost overnight the Eleocharis becomes a thick turf, so lush and so dense that the meadow mice from the adjoining upland cannot resist the temptation. They move *en masse* to the green pasture, and apparently spend the nights rubbing their ribs in its velvety depths. A maze of neatly tended mousetrails bespeaks their enthusiasm. The deer walk up and down in it, apparently just for the pleasure of feeling it underfoot. Even a stay-at-home mole has tunneled his way across the dry bar to the Eleocharis ribbon, where he can heave and hump the sod to his heart's content.

At this stage the seedlings of plants too numerous to count and too young to recognize spring to life from the damp warm sand under the green ribbon.

Three weeks later (pp. 55–56):

The Eleocharis sod, greener than ever is now spangled with blue mimulus, pink dragonhead, and the milk-white blooms of Sagittaria. Here and there a cardinal flower thrusts a red spear skyward. At the head of the bar, purple ironweeds and pale pink joepyes stand tall against the wall of willows. And if you have come quietly and humbly, as you should to any spot that can be beautiful only once, you may surprise a fox-red deer, standing knee-high in the garden of his delight (pp. 55–56).

HUMAN OBLIGATIONS TO ECOSYSTEMS

Let us now consider whether or not we, you and I, have *prima facie* obligations towards ecosystems, in particular, the obligation to avoid destroying them, apart from any human advantage that might be gained by their continued existence. My argument consists in the elaboration of two examples, followed by appeals to the reader's intuition. The second, Case II, is designed to function as a counter-example to the claim that human beings have no obligations to preserve ecosystems except when doing so serves human interests or prevents the unnecessary suffering of other sentient beings.

Some clarifications are needed at the start. By "*prima facie* obligation" I mean an obligation that would exist in the absence of other, countervailing moral considerations. So I will construct cases in which such other considerations are designedly absent. A common consideration of this sort is the effect our actions have on intelligent beings, whether they be humans, extraterrestrials, or (should they be considered intelligent enough) apes and aquatic mammals. Accordingly, I will construct my cases so that the destruction of the environment affects none of these. Finally, the obligation in question is not to preserve ecosystems from any and every threat to their health and existence. Rather, the obligation for which I am contending is to protect ecosystems from oneself. The differences here may be important. A duty to protect the environment from any and every threat would have to rest on some principle concerning the duty to bring aid. Such principles concern positive duties, which are generally considered less stringent than negative duties. The duty to protect the environment from oneself, on the other hand, rests on a principle concerning the

---

*Editor's note: Eleocharis is a type of sedge.

duty to do no harm, which is a negative duty. Those not convinced that we have a duty to bring aid may nevertheless find a *prima facie* duty not to harm the environment easy to accept.

Case I

Consider the following situation. Suppose that you are a pilot flying a bomber that is low on fuel. You must release your bombs over the ocean to reduce the weight of the plane. If the bombs land in the water they will not explode, but will, instead, deactivate harmlessly. If, on the other hand, any lands on the islands that dot this part of the ocean, it will explode. The islands contain no mineral or other resources of use to human beings, and are sufficiently isolated from one another and other parts of the world that an explosion on one will not affect the others, or any other part of the world. The bomb's explosion will not add to air pollution because it is exceedingly "clean." However, each island contains an ecosystem, a biotic pyramid of the sort described by Aldo Leopold, within which there are rivers, sandbars, Eleocharis, meadow mice, cardinal flowers, blue mimulus, deer, and so forth, but no intelligent life. (Those who consider mice, deer, and other such animals so intelligent as to fall under some ban against killing intelligent life are free to suppose that in their wisdom, all such creatures have emigrated.) The bomb's explosion will ruin the ecosystem of the island on which it explodes, though it will not cause any animals to suffer. We may suppose that the islands are small enough and the bombs powerful enough that all animals, as well as plants, will be killed instantly, and therefore painlessly. The island will instantly be transformed from a wilderness garden to a bleakness like that on the surface of the moon.

Suppose that with some care and attention, but with no risk to yourself, anyone else or the plane, you could release your bombs so as to avoid hitting any of the islands. With equal care and attention you could be sure to hit at least one of the islands. Finally, without any care or attention to the matter, you might hit one of the islands and you might not. Assuming that you are in no need of target practice, and are aware of the situation as described, would you consider it a matter of moral indifference which of the three possible courses of action you took? Wouldn't you feel that you ought to take some care and pay some attention to insure that you avoid hitting any of the islands? Those who can honestly say that in the situation at hand they feel no more obligation to avoid hitting the islands than to hit them, who think that destroying the balanced pyramidal structure of a healthy ecosystem is morally indifferent, who care nothing for the islands' floral displays and interactions between flora, fauna, soil, water, and sun need read no further. Such people do not share the intuition on which the argument in this paper rests.

I assume that few, if any readers of the last paragraph accepted my invitation to stop reading. I would have phrased things differently if I thought they would. Many readers may nevertheless be skeptical of my intuitive demonstration that we feel a *prima facie* obligation to avoid destroying ecosystems. Even though no pain to sentient creatures is involved, nor the destruction of intelligent life nor pollution or other impairment of areas inhabited by human beings or other intelligent creatures, some readers may nevertheless explain their reluctance to destroy such an ecosystem by reference, ultimately, to human purposes. They can thereby avoid the inference I am promoting. They might point out that the islands' ecosystems may be useful to scientists who might someday want to study them. No matter that there are a great many such islands. The ecosystem of each is at least slightly different from the others, and therefore might provide some information of benefit to human beings that could not be gleaned elsewhere. Alternatively, though scientists are studying some, it might be to the benefit of humanity to establish Holiday Inns and Hilton Hotels on the others. Scientists have to relax too, and if the accommodations are suitable they will be more likely to enjoy the companionship of their families.

I believe that such explanations of our intuitive revulsion at the idea of needlessly destroying a healthy ecosystem are unhelpful evasions. They represent the squirming of one who intellectually believes ethics to concern only humans and other intelligent creatures, perhaps with a rider that one ought not to cause sentient creatures unnecessary suffering, with the reality of his or her own moral intuitions. The next case will make this clearer.

Case II

Suppose that human beings and all other intelligent creatures inhabiting the earth are becoming extinct. Imagine that this is the effect of some cosmic ray that causes extinction by preventing procreation. There is no possibility of survival through emigration to another planet, solar system or galaxy because the ray's presence is so widespread that no humans would survive the lengthy journey necessary to escape from its influence. There are many other species of extraterrestrial, intelligent creatures in the universe whom the cosmic ray does not affect. Nor does it affect any of the non-intelligent members of the earth's biotic community. So the earth's varied multitude of ecosystems could continue after the extinction of human beings. But their continuation would be of no use to any of the many species of intelligent extraterrestrials because the earth is for many reasons inhospitable to their forms of life, and contains no mineral or other resources of which they could make use.

Suppose that you are the last surviving human being. All other intelligent animals, if there were any, have already become extinct. Before they died, other humans had set hydrogen explosives all around the earth such that, were they to explode, all remaining plant and animal life on the earth would be instantly vaporized. No sentient creature would suffer, but the earth's varied multitude of ecosystems would be completely destroyed. The hydrogen explosives are all attached to a single timing mechanism, set to explode next year. Not wishing to die prematurely, you have located this timing device. You can set it ahead fifty or one hundred years, insuring that the explosion will not foreshorten your life, or you can, with only slightly greater effort, deactivate it so that it will never explode at all. Who would think it a matter of moral indifference which you did? It seems obvious that you ought to deactivate the explosives rather than postpone the time of the explosions.

How can one account for this "ought"? One suggestion is that our obligations are to intelligent life, and that the chances are improved and the time lessened for the evolution of intelligent life on earth by leaving the earth's remaining ecosystems intact. But this explanation is not convincing. First, it rests on assumptions about evolutionary developments under different earthly conditions that seem very plausible, but are by no means certain. More important, as the case was drawn, there are many species of intelligent extraterrestrials who are in no danger of either extinction or diminished numbers, and you know of their existence. It is therefore not at all certain that the obligations to intelligent life contained in our current ethical theories and moral intuitions would suggest, much less require, that we so act as to increase the probability of and decrease the time for the development of another species of intelligent life on earth. We do not now think it morally incumbent upon us to develop a form of intelligent life suited to live in those parts of the globe that, like Antarctica, are underpopulated by human beings. This is so because we do not adhere to a principle that we ought to so act as to insure the presence of intelligent life in as many earthly locations as possible. It is therefore doubtful that we adhere to the more extended principle that we ought to promote the development of as many different species of intelligent life as possible in as many different locations in the universe as possible. Such a problematic moral principle surely cannot account for our clear intuition that one obviously and certainly ought not to reset the explosives rather than deactivate them. It is more plausible to suppose that our current morality includes a *prima facie* obligation to refrain from destroying good ecosystems irrespective of both the interests of intelligent beings and the obligation not to cause sentient beings unnecessary suffering.

It is not necessary to say that ecosystems have rights. It is a commonplace in contemporary moral philosophy that not all obligations result from corresponding rights, for example, the obligation to be charitable. Instead, the obligation might follow from our concept of virtuous people as ones who do not destroy any existing things needlessly. Or perhaps we feel that one has a *prima facie* obligation not to destroy anything of esthetic value, and ecosystems are of esthetic value. Alternatively, the underlying obligation could be to avoid destroying anything that is good of its kind—so long as the kind in question does not make it something bad in itself—and many of the earth's ecosystems are good.

Our intuition might, on the other hand, be related more specifically to those characteristics that make good ecosystems good. Generally speaking, one ecosystem is better than another if it incorporates a greater diversity of life forms into a more integrated unity that is relatively stable, but not static. Its homeostasis allows for gradual evolution. The leading concepts, then, are diversity, unity, and a slightly less than complete homeostatic stability. These are, as a matter of empirical fact, positively related to one another in ecosystems. They may strike a sympathetic chord in human beings because they correspond symbolically to our personal, psychological need for a combination in our lives of both security and novelty. The stability and unity of a good ecosystem represents security. That the stability is cyclically homeostatic, rather than static, involves life forms rather than merely inorganic matter, and includes great diversity, corresponds to our desires for novelty and change. Of course, this is only speculation. It must be admitted that some human beings seem to so value security and stability as to prefer a purely static unity. Parmenides and the eastern religious thinkers who promote nothingness as a goal might consider the surface of the moon superior to that of the earth, and advocate allowing the earth's ecosystems to be vaporized under the conditions described in Case II.

My intuitions, however, and I assume those of most readers, favor ecosystems over static lifelessness and, perhaps for the same reason, good ecosystems over poorer ones. In any case, the above speculations concerning the psychological and logical derivations of these intuitions serve at most to help clarify their nature. Even the correct account of their origin would not necessarily constitute a justification. Rather than try to justify them, I will take them as a starting point for further discussion. So I take the cases elaborated above to establish that our current morality includes a *prima facie* obligation to avoid destroying good ecosystems, absent considerations of both animal torture and the well-being of intelligent creatures. . . .

REFERENCES

1 Leopold, A. 1970. *A Sand County Almanac, with essays on conservation from Round River.* New York: Ballantine Books.

QUESTIONS

1 Do you agree with Wenz's moral intuitions about the intrinsic value of ecosystems?
2 If you recognize the intrinsic value of ecosystems as well as other natural nonsentient objects, how would that change your perception of the relation between you and the rest of the natural world?

Why Do Species Matter?

Lilly-Marlene Russow

Lily-Marlene Russow is associate professor of philosophy at Purdue University. She specializes in philosophy of mind and phenomenology. Her published articles include "Regan on Inherent Value" and "Unlocking the Chinese Room."

Russow's purpose is to provide an acceptable foundation for claims about our obligations to protect species. In the first section, Russow describes several test cases intended to show some of the complexities involved in any attempt to articulate these obligations. In the second section, she criticizes and rejects various attempts to provide the appropriate foundation. The rejected approaches include both anthropocentric ones and those that ascribe inherent value to *species.* On Russow's analysis, any attempt to ascribe inherent value to a species involves conceptual confusion. In the final section, Russow argues that (1) it is individual

Reprinted with permission of the author and the publisher from *Environmental Ethics,* vol. 3 (Summer 1981), pp. 103–112.

members of a species that have value and (2) that value is aesthetic. In her discussion, Russow, unlike Rollin, treats aesthetic value as an inherent characteristic of animals rather than as an instrumental value for human beings.

I   SOME TEST CASES

If we are to find some intuitively acceptable foundation for claims about our obligations to protect species, . . .[it is useful to begin with] a description of some test cases. . . .

Case 1   The snail darter is known to exist only in one part of one river. This stretch of river would be destroyed by the building of the Tellico dam. Defenders of the dam have successfully argued that the dam is nonetheless necessary for the economic development and well-being of the area's population. To my knowledge, no serious or large-scale attempt has been made to breed large numbers of snail darters in captivity (for any reason other than research).

Case 2   The Pére David deer was first discovered by a Western naturalist in 1865, when Pére Armand David found herds of the deer in the Imperial Gardens in Peking: even at that time, they were only known to exist in captivity. Pére David brought several animals back to Europe, where they bred readily enough so that now there are healthy populations in several major zoos. There is no reasonable hope of reintroducing the Pére David deer to its natural habitat; indeed, it is not even definitely known what its natural habitat was.

Case 3   The red wolf *(Canis rufus)* formerly ranged over the southeastern and south-central United States. As with most wolves, they were threatened, and their range curtailed, by trapping, hunting, and the destruction of habitat. However, a more immediate threat to the continued existence of the red wolf is that these changes extended the range of the more adaptable coyote, with whom the red wolf interbreeds very readily; as a result, there are very few "pure" red wolves left. An attempt has been made to capture some pure breeding stock and raise wolves on preserves.

Case 4   The Baltimore oriole and the Bullock's oriole were long recognized and classified as two separate species of birds. As a result of extensive interbreeding between the two species in areas where their ranges overlapped, the American Ornithologists' Union recently declared that there were no longer two separate species; both ex-species are now called "northern orioles."

Case 5   The Appaloosa is a breed of horse with a distinctively spotted coat; the Lewis and Clark expedition discovered that the breed was associated with the Nez Percé Indians. When the Nez Percé tribe was defeated by the U.S. Cavalry in 1877 and forced to move, their horses were scattered and interbred with other horses. The distinctive coat pattern was almost lost; not until the middle of the twentieth century was a concerted effort made to gather together the few remaining specimens and reestablish the breed.

Case 6   Many strains of laboratory rats are bred specifically for a certain type of research. Once the need for a particular variety ceases—once the type of research is completed—the rats are usually killed, with the result that the variety becomes extinct.

Case 7   It is commonly known that several diseases such as sleeping sickness, malaria, and human encephalitis are carried by one variety of mosquito but not by others. Much of the disease control in these cases is aimed at exterminating the disease carrying insect; most people do not find it morally wrong to wipe out the whole species.

Case 8   Suppose that zebras were threatened solely because they were hunted for their distinctive striped coats. Suppose, too, that we could remove this threat by selectively breeding zebras that are not striped, that look exactly like mules, although they are still pure zebras. Have we preserved all that we ought to have preserved?

What does an examination of these test cases reveal? First, that our concept of what a species *is* is not at all unambiguous; at least in part, what counts as a species is a matter of current fashions in taxonomy. Furthermore, it seems that it is not the sheer diversity or number of species that matters: if that were what is valued, moral preference would be given to taxonomic schemes that separated individuals into a larger number of species, a suggestion which seems absurd. The case of the orioles suggests that the decision as to whether to call these things one species or two is not a moral issue at all. Since we are not evidently concerned with the existence or diversity of species in *this* sense, there must be something more at issue than the simple question of whether we have today the same number of species represented as we had yesterday. Confusion sets in, however, when we try to specify another sense in which it is possible to speak of the "existence" of a species. This only serves to emphasize the basic murkiness of our intuitions about what the object of our concern really is.

This murkiness is further revealed by the fact that it is not at all obvious what we are trying to preserve in some of the test cases. Sometimes, as in the case of the Appaloosa or attempts to save a subspecies like the Arctic wolf or the Mexican wolf, it is not a whole species that is in question. But not all genetic subgroups are of interest—witness the case of the laboratory rat—and sometimes the preservation of the species at the cost of one of its externally obvious features (the stripes on a zebra) is not our only concern. This is not a minor puzzle which can be resolved by changing our question from "why do species matter?" to "why do species and/or subspecies matter?" It is rather a serious issue of what makes a group of animals "special" enough or "unique" enough to warrant concern. And of course, the test cases reveal that our intuitions are not always consistent: although the cases of the red wolf and the northern oriole are parallel in important respects, we are more uneasy about simply reclassifying the red wolf and allowing things to continue along their present path.

The final point to be established is that whatever moral weight is finally attached to the preservation of a species (or subspecies), it can be overridden. We apparently have no compunction about wiping out a species of mosquito if the benefits gained by such action are sufficiently important, although many people were unconvinced by similar arguments in favor of the Tellico dam.

The lesson to be drawn from this section can be stated in a somewhat simplistic form: it is not simply the case that we can solve our problems by arguing that there is some value attached to the mere existence of a species. Our final analysis must take account of various features or properties of certain kinds or groups of animals, and it has to recognize that our concern is with the continued existence of individuals that may or may not have some distinctive characteristics.

II SOME TRADITIONAL ANSWERS

There are, of course, some standard replies to the question "Why do species matter?" or, more particularly, to the question "Why do we have at least a *prima facie* duty not to cause a species to become extinct, and in some cases, a duty to try actively to preserve species?" With some tolerance for borderline cases, these replies generally fall into three groups: (1) those that appeal to our role as "stewards" or "caretakers," (2) those that claim that species have some extrinsic value (I include in this group those that argue that the species is valuable as part of the ecosystem or as a link in the evolutionary scheme of things), and (3) those that appeal to some intrinsic or inherent value that is supposed to make a species worth preserving. In this section, with the help of the test cases just discussed, I indicate some serious flaws with each of these responses.

The first type of view has been put forward in the philosophical literature by Joel Feinberg, who states that our duty to preserve whole species may be more important than any rights had by individual animals.[1] He argues, first, that this duty does not arise from a right or claim that can properly be attributed to the species as a whole . . . and second, while we have some duty to unborn generations that directs us to preserve species, that duty is much weaker than the actual duty we have to preserve species. The fact that our actual duty extends beyond our duties to future generations is explained by the claim that we have duties of "stewardship" with respect to the world as a whole. Thus, Feinberg notes that his "inclination is to seek an explanation in terms of the requirements of our unique station as rational custodians of the planet we temporarily occupy."[2]

The main objection to this appeal to our role as stewards or caretakers is that it begs the question. The job of a custodian is to protect that which is deserving of protection, that which has some value or worth. But the issue before us now is precisely *whether* species have value, and why. If we justify our obligations of stewardship by reference to the value of that which is cared for, we cannot also explain the value by pointing to the duties of stewardship.

The second type of argument is the one which establishes the value of a species by locating it in the "larger scheme of things." That is, one might try to argue that species matter because they contribute to, or form an essential part of, some other good. This line of defense has several variations.

The first version is completely anthropocentric: it is claimed that vanishing species are of concern to us because their difficulties serve as a warning that we have polluted or altered the environment in a way that is potentially dangerous or undesirable for us. Thus, the California condor whose eggshells are weakened due to the absorption of DDT indicates that something is wrong: presumably we are being affected in subtle ways by the absorption of DDT, and that is bad for us. Alternatively, diminishing numbers of game animals may signal overhunting which, if left unchecked, would leave the sportsman with fewer things to hunt. And, as we become more aware of the benefits that might be obtained from rare varieties of plants and animals (drugs, substitutes for other natural resources, tools for research), we may become reluctant to risk the disappearance of a species that might be of practical use to us in the future.

This line of argument does not carry us very far. In the case of a subspecies, most benefits could be derived from other varieties of the same species. More important, when faced with the loss of a unique variety or species, we may simply decide that, even taking into account the possibility of error, there is not enough reason to think that the species will ever be of use; we may take a calculated risk and decide that it is not worth it. Finally, the use of a species as a danger signal may apply to species whose decline is due to some subtle and unforseen change in the environment, but will not justify concern for a species threatened by a known and forseen event like the building of a dam.

Other attempts to ascribe extrinsic value to a species do not limit themselves to potential human and practical goods. Thus, it is often argued that each species occupies a unique niche in a rich and complex, but delicately balanced, ecosystem. By destroying a single species, we upset the balance of the whole system. On the assumption that the system as a whole should be preserved, the value of a species is determined, at least in part, by its contribution to the whole.

In assessing this argument, it is important to realize that such a justification (a) may lead to odd conclusions about some of the test cases, and (b) allows for changes which do not affect the system, or which result in the substitution of a richer, more complex system for one that is more primitive or less evolved. With regard to the first of these points, species that exist only in zoos would seem to have no special value. In terms of our test cases, the David deer does not exist as part of a system, but only in isolation. Similarly, the Appaloosa horse, a domesticated variety which is neither better suited nor worse than any other sort of horse, would not have any special value. In contrast, the whole cycle of mosquitoes, disease organisms adapted to these hosts, and other beings susceptible to those diseases is quite a complex and marvelous bit of systematic adaptation. Thus, it would seem to be wrong to wipe out the encephalitis-bearing mosquito.

With regard to the second point, we might consider changes effected by white settlers in previously isolated areas such as New Zealand and Australia. The introduction of new species has resulted in a whole new ecosystem, with many of the former indigenous species being replaced by introduced varieties. As long as the new system works, there seem to be no grounds for objections.

The third version of an appeal to extrinsic value is sometimes presented in Darwinian terms: species are important as links in the evolutionary chain. This will get us nowhere, however, because the extinction of one species, the replacement of one by another, is as much a part of evolution as is the development of a new species.

One should also consider a more general concern about all those versions of the argument which focus on the species' role in the natural order of things: all of these arguments presuppose that "the natural order of things" is, in itself, good. As

William Blackstone pointed out, this is by no means obvious: "Unless one adheres dogmatically to a position of a 'reverence for all life,' the extinction of some species or forms of life may be seen as quite desirable. (This is parallel to the point often made by philosophers that not all 'customary' or 'natural' behavior is necessarily good)."[3] Unless we have some other way of ascribing value to a system, and to the animals which actually fulfill a certain function in that system (as opposed to possible replacements), the argument will not get off the ground.

Finally, then, the process of elimination leads us to the set of arguments which point to some *intrinsic value* that a species is supposed to have. The notion that species have an intrinsic value, if established, would allow us to defend much stronger claims about human obligations toward threatened species. Thus, if a species is intrinsically valuable, we should try to preserve it even when it no longer has a place in the natural ecosystem, or when it could be replaced by another species that would occupy the same niche. Most important, we should not ignore a species just because it serves no useful purpose.

Unsurprisingly, the stumbling block is what this intrinsic value might be grounded in. Without an explanation of that, we have no nonarbitrary way of deciding whether subspecies as well as species have intrinsic value or how much intrinsic value a species might have. The last question is meant to bring out issues that will arise in cases of conflict of interests: is the intrinsic value of a species of mosquito sufficient to outweigh the benefits to be gained by eradicating the means of spreading a disease like encephalitis? Is the intrinsic value of the snail darter sufficient to outweigh the economic hardship that might be alleviated by the construction of a dam? In short, to say that something has intrinsic value does not tell us *how much* value it has, nor does it allow us to make the sorts of judgments that are often called for in considering the fate of an endangered species.

The attempt to sidestep the difficulties raised by subspecies by broadening the ascription of value to include subspecies opens a whole Pandora's box. It would follow that any genetic variation within a species that results in distinctive characteristics would need separate protection. In the case of forms developed through selective breeding, it is not clear whether we have a situation analogous to natural subspecies, or whether no special value is attached to different breeds.

In order to speak to either of these issues, and in order to lend plausibility to the whole enterprise, it would seem necessary to consider first the justification for ascribing value to whichever groups have such value. If intrinsic value does not spring from anything, if it becomes merely another way of saying that we should protect species, we are going around in circles, without explaining anything. Some further explanation is needed.

Some appeals to intrinsic value are grounded in the intuition that diversity itself is a virtue. If so, it would seem incumbent upon us to create new species wherever possible, even bizarre ones that would have no purpose other than to be different. Something other than diversity must therefore be valued.

The comparison that is often made between species and natural wonders, spectacular landscapes, or even works of art, suggests that species might have some aesthetic value. This seems to accord well with our naive intuitions, provided that *aes-*

thetic value is interpreted rather loosely; most of us believe that the world would be a poorer place for the loss of bald eagles in the same way that it would be poorer for the loss of the Grand Canyon or a great work of art. In all cases, the experience of seeing these things is an inherently worthwhile experience. And since diversity in some cases is a component in aesthetic appreciation, part of the previous intuition would be preserved. There is also room for degrees of selectivity and concern with superficial changes: the variety of rat that is allowed to become extinct may have no special aesthetic value, and a bird is neither more nor less aesthetically pleasing when we change its name.

There are some drawbacks to this line of argument: there are some species which, by no stretch of the imagination, are aesthetically significant. But aesthetic value can cover a surprising range of things: a tiger may be simply beautiful; a blue whale is awe-inspiring; a bird might be decorative; an Appaloosa is of interest because of its historical significance; and even a drab little plant may inspire admiration for the marvelous way it has been adapted to a special environment. Even so, there may be species such as the snail darter that simply have no aesthetic value. In these cases, lacking any alternative, we may be forced to the conclusion that such species are not worth preserving.

Seen from other angles, once again the appeal to the aesthetic value of species is illuminating. Things that have an aesthetic value [may be] compared and ranked in some cases, and commitment of resources may be made accordingly. We believe that diminishing the aesthetic value of a thing for mere economic benefit is immoral, but that aesthetic value is not absolute—that the fact that something has aesthetic value may be overridden by the fact that harming that thing, or destroying it, may result in some greater good. That is, someone who agrees to destroy a piece of Greek statuary for personal gain would be condemned as having done something immoral, but someone who is faced with a choice between saving his children and saving a "priceless" painting would be said to have skewed values if he chose to save the painting. Applying these observations to species, we can see that an appeal to aesthetic value would justify putting more effort into the preservation of one species than the preservation of another; indeed, just as we think that the doodling of a would-be artist may have no merit at all, we may think that the accidental and unfortunate mutation of a species is not worth preserving. Following the analogy, allowing a species to become extinct for *mere* economic gain might be seen as immoral, while the possibility remains open that other (human?) goods might outweigh the goods achieved by the preservation of a species.

Although the appeal to aesthetic values has much to recommend it—even when we have taken account of the fact that it does not guarantee that all species matter—there seems to be a fundamental confusion that still affects the cogency of the whole argument and its application to the question of special obligations to endangered species, for if the value of a species is based on its aesthetic value, it is impossible to explain why an endangered species should be more valuable, or more worthy of preservation, than an unendangered species. The appeal to "rarity" will not help, if what we are talking about is species: each species is unique, no more or less rare than any other species: there is in each case one and only one species that we are talking about.

This problem of application seems to arise because the object of aesthetic appreciation, and hence of aesthetic value, has been misidentified, for it is not the case that we perceive, admire, and appreciate a *species*—species construed either as a group or set of similar animals or as a name that we attach to certain kinds of animals in virtue of some classification scheme. What we value is the existence of individuals with certain characteristics. If this is correct, then the whole attempt to explain why species matter by arguing that *they* have aesthetic value needs to be redirected. This is what I try to do in the final section of this paper.

III VALUING THE INDIVIDUAL

What I propose is that the intuition behind the argument from aesthetic value is correct, but misdirected. The reasons that were given for the value of a species are, in fact, reasons for saying that an individual has value. We do not admire the grace and beauty of the species *Panthera tigris;* rather, we admire the grace and beauty of the individual Bengal tigers that we may encounter. What we value then is the existence of that individual and the existence (present or future) of individuals like that. The ways in which other individuals should be "like that" will depend on why we value that particular sort of individual: the stripes on a zebra do not matter if we value zebras primarily for the way they are adapted to a certain environment, their unique fitness for a certain sort of life. If, on the other hand, we value zebras because their stripes are aesthetically pleasing, the stripes do matter. Since our attitudes toward zebras probably include both of these features, it is not surprising to find that my hypothetical test case produces conflicting intuitions.

The shift of emphasis from species to individuals allows us to make sense of the stronger feelings we have about endangered species in two ways. First, the fact that there are very few members of a species—the fact that we rarely encounter one—itself increases the value of those encounters. I can see turkey vultures almost every day, and I can eat apples almost every day, but seeing a bald eagle or eating wild strawberries are experiences that are much less common, more delightful just for their rarity and unexpectedness. Even snail darters, which, if we encountered them every day would be drab and uninteresting, become more interesting just because we don't—or may not—see them every day. Second, part of our interest in an individual carries over to a desire that there be future opportunities to see these things again (just as when, upon finding a new and beautiful work of art, I will wish to go back and see it again). In the case of animals, unlike works of art, I know that this animal will not live forever, but that other animals like this one will have similar aesthetic value. Thus, because I value possible future encounters, I will also want to do what is needed to ensure the possibility of such encounters—i.e., make sure that enough presently existing individuals of this type will be able to reproduce and survive. This is rather like the duty that we have to support and contribute to museums, or to other efforts to preserve works of art.

To sum up, then: individual animals can have, to a greater or lesser degree, aesthetic value: they are valued for their simple beauty, for their awesomeness, for their intriguing adaptations, for their rarity, and for many other reasons. We have moral obligations to protect things of aesthetic value, and to ensure (in an odd sense) their continued existence; thus, we have a duty to protect individual animals (the duty may be weaker or stronger depending on the value of the individual), and to ensure that there will continue to be animals of this sort (this duty will also be weaker or stronger, depending on value).

NOTES

1 Joel Feinberg, "Human Duties and Animal Rights," in *On the Fifth Day: Animal Rights and Human Ethics,* Richard Knowles Morris and Michael W. Fox, eds. (Washington: Acropolis Books, 1978), p. 67.
2 *Ibid,* p. 68.
3 William Blackstone, "Ethics and Ecology," in *Philosophy and Environmental Crisis,* ed. William Blackstone (Athens: University of Georgia Press, 1974), p. 25.

QUESTIONS

1 If Rollin is correct, and aesthetic value is an instrumental value, is Russow's position ultimately anthropocentric?
2 Is there an obligation to preserve a species threatened with extinction even if meeting that obligation means the loss of a livelihood for some human beings?

Radical American Environmentalism and Wilderness Preservation: A Third World Critique

Ramachandra Guha

Ramachandra Guha is reader in sociology at the Institute of Economic Growth in Delhi, India. A sociologist and historian, he has written extensively on the historical roots of ecological conflict and on environmental ideas in East and West. Guha wrote this essay while serving as a visiting lecturer at the Yale School of Forestry and Environmental Studies. He is the author of *The Unquiet Woods: Ecological Change and Peasant Resistance in the Himalaya* (1990).

Guha advances a critique of the American deep ecology movement from a Third World perspective. He states and criticizes three of the central tenets he identifies with American deep ecology: (1) its distinction between anthropocentric and biocentric approaches to environmental issues, (2) its focus on wilderness preservation, and (3) its conviction that the American version of deep ecology represents the most radical trend in environmentalism. In respect to (1), Guha argues that this distinction is of little use in helping us to understand the dynamics of environmental degradation. In respect to (2), he maintains that the implementation of the wilderness agenda is causing serious deprivation in Third

Reprinted with permission of the author and the publisher from *Environmental Ethics,* vol. 11 (Spring 1989), pp. 71–76, 78–83.

World countries. In respect to (3), Guha points out that American deep ecologists fail to seriously question the ecological and sociopolitical basis of the consumer society, even though its consumerism is responsible for so much environmental degradation. He gives examples from other cultures (Germany and India) to illustrate what he considers a far more radical environmentalism—one that emphasizes equity and the integration of ecological concerns with livelihood and work.

I INTRODUCTION

The respected radical journalist Kirkpatrick Sale recently celebrated "the passion of a new and growing movement that has become disenchanted with the environmental establishment and has in recent years mounted a serious and sweeping attack on it— style, substance, systems, sensibilities and all."[1] The vision of those whom Sale calls the "New Ecologists"—and what I refer to in this article as deep ecology—is a compelling one. Decrying the narrowly economic goals of mainstream environmentalism, this new movement aims at nothing less than a philosophical and cultural revolution in human attitudes toward nature. In contrast to the conventional lobbying efforts of environmental professionals based in Washington, it proposes a militant defence of "Mother Earth," an unflinching opposition to human attacks on undisturbed wilderness. With their goals ranging from the spiritual to the political, the adherents of deep ecology span a wide spectrum of the American environmental movement. As Sale correctly notes, this emerging strand has in a matter of a few years made its presence felt in a number of fields: from academic philosophy (as in the journal *Environmental Ethics*) to popular environmentalism (for example, the group Earth First!).

In this article I develop a critique of deep ecology from the perspective of a sympathetic outsider. . . . I speak admittedly as a partisan, but of the environmental movement in India, a country with an ecological diversity comparable to the U.S., but with a radically dissimilar cultural and social history.

My treatment of deep ecology is primarily historical and sociological, rather than philosophical, in nature. Specifically, I examine the cultural rootedness of a philosophy that likes to present itself in universalistic terms. I make two main arguments: first, that deep ecology is uniquely American, and despite superficial similarities in rhetorical style, the social and political goals of radical environmentalism in other cultural contexts (e.g., West Germany and India) are quite different; second, that the social consequences of putting deep ecology into practice on a worldwide basis (what its practitioners are aiming for) are very grave indeed.

II THE TENETS OF DEEP ECOLOGY

While I am aware that the term *deep ecology* was coined by the Norwegian philosopher Arne Naess, this article refers specifically to the American variant.[2] Adherents of the deep ecological perspective in this country, while arguing intensely among themselves over its political and philosophical implications, share some fundamental premises about human-nature interactions. As I see it, [the following are three of] the defining characteristics of deep ecology:

First, deep ecology argues, that the environmental movement must shift from an "anthropocentric" to a "biocentric" perspective. In many respects, an acceptance of the primacy of this distinction constitutes the litmus test of deep ecology. A considerable effort is expended by deep ecologists in showing that the dominant motif in Western philosophy has been anthropocentric—i.e., the belief that man and his works are the center of the universe—and conversely, in identifying those lonely thinkers (Leopold, Thoreau, Muir, Aldous Huxley, Santayana, etc.) who, in assigning man a more humble place in the natural order, anticipated deep ecological thinking. In the political realm, meanwhile, establishment environmentalism (shallow ecology) is chided for casting its arguments in human-centered terms. Preserving nature, the deep ecologists say, has an intrinsic worth quite apart from any benefits preservation may convey to future human generations. The anthropocentric-biocentric distinction is accepted as axiomatic by deep ecologists, it structures their discourse, and much of the present discussion remains mired within it.

The second characteristic of deep ecology is its focus on the preservation of unspoilt wilderness—and the restoration of degraded areas to a more pristine condition—to the relative (and sometimes absolute) neglect of other issues on the environmental agenda. I later identify the cultural roots and portentous consequences of this obsession with wilderness. For the moment, let me indicate three distinct sources from which it springs. Historically, it represents a playing out of the preservationist (read *radical*) and utilitarian (read *reformist*) dichotomy that has plagued American environmentalism since the turn of the century. Morally, it is an imperative that follows from the biocentric perspective; other species of plants and animals, and nature itself, have an intrinsic right to exist. And finally, the preservation of wilderness also turns on a scientific argument—viz., the value of biological diversity in stabilizing ecological regimes and in retaining a gene pool for future generations. Truly radical policy proposals have been put forward by deep ecologists on the basis of these arguments. The influential poet Gary Snyder, for example, would like to see a 90 percent reduction in human populations to allow a restoration of pristine environments, while others have argued forcefully that a large portion of the globe must be immediately cordoned off from human beings.[3] . . .

Third, deep ecologists, whatever their internal differences, share the belief that they are the "leading edge" of the environmental movement. As the polarity of the shallow/deep and anthropocentric/biocentric distinctions makes clear, they see themselves as the spiritual, philosophical, and political vanguard of American and world environmentalism.

III TOWARD A CRITIQUE

Although I analyze each of these tenets independently, it is important to recognize, as deep ecologists are fond of remarking in reference to nature, the interconnectedness and unity of these individual themes.

1 Insofar as it has begun to act as a check on man's arrogance and ecological hubris, the transition from an anthropocentric (human-centered) to a biocentric (humans as only one element in the ecosystem) view in both religious and scientific traditions is only to be welcomed. What is unacceptable are the radical conclusions drawn by deep ecology, in particular, that intervention in nature should be guided primarily by the need to preserve biotic integrity rather than by the needs of humans. The latter for deep ecologists is anthropocentric, the former biocentric. This dichotomy is, however, of very little use in understanding the dynamics of environmental degradation. The two fundamental ecological problems facing the globe are (i) overconsumption by the industrialized world and by urban elites in the Third World and (ii) growing militarization, both in a short-term sense (i.e., ongoing regional wars) and in a long-term sense (i.e., the arms race and the prospect of nuclear annihilation). Neither of these problems has any tangible connection to the anthropocentric-biocentric distinction. Indeed, the agents of these processes would barely comprehend this philosophical dichotomy. The proximate causes of the ecologically wasteful characteristics of industrial society and of militarization are far more mundane: at an aggregate level, the dialectic of economic and political structures, and at a micro-level, the life style choices of individuals. These causes cannot be reduced, whatever the level of analysis, to a deeper anthropocentric attitude toward nature; on the contrary, by constituting a grave threat to human survival, the ecological degradation they cause does not even serve the best interests of human beings! If my identification of the major dangers to the integrity of the natural world is correct, invoking the bogy of anthropocentricism is at best irrelevant and at worst a dangerous obfuscation.

2 If the above dichotomy is irrelevant, the emphasis on wilderness is positively harmful when applied to the Third World. If in the U.S. the preservationist/utilitarian division is seen as mirroring the conflict between "people" and "interests," in countries such as India the situation is very nearly the reverse. Because India is a long settled and densely populated country in which agrarian populations have a finely balanced relationship with nature, the setting aside of wilderness areas has resulted in a direct transfer of resources from the poor to the rich. Thus, Project Tiger, a network of parks hailed by the international conservation community as an outstanding success, sharply posits the interests of the tiger against those of poor peasants living in and around the reserve. The designation of tiger reserves was made possible only by the physical displacement of existing villages and their inhabitants; their management requires the continuing exclusion of peasants and livestock. The initial impetus for setting up parks for the tiger and other large mammals such as the rhinoceros and elephant came from two social groups, first, a class of ex-hunters turned conservationists belonging mostly to the declining Indian feudal elite and second, representatives of international agencies, such as the World Wildlife Fund (WWF) and the International Union for the Conservation of Nature and Natural Resources (IUCN), seeking to transplant the American system of national parks onto Indian soil. In no case have the needs of the local population been taken into account, and as in many parts of Africa, the designated wildlands are managed primarily for the benefit of rich tourists. Until very recently, wildlands preservation has been identified with environmentalism by the state and the conservation elite; in consequence, environmental problems that impinge far more directly on the lives of the poor—e.g., fuel, fodder, water shortages, soil erosion, and air and water pollution—have not been adequately addressed.[4]

Deep ecology provides, perhaps unwittingly, a justification for the continuation of such narrow and inequitable conservation practices under a newly acquired radical guise. Increasingly, the international conservation elite is using the philosophical, moral, and scientific arguments used by deep ecologists in advancing their wilderness crusade. A striking but by no means atypical example is the recent plea by a prominent American biologist for the takeover of large portions of the globe by the author and his scientific colleagues. Writing in a prestigous scientific forum, the *Annual Review of Ecology and Systematics,* Daniel Janzen argues that only biologists have the competence to decide how the tropical landscape should be used. As "the representatives of the natural world," biologists are "in charge of the future of tropical ecology," and only they have the expertise and mandate to "determine whether the tropical agroscape is to be populated only by humans, their mutualists, commensals, and parasites, or whether it will also contain some islands of the greater nature—the nature that spawned humans, yet has been vanquished by them." Janzen exhorts his colleagues to advance their territorial claims on the tropical world more forcefully, warning that the very existence of these areas is at stake: "if biologists want a tropics in which to biologize, they are going to have to buy it with care, energy, effort, strategy, tactics, time, and cash."[5]

This frankly imperialist manifesto highlights the multiple dangers of the preoccupation with wilderness preservation that is characteristic of deep ecology. As I have suggested, it seriously compounds the neglect by the American movement of far more pressing environmental problems within the Third World. But perhaps more importantly, and in a more insidious fashion, it also provides an impetus to the imperialist yearning of Western biologists and their financial sponsors, organizations such as the WWF and IUCN. The wholesale transfer of a movement culturally rooted in American conservation history can only result in the social uprooting of human populations in other parts of the globe. . . .

3 How radical, finally, are the deep ecologists? Notwithstanding their self-image and strident rhetoric (in which the label "shallow ecology" has an opprobrium similar to that reserved for "social democratic" by Marxist-Leninists), even within the American context their radicalism is limited and it manifests itself quite differently elsewhere.

To my mind, deep ecology is best viewed as a radical trend within the wilderness preservation movement. Although advancing philosophical rather than aesthetic arguments and encouraging political militancy rather than negotiation, its practical emphasis—viz., preservation of unspoilt nature—is virtually identical. For the mainstream movement, the function of wilderness is to provide a temporary antidote to modern civilization. As a special institution within an industrialized society, the national park "provides an opportunity for respite, contrast, contemplation, and affirmation of values for those who live most of their lives in the workaday world."[6] Indeed, the rapid increase in visitations to the national parks in postwar America is a direct consequence of economic expansion. The emergence of a popular interest in wilderness sites, the historian Samuel Hays points out, was "not a throwback to the primitive, but an integral part of the modern standard of living as people sought to add new 'amenity' and 'aesthetic' goals and desires to their earlier preoccupation with necessities and conveniences."[7]

Here, the enjoyment of nature is an integral part of the consumer society. The private automobile (and the life style it has spawned) is in many respects the ultimate ecological villain, and an untouched wilderness the prototype of ecological harmony; yet, for most Americans it is perfectly consistent to drive a thousand miles to spend a holiday in a national park. They possess a vast, beautiful, and sparsely populated continent and are also able to draw upon the natural resources of large portions of the globe by virtue of their economic and political dominance. In consequence, America can simultaneously enjoy the material benefits of an expanding economy and the aesthetic benefits of unspoilt nature. The two poles of "wilderness" and "civilization" mutually coexist in an internally coherent whole, and philosophers of both poles are assigned a prominent place in this culture. Paradoxically as it may seem, it is no accident that Star Wars technology and deep ecology both find their fullest expression in that leading sector of Western civilization, California.

Deep ecology runs parallel to the consumer society without seriously questioning its ecological and socio-political basis. In its celebration of American wilderness, it also displays an uncomfortable convergence with the prevailing climate of nationalism in the American wilderness movement. For spokesmen such as the historian Roderick Nash, the national park system is America's distinctive cultural contribution to the world, reflective not merely of its economic but of its philosophical and ecological maturity as well. In what Walter Lippman called the American century, the "American invention of national parks" must be exported worldwide. Betraying an economic determinism that would make even a Marxist shudder, Nash believes that environmental preservation is a "full stomach" phenomenon that is confined to the rich, urban, and sophisticated. Nonetheless, he hopes that "the less developed nations may eventually evolve economically and intellectually to the point where nature preservation is more than a business."[8]

The error which Nash makes (and which deep ecology in some respects encourages) is to equate environmental protection with the protection of wilderness. This is a distinctively American notion, born out of a unique social and environmental history. The archetypal concerns of radical environmentalists in other cultural contexts are in fact quite different. The German Greens, for example, have elaborated a devastating critique of industrial society which turns on the acceptance of environmental limits to growth. Pointing to the intimate links between industrialization, militarization, and conquest, the Greens argue that economic growth in the West has historically rested on the economic and ecological exploitation of the Third World. Rudolf Bahro is characteristically blunt:

> The working class here [in the West] is the richest lower class in the world. And if I look at the problem from the point of view of the whole of humanity, not just from that of Europe, then I must say that the metropolitan working class is the worst exploiting class in

history. . . . What made poverty bearable in eighteenth or nineteenth-century Europe was the prospect of escaping it through exploitation of the periphery. But this is no longer a possibility, and continued industrialism in the Third World will mean poverty for whole generations and hunger for millions.[9]

Here the roots of global ecological problems lie in the disproportionate share of resources consumed by the industrialized countries as a whole *and* the urban elite within the Third World. Since it is impossible to reproduce an industrial monoculture worldwide, the ecological movement in the West must begin by cleaning up its own act. The Greens advocate the creation of a "no growth" economy, to be achieved by scaling down current (and clearly unsustainable) consumption levels. This radical shift in consumption and production patterns requires the creation of alternate economic and political structures—smaller in scale and more amenable to social participation—but it rests equally on a shift in cultural values. The expansionist character of modern Western man will have to give way to an ethic of renunciation and self-limitation, in which spiritual and communal values play an increasing role in sustaining social life. This revolution in cultural values, however, has as its point of departure an understanding of environmental processes quite different from deep ecology.

Many elements of the Green program find a strong resonance in countries such as India, where a history of Western colonialism and industrial development has bene-fited only a tiny elite while exacting tremendous social and environmental costs. The ecological battles presently being fought in India have as their epicenter the conflict over nature between the subsistence and largely rural sector and the vastly more powerful commercial-industrial sector. Perhaps the most celebrated of these battles concerns the Chipko (Hug the Tree) movement, a peasant movement against defor-estation in the Himalayan foothills. Chipko is only one of several movements that have sharply questioned the nonsustainable demand being placed on the land and vegetative base by urban centers and industry. These include opposition to large dams by displaced peasants, the conflict between small artisan fishing and large-scale trawler fishing for export, the countrywide movements against commercial for-est operations, and opposition to industrial pollution among downstream agricultural and fishing communities.[10]

Two features distinguish these environmental movements from their Western counterparts. First, for the sections of society most critically affected by environmen-tal degradation—poor and landless peasants, women, and tribals—it is a question of sheer survival, not of enhancing the quality of life. Second, and as a consequence, the environmental solutions they articulate deeply involve questions of equity as well as economic and political redistribution. Highlighting these differences, a leading In-dian environmentalist stresses that "environmental protection per se is of least con-cern to most of these groups. Their main concern is about the use of the environment and who should benefit from it."[11] They seek to wrest control of nature away from the state and the industrial sector and place it in the hands of rural communities who live within that environment but are increasingly denied access to it. These commu-nities have far more basic needs, their demands on the environment are far less intense, and they can draw upon a reservoir of cooperative social institutions and local ecological knowledge in managing the "commons"—forests, grasslands, and the waters—on a sustainable basis. If colonial and capitalist expansion has both accentuated social inequalities and signaled a precipitous fall in ecological wisdom, an alternate ecology must rest on an alternate society and polity as well.

This brief overview of German and Indian environmentalism has some major implications for deep ecology. Both German and Indian environmental traditions allow for a greater integration of ecological concerns with livelihood and work. They also place a greater emphasis on equity and social justice (both within individual countries and on a global scale) on the grounds that in the absence of social regeneration environmental regeneration has very little chance of succeeding. Finally, and perhaps most significantly, they have escaped the preoccupation with wilderness perservation so characteristic of American cultural and environmental history.

IV   A HOMILY

In 1958, the economist J. K. Galbraith referred to overconsumption as the unasked question of the American conservation movement. There is a marked selectivity, he wrote, "in the conservationist's approach to materials consumption. If we are concerned about our great appetite for materials, it is plausible to seek to increase the supply, to decrease waste, to make better use of the stocks available, and to develop substitutes. But what of the appetite itself? Surely this is the ultimate source of the problem. If it continues its geometric course, will it not one day have to be restrained? Yet in the literature of the resource problem this is the forbidden question. Over it hangs a nearly total silence."[12]

The consumer economy and society have expanded tremendously in the three decades since Galbraith penned these words; yet his criticisms are nearly as valid today. I have said "nearly," for there are some hopeful signs. Within the environmental movement several dispersed groups are working to develop ecologically benign technologies and to encourage less wasteful life styles. Moreover, outside the self-defined boundaries of American environmentalism, opposition to the permanent war economy is being carried on by a peace movement that has a distinguished history and impeccable moral and political credentials.

It is precisely these (to my mind, most hopeful) components of the American social scene that are missing from deep ecology. In their widely noticed book, Bill Devall and George Sessions make no mention of militarization or the movements for peace, while activists whose practical focus is on developing ecologically responsible life styles (e.g., Wendell Berry) are derided as "falling short of deep ecological awareness."[13] A truly radical ecology in the American context ought to work toward a synthesis of the appropriate technology, alternate life style, and peace movements. By making the (largely spurious) anthropocentric-biocentric distinction central to the debate, deep ecologists may have appropriated the moral high ground, but they are at the same time doing a serious disservice to American and global environmentalism.

NOTES

1 Kirkpatrick Sale, "The Forest for the Trees: Can Today's Environmentalists Tell the Difference," *Mother Jones* 11, no. 8 (November 1986): 26.

2 One of the major criticisms I make in this essay concerns deep ecology's lack of concern with inequalities *within* human society. In the article in which he coined the term *deep ecology,* Naess himself expresses concerns about inequalities between and within nations. However, his concern with social cleavages and their impact on resource utilization patterns and ecological destruction is not very visible in the later writings of deep ecologists. See Arne Naess, "The Shallow and the Deep, Long-Range Ecology Movement: A Summary," *Inquiry* 16 (1973): 96 (I am grateful to Tom Birch for this reference).

3 Gary Snyder, quoted in Sale, "The Forest for the Trees," p. 32. See also Dave Foreman, "A Modest Proposal for a Wilderness System," *Whole Earth Review,* no. 53 (Winter 1986–87): 42–45.

4 See Centre for Science and Environment, *India: The State of the Environment 1982: A Citizens Report* (New Delhi: Centre for Science and Environment, 1982); R. Sukumar, "Elephant-Man Conflict in Karnataka," in Cecil Saldanha, ed., *The State of Karnataka's Environment* (Bangalore: Centre for Taxonomic Studies, 1985). For Africa, see the brilliant analysis by Helge Kjekshus, *Ecology Control and Economic Development in East African History* (Berkeley: University of California Press, 1977).

5 Daniel Janzen, "The Future of Tropical Ecology," *Annual Review of Ecology and Systematics* 17 (1986): 305–06; emphasis added.

6 Joseph Sax, *Mountains Without Handrails: Reflections on the National Parks* (Ann Arbor: University of Michigan Press, 1980), p. 42. Cf. also Peter Schmitt, *Back to Nature: The Arcadian Myth in Urban America* (New York: Oxford University Press, 1969), and Alfred Runte, *National Parks: The American Experience* (Lincoln: University of Nebraska Press, 1979).

7 Samuel Hays, "From Conservation to Environment: Environmental Politics in the United States since World War Two," *Environmental Review* 6 (1982): 21. See also the same author's book entitled *Beauty, Health and Permanence: Environmental Politics in the United States, 1955–85* (New York: Cambridge University Press, 1987).

8 Roderick Nash, *Wilderness and the American Mind,* 3rd ed. (New Haven: Yale University Press, 1982).

9 Rudolf Bahro, *From Red to Green* (London: Verso Books, 1984).

10 For an excellent review, see Anil Agarwal and Sunita Narain, eds., *India: The State of the Environment 1984–85: A Citizens Report* (New Delhi: Centre for Science and Environment, 1985). Cf. also Ramachandra Guha, *The Unquiet Woods: Ecological Change and Peasant Resistance in the Indian Himalaya* (Berkeley: University of California Press, 1990).

11 Anil Agarwal, "Human-Nature Interactions in a Third World Country," *The Environmentalist* 6, no. 3 (1986): 167.

12 John Kenneth Galbraith, "How Much Should a Country Consume?" in Henry Jarrett, ed., *Perspectives on Conservation* (Baltimore: Johns Hopkins Press, 1958), pp. 91–92.

13 Devall and Sessions, *Deep Ecology,* p. 122. For Wendell Berry's own assessment of deep ecology, see his "Amplications: Preserving Wildness," *Wilderness* 50 (Spring 1987): 39–40, 50–54.

QUESTIONS

1 Is overconsumption by the industrialized world and by urban elites in the Third World one of the most serious ecological problems we face today? If yes, what changes would you be willing to make in your life to help solve the problem?

2 Should the overcoming of inequalities in a society have priority over concerns such as the preservation of wilderness areas?

SUGGESTED ADDITIONAL READINGS FOR CHAPTER 11

CALLICOTT, J. BAIRD: *In Defense of the Land Ethic: Essays in Environmental Philosophy.* Albany: State University of New York Press, 1989. In this collection of essays, originally published between 1979 and 1987, Callicott articulates, defends, and extends Aldo Leopold's seminal environmental philosophy.

Environmental Ethics. This journal, identifying itself as "An Interdisciplinary Journal Dedicated to the Philosophical Aspects of Environmental Problems," began publication in 1979. It is an invaluable source of material relevant to the issues under discussion in this chapter.

JOHNS, DAVID M.: "The Relevance of Deep Ecology to the Third World: Some Preliminary Comments," *Environmental Ethics,* vol. 12, Fall 1990, pp. 233–252. Johns discusses and criticizes some of Ramachandra Guha's major contentions regarding the American deep ecology movement.

LEOPOLD, ALDO: "The Land Ethic." In *A Sand County Almanac.* New York: Oxford University Press, 1966, pp. 217–241. In this essay, a frequent reference point of contemporary discussions, Leopold calls for an extension of the ethical community beyond its traditional anthropocentric limits.

NAESS, ARNE: *Ecology, Community and Lifestyle,* translated and edited by David Rothenberg. Cambridge: Cambridge University Press, 1989. This book explains the philosophical ideas of one of the foremost defenders of a deep ecology approach to environmental ethics.

REGAN, TOM, ed.: *Earthbound: New Introductory Essays in Environmental Ethics.* New York: Random House, 1984. In this collection of original essays, a wide range of issues in environmental ethics is addressed.

SAGOFF, MARK: *The Economy of the Earth: Philosophy, Law, and the Environment.* Cambridge: Cambridge University Press, 1988. Sagoff criticizes and rejects the conceptual vocabulary of resource and welfare economics, with its emphasis on cost-benefit analysis, which is often used in justifications of environmental policies. He argues for an alternative, more morally sensitive approach to environmental policy.

SCHERER, DONALD, and THOMAS ATTIG, eds.: *Ethics and the Environment.* Englewood Cliffs, N.J.: Prentice-Hall, 1983. Part One of this anthology organizes material under the heading of "Defining an Environmental Ethic." Part Two deals with "Specific Environmental Problems."

STONE, CHRISTOPHER D.: *Earth and Other Ethics: The Case for Moral Pluralism.* New York: Harper & Row, 1987. Arguing for a need to rethink some of the most basic assumptions of ethics, Stone argues that no one ethical framework can provide answers to all our ethical dilemmas, including those centered on the environment.

TAYLOR, PAUL W.: *Respect for Nature: A Theory of Environmental Ethics.* Princeton, N.J.: Princeton University Press, 1986. Rejecting both speciesism and sentientism, Taylor puts forth and defends a biocentric ethical system.

VANDEVEER, DONALD, and CHRISTINE PIERCE, eds.,: *People, Penguins, and Plastic Trees*. Belmont, Calif.: Wadsworth, 1986. This very useful anthology provides readings organized around four questions: (1) "The Other Animals: Mere Resources?" (2) "The Broader Environment: Other Lives of Value?" (3) "Constructing an Environmental Ethic: Which Foundation?" and (4) "Economics, Ethics, and Ecology: How Much Common Ground?"